C OCEAN

RWAY

SWEDEN
FINLAND

ESTONIA
LATVIA
LITHUANIA
BELARUS
CZECH REPUBLIC
SLOVAK REPUBLIC
SLOVENIA
HUNGARY
CROATIA

DARK
NDS

GERMANY POLAND
UX
AUS
ITALY ROMANIA
ALBANIA MOLDOVA
GREECE MACEDONIA

UKRAINE
BOSNIA-
HERZEGOVINA
SERBIA
BULGARIA

GEORGIA
ARMENIA

RIA

TUNISIA
CYPRUS
LEBANON
ISRAEL

TURKEY

SYRIA
IRAQ

AZERBAIJAN

IRAN

LIBYA

JORDAN

EGYPT
BAHRAIN

SAUDI
ARABIA

YEMEN

OMAN

KUWAIT
QATAR

UNITED
ARAB
EMIRATES

NIGER

CHAD

SUDAN

NIGERIA

ERITREA

CAMEROON

UGANDA

ETHIOPIA

DJIBOUTI

SOMALIA

RWANDA
BURUNDI
ZAIRE

KENYA

ANGOLA

TANZANIA MALAWI
COMOROS
MOZAMBIQUE

ZAMBIA

NAMIBIA

BOTSWANA

MADAGASCAR

MAURITIUS

SOUTH
AFRICA

ZIMBABWE
SWAZILAND
LESOTHO

RUSSIA

KAZAKHSTAN

MONGOLIA

UZBEKISTAN

TURKMENISTAN

KYRGYZSTAN
TAJIKISTAN

AFGHANISTAN

CHINA

NORTH
KOREA

SOUTH
KOREA

JAPAN

PAKISTAN

NEPAL
BHUTAN

INDIA

BANGLADESH

MYANMAR
(BURMA)

LAOS

TAIWAN

VIETNAM

PHILIPPINES

THAILAND
SRI LANKA

MALDIVES

CAMBODIA (KAMPUCHEA)

BRUNEI
MALAYSIA

SINGAPORE

I N D O N E S I A

SEYCHELLES

INDIAN
OCEAN

NORTH
PACIFIC
OCEAN

MARSHALL
ISLANDS

MICRONESIA

KIRIBATI

NAURU

PAPUA
NEW GUINEA

SOLOMON
ISLANDS

TUVALU

VANUATU

FIJI

Equator

Tropic of Cancer

Tropic of Capricorn

AUSTRALIA

NEW ZEALAND

Antarctic Circle

20° 40° 60° 80° 100° 120° 140° 160°

80°

60°

40°

20°

20°

40°

60°

80°

0   1000   2000 Miles

0   1000   2000   3000 Kilometers

The World's Religions

The World's Religions:
Worldviews and Contemporary Issues

William A. Young
Westminster College

Prentice Hall, Englewood Cliffs, New Jersey 07632

Library of Congress Cataloging-in-Publication Data

Young, William A.,
  The world's religions : worldviews and contemporary issues / by
William A. Young.
    p.   cm.
  Includes bibliographical references and index.
  ISBN 0-13-032806-5
  1. Religions. 2. Religion. 3. Sects. 4. Cults. I. Title.
BL80.2.Y68 1995   94-19431
291—dc20   CIP

Acquisitions Editor: Ted Bolen
Production Editor: Shelly Kupperman
Editorial Director: Charlyce Jones Owen
Art Director: Anne Bonanno Nieglos
Interior Designer: Donna M. Wickes
Cover Designer: Anthony Gemmellaro
Buyer: Lynn Pearlman
Photo Director: Lorinda Morris Nantz
Photo Researcher: Anita Dickhuth
Editorial Assistants: Nicole Gray and Meg McGuane
Cover Illustration: Alice B. Thiede and William A. Thiede
Cover Photos: (left) G. Colliva/The Image Bank
              (center) Russell Kord/The Image Bank
              (right) Obremski/The Image Bank

©1995 by Prentice-Hall, Inc.
A Simon & Schuster Company
Englewood Cliffs, New Jersey 07632

Printed in the United States of America
10 9 8 7 6 5 4 3 2 1

ISBN 0-13-032806-5

Prentice-Hall International (UK) Limited, *London*
Prentice-Hall of Australia Pty. Limited, *Sydney*
Prentice-Hall Canada Inc., *Toronto*
Prentice-Hall Hispanoamericana, S.A., *Mexico*
Prentice-Hall of India Private Limited, *New Delhi*
Prentice-Hall of Japan, Inc., *Tokyo*
Simon & Schuster Asia Pte. Ltd., *Singapore*
Editora Prentice-Hall do Brasil, Ltda., *Rio de Janeiro*

Contents

Preface

In two decades of teaching college courses on the world's religions, I have found that students most want to know how religions answer basic human questions such as "Why are we here?" and "What happens after death?" In addition, they wish to learn how religions respond to contemporary ethical issues such as the ecological crisis, war, capital punishment, abortion, economic justice, gender roles, and sexual orientation. They also want to learn about the early history and development of religions, their basic teachings, and the major branches within religions. They want to familiarize themselves with the major religions of the world such as Hinduism, Taoism, and Islam. But they also want to know about the religions of indigenous peoples, such as Native Americans, as well as more recently established religious movements, such as Christian Science and the Nation of Islam. Finally, they want to be able to compare and contrast both older and more recent religions openly and fairly.

Instructed by my students' concerns, I have written a "student-friendly" introduction to the world's religions. The text is intended for use in surveys of the world religions, as well as for interested general readers who want to become acquainted with religions and how they respond to basic human questions and contemporary issues.

Chapter One establishes a framework for understanding religion, with a definition that distinguishes religion from other human phenomena and structures the analysis of religion in this book. It also discusses general questions such as "Why are people religious?" and "What is the relationship between religion and science?" Chapter Two is an important and unique chapter that introduces readers to the basic human questions as religions address them and some of the contemporary ethical issues to which the religions of the world are responding.

Chapters Three through Fourteen provide an overview of the histories of the major religions of the world and their basic teachings within a framework that allows for objective and fair comparisons among religions. The religions surveyed include indigenous religions of Africa and North America (focusing on the religions of the Yoruba of West Africa and the Oglala Lakota [Sioux] of the American Great Plains as case studies), Hinduism, Buddhism, Jainism, Sikhism, Taoism, Confucianism, Shinto, Zoroastrianism, Judaism, Christianity, and Islam. Each chapter highlights selections from the sacred texts of the appropriate religion, illustrating their responses to basic human questions. A special feature of this book is that each chapter samples the religions' responses to the timely ethical issues listed above. Chapter-ending summaries and questions help students to learn the essential features of the religions and to engage in reflection and discussion about them. Suggestions for further study point the way for those readers who wish to delve deeper. The intent is to encourage students to enter into a dialogue with the world's religions and with one another about the most important issues humanity faces today.

Chapter Fourteen introduces readers to a representative sampling of the world's new religions—religions that either emerged during the nineteenth or twentieth centuries from the traditional religions covered in earlier chapters or sprang up independently. In this chapter students will encounter some of the more controversial new religions, such as Satanism and the Unification Church, as well as religions that are widely identified with the religious "mainstream," such as the Baha'i Faith and the Church of Jesus Christ of Latter-day Saints (the Mormons). In this chapter we will also treat movements that some consider "secular" religions, such as Marxism and capitalism. In all cases, the approach taken to these religions is descriptive.

The final chapter of the text looks to the future, raising the questions of how religions may relate to one another in the future and whether and how they may cooperate in addressing contemporary ethical issues (using the ecological crisis as an example). A glossary concludes the text.

Readers have a right to know the background and basic point of view of a book's author. I intend for my perspective to be one of empathy for and identification with each of the religions I am presenting. As I will try to make clear in Chapter One, I believe that in the study of religion understanding should precede evaluation. In this text my task is to facilitate readers' understanding and, as much as possible, to bracket off my own opinions and preferences. Nonetheless, no treatment is completely objective, for that is not humanly possible. My situation is as follows. I am a college professor who teaches in a small liberal-arts college. I have also served as a college chaplain; I am an ordained Christian minister, and I

regularly lead Christian worship in a collegiate setting as well as in a rural community. I am also committed to and have been involved in the movement that is seeking to break down barriers between Christian churches and the emerging interfaith dialogue that is seeking to promote greater tolerance among different religions. I realize that as I look at other religions, my Western, Christian perspective is at work. For example, by seeking to abstract and compare the fundamental principles of the world's religions and their positions on basic human questions and contemporary ethical issues, I am imposing a perspective foreign to many of the religions I am studying and therefore distorting them somewhat. My hope is that this approach will enable students to frame initial pictures of the world's religions so that they will then move on to deeper study of the religions.

ACKNOWLEDGMENTS

Writing a book of this scope is not a solitary enterprise, even though it is sometimes a lonely one. I am indebted to a host of teachers, colleagues, friends, and family members who have encouraged and challenged me over the years. My parents awakened in me a curiosity about the world, and modeled for me lives of commitment to their own spiritual heritage, but with respect for other religious traditions. My first course in world religions, with the late Professor John Gammie at the University of Tulsa, awakened in me a fascination with the study of religion that has never abated. My understanding of the world's religions and methods of studying them was refined under the guidance of several of my teachers at McCormick Theological Seminary and the University of Iowa. I would especially like to acknowledge my Ph. D. advisor at the University of Iowa, Professor J. Kenneth Kuntz, and Professor Robert Baird, who shared with me his helpful insights about methodology in the study of religion. Willamette University in Salem, Oregon, gave me my first opportunity to try my hand at teaching. For nearly twenty years I have benefited from my association with faculty and students at Westminster College in Fulton, Missouri.

Among the many Westminster colleagues who have affected my own intellectual development I will single out only one: Professor Chris Hauer, my colleague in religious studies, whose breadth of knowledge and insight have been a constant source of stimulation. I have also benefited from my association with colleagues too numerous to mention, who have given me an opportunity to try out new ideas and to listen to theirs in a variety of settings, both formal and informal

The various scholars who have reviewed the manuscript of this text at various stages have provided a number of very helpful suggestions for improving it. Julius J. Jackson, Jr., San Bernandio Valley College; James Cook, Oakland Community College; James S. Dalton, Siena College; Dale Bengtson, Southern Illinois University; Martin S. Jaffee, University of Washington; Adele B. McCollum, Montclair State University; Catherine Wessinger, Loyola University; Roger E. Olson, Bethel College; David L. Barnhill, Guilford College; George E. Saint-Laurent, California State University-Fullerton; David Carrasco, University of Colorado; Daniel A. Brown, California State University-Fullerton; Steven Heine, Penn State University; Diana L. Hayes, Georgetown University; Gary Alexander, University of Wisconsin-Stevens Point; John H. Cartwright, Boston University; Francis Cook, University of California-Riverside; Zev Garber, Los Angeles Valley College; Peter Ochs, Drew University; Robert C. Monk, McMurry University; and Diane Bell, College of the Holy Cross. I am grateful for their careful reading and proposals, many of which I have adopted. They are, of course, not responsible for any errors of fact or problematic interpretations that remain.

A number of people at Prentice Hall deserve acknowledgment for their efforts in behalf of this work. In particular, Ted Bolen, Religion Editor, and assistants, Nicole Gray and Meg McGuane, Wayne Spohr (Field Representative), and Production Editor, Shelly Kupperman have been most supportive from the formulation of this project through its completion. They and their colleagues make writing a textbook not nearly as onerous a task as it could well be.

My family has encouraged me to pursue this project and they have endured with patience the many hours when Dad was lost in the world of writing about the world's religions. This book is dedicated to my wife, Sue, who most had to tolerate "the absorbedness of work" (as poet Donald Hall calls it), which tends to create a world of its own. It is also dedicated to the hundreds of students in scores of classes who have given me the privilege of introducing them to the world's religions. Without them this book would not exist, and for them I have written it.

William A. Young

 **ABC News/PH Video Library for Issues in World Religions**
Video is the most dynamic of all the supplements you can use to enhance your class. But the quality of the video material and how well it relates to your course can still make all the difference. For these reasons, Prentice Hall and ABC News have decided to work together to bring you the best and most comprehensive video ancillaries available in the college market.

Through its wide variety of award-winning programs—*Nightline, Business World, On Business, This Week with David Brinkley, World News Tonight,* and *The Health Show*—ABC offers a resource for feature and documentary-style videos related to text concepts and applications. The programs have extremely high production quality, present substantial content, and are hosted by well-versed, well-known anchors. Prentice Hall, its authors, and its editors provide the benefit of having selected videos on topics that will work well with this course and text and give the instructor teaching notes on how to use them in the classroom.

"The ABC News/PH Video Library for Issues in World Religions" offers video material for almost every chapter in the text. An excellent video guide is included in the Instructor's Manual and carefully and completely integrates the videos into your lecture.

The World's Religions

SECTION I

Introduction

Before we begin our study of particular religions, we must first answer some general questions. What is religion? Why are people religious? Why are there so many religions? Why is the study of religion so important today? What is the relationship between science and religion? What are the various ways religion may be studied, and how will religion be studied in this text? These are among the questions to be discussed in Chapter One.

Since the particular focus of this text is how religions respond to basic human questions and contemporary ethical issues, we also need to set the stage for an examination of the ways in which religions respond to these matters. In Chapter Two we will clarify the nature of the following basic human questions: Who are we as humans? What is the basic human dilemma? Why are we here? What happens after death? How did the world come into being? What is the destiny of the universe? What is right living? What is our obligation to others? What are our obligations to non-human life? Is there a basic moral law? What is the sacred? How is the sacred made known? We will also take a preliminary look at the following ethical issues: the ecological crisis, war, capital punishment, abortion, euthanasia, economic justice, gender roles and the status of women, and homosexuality.

CHAPTER 1

An Introduction to Religion and the Study of Religion

WHAT IS RELIGION?

The Problem of Defining Religion

One person joins the army of her country and enthusiastically kills enemy soldiers. Another refuses to become a soldier and spends time in prison for violating the compulsory-service law of his country. One person dances with abandon, holding poisonous snakes and gesticulating wildly. Another sits quietly for hours, seemingly frozen like a statue. One person talks about the earth as her mother and the birds, fish, and land animals as her sisters and brothers. Another speaks majestically of the human sovereignty over nature and implies that other animals are subordinate to humans. One person says that mankind's only hope is through faith in the mercy of the one and only God. Another asserts that many gods exist, but they are powerless to help humans reach the highest goal. Still another denies the existence of God or gods, but seems to have an all-encompassing worldview that takes the place of faith in God or gods.

All of these seemingly contradictory behaviors and beliefs have been identified as "religious" by scholars in the field of religious studies, illustrating the difficulty of identifying the object of their study. If such diverse phenomena are religious, is there any common denominator that enables us to distinguish religion from other human endeavors?

Scholars are frankly divided on this most basic question. Some argue that it is impossible to define religion in general. Any attempt to define religion as a whole inevitably falls victim, they say, to the bias of a particular religious or non-religious point of view. Others think that given the basic diversity among religions, no single definition encompassing all religions is possible.

Other interpreters, including the author of this text, think that a definition of religion in general is not only possible, but essential to the study of religion. A definition may reflect the bias of its author, but readers have a right to know the basic perspective taken in a presentation on a subject, especially one as controversial as religion. Therefore, we will begin this study of the world's religions with a definition that we will use throughout our discussion.

Is a Dictionary Definition Adequate for the Study of Religion?

We could simply adopt one of the definitions of religion found in a good dictionary. However, a glance at one popular dictionary's definitions of religion (*The Random House Dictionary*) suggests that such definitions are not adequate for a thorough study. The *Random House* entries under "religion" are typical of those in modern American dictionaries. This dictionary says religion is:

1. a set of beliefs concerning the cause, nature, and purpose of the universe, especially belief in or the worship of God or gods.
2. an organized system of belief in and worship of God or gods.
3. something one believes in or follows devotedly.

These definitions may have the virtue of simplicity and clarity, but they are not adequate for our study. The problem with the first two is that they are too narrow, reflecting an unnecessarily strong Western cultural bias. The first definition limits religion to "beliefs," and, as we shall see, religion encompasses a much wider range of human activity. While all religions may involve the quest for understanding the universe, they do not all express themselves as a "set of beliefs."

By naming God or gods as *essential* to religion, the second definition is much too limiting. In some religions, such as Judaism, Christianity, Islam, and devotional Hinduism, belief in and worship of a God or gods are critically important. However, in other religions, such as Theravada and Zen Buddhism and Jainism, not to mention "secular religions" such as Marxism, gods are not central. The first definition attempts to be more inclusive on this issue, but still implies that religions that do not focus on gods are somehow not quite as fully religious as those that do.

The term "worship" is mentioned in both definitions. For most readers of this text, "going to church" may be what first comes to mind when the word "religion" is mentioned. Hence, a definition of religion that names worship alongside belief as essential probably seems appropriate. While worship may be an exceedingly common ingredient in religion, it is not, as we will see, *essential* to religion. In fact, some movements, like philosophical Taoism and Zen Buddhism, explicitly distance themselves from such acts.

The third definition seems to fit the criterion of breadth, by defining religion as "something one believes in or follows devotedly." The key word is "devotedly." I may believe in and follow an exercise regimen devotedly. Does that mean my religion is exercise? What about the person who devotedly watches a particular television show each week, or the group that gathers devotedly to study and re-enact Civil War battles? Today, we use the term "religion" in this vague way, to name an activity or belief to which we are firmly committed. We may be religious in this sense about a number of things, but does that mean they are all our religion? A definition to be used in the study of the world's religions needs to be more precise. We are looking for a definition that goes beyond common usage for the sake of meeting the goal of guiding a serious study of the varied religions in the world.

Adopting a Working Definition of Religion

Many scholars have been sensitive to this problem, and have developed what they call "functional" or "working" definitions of religion. A functional definition is one designed for a particular use, in this case the broad study of religion. Such definitions are intended not to capture the "true" essence of religion, but rather to outline only a framework for distinguishing and understanding religion. There is no *one* right working definition of religion. Each interpreter should stipulate and explain the definition adopted in his or her study. The reader may then decide whether the definition chosen has proved helpful in guiding the study or has merely confused matters.

The definition of *religion* developed for this analysis is:

Religion is human transformation in response to perceived ultimacy.

At first reading this definition may seem remote, perhaps even nonsensical. My task now is to convince you that it is appropriate and helpful for the purpose at hand, a study of the world's religions in an academic setting. To that end, we will first look at the three key words in the definition (human, transformation, and ultimacy), then explain the definition as a whole.

Human   The first decision one must make is whether to limit religion to humanity, or to include other, non-human life as religious creatures. Are dogs religious? What about plants? As we shall see, some people steadfastly believe that the answer to these questions is "yes." Others believe just as firmly that only humans may be religious. Our approach to this question is that if non-human beings *are* religious, we have not yet found a sufficiently open form of communication to be able to understand and describe their religions in an academic setting. Therefore, for the purposes of this study, we will stipulate that religion is a *human* phenomenon.

It should be noted that the definition leaves open the issue of whether religion is something humans engage in as individuals or groups. In fact, religion involves humans acting both in isolation and as communities, with some religions seeming to stress one over the other. A definition of religion adopted for a general study should not limit itself to either.

The inclusion of the term "human" in the definition also makes clear that religion is being understood as a *human* activity. This is important because some may wish to stipulate that the focus of activity in a definition of religion must be on the non-human, as in the definition of religion as *"God's"* reaching out to humans." For the purposes of this study, religion is human behavior *in response to* some sort of perceived ultimacy such as God. This enables us to deal with what can be directly observed (that which humans say and do) rather than what is beyond our direct observation (for example, God).

Finally, the word "human" implies that in any religion the observer will find a particular understanding of what it means to be human. We tend to assume that there is one self-evident view of the nature of humanity (which usually reflects our own particular religious perspective). In fact, we will find a diversity of teachings about the essential elements of humanity. Do humans have souls? If so, are these souls unique? Do humans survive physical death? If so, how? What is the relationship between soul and matter in humans? Are humans fundamentally distinct from other living beings? As we study religions we need to be sensitive to the diversity of understandings of "humanity" we are encountering.

Transformation   Our definition emphasizes the dynamic quality of religion. Virtually every sort of human thought, feeling, or action *may* be religious. In order for anything human to qualify as religious, according to our definition, it must be related to a process of *transformation,* meaning *change* from one state of being to another. Transformation implies a situation prior to the change, the process of change itself, and the state that follows the change. Therefore, the single word "transformation" points us to three distinct aspects of religion.

First, religion identifies for individuals and/or groups a situation of life from which change is necessary. Such a state might be called the problem or predicament or, simply, the human situation. One religion might identify "attachment to the material world" as this basic problem; another, "an absence of harmony with the spirit world." We will maintain that a common feature of all religions is the explicit or implicit naming of a state *from* which transformation occurs.

Second, religion implies a state of existence that follows the process of transformation. This end may be expressed as an essentially individual phenomenon, as when a Buddhist monk experiences the blissful state called nirvana. Or it may be a communal situation, such as the new age that some branches of Judaism associate with their belief in the coming of the Messiah. The state may be said to occur for individuals before death, after death, or both. It may come as a result of divine or human

A scribe repairs an ancient Biblical scroll used in Jewish worship, illustrating the reverence for written texts characteristic of many religious traditions.

initiative. All that can be said in general is that religious transformation involves a goal, an ideal state toward which the transformation is directed.

Third, religion involves a process, a means through which the transformation occurs. The "means of transformation" is at the heart of religion. The means often involves identification with myths and legends that tell the story of the religion and the acting out of these myths and legends in the form of rituals. In a religious context, language has transformative power. When invoked properly, or dramatically enacted by those entrusted with authority to do so, the "words of religion" enable people to participate in the process of change. As we shall see, in virtually all religions myth and ritual are present. We will spend more time below discussing these terms because they have specialized meanings, different (especially in the case of myth) from popular usage. At this point, it is sufficient to acknowledge them as critical components in the means of religious transformation.

In addition to narratives and ritual acts, the means may also include direct experiences of that which inspires the transformation (mysticism). The transformation often entails the enactment of a "right" way of relating to others, the world, and one's self (ethics). The means could also involve assent to certain teachings and assertions (belief).

To reiterate a point made earlier, virtually any human activity may become part of the means of transformation. In a real sense, the study of religion is the study of everything, because nothing can be ruled out *a priori* as non-religious. And what is religious in one context may be considered not religious in another. For example, in one setting killing an animal may be a matter of obtaining food, with no religious meaning. However, in other contexts killing an animal may have deeply religious significance, either positive or negative. So, what *are* the criteria for distinguishing a religious phenomenon from other, non-religious human endeavors?

Ultimacy   There is a fairly broad consensus among scholars today that the critical factor in naming something religious is *ultimacy*. Religious phenomena are those associated with that which a person or group perceives as ultimate in their individual and/or communal life. That which is ultimate means whatever is at the focus of life, which defines what life or true reality is for a person or community. We commonly associate religion with ultimacy that people experience or believe in as coming from a higher plane of existence than ordinary, earthly reality. We will call this perceived extraordinary reality "spiritual," as opposed to the "material" reality of the world directly accessible to the physical senses and the rational mind.

Spiritual ultimacy may be expressed in personal language, the language of gods and goddesses. Those religions whose ultimacy is spiritual and personal speak of the ultimate as one or more gods or spirits. Christianity, for example, is such a religion, for its transformation is in response to an ultimacy perceived as a personal deity. Other religions may have a spiritual sense of ultimacy, but view gods and spirits as either non-existent or not supreme. The Tao of Taoism, for example, although ultimate, is not perceived as a god.

The terminology that has developed in Western cultures to describe the various perceptions of spiritual ultimacies reflects a bias in favor of personal description. Belief in the existence of personal gods is called in general *theism*. Belief in the existence of one all-powerful god, to the exclusion of other gods, is called *monotheism*. The belief in the existence of a plurality of personal gods is called *polytheism*. The rejection of belief in personal gods (and, by extension, spiritual reality in general) is known as *atheism*. Less common examples of theism are *henotheism* (belief that many gods exist, but that one is the dominant god) and *pantheism* (the belief that all reality is god). The belief that all reality is infused with spiritual power (either an impersonal spiritual force or personal beings) is called *animism*.

The term "perceived" is used advisedly in our definition of religion. It is present to clarify that the definition is not claiming to identify the *true* ultimacy, only that which different people have responded to as ultimate. A perceptive (no pun intended) reader might object that perception is an exercise of the human mind in relation to this world. How can one perceive that which is, by definition, beyond the realm of ordinary existence? In order to attempt to understand religions with spiritual ultimacies we must be willing to assume, for the purpose of the study, the possibility of perception of *spiritual* reality. At some point each person in our modern, secular culture must decide for herself or himself whether such claimed perception actually occurs, or whether it is merely a misconstruction of some experience susceptible to ordinary explanation. However, the following study will be more engaging and interesting if the reader tries to "bracket off" his or her own assumptions about whether particular kinds of spiritual perception are possible. As we shall see below, such an approach is an aspect of what is called a "phenomenological" study of religion.

Secular Religions?

For most of human history the vast majority of people have responded to what they perceive as spiritual ultimacy, whether personally or impersonally expressed. A characteristic of the modern world is the emergence of perceived ultimacies that are not spiritual, but of the physical or mental world we experience and express as humans. Since "spiritual" is not a necessary component of our definition, we may include such secular ultimacies in the scope of our study and identify them as "secular religions". One of the most prevalent twentieth-century secular religions is Marxism, named after the nineteenth-century economic and social theorist Karl Marx (1818-1883). Although now in serious decline, from the Bolshevik Revolution in Russia in 1917 until the early 1990s Marxism *was* an important and influential secular religion. Marxists perceived ultimacy not as a god or some impersonal spiritual reality or force, but as material reality understood in terms of the laws Karl Marx described. They sought a transformation of society from a state of alienation, caused by economic oppression, to the communal utopia of the classless society. This would inevitably arise, Marxists believed, under the stewardship of the Communist Party. Marxism is perhaps the most famous secular religion, but there are others, now more influential as we move to the end of the twentieth century and beyond. Some would argue that the economic and social theory most directly opposed to Marxism, *laissez-faire* capitalism, is a secular religion now more threatening to spiritual religions than Marxism. Advocates of this position argue that under unrestrained capitalism the pursuit of material wealth can become for some a pattern of ultimacy, which drives out a meaningful sense of spirituality for individuals and societies.

Our contention is that the definition of religion as human transformation in response to perceived ultimacy provides a framework for the objective study of the world's religions. It is inclusive enough to encompass the breadth of spiritual religions, as well as the secular religions we find in the modern world. But it is also narrow enough to provide a series of specific characteristics that enable us to distinguish religious from non-religious phenomena. It would be a good idea for readers to pause now and evaluate this definition. Is it clear? What are its strengths and limitations?

WHY ARE PEOPLE RELIGIOUS?

Many people, probably most people in the world as a whole, *are* religious. Given our definition, one could easily argue that *all* people and groups are religious, for everyone seems to engage in transformation in response to some perceived secular or spiritual ultimacy. Readers may wish to reflect on or discuss the question of the universality of religion now or later in their study. An equally interesting question is *"Why* are people religious?"

One way to answer this question is in terms of the human needs religions meet. First, religion meets psychological needs. Perhaps the most basic need a person has is to feel a sense of identity and belonging. The perception of ultimacy gives an individual an underlying focus, a fundamental awareness of what is, for that person, the truly real. Religion orders life, and gives life a meaning and purpose that conditions all other experiences. Religion helps people cope with the human anxiety of feeling alone and unattached in the world, by linking one's own existence with that which is perceived as the foundation of existence. Some critics, most notably Sigmund Freud (1856-1939), have charged that religion causes people to deal with psychological needs in an unhealthy, immature manner. However, religious people themselves typically believe that without their response to perceived ultimacy, life would be much less fulfilling.

Second, religion meets social needs. Religion is the foundation not only of individual life, but of communal life, creating "ordered reality" for groups who share the same perception of ultimacy. Religions are the most common source of the shared values that are essential to a society.

Religion orders life at all levels of society, from the family to the nation-state. This is most evident in self-consciously religious societies, such as modern Iran. However, even in avowedly secular societies, such as contemporary China, it may be argued that a perceived secular ultimacy is the source of the ordering of national life. Critics, such as those influenced by Karl Marx's view of religion, have charged that religion actually functions as an oppressive force in societies, causing oppressed people to be unaware of their plight or to feel powerless to change it. Others think that religion has been proven to be a powerful agent of social change, creating more just societies. Regardless, religion is indeed a "sacred canopy" that encompasses all levels of a society.

Another way to answer the question of why people are religious is to look not to the *functions* of religion, but to ultimacy itself. People seem to be religious because they feel compelled to be so. They have no choice. They perceive ultimacy and they respond. Asking many religious persons why they are religious is like asking them why they breathe: It is not something about which they feel they have made a voluntary decision. It would seem that if we are to take seriously religious people, we must avoid the temptation to reduce religion to an examination of its psychological or social function. From this perspective, "religion" is a phenomenon in its own right, which has its own reason for being.

WHY SO MANY RELIGIONS?

We have attempted to account for the incredible variety of religions in the world by including in our definition the word "perceived." Peoples' perceptions are conditioned by the times and places in which they live, and especially by their languages. Their perceptions of ultimacy, therefore, are inevitably colored by these and other factors. For example, it is not surprising that when expressing the idea of a "paradise," religions that developed in a desert environment pictured an oasis, with lush trees and plenty of life-giving water. The language of imagery is metaphorical, with words drawn from everyday or extraordinary experience pointing us toward that which is ultimate. For example, in a culture whose form of government is monarchical, the ultimate may be expressed using royal language. God is a king, who rules. Recognizing the metaphorical quality of the language of religions is a key step in understanding, and not being threatened by, the diversity of religions in the world.

Is it possible to penetrate to a deeper level than the metaphorical to find a common *essence* to all religions? Or are the metaphors of religion so essential to the religion's identity that at the most basic level religions are fundamentally different? As you study the religions described in this text, you are invited to develop your own theories about the basic unity or diversity of religions in the world.

Sikh worshippers gather to affirm the shared values that create "ordered reality" for their community.

The conflict in Northern Ireland is one of many in the world with religious roots.

WHY IS THE STUDY OF RELIGION SO IMPORTANT TODAY?

When asked why the study of religion is important, most of us engaged professionally in the field are tempted to give the "Why climb Mount Everest?" answer: because it's there. Religion is pervasive and, from what we are able to gather about the earliest evidence of human life, it always has been. Anyone seeking to understand the world in which he or she lives must confront religion.

More specifically, the study of religion is critical today because of its role in a variety of areas of human life: political, artistic, and economic, to mention a few. Politically, one has only to look at a daily newspaper to see the influence of religion. Whether it be Islam and Judaism in the Middle East, Hinduism and Sikhism in India, or branches of Christianity in Europe and the Americas, the political conflicts of the world have a distinctly religious tone. In the important political question of population control, differing attitudes on the per-

missibility of abortion and forms of birth control, rooted in varying religious perspectives, are a prime ingredient in the debate.

In the arts religion is also a driving force. The clearest examples are in traditionally religious cultures. One has only to stroll through a museum featuring European paintings from the Middle Ages to witness how pervasive was the influence of religion on art in that place and era. Today, the artistic influence of religion is less obvious, but it should not be ignored. Listen to any type of contemporary music and ask how varying perceptions of ultimacy are being expressed in the songs you are hearing!

Economic decisions are rooted in peoples' perceptions of ultimacy. How resources are viewed and used in a society depends on a people's religion. For example, an indigenous society views and relates to non-human animals in a very different way than a materialistic society. The difference in the resource use is rooted in religion. Indigenous people perceive ultimacy as present in all of nature, so the maintenance of harmony with nature is critical to how they draw upon nature to meet their daily needs. In a society where material ultimacy dominates, nature is typically viewed as "stuff" to be used however humans wish. As demonstrated by the early-twentieth-century students of the relationship between religion and economic life, Max Weber and R. H. Tawney, the rise of capitalism in Europe was linked to the emergence of Protestant Christianity. One can hardly understand economic issues without attention to their religious underpinnings!

Throughout this text, as we study the religions of the world, we will focus particular attention on how religions respond to some of the major political, social, ethical, and economic issues of the modern world.

In addition to these objective reasons for studying religion, there are subjective factors to consider. Why is it important for *you* to study religion? You may or may not consider yourself a religious person; you probably make that determination on the basis of your participation in a structured religious organization. Even if you think of yourself as non-religious, it is nearly impossible for you to avoid religious questions. Who does not contemplate his or her place in the universe? Who does not wonder what "life" is and whether it extends beyond physical death? This study will enable you to confront how people throughout history have answered these and other fundamental issues. If you are a self-consciously religious person, you will have the opportunity to compare your answers to the basic questions of life with those of other religious people. The process may not be comfortable, but it will be educational in more than a detached way.

Finally, we should consider what might be called the "moral imperative" for studying religion. We live on an ever-smaller planet, which is shrinking because of both the growing numbers of humans inhabiting the earth and the amazing communications technology that links even the most remote regions. If the human species is to survive we must learn to live together and cooperate in solving the environmental and political problems we face. The key to cooperation is understanding the "other." How can we hope to understand other peoples unless we are willing to study their religions, their responses to perceived ultimacy? It may sound melodramatic, but it is arguably true that our future depends on peoples' willingness to understand sympathetically other peoples' religions.

WHAT IS THE RELATIONSHIP BETWEEN SCIENCE AND RELIGION TODAY?

A commonly held perspective in the late twentieth century in the West (particularly in academic circles) is that science has replaced religion. While one may want to make the case that science should supplant religion, the pervasiveness of religion shows that this has not yet happened for the vast majority of humans. In the modern world, then, both science and religion are present. Here we will summarize only a few of the different perspectives on how science and religion relate.

Many people believe that religion and science are incompatible ways of approaching the world. Some religious people stubbornly reject scientific explanations that they believe conflict with the religious. Some Christians, for example, reject the biological theory of evolution; they believe it contradicts the Biblical teaching of creation in six days, which they believe to be a true description of how life originated. On the other side, some scientists refuse to acknowledge the legitimacy of religion because of their perception that religion always depends on supernatural explanations. Because science assumes natural explanations, they contend that those who seek to be scientific in their outlook must reject religion. For example, some scientists argue that because the Bible represents a pre-scientific view of the world, the Bible is at best antiquated and at worst dangerous because it thwarts the scientific work necessary to cope with the complex problems of life today.

Others stake out different territories for science and religion. "Good fences make good neighbors," and so it is with these two different ways of looking at the world, some would say. Religion begins where science ends, it might be argued. Science helps us understand the world naturally;

religion examines the underlying causes and purposes of existence. For example, the Biblical story of creation deals with questions such as "Why does the universe exist?" and "What is the fundamental relationship between God and life?" Scientists studying origins are silent on these questions, focusing instead on issues such as "How did the universe come into existence?"

A third position is that science and religion are neither opposed nor separate, but are rather interrelated and complementary ways to approach life. From this point of view, both science and religion are trying to respond to the mysteries of existence. At some points, the responses may diverge, but increasingly, advocates of this position would argue, science and religion are coming to the same basic insights from their different directions. For example, some modern physicists think that their discoveries about the basic state of indeterminacy or flux in nature accord with the teaching of religions such as Buddhism and Taoism about the fundamentally fluid nature of reality. On the other hand, some religious thinkers (especially in Judaism and Christianity) are drawing on scientific theories such as evolution to explore new ways of perceiving ultimacy. The recent discovery of evidence corroborating the "big bang" theory has suggested to some in both the scientific and religious communities that there must have been a spiritual force that caused the cosmos to begin in a primordial explosion.

WHAT SPECIAL TERMS ARE USED IN THE STUDY OF RELIGION?

Every discipline has its own specialized language into which those experiencing the field for the first time must be initiated. Religious studies is no different. While we will try to avoid unnecessary "jargon" in this work, we will utilize some of the key terms scholars in the field have developed. Here is a list of terms associated with the study of religion in general. They will be used throughout our discussion. All are defined in the glossary at the end of the book. It would be wise at this point to check the meanings of those terms which may not be familiar to you.

agnosticism	heretic	reality
asceticism	immanent	revelation
atheism	immortality	rites of passage
canon	liberalism	ritual
conversion	magic	sacred
cosmology	meditation	sacrifice
cosmos	modernism	salvation
demons	monasticism	secular
divination	monism	soul, spirit
doctrine	monotheism	spiritual
dogma	mysticism	symbol
dualism	myth	theism
eschatology	orthodox	theology
ethics	pantheism	tradition
fatalism	polytheism	traditionalism
fundamentalism	profane	transcendent

WHAT ARE SYMBOLS, MYTHS, AND RITUALS?

Because of their central importance in the study of religion we need to clarify more fully three related terms: symbol, myth, and ritual.

Symbols

In general, a *symbol* is something that stands for something else. Drivers in the United States know that an octagonal red sign at an intersection means "Stop!" The sign symbolizes the concept of "stopping" within the rules established for driving. Symbols may be objects, like the sign, or they may be gestures or sounds. When a baseball umpire raises his or her right hand, a strike is being called. When a movie director says "Cut!," the actors know that they should stop the scene. Religion is full of symbols in this general sense: objects, gestures, and sounds that reveal some aspect of whatever is ultimate in the religion. For example, in Hinduism pictures of deities often show the god as having a number of arms as a visual way of expressing the power of the god. In Buddhism, pictures or statues of the Buddha often show him raising his hand in a distinctive gesture that communicates the idea that those who follow his path need not be afraid. When a Jew says *"Shema' yisrael..."* ("Hear, O Israel..."), he or she is articulating a belief in the unity of God.

However, many students of religion suggest a somewhat more specialized meaning for the term "symbol" when applying it to religion. More than simply representing something else, a religious symbol enables people to participate in that to which the symbol points. For example, when Hindus walk around (circumambulate) the object that symbolizes a particular deity, they are actually experiencing the sacred reality of that god. When a Roman Catholic priest lifts the host and says the prescribed words, the wafer is not a mere *representation* of the body of Christ. When worshippers take the bread, they believe they are actually receiving Christ. Although religious people often disagree on the precise meaning of symbolic "participation," the belief that symbols (whether simple or elaborate) are essential to their having contact with that which they deem ultimate is held in common. In studying a religion, awareness of the rich symbols present and their particular usage is critical to understanding.

Myths

The dominant usage of the term "myth" today and its specialized meaning in the study of religion are very different. In current general usage, myths are "false stories" because they conflict with what we know empirically to be true. For example, we might say that the belief that casual contact spreads the AIDS virus is a "myth," because scientific research has shown that to be untrue. To say in response to someone's story "That's a myth!" is to denigrate the account, relegating it to the realm of the unbelievable.

In the study of religion the term *myth* has a specialized meaning. In our study we will use myth for stories about whatever people perceive to be ultimate, which they therefore accept without question as *true* reality. Since myths deal with ultimacy, they stand outside ordinary, profane space and time. Myths are often called "foundational stores" because they typically function to create the basic patterns of order (cosmos) for those who believe them. They are paradigmatic, meaning that they reveal the way life is to be understood and lived by those who are grasped by the particular ultimacy with which the myth is concerned.

In the popular understanding, only "primitive," now discredited religions had myths. They may be interesting to study (as are the myths surrounding the Olympian gods) but they are now "dead." Contemporary students of religion typically take the position that *every* religion (whether spiritual or secular) has myths, for every religion has narratives about that which is ultimate—foundational stories that are at the heart of the religion.

One of the most common types of myths is the "myth of origins" (cosmogonic myth), which recounts the story of how that which is ultimate gave rise to all experienced reality. For example, for Judaism and Christianity the first two chapters of Genesis are a myth of origins, a story about the beginnings of space and time that reveals the nature of the cosmos created by God. Virtually every religion has a myth of origins that fulfills a similar function.

Other myths relate to that toward which ordinary time is moving, rather than that from which it comes. They are called "eschatological myths," and they are particularly common in the religions that hold a linear view of time. For example, the Christian Bible ends with a book that tells the myth of the end time. Like the Book of Revelation, most end-time myths tell of how the order present in the time of origins will be completely restored at the end of time. Religions that take a cyclical view of time, like Hinduism, still have mythic accounts of the end of the current age, which will be destroyed before the next cosmic cycle begins.

Because they "stand outside ordinary time," myths speak of a time that is eternally present and repeatable (see Eliade 1959: 68–113). That is, if the story of the myth is not limited to a particular time, then it is equally true and real at the particular moment at which it is told. The telling of a myth does not relate to something that happened within time (although myths may relate to historical events) as much as it draws the eternal into the present reality. For example, for Jewish people the story of the deliverance of the people of ancient Israel from slavery in Egypt (told in the Book of Exodus in the Hebrew Bible) is a foundational story or myth. Although the story of the deliverance presumably occurred in some form within time, the story about these events is a myth, which speaks of how God interacts with his people at all times. When the story is recounted, those who accept it as myth experience it not only as an account of what "happened," but what continually "happens."

One of the critical steps in the study of any religion, spiritual or secular, is to ask "What are the myths?" Myths are not confined to religions with spiritual ultimacies. So-called secular religions have foundational stories that order the cosmos they inhabit, and eschatological stories that reveal that toward which time is moving. For example, Marxism tells mythic versions of historical events to show how the phenomenon of class struggle keeps repeating itself. It also envisions the "classless society," which will represent the culmination of ordinary, class-conscious history. The vibrancy of a religion can be measured in part by the power of the religion's myths to continue to lay the foundations for ordered reality for the people who tell them. Living myths are not only stories told but realities lived. They provide the models for living, for groups as a whole as well as for individuals.

The final point to be made about myths for now is that they are not fixed. Myths take on new aspects as they are told and retold. For example, the myth of origins in the first book of the Hebrew Bible (Genesis 1) was retold with new nuances by a Christian writer in the first chapter of the Gospel of John in the Christian New Testament.

Rituals

A term equally important in the study of religion in general is *ritual*. If myths are stories outside time and space, which order reality for those who accept them as true, then rituals are those actions within time and space that bring the power of myth into the lives of the people. We may define ritual as symbolic action that enables persons to participate in transformation in response to ulti-

macy. The source of ritual is myth. Rituals are often, one might say, "myths enacted." Myths express in word and image; rituals dramatize the ordering of cosmos in terms of performance. For example, if the story of the deliverance of Egypt is a basic Jewish myth, then the Passover celebration is the ritual through which the myth is enacted and the people may participate in the transformation in response to the ultimacy perceived in the myth. Through participation in the ritual the individual or community steps outside ordinary time and space and enters, during the ritual, into sacred, ordered time and space.

Rituals create "sacred space," areas recognized or set apart temporarily or permanently from ordinary usage to become arenas for the experience of the ultimate. Whether a magnificent cathedral or a small home shrine, it is the conducting of rituals that transforms these spaces into "true space," where encounters with ultimacy order and give meaning to life.

Rituals order time, creating moments amidst ordinary time when the sacred enters in to create cosmos. Some ritual observances are recurrent, creating a calendar for those who share the same perception of ultimacy. For example, in traditional Christian cultures the year is ordered according to the series of festivals that enact the Christian myth (such as Easter and Christmas). "The periodicity of ritual time...ensures the perpetual grounding of world in its myth. Through daily, weekly, monthly, or annual ritual time, myth is recoverable" (Paden 1988: 101). In most religions there are "great" festivals that order the entire year at the time of transition from one year to another. Typically, there is a time of purification, involving restriction and denial, followed by a time of celebration and rebirth. For example, the Christian "new year" is created by the combination of the purificatory period called Lent, climaxing in death on Good Friday, followed by the time of rebirth at Easter.

In addition, there are other festivals of renewal on a monthly, weekly, or daily basis. In many indigenous religions, and in traditional practice in other religions, all of time is sacralized through the daily repetition of rituals.

Periodic rituals are for groups, but also for individuals. In most religions individuals celebrate their birthday, marriage day, or the death of a family member as recurrent times of renewal. For the times of transition in the life of the individual (birth, adulthood, marriage, death) there are "rites of passage" to mark as well as order these moments.

Today rituals are often dismissed as a waste of time by those for whom the associated myths have no power. However, look at your own life or the lives of others and ask yourself if you and they do not have certain "rituals" that order life. For some people in modern, materialistic society the weekend is ritual time, with the Friday or Saturday night party serving as a focus and frame for the experience of "true reality." At the party they "step outside ordinary time" and enter into a transformed reality that creates a sense (at least for a time) of meaningfulness.

WHAT IS THE APPROACH TO RELIGION IN THIS TEXT?

The Phenomenological Approach: The Quest for Understanding

Earlier we identified this text's approach to religion as essentially phenomenological. We will now explain the phenomenological method more fully as it will be implemented in this study and compare it to other ways religion may be studied.

Simply stated, the phenomenological approach to religion is a method that attempts to understand religion from the perspective of religious persons themselves. Perhaps you have heard the popular saying, derived from a Native American proverb, that you should not judge a person until you have walked a mile in his or her moccasins. The phenomenological method, in the sense used here, holds that "understanding" precedes "evaluation," and that a primary goal when studying religion is to understand the religion as much as possible "from the inside." That is an idealistic, perhaps utopian, objective. How can we possibly perceive ultimacy as others do? Because we cannot fully attain the phenomenological goal does not mean we should not try. What is required is a willingness to "bracket off" one's own assumptions about religion in general and other religions in particular long enough to see the world from another point of view. We must attempt to let religions speak for themselves and listen sensitively to what we hear.

However, it is important to realize that the phenomenological method, and others to be introduced below, all reflect a modern, Western bias of seeking to abstract the fundamental principles about religions as a way of understanding them. No matter how sympathetic our portrayal may be, what you will be reading is one author's attempt to interpret religious phenomena *in terms meaningful to him and, ideally, to his readers.* Although I have attempted to bracket off my own perspective on the issues being addressed, it will inevitably affect my descriptions. Readers should be sensitive to how the author's and their own ways of looking at the world are shaping their understanding.

A Framework for Understanding

The phenomenological approach seeks more than a superficial awareness of religions; it is not merely the accumulation of raw data about what religious people say and do. Gathering data about religions is the starting point, and in the pages that follow you will find a great deal of information about the world's religions. However, to understand religion we must try to penetrate the surface and look for the structures of meaning, the patterns that organize the facts into coherent "worlds."

We will contend that when an observer looks for such patterns, what emerges is a framework that is present in all religions. The framework includes the religion's responses to a variety of questions raised by the perception of ultimacy. That framework forms the basis we will use in attempting to understand the distinctive nature of each religion. These are the six dimensions of the framework we will use in trying to understand religions:

1. problem—each religion expresses a fundamental human dilemma posed by the perception of ultimacy.

2. cause—for each religion there is a basic source of the underlying human problem.

3. reality—given its perception of ultimacy, each religion has a particular way of ordering the world. "Time" and "space" can have different meanings in different religions, as we will see.

4. end—each religion identifies an ideal state, toward which the transformation occasioned by perceived ultimacy moves.

5. means—what, in each religion, enables transformation to occur? How do people respond to perceived ultimacy? What are the symbols, myths, and rituals through which ultimacy is experienced?

6. sacred—this is, in our usage, a synonym for "the ultimate." At the heart of any religion is that which is perceived as ultimate or sacred. Thus, the question of the expression of what is sacred is at the heart of our study.

Because an understanding of human nature is present in each of these elements separately, and in all of them together, we will give attention to this important issue at various points in our analysis.

Our approach to these topics will be twofold. On the one hand, when we summarize the basic teachings of each religion, we will use the above framework. On the other hand, included as inserts in each of the chapters are selections from the sacred texts of the religions that respond to many of these topics. In Chapter Two we will clarify more fully some of the basic human questions implied in this framework.

Other Approaches to the Study of Religion

How does the phenomenological approach differ from other methods of study? The study of religion may be divided into two basic branches, based on the fundamental purpose being pursued: evaluation or understanding. The purpose of evaluation is to ascertain the "truth" about religion in general or religions in particular.

One method of study that seeks as its primary goal the truth about religions might be called the *"religious approach to the study of religion."* As we have already acknowledged, any observer inevitably looks

at other religions from the perspective of his or her own perception of ultimacy. In this method, however, the student has as a fundamental goal of the study an assessment of the truth of other religions from this point of view. For example, if I am a Christian I might examine other religions without bracketing off my own assumptions about what is true in religion. I then study other religions to see the degree to which they accord with Christian truth as I understand it. The same approach may be taken with any religion as a starting point. Or I might start my study from the perspective that the assumption that spiritual reality exists is not true. I then study religions that claim spiritual ultimacies in order to refute their claims. Since I hold as ultimate the assertion that there is no spiritual reality, this perspective still falls under the heading of a religious approach to religion (using our definition of religion).

Another approach with an evaluative goal is the *"philosophy of religion."* Here, however, the truth claims of religions are assessed from the standpoint of their susceptibility to being proven or disproven on the basis of rational argument. Does God (or any spiritual ultimacy) exist? A philosopher of religion will carefully analyze each of the terms of this assertion to determine the degree to which the assertion may be said to have a rational meaning. Like other disciplines, philosophy has a variety of schools of interpretation, each of which approaches religion from a different perspective. What they hold in common is an interest in whether religion or religions may be said to be "true" (whatever "truth" might mean, according to the particular philosophical school). A philosophical approach to the study of religion is fascinating, but it is not the task we have set for ourselves in this work.

Other methods besides the phenomenological have as a primary goal understanding, rather than evaluating, religion. They are the historical, the functional, and the comparative approaches. The *historical approach* seeks to understand the religions as they have come into existence and developed through time. A historical study will typically examine the origins of a particular religion, its earliest expression, its spread and often divisions, up to the present.

A *functional study* seeks to understand the function or role religion plays in another human context. Psychologists of religion typically study the function of religion in the makeup and development of individuals. Sociologists of religion examine the role religion plays in human groups, from the family to the entire society. Anthropologists of religion engage in a method of study functional in intent, but often phenomenological in spirit. They typically focus on the place of religion in the cultures of indigenous peoples, through a process of participation in and observation of the people of that culture. Anthropologists also apply their observational and interpretive skills to other existing cultures. The common denominator in the functional approach is that the primary interest is in understanding the role of religion in the life of an individual, a society, or a culture. The functional approach overlaps with the evaluative when the question of whether religion is functional or dysfunctional in the various contexts is raised.

By contrast, the phenomenological approach focuses on religion per se, seeking an understanding of the structures of meaning within the religion. This is seen by those who take this approach as a necessary prerequisite to the study of the function of religion, or an analysis of the truth of religion.

The *comparative method* of studying religion seeks to understand religion by looking for that which is common among religions. Its basic question is whether there is an "essence" that all religions share. The method also seeks to penetrate differences in imagery to determine the ways in which the fundamental patterns of religious expression are the same.

An Overview of the Rest of the Text

In the present study our basic approach *is* phenomenological. Our goal is to let each religion speak for itself, presenting it in a way that could be affirmed by the people who themselves perceive ultimacy in this manner. However, we will draw on other methods, especially the historical and comparative, in the process.

In each chapter we will use the historical approach in telling the basic story of each religion, following (for the most part) its chronological development. We will also use the comparative

framework presented above as we seek to understand the basic teachings of each religion and their responses to essential human and contemporary ethical issues.

We have organized our presentation of the religions of the world in the following manner. First, we will examine the "indigenous religions," which find expression throughout the world as the earliest form of religion. Fortunately, some indigenous religions survive, and so we study them not only as the original and most basic type of religion, but in their contemporary expression. We will therefore look at the characteristics of indigenous religions in general, give an overview of indigenous religions in Africa and North America, focus on the religions of the

FIGURE 1.1

Adherents of the World's Religions and Non-Religious Population

RELIGION	NUMBER OF ADHERENTS
Christianity	1.83 billion
Roman Catholics	1.03 billion
Protestant	374 million
Orthodox	170 million
Anglican	74.9 million
Other	188 million
Islam	971 million
Non-Religious	876 million
Hinduism	733 million
Buddhism	315 million
Atheism	240 million
Chinese Folk Religion	187 million
New Religions	143 million
Tribal Religions˙	96.6 million
Sikhism	18.8 million
Judaism	17.8 million
Shamanism˙	10.5 million
Confucianism	6 million
Jainism	3.8 million
Shinto	3.2 million
Other	18.6 million
˙Combined in this work as "Indigenous Religions"	

Excerpt from 1993 Britannica Book of the Year. *Copyright © 1993 by Encyclopaedia Britannica, Inc. Reprinted with permission.*

Yoruba people of Africa and the Oglala Lakota of North America, and finally discuss the impact of indigenous religions on other religions.

Next, we will turn to the major geographic areas of the world to study the religions that originated in and dominated these regions in the historical period: the religions of South and Southeast Asia (Hinduism, Theravada Buddhism, Jainism, and Sikhism); the religions of East Asia (Taoism, Confucianism, Mahayana Buddhism, and Shinto); and the religions of the Middle East, Europe, and the Americas (Zoroastrianism, Judaism, Christianity, and Islam).

Finally, we will examine the "new religions" of the world; that is, religions that have developed in the last century in the context of the major religious traditions discussed above or that have emerged afresh. In this section we will give attention to the controversial issue of "secular religions" such as Marxism and capitalism. Unfortunately, we will be able to treat only a few of the myriad of new religions present in the world today, but enough to give a sense of their variety. We will conclude with various views of what the future holds for the world's religions.

Throughout our survey of the world's religions, we will intersperse excerpts from the recorded oral traditions and sacred writings of the world's religions that respond to basic human questions of identity, destiny, reality, and morality.

In the final section of each chapter we will present how the world's religions have responded and are responding to some of the major issues of the modern world: the ecological crisis, war, capital punishment, abortion, economic justice, gender roles and the status of women, and homosexuality.

At the end of each chapter we will raise a series of questions for group discussion and/or individual reflection. They are not review or study questions. Instead, these are questions with no right or wrong answers. They are intended to provoke thought and conversation. If they work, this text will become a dialogue between the reader and the religions being studied, or a "town meeting" of readers, rather than just a monologue by the author.

There is nothing more fascinating and rewarding than a serious, open conversation about religion! There is also nothing more fraught with the potential for misunderstanding and personal animosity. Please be respectful and gentle with one another if you are using this text as the basis for talking about religion in a group of persons with diverse attitudes about religion.

Two concluding comments about this study of religion are necessary before we actually embark on it. First, to reiterate an important point: No student may step fully outside his or her own religious identity when examining others! None of us is able to shed the cultural, social, and psychological influences that have been a part of the formation of our experience of the world. That holds true for the author as well as for readers. I am aware that my decision to approach religion phenomenologically, with support from the historical and comparative methods, has been shaped by my own particular journey.

Your response to what you have read so far and what is to come will be guided by your own set of experiences with religion. The only real antidotes for the inadvertent blindness sometimes caused by preconditioning are self-awareness, self-criticism, and humility. If we allow ourselves to be aware of how our own presuppositions are affecting our understanding, if we constantly ask ourselves whether we are being fair in our statements about what we are studying, and if we acknowledge that we ourselves do not yet have a complete grasp of the truth, the study will be an effective and rewarding one.

Second, establishing understanding as the primary goal does not mean that evaluation is not important. In fact, we could not avoid evaluating what we are studying even if we wanted to. My perspective as the author is that I should not do the work of evaluation for the reader. If this text is being used in the setting of a classroom, I hope that evaluative discussions will be allowed by the teacher. The class will be much more interesting if you not only seek to understand religion, but engage in an open and frank (but respectful) discussion about the truth of religion and religions. However, I encourage you not to short-circuit the process. Before you move to the stage of evaluation, make sure you have first tried hard to understand the religion you are judging!

CHAPTER SUMMARY

The legendary founder of Taoism (see Chapter Eight), Lao Tzu, is reputed to have said, "The journey of a thousand miles must begin with a single step." If you complete a study of the world's religions, even an introductory one such as this book intends, you will feel as though you have journeyed at least a thousand miles by foot! There is much ground to cover! The purpose of this first chapter has been to help you get started in your journey.

In this chapter we first discussed the problems associated with defining religion and whether developing a definition of religion is a necessary starting point for a study of religion. We adopted as our working definition of religion for this study "human transformation in response to perceived ultimacy," briefly explaining each of its elements.

We then asked: "Why are people religious?" "Why so many religions in the world?" "Why is the study of religion so important today?" and "What is the relationship between religion and science today?" In each case we reflected on various possible answers. Next we listed some of the most important terms used in the study of religion. We then focused special attention on three concepts

central to the study of religion: symbol, myth, and ritual.

We next turned our attention to the method of study employed in this text, explaining that the basic approach is phenomenological (which entails trying to let the religions speak for themselves as much as possible). Using our definition of religion as a basis, we also developed a framework for understanding religion, which identifies the following elements: the problem or basic human dilemma; the cause or source of this dilemma; the perception of reality or way of ordering the world of time and space; the end or ideal state; the means of transformation; and the description of the sacred or ultimacy perceived in the religion.

We distinguished between study of religion for the purpose of evaluation and understanding. Approaches that focus on understanding include the phenomenological, functional (psychological, sociological, or anthropological), historical, and comparative methods. We explained that we will draw on the latter two to complement the phenomenological approach in this text.

The chapter concluded with an overview of the rest of the text. You are ready now to embark on what will be a fascinating journey, if you go into it with curiosity and an open mind.

QUESTIONS FOR DISCUSSION AND REFLECTION

1. As you begin a study of the religions of the world, what is your basic attitude toward religion? Do you consider yourself a religious person? Why or why not? Write down a brief sketch of your experiences with religion (including both positive and negative experiences). How have these experiences shaped the attitude you have toward religion now? Now try to explain your attitude to someone else and try to understand that person's understanding of religion. Discuss various attitudes in a group.

2. How many different religions have you *directly* encountered? What was the nature of your

encounter(s)? Discuss with others these encounters and what you feel you learned from them.

3. What do you hope or expect to derive from a serious study of religion? Jot down the general and specific questions you have right now about religion. In a group situation, share these questions and discuss why you want to pursue them. Keep a record of the questions generated for reference during your study.

4. Do you think that a study of religion should include "secular religions," as we have proposed in this chapter? Why or why not?

5. Are science and religion in opposition to one another, concerned with different things, or complementary? Take a provisional point of view on this question and defend it in a discussion with others.

6. Pick up a major newspaper or a weekly news magazine and make a list of the stories that reflect the influence of religion. Share what you discovered in a group setting, using it as a basis for discussing the extent and depth of the role religion plays in the modern world. Is the role of religion today essentially positive or negative, in your estimation? How well does the media cover religion?

7. Consult the "framework for understanding religion" in this chapter and give your own provisional responses to each of the elements. What, for example, do *you* think is the basic human problem and the cause of that problem? If you find you do not have clear responses, why do you suppose that is the case?

SOURCES AND SUGGESTIONS FOR FURTHER STUDY

CAMPBELL, JOSEPH (WITH BILL MOYERS), 1988 *The Power of Myth.* New York: Doubleday. Based on the PBS television series of the same name; a reflection on the universality of spiritual themes by one of the exponents of the cross-cultural study of myth and ritual as a way to probe the psychological depths of human nature. Other popular works by Campbell include *The Hero with a Thousand Faces* and *The Masks of God.*

CUNNINGHAM, LAWRENCE, ET AL., 1991 *The Sacred Quest: An Invitation to the Study of Religion.* New York: Macmillan. A very accessible introduction to the phenomenological study of religion.

ELIADE, MIRCEA, 1959 *The Sacred and the Profane: The Nature of Religion,* tr. Willard Trask. New York: Harper & Row. The basic work of one of the most important proponents of the phenomenological approach to religion. Other works by this leading figure in the twentieth-century study of religion include *Cosmos and History* (1954), *Myth and Reality* (1963), *Patterns in Comparative Religion* (1963), and *Rites and Symbols of Initiation* (1965).

1987 *The Encyclopedia of Religion.* New York: Macmillan. Eliade served before his death as general editor of this most important reference work for the study of religion. Full of articles on all aspects of religion in general and of particular religions, it should be in the reference section of all libraries!

HICK, JOHN, 1989 *An Interpretation of Religion: Human Responses to the Transcendent.* New Haven, Conn.: Yale University Press. A study of the function of religion in individual transformation from ego-centeredness to reality-centeredness.

PADEN, WILLIAM, 1988 *Religious Worlds: The Comparative Study of Religions.* Boston: Beacon Press. A competent overview of the comparative method, with attention to basic categories in the study of religion.

STRENG, FREDERICK J., 1985 *Understanding Religious Life,* 3rd ed. Belmont, Calif.: Wadsworth. An introduction to religion focusing on the ways in which people are religious (personally and socially) and how religious meaning is expressed.

CHAPTER 2

An Orientation to Religious Responses to Basic Human Questions and Contemporary Ethical Issues

INTRODUCTION: WHY?

What distinguishes humans from other animals? Like other animals, we are mortal—we are born, we live, and we die. Close observers of other primates tell us that in many ways (perhaps most), we humans are no different from chimpanzees or gorillas. We are social creatures who develop strong ties to other members of our species. We have emotions and thoughts, and we have learned to adapt to changing environments. What apparently makes humans unique is our ability to reflect on our condition, to ask the question "Why?" We ask why things are as they are, and we reflect on how they might be different.

Our uniquely human capacity to raise and reflect on questions of meaning and purpose may be understood from the perspective of religion. Our perception of ultimacy is intimately related to the way we respond to what might be called "basic human questions" such as these:

Questions of Human Identity
  1. *Who are we as humans?*
  2. *What is the basic human dilemma?*

Questions of Human Destiny
  1. *Why are we here?*
  2. *What happens after death?*

Cosmic Questions
  1. *How did the world come into being?*
  2. *What is the destiny of the universe?*

Questions of Morality
  1. *What is right living?*
  2. *What is our obligation to others?*
  3. *What are our obligations to non-human life?*

Questions about the Sacred
  1. *What is the sacred?*
  2. *How is the sacred made known?*

In the sacred traditions, oral and written, of the world's religions these questions nearly always form the background of the teaching passed from generation to generation. One fruitful way to penetrate to the core of each religion and to compare religions is to sample the various ways sacred legends and writings respond to these questions. As we survey the various religions found in the world today, we will include selected excerpts from the sacred texts (written or oral) of each religion which respond to these questions. In this chapter we will introduce each of the basic human questions and the range of responses you will encounter as you study each of the world's religions.

Religions respond not only to timeless questions such as these but also to the issues raised by the circumstances in which they find themselves, to contemporary ethical issues. Among the many such questions we might consider late in the twentieth century, we will examine how the living religions of the world address the following current issues:

the ecological crisis	euthanasia
war	economic justice
capital punishment	gender roles and
abortion	the status of women
	homosexuality

In this chapter we will offer a broad analysis of the dimension of each of these basic human questions and contemporary issues to set the stage for our discussion in subsequent chapters of how specific religions are responding to them.

BASIC HUMAN QUESTIONS

Questions of Human Identity

We might call our uniquely human ability to reflect on ourselves the blessing and curse of our human nature. Without the ability for self-reflection, we would not be able to imagine ourselves differently than we are. We would probably not have been able to develop in the amazing way we have in the relatively short time we have been on planet Earth. We would not have produced the diverse cultures and religions that make human life so rich. However, self-reflection leaves us with a gnawing sense of uncertainty. The more advanced we become materially, the less certainty we seem to have about our identity as humans.

Religions have always wrestled with just these sorts of questions of human identity, providing an array of responses that ground them in a sense of ultimacy about life. In the chapters that follow you will encounter many of the answers religions have given to two of the many basic questions of human identity: Who are we? What is the basic human dilemma? In an age of increasing uncertainty, they may provide some helpful insights for readers who are confronting these questions for the first time or readers who are reassessing their perspectives.

The religions we call "spiritual religions" share a sense that we are more than a collection of molecules, that we have a dimension to our identity as humans that is not reducible to our physical bodies. For many spiritual religions, such as many of the indigenous religions, that dimension is best understood as a spiritual nature, a "soul" or "spirit" that shares in some way or reflects the nature of the spiritual reality that is ultimate in the cosmos. Some spiritual religions (for example, Jainism) maintain that each soul (human and non-human) is unique; others, such as some schools of Hinduism, claim that once we penetrate to the essence of our nature we discover that our true identity manifests the spiritual nature of all reality. Buddhism is unique in the claim that teachings of an "eternal self" actually inhibit our spiritual advancement; at our core there is "no eternal self." That may seem a paradoxical assertion for a spiritual religion, but such ambiguities are part of what makes religions so fascinating!

While "secular religions" typically dismiss the notion of a soul, they too have teachings about our fundamental identity as humans. Marxism, for example, maintains that our basic identity is economic; we derive meaning from our capacity to create material value.

As with other basic human questions, we will not be able to include an excerpt from every religion studied on the question "Who are we?" But you will find enough to sample the variety of religious responses to this very fundamental issue.

Questions of Human Origins and Destiny

Why are we humans here on earth and where are we headed? Each religion directly or indirectly responds to the mystery of our beginning and our ending. The stories of why we exist as humans are some of the most intriguing found in sacred oral and written literature. We will sample myths of humankind coming into existence when the creator god forms the first human from the earth and breathes life into the creature; or the tale of humans emerging from another world, beneath and prior to the present world; and many others.

In a variety of ways the religions of the world describe a joy and bliss that are the culmination of human existence transformed in response to ultimacy. Most religions describe this state as manifest in earthly existence, but with an important component beyond this life.

Spiritual religions speak of an ultimacy not limited by ordinary time and space. Whatever is ultimate in these religions is not terminated by human death. To be transformed in response to this ultimacy is to experience a state of being beyond death. However, each religion has its own way of expressing what happens after death. Is there a soul that survives our demise? If so, what state or states of existence await this soul? Is life beyond death a reward or punishment for behavior in this life? If there is no unique soul that survives death, what happens? From the mammoth quantity of sacred literature dealing with the afterlife we have selected a small but representative sampling.

Cosmic Questions

Religions not only respond to questions of human identity and destiny, they also address questions of cosmic origins and ends. Virtually every religion has its own story or stories that tell of the ultimate beginnings of the universe. Students of religion call these accounts "cosmogonies," for they relate the origins of the known cosmos. Most religions also look to the future of the cosmos and envision what will happen when the world as it is now experienced comes to an end.

The religions of the world are fairly clearly divided on questions of cosmic origins and ends. Is there just one beginning and one end? Or is there a cosmic process in which after each end of the cosmos, another beginning follows in an eternal cycle? Religions that originated in India view the cosmos as a continuing circle in which all life participates until liberation from the cycle is attained. Religions that originated in the Middle East speak of just one beginning, when God created the heavens and the earth, and one fulfillment, in which the cosmic process will be brought to completion and the final age of harmony begins. Indigenous religions and the religions that originated in China are not so easily classified, although they tend more toward the cyclical than the linear understanding.

As many observers have noted, the stories of origins and endings establish patterns that structure life in the present. Sacred time and space are formed by accounts of cosmic creation and completion. Humans seeking to order their lives in response to ultimacy inevitably look to these stories for guidance, so that in their own acts of creation and culmination they follow the models established at the beginning or those that will be followed at the end.

Throughout the survey in the following chapters, the religions will speak themselves in response to the fundamental questions of how the world came into being and how it will end. The natural question is "How can we know which story is the true one, with so many different versions of where the cosmos came from and where it is going?" Perhaps we should ask instead "Must one choose among the stories?" If the stories are read as literal descriptions of events, then one must choose. But, what if we considered their "truth" not to be a function of their facticity or historicity? What if we evaluated their truth as being their power to reveal to us basic insights about life and their ability to deepen our understanding of the mysteries of the cosmos? Then we could draw an unlimited number of truths from them, without having to decide which *one* is true and which others are false.

Questions of Morality

Religions teach people how to live rightly in the world. "Rightly," from a religious perspective, means in harmony with or as instructed by perceived ultimacy. Each religion identifies ways of relating to other people and to the world in general that are based on its perception of ultimacy. For those religions in which the ultimate is impersonal, the way of living rightly is determined by a sense of order (a cosmic law, principle, or process, such as the Tao of Taoism). The religions that relate to a personal ultimacy (God or gods) speak of a path of life revealed by the deity or deities as the right way to live. These religions may also identify a fundamental moral law, but it is the deity who makes known what constitutes that law.

In excerpts from the sacred stories of the world's religions we will learn what religions teach about the following moral questions: What is right living? How should we act in relationship to others? How should we act in relationship to the non-human world?

Questions About the Sacred

That which religions perceive as ultimate we have called in this work the "sacred." In most religions the sacred is spiritual, meaning the sacred is perceived to be a reality that goes beyond or underlies the material world. In this work we have extended the range of meaning of sacred to include non-spiritual or secular patterns of ultimacy.

In a series of excerpts in the following chapters we will focus on those sacred writings which speak of a spiritual sacred. However, not all describe the spiritual in the same way. In the indigenous religions to be discussed in the next two chapters, everything is spiritual. The world is full of spirit beings and forces, as well as deities that created and watch over the world. In Hinduism we encounter one perspective that views the sacred as a unitary ultimate reality (Brahman), a oneness that encompasses everything spiritual and material. From another Hindu perspective, the sacred is a personal Supreme Lord, from whom emanates the entire spiritual and material universes. Both

Theravada Buddhism and Jainism are "atheistic" religions, denying that any personal God is supreme. The highest reality is the state of liberation experienced by the individual seeker. Philosophical Taoism points toward the mysterious Tao, the source and end of all reality and the process of its coming to be and passing away. For Shinto the world was created by and is full of *kami*: beings, forces, objects, even ideas that inspire reverence and awe. Mahayana Buddhism includes a variety of conceptions of the spiritual, ranging from Buddhas and Bodhisattvas, which are treated as personal deities, to the impersonal Buddha-nature, which (like Brahman) is present in all reality. Zoroastrianism, Judaism, Christianity, and Islam are monotheistic religions, asserting that God is both one and personal, the Supreme Lord who created the world and will bring it to culmination at a final judgment. The "new religions" reflect a diversity of perceptions of the sacred.

Sacred writings do not explain or prove the spiritual. Rather, these texts provide images, metaphors, and symbols that point toward and allow the faithful to experience spiritual reality. We include selections that respond to two questions: What is the sacred? How is the sacred made known to humans?

CONTEMPORARY ETHICAL ISSUES

The Ecological Crisis

> *The pollution and destruction of [the] environment are religious and ethical problems that derive basically from irreverent and immoral attitudes toward nature, rather than from technological inadequacy alone.*
> —*Harold Schilling, Physicist*
> *(cited in Barbour 1972: 100)*

Many people today believe that the fundamental ethical issue of the contemporary world is the well-being of the planet as a whole. Many contend that the ecological crisis conditions all other concerns we face. If we do not find ways to keep from destroying the balance of life, all other issues are irrelevant.

As we approach the end of the twentieth century, there is wide agreement that the balance of life on planet Earth is in danger. The issues are familiar:

- ozone depletion releasing ultraviolet radiation, which threatens to severely damage humans, other animals, and plants;
- carbon emissions resulting in the "greenhouse effect" and the dangerous elevation of the Earth's temperature, with a host of negative consequences;
- deforestation, including, but not limited to, the important tropical rain forests;
- pollution of the air, earth, and water;
- desertification, caused by depletion of the Earth's soils through current agricultural practices;
- population growth that threatens to exceed the carrying capacity of the Earth, unless we learn to distribute resources more equitably;
- consumption of natural resources faster than they can be replenished;
- the decreasing but still present threat of nuclear war.

The scope of the crisis is shown each year in a publication by the World Watch Institute called "State of the World." The 1992 edition of that annual study includes the following assessment (Postel 1992: 3):

- the protective ozone shield in heavily populated latitudes of the northern hemisphere is thinning twice as fast as scientists thought just a few years ago;
- a minimum of 140 plant and animal species are condemned to extinction each day;
- atmospheric levels of heat-trapping carbon dioxide are now 26 percent higher than the preindustrial concentration, and continue to climb;
- the Earth's surface was warmer in 1990 than in any year since record keeping began in the mid–nineteenth century; six of the seven

warmest years on record have occurred since 1980;

- forests are vanishing at a rate of some 17 million hectares a year, an area about half the size of Finland;
- world population is growing by 92 million people annually, roughly equal to adding another Mexico each year; of this total, 88 million are being added in the developing world.

As we shall see, most religions teach that humans have a special responsibility to preserve the balance of life. Does the ecological crisis demonstrate a fundamental failure of the world's religions to follow their own teachings? For a number of years many interpreters have argued that the roots of the environmental crisis are found in the teaching of Western religions that humans are distinct from nature and have a divinely sanctioned right to exploit nature (see, for example, White 1967). Many today are saying that since the roots of the present environmental crisis are spiritual, the solutions must come from religious sources as well. At the least, it is clear that any analysis of the ecological crisis must include attention to the possible role religions have played in creating it, and their potential for resolving it.

In the chapters that follow we will examine the ecological teachings of the world's religions and their response to the current ecological crisis.

War

Today wars are raging around the world. From the intractable conflict in the former Yugoslavia to the continuing violence in the Middle East to smoldering hostilities in more than two dozen other countries, war is a sad but seemingly inevitable fact of human relations.

To set the stage for discussion of how religions are responding to wars, let us first be clear about the cost of war. It should first of all be measured in

Freshly dug Muslim graves fill a former football (soccer) field in the Bosnian capital of Sarajevo.

human lives. How many people have been killed in wars in this century? The numbers of combatants and non-combatants killed is staggering: tens of millions of men, women, and children. The cost of war is also economic. In the United States alone, what has been the cost of the Cold War since 1945? By 1989 over $10 trillion had been spent. According to scientist Carl Sagan, "What could you buy with $10 trillion? The answer is everything— everything in the United States except the land; every skyscraper, house, ship, train, airplane, automobile, baby diaper, pencil. Everything could be purchased for $10 trillion." (Vittachi 1989: 30)

Given the immensity of the cost of war, is war ever justified? The story of the relationship between religion and war has not been a happy one. Religion has been and continues to be used to justify some of the most terrible conflicts in human history. Yet religions have also inspired great sacrifice by those who have fought in wars now widely accepted as just wars against oppressors who had to be stopped. As we shall see, religions have also encouraged many to work tirelessly to find non-violent solutions to the conflicts that cause wars.

Capital Punishment

As these words are written, a man is being strapped into the gas chamber at San Quentin prison in California. He was convicted of the murder of two teenage boys in 1978. Robert Harris is the first inmate on California's Death Row to be executed in a quarter-century. Over 300 wait to follow him. Outside San Quentin, as Harris dies, opponents of the death penalty argue that the state should not take a life. They point out that the United States is the last major democracy that still has capital punishment. Some appeal to religious teachings to voice their disapproval. Meanwhile, the families of the two boys Harris killed speak of their desire to see justice done and the lack of mercy that he showed to his victims. Supporters of the death penalty also cite religious grounds such as the Biblical injunction, "A life for a life, an eye for an eye, and a tooth for a tooth," to defend their position.

In 1972 the U.S. Supreme Court ruled that the death penalty as it was then being imposed was unconstitutional. However, the Court also held that the death penalty would meet constitutional standards if it were designated for certain crimes and applied uniformly. Since 1976 about forty states have passed new laws, and the number of executions has slowly but steadily risen. Most European and Latin American countries have abolished the death penalty. For example, Great Britain ended capital punishment in 1965 and Canada abolished it in 1976. The largest countries in which capital punishment is still imposed, outside the United States, are Russia and China. South Africa also has the death penalty.

Our purpose in this work will not be to review all the arguments in the general moral debate on the death penalty, but to examine the specific teachings of the world's religions that have addressed this issue.

Abortion

In Buffalo, New York, "pro-life" and "pro-choice" forces gather for yet another round in one of the most intractable ethical disputes of modern times. Both sides claim that their positions have religious validity. The U.S. Supreme Court prepares to review a Pennsylvania statute restricting abortion, and the debate goes on. Does a woman have a right to choose to terminate a pregnancy through abortion? If so, in what circumstances? Does an unborn child have a "right to life"? If not, why not? When does life begin? Is abortion a symbol of the deterioration of modern society's values or of the growing recognition of the autonomy and dignity of women? In this work our concern is the teachings of the world's religions regarding abortion.

However, before we turn to the teachings of some of the world's religions on this topic, let us clarify what abortion is and the situation concerning abortion in the United States. There are two types of abortion: spontaneous and induced. A spontaneous abortion is commonly called a miscarriage, and refers to the natural or accidental termination of a pregnancy resulting in the death and expulsion of the embryo or fetus from a woman's body.

"Pro-choice" protesters confront "Pro-life" marchers demonstrating against the Roe v. Wade decision. Both sides in the abortion debate draw upon religious teachings.

Other abortions are induced. Induced abortions may be either therapeutic or elective. Therapeutic abortions are those performed because the mother's life or health is judged to be at risk. In extreme circumstances, the physical life of the mother is in jeopardy unless an abortion is performed. In other cases, continuing the pregnancy may be deemed a serious risk to the physical or mental health of the mother. A woman's psychological well-being may be a factor when the pregnancy has resulted from rape or incest. When the woman's physical or mental well-being is not at risk, and an induced abortion occurs, it is said to be "elective." Eugenic factors can come into play as a basis for an elective abortion. For example, a woman may choose to have an abortion to avoid giving birth to a child with a severely limiting physical or mental disease. The social situation of the mother and her family are sometimes factors in elective abortions, with the mother deciding to end the pregnancy because of the strain having another child would place on her family and /or herself. Some elective abortions are motivated by a desire to give birth to a male or female child. Finally, a woman may not want to have a child because she

deems it impractical or inconvenient and thus elects an abortion.

Before 1973 abortions in the United States were regulated by state law. Some states had liberalized their laws, allowing women to have elective abortions with limited restrictions. Most states, however, allowed abortions only in strictly regulated situations, when the life or physical health of the mother was clearly at risk.

In 1969 there were approximately 20,000 abortions performed in the United States. Many physicians were reluctant to perform abortions because the Hippocratic Oath, which guides the practice of medicine, says: "I will follow that system of regimen which, according to my ability and judgment, I consider for the benefit of my patients, and abstain from whatever is deleterious and mischievous. I will give no deadly medicine to anyone if asked, nor suggest any counsel; and in like manner I will not give to a woman a pessary to produce abortion. With purity and holiness I will pass my life and practice my art."

On January 22, 1973, the U.S. Supreme Court ruled, in a decision known as *Roe* v. *Wade*, that states could not forbid a woman from having an abortion during the first three months of her pregnancy (called the first trimester) if her physician approved. During the second trimester, states were allowed to regulate abortions only as they affected the mother's health. During the third trimester, after the fetus becomes "viable" (able to live outside the womb), the Court ruled that abortions could be performed only to protect the life or health (including mental health) of the mother.

Within two years of the Court's ruling the number of abortions in the United States had risen to 1 million, and the number has continued to increase. Most abortions being performed in the United States were elective. Some opponents of abortion were becoming increasingly aggressive in their attempts to end what they called a "slaughter of innocents." In 1993 a physician who performed abortions was shot and killed, and another was seriously wounded. Advocates of abortion rights tried to use the courts to restrict the tactics of pro-life groups.

In the chapters that follow we will step back from the immediacy of the abortion debate as it rages today and seek to understand the full range of the world's religions' teachings concerning this controversial issue.

Euthanasia

The marvels of modern medicine have transformed euthanasia from a theoretical ethical question to a practical matter for increasing numbers of people. All of us are familiar with stories of terminally ill people crying out for assistance in ending their suffering and the debate over those who, like Dr. Jack Kevorkian, have chosen to respond to their appeals by assisting in their suicides. We also probably know of instances where families were forced to decide whether to authorize the administering or withholding of treatment of family members who were seemingly in the final stages of life.

"Euthanasia" comes from the Greek words that mean "good" and "death." The term was

Women and children during a drought in India wait to receive food.

coined by Sir Thomas More (1478–1535) to describe "the painless and merciful killing of incurables" (Goldman 1978: 171). In general usage, euthanasia refers to the ending of the life of someone because of a belief that death is preferable to life. Suicide can be considered self-imposed euthanasia, but the term usually is limited to cases in which a second party either takes action or refrains from action, which results in the death of another person. The popular term "mercy killing" is frequently used as a synonym for euthanasia.

Euthanasia may be either voluntary or involuntary. Voluntary euthanasia occurs when the person who dies asks someone else to enable death to occur. For example, a person unable to move, but still alert, asks a friend to help him take an overdose of sleeping pills. Involuntary euthanasia means that the person whose life is taken is not an active decision maker in the process. It usually occurs when a person is incapacitated and unable to make his or her wishes known. For example, a husband takes a gun and shoots his wife who is suffering from Alzheimer's disease, her brain function having atrophied to the point that she is unable to make her will known.

Euthanasia is also either passive or active. Passive euthanasia (sometimes called anti-dysthanasia) refers to a situation in which action is withdrawn or withheld and the person is allowed to die. In a recent case that received national attention, the parents of Nancy Cruzan, a Missouri woman diagnosed to be in a "persistent vegetative state," received court approval (after a long legal battle) to have the feeding tubes that were keeping her alive removed. The act was one of passive euthanasia, for Ms. Cruzan was "allowed to die" rather than killed.

Active euthanasia means that an action occurs which causes the person to die. The previous case of a husband shooting his wife is a clear example of active euthanasia. Another is when a medical practitioner administers a drug that results in the early death of a terminally ill person, in an attempt to alleviate the suffering of the patient and/or the patient's family. The line between active and passive euthanasia can easily blur, however. When a plug is pulled from a respirator and the patient, who was being kept alive on the machine, dies, is this passive or active? It is active in the sense that a concrete action (pulling the plug) occurred. It is passive because the "action" simply allowed the natural process of dying to continue; the person was not actively killed.

This is an important distinction, because passive euthanasia is widely viewed as ethical, while active euthanasia is still considered homicide. Those who engage in active "mercy killing" are often tried and sometimes (but rarely) convicted of a serious crime. Some today argue, however, that the distinction between the two is morally irrelevant, since the end (a "good death") is the same, and may be much more humane when active steps are taken to accomplish it.

The world's religions, as we shall see in the following chapters, have been deeply involved in the attempt to respond to the issues raised by euthanasia.

Economic Justice

The basic reality of the world today is staggering poverty amidst eye-popping affluence. In 1988 the World Bank estimated that nearly 20 percent of the world's population (which in the early 1990s means 1 billion people) lived in a state of "absolute poverty," which is defined as a condition characterized by "malnutrition, illiteracy, disease, short life expectancy, and high rates of infant mortality." Another billion people probably lived a subsistence lifestyle which, although not life-threatening, condemns people to having little more than the very minimal necessities. Eighty-five percent of the world's poor live in the "developing" countries of Africa, Asia, and Latin America. The life of the poor involves inadequate nutrition, poor shelter, lack of hygiene and health care, and a lack of material resources or the basic skills to transcend their situation (Leonard 1989: 9–10).

"Today, 85 percent of the world's income goes to 23 percent of its people—the affluent consumers. By contrast, more than 1 billion people, the absolute poor, survive on less than $1 a day" (Postel 1992: 4). In human terms this maldistribution of the world's resources means that (Postel 1992: 4–5):

- One in three children is malnourished.
- Some 1.2 billion people lack water safe to drink.
- Nearly 3 million children die annually from diseases that could be averted by immunizations.
- 1 million women die each year from preventable reproductive health problems.
- About 1 billion adults cannot read or write.

In 1981, among the countries with the highest per capita incomes, thirteen of seventeen were Protestant Christian (the other were oil-producing states, mostly Muslim). The high middle range ($2,000 to $7,000) were Roman Catholic. The low middle ($500 to $2,000) were Roman Catholic and Muslim. The lowest (below $500) were Hindu, Muslim, Buddhist, and indigenous. Interestingly, Israel, Singapore, and Hong Kong also rated highly. Early in this century two social scientists, Max Weber and R.H. Tawney, developed a theory that these statistics would seem, at least in part, to confirm. They theorized that the particular dynamics of Protestant Christianity (especially in its Calvinist form) sparked disciplined economic action that facilitated the development and success of the capitalist system. Weber said that this "Protestant ethic" provided the motivation for the development of capitalism through emphasizing (1) work as a way of life, (2) worldly asceticism, and (3) rationalism (see Robertson 1987: 4–8).

Turning his attention to Eastern religions, Weber tried to show that the religions that originated in India had a far greater concern with nonmaterial ends and the maintenance of an organically ordered society than the economic development characteristic of societies imbued with Protestant principles. They created a climate not conducive to the development of capitalism, he maintained.

Weber recognized that in East Asia Confucianism, if it could be taken out of the feudal context, would provide the values conducive to the development of capitalist economies. Indeed, as others have observed, "Confucian teaching provides an economic ethic conducive to perseverance and accumulation" (Palanca 1985: 66–67). Since World War II, Japan, Taiwan, Korea, and other Asian countries have developed the political contexts in which Confucian social values have helped to create vibrant market economies.

In any event, Weber's thesis that religion plays a central role in shaping economic life has widespread acceptance today. If we are to understand such economic issues as the distribution of wealth and the growing disparity between rich and poor, and how to respond to them, we must examine religious teachings.

Gender Roles and the Status of Women

Gender is unavoidably an issue all religions and students of religion today must face. As one scholar has put it, "It is no longer possible to study religious practice or religious symbols without taking gender—that is, the cultural experience of being male or female—into account" (Bynum 1986: 1–2). Gender is an inevitable ingredient in the human attempt to portray the sacred and the human experience of the sacred.

We need first to distinguish between "sex" and "gender" as the terms are used in academic discussions today. Sex refers to the differences attributable to biology, while gender refers to the distinctions between male and female human beings "that are created through psychological and social development within a familial, social, and cultural setting" (Bynum 1986: 7). Gender, therefore, is to a significant degree "culturally constructed" and may have considerably different meanings in different cultural settings.

Historically, the separate but complementary functions of male and female in various cultures have provided an important model for religious images of reality as a whole (as in the *yin/yang* conception in East Asian cultures) and sacred reality in particular (as in the Hindu understanding of paired deities and the masculine/feminine balance of the major gods). The issue of the relationship between gender and language about the sacred will be one of the concerns we will address in subsequent chapters.

In broad terms, indigenous religions (see Chapters Three and Four) have drawn more heavily on the spiritual power associated with the feminine and do not manifest a gender hierarchy (in which one gender is thought to be superior to the other) in religious roles. However, the opposition of female and male has been used in most of the major religions as a basis for the establishment of clearly separate roles for the genders, with the woman's often being subordinate. In general, the predominance of masculine language and imagery for the sacred in Western religions has reinforced the attitude that women have a lesser spiritual role than men.

The tendency toward male domination in the world's religions (called *patriarchy*) has inspired movements that have touched virtually all religions in an effort to liberate women from what are considered oppressive religious structures. These movements have also sparked resistance among traditionalists, who view attempts to elevate the status of women as an assault on an ordering of life and gender relations that has sacred sanction.

A full appreciation of the world's religions requires that we look at what they teach about gender and how they respond to the current controversies surrounding gender.

Homosexuality

"Homosexuality" has been defined as "a predominant, persistent, and exclusive psychosexual attraction toward members of the same sex" (Kanoti and Kosnik 1978: 671). Before we proceed, we must acknowledge that homosexuality was "constructed" as a concept in nineteenth-century Europe, and its helpfulness in understanding same-sex relations in other cultures is, as we shall see, limited. The same might be said of the more recent concept of "sexual orientation." This is yet another example of how the conceptual tools we use to study the world reflect our own particular cultural experience. We must try to do our best to understand how same-sex relations are understood within the context of the religions and cultures we are studying, rather than imposing our own values on that culture as a vehicle of analysis.

Same-sex relations are found in all cultures and have been a part of human experience since the beginning of recorded history. A recent study (Greenberg 1988: 25–26) has identified four types of homosexual relations found in all major culture areas. They are *transgenerational homosexuality*, which is found primarily among males, and between an older, more assertive male and a younger partner; *transgenderal homosexuality*, in which one of the partners assumes a gender role that does not correspond with his/her biological sex; *egalitarian homosexual relations* between two members of the same sex, sometimes in association with a particular life phase; and *class-distinguished homosexuality*, involving same-sex relations between members of different social classes.

As we will see, in a number of religions various expressions of homosexuality are accepted as normal. However, in Western societies homosexuality has been judged negatively since about the eleventh century, to a significant degree because of the way homosexuality is viewed in the Western religions.

The debate about homosexuality has become particularly heated in recent decades in the West as more scientists and physicians have expressed the view that homosexuality is much more a matter of genetic determination than psychosocial conditioning or free choice, and is therefore not abnormal and need not be "treated" (see Burr 1993). This has put increasing pressure on religions to renounce traditions that say that homosexuality departs from the sacred ordering of human life. Many "modernists" among Western religious traditions (especially in Judaism and Christianity) have accepted this challenge and have taken the position that homosexuality is as valid an expression of human sexuality as heterosexuality. In response, "traditionalists" have vigorously defended classical teachings that portray homosexual behavior as wicked. Our purpose will not be to try to resolve this complicated issue, but to provide readers with various points of view represented in the world's religions so that they may be better informed as they confront the controversy themselves.

CHAPTER SUMMARY

In this chapter we set the stage for the examination of the teachings of the world's religions on some basic human questions and contemporary ethical issues.

The basic human questions we chose for examination involve human identity, human destiny, cosmic origins and destiny, morality, and the sacred. Human identity includes the questions "Who are we as humans?" and "What is the basic human dilemma?" Human destiny includes the questions "Why are we here?" and "What happens after death?" Cosmic questions to be discussed will include "How did the world come into being?" and "What is the destiny of the universe?" Questions of morality are "What is right living?" "What is our obligation to others?" and "What are our obligations to non-human life?" By questions about the sacred we mean "What is the sacred?" and "How is the sacred made known?" Our approach to these questions in the subsequent chapters will be to include relevant excerpts from the sacred literature (oral and written) of the world's religions.

From among the many ethical issues that rightly concern thoughtful people around the world today, we have selected the following to examine: the ecological crisis, war, capital punishment, abortion, euthanasia, economic justice, gender roles and the status of women, and homosexuality. In this chapter we clarified the extent of each of these issues and identified the ways in which the world's religions have related to them in general. In the chapters that follow we will examine more specifically how many religions are responding to these issues today.

We are now almost ready to begin our survey of the world's religions, looking at their histories and basic teachings as well as their responses to some of the basic human questions and contemporary ethical issues. However, before we do, readers should clarify the perspectives they bring to this enterprise by thinking and talking about the following questions, which relate to the topics of this chapter.

QUESTIONS FOR DISCUSSION AND REFLECTION

Basic Human Questions

Who Are We?

1. Are human beings "microcosms" of the "cosmos"? Do we have in our nature in miniature the basic structure of the entire universe? Try to approach this question both scientifically and spiritually.

2. Some religions teach that humans have a permanent spiritual nature (a soul) and others do not. Do you believe that humans have "souls"? On what do you base your belief?

3. Do you believe in reincarnation? If so, why? If not, why not? What are the implications of your attitude toward reincarnation on the way you choose to live your life?

What Is the Basic Human Dilemma?

1. Does this question make assumptions about human nature with which you agree or disagree? Do you think we *should* spend time reflecting on "what is wrong with us"?

2. If you agree that thinking about this issue is worthwhile, what comes to mind as the basic "problem" all humans face and from which they need to be transformed?

Why Are We Here?

1. Have you ever wondered why you are here? If so, what were your thoughts when you found yourself reflecting on this question?

2. What is the value of stories that tell of human

origins? There are a variety of such stories. Does that mean one is true and the others are false, that all are false, that all are true in their own way?

What Happens after Death?

1. React to the teaching common among indigenous religions that the spirits of our ancestors remain with us, until the proper rituals are conducted to assist them in their journey to the spirit world. Does it have a place in the modern world, or is it a naive notion best left behind?
2. Do you believe that the dead live on in nature?
3. Do you believe in "heaven" and/or "hell"? If so, what do these concepts mean to you?

How Did the World Come into Being?

1. In your opinion, what should constitute "truth" for religious stories of cosmic origins? Are they to be considered literally or symbolically true?
2. Is there a particular story of cosmic origins you have heard to which you are most attracted? If so, what is it? Why are you drawn to it?
3. Try imagining and writing down a new story of cosmic origins.

What Is the Destiny of the Cosmos?

1. Do you believe that there will be an end of the cosmos or that the cosmos is eternal? On what do you base your belief?
2. Is there a particular story of cosmic destiny you have heard to which you are most attracted? If so, what is it? Why are you drawn to it?
3. Try imagining and writing down a new story of cosmic destiny.

What Is Right Living?

1. Jot down the qualities of "right living" as they occur to you. What is the source of these ideas? How many are influenced by your exposure to religion?
2. What is the relationship between personal piety and active concern for others? Is one possible without the other?

What Is Our Obligation to Others?

1. Do you believe human beings have obligations to one another? If so, what are they? To whom do they extend: immediate family, larger family, members of your religious or other community, citizens of your nation, all people?
2. If you do not believe we have obligations to one another, what is the basis of your belief.

What Is Our Obligation to Non-Human Life?

1. Is all of nature alive? How does your response to that question affect how you treat nature?
2. Does respect for nature logically lead to vegetarianism? Why or why not?
3. Do non-humans have "rights"? If so, what are they? If not, why not?

What Is the Sacred?

1. Do you believe that "sacred" reality exists? On what do you base your belief?
2. If you believe in the reality of the sacred, do you find yourself drawn more to the images of the sacred that are personal or impersonal? Can the two be reconciled, or must one choose between them?
3. If you believe in a personal conception of the sacred, are you drawn more to masculine or feminine images of the sacred? Why?
4. Given the mystery of the sacred, can we really say *anything* about the sacred, or should we simply be silent?

How Is the Sacred Made Known?

1. Is the best place to look for the sacred within yourself? Why or why not?
2. Do you agree that if you try *too hard* to know the sacred, you will fail?
3. Have you had any experiences that you consider to be encounters with the sacred? What are they? If you have shared your experiences with others, how have they responded? Is it possible to "know the sacred" without having had such experiences?

Contemporary Ethical Issues

The Ecological Crisis

1. In your opinion, are human beings by nature "abusers of nature," or is this behavior culturally determined?

2. Does nature have legal standing? Discuss the importance and implications of accepting the principle that non-human beings and objects have "rights" that deserve legal protection. What would the implications be for society?

3. What steps are you willing to take voluntarily to restore the "balance of life"? What should be the role of national governments? What should be the role of the United Nations?

War

1. In general, do you think religion has done more to cause war or peace in the world?

2. Are there any circumstances in which the use of nuclear weapons is morally justifiable?

3. Do people in situations of oppression have a right to engage in a violent struggle against their oppressors? Do they have a moral right to attack civilian targets?

4. What might religions today do to bring an end to the use of war as a means for solving political disputes?

Capital Punishment

1. Would the world be a better place if capital punishment were more widely applied or abolished?

2. Make a list of arguments for and against capital punishment. Which have a relationship to religion? Are these among the reasons you find most compelling?

Abortion

1. Do you agree that abortion is a religious issue? Would our society be better off if religious people were less involved or more involved in the dispute over abortion?

2. A nineteen-year-old college student has become pregnant. You share her religious affiliation and she has approached you for advice on whether she should obtain an abortion. What would you tell her?

3. Should issues of population control and poverty have any bearing on the abortion issue?

4. Have you joined or would you take part in a protest at an abortion clinic, either to try to stop abortions or to protect access for those seeking them? How politically active have you been or do you feel you should be on this issue?

5. Is there a role for religious people in trying to find a middle ground between the "pro-life" and "pro-choice" positions on abortion?

Euthanasia

1. A 20-year-old man suffered brain damage in an automobile accident. For four years he has been in an irreversible coma, kept alive by artificial feeding. He could live for another thirty or more years like this, although he is not able to interact with other people and never will be, his physicians say. His parents have sought guidance from religious teachers on whether they have the moral right to have the feeding tube removed so that their son may be allowed to die. Would such an action be active or passive euthanasia? Is it morally justified? What should be the role of religion in making this determination?

2. In 1972 Gary Stocks was severely beaten; for six weeks he remained paralyzed and in a coma. His doctors predicted he would never be more than a "vegetable." Yet he recovered and resumed his doctoral studies. How should a case like this affect the discussion of euthanasia?

3. Research the case of Dr. Jack Kevorkian, the Michigan physician who has helped a number of people to use various devices he has designed to end their lives. In your view, are his actions in these situations morally justifiable?

4. If a terminally ill friend or relative asked for your assistance if he or she decided to end the suffering through artificial means, what would you do? What role would religion play in your decision?

Economic Justice

1. Do you agree that the disparity between rich and poor in the world is a serious problem? If so, is it the most critical problem the world faces? If not, why not?

2. Would you favor the development of a world government that would take steps to ensure that the wealth of the world is distributed more equitably? Why or why not? What other measures can be taken to overcome the problems associated with the absolute poverty of so many in the world today?

Gender Roles and the Status of Women

1. Do you agree that gender is a culturally constructed phenomenon? Or do you subscribe to the more traditional attitude that "male" and "female" are biologically determined realities? What evidence do you consider in choosing between these two approaches to sex and gender?

2. Have you ever experienced "patriarchy"? Do you think the society in which you live is patriarchal?

3. How important do you think it is to include both masculine and feminine images in describing the sacred?

4. Should women and men have equal access to initiation and ordination as religious leaders? Why or why not?

5. Try to put yourself in the position of a woman who has come to the conclusion that religion is hopelessly patriarchal. What would cause her to believe this? Is she right? What should she do?

Homosexuality

1. Why do you think homosexuality is such a controversial issue among many religious people today?

2. Why do some homosexual persons form their own separate groups within religions?

3. Has your attitude toward homosexuality changed in recent years? If so, how and why?

4. What should be the role of religion in shaping attitudes toward homosexuality?

SOURCES AND SUGGESTIONS FOR FURTHER STUDY

Basic Human Questions

The following anthologies of sacred writings from the world's religions are helpful resources for studying the religious responses to the basic human questions introduced in this chapter.

ELIADE, MIRCEA, 1992 *Essential Sacred Writings from around the World.* San Francisco: HarperSanFrancisco.

SMART, NINIAN AND RICHARD D. HECHT, ED., 1982 *Sacred Texts of the World: A Universal Anthology.* New York: Crossroad.

VAN VOORST, ROBERT E., 1994 *Anthology of World Scriptures.* Belmont, Calif.: Wadsworth Publishing Company.

WILSON, ANDREW, ED., 1991 *World Scripture: A Comparative Anthology of Sacred Texts.* New York: Paragon House.

Contemporary Ethical Issues

General

CARMODY, DENISE LARDNER, AND JOHN TULLY CARMODY, 1988 *How to Live Well: Ethics in the World Religions.* Belmont, Calif.: Wadsworth.

CRAWFORD, S. CROMWELL, ED., 1989 *World Religions and Global Ethics.* New York: Paragon House.

CROTTY, ROBERT B., MARIE T. CROTTY, AND ARNOLD D. HUNT, EDS., 1991 *Ethics of the World Religions.* San Diego: Greenhaven Press.

The Ecological Crisis

BARBOUR, IAN, 1972 *Earth Might Be Fair: Reflections on Ethics, Religion, and Ecology.* Englewood Cliffs, N.J.: Prentice Hall.

BROWN, LESTER, 1992 "Launching the Environmental Revolution," in *State of the World 1992: A Worldwatch*

Institute Report on Progress Toward a Sustainable Society, ed. Linda Starke (New York: W.W. Norton), 174–190.

CHAPPLE, CHRISTOPHER KEY, 1993 *Ecological Prospects: Science, Religion, and Aesthetic Perspectives.* Albany: State University of New York Press.

HARGROVE, EUGENE, ED., 1986 *Religion and Environmental Crisis.* Athens: The University of Georgia Press.

LOVELOCK, JAMES E., 1982 *Gaia: A New Look at Life on Earth.* New York: Oxford University Press.

NASH, RODERICK, 1989 *The Rights of Nature: A History of Environmental Ethics.* Madison: The University of Wisconsin Press. See especially "The Greening of Religion," 87–120.

POSTEL, SANDRA, 1992 "Denial in the Decisive Decade," in *State of the World 1992*, 3-8.

SPRING, DAVID, AND EILEEN SPRING, EDS., 1974 *Ecology and Religion in History.* New York: Harper & Row.

WHITE, LYNN, JR., 1967 "The Historical Roots of Our Ecological Crisis," *Science* 155 (1967): 1203–07. (Included in Spring 1974: 15–31.)

War

FERGUSON, JOHN, 1977 *War and Peace in the World's Religions.* London: Sheldon Press.

LACKEY, DOUGLAS, 1989 *The Ethics of War and Peace.* Englewood Cliffs, N.J.: Prentice Hall.

Capital Punishment

BEDAU, HUGO A., ED., 1982 *The Death Penalty in America.* New York: Oxford University Press.

HOOK, DAVID, AND LOTHAR KALIN, 1989 *Death in the Balance: The Debate over Capital Punishment.* Lexington, Mass.: Lexington Books.

MACKEY, VIRGINIA, 1993 *Punishment: In the Scripture and Tradition of Judaism, Christianity, and Islam.* Albany, N.Y.: State University of New York.

SORRELL, TOM, 1988 *Moral Theory and Capital Punishment.* New York: Oxford University Press.

Abortion

BRODY, BARUCH, 1975 *Abortion and the Sanctity of Life.* Cambridge, Mass: MIT Press.

GREGORY, HAROLD, ED., 1983 *The Religious Case for Abortion.* Asheville, N.C.: Madison and Polk.

SCHWARTZ, STEPHEN, 1990 *The Moral Question of Abortion.* Chicago: Loyola University Press.

Euthanasia

HAMEL, RON P., ED., 1991 *Choosing Death: Active Euthanasia, Religion, and the Public Debate.* Valley Forge, Pa.: Trinity Press International.

HORAN, DENNIS J., AND DAVID MALL, 1977 *Death, Dying, and Euthanasia.* Washington, D.C.: University Publications of America.

LARUE, GERALD A., 1985 *Euthanasia and Religion: A Survey of the Attitudes of World Religions to the Right-to-Die.* Los Angeles: The Hemlock Society.

TROWELL, H.C., 1973 *The Unfinished Debate on Euthanasia.* London: SCM Press.

Economic Justice

BARBOUR, IAN, 1980 *Technology, Environment, and Human Values.* New York: Praeger.

FERRÉ, FREDERICK, AND RITA H. MATARAGNON, EDS., 1985 *God and Global Justice: Religion and Poverty in an Unequal World.* New York: Paragon House.

GILDER, GEORGE, 1980 *Wealth and Poverty.* New York: Basic Books.

POSTEL, SANDRA, 1992 "Denial in the Decisive Decade," in *State of the World 1992*, 3–8.

ROBERTSON, ROLAND, 1987 "Economics and Religion," in *The Encyclopedia of Religion*, vol. 5, ed. Mircea Eliade (New York: Macmillan), 1–11.

TAWNEY, R.H., 1962 *Religion and the Rise of Capitalism.* Gloucester, Mass.: P. Smith.

WEBER, MAX, 1930 *The Protestant Ethic and the Spirit of Capitalism*, trans. Talcott Parsons. London: G. Allen and Unwin.

Gender Roles and the Status of Women

ATKINSON, CLARISSA, ET AL., 1985 *Immaculate and Powerful: The Female in Sacred Image and Social Reality.* Boston: Beacon Press.

BYNUM, CAROLINE WALKER, STEVAN HARRELL, AND PAULA RICHMAN, 1986 *Gender and Religion: On the Complexity of Symbols.* Boston: Beacon Press.

CARMODY, DENISE, 1989 *Women and World Religions.* 2nd ed. Englewood Cliffs, N.J.: Prentice Hall.

ECK, DIANA L., AND DEVAKI JAIN, 1987 *Speaking of Faith: Global Perspectives on Women, Religion, and Social Change.* Philadelphia: New Society.

FALK, NINA AUER, AND RITA M. GROSS, 1989 *Unspoken Worlds: Women's Religious Lives.* Belmont, Calif. Wadsworth.

HADDAD, YVONNE YAZBECK, AND ELLISON BANKS FINDLY, 1985 *Women, Religion, and Social Change.* Albany: State University of New York Press.

PLASKOW, JUDITH, AND CAROL CHRIST, 1989 *Weaving the Visions: New Patterns in Feminist Spirituality.* San Francisco: HarperSanFrancisco.

SHARMA, ARVIND, ED., 1987 *Women in World Religions.* Albany: State University of New York Press.

1994 *Today's Woman in World Religions.* Albany: State University of New York Press.

Homosexuality

BATCHELOR, EDWARD, 1980 *Homosexuality and Ethics.* New York: Pilgrim Press.

BLACKWOOD, EVELYN, 1986 *The Many Faces of Homosexuality: Anthropological Approaches to Homosexual Behavior.* New York: Harrington Park Press.

BULLOUGH, VERN, 1979 *Homosexuality: A History.* New York: New American Library.

BURR, CHANDLER, 1993 "Homosexuality and Biology," *The Atlantic Monthly* 271: 47–65.

CARRIER, J. M., 1980 "Homosexual Behavior in Cross-Cultural Perspective," in *Homosexual Behavior: A Modern Reappraisal,* ed. J. Mormer (New York: Basic Books), 100–122.

DYNES, WAYNE, ED., 1990 *The Encyclopedia of Homosexuality.* New York: Garland Press.

GREENBERG, DAVID F., 1988 *The Construction of Homosexuality.* Chicago: University of Chicago Press.

HASBANY, RICHARD, ED., 1989 *Homosexuality and Religion.* New York: Harrington Park Press.

HERDT, GILBERT, 1987 "Homosexuality," in *The Encyclopedia of Religion,* vol. 6, ed. Mircea Eliade (New York: Macmillan), 445–453.

KANOTI, GEORGE A., AND ANTHONY R. KOSNIK, 1978 "Homosexuality: Ethical Aspects," in *Encyclopedia of Bioethics,* vol. 2 (New York: Free Press), 671.

PARRINDER, GEOFFREY, 1980 *Sex in the World's Religions.* London: Sheldon Press.

SWIDLER, ARLENE, ED., 1993 *Homosexuality and World Religions.* Valley Forge, Pa.: Trinity Press International.

Indigenous Religions

Indigenous means "pertaining to a particular area." Indigenous religions are those religions native to a specific geographic area, such as North America, Africa, or Australia. In each region of the world we find religions that were present when modern people first entered the area and/or that reflect an earlier stage of cultural development than the state-level societies that dominate the world today. For example, in North America the religious teachings and practices of the inhabitants of the land present when Europeans first made contact in the fifteenth century continue today in many traditional Native American religions. This does not mean that indigenous religions have not changed over time. *All* religions change, as do all human activities and institutions. However, many of the religions of contemporary indigenous peoples in their traditional manifestations are, to a significant degree, in continuity with the basic beliefs and practices of the religions of their ancestors. Such religions are fascinating in their own right. They can also help us become aware of basic religious patterns that are found in the religions we will study in subsequent chapters.

In the next two chapters we will survey the general characteristics of the indigenous religions of Africa and North America, and treat as case studies the religion of the Yoruba people of West Africa and the Oglala Lakota of North America.

CHAPTER 3

Introduction and Indigenous Religions of Africa

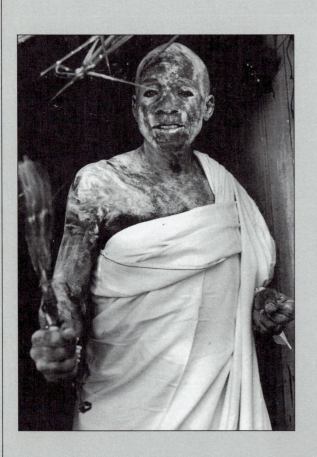

TUNISIA

MOROCCO

ALGERIA

S A H A R A

NIA

MALI

Niger River

N

NIG

COAST

NA FASO

GHANA

TOGO
BENIN

EQUATORIAL
GUINEA

Gulf
of
Guinea

ATLANTIC

OCEAN

PROBLEMS IN STUDYING INDIGENOUS RELIGIONS

We must acknowledge the serious problems facing any outsider who tries to describe indigenous religions today. The first is with the word "religion" itself. *Religion* is a Western term, which usually implies an organized set of beliefs and practices to be distinguished from a "non-religious" sphere of life. As we shall see, indigenous peoples make no such distinction. An Oglala Lakota leader told the author, "We have no word 'religion' in our language. It is not a word appropriate to our traditional way of life." Many scholars have begun to use the term "spirituality" instead of "religion" when speaking of the sacred ways of indigenous peoples. We have chosen to use the word "religion" in this chapter because we are committed to using a broader definition of religion ("human transformation in response to perceived ultimacy"), which, we believe, applies to non-Western patterns of ultimacy or spirituality as much as it does to Western patterns. Although indigenous peoples typically have no word for "religion," they do have patterns of ultimacy that are central to their cultures.

The second problem reflects an even more blatant bias. Until quite recently scholars seeking to describe these religions often called them "primitive" religions, adopting the stereotype that religions that developed subsequently are "advanced." However, the intricate and sophisticated teachings and practices of these religions show them to be as developed as any other religions.

Other appellations are more descriptive, but still reflect a modern, Western bias and suggest a third problem—"naming" this group of religions. These religions have been called "preliterate" or "non-literate" religions, indicating that they do not have written scriptures. The above designations imply a lack of a literature, but that is not the case. Instead, their myths and legends are transmitted orally: Sacred traditions are revered and preserved orally in virtually every indigenous culture. Other interpreters have called these religions "prehistoric," but this is misleading because they have continued into and, in many cases, show the influences of the historical era.

The search for a more descriptive name has led some scholars to call the indigenous religions "basic" or "primal" religions, reflecting their status as the original religions and in some ways the foundation for later religions. These designations are not themselves prejudicial, but they risk misunderstanding by those who assume that "basic" or "primal" means simple or not complex. Others have adopted the term used for the level of social organization most common in these religions, calling the religions "tribal" or "small-scale traditional." "Native" religions is a term that has also been used. However, both "tribal" and "native" have taken on misleading, stereotypical meanings in modern societies, and "small-scale traditional" is misleading because many of these religions were associated with very large groups of people.

In our discussion we will use the designations "indigenous" or "traditional" religions, because these terms seem the most descriptive and the most neutral of the titles so far suggested.

Of course, *any* "naming" of these religions as a group has serious limitations. Each of the indigenous religions of the world is unique. Penetrating the complexities and mysteries of any one indigenous religion is nearly impossible for outsiders; it is even harder to generalize about indigenous religions as a group. Even initiates into these religions typically receive only a portion of the full panoply of sacred knowledge associated with the religion. Outsiders, even those who spend much time with the people, have access to isolated bits of information that they must try to put together into a meaningful whole. Moreover, these religions depend on oral rather than written traditions, and these must be passed from generation to generation. Despite these difficulties, much progress has been made toward an understanding that can be communicated at least partially to outsiders. Anthropologists and ethnographers have documented hundreds of indigenous cultures, writing down the rich oral traditions and variegated beliefs and practices they exhibit.

Some interpreters would argue that any attempt to generalize about the indigenous religions is misguided, loaded with the (typically

Western) biases of the interpreter. For example, terms we will use, such as "animism," "totem," and "fetish," were invented by Western scholars to classify the beliefs and practices they were observing. Many today would say that those terms should not be used at all because they are foreign to the groups being studied. However, phenomenological study has identified common patterns that support our speaking of indigenous religions collectively. Assuming, for the purposes of this study, the validity of identifying common patterns, we will review some of the most important shared qualities, which together point toward a distinctive "worldview" for this family of religions, and some of the characteristics of the indigenous religions of two regions: Africa and North America.

In addition to surveying this shared worldview and the general characteristics of such religions in Africa and North America, we will focus on two specific indigenous religions: the Yoruba of West Africa and the Oglala Lakota of the Great Plains of North America.

THE TRADITIONAL WORLDVIEW OF INDIGENOUS PEOPLES

The pattern we have selected for understanding the basic teachings of religions (see Chapter One) also serves as a framework for introducing the traditional worldview of families of religions. Here we will examine the shared worldview of indigenous religions. In subsequent sections we will encounter the shared worldviews of the religions of South and Southeast Asia (Section Three), the religions of East Asia (Section Four), and the religions of the Middle East and beyond (Section Five). Comparing and contrasting these basic worldviews is a helpful way of establishing contexts for understanding the complexity of the world's religions. As with all generalizations, they are intended as learning tools rather than as final, definitive descriptions.

Problem: Lack of Balance

For indigenous peoples, *all* life is spiritual. The spiritual world is not separate from us; we live in a spir-

itual world at all times, whether we are aware of it or not. Indeed, as must be stressed, indigenous peoples believe there is but one world. We are spiritual beings ourselves and we live amidst spiritual beings and forces, seen and unseen. As humans we are certainly not superior to other spiritual beings. The basic human problem is failure to respect the intended spiritual equilibrium of all life, human and non-human, and to live within it. Often, indigenous peoples will speak of a path of harmony that they are intended to walk, and the problem as departing from that path onto a road of disharmony or error.

The problem is usually expressed collectively. At issue is the spiritual balance of the community as a whole (family, clan, tribe, or nation) in the context of the balance of all life. An individual's spiritual imbalance is problematic because it undermines the harmony of the group, not merely because of the consequences for the person alone. The effects of spiritual imbalance are manifest in the material status of the group and on the individual, so social chaos and individual disease or dislocation are assumed to be fundamentally spiritual problems.

Cause: Loss of Balance

For indigenous peoples, balance does not have to be *created*; it is already and everywhere present for those who learn to be attentive. Imbalance is caused by forgetting the way of life patterned after the spiritual and turning to a false, error-filled path. Forgetfulness may be brought on when people become too enamored with inappropriate activities, such as the pursuit of one's own or one's family's material well-being at the expense of the group as a whole, often extending to the community of all living beings.

Reality: Sacred Words, Time, and Space

Language today is typically thought of as a "symbolic activity." We recognize that when we speak a word, the word is different from the thing about which we have spoken. However, for indigenous peoples, "words have a special potency or force that is integral to their specific sounds: What is named is therefore understood to be really present in the name in unitary manner, not as a 'symbol' with dualistic implication, as is generally the case with modern languages. . . . Recitation of a myth of creation, for example, is understood to be an actual, not a symbolic recapitulation of that primordial creative process or event, which is not bound by time" (Brown 1988: 3; see also 88–89). Therefore, when an indigenous person skilled in sacred matters speaks of the sacred, the sacred is experienced as present. In general, the desire to experience sacred reality in order to be a part of that which is perceived as true reality is a pattern found in all religions (see Eliade 1959).

Indigenous peoples also view time differently than is typical in the modern world. Under the influence of the Western religions and with the rise in the nineteenth century of historicism, most persons in "developed" countries have come to view time as a linear process. What has happened in the past will not be repeated in the future in any literal sense. By contrast, for indigenous peoples time is rhythmic and cyclical rather than a straight line. Traditional indigenous people do not seek progress in life. They seek to experience the true reality of the spiritual amidst the cyclical patterns of life. They typically look to a sacred time of origins, which stands outside the circle of profane time.

Through a panoply of rituals indigenous peoples order the circle of life in a sacred manner. For example, in the cycle of an individual's life there are special moments, times of passage from one stage to another—birth, infancy and early childhood, entering adulthood, marriage, and death. By ordering these times in a sacred manner through carrying out *rites of passage,* the individual's life cycle becomes a manifestation of the sacred. These rites of passage involve typical stages (see Van Gennep), as in, for example, the actions typical of the funeral rituals associated with death. First comes separation from the preceding status, as when a corpse is removed from its place of living to be prepared for passage to the next stage. Next comes the stage of "liminality," the passage itself, as when the body is placed in a carrier (for instance, a casket) and taken

in a procession on a symbolic journey to its next stage of existence. At this stage the change in status is accomplished, as when the deceased person becomes an ancestor. Finally comes reincorporation, as when the corpse, now having passed into a new status, reenters the social world in its new identity through being burned, buried, or exposed to the elements.

Many observers have pointed out that modern cultures maintain rites of passage for the fundamental transitions of life, whether in spiritual or secularized fashion. For example, groups ranging from college fraternities and sororities to urban gangs often reflect the pattern of separation, transition, and incorporation associated with rites of passage in their rituals of initiation. It would be good at this point for you to reflect on and discuss with others the rites of passage you have participated in or observed.

Similarly, the yearly cycle of the seasons may be approached in a sacred manner. The Christian adaptation of the seasonal rituals of indigenous European peoples to the special historical moments in the life of Christ (as with the celebration of Christmas and Easter) is an indication of the continuing influence of indigenous religions.

Just as sacred time may be "made present," sacred space may also be created. This is apparent in the structures built for ritual purposes. However, it is true in "ordinary" life as well. For example, the building of a village or a dwelling is, for indigenous peoples, a sacred act that must be done according to the pattern revealed in myth. When indigenous peoples enter sacred space, whether during a special ritual time or during daily existence, they perceive themselves in a reality ordered by the spiritual and thus "truly real."

End: Balance

The fundamental transformation indigenous peoples realize is necessary is to maintain equilibrium with the spiritual and restore that balance when it is lost. Although indigenous religions usually speak of an existence after the present life, it is not often thought of as the principal goal to be sought. Rather, indigenous peoples seek to experience

Uniquely empowered to communicate with the spirit world, a shaman here calls upon the power of the spirit beings by uttering special words and beating a sacred drum

"true reality" wherever and whenever they are. It is a state primarily understood as collective. When the group is living in harmony with the spiritual, the individual is also. Since the spiritual is everywhere potentially present, balance must be sought with everyone and everything, at all times. When spiritual equilibrium is present, that which the group needs for its material well-being will follow.

Means: The Spiritual Pattern

Indigenous religions typically have no written "scriptures," but oral myths and legends that reveal the spiritual paradigms the group is to follow are passed from generation to generation. As we have noted, the spiritual patterns involve individual rituals (the rites of passage, for example). There are also many prescribed group rituals that must be carried out in order to preserve or restore harmony.

Some indigenous religions may have priests who carry out the rituals. Another typical religious leader is the *shaman*. The term comes from Siberian indigenous religion, but is now widely used for a

"sacred person" who has entered fully into the spirit world and thereafter is gifted with the ability to make journeys there for the sake of the spiritual well-being of his or her people. Through these ecstatic journeys the shaman acquires a knowledge used to heal sicknesses, instruct a person or group on proper courses of action, and even cause good things to happen. Typically a shaman not only has had a spontaneous, powerful spiritual experience that has empowered the specialist, but also has studied sacred lore with another shaman. Someone who has been called to be a shaman and has accepted the status by passing through the process of apprenticeship is particularly venerated and retains the position throughout his or her life.

A shaman often uses and sometimes gives to others special sacred objects, which indigenous peoples believe can assist them in their pursuit of harmony. An example would be the feathers often worn by indigenous religious leaders, or the special rattles or drums often used in ceremonies. These have been called by Western scholars of earlier generations "fetishes," but the corruption of the term *fetish* in modern psychological usage makes it of dubious value in phenomenological study. The sacred pipe so prevalent among Native Americans is an example of a sacred object.

The term *magic* is usually associated with indigenous religions, and is popularly thought of as a manipulation of objects or persons by someone who knows the proper formula or ritual. Indigenous peoples often use what interpreters call *imitative magic*, when they behave ritually like whatever they are seeking to influence. For example, to try to ensure fertility intercourse is sometimes feigned in ritual. To the outside observer such practices may *seem* to be designed to try to force an outcome. Indigenous peoples themselves presumably view these practices as their following a pattern that the spirits have prescribed.

Another widely misunderstood practice common among indigenous religions as part of the effort to live in harmony with the spiritual has been given the name *taboo* by outside observers. If something or someone is "taboo," it is thought to be so spiritually potent that touching the object or person, or engaging in the prohibited behavior, will have disastrous consequences. In most indigenous cultures menstruating women are taboo, as are warriors before and after a battle (until they have been ritually purified). It is often considered a taboo to speak the names of the dead or for men to eat certain foods during initiation. It should be noted that taboos like that regarding menstruation have been used by women in indigenous cultures to develop solidarity among women. The menstrual huts in which women are confined often become places where they may communicate freely without intrusion by males.

Because violating a taboo is not the only source of ritual impurity, indigenous religions typically have a standard rite of purification. Water and smoke are frequently used in these rituals to create cleansing and to restore harmony.

Some, but not all, indigenous religions prescribe sacrifices, in which something animate or inanimate is offered to the spirits or God. Offerings may be made to placate spirits that the groups believe have been offended, or to propitiate spirits for some particular blessing.

Because of the attitude toward nature in indigenous religions, it is not surprising that groups develop spiritual relationships with particular animals, plants, or even inanimate objects. Spiritual bonds between groups (typically subgroups within a larger group) and animals are most common. The animal (sometimes called a *totem* by Western scholars) is thought to be the special protector of the group, and the group shows reverence for the animal. In some groups images of the totems are carved on ritual poles (hence a "totem pole"). Totemic groupings are a common way of distinguishing members for particular ritualistic functions. Each group has its own specialized rituals and mysteries that are not revealed to those outside the group, although knowledge may be shared among such groups. To become a part of a totemic group requires a ritual of initiation, in which the member's ordinary identity is stripped away and a new identity is ritually assumed.

Many interpreters have pointed out that totemism and other practices and beliefs of indigenous peoples persist in modern cultures, often in camouflaged form. (See Eliade 1959: 201–13.) We have already noted the continuation of rites of passage in religious and non-religious settings. A school mascot could be considered a vestige of the totemic practice. A rabbit's foot or even an item of clothing believed to bring luck is an example of a sacred object thought to have special powers.

Sacred: Everything Is Spiritual

In the major religions of the world today, participants typically draw a clear distinction between the spiritual realm and the material or profane world. Most Jews, Christians, and Muslims, for example, speak of God as separate from the world, viewing the deity as the transcendent creator, sustainer, and judge. Most Hindus, as we shall see, call material reality *maya* (illusion), and differentiate between the eternal, spiritual reality and the temporal, material reality of this world.

There is no such strict distinction between the spiritual and material in the worldview common among indigenous peoples, for whom "everything is alive" and therefore everything is potentially spiritual. Indigenous peoples believe that all reality is infused with spirituality. Humans are spiritual beings, but so are birds, deer, trees, lakes and streams, the sky, and the earth as a whole. In many indigenous cultures, humans and other animals are called together "people." Modern Western interpreters, with their penchant for labeling things, call the attitude that all reality is infused with spirits, and therefore alive, by the name *animism* (from the Latin word *anima*, "spirit" or "soul").

If the spiritual is everywhere and at all times potentially present, then what we might call ordinary activities are, for indigenous peoples, by nature spiritual. For example, the life-sustaining act of hunting or farming is seen as a spiritual activity by many indigenous peoples, and is undertaken with the same care and reverence as any other ritual. The same could be said of making a basket from plants or a blanket from a skin.

If *everything* is potentially spiritual, then *all* life must be lived as a ritual. Everyday activities are patterned after myths that tell the story of how the world and its inhabitants came into existence. By recapitulating the myth in a ritualized action, the people participate in the creation of the cosmos in which they find harmonious life. As one native person remarked, "We do not believe our religion, we dance it!" (cited by Brown 1988: 123).

The attitude toward spiritual beings is quite complex, because if all life is spiritual, then spiritual beings are everywhere potentially present. Western missionaries typically attacked indigenous peoples as "heathens" or "idolaters" because they seemed to worship material objects and a plethora of spirits rather than "the one true god." From a phenomenological perspective, this reflects judgment before understanding. In fact, examination of a variety of indigenous religions suggests that many recognize a *high god,* who is perceived as a transcendent creator, just as in Western religions.

However, in indigenous religions the high god is but one dimension of the spiritual, and, on a day-to-day basis, not necessarily the most important. Veneration is due not only the creator but the other

divine beings who are also active in creating and maintaining the world, as well as the spirits with whom one comes into contact daily or periodically. Spirits are present and deserve awe and respect amidst the daily routine, meaning that there is no underlying or rigid distinction between the routine and the sacred. However, particular spirits may appear at times (in some groups in the form of masked members of the tribe) and a special ritual may occur. Modern observers sometimes say that indigenous peoples seem to live in fear of the spirits they perceive all around them. It would be more accurate to say that they live with reverence for these spirits, recognizing that harmony in life depends on maintaining good relations with other spiritual beings, seen and unseen.

Let us turn now to specific indigenous religions in their own contexts. In this chapter we will introduce the religion of the Yoruba people of West Africa in the context of a discussion of the general

In this scene from a Voodoo ceremony, a woman leaves the altar where she has just experienced a god entering into her, in order to express her joy in an ecstatic dance.

FIGURE 3-1

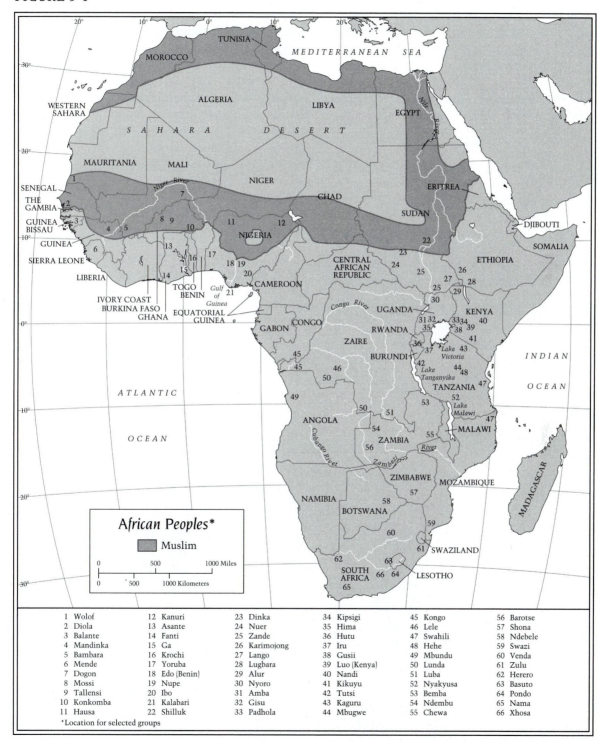

African Peoples*

▨ Muslim

0   500   1000 Miles

0   500   1000 Kilometers

1 Wolof	12 Kanuri	23 Dinka	34 Kipsigi	45 Kongo	56 Barotse
2 Diola	13 Asante	24 Nuer	35 Hima	46 Lele	57 Shona
3 Balante	14 Fanti	25 Zande	36 Hutu	47 Swahili	58 Ndebele
4 Mandinka	15 Ga	26 Karimojong	37 Iru	48 Hehe	59 Swazi
5 Bambara	16 Krochi	27 Lango	38 Gusii	49 Mbundu	60 Venda
6 Mende	17 Yoruba	28 Lugbara	39 Luo (Kenya)	50 Lunda	61 Zulu
7 Dogon	18 Edo (Benin)	29 Alur	40 Nandi	51 Luba	62 Herero
8 Mossi	19 Nupe	30 Nyoro	41 Kikuyu	52 Nyakyusa	63 Basuto
9 Tallensi	20 Ibo	31 Amba	42 Tutsi	53 Bemba	64 Pondo
10 Konkomba	21 Kalabari	32 Gisu	43 Kaguru	54 Ndembu	65 Nama
11 Hausa	22 Shilluk	33 Padhola	44 Mbugwe	55 Chewa	66 Xhosa

*Location for selected groups

characteristics of indigenous religions of Africa. In Chapter Four we will focus on the religion of the Oglala Lakota people of the Great Plains in the context of the recurrent patterns particular to Native American indigenous religions.

AN ORIENTATION TO THE INDIGENOUS RELIGIONS OF AFRICA

The Land and Peoples

The immense continent of Africa (see Figure 3.1 on page 47), the world's second largest, is divided by the world's largest desert, the Sahara, which stretches across northern Africa. Geographically Africa is amazingly diverse. The tropical rain forests of western and central Africa are the image most foreigners have had of what has been called the Dark Continent. However, most of Africa is actually grassland (savannah), inhabited in increasingly restricted areas by the famous animals of the continent—among them elephants, lions, zebras, and giraffes.

The total human population of Africa is nearly a half-billion. North of the Sahara the religions of Islam and Christianity dominate. Christianity (see Chapter Twelve) and Islam (see Chapter Thirteen) have swept through the region south of the Sahara (in what is called sub-Saharan Africa), converting millions, but the traditional, indigenous religions of Africa continue to flourish. Approximately one-quarter of the sub-Saharan African peoples are still associated with the indigenous religions that are our concern in this chapter. About one-fifth are Muslim, with a similar number Christian. With more than 800 separate ethnic groups, there are hundreds of separate religions.

A Brief History of Africa South of the Sahara

Africa is the birthplace of humanity. The earliest remains of the probable ancestors of our species have been unearthed in eastern and southern Africa (in such finds as the famous "Lucy"), dating to a time about 3 million years ago.

Until about 7,000 years ago, Africans lived mostly in small bands of hunters and gatherers. Then, with the advent of agriculture and the later discovery of ironmaking, larger, more integrated

Caravans such as this one through the modern nation of Niger, helped spread the non-indigenous religions of Islam and Christianity to sub-Saharan Africa.

Participants in an indigenous ritual in Cameroon, West Africa.

Dancers from the Dogon people of West Africa. When wearing the stylized masks, the dancers embody the presence of spiritual powers.

societies emerged. Near the beginning of the common era (abbreviated as C.E., as an alternative to A.D.), Bantu-speaking peoples began a southward migration from the eastern coast into the central forests and throughout eastern and southern Africa.

Christianity and Islam were introduced into northern Africa early in their histories, with Islam coming to dominate most of the north by the eighth century. Both religions then spread south with camel caravans through the Sahara Desert. Islam especially helped contribute to the development of a series of great sub-Saharan empires.

Long before European contact, which began in earnest in the 1400s, many highly developed cultures arose in Africa, such as the Benin in the west, Buganda in the east, the Kongo in west central Africa, and the Zimbabwe of the south. The notion that civilization only came to Africa with the arrival of the first Europeans about 500 years ago reflects the cultural arrogance of the invaders. Nevertheless, with the coming of Europeans the face of the continent *was* dramatically altered. The wealth of Africa was exploited, with human slaves and gold the major losses. By the 1800s about 500,000 Africans had been shipped to North America as slave laborers. At the beginning of the twentieth century virtually all of Africa was in the hands of European nations, which created colonies that often cut across ethnic boundaries.

Revolutions against the colonial powers sprang up across the continent, sometimes resulting in bloody conflicts and ultimately, after World War II, in independence. At present, there are over fifty independent African nations. Ethnic rivalries, suppressed during the colonial period, have re-emerged, and economic dependence on the rapidly changing markets in a few resources developed by the colonial powers continues as a significant threat to the well-being of the peoples of Africa.

Common Spiritual Patterns

One of the first Portuguese to land on the southern coast of Africa reported that "The people … have no religion" (Booth 1977: 1). Unfortunately, most of the rest of the world still has little awareness of traditional African religions. Those who do are most likely to have a distorted impression, with images of wicked "witch doctors" casting evil spells and cannibals preparing dinners of boiled missionaries. Our goal here is to counter this lack of understanding and misrepresentation of indigenous African religions.

Methods of Studying African Religions Two ways of introducing traditional African religions are found among modern interpreters. One approach is to identify the patterns common to most, although by no means all, of the indigenous religions of Africa (e.g., Ray 1976 and 1987: 62–69; Mbiti 1970; Parrinder 1976). Another, which is more common today, is to avoid generalizations and describe instead particular religions (e.g., King 1986; Lawson 1985). Here we will give a sampling of both methods, surveying briefly some of the shared characteristics of indigenous African religions that scholars have noticed, but also examining in some detail the religion of the Yoruba people of West Africa. A few of the other well-documented African peoples whom we could have selected (and the modern nations where they are found) include the Nuer (Sudan), the Zulu (South Africa), the Azande (Sudan), the Dinka (Sudan), the Lugbara (Uganda, Zaire), the Maasai (Kenya and Tanzania), and the Ashanti (Ghana and Ivory Coast).

Although traditional African religions are sometimes called "tribal," that is a misnomer. Within the traditional cultures of Africa can be found bands of hunters and gatherers where the tribal concept does not readily apply, and urbanized empires that consist of a variety of tribes, with boundaries among them somewhat blurred.

Myths of Origins Many African societies have myths of origins that portray an original time in which humans were immortal, enjoying an eternal bliss; then they go on to describe why suffering, sickness, and death entered into the human situation. In some of these myths humans disobeyed some divine law. In others a trickster god became involved and led humans astray. In still others humans' pleas to the chief god became so obnoxious that the creator withdrew. In still others

COSMIC QUESTIONS: HOW DID THE WORLD COME INTO BEING?

A Boshongo Creation Legend

In this myth of origins, the creator god (here Bumba) creates by vomiting. Note the explanation of the kinship between humans and other animals. The Boshongo are a part of the Central Bantu of the Lunda Cluster (Leach 1956: 145–46).

In the beginning, in the dark, there was nothing but water. And Bumba was alone.

One day Bumba was in terrible pain. He retched and strained and vomited up the sun. After that light spread over everything. The heat of the sun dried up the water until the black edges of the world began to show. Black sandbanks and reefs could be seen. But there were no living things.

Bumba vomited up the moon and then the stars, and after that the night had its light also.

Still Bumba was in pain. He strained again and nine living creatures came forth: the leopard named Koy Bumba, and Pongo Bumba the crested eagle, the crocodile, Ganda Bumba, and one little fish named Yo; next, old Kono Bumba, the tortoise, and Tsetse, the lightning, swift, deadly, beautiful like the leopard, then the white heron, Nyany Bumba, also one beetle, and the goat named Budi.

Last of all came forth men. There were many men, but only one was white like Bumba. His name was Loko Yima.

The creatures themselves then created all the creatures. The heron created all the birds of the air except the kite. He did not

---

unforeseen problems cause the breakdown of the original situation.

Gods and Spirits   Most of the indigenous religions of Africa have both monotheistic and polytheistic elements in their conceptions of the sacred. In addition, belief in an impersonal force is not uncommon. Like indigenous religions in other parts of the world, African religions often affirm a "high god" who is the ultimate power behind all things and who is understood to be the creator and sustainer of all life. One such god is Mulungu, the supreme god in some East African societies, who is described both as a personal god and as an impersonal spirit. Mulungu is all-powerful and everywhere present; Mulungu's voice is heard in the lightning and Mulungu's power is apparent in the thunder. Another is the chief god Amma of the Dogon, who created the heavens and earth, and then entered into the earth. Without this central deity the world would cease to be, but this god does not often, if ever, become directly involved in human affairs. That is left to the other spiritual beings.

The so-called "lesser gods" and spirits (including the ancestors) usually receive the most attention, since they have the power to influence the course of daily life for the people. They derive their power from the chief god, and sometimes are the messengers of the high god. The spirits are manifest in the objects and forces of nature: thunder, lightning, mountains, forests, lakes and streams, trees, and animals. The earth itself is often pictured as a god, the mother of all life. Some interpreters distinguish among totemic spirits, who are guardians of family and other groups; territorial spirits, who are the spirits of recognized leaders in a particular area, invoked by larger social groupings; and the ancestor spirits, who are revered by families and villages.

Rituals   Typically, rituals in African religions are the means through which relief comes from this-worldly problems. The actions that cause misfortune are typically deeds that insult the gods or spirits (including the ancestors). After consultation

make the kite. The crocodile made serpents and the iguana. The goat produced every beast with horns. Yo, the small fish, brought forth all the fish of all the seas and waters. The beetle created insects.

Then the serpents in their turn made grasshoppers, and the iguana made the creatures without horns.

Then the three sons of Bumba said they would finish the world. The first, Nyone Ngana, made the white ants; but he was not equal to the task, and died of it. The ants, however, thankful for life and being, went searching for black earth in the depths of the world and covered the barren sands to bury and honour their creator.

Chonganda, the second son, brought forth a marvellous living plant from which all the trees and grasses and flowers and plants in the world have sprung. The third son, Chedi Bumba, wanted something different, but for all his trying made only the bird called the kite.

Of all the creatures, Tsetse, lightning, was the only troublemaker. She stirred up so much trouble that Bumba chased her into the sky. Then mankind was without fire until Bumba showed the people how to draw fire out of trees. "There is fire in every tree," he told them, and showed them how to make the firedrill and liberate it. Sometimes today Tsetse still leaps down and strikes the earth and causes damage.

When at last the work of creation was finished, Bumba walked through the peaceful villages and said to the people, "Behold these wonders. They belong to you." Thus from Bumba, the Creator, the First Ancestor, came forth all the wonders that we see and hold and use, and all the brotherhood of beasts and man.

Excerpt from From the Beginning: Creation Myths from Around the World *by Maria Leach. Copyright © 1956 by Harper & Row, Publishers, Inc. Reprinted by permission of HarperCollins Publishers.*

with a priest or priestess, an offering to appease the offended deity or other member of the spirit world is brought.

Places of worship in traditional African religions range from natural phenomena, such as a rock, river, or grove of trees, to elaborate structures made by human hands. Regardless of their origin, they serve as avenues of communication for humans with the spirit world.

Offerings, and priests to manage them, are necessary to maintain peaceful relations with spiritual beings and forces. Shrines are built to honor the spirits and house images associated with them. Special societies form around various deities and spirits. The spirits also have the power to possess humans. Some people, chosen by the spirit beings, enter into special, continuing relationships. The spirits, when properly propitiated, work through them to cure illnesses and bring solutions to other problems.

Virtually every traditional African family has an ancestor shrine. Once an ancestor has entered into the spirit world through the conducting of the proper funeral ritual, that ancestor is thought to be immortal, existing beyond historical time. Therefore, ancestors may appear in myths of origins. Ancestral images in the shrines are not accurate portrayals of the deceased ancestor but are intended to evoke the ancestor's continued presence. Not everyone who dies may become an "ancestor"—only persons who had prominent positions in the family or society. More ordinary people become spirits who must be properly venerated so that they will pass on to the spirit world and cease to take an active role in ongoing communal life. By contrast, the ancestors are very much involved in the affairs of the community and must be consulted for advice on important occasions. They are offended when not properly venerated, and offended ancestors can be a source of great trouble in a family, village, or nation.

Divination is also a common element of traditional African religions, as specialists use items such as animal entrails or shells to ascertain the nature of a person's situation and project what will occur in

QUESTIONS ABOUT THE SACRED: WHAT IS SACRED?

An African Poem about God

This African poem challenges the commonly held view that indigenous peoples have a simplistic or naive conception of the spiritual. This poem evokes the mystery of the sacred (Mbiti 1969: 34–35).

> *In the beginning was God,*
> *Today is God*
> *Tomorrow will be God.*
> *Who can make an image of God?*
> *He has no body.*
> *He is as a word which comes out of your mouth.*
> *That word! It is no more,*
> *It is past, and still it lives.*
> *So is God.*

Excerpt from **African Religions and Philosophy** *by John Mbiti. Reprinted by permission of Heinemann Educational Books Limited.*

the future. Dreams and their interpretation are also important. The view that a person's larger destiny is determined before his or her birth is particularly common in West African religions. Through divination a person can receive knowledge about the direction of this destiny and use that information to help seek the assistance of spirits to ensure a positive rather than a negative outcome.

Sacrifices are quite common in African religions. Vegetable offerings or animal victims (such as the ox sacrifice of the Nuer) are given to the spirits and gods, with the expectation that they will return the favor by bestowing some blessing on the worshipper. Sacrifices are offered on a regular, seasonal basis, or in response to some special personal, family, or societal situation. The one bringing the sacrifice often participates in the consumption of the offering, sharing the meal with the honored god or ancestral spirit and reaffirming the communal bonds that join them. Although human sacrifices did occur on rare occasions in some traditional African religions, their presence and importance have been grossly exaggerated.

As with other indigenous religions, rites of passage (especially at birth, puberty, marriage, and death) play an exceedingly important role in African traditional religions. The ritual marking birth often begins after the first week, when the baby's survival is more certain. At this point the baby's name is chosen, frequently through the use of divination. In a number of African societies the infant is then symbolically presented to the moon as a member of the family of all living beings.

During childhood boys and girls receive instruction on the values of the society and their proper roles within it. As puberty approaches boys and girls are separated and given special instruction in the roles they will have as adults and as to their expected behavior sexually. Through this ritual the young person passes out of childhood into adulthood and full membership in the society. This permanent change in status is often symbolized by indelible marks made on the body of the initiate. Circumcision of males and clitoridectomies of females (see below) are widely practiced, although the latter is coming under strong opposition.

Indigenous African religions are particularly noted for their magnificent works of arts, including carved figures of the gods, spirits, and ancestors; masks and headdresses; staffs; and other ceremonial instruments. The figures serve both to embody the divine beings and as a means through which they may be propitiated by worshippers. Although stylized, the figures are typically in human form. As is typical in most religions, shrines are built to house the images, with two areas—one for worshippers and priests and another where the spirit "dwells." The distinctive masks are frequently worn in communal dances.

New Religious Movements

In the last century, primarily as a result of contact with Christian and Muslim missionaries and in response to colonial domination, over 7,000 new religious movements, with more than 32 million adherents, have emerged in sub-Saharan Africa. These religions combine some of the above elements of traditional African religions with features of Christianity and Islam. Particularly active since the 1920s, these religions began as movements

---

QUESTIONS OF MORALITY: WHAT ARE OUR OBLIGATIONS TO OTHERS?

Instructions to Yamana Initiates

These instructions are given to initiates at the initiation ritual of the Yamana people, according to anthropologist Martin Gusinde (Gusinde 1961 [vol. 3]: 740).

Do not seek to benefit only yourself, but think of other people also. If you yourself have an abundance, do not say: "The others do not concern me, I need not bother about them!" If you were lucky in hunting, let others share it. Moreover, show them the favorable spots where there are many sea lions which can easily be slain. Let others have their share too occasionally. If you want to amass everything for yourself, other people will stay away from you and no one will want to be with you. If you should one day fall ill, no one will visit you because, for your part, you did not formerly concern yourself about others.

If you come into the region where you were born and you want to set up camp with several other people, give them [the ones who are unfamiliar with the site] the sheltered place. Do not think, "What do I care if these strangers lose their canoe." Rather, take good care of the visiting strangers, for they will return home and there they will praise you.

If you know of a favorable hunting ground there [where you were born], encourage the visitors and say: "Go to that place, there you will surely find rich booty." Point the place out to them exactly so that they can obtain large amounts of meat to take on their journey.

Grant other people something also. The Yamana do not like a person who acts selfishly.

No one likes a perverse, obstinate person: everyone speaks scornfully of him and avoids him.

Excerpt from The Yamana *by Martin Gusinde. Reprinted by permission of Human Relations Area Files Press.*

---

among oppressed peoples, offering them ways of expressing hope for freedom from colonial domination and a renewed sense of community within a transformed social situation.

One type of the new African religious movements is called "neotraditional," because of an emphasis on "aspects of traditional religion in the new social and cultural context" (Jules-Rosette 1987: 85). Examples of such neotraditional movements include the Bwiti of Gabon and the Church of the God of Our Ancestors of Zaire. Other types of new movements are the "indigenous churches" (such as the Harris Movement of the Ivory Coast or the Aladura Movement of Nigeria, which will be discussed below). They were started by African leaders in direct response to colonialism. A third type, the "separatist movements," broke off from established Christian churches or Islamic groups.

Examples include the Jamaa Movement of Zaire and Legion of Mary of Kenya, which originated within Roman Catholicism; and Balokole ("the Saved Ones"), also known as the East African Revival Movement, a Protestant separatist group.

CASE STUDY—THE YORUBA OF WEST AFRICA

Introduction: Who Are the Yoruba?

Numbering as many as 15 million, the Yoruba are descendants of one of the most influential cultures of West Africa. Most Yoruba live in the southwestern region of the modern nation of Nigeria, but a number reside in surrounding countries such as Benin, Ghana, and Togo. About twenty subgroups within Yoruba culture have been identified, each

HUMAN DESTINY: WHAT HAPPENS AFTER DEATH?

An African Poem on Life after Death

In the indigenous worldview the human spirit is one with nature, for all nature is alive spiritually. This African poem, by Birago Diop, a Senegambian author, expresses an understanding of the afterlife in which the human spirit lives on as part of nature (Jahn 1961: 108).

> Hear more often things than beings,
> the voice of the fire listening,
> hear the voice of the water.
> Hear in the wind
> the bushes sobbing,
> it is the sign of our forebears.
>
> Those who are dead are never gone:
> they are there in the thickening shadow.
> The dead are not under the earth:
> they live in the tree that rustles,
> they are in the wood that groans,
> they are in the water that runs,
> they are in the water that sleeps,
> they are in the hut, they are in the crowd,
> the dead are not dead.
>
> Those who are dead are never gone:
> they are in the breast of the woman,
> they are in the child who is wailing,
> and in the firebrand that flames.
> The dead are not under the earth:
> they are in the fire that is dying,
> they are in the grasses that weep,
> they are in the whimpering rocks,
> they are in the forest, they are in the house,
> the dead are not dead.

Excerpt from **Muntu: An Outline of the New African Culture** *by Janheinz Jahn. Coopyright © 1961, 1989 by Faber and Faber. Reprinted by permission of Grove Press.*

nificant presence in Brazil, Cuba, Jamaica, and North America. A significant, but hard to estimate, number of contemporary African-Americans are descended from Yoruba slaves.

Archaeological and religious evidence suggests that the Yoruba have lived in their West Africa homeland since the fifth century before the Common Era (B.C.E.). Before the end of the first millennium the Yoruba had developed a complex urban society, with the important city of Ile-Ife dating from the ninth century. While other cities such as Oyo have been more important politically, over a thousand years later Ile-Ife continues as the center of Yoruba religious life.

There is a vast collection of Yoruba poetry, organized into collections called *odu*. They provide great insight into the basic values of Yoruba culture.

Gods and Spirits

According to the Yoruba worldview the cosmos has two levels, *Orun* and *Aiye*. Orun is heaven or sky, and is the abode of the Supreme God and the other gods (*orisa*) and ancestors. Aiye is the place of habitation for humans and other animals, as well as the home of the *omoraiye* (the children of the world), the beings responsible for witchcraft and sorcery.

The Yoruba name for the Supreme God is *Olorun Olodumare*. *Olorun* (Owner of the Sky) is the Lord above all, who dwells in the heavens and is the source of all life. He is also known as *Alaaye* (The One Who Lives) or *Elemii* (The Lord of Life). Another title is *Eledaa* (Creator). Although people may pray to Olorun, there are no shrines in Olorun's honor, and no rituals or sacrifices to influence Olorun.

According to one version of the Yoruba myth of origins, at the beginning Olorun lived in the heavens with other deities. The heavens and the earth were close together, and the earth was a desolate marsh. The heavenly beings at times came to earth to hunt. When Olorun decided to make the land firm, he commanded *Orisa-nla* (Great Divinity) to carry out the plan. When Orisa-nla came to earth, he threw down soil and released a five-toed hen and pigeon. When the hen spread the soil the marshy waters were forced back and dry land

with its own distinctive linguistic, political, and religious patterns. In fact, the use of the term "Yoruba" to designate these related peoples collectively may very well be a nineteenth-century development. Many Yoruba were forcefully taken to the Americas as slaves, where they have become a sig-

appeared. Then trees were planted, and Olorun breathed life into sixteen humans and sent them to earth. He taught Orisa-nla to make human forms, and then he breathed life into them. In other versions of the myth, Orisa-nla became drunk on palm wine and *Oduduwa,* his rival in the myth, is the creator. In this version Ile-Ife is the place of creation. Yoruba oral history remembers Oduduwa (or *Odua*) as the original king and creator of the Yoruba people, ruling from Ile-Ife.

Humans consist of *ara* (matter) formed by Orisa-nla, into which Olorun breathes *emi,* spirit. When a Yoruba dies, the body returns to the earth (see below) and the spirit is reincarnated as a new child.

The orisa in general are projections of the power of Olorun, found in elements of nature and among the distinguished ancestors. According to some Yoruba legends, there are 401 orisa, all of whom were once humans who lived especially notable lives. This is a way of symbolizing the variety of orisa and ways of responding to them ritually. Orisa-nla (also called *Obatala*) is but one of the orisa, although as the one who forms babies in their wombs, he is the most important. He is worshipped throughout the Yoruba homeland. To mock infants, including those who are disformed, is to insult Orisa-nla their creator. He is worshipped with offerings of pure water, and his color is white. His followers often wear white clothes. The two main taboos associated with Orisa-nla are drinking palm wine and having contact with dogs. In one tradition Obatala and Oduduwa are portrayed androgynously, combining male and female elements.

In Yoruba mythology the deity to whom diviners turn most for guidance is *Orunmila,* for he was present at creation and knows the destinies of human beings. With the belief that humans have a destiny given by Olorun that they have forgotten, the practice of *ifa* or divination is particularly important.

The trickster figure in the Yoruba pantheon is *Esu.* He traverses the earth, reporting on people to the orisa, and deceiving people into wrong actions (without which the deities would not receive offerings from people seeking to win back their favor). Sacrifices to the orisa must include a portion for

A drummer in one of the many festivals of the Yoruba people of West Africa.

Esu, to ensure that the offering reaches the intended divine recipient. Esu mediates the conflicting qualities of reverence and irreverence, good and evil, allowing him to serve as a mediator between heaven and earth. The association of Esu with the devil by Christians is an example of the imposition of a foreign understanding that distorts the meaning within the culture's own religious context.

Different orisa are popular in different areas. *Sango* (King and Thunderer), once the demonic king of Oyo, is worshipped in towns that once were part of the Oyo empire. He guarantees the moral order, punishing those who violate social norms. He is also one of the deities who most frequently "mounts" (takes possession of) worshippers. Another popular orisa is *Ayelala*, once a slave girl who was sacrificed in place of a man who had done a wicked deed. She is now the deity who punishes immorality.

Ogun, the most widely worshipped orisa, is the Yoruba god of war and iron, with associated powers of both formation and destruction. He lives at the fringes of society and is feared, because he can inflict his power to kill or destroy on his own people without warning. He also watches over the hunter and forester. Like other orisa he specializes in particular areas of life: in his case, violence and, through his patronage of iron, culture. He is also viewed as the guarantor of justice; in court, traditional Yoruba swear to speak the truth by kissing a piece of iron in the name of Ogun. Drivers often carry a representation of Ogun as an amulet to ward off accidents. Here is an example of a song sung seeking Ogun's protection of the iron objects owned by the petitioner (Ray 1976: 80):

> *Ogun, here are Ehun's kola nuts;*
> *He rides a bicycle,*
> *He cultivates with a machete,*
> *He fells trees with the axe.*
> *Do not let Ehun meet your anger this year,*
> *Take care of him.*
> *He comes this year,*
> *Enable him to come next season.*

Another Yoruba deity who possesses both male and female qualities is *Orisa-oko*, patron of farmers. *Ile*, the earth, is the dry land of the creation myth. When a Yoruba child is born, the baby is laid on the earth, and at death the deceased is returned to the womb of the earth. According to a legend, when Ile became angry she caused crops to fail and living beings to become sterile.

Yoruba do not exclusively worship one orisa. Instead, a particular family or village is under the sway of an assemblage of orisa, evident in the variety of orisa images in their shrines. Each person has his or her own personal *orisa* (or *ori inun*, inner head), symbolic of a personal destiny, an array of possibilities and limitations, which cannot be altered. At birth one loses memory of this des-

tiny. A person must pass through life, acknowledging the ori as an orisa who must be called upon in order to realize the fullest potential of this given destiny.

As with other indigenous religions, ancestors play an important role in Yoruba religion. Certain ancestral spirits may return through masked dancers, who appear at popular yearly festivals with special messages for those left behind. Within families the head of the family is charged with seeing that the ancestors are properly venerated. In addition to the family ancestors, there are also "deified ancestors," leaders who because of their particular contributions are now venerated. They are worshipped within a particular locality rather than within a family.

Also important to understand is the Yoruba conception of *ase*, the divine energy that causes things to come into existence and to pass away. Orisa manifest ase, yet it is present in all things. In all situations it is the force that opposes chaos.

Religious Leaders

There are a number of different practitioners within Yoruba religion. At the family level the responsibility for maintaining the proper rituals and ensuring that all members are following the basic guidelines of balanced life falls on the *olori ebi*, the head of the family. In towns or cities the *oba* (chief, leader) is in charge of the proper conducting of rituals. In the Yoruba worldview, all leaders originally came from Ile-Ife, where the gods established the earthly kingdom. In addition, there are priests associated with the shrines of Ife and those throughout the Yoruba homeland. Each of the many deities has its own priesthood. For example, the *aworo* (or *babalawo*, father of secret things) priesthood is associated with Orunmila, and they are therefore the religious functionaries most often consulted for advice through an elaborate process of divining. Such advice is sought both for individual concerns and to determine the course of events affecting the family or larger group. Becoming a priest requires a long period of training and apprenticeship.

In addition to the priests who conduct the sacrifices and other aspects of ordered religious practice, there are *elegun*, shamans who are sponta-neously possessed by spirits and become intermedi-aries for them. However, any Yoruba, most often in the context of one of the festivals, may be possessed and enter into an ecstatic state. In fact, such pos-sessions are typical.

The *oloogun* is the Yoruba religious func-tionary who specializes in healing, often working in cooperation with a priest. Because healing comes from the gods and spirits, the oloogun are viewed merely as channels for the rejuvenating power.

Rituals

The most important annual Yoruba festival is *Odun Egungun*, which focuses on the ancestors of the father's family. The *egungun* are masks created from layers of cloth, made of dark colors with white edges, and also the Yoruba males who wear them. The masked dancers enter with dignified pace, then engage in whirling motions that cause the cloth lay-ers to fly out in various patterns. The dancers embody the presence and power of the ancestors. Their masks are handed down from generation to generation.

Another important yearly Yoruba festival is known as *Eje*, the new yam festival. Yams are a sta-ple of the Yoruba diet, and their successful cultiva-tion and harvesting is essential to the well-being of the people.

The *Gelede* festival at the time of the spring rains is given in honor of the female "mothers" (*awon iya wa*). All women are recognized as possess-ing awesome creative and destructive power, but this festival particularly honors women elders and ancestors. It is a joyous, though reverential celebra-tion. It takes place in the market, where transitions occur, and where women dominate. (The men who dance are seen as agents of the women.) At night masked dancers enter the market, with the white and bearded Spirit of the Ancestresses as Great Mother and the Spirit Bird, with a long and pointed red beak, prominent in the masquerade. They rep-resent the foremothers. During the night ceremony the various gods are called upon, Ogun as the virile one and Esu as the deceiver and messenger. The particular concerns of the people are voiced, and prayers are made for long life and many children.

The next afternoon children dance, so that they may learn the proper steps and ways to wear the masks. Later adults take over, creating a huge gath-ering. The culmination is a dancer representing a female ancestor, promising blessing and joy.

Sacrifices are very important in Yoruba ritual, with offerings of prayers, nuts, or animals. Sacrifices are chosen that reflect the character of the orisa; so, for example, the war god Ogun receives the carniv-orous dog as his sacrificial food. In return, the power of the orisa passes to the worshipper.

Yoruba rites of passage have their own distinc-tive characteristics. Before birth a mother visits a babalawo so that the priest may divine the new-born's destiny and ascertain (with a healer's assis-tance) which medicines to take to ensure a good birth and what taboos to practice. After the birth of the child the mother returns to the priest, who again divines the child's destiny. The parents then make an offering at the shrine of the orisa most important to the family. If the child is a girl, a naming ceremony is held on the seventh day; a boy's naming ceremo-ny occurs on the ninth day. Twins are named on the eighth day. A name is chosen that honors the orisa with which the family is specially related.

Yoruba children receive instruction through-out their early years about the rituals and customs of the family and larger community. Males are typ-ically circumcised early in life in preparation for marriage. After intricate negotiations between the two families, carried out by a mediator and includ-ing divination, the wedding takes place. After elab-orate preparations in the homes of both bride and bridegroom, the bride is led in procession to the bridegroom's home for the marriage ceremony.

Upon a Yoruba's death, particularly when the deceased is the head of a family or another impor-tant person, an elaborate funerary rite occurs. The dead person is thoroughly washed and laid out in the dwelling. A bed made out of the finest wood is made, and the person is buried in the family com-pound, with appropriate sacrifices so that the per-son will be received into *orun rere* (good heaven). Masked dancers then emerge from the dead per-son's home, beginning a time of feasting and danc-ing. If the person is worthy of the status of an ancestor, a shrine marks the place of burial and becomes a place of worship for the family, who consider the ancestor to be present with them.

As with other indigenous religious traditions, the Yoruba have distinct religious societies. One of the principal Yoruba secret societies is the *Osugbo* or *Ogboni* society. Initiates are taught to understand their special house as a microcosm of the universe. Thus the mystery seems to be, as it often is in such groups, the original unity of all reality, which goes beyond all the opposites of ordinary human experience.

Amulets and other magic objects are used for protection against hostile powers. Small objects, made potent by incantations, may also be used to negatively influence enemies.

Islam was introduced to the Yoruba centuries ago, but was not widely embraced until the Yoruba began to be victimized by slave traders and came under the control of the British in the nineteenth century. Then many Yoruba converted to Islam, perhaps in part as a form of protest against the efforts of Christian missionaries endorsed by the British (beginning about 1840).

Aladura: A Modern Religious Movement

Other Yoruba have affiliated with some of the modern movements that have arisen in the last century. Particularly influential among the Yoruba is the *Aladura* (People of Prayer) movement, which began in response to the missionary activity of the Church of England (the Anglican Church). It originated not as a separate movement, but as a supplement to the rituals and organization of the Anglican Church. However, groups within the Aladura movement began to create their own distinct identities. One such group is the *Egbe Serafu* (Seraphim Society), inspired by the vision of angels received by a young woman named Abiodun Akinsowon during a Christian ritual in 1925. The appeal of the groups that make up the Aladura movement is their emphasis on charismatic leadership, visionary interpretation of the Christian Bible, inspired prayer, and healing. It has grown and now can be found throughout Africa and in other parts of the world where Yoruba people live.

RESPONSES TO CONTEMPORARY ETHICAL ISSUES

The Ecological Crisis

A traditional Yoruba proverb expresses the most widely held attitude among those who participate in African traditional religions toward how humans should relate to the non-human world: One going to take a pointed stick to pinch a baby bird should first try it on himself to see how it hurts. In other words, humans should not see themselves as lords over nature, empowered to treat other living beings however they feel. We are all related, and as members of one living community we must treat animals as well as other humans with respect and reverence.

As in other areas of the world, the tension between pressures to modernize that take a toll on the balance of life and this traditional reverence is one of the most significant issues facing African leaders.

War

The Akan and Ewe people of the African country of Ghana are committed to peace. The Ewe idealize persons who are peace-loving and calm. Two of the four days of their week are designated as "cool days," set aside for ritual activities that instill values of peace. "In the event that disputes and disagreements arise between individuals, family members, and in society, efforts are made to solve the conflicts quickly by the head of the family or clan by summoning the disputing parties and some kinsfolk for arbitration" (Ansah 1989: 259).

Abortion

For indigenous religions in general, all life is sacred, for all life is the realm of the spiritual. The Akan and Ewe people of Ghana reflect an awareness of the sanctity of life in the frequency of the term "life" in personal names and common greetings. Since abortion results in the taking of life, it is viewed as a "bad act." During pregnancy a variety of rituals surround the expectant mother to protect both her and the unborn child (Ansah 1989: 261–62).

The indigenous attitude toward marriage and family life also supports a negative attitude toward abortion. Prosperity is measured by the number of children in the family, and a large family is necessary to provide for the welfare of elders. Therefore, abortion is thought to be a maladaptive behavior, and is discouraged on those grounds.

In most indigenous societies abortion was not a significant issue until modern times. Now it is a frequent concern, as young women are less willing to abide by the taboos against intercourse before marriage and more concerned about protecting their own futures despite the proscriptions against abortion.

Euthanasia

The Akan and Ewe people of Ghana are opposed to euthanasia because of a firm belief that life itself is the highest of human values. Since the end of euthanasia is the destruction of life, it cannot be permitted. One proverb puts it this way: "No form of life should be considered unworthy of living" (Ansah 1989: 262).

However, in other indigenous cultures euthanasia is practiced. Allowing an elderly person to go off alone and die is sanctioned by some groups as an acceptable way of putting the well-being of the group before one's own "right to life."

Economic Justice

The Yoruba have a number of proverbs that teach the dignity of hard work: "weeping will not save anyone from penury," "the pretended illness of the indolent is incurable," "labor is the cure of poverty" (Abogunrin 1989: 282–83). However, Yoruba tradition also teaches that those who by their labor acquire wealth are expected to share their resources with others. Riches pass away ("money comes and goes like the showers of rain"), so what a person should strive for is a good name. A reputation is gained not by the accumulation of wealth but by generosity. Giving freely to the poor is rewarded in life beyond death.

Unfortunately, both Western economic-growth models and indigenized socialist models have proven ineffective in helping the economic

The Bantu-speaking Zulu people of South Africa have a proud military tradition, re-enacted in this warriors' dance. Violence between Zulus and supporters of the African National Congress plagued the transition to majority rule in South Africa, but subsequently subsided.

plight of many indigenous peoples. The poor have become poorer and the rich richer. According to the World Bank, by 1980 70 percent of Africans lived in absolute poverty (Turner 1985: 84).

According to Turner, indigenous cultures must adapt if economic development is to occur. They must turn from a cosmos based on necessary internal relations to one revealing contingent relationships. They must cease trying to deal with power through magic and ritual, and turn instead to dependence on science and faith. By the addition of history to myth, they need to develop a new category for dealing with time. They must move from a *society* that is closed, unitary, and sacral, to one that is open, pluralist, and secular. They must view *evil* as involving moral rather than ritual pollution, and as located internally in the individual as well as externally in evil forces (Turner 1985: 93).

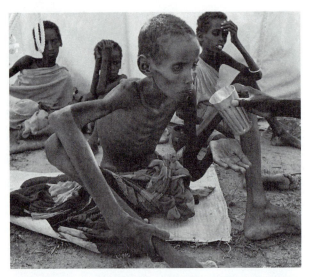

A 1992 famine in the African nation of Somalia was caused not by natural disaster, but by a protracted civil war. Here a child receives oral rehydration at a Red Cross feeding center.

Are these the changes necessary in indigenous religions if the abject poverty in which so many peoples are forced to live is to change? If these changes were adopted, could indigenous peoples preserve their identity? Is there some way in which the traditional values can be preserved without condemning the people to poverty?

Many of the new religious movements of Africa (which now number in the thousands) provide an institutional matrix for economic development. The Harris movement in West Africa is an example. The largest derivative of this movement, Deima or Dahima, is credited with being the principal factor for the relative economic success in Ivory Coast (Turner 1985: 91–92).

Gender Roles and the Status of Women

Among the Akan and Ewe peoples of modern Ghana, traditional roles for women persist (Ansah 1989: 256–57). A growing number of women have pursued educations and achieved considerable social equality in the cities. However, traditional society is clearly patriarchal, and women who do not break away from these patterns of male dominance entirely rarely challenge them from within.

Gender inequality in Akan and Ewe cultures is manifest in a number of ways. For example, widows must maintain a period of ceremonial mourning after the death of a husband for twelve to eighteen months, while a man's prescribed period of grief ranges from seven to twenty-four days. Severe restrictions are placed on menstruating women, who are considered ritually impure.

Within Ewe tradition women are treated as spiritual, if not social and economic, equals. The deity is conceived of as both male and female, and in the hierarchy of deities many are feminine. Women may assume priestly duties. However, among some of the Ewe only a woman who has reached menopause (and symbolically become a man) is eligible for the highest priestly office, while a male priest of any age may be elevated.

In Yoruba culture women as well as men are expected to have a vocation, often tending their own farms or engaging in other money-raising activities. However, the husband is considered the head of the home and the principal breadwinner. Women are priests in many religious groups, with men worshiping under their leadership. However, some groups that focus on ancestral spirits bar women's participation. Despite these leadership roles, women are still stereotyped in Yoruba society as too emotional and unable to keep secrets (Abogunrin 1989: 280).

In African and other indigenous religions, special rites of passage for women relating to fertility play an important role. Specific rituals for women, for puberty, marriage, birth, menopause, and death, are found in virtually all indigenous cultures. The seclusion rites associated with menstruation also symbolize the power associated with the feminine in indigenous religions. All of these enable women in indigenous cultures to feel a sacral importance tied to gender, and a special empowerment separate from men. Women's societies typically oversee all these gender-specific rituals for women, creating an independent source and arena of sacral influence for women, as well as a special sense of community among women.

The disfiguring clitoridectomy common in a number of cultures in Africa and Asia is an ongoing concern. The external genitalia of girls as young as infants, but usually older, are removed or mutilated and their vulvas sewn shut, leaving an opening only large enough for urination and menstruation. It is estimated that about 2 million girls in Africa are made to endure clitoridectomies each year. The purpose is to ensure virginity and to eliminate sexual sensation. It may also be that the clitoridectomy is thought to remove any signs of maleness in the girl (the clitoris being perceived as a type of penis). In any event, an international movement in the developed world, championed by Pulitzer Prize–winning African-American novelist Alice Walker, has emerged to try to force an end to the practice. Many educated Africans also want to end female genital mutilation, but many others join traditionalists in viewing the efforts of Walker and others as examples of "cultural condescension." One Kenyan women's rights leader made the point this way: "Let indigenous people fight it according to their own traditions. It will die faster than if others tell us what to do." In response, Walker has said, "Torture is not culture" (Kaplan 1993: 124).

Homosexuality

With regard to homosexuality among peoples who practice indigenous African religions, the evidence is ambiguous. There seems to be both condemnation and acceptance, depending on the culture and the observer reporting.

Among many traditional African peoples, like the Akan and Ewe of Ghana, homosexuality is simply outside the normal frame of reference. To them it is simply inconceivable "that a person can have sexual desire toward another person of his own sex. Even animals, they contend, distinguish between male and female in their sex life" (Ansah 1989: 257). Among the Yoruba, "homosexuality, lesbianism, and having sex with animals are not only taboos, but are regarded as mental illnesses that require as much treatment as those who eat sand or potsherd" (Abogunrin 1989: 280).

These negative attitudes may very well reflect the influence of Western cultural incursions.

Awareness that most Europeans and Americans did not approve of homosexuality probably led to the concealment of more positive perspectives. A recent study (Baum 1993) has found information about the practice of homosexuality in about fifty African societies and evidence that various forms of homosexuality are accepted in many of them. For example, egalitarian homosexuality was found in 20 percent of the societies. In most cases these relations developed during adolescence among young men, sometimes during rites of passage, and were abandoned at marriage. Reciprocal homosexual relations during adulthood were found to be more common among women. In part, this may result from the existence of polygynous households in which the wives live separately from their husband and in close social interaction with one another.

Transgenerational homosexuality is present in some societies in association with the rite of initiation to adulthood for males. The older partner takes on the role of mentor of the initiate, and the sexual relationship is seen as a crucial part of the young man's preparation for life as an adult.

The Azande practice an "age-structured, military" homosexuality. The king's household includes not only hundreds of wives but some boys who are "married" to him. Warriors also "married" boys, who travelled with them and were addressed as "my love" (Herdt 1987: 448).

In South Africa transgenerational homosexuality is found in mining communities, where older men take junior partners as their "wives." This is a result of the male migrant labor under apartheid, which has forced men to live apart from their families in same-sex communities.

Transgenderal homosexuality is found among the peoples of southern and central Africa. It is often associated with religious roles, as the person in the transgenderal role is seen to combine both male and female spiritual power. For example, in the religion of the Ila of Zambia the male *mwaami* (prophet) might dress as and live among women (although there is no indication that this meant engaging in sexual relations with men). The transgenderal role is taken typically as the result of a dream or vision.

CHAPTER SUMMARY

 The purpose of this chapter was to introduce readers to the religions of indigenous peoples of the world, people who have lived in regions of the world since before the beginning of the historical era and who practice their own native religious traditions. We discussed some of the problems associated with studying indigenous religions, especially the issue of whether outsiders may hope to come to understand the complexities of these religions without badly distorting them. In the past scholars have labelled these religions as "primitive," "preliterate," and "basic," among other names. We chose "indigenous" because it is more descriptive, and because it is increasingly being used by representatives of these religions as a self-designation.

Our approach to a description of the indigenous religions was twofold. First, we identified some shared characteristics of these religions as a whole. Using the "framework for understanding" developed in Chapter One, we examined what might be called the general indigenous worldview.

In this chapter we turned to the indigenous religions of Africa. First, we identified some of the common patterns found in most (but by no means all) of the traditional religions of Africa. We then examined in some detail the religion of the Yoruba people of West Africa. The chapter concluded with the discussion of responses to contemporary ethical questions among indigenous African religions.

QUESTIONS FOR DISCUSSION AND REFLECTION

1. Indigenous peoples believe that "everything is alive; everything is sacred." What would be the impact if this belief were more widely embraced?

2. Are you a member of a group that has some of the characteristics of indigenous religions, such as "totems," "taboos," and rites of initiation into the "mysteries" of the group? Do these groups play a similar function as that of "totemic clans"?

3. What was your attitude toward indigenous religions before studying this chapter? Has reading this chapter affected your attitude? If so, how? If not, why not?

4. What will be lost if indigenous religions vanish? Should people in the "developed" world work to preserve indigenous religions? If so, how? If not, why not?

5. The accumulation of individual wealth over an extended period is frowned on in many indigenous cultures. Why is that the case? Would you like to live in such a culture? Could you adapt?

6. Is there evidence today to support the indigenous religions' teaching that failure to live in harmony with all the beings of the earth will lead humans to destruction? Is it feasible to restore a way of life characterized by this way of harmony?

7. What about the religion of the Yoruba people most intrigues you? If you are or were a descendant of the Yoruba people who were taken as slaves to the Americas, would you want to learn more about the religion of your ancestors? Of what value would such a study be to you? Why should people with no contact with the Yoruba be interested in their religion?

SOURCES AND SUGGESTIONS FOR FURTHER STUDY

Indigenous Religions in General

CAMPBELL, JOSEPH, 1970 *The Masks of God: Primitive Mythology*. New York: Viking.

ELIADE, MIRCEA, 1959 *The Sacred and the Profane: The Nature of Religion*, tr. Willard R. Task. New York: Harper & Row.

   1964 *Shamanism: Archaic Techniques of Ecstasy*, tr. Willard Trask. Princeton, N.J.: Princeton University Press.

GILL, SAM, 1982 *Beyond "The Primitive": The Religions of Nonliterate People*. Englewood Cliffs, N.J.: Prentice Hall.

Lewis, I.M.,1989 *Ecstatic Religion: A Study of Shamanism and Spirit Possession*, 2nd ed. New York: Routledge.

VAN GENNEP, ARNOLD, 1960 *Rites of Passage*, tr. Monika B. Vizedom and Gabrielle L. Caffe. London: Routledge.

African Indigenous Religions

General

BOOTH, NEWELL S., JR., 1977 *African Religions: A Symposium*. New York: NOK Publishers.

GUSINDE, MARTIN, 1961 *The Yamana: The Life and Thought of the Water Nomads of Cape Horn*, tr. Frieda Schutze. New Haven, Conn.: Human Relations File [1932].

IDOWU, E. BOLAJI , 1973 *African Traditional Religion*. Maryknoll, N.Y.: Orbis.

JAHN, JANHEINZ , 1961 *Muntu: An Outline of the New African Culture*, tr. Marjorie Greene. New York: Grove Press.

JULES-ROSETTE, BENNETTA, 1987 "African Religions: Modern Movements," in *The Encyclopedia of Religion*, vol. 1, ed. Mircea Eliade (New York: Macmillan), 82–89.

KING, NOEL Q., 1986 *African Cosmos: An Introduction to Religion in Africa*. Belmont, Calif.: Wadsworth.

LAWSON, E. THOMAS, 1985 *Religions of Africa: Traditions in Transformation*. San Francisco: Harper & Row.

MBITI, JOHN S., 1969 *African Religions and Philosophy*. New York: Praeger.

PARRINDER, GEOFFREY, 1976 *African Traditional Religion*, 3rd ed. New York: Harper & Row.

RAY, BENJAMIN C., 1976 *African Religions: Symbol, Ritual, and Community*. Englewood Cliffs, N.J.: Prentice Hall.

   1987 "African Religions: An Overview," in *The Encyclopedia of Religion*, vol. 1, 62–69.

The Religion of the Yoruba

AWOLALU, J. OMOSADE, 1979 *Yoruba Beliefs and Sacrificial Rites*. London: Longman.

DREWAL, MARGARET, 1983 *Gelede: A Study of Art and Feminine Power Among the Yoruba*. Bloomington: Indiana University Press.

EADES, J.S. 1980 *The Yoruba Today*. Cambridge: Cambridge University Press.

IDOWU, E. BOJALI 1962 *Olodumare: God in Yoruba Belief*. London: Longman.

PEEL, J.D.Y. 1968 *Aladura: A Religious Movement Among the Yoruba*. Oxford: Oxford University Press.

PEMBERTON, JOHN III 1987 "Yoruba Religion," in *The Encyclopedia of Religion*, vol. 15, 535–38.

Ethical Issues

General

ABOGUNRIN, SAMUEL O., 1989 "Ethics in Yoruba Religious Tradition," in *World Religions and Global Ethics*, ed. S. Cromwell Crawford (New York: Paragon House), 266–96.

ANSAH, JOHN K., 1989 "The Ethics of Traditional African Religions," in *World Religions and Global Ethics*, 241–65.

Economic Justice

TURNER, HAROLD W., 1985 "The Relationship Between Development and New Religious Movements in the Tribal Societies of the Third World," in *God and Global Justice: Religion and Poverty in an Unequal World*, ed. Frederick Ferré and Rita H. Mataragno (New York: Paragon House), 84–110.

Gender Roles and the Status of Women

KAPLAN, DAVID A., 1993 "Is It Torture or Tradition? The Genital Mutilation of Young African Girls Sparks an Angry Intellectual Debate in the West." *Newsweek*, December 20: 124.

Homosexuality

BAUM, ROBERT, 1993 "Homosexuality and the Traditional Religions of the Americas and Africa," *Homosexuality and World Religions*, ed. Arlene Swidler. Valley Forge, Pa.: Trinity Press International.

HERDT, GILBERT, 1987 "Homosexuality," in *The Encyclopedia of Religion*, vol. 6, 445–53.

Other References

BROWN, JOSEPH EPES, 1988 *The Spiritual Legacy of the American Indian*. New York: Crossroad.

LEACH, MARIA , 1956 *The Beginning: Creation Myths Around the World*. New York: Funk and Wagnalls.

CHAPTER **4**

Indigenous Religions of North America

INTRODUCTION

When Europeans first encountered the native inhabitants of what we now call North America, they, like the Europeans who first visited Africa, thought they had discovered a people with no religion. Christopher Columbus wrote of the people he found on the first islands he "discovered" in the new world in 1492: "They have no religion and I think that they would be very quickly Christian-ized; for they have a very ready understanding" (cited by Gill 1982: 3).

Prejudice closes the eyes of the observer to the reality and value of those who are different. Columbus thought the peoples of the lands to which he had come had no religion, because what he observed had no parallel with his own experience of religion. He assumed that to be "religious" a people must follow the same patterns he had known.

Regrettably, the attitude represented by Columbus dominated the European response to the indigenous peoples of the "new world" for centuries. In some quarters it continues today. On the day I am writing these words a television commercial for a brand of cough drops is being shown. It shows three Eskimo (Inuit) men, each with a different remedy. The younger man contrasts the effectiveness of the drops he uses with the "traditional remedies" of his father and uncle. The seemingly inoffensive commercial is, at one level, a parody of the "silliness" of the rituals of the indigenous peoples of the Arctic.

The purpose of this chapter is to identify and understand the family of religions Columbus could not recognize. First, we will describe the variety of indigenous peoples found in North America and some of the common patterns of their religions. Then we will examine in detail the sacred ways of the Oglala Lakota of the Great Plains.

AN ORIENTATION TO THE INDIGENOUS RELIGIONS OF NORTH AMERICA

The Land and Peoples

Sometime between twenty and forty thousand years B.C.E., the ancestors of the native peoples of North America crossed the Bering Strait and began a process of settlement, which by 6000 B.C.E. had carried their descendants south to the very tip of South America. A full introduction would cover the religions of the indigenous peoples of Central and South as well as North America, with discussions of what is known of the religions of peoples such as the Aztecs and Mayas of Central America and the Incas of South America. However, we have space in this work to concentrate only on the indigenous peoples of North America.

By the time of European contact there were about a million native North Americans, living in six separate culture areas: the far North, the Eastern woodlands, the Great Plains, the Northwest coast, the Southeast, and the Southwest (see Figure 4-1). Together there were perhaps as many as 2,000 separate cultures. We will touch here on the peoples of several of these areas.

In the Eastern woodlands a number of groups had reached a sophisticated level of political organization before the arrival of Europeans. By 1400 five groups (the Cayuga, Onondaga, Oneida, Mohawk, and Seneca) had formed an alliance known as the Iroquois League. In the Southeast the Cherokee, Chickasaw, Choctaw, Creek, and Natchez had formed the Creek Confederacy. However, despite early cooperation, the long-term effect of the coming of Europeans was the decimation of these once proud peoples. With the passage of the Indian Removal Act of 1830 most of the Eastern tribes that had not yet been forced westward were moved to make way for European settlers.

When the Spanish brought the horse and gun north from Mexico in the seventeenth century, a new way of life was made possible for Native Americans on the sparsely populated Central and Northern Plains. Some of the groups that established themselves on the Plains were the Arapaho, Cheyenne, Comanche, Crow, Mandan, Pawnee, and the Lakota/Nakota/Dakota (better known as the Sioux). They had a range of forms of social and political organization, but roving bands of families that depended on their hunting of the then ubiquitous buffalo were most common. As we will see

In this revealing drawing, executed about a century after the 1492 voyage of Christopher Columbus, the artist expresses the dominant European perception of indigenous peoples at the time.

Source: Mary Evans Picture Library/ Photo Research.

when we discuss the history of the Oglala Lakota, the European incursion into the Plains resulted in a series of broken treaties, bloody conflicts, and seized lands, which forced the Plains Indians onto inhospitable reservations and condemned them to a marginal existence which, for many, continues to this day.

The Native Americans of the Southwest include such groups as the Apache, Navajo, Pima, Hopi, Zuni, and Yaqui. The predecessors of the peaceful Pueblo Indians (among them the Hopi and Zuni) included the famous and mysterious Anasazi, who lived in cliff houses. They had a highly developed culture that was well established several hundred years before the Spanish arrived. Like the Plains Indians, after wars with the U.S. government the Navajo and Apache were forced onto reservations, as were the other groups. Today the Navajo are the largest Native American group, numbering close to 150,000.

Today there are approximately 1.5 million Indians living in the United States. Many live on the 285 official reservations, where many believe they can more effectively practice and preserve their traditional ways of life. Others have migrated to urban areas, creating their own communities in places such as Minneapolis and Chicago. Still others have fully assimilated into "American" culture. Assimilation has come in part as the result of the policies of government and private agencies that have sought to encourage (and, in some cases, force) Native Americans to give up their traditional ways and "fit in" to the dominant cultural patterns.

Common Religious Patterns

While generalizations about the religions of such widely diverse peoples are dangerous, it is possible to identify some common patterns present in many

FIGURE 4-1

Traditional Locations of Selected Native American Nations

of the traditional religions of the indigenous peoples of North America.

Gods and Spirits Like other indigenous peoples, traditional Native Americans consider all nature to be spiritually alive. There are spirits of other animals, spirits of natural phenomena such as thunder and lightning, spirits of the dead. The earth is alive, the Mother of all. Native American peoples also typically envision a supreme god—the Lakota *Wakan Tanka* or the Pawnee *Tirawa*—the source of all life, above all other deities, but remote from the everyday

COSMIC QUESTIONS: HOW DID THE WORLD COME INTO BEING?

The Lakota Story of Creation

In 1895 Dr. James Walker came to the Pine Ridge Reservation as a physician. Unlike other doctors, he worked cooperatively with Oglala healers in combatting disease. As a result, some of the elders took him into their confidence, and taught him the lore of their people. Dr. Walker transcribed and translated what he was told, and his records are the principal source for our understanding of Oglala mythology, including the creation account, from which the following is excerpted (Dooling 1984: 3–5).

In the beginning was Inyan [stone], who had no beginning, for he was there when there was no other, only Hanhepi, the Darkness. Inyan was soft and shapeless, but he was everywhere and he had all the powers. These powers were in his blood, and his blood was blue. His spirit was Wakan Tanka.

Inyan desired that there be others so that he might exercise his powers. But there could be no others unless he created them from himself. To do so he would have to give part of his spirit and part of his blood, and the powers that were in the blood. So he decided to create another but only as part of himself, so that he could keep control over the powers. He took part of himself and spread it over and around himself in the shape of a great disk. He named the disk Maka, the Earth, and he gave Maka a spirit, Maka-akan, Earth Spirit, and she is part of Inyan. But in creating her, he took so much from himself that his veins opened and all his blood flowed from him, and he shrank and became hard and powerless.

As Inyan's blood flowed, it became the blue waters which are on the earth. Because powers cannot live in water, they separated

affairs on earth. In a sense, the high god is present in all things, yet removed from them all. There is also the common pattern of a sacred power, a force present everywhere—for example, the Lakota *wakan* or the Algonquin *orenda.*

Also common in Native American mythology is the Trickster, who brings both order and disorder. The Trickster is often a participant in the creative process, carrying out the plan of creation of the Creator. However, the Trickster also cunningly confronts people and exploits their own instincts toward disharmony. An example is the Spider Grandmother of Hopi and other mythologies.

Rituals   Native Americans seek as their primary goal to live in balance in the present with the spirits everywhere present (rather than to prepare for life in a world beyond death). One of the most common patterns among indigenous North Americans is the use of dance as a means of interacting with the spirit world. Dances are held to prepare people for a special event, to celebrate some significant happening, and during rites of passage. Drums beat out a steady rhythm and the repetition of short songs usually accompanies the dancing. Dances can last for hours, even days. They are also a means of drawing the community together and revitalizing it, and of maintaining the harmony of the cosmos. Ceremonial masks worn to personify particular spirits are a particular method of bringing about harmony with the spirit world. Dances to influence the spirits to bring fertility are particularly common.

In a number of Native American religions visions play an important role. For example, in preparation for the rite of passage at puberty, a young person must go into the wilderness to fast and wait for a vision that will provide guidance for the

themselves and became a great blue dome whose edge is near the edge of Maka. This blue dome of the powers of the blood of Inyan is now the sky and is not material but is the spirit of Taku Skanskan, the Great Spirit. When these powers assumed one shape, they said a voice spoke, saying: "I am the source of energy, I am Skan." This was the beginning of the third of the Sacred Beings who is the highest of all because he is spirit. Inyan and Maka are material, and the world of matter has no powers except what are given by Skan.

[Skan then creates Light (Anpetu) and the fourth Sacred Being, Wi, the Sun. He gathers the other Sacred Beings and says to them:]

I, Skan, and you, Inyan, Maka, and Wi, are four, but we are only one, and that one is Wakan Tanka, which no one can understand. Each of us is part of Wakan Tanka which is the Great Incomprehensible.

[Each of the Sacred Beings is given a realm.] Wi, whose color is red, is the chief of the Sacred Beings, because he is above all. Skan (blue) is the source of all power and spirit and has domain over all. Maka (green) has dominion over all the lands except the mountains and high hills. Inyan (yellow) is given the mountains, rocks, and high hills. Each of the beings creates a companion. Wi creates the Moon. Maka creates Passion, but throws her into the

waters because she became jealous of her. Skan creates Wind. Inyan makes Thunderstorm. From a huge egg made by Thunderstorm and fertilized by Skan comes Ksa, Wisdom, who invented language, told stories, and gave names to all creatures and things. [The elaborate tale continues with the creation of Pte Oyate, the "Buffalo People," the animals, four times and directions, and the Ikce Oyate, the "Real People," the Oglala name for themselves. At the conclusion of the tale the Ikce Oyate receive the sacred pipe from White Buffalo Calf Woman.]

Excerpt from The Sons of the Wind *by D.M. Dooling. Copyright © 1984 by The Society for the Study of Myths and Tradition. Reprinted by permission of HarperCollins Publishers.*

future. Hunters and warriors might prepare for the difficult tasks before them through seeking visions.

Usually at about age 7 or 8 a child is initiated into the group. The ritual often involves a period of gradually increased solitary fasting and a time of separation from the family and village. As we have noted, seeking visions that reveal to the child his or her role in the group is often associated with this ritual.

Courtship rituals in some groups involve the male attracting the attention of his desired mate through serenading her with a flute. The marriage ceremony itself is usually quite simple, with an exchange of gifts between the two families, followed by a dance for the entire group.

Native Americans typically have a great deal of respect for elders in the group. It is accepted that they have accumulated a great deal of sacred knowledge, from which other members should

eagerly learn. However, when the cycle of life is complete, elders willingly wait for death either in their dwellings or, in some cases, at a place separate from the village.

Many Native American groups consider the number "four" to be particularly sacred. Time and space seem to be structured in fours: four seasons, four directions, most animals walking on four feet, and four states of life (infancy, youth, adulthood, and old age). As with other religions, each of these stages is marked by a rite of passage. Customs differ in each society. At birth, for example, among traditional Apaches the child's umbilical cord is dried, placed in a special bag, and put on the cradle. As with African religions, naming ceremonies are a common part of rituals associated with birth and infancy.

Traditional Native Americans share many of the same "taboos" as other indigenous peoples, such as menstruating women and dead bodies.

Religious Leaders   Unlike African religions, Native American religions do not usually have priests, in part because sacrifices play only a minor role and because individuals typically sought direct rather than mediated contact with the spirit world. Healers (called by outsiders medicine men or women) play a significant role in many indigenous North American religions. It is believed that healers are anointed with their special power over sickness by spirits who come to them in visions. Particular rituals such as the sucking out of foreign objects thought to be implanted in the victim's body are part of a healer's methods.

Another important, and related, type of religious leader is the shaman, who is empowered to take spirit journeys in order to bring healing or to see into the future.

CASE STUDY—THE OGLALA LAKOTA (SIOUX): THE SACRED HOOP OF THE NATION

Introduction

Outsiders know the people whose religion we will now study as one group within the Sioux nation. However, "Sioux" is a French corruption of the Algonquian *nadowesiih* ("little adders"), which was applied to this nation by the Ojibwa, and adopted by the French missionaries and traders. "Sioux" has been adopted as a self-designation, particularly when speaking to outsiders, despite its originally pejorative connotation. However, increasingly many Sioux wish to be known by the term in their own language e.g. *Lakota* (perhaps best translated as "allies").

The Oglala Lakota are one group within a nation that originally called itself *Oceti Sakowin*, which means "the seven fireplaces," reflecting the traditional social/political divisions. The nation has also been known by the terms that represent the three related dialects they speak: Lakota, Dakota, and Nakota. The political designation of those who speak the Lakota dialect is the Teton or Western Sioux, while those who speak Nakota are called the Yankton Sioux, and Dakota speakers are the Santee

Sioux. Within the Teton Sioux (Lakota) there are seven subdivisions: *Oglala* ("they scatter their own"), *Sicangu* ("burned thighs," better known by the French term Brule), *Hunkpapa* ("end of the circle"), *Mnikowoju* ("planters beside the stream," often transliterated Mineconjou), *Sihasapa* ("black foot"), *Oohenunpa* ("two boilings," better known as the Two Kettle), and *Itazipca* ("without bows," better known by the French term Sans Arc).

The Sioux have been the subject of many Hollywood movies, mostly quite stereotypical treatments ranging from the vicious savages of the Westerns of the 1940s and 1950s to the "noble savages" of the 1990 Oscar-winning film "Dances with Wolves." While the latter film gives a very sympathetic portrayal of this group of Native Americans, they deserve more in-depth and realistic attention than the Hollywood movie genre allows.

Our concern in this section is with the Oglala Lakota, whose principal home is now the Pine Ridge Indian Reservation of South Dakota, near the Black Hills (see Figure 4-2). We will first trace the history of the Oglala. We will then describe the classical spiritual ways of the Lakota and what has happened to the Oglala and their spirituality in recent decades.

A Brief History of the Oglala

According to some historians, the ancestors of the Lakota migrated to Minnesota after being forced out of their original homelands on the East Coast, perhaps in the Carolinas. By the 1600s the Sioux had settled in villages in the forests of Minnesota. They gathered wild rice, hunted, practiced limited horticulture, and engaged in trade with other Native Americans. Many Lakota, however, believe that some of their ancestors were already living near the Black Hills by 900 C.E.

Modern historians contend that in the early to mid-1700s many, but not all, of the Sioux were forced out of Minnesota by the Crees and Chippewas, who had been armed by the British and the French. The Teton Sioux (Lakota) were at the western edge of the migration. In the Plains they formed groups of extended families, called "bands" (*tiyospaye*). Each was led by a chief, who had distinguished himself as a hunter/warrior, and a council of elders. Within band there were camps (*wicoti*) of twenty-five or more, headed by an elected leader. Leaders remained in their roles as long as they could provide for the needs of the group and protect them (Powers 1986: 26–27). These leadership roles were not necessarily confined to men, as evidence has been found that there were women leaders, women's societies, and women warriors. The bands were largely autonomous. The Oglala adapted well to the prairie environment: During most of the year they lived in encampments of *tipis* alongside rivers and streams. The tipis could be moved to follow the buffalo herds. The buffalo provided the basis for lifestyle that was subsistence-level but adequate. In the winter the Oglala established camps in more sheltered areas often near the Black Hills.

By 1750 the Oglala had obtained their first horses, increasing their mobility as well as their hunting and war-making ability. A hunter/warrior could show his valor and earn "coup points" by riding into a buffalo herd and striking the lead animal a blow on the nose, or into an enemy camp and hitting a foe with a glancing blow.

By 1775 the Lakota had crossed the Missouri River and reached the Black Hills, driving out the Kiowas and Crows. The Lewis and Clark expedition encountered the Lakota in September 1804 and made the first of what was to become a series of treaties with them, guaranteeing them the right to live where they were without restrictions.

This began a period of uneasy, sometimes violent interactions between the Oglala and other branches of the Teton Sioux and European settlers and the soldiers sent to protect them. War broke out in 1854, and the Lakota distinguished themselves as brave warriors in conflicts, especially in the Red Cloud Wars of the 1860s. Some of the most renowned leaders of the "Indian Wars" were the Oglala warriors Red Cloud and Crazy Horse. Their power was sufficient to force the Fort Laramie Treaty of 1868, in which the U.S. government agreed to close the Bozeman Trail and promised that the Black Hills were "for the absolute and undisputed occupation of the Sioux." However, when gold was discovered in the Black Hills in

FIGURE 4-2

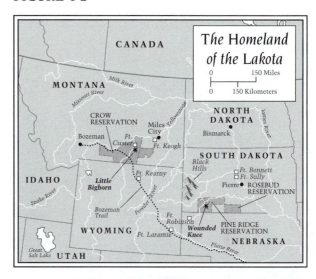

1874, the treaty was broken and whites flooded onto Lakota land. This set the stage for the last great Lakota victory. Oglala were a part of the coalition that attacked and slaughtered General George ("Long Hair") Custer's forces at the Battle of the Little Big Horn on June 25, 1876.

Their victory was shortlived, however. By 1880 the Oglala and other Sioux had been subjugated and forced onto reservations–"the natural and best home of all red men," said one white leader of the time. The Pine Ridge Reservation was established in 1878. Although it had only one small area of farmable land (which was excised from the reservation in 1911), the Oglala were told to become self-sufficient farmers, following the European model. Some Euroamerican leaders recognized what this meant to the Lakota. Thomas J. Morgan, U.S. Commissioner of Indian Affairs under President Benjamin Harrison, said (Mooney 1896: 825):

> *The buffalo had gone and the Sioux had left to them alkali land and government rations. . . . Suddenly, almost without warning, they were expected at once and without previous training to settle down to the pursuits of agriculture in a land largely unfitted for such use. The freedom of the chase was to be exchanged for the idleness of the camp. The boundless range was to be abandoned for the circumscribed reservation, and*

Nineteenth century artist George Catlin captures the harmony of horse and rider displayed in the buffalo hunts essential for the way of life of the Oglala Lakota and other native American people of the Great Plains.

Source: George Catlin, **Self-Torture In A Sioux Religious Ceremony, The Sun Dance,** 1835–1837. *National Museum of American Art, Washington, DC/Art Resource, NY.*

abundance of plenty to be supplanted by limited and decreasing government subsistence and supplies. Under these circumstances it is not in human nature not to be discontented and restless, even turbulent and violent.

The great Sioux leaders were systematically humiliated or murdered. The great Oglala leader Red Cloud (the first leader to win a war against the United States!) was captured and confined, and Crazy Horse had already been killed in 1877. The Hunkpapa chief Sitting Bull became the symbol of the "domesticated" Indian, travelling with "Wild West shows" throughout the United States and Europe. Finally, in 1890, Sitting Bull too was killed while resisting arrest. As one U.S. senator said in 1881, "These Indians must either change their modes of life or they will be exterminated" (Hughes 1983: 117). Before he died, according to tradition, Crazy Horse had this to say to the victors (cited by Matthiesen 1992: ix):

We did not ask you white men to come here. The Great Spirit [Wakan Tanka] gave us this country as a home. You had yours. We did not interfere with you. The

Great Spirit gave us plenty of land to live on, and buffalo, deer, antelope and other game. But you have come here; you are taking my land from me; you are killing off our game, so it is hard for us to live. Now, you tell us to work for a living, but the Great Spirit did not make us to work, but to live by hunting. You white men can work if you want to. We do not interfere with you, and again you say, why do you not become civilized? We do not want your civilization! We would live as our fathers did, and their fathers before them.

In 1883, at the insistence of Secretary of the Interior H.M. Teller, who said that the Sun Dance was "hindering the civilization of the Indians" and stimulating the violent tendencies of young warriors, a concerted effort began to annihilate traditional Lakota religion. As a result the sacred ways described below nearly vanished entirely. This prohibition continued as official government policy until 1934. It continues unofficially even now, despite a 1978 Act of Congress guaranteeing all Native Americans the right to practice their traditional religions.

The death of Sitting Bull, combined with government hysteria about Sioux participation in the

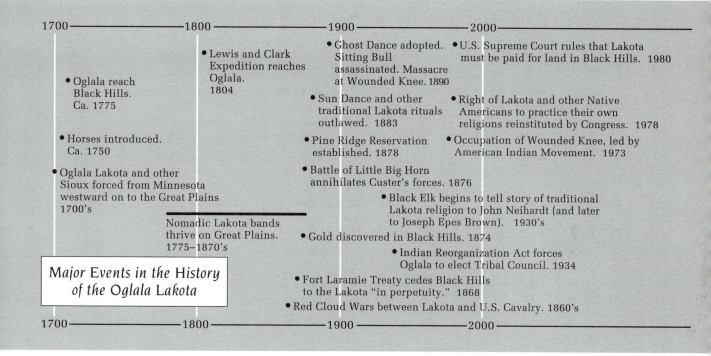

1700 ———————— 1800 ———————— 1900 ———————— 2000

• Lewis and Clark
Expedition reaches
Oglala.
1804

• Ghost Dance adopted.
Sitting Bull
assassinated. Massacre
at Wounded Knee. 1890

• U.S. Supreme Court rules that Lakota
must be paid for land in Black Hills. 1980

• Oglala reach
Black Hills.
Ca. 1775

• Sun Dance and other
traditional Lakota rituals
outlawed. 1883

• Right of Lakota and other Native
Americans to practice their own
religions reinstituted by Congress. 1978

• Horses introduced.
Ca. 1750

• Pine Ridge Reservation
established. 1878

• Occupation of Wounded Knee, led by
American Indian Movement. 1973

• Oglala Lakota and other
Sioux forced from Minnesota
westward on to the Great Plains
1700's

• Battle of Little Big Horn
annihilates Custer's forces. 1876

Nomadic Lakota bands
thrive on Great Plains.
1775–1870's

• Black Elk begins to tell story of traditional
Lakota religion to John Neihardt (and later
to Joseph Epes Brown).   1930's

• Gold discovered in Black Hills. 1874

**Major Events in the History
of the Oglala Lakota**

• Indian Reorganization Act forces
Oglala to elect Tribal Council. 1934

• Fort Laramie Treaty cedes Black Hills
to the Lakota "in perpetuity." 1868

• Red Cloud Wars between Lakota and U.S. Cavalry. 1860's

1700 ———————— 1800 ———————— 1900 ———————— 2000

Ghost Dance movement, set in motion a tragic set of events. The climax came on December 29, 1890, with the massacre of 300 Lakota men, women, and children by soldiers from Custer's Seventh Cavalry regiment at a settlement called Wounded Knee on the Oglala's Pine Ridge Reservation.

After Wounded Knee the Oglala and the other Lakota tribes were crushed, not only physically but spiritually. Since 1890 most Oglala have lived in poverty on the Pine Ridge Reservation, dependent on the few jobs and welfare allotments provided by government agencies, especially the Bureau of Indian Affairs.

The 1934 Indian Reorganization Act forced the Oglala to elect a central tribal council and chief, in violation of their traditional political organization into autonomous bands. Isolated holy men kept alive the traditional Oglala ceremonies and values, but, under intense pressure from government agents and missionaries, many Oglala gave up their distinctive ways, taking European names and lifestyles. In recent years, many Oglala have attempted to find a balance between adapting to modern society and preserving their Oglala identity. Oglala Lakota College in Kyle, South Dakota, is committed to educating Lakota students with skills appropriate for modern life, but with the foundation of traditional Lakota values. A resurgence of interest in traditional Lakota spirituality is very much in evidence today.

In 1973 Wounded Knee became the site of a seventy-one-day occupation led by the intertribal American Indian Movement (see Matthiessen 1992: 58–82). Unfortunately, Wounded Knee once again became a place of violence between Native Americans and government forces.

Some Oglala have been leaders in the legal movement to force the U.S. government to honor treaties made with the Lakota and other Native Americans. In 1976 an Oglala holy man, Frank Fools Crow, testified before a congressional committee on the matter. In his testimony he said, "The Black Hills is our church, the place where we worship. The Black Hills is our burial grounds. The

The Oglala Lakota leader, Red Cloud, hero of the successful campaign to close the Bozeman Trail in the 1860s.

bones of our grandfathers lie buried in those hills. How can you expect us to sell our church and our cemeteries for a few token white-man dollars? We will never sell" (Mails 1979: 212). In 1980 the Supreme Court awarded the Lakota $105 million in compensation for the Black Hills, in return for Lakota abandonment of their legal claim. Those who filed the suit refused, however, to accept the financial settlement. One Lakota leader put it this way: "How can we put a price on our Mother?"

By 1984 100,000 Lakota were left on the Oglala Pine Ridge Reservation and on other reservations in South and North Dakota, Montana, and Saskatchewan in Canada (Powers 1987: 434).

Patterns of Traditional Oglala Spirituality

Central Concepts and Symbols   Until recently most non–Native Americans grew up with a few stereotypical ideas about Native American religion: the Great Spirit, the peace pipe, and the happy hunting ground. All are distortions of aspects of the religions of the people who, like the Oglala, inhabited the

Great Plains in the nineteenth century. Our task here is to attempt to understand—as best we can, given our status as outside observers—the spiritual ways of the Oglala. We will first clarify basic spiritual concepts, symbols, and leaders and then turn to the rituals of Oglala religion.

HOLINESS   The Lakota conception of the sacred (*wakan*) or holiness (*wakana*) defies easy classification. On the one hand, there seems to be a central deity, *Wakan Tanka,* to whom the Oglala pray. When addressed as "Grandfather" (*Tunkashila*), *Wakan Tanka* is not manifest; when invoked as "Father," *Wakan Tanka* is manifest, as, for example, through the sun. The feathers of the highest flying bird, the eagle, symbolize *Wakan Tanka.* It must be acknowledged, however, that some authorities on Lakota religion contend that the conception of *Wakan Tanka* as a personal deity did not develop until Christian missionaries began to influence Lakota beliefs, using *Wakan Tanka* to speak of the one Christian God.

The single name *Wakan Tanka* can also represent "sixteen important supernatural beings and powers, half of which existed prior to the creation of the earth, half as a result of it" (Powers 1987: 436). As one expert has said, "Rather than a single being, *Wakan Tanka* embodied the totality of existence ... " (DeMaillie 1987: 28; see also Powers 1986: 118). According to Fools Crow, the best translation into English is not the common "Great Spirit," but "Holiest of Everything" (Mails 1979: 120). Another scholar has expressed the ambiguity by saying that *Wakan Tanka* includes "both the conception of a vaguely personified supreme divinity that the natives believe they recognized in the different phenomena, e.g., the sun and the thunder, on the one hand, and the conception of independent divinities behind these phenomena on the other" (Hultkrantz; cited in Steinmetz 1990: 41). In the sacred language of *wakan* persons, *Wakan Tanka* is called *Tobtob* ("four times four"), symbolic of the fact that all sacred things come in fours (Powers 1987: 436).

As with the Hopi and many other indigenous peoples, the earth is understood as Mother (*maka ina*) or, when unmanifest, as Grandmother. Marla

Powers (1986: 35) records a typical Oglala prayer to Mother/Grandmother Earth:

> *O You, Grandmother, from whom all earthly things come, and O You, Mother Earth, who bear and nourish all fruits, behold us and listen: Upon You there is a sacred path which we walk, thinking of the sacredness of all things.*

Wakan is not confined to "deities." Everything has a *wakan* or spirit. Indeed *wakan* is "a dynamic concept indicating the potentiality of anything to become transformed from a secular to a sacred state" (Powers 1987: 436). Birds and animals have spirits, just as humans, so they are called the "winged people" and the "four-legged people" to distinguish them from the human "two-legged people." Humans must learn to humble themselves before the smallest ant, for even there *Wakan Tanka* is present. Every being has a *wochangi* or sacred influence. Humans must learn to be attentive, so that they can receive the *wochangi* of other beings. Sometimes holiness is spoken of as an impersonal force (*wakana*), which is everywhere potentially present. The Oglala also speak of *wakan* beings, spirits of ancestors and other "ghosts," which though invisible are believed to be present with the Oglala and can appear to "sacred persons" or others during visions.

THE CIRCLE AND ITS CENTER   A principal Oglala symbol for holiness is the circle. Like *Wakan Tanka* the circle has no end (Black Elk 1932: 164–65):

> *… The Power of the World always works in circles, and everything tries to be round. In the old days when we were a strong and happy people, all our power came to us from the sacred hoop of the nation, and so long as the hoop was unbroken the people flourished. The flowering tree was the living center of the hoop and the circle of the four quarters nourished it. . . . Everything the Power of the World does is done in a circle. The sky is round, and I have heard the earth is round like a ball, and so are the stars. The wind. . . whirls. Birds make their nests in circles, for theirs is the same religion as ours. The sun [moves in a circle as does the moon]. Even the seasons form a great circle [and so does the life of each human being].*

Each year in the early summer, the Lakota gathered for a "camp circle," reflecting the symbol-ism of the nation as a *sacred hoop*. In the nineteenth century the circle was often concentric, with younger married couples placing their tipis in front of their parents'. In the middle was an area for dances, with a tree at the center. The circle created Oglala cosmos, a sacred space that gave the Oglala an experience of true reality. The entrance to the circle was always at the east, nearest the rising sun. During the camp circle the Sun Dance was performed. The loss of tribal unity was expressed in the imagery of the sacred hoop being broken, and the flowering tree at its center dying.

The Oglala's home, the tipi, also manifested the circle symbolism. Viewed from above, a tipi forms a circle. The crossed poles of the tipi formed a center.

CARDINAL DIRECTIONS   For the Oglala, the four cardinal directions (north, south, east, and west) and the two central directions (up and down) were very important. According to Fools Crow, "in these six directions is found everything needed for renewal, physical and intellectual growth, and harmony." The sacred powers given by the directions include, he says, "joy, good health, growth, endurance, wisdom, inner peace, warmth, and happiness." In the important pipe ceremony, the pipe is smoked and pointed with its stem pointing out in a clockwise circle, to the west, north, east, and south; then down to Grandmother Earth, up to Grandfather, and "in an almost imperceptible higher movement to *Wakan Tanka*" (Mails 1979: 58).

Also very important in Lakota symbolism are the "two roads": the black road of destruction, which stretched symbolically from west to east; and the red road of goodness, which goes from north to south.

CHARISMATIC LEADERS   The Oglala placed great importance on strong political and social leaders. Political leaders were designated by visions, and were often given names representative of the visions. For example, the vision of a dancing horse showed "Crazy Horse" that his destiny was to be a leader of his people, and it gave him his name.

The spiritual leaders of the Oglala are known as *wicasa wakan* (sacred man) or *winyan wakan* (sacred woman). They are distinct from the so-called medicine men and women who have a special knowledge of medicinal plants and how to set fractures. The sacred men and women are intermediaries for the people to the spirit beings and their powers. They can speak with animals. They are able to call on the power of *wakana* for healing individuals as well as for the well-being of the people as a whole. Before the annihilation of the buffalo, they could determine where buffalo would be found through mystical means. They could also predict the outcome of wars. The process of becoming a sacred person usually involved overcoming some misfortune, receiving instruction from another *wakan* person, crying for a vision (see below), serving an apprenticeship, and finally "ordination" (Powers 1975: 59–63; see also Black Elk 1990; Lewis 1990: 39–42, 178–84). The Lakota shaman John Fire Lame Deer describes the *wicasa wakan* in this way (Lame Deer 1972: 145–46):

> *The wicasa wakan loves the silence, wrapping it around himself like a blanket—a loud silence with a voice like thunder which tells him of many things. Such a man likes to be in a place where there is no sound but the humming of the insects. He sits facing the West, asking for help. He talks to the plants and they answer him. He listens to the voices of all those who move upon the Earth, the animals. He is at one with them. From all living beings something flows into him all the time, and something flows from him. I don't know where or what, but it's there. I know.*

RITUAL CLOWNS (HEYOK'A)   Oglala society included an important role for "ritual clowns," called by the Oglala *heyok'a* (Lewis 1990: 140–52; Walker 1980: 14, 155–57; DeMallie 1984: 232–35). They are also known as the "contraries." The *heyok'a* clan is a loosely organized, somewhat secretive society, whose members claim magical powers. By systematically breaking the accepted customs and taboos of the society, they relieve the pressure that builds up under the strict Oglala moral code. No one chooses to be a contrary. A *heyok'a* is designated by a vision of Thunder Beings. Thereafter, the contrary is obligated to do everything in reverse, to ward off the dangers of lightning and storm. On dance days they engage in disorderly, even deviant behavior,

in ways similar to their Hopi counterparts. The effect is a comic relief, especially appreciated at times of stress and despair, balancing the solemnity of the occasion. For example, a masked contrary might wear a costume with an exaggerated penis-like nose and feign lewd, even disgusting behaviors. Contraries sometimes urinate on their clothes, throw excrement on the crowds, and pretend ejaculations. Their "deviant" behavior is thought to be a source of curative power, and *heyok'a* are considered potent healers.

It may very well be that the more extreme behaviors of the *heyok'a* were in response to the attacks by European missionaries and others on what they regarded as a pagan perversion of gender roles. In any event, the *heyok'a* were accepted and valued in traditional Oglala society.

THE GIVEAWAY CEREMONY   We should mention the traditional phenomenon of the "giveaway ceremony," similar to a phenomenon found in a number of indigenous groups worldwide. To avert some misfortune, to seek renewal and to offer thanksgiving after one, or to prepare for some special occasion, an Oglala family may give away some, even all, of its most valued possessions to others. Economically, this allowed for a ritualized avoidance of the concentration of wealth in one family, and stressed the positive values of sharing and concern for the well-being of the group as a whole. Fools Crow describes a giveaway ceremony he and his wife, Fannie, held in 1928, after the death of his daughter Grace (Mails 1979: 117):

> *We ... invited the poorest people in our district. Of our 183 horses, we gave away nearly half. We had 42 cows, and we gave half of them away. We gave away all of our poultry. We gave away our clothing. . . . All we kept of our furniture was the kitchen stove and the cooking utensils.*

THE SACRED PIPE   The most important sacred implement for Oglala religion, as it is for many other Native American groups, is the *cannunpa* (also chanunpa) *wakan,* or *sacred pipe* (see Powers 1975: 81–83, 86–88; Brown 1953: 3–10; Black Elk 1990: 49–67; Steinmetz 1990: 53–57; Lewis 1990:

44–47; Mails 1979: 55–59; Powers 1986: 42–49). The sacred pipe is used in all Oglala rituals, and it symbolizes the cosmos as a whole.

The myth of the gift of the sacred pipe is one of the most commonly recorded Oglala narratives. According to this myth, the pipe was brought to the people by *Ptehincalasan Win* (White Buffalo Calf Woman). Today the pipe venerated as the original pipe is kept at Green Grass on the Cheyenne River Reservation in northern South Dakota (Steinmetz 1990: 15–16). A shaman might bring his own *cannunpa* to touch the original Calf Pipe Bundle. In presenting the pipe, White Buffalo Calf Woman said, "With this sacred pipe you will walk upon the Earth; for the Earth is your Grandmother and Mother, and She is sacred. Every step that is taken upon Her should be a prayer." She told them that the pipe bowl was red catlinite stone, representing the earth. Carved in the stone was a buffalo calf, representing all the four-leggeds. The wooden stem symbolized all that grows on the earth. The twelve feathers stood for the spotted eagle and all the winged creatures. Those who smoke the pipe are joining themselves with everything in the universe. When you pray with this pipe, she said, you are praying for and with everything. The seven circles on the round stone, she said, were the seven rites in which the pipe would be used. When she left, the woman said that she would look back at the people in each of the four ages to come, and at the end she would return. As she walked away she turned into a buffalo calf, then into a white buffalo, and then a black buffalo, which bowed to each of the four directions and disappeared. (See also Fools Crow's version of the story in Mails 1979: 142–45.)

When the pipe is to be used in a ceremony, it is taken from its special pouch by the sacred person to whom it has been entrusted. The *wakan* person raises the pipe with both hands above his head, or points the stem of the pipe in the direction to be invoked. Tobacco, sealed in the bowl of the pipe during its consecration, is then lit. Those smoking the pipe sit in a circle, each repeating the pointing of the pipe in the four directions and puffing on it four times. Smoking or even touching this special pipe in

The cannunpa *or sacred pipe, here displayed with the decorated pouch in which it is kept.*

any but the prescribed manner or by anyone but those of the highest integrity is taboo. However, non-specialists may use their own individual sacred pipes, praying with them in the four directions.

The Traditional Rituals of the Oglala   According to some traditions, with the sacred pipe White Buffalo Calf Woman gave the Oglala seven rituals that form the core of the spirituality of the tribe. The following description is based on the accounts of Powers (1975: 89–103) and the holy man Black Elk, as told to Brown (1952: 10–138).

There are other important Lakota rituals that would need to be discussed in a full survey, such as the Kettle Dance, Horse Dance, and Buffalo Dance, to name a few (see Fools Crow's description in Mails 1979: 60–82). In any event, through these seven rituals we receive a sense of the types of rituals performed during the first half of the nineteenth century, as well as an introduction to the practices of Lakota traditionalists today.

THE SWEAT LODGE (*INIKAGAPI*, "TO RENEW LIFE") This ritual of purification or renewal is often conducted in preparation for participation in other rites or for a great endeavor. It may also be done as a ceremony in itself, as a means of petitioning for a need or offering thanksgiving for a blessing.

The "sweat lodge" itself is a domed structure of bent willows covered with buffalo robes and

QUESTIONS ABOUT THE SACRED: HOW IS THE SACRED MADE KNOWN?

An Oglala Power Vision

In this passage, Oglala holy man Black Elk describes to John Neihardt a "power vision" of sacred beings he had during an illness as a child. In indigenous religions the shaman has access to the spirit world, where he or she is empowered by the sacred to bring healing or guidance to the people (Black Elk 1932: 17–39).

It was the summer when I was nine years old, and our people were moving slowly towards the Rocky Mountains. We camped one evening in a valley beside a little creek. . . .

The next morning the camp moved again, and I was riding with some boys. We stopped to get a drink from a creek, and when I got off my horse, my legs crumpled under me and I could not walk. So the boys helped me up and put me on my horse; and when we camped again that evening, I was sick. The next day the camp moved on to where the different bands of our people were coming together, and I rode in a pony drag, for I was very sick. Both my legs and both my arms were swollen badly and my face was all puffed up.

When we had camped again, I was lying in our tepee and my mother and father were sitting beside me. I could see out through the opening, and there two men were coming from the clouds, headfirst like arrows slanting down, and I knew they were the same that I had seen before. Each now carried a long spear, and from the points of these a jagged lightning flashed. They came clear down to the ground this time and stood a little way off and looked at me and said: "Hurry! Come! Your Grandfathers are calling you!"

[Black Elk says he was taken into the sky on a cloud, where he is led by dancing horses to a council of the Grandfathers, who are the Powers of the Four Directions of the World and of the Sky and the Earth. From each he receives a power to use to lead his people that they might walk in a wakan way. He sees into the future the fate of his people, as they walk, in four ascents, on both the black road of destruction and the red road of harmony. He sees the sacred hoop of the nation with the flowering tree at the center, and is told that he will restore the nation. At the climax of the vision he is taken to the Oglala center of the world, Harney Peak in the Black Hills, where he sees the whole world as a sacred hoop.]

Then I was standing on the highest mountain of them all, and round about beneath me was the whole hoop of the world. And while I stood there I saw more than I can tell and I understood more than I saw; for I was seeing in a sacred manner the shapes of all things in the spirit, and the shape of all shapes as they must live together like one being. And I saw that the sacred hoop of my people was one of many hoops that made up one circle, wide as daylight and as starlight, and in the center grew one mighty flowering tree to shelter all the children of one mother and one father. And I saw that it was holy.

Excerpts from Black Elik Speaks *by John G. Neihardt. Copyright © 1932, 1959, 1972, by John G. Neihardt. Copyright © 1961 by the John G. Neihardt Trust. Reprinted by permission of the University of Nebraska Press.*

other skins, with hot stones in the center. The lodge is the cosmos and the rocks are Grandmother Earth. The fire is the life-giving power of *Wakan Tanka*. The water symbolizes the Thunder Beings, who come fearfully but bring goodness. The round pit in the center of the lodge is the center of the universe where *Wakan Tanka* comes to the worshippers. From the entrance of the lodge, a path of eight paces is made, running east and west. At the eastern end is a mound of earth dug from the pit inside the lodge. The mound is an altar, called "Grandmother." Two paces further is the "fire without end," in which the stones are heated. Both men and women may participate in the sweat lodge ritual, but usually not together.

As the fireplace is being prepared, the participants pray, "O Grandfather and Father *Wakan Tanka,* maker of all that is, who always has been, behold me! And You, Grandmother and Mother Earth, You are *wakan* and have holy ears; hear me! We have come from You, we are a part of You, and we know that our bodies will return to You. . . . By purifying myself in this way, I wish to make myself worthy of You, O *Wakan Tanka,* that my people may live!" The worshippers leave behind in the lodge (sometimes called the stonepeople's lodge) all that is impure and come away having known the "real world," which lies behind the world of experience. As one shaman put it, "We go into that sacred Lodge to purify ourselves. We go in there to see just who we really are, and in the darkness to see how we go on this Earth. We make ourselves really humble, like the littlest creature, and we pray to the Spirit that we may be healed, that all may be healed. We see that we are not separate from anything. We are all in this together. And we always say *mitakuye oyasin,* all my relations" (Halifax 1990: 26).

THE VISION QUEST (*HANBLECHEYA,* "CRYING FOR A VISION") Under the guidance of a *wakan* person, any person may seek to enter the spirit world. A young person might undertake a *vision quest* in order to receive guidance for his or her life. A warrior might go before a battle or in preparation for the Sun Dance. A family member might go to request healing for a sick or dying relative. A person might also "cry for a vision" as a way of giving thanks to *Wakan Tanka* for some special blessing.

After purification through fasting, typically lasting four days, and participation in the sweat lodge ritual, the person seeking a vision is led by his guide to a sacred hill. The only thing taken is a blanket. No food or water is allowed. The seeker is given a sacred pipe to have throughout the ritual. A pit is dug in the ground at the center. At times the worshipper will climb into this pit, covered with brush. The cardinal directions are marked. The person walks to each of the points, returning to the center, crying for a vision, all day long. The ritual

lasts from two to four days. The seeker may neither eat nor drink while lamenting. When the person finally lies down, exhausted, a vision may come. The seeker may be spoken to by animals or visited by Thunder Beings. Often the vision reinforces our sense of "nothingness" in comparison to holiness.

Sometimes visions come to persons spontaneously, often during a time of illness, as was the case with the "Great Vision" of Black Elk. These are "visions without crying" or "power visions," and they are commissions to a special leadership role in the tribe.

THE KEEPING OF THE SOUL (*WANAGI YUHAPI*) When an Oglala dies, his or her "ghost" (*wanagi*) normally travels south along the "ghost road" (the milky way) until an old woman decides its fate, either sending it on its way to the spirit world or returning it to the earth where it lives as a shade.

However, at times the family may elect to "keep the soul," particularly if the deceased is a beloved son. The ghost is kept for a specified period, now usually six months to a year. Then it is ritually released. The ritual ensures that the ghost will make it to the spirit world when released and keeps the family and tribe mindful of the fragility of life.

The ritual itself involves a *wakan* person cutting a lock of hair from the dead person and wrapping it. The hair is put in a buckskin bag, and, with a sacred pipe, is rolled into a bundle. The soul has its own tipi, and is placed on a special tripod opposite the entrance.

On the final day of the ghost keeping, when the spirit is released, the family holds a great feast, and all the family's possessions are given to the needy in honor of the departing ghost.

THE SUN DANCE (*WIWANYANG WACHIPI,* "DANCING WHILE GAZING AT THE SUN") The *Sun Dance* is "a way in which the people express their participation in the great cycles of nature; ... a world renewal rite associated with the appearance of new green vegetation and the increase of animals, particularly the buffalo" (Hughes 1983: 89). When the Oglala still lived freely on the prairie, it occurred over a four-day period when the bands gathered in June for a

*An 1874 painting of a Lakota
Sun Dance by Jules Tavernier.*

Source: Art Resource.

camp circle and a common buffalo hunt. In the
1870s so many Lakota gathered for the ceremony
that the diameter of the encampment was up to
four miles, with forty groups of from six to twelve
dancers, each with a holy man. In 1880 Red Cloud
led a Sun Dance in which 700 lodges were pitched,
in a circumference of six miles (Steinmetz 1990: 27;
for a full description of a traditional Sun Dance, see
Walker 1917; for Fools Crow's description, see
Mails 1979: 118–38).

The role of the sun needs to be clarified.
According to Fools Crow, the sun, like the sacred
pipe and the cardinal directions, is an instrument of
Wakan Tanka. "We respect it and pray to it," he
says, "because it watches over the world and sees
everything that is going on. It also serves God by
bestowing special gifts that it has upon the world.
But the sun is not God." During the ritual, dancers
are able to see the sun with their eyes open
(although they do not stare constantly at the sun,
as is sometimes reported). Fools Crow says that "in
it we see visions" (Mails 1979: 119).

On the first day of the ceremony, a hole is dug
in the center of the camp circle, and a large lodge is
built around it. On the second day a cottonwood

pole is ritually selected and brought by procession
into the camp. On the third day the pole is raised at
the center of the lodge. In making the lodge with
the sacred pole at the center, the Oglala are creating cosmos.

During these three days those who have
taken a vow to participate in the dance prepare
themselves under the guidance of a *wakan* person.
They must decide whether to dance gazing at the
sun, pierced, suspended, or dragging buffalo skulls.
In the latter three forms, the dancer is pierced by
the sacred person and rawhide thongs are attached
to the dancer's flesh.

On the fourth day the dancers who have chosen to gaze at the sun do so throughout the day. The
pierced dancers continue until the pressure causes
the thongs to break free. If they are having trouble,
friends and family may help them by increasing the
pressure on the thongs. The dance ends when the last
dancer has succeeded in breaking the hold of the
thongs. The lodge and pole are left in place, until they
deteriorate and return to Mother Earth.

According to Black Elk, the Sun Dance was
introduced as a rite of penance, when the people
had begun to forget *Wakan Tanka.* At the conclu-

Artist John Innes (1868-1941) portrays a buffalo hunt on the Great Plains.

Source: "The Buffalo Hunt" John Innes, 1868-1941. Photo by: Photo Researchers, Inc.,/Tom McHugh, 1974. Luxton Museum, Glenbow-Alberta Institute.

Six "totem poles" in Stanley Park, Vancouver, Canada. The carved figures symbolize a spiritual relationship between particular animals and the group for whom the pole has been erected.

> ## COSMIC QUESTIONS:
> ## WHAT IS THE DESTINY OF THE COSMOS?
>
> ### The Ghost Dance
>
> *This passage, from an 1891 document called the "Messiah Letter," is based on oral instructions given by Jack Wilson (Wovoka), to a group of Cheyenne and Arapaho leaders who had visited him (Mooney 1896: 781).*
>
> I, Jack Wilson, love you all, and my heart is full of gladness for the gifts you have brought me. When you get home I shall give you a good cloud [rain?] which will make you feel good. I give you a good spirit and give you all good paint. I want you to come in three months, some from each tribe there [the Indian Territory]. . . .
>
> Grandfather says, when your friends die you must not cry. You must not hurt anybody or do harm to anyone. You must not fight. Do right always. It will give you satisfaction in life. . . .
>
> Do not tell the white people about this. Jesus is now upon the earth. He appears like a cloud. The dead are all alive again. I do not know when they will be here; maybe this fall or in the spring. When the time comes there will be no more sickness and everyone will be young again.
>
> Do not refuse to work for the whites and do not make any trouble with them until you leave them. When the earth shakes [at the coming of the new world] do not be afraid. It will not hurt you.
>
> I want you to dance every six weeks. Make a feast at the dance and have food that everybody may eat. Then bathe in the water. That is all. You will receive good words again from me some time. Do not tell lies.
>
> *Excerpts from* Black Elik Speaks *by John G. Neihardt. Copyright © 1932, 1959, 1972, by John G. Neihardt. Copyright © 1961 by the John G. Neihardt Trust. Reprinted by permission of the University of Nebraska Press.*

sion of the dance, the dancers are told: "By your actions you have strengthened the sacred hoop of the nation. You have made a good center which will always be with you, and you have created a closer relationship with all things of the universe" (Brown 1971: 99–100).

THE MAKING OF RELATIVES (*HUNKAPI*) This ritual creates a special bond between two people stronger than kinship. The two people promise to die for one another, if necessary. One of the two is always older and is referred to as "*Hunke* father." As with the other rituals, it occurs in an especially erected structure, and is presided over by a *wakan* person.

PREPARING A GIRL FOR WOMANHOOD (*ISHNATI AWICALOWAPI*, "THEY SING OVER HER MENSES") This puberty ritual occurs after a young woman's first menstruation, and marks a girl's becoming a woman. It is also called the Buffalo Ceremony, because of the belief that the buffalo guards a woman's chastity and fertility. In the ceremony the young woman is told that like Mother Earth she will be able to bear children. She is also instructed that during her menstruation she possesses an especially potent sacred influence, which must be carefully guarded. She is taught the rituals of purification in which she will need to engage during her menstrual cycle throughout her period of fertility.

THE THROWING OF THE BALL (*TAPA WANKAYEYAPI*, "THROWING THE BALL UPWARD") In this ritual a young girl stands in a field surrounded by many people standing at the four directions. She throws a ball made from buffalo skin (symbolizing the universe and *Wakan Tanka*) to each of the four directions, and persons at each direction attempt to catch it. The ball also represents knowledge, and whoever catches it is considered fortunate.

The god Shiva as Nataraja, Lord of the Cosmic Dance.

ticular abilities, they can be offered to God as a sacrifice. According to the *Gita*, God loves humans and is concerned about them, taking various forms (*avatars*) to express this compassion. To respond to God's compassion with a life of devotion to God is to take the path to ultimate communion with God.

The *Gita* also teaches readers about the nature of the Ultimate. Like humans, the Ultimate has two natures: a lower, material nature (*prakriti*) and a higher, spiritual nature (*purusha*). One of the enticements of the *Gita* is its ambiguity. Is the Ultimate impersonal, the *Brahman* of the *Upanishads?* Or is the Ultimate the Supreme Lord, a personal god? Which is the superior spiritual path, selfless action guided by *dharma*, meditation on the Impersonal Absolute, or devotion to a personal God? If the Ultimate *is* personal, is Vishnu or Krishna the Supreme Lord? Is the *Gita's* last word about the nature of the Ultimate monistic, monotheistic, or pantheistic? This ambiguity has inspired commentators to write volumes on the *Gita*, without generating definitive answers to any of these questions. Perhaps the ambiguity is intentional, to make us aware that as humans we cannot pin down the nature of the Ultimate, or the best

means of ultimate transformation! If this is the case, then the *Gita* offers support for tolerance among differing religious positions.

Like all religious classics, the *Bhagavad-Gita* can be read on a variety of levels. This brief summary of its major teachings is meant to inspire the reader to explore its depths more fully. For those who would like to read the *Gita* as a whole, a variety of inexpensive English translations are readily available.

"Devotional" Hinduism and the Major Deities: The Puranas

Although their precise time of origin is unknown, the set of writings called the *puranas* came into prominence in the period after the *Bhagavad-Gita* (about 400 through 900 C.E.), called by many scholars the postclassical phase in the development of Hinduism. The *puranas* are stories and teachings primarily concerned with the personalities and exploits of three gods (called, as a group, the *trimurti*) and their accompanying goddesses. The gods are *Brahma* (the creator), *Vishnu* (the preserver), and *Shiva* (the destroyer). *Brahma's* principal consort is *Sarasvati* (goddess of wisdom and learning); *Vishnu's* is *Laksmi* (goddess of fortune); and *Shiva's* traditional consort is *Parvati*, although other goddesses are more prominently associated with *Shiva*, as we shall see.

Although the creator god figures in many stories in the *puranas*, *Brahma* is the least important of the three major deities. Unlike *Shiva* and *Vishnu*, no devotional movements focusing on *Brahma* developed. Like other deities, however, *Brahma* has a special animal on which he rides. In *Brahma's* case it is the swan. *Brahma* is depicted as red, with four bearded faces (symbolizing his all-knowing nature) and four arms (many arms symbolize the power of the deity).

Vishnu, whom we have already encountered in the *Bhagavad-Gita*, is the god of love, compassion, and forgiveness. As revealed in the *Bhagavad-Gita*, Vishnu comes to earth in many forms (*avatars*) to help humanity at times of trouble. The *Bhagavata Purana* speaks of nine current incarnations of *Vishnu*. Besides *Krishna* in the *Bhagavad-Gita*, the incarnations include several animals such as a boar who

A Hindu sadhu (holy man) sits on the banks of the Ganges River as worshippers bathe in the waters of this most sacred of rivers.

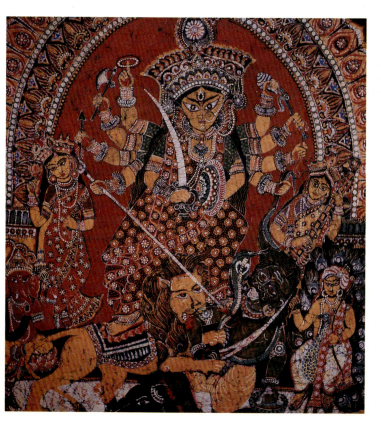

A painting of the Hindu goddess, Durga, consort of the God Shiva. Her multiple arms symbolize her awesome power. Durga is revered as the destroyer, whose work leads to regeneration.

raised the earth at the time of the primordial waters, and creatures such as a man-lion. Notably, *Gautama Buddha* (the founder of Buddhism) is one of the classic *avatars* of Vishnu, reflecting the Hindu absorption of Buddhism into its own teachings. The literature also looks toward a tenth *avatar, Kalkin,* who will appear at the end of the present age on a white horse to punish the wicked and reward the righteous.

In addition to his earthly incarnations, *Vishnu* is the preserver of the entire cosmos. For his devotees, *Vishnu* is the Supreme Person who transcends, yet is the source of all reality. The coming into existence of the material world is but his *lila* (sport or play), which has no effect on his ultimate nature. As Arjuna learns in the *Bhagavad-Gita,* everything (including the rest of the gods) will be absorbed into *Vishnu* at the end of the present age.

The religious movement focusing on devotion to *Vishnu* is known as Vaishnavism, and devotees are called Vaishnavites. They express their love for *Vishnu* in poems and songs, and seek liberation by responding to *Vishnu's* love for humanity with a life of devotion to their Lord, the one Supreme God.

Shiva is the most popular of the three major deities of devotional Hinduism. Known principally as "the destroyer," *Shiva* is the god of death, disease, and destruction. However, he is also the god of regeneration. Given the Indian view of cyclical life, these two functions are not contradictory. Before renewal can take place, there must first be destruction. Therefore, like *Vishnu, Shiva* takes the role of the Supreme Lord, who rules over the cosmic process.

Shiva's association with reproduction leads to his portrayal in pictures with a constantly erect penis. Two of the principal symbols associated with Shiva are the *lingam* and *yoni,* the male and female sexual organs, respectively. These symbols are usually found in stylized form in shrines associated with *Shiva.*

Among the popular epithets of *Shiva* are Lord of Creatures and Lord of the Dance. Portrayed as *Nataraja* (Lord of the Dance), *Shiva* is shown in a dancing pose, maintaining the rhythm of the universe through his exuberance. Yet his face is in calm repose, because he is not affected by or attached to his cosmic dance.

The devotional movement that identifies *Shiva* as the Supreme Lord is called Shaivism and its devotees, Shaivites.

In addition to *Parvati,* other goddesses are more prominently associated with *Shiva.* One of them, *Kali,* is one of the most well-known deities in Hinduism. In the popular pictures of *Kali,* used like the portrayals of other deities as objects of devotion, she is often depicted wearing human skulls around her neck, ripping the flesh of her victims, and drinking blood. Her bloodthirsty habits are legend. One group of followers of *Kali,* the *thagi* (from which we derive the English word "thug"), were a secret society in northern and central India. They robbed and strangled victims as a way of showing devotion to *Kali.* (The practice was outlawed in British India.) As with *Shiva,* the more horrific side of *Kali* must be understood in the context of her role in regenerating the cosmos. Without destruction, there can be no regeneration.

One of the most popular legends from the *Puranas* is the story of *Ganesha,* the elephant-headed son of *Shiva* and *Parvati.* According to many versions of the tale, *Ganesha* received his elephant head in an unusual way. Not recognizing *Ganesha* as his son, *Shiva* beheads him. The enraged *Parvati* threatens to destroy the universe and all the gods unless her son's head is restored. *Shiva* sends his attendants to bring the first suitable head they can find. They return with the head of an elephant, and *Shiva* restores his son with the new head. *Ganesha* is worshipped in his own right as a god who overcomes obstacles and upholds *dharma.* Shrines with images of the elephant-headed god can be found throughout India. His popularity is increasing in modern India, as persons turn to him to help them adapt to changing times.

For most Hindus today the means of ultimate transformation is devotion (*bhakti*) to a personal god (often called *bhakti yoga* or *bhakti marga*). By far the two most prominent deities are *Vishnu* and *Shiva,* and the two principal movements Vaishnavism and Shaivism. However, other deities, principal among them *Krishna* and *Rama* (both considered within the Vaishnavite branch of the *bhakti* movement), have inspired separate religious movements. The fact that each movement considers its deity supreme is accepted within Hinduism, and has not led to the internecine conflict among claims of supremacy for different deities found elsewhere.

Within *bhakti* Hinduism we find two orientations, which reflect different "goals." For most Indians the concerns of family and home take precedence over more refined spiritual concerns, as they do for most of the world's peoples. In India full commitment to spiritual matters is popularly reserved for *sadhus* (holy persons) and those who have taken the vow of *sannyasin* (renunciation of all worldly attachments). For them, the issues of acquiring sufficient food for the family, carrying out daily responsibilities, and dealing with sicknesses and other family problems are the primary concerns of others. Thus, they look to a deity for help in facing mundane matters, and tend to approach *bhakti* from this perspective. Their acts of devotion (*puja*) to a god are for the purpose of seeking divine assistance and comfort in meeting the challenges of daily living and confronting the tragedies of life. Through their acts of devotion they may hope to attain a higher birth in a subsequent life, but their primary focus is this-worldly. This approach is sometimes called "lower *bhakti*."

"Higher *bhakti*" refers to devotion to a personal god for the purpose of seeking liberation (*moksha*) from the cycle of rebirth after one's current life. In this approach, devotees will typically divorce themselves as much as possible from the attachments of daily living and treat all their activities as an expression of love for the deity. Some will take the vow of a *sannyasin* either at the fourth stage of life or earlier, in order to practice the total devotion associated with "higher *bhakti*."

While the distinction between "higher" and "lower" *bhakti* may be helpful in understanding the different types of transformation sought within devotional Hinduism, it should not be drawn too sharply. For many devotional Hindus, as for persons in the devotional traditions of other religions, both motivations are present in their worship of a personal god.

A particular kind of practice found in devotional Hinduism is called "*shaktism*" (*shakti* means "power, might"). *Shakti* is the active energy of a god, usually depicted as the feminine aspect (bal-anced with the passive side, depicted as masculine). In Hindu mythology and iconography, *shakti* is often depicted as a goddess (as in the expression by Shaivites of *shakti* in the person of *Kali*), and these goddesses are called *shaktis*. *Shaktism* is the practice of seeking to identify with this active power and draw upon it for material or spiritual pursuits. "Right-handed" *shaktism* is the more philosophical expression of this belief in the union of the two powers, while "left-handed" *shaktism* is the more magical and esoteric.

Related to left-handed *shaktism* is the religious phenomenon known as *tantrism*. It is an unorthodox practice found in Tibetan Buddhism, Jainism, and Sikhism as well as Hinduism. *Tantra* is the Sanskrit word for "that which extends, spreads." In a broad sense, *tantrism* is religious practice outside the Vedic tradition, including rituals open to persons not of the Brahmin class. *Tantras* themselves are manuals of magical words and spells used in this unorthodox practice. Hindu *tantrism* refers more specifically to the worship of deities for worldly purposes, but also to a mysterious, radical method (involving occult practices) for seeking *moksha*. *Tantrics* are known for cultivating the more sensual aspects of human nature as a way of seeking spiritual advancement. Hindu *tantrics* emphasize the union between the masculine and feminine in divinity. The universe comes into existence through the union of the male god's potency and the female *shakti*. Rather than the ascetic renunciation of the sensual, as in mainstream Hinduism, *tantrism* attempts to harness sensual energy for spiritual (or mundane) purposes. The practitioner learns to draw upon the "dormant power" (*kundalini*) within himself or herself, and is then initiated into a "circle" (*cakra*) of other *tantrics*, equally divided among males and females. The males symbolize *Shiva* and the females *shakti*. In a highly stylized ritual, the worshippers engage in sensual behavior, consuming intoxicants and finally engaging in sexual union. Key to the final step is the retention of semen by the male, demonstrating control over mind, breath, and ejaculation. This symbolizes the experience of cosmic withdrawal into oneness, rather than the creative extension of power, and is seen as an abbreviated but risky path to *moksha*. The practice, therefore, has an element of philosophical monism. Needless to say, Hindu *tantrism* as a spiritual path is a practice reserved for a very few highly committed (and unorthodox) seekers. Its practice has been in decline in modern Hinduism. *Tantrism* is visible to the general population in the erotic art often seen on Hindu temples. *Tantric* literature was compiled between 500 and 1500 C.E.

In addition to the *puranas* other texts, called *agamas*, arose in the devotional tradition. Their development coincides with growth of temples housing images of the gods, between about 400 and 900 C.E. They are principally ritual texts that regulate the *puja* and other devotional practices associated with the deities in temples and home shrines. The "seeing" (*darshana*) of the god, as manifest in the image, is often the goal for those who go on pilgrimage to one of the temples. *Agamas* also appears as a term for scriptures in Buddhism and Jainism, so the Hindu *agamas* are to be distinguished from the Buddhist and Jain texts of the same name.

"Philosophical" Hinduism: The Commentaries

The other major branch of Hinduism, which inspired a number of movements in the postclassical period, is often called "philosophical" because the ultimate focus is on knowledge of the spiritual rather than devotion to a personal god. We should note here that in Asian traditions we do not find the distinction between "philosophy" and "religion" found in the West (especially since the Enlightenment). The knowledge sought in Hindu philosophy is not "objective" knowledge about the world, but a direct, experiential knowledge of the sacred. In this branch the term *darshana* ("seeing") refers to the various philosophical schools. Although the most popular tradition identifies six philosophical systems within Hinduism, there are in fact a myriad of positions. The divergent schools arose from distinct commentaries on Vedic texts, especially the *Upanishads*. We will restrict our attention to two of the more prominent systems of thought: the *yoga* school and *Advaita Vedanta*.

Yoga is probably the one Hindu term known to most persons outside India. However, it is often misunderstood. It is usually thought of only as a form of physical exercise involving strange postures. In fact, physical (*hatha*) *yoga*, in which various physical exercises involving unusual positions are practiced, is but one aspect of the broader phenomenon. In its widest sense in Hinduism, *yoga* (from the Sanskrit term for "to yoke or join") refers to a variety of methods that seek to join the individual soul to the Ultimate, and thus achieve liberation from rebirth. Thus, *bhakti yoga* is the spiritual path that emphasizes devotion to gods or goddesses, or both. More narrowly, *yoga* refers to a particular philosophical school developed by the fourth-century-C.E. sage Patanjali, who wrote a philosophical treatise on meditation in the form of a commentary on the *Yoga Sutra* (*sutras* are collections of aphorisms). The meditative discipline based on his work became known as *raja yoga* (meaning the "king" or supreme *yoga*). Its practice involves working through a series of defined stages, including the following:

1. *Yamas*—vows of restraint, pledging chastity and pledging not to hurt living creatures.
2. *Niyama*—internal control, calmness.
3. *Asamas*—bodily postures, including the popular lotus position, to assist concentration and control.
4. *Pranayama*—breath control.
5. *Pratyahara*—control of senses.
6. *Dharana*—extreme concentration on a single object
7. *Dhyana*—withdrawal from all attachments through meditation.
8. *Samadhi*—entering into a trance in which oneness with *Brahman*, and therefore liberation, is experienced.

Those engaged in *raja yoga* sometimes perform remarkable physical feats such as reclining calmly on a bed of nails or walking on hot coals, demonstrating their control over their bodies. Philosophically, the school is "dualistic," emphasizing that the universe has two basic principles—the

The "father of modern India," Mohandas K. Gandhi (with walking stick) leaves unsuccessful negotiations with the British Viceroy of India during the Indian struggle for independence.

material (*prakriti*) and the spiritual (*purusha*). Attachment to the material must be overcome through the preceding steps, so that the *Atman* may experience union with the spiritual.

Another important Hindu philosophical system is *Advaita Vedanta,* one of the three *vedanta* schools (all of which are based on commentaries on the *Upanishads*). *Advaita Vedanta* literally means the "non-dual or monistic system based on the *Upanishads.*" The other *Vedanta* schools are *Dvaita* (meaning "dualistic," and therefore recognizing the distinction between material and spiritual reality) and *Vishishtadvaita* (a "qualified non-dualism" in which both the distinction of the material and spiritual and their ultimate unity are expressed). *Advaita Vedanta* developed in the ninth century C.E. when a philosopher named Shankara (788–820) wrote a commentary on an earlier work known as the *Vedanta Sutra.* The *Advaita Vedanta* school emphasizes the absolute oneness of *Brahman.* All else is illusion (*maya*). To illustrate this point, Shankara used the example of a person seeing a coiled object on the ground and jumping back,

thinking it to be a snake. On closer examination he found it to be only a piece of rope. According to Shankara, our minds, overcome with desire, interact with the energy of the truly real to create the illusion that the material world is real, as a person in the desert driven by thirst sees an oasis that is not there. Until we penetrate the veil of illusion, we will assume that the world of diversity we see and experience is the true reality. Shankara spoke of the path to liberation as having two phases. In the first phase, we worship a personal god (for Shankara it was *Shiva*) in order to bring spiritual reality into focus and to begin our spiritual quest. In the second phase, we move beyond a personal god to the higher experience of oneness. For Shankara personal gods are nothing more than the supreme oneness (*Brahman*) *with* attributes, not to be confused with the impersonal reality or *Brahman without* attributes.

This monistic interpretation of Hinduism—in which a personal god is understood as the provisional manifestation of impersonal *brahman*, rather than as the highest spiritual reality (as is the case in the *bhakti* movements)—has been popularized in the West by modern Indian intellectuals who hold the *Advaitan* position. It is sometimes mistakenly presented *as* Hinduism, rather than as one major branch within the Hindu tradition.

Reactions to Outside Influences

Beginning in the eighth century C.E., Hinduism had to respond to the religions brought by those who invaded South Asia. First it was Islam, a religion with teachings in some cases diametrically opposed to Hindu views (see Chapter Thirteen). As a result, for over a thousand years Hindus and Muslims have maintained a sometimes violent, but usually peaceful, coexistence. The most striking religious effect of the introduction of Islam into India was the development in the fifteenth century C.E. of the new religion of Sikhism, which sought to synthesize the best of the two traditions (see Chapter Seven).

The coming of Christianity to India has had a more profound effect on the development of Hinduism in the modern world. This was especially true after the British allowed Christian missionaries to enter India in the nineteenth century. They brought not only the Christian gospel, but also schools and other institutions that introduced Indians to Western values and customs. As a result arose movements and teachers who sought to blend what they considered the best of Christian and Western views with their own Hindu traditions.

The first such Hindu reform school was the *Brahmo Samaj* (Society of God), founded in 1828 by Ram Mohan Roy (1774–1833), a *Brahmin* who had studied a variety of religions. He became convinced that the truth behind all religions was that there is one personal God. He accepted the ethical teaching and congregational worship of Christianity (but not the divinity of Jesus), and sought to purge all polytheistic practices and references from Hinduism. His goal was universal religion and a reform of society based on belief in the one God and the highest ethical principles. He joined with the British in opposing practices such as *sati,* the custom of a widow placing herself on the funeral pyre of her husband to be consumed with him.

In response to reform movements that leaned heavily on Western teachings and sought to move beyond Hinduism to a "universal religion," others sought to reform Indian society by returning to Vedic values. One such movement was the *Arya* (from Aryan) *Samaj,* created in 1875.

Another influential nineteenth-century reformer was Sri Ramakrishna (1835–1886). Ramakrishna was a *Brahmin* and a priest of the goddess *Kali.* He longed for a mystical experience and attained union with the divine (*samadhi*) through concentration on an image of *Kali,* whom he called Mother. He then undertook a twelve-year spiritual journey, during which he had religious experiences following the disciplines of Jainism, Buddhism, Islam, and Christianity. He became convinced that all religions were simply different paths to the same summit. Ramakrishna's disciple, Vivekananda (1862–1902), became one of the first Hindu missionaries to the West, carrying the philosophy of *Advaita Vedanta* to the first Parliament of Religions at Chicago in 1893. He spoke of the oneness of all religions, and the highest spiritual experience of the oneness of all reality. In India the Ramakrishna Order was established among his disciples. They were often highly educated Indians who founded schools, hospitals, and other institutions for the betterment of the poor.

In more recent times one of the most articulate interpreters of Hinduism to the West was Sarvepalli Radhakrishnan (1888–1975). He was a philosopher, schooled in both Western and Indian thought, and a politician who served his country as president (1962–1967). Radhakrishnan became convinced that the materialism and skepticism generated by modern science and technology needed to be tempered by a renewal of spirituality. He thought that all of the world's religions had the same spiritual core, an insight best expressed, he felt, by *Advaita Vedanta.* In his writings and in his life, Radhakrishnan committed himself to service and sacrifice. His plea for cooperation among the world's religions has had a strong influence on many people.

In the arts Rabindranath Tagore (1861–1941) stands out as the principal Indian voice for a reconciliation between Western and Indian spirituality.

QUESTIONS OF HUMAN IDENTITY: WHO ARE WE?

The *Atman*

The common Hindu view of our human nature is that we have two "souls" or basic "selves." One is the eternal, indestructible, spiritual Atman. *The other is the material nature (often called the* jiva*), which constitutes the "self" that acts and therefore accumulates the effects of* karma. *Sometimes the eternal* Atman *is called in English translations the "Self," while the changing* jiva *is described simply as the "self." From the Hindu perspective, the* Atman *is one with the spiritual essence and source of the entire cosmos, either the impersonal* Brahman *or a personal Supreme Lord.*

In this selection, from the Chandogya Upanishad, the sage speaks of the Self [Atman] that is not yet visible to the eye, yet is greater than the whole of the physical cosmos (3.14.2,4; Radhakrishnan and Moore 1957: 64).

He who consists of mind, whose body is life, whose form is light, whose conception is truth, whose self is space, containing all works, containing all desires, containing all odors, containing all tastes, encompassing this whole world, the unspeaking, the unconcerned—this Self of mine within the heart is smaller than a grain of rice, or a barley-corn, or a mustard seed, or a grain of millet, or the kernal of a grain of millet; this Self of mine within the heart is greater than the earth, greater than the atmosphere, greater than the sky, greater than these worlds.

Containing all works, containing all desires, containing all odors, containing all tastes, encompassing this whole world, the unspeaking, the unconcerned—this is the Self of mine within the heart, this is Brahman. Into him I shall enter on departing hence. ...

The son of a leader of *Brahmo Samaj,* Tagore received an education in both Indian and Western culture. In his writings he speaks eloquently of the universal search for God, emphasizing the process of the search over static beliefs and practices. In 1913 Tagore became the first Asian to win the Nobel Prize for literature.

Sri Aurobindo Ghose (1872–1950) was the son of an Indian physician who had become convinced of the inferiority of Indian culture. Aurobindo's father sent him to European schools, where he received many academic awards. Ghose had no exposure to the classical texts of India until he returned home to begin an academic career. He taught himself Sanskrit and became enthralled with the spiritual depth of the Hindu classics and the value of Indian culture. After a period of political activity in support of Indian nationalism, Ghose withdrew to form an *ashram* (spiritual center) in southern India, which continues to attract students from all over the world. He spent the rest of his life practicing and teaching a form of *yoga.* He wrote a number of highly acclaimed works, including the epic poem *Savitri,* reflecting his own spiritual odyssey, and the philosophical work *The Divine Mind,* in which he related the spiritual progress of the individual to a cosmic evolution. Synthesizing his education in Western science with his own spiritual heritage, he spoke of the phases of evolution as life out of matter, mind out of life, and ultimately spirit out of mind. Our purpose as humans, he wrote, is to facilitate this final stage, bringing union to matter, life, mind, and spirit.

The last Hindu reformer we will discuss is the best known and historically the most important—Mohandas K. (Mahatma) Gandhi (1869–1948). Educated to be a lawyer in England, the young Gandhi found when he began a legal practice in South Africa that he could not shed the stigma of his Indian heritage. He experienced discrimination against people considered to be inferior, and he committed his life to the liberation of people from such injustices. He drew on his Hindu background, especially the teaching on *dharma* and non-attached action in the *Bhagavad-Gita;* the ideals of the Sermon on the Mount of Jesus in the Christian New Testament; and the teaching of *ahimsa* (non-injury to life) from Jainism. Gandhi returned to his homeland to lead a non-violent struggle for independence. He challenged the traditional caste system, especially the degrading treatment of persons in the "scheduled classes," the *untouchables* who were thought to be so low they were not even a part of the traditional fourfold class division. Gandhi called the untouchables *harijan* ("children of God") and was influential in the adoption of a constitution that prohibited discrimination on the basis of caste. Some orthodox Hindus viewed Gandhi as a heretic because of his renunciation of caste and his willingness to cooperate with Muslims. Gandhi was assassinated by an orthodox Hindu, but his influence continued. The American civil rights leader of the 1960s, Dr. Martin Luther King, Jr., cited Gandhi's non-violent teachings as an inspiration in his campaign to win justice for black Americans.

Hinduism Today

The modern state of India is a secular nation, the largest democracy in the world. In its 1948 constitution, India adopted the Western ideas of freedom of religion and equal protection under the law. Special efforts continue to redress past injustices by reserving jobs and scholarships for lower caste persons, especially members of the scheduled castes. These efforts have brought cries of "reverse discrimination" from persons in the middle castes who think they have lost opportunities because of efforts to help outcasts. Despite a political commitment to human rights, the traditional Hindu teaching of *karma* makes it very difficult to overcome the inherent inequalities and injustices of the caste system. This has caused some Indian intellectuals to renounce Hinduism altogether, claiming that it

is incompatible with the development of a modern, secular society. On the other extreme, Hindu traditionalists have decried the excesses and social instability brought on by the adoption of Western ideals. They call for a return to a society strictly based on the values of the Vedic tradition, such as those expressed in the Laws of Manu. In the middle are those who seek to maintain the best of Hindu spirituality, integrating these values with the respect for individual freedoms introduced by Westerners.

In the last century, numerous Hindu teachers have come to the United States. Some have begun movements that continue today as expressions of the Hindu tradition in North America. Several, including the well-known International Society for Krishna Consciousness (better known as the "Hare Krishnas" and the less-well-known Vedanta Society), will be discussed in Chapter Fourteen: New Religions.

DISTINCTIVE TEACHINGS

Why are there so many gods in Hinduism? Is one god better than the others? Why do Hindus worship cows? Why do Hindus believe that after they die they will be reborn in another life? What controls the kind of birth they will experience? Why is Hindu society divided into "castes"? Is the caste system as restrictive now as it once was? These are the questions often raised about Hinduism. We have touched on some of them already. In this section we will answer the others as we summarize the distinctive teachings of Hinduism as it is practiced today.

Problem: The Eternal Soul Trapped by Karma

All branches of Hinduism share an understanding of the basic dilemma humans face. Our true nature is *Atman,* eternal soul, but the *Atman* is trapped in a cycle of rebirth (*samsara*) because of the law of *karma.* The law of *karma* stipulates that we are inevitably determined in our future actions by the effects of our past actions. Until the inexorable enchainment of

QUESTIONS OF HUMAN IDENTITY: WHAT IS THE BASIC HUMAN DILEMMA?

Trapped in the Cycle of Rebirth

All the religions that originated in India share the understanding that humans are trapped in a cycle of rebirth because of attachment caused by desire. As this passage from the Upanishads *illustrates, for Hin-duism the attachment is to the self* (jiva), *which results in our being ignorant of our spiritual nature* (Atman, *here translated as Self*) (Chandogya Upanishad *8.12.1;* Prabhavananda 1963: 51).

This body [*jiva*] is mortal, always gripped by death, but within it dwells the immortal Self [*Atman*]. This Self, when associated in our consciousness with the body, is subject to pleasure and pain; and so long as this association continues, freedom from pleasure and pain can no man find.

But as this association ceases, there cease also the pleasure and the pain. Rising above physical consciousness, knowing the Self to be distinct from the senses and the mind—knowing it in its true light—one rejoices and is free.

Excerpt from The Spiritual Heritage of India, *ed. Swami Prabhavananda. Reprinted with permission of Vedanta Press.*

karma is broken, the *Atman's* journey through unending rounds of rebirth will continue. The level of existence of the *Atman* is controlled by the actions of prior lives. Each action tends toward a particular effect, and that effect will be realized whether in the current life or another. For example, a person whose actions are slovenly may cause the *Atman* to experience rebirth as a sloth.

If someone is born as a human, his or her social level ("caste") is dependent on past *karma*. As noted above, originally Hindu tradition recognized four social levels (*varna*): *Brahmins* (priests and sages), *Kshatriyas* (warriors), *Vaisyas* (merchants or farmers), and *Shudras* (servants). However, over time an elaborate system of several thousand "functional castes" (*jati*), groups of similar occupations in the same area, developed. In addition, divisions of race, sect, and immigration have created new *jati* groups. The lowest *jati* became known as "outcasts" or "untouchables," because their occupations involved them in traditionally ritually impure activities (e.g., contact with dead bodies, whether animal or human). Despite decades of attempts to end discrimination against untouchables and to reform the *jati* system, the complex caste system still dominates life in India, especially in rural areas. Some tradi-

tional Hindus believe that only male *Brahmins* may escape rebirth. The most persons born in other castes (and women) can hope for, they believe, is to be born as a male *brahmin* in the next life. Most Hindus, however, influenced by the teaching of the *Bhagavad-Gita*, believe that one's caste or gender is not a detriment to attaining liberation.

Despite differences in understanding of the spiritual importance of caste, all Hindu schools emphasize that the principal issue humans must address is how the *Atman* may escape *karmic* entrapment.

Cause: Ignorance Resulting in Attachment

The entrapment of the *Atman* by *karma* is a result of *avidya* (ignorance). The Hindu understanding of "ignorance" is different from the ordinary meaning of the concept in the West. *Avidya* is not a lack of knowledge; it is spiritual confusion about our true human nature and the true nature of all reality. It is delusion, believing that the changing world in which we live day to day is the only reality.

Hinduism teaches that because of our ignorance, we inevitably assume that the material

QUESTIONS OF HUMAN DESTINY: WHAT HAPPENS AFTER DEATH?

The Destiny of the *Atman*

According to this first passage, from the Bhagavad-Gita, *whatever is on a person's mind at the time of death will be his or her destiny in the next life (because the person's* karma *will dictate it). Therefore, Lord Krishna urges Arjuna to have Him on his mind at death, so that he will live eternally on the spiritual plane of existence, enjoying Krishna forever (8:5–7, 12–13; Prabhupada, trans. 1983: 419–21, 427–28).*

The second text, from the Garuda Purana, speaks of a hell, a terrible place where souls that need to be purified are sent before continuing their journeys. Hell, therefore, is a frightening place, but not an eternal one (3.49–53, 71; Wood and Subrahmanyam 1974: 26–27, 29).

And whoever, at the end of his life, quits his body, remembering Me alone, at once attains My nature. Of that there is no doubt. Whatever state of being one remembers when he quits his body, O son of Kunti, that state he

will attain without fail. Therefore, Arjuna, you should always think of Me in the form of Krishna and at the same time carry out your prescribed duty of fighting. With your activities dedicated to Me and your mind and intelligence fixed on Me, you will attain Me without doubt. ... The yogic situation is that of detachment from all sensual engagements. Closing all the doors of the senses and fixing the mind on the heart and the life are at the top of the head, one establishes himself in yoga.

After being situated in this yoga practice and vibrating the sacred syllable om, the supreme combination of letters, if one thinks of the Supreme Person-ality of Godhead and quits his body, he will certainly reach the spiritual planets.

Some of the sinful are cut with saws, like firewood, and others thrown flat on the ground, are chopped into pieces with axes. Some, their bodies half buried in a

pit, are pierced in the head with arrows. Others, fixed in the middle of a machine, are squeezed like sugar cane. Some are surrounded closely with blazing charcoal, enwrap-ped with torches, and smelted like a lump of ore. Some are plunged into heated butter, and others into heated oil—and like a cake thrown into the frying pan they are turned about. Some are thrown in the way, in front of huge maddened elephants, and some with hands and feet bound are placed head downwards. Some are thrown into wells; some are hurled from heights; others, plunged into pits full of worms, are eaten away by them. . . .

Having experienced in due order the torments below, he comes here again, purified.

Excerpts from Bhagavad-Gita As It Is, *trans. A.C. Bhaktivedanta Swami Prabhupada. Copyright © 1972 by The Bhaktivedanta Book Trust International. Used with permission.*

Excerpt from The Garuda Purana: Saroddhara ed. by Ernest Wood and S.V. Subrahmanyam. Reprinted by permission of AMS Press.

world is the only reality, and we become attached to that world. We seek ultimate fulfillment in the activities of the material world—such as relations with other persons, work, leisure activities, eating—unaware that attachment to these is entrapping us. We assume that the "self" that acts is the only self, and we fail to realize that beneath this changing, acting "self" is the eternal *Atman*. Therefore, for Hinduism as for other religions that share the common Indian worldview, at the heart

of the issue is desire, which causes us to act and which leaves us deluded about that which should be our principal concern—spiritual liberation.

Reality: Penetrating the Veil of Maya

The most common term associated with the Hindu understanding of the material world is *maya* (illusion). The various branches of Hinduism share the belief that the material world

Bathers in the sacred Ganges River at the holy city of Benares.

obscures the spiritual. Because of our ignorance, we fail to see that we must penetrate through this "veil" to the unchanging spiritual reality. Where they differ is whether the world of *maya* is real in some sense, or actually "unreal." Some schools say that *maya* results from the creative energy of the Supreme Lord (a personal god), through which God brings the material world into existence. *Maya* is real, but should not be confused with God's higher, eternal nature. Other schools believe that *maya* results from human ignorance; when we "wake up" we will discover that there is but one true Reality and that all else has only a temporary, provisional existence. A variety of other views can be found among other schools.

Despite these rather technical philosophical differences, Hinduism in general teaches that the material world comes into existence and is dis-

solved in a cosmic process of rebirth and is therefore without beginning and without end.

End: Liberation from the Cycle of Rebirth

According to classical Hinduism, life has four aims: *dharma* (right conduct), *artha* (material gain), *kama* (pleasure, mainly thought of in sexual terms), and finally *moksha* (liberation from the cycle of rebirth). This clearly shows that Hinduism is not the world-denying religion some have accused it of being. With these four aims, Hinduism recognizes that there is a time and a place for pursuing material gain and enjoying sexual pleasure, insofar as both are within the context of right conduct. There is even a well-known handbook, the *kama sutra*, to guide couples in the pursuit of sexual pleasure. Within classical formulation, the proper context to pursue material wealth and sexual pleasure is at the "householder" stage, when a person is married and fulfilling familial responsibilities. However, there is a higher goal in life—the fourth aim, *moksha*, the culmination of life. It may be realized within this life; it is *not* merely a state of existence after death.

The branches of Hinduism share *moksha* as the ultimate goal. However, they differ on the nature of the liberated state. The *bhakti* movements speak of the communion of the *Atman* with a personal deity in an eternal state of "enjoyment or bliss." The philosophical schools tend toward a more impersonal view. They typically emphasize that *moksha* is beyond description. All that we can say is that once the *Atman* experiences liberation, there is no more rebirth, only a state of complete and total release. The monistic school (*Advaita Vedanta*) speaks of *moksha* as coming to awareness of the identity of the *Atman* with the cosmic oneness (*Brahman*), a state of absorption often called *samadhi*.

Means: The Various Paths to Liberation

The most common way of designating the different paths to liberation within Hinduism is to speak of *karma yoga* (the way of action), *bhakti yoga* (the way of devotion), and *jnana yoga* (the way of knowledge).

QUESTIONS ABOUT THE SACRED: WHAT IS SACRED?

Personal or Impersonal?

The Upanishads *use both personal and impersonal language to speak of* Brahman, *the ultimate reality. In the first passage, from the* Svetastavara Upanishad, *the language is personal but the image is somewhat impersonal. This creates an ambiguity exploited by interpreters who want to emphasize the personal over the impersonal dimension, or vice versa. Hinduism addresses the Supreme Lord as both masculine and feminine (6.11–13; Macnicol 1938: 219–20).*

The second passage from the Bhagavad-Gita *reflects this duality. Krishna is speaking. Like the* Upanishads, *the* Gita *mixes personal and impersonal imagery (9:17–19; Prabhupada 1983: 477–80).*

He [Brahman] is the one God, hidden in all beings, all-pervading, the Self within all beings, watching over all works, dwelling in all beings, the perceiver, the only one, free from all qualities.

He is the one ruler of many who [seem to act, but really] do not act; he makes the one seed manifold. The wise who perceive him within their self, to them belongs eternal happiness, not to others.

He is the eternal among eternals, the thinker among thinkers, who, though one, fulfills the desires of many....

I am the father of this universe, the mother, the support and the grandsire. I am the object of knowledge, the purifier and the syllable om. I am also the Rig, the Sama, and the Yajur Vedas.

I am the goal, the sustainer, the master, the witness, the abode, the refuge and the most dear friend. I am the creation and the annihilation, the basis of everything, the resting place and the eternal seed.

O Arjuna, I give heat, and I withhold and send forth the rain. I am immortality, and I am also death personified. Both spirit and matter are in Me.

Excerpts from Hindu Scriptures, *ed. Nicol Macnicol (1938) and R.C. Zaehner (1966). Reprinted with permission of Everyman's Library, David Campbell Publishers Ltd.*

Excerpts from Bhagavad-Gita As It Is, *trans. A.C. Bhaktivedanta Swami Prabhupada. Copyright © 1972 by The Bhaktivedanta Book Trust International. Used with permission.*

Sometimes the term *marga* (which literally means "path") is used instead of *yoga*. Although a variety of other *yoga* (referring to the process of joining or yoking the *Atman* with the spiritual source) are found in Hinduism, these three are the most widely recognized.

Karma yoga is the path followed by most Hindus, although it is often combined with others. It simply means living in accord with *dharma* (duty, determined principally in Hinduism by gender, caste, and stage of life). For traditionalists the Laws of Manu set forth the guidelines for living. They include the rituals one must perform, the occupations one may enter, and the ways one should interact with others. The *Bhagavad-Gita* added the notion of carrying out one's caste *dharma* with an attitude of detachment, and treating all of one's actions as sacrifices to the Supreme Lord. *Karma yoga* has the virtue of simplicity and accessibility. Traditionalists believe that through *karma yoga*, lower-caste individuals can only improve their rank in the next life, while others believe *karma yoga* opens the door to *moksha* for any, regardless of caste and gender.

Bhakti yoga is the path of devotion to a personal deity. Rooted in the Vedic practice of sacrifice to various gods, it came into prominence with the *Bhagavad-Gita* and increased in popularity with the emergence of Shiva and Vishnu as the principal deities in the Hindu pantheon. Hindus are remarkably tolerant of people's right to choose different deities as the object of their devotion. One common way of explaining the diversity of gods is to recognize them as manifestations of the one Supreme Lord, who gladly accepts being worshipped by a variety of names.

Reverence for the cow as sacred Mother is a basic teaching of the Hindu tradition.

This tolerance is extended beyond the Hindu names for gods to the ways of knowing the divine in other religions. Nevertheless, different *bhakti* movements recognize their particular God (Shiva, Vishnu, Kali, or Krishna, for example) as ultimate. For philosophical schools, which speak of an ultimacy that goes beyond personal identity, this path is often considered a preliminary to the highest form of spiritual attainment—knowledge.

In Hinduism there is no day of the week set aside for worshipping the gods. Expressions of devotion (*puja*) are to be a part of one's daily routine. However, each deity has temples, to which the faithful make pilgrimages as a way of showing devotion, and special days during the year set aside for festivals. One of the most famous is the Jagannatha Temple at Puri, which houses an image of Vishnu. Once a year the image is taken from the temple and moved by a special vehicle (called a "juggernaut"). However, thousands of other temples and shrines dot the Indian landscape.

The most popular pilgrimage spots for all Hindus are found along the banks of the River Ganges. Known as Mother Ganges, the river (first among the seven holy rivers of India) is thought to

be a goddess herself, related mythologically to both Shiva and Vishnu. To bathe in the life-giving and purifying waters of Mother Ganges is a source of inestimable joy for virtually all Hindus. To be cremated along her banks is the hope of all Hindus. Of the many sacred cities along the Ganges, the most prominent is Benares (today known as Varanasi or simply Kasi) in north-central India.

Jnana yoga (the way of knowledge) is the path of meditation that leads ultimately to an intuitive experience of the Ultimate, usually spoken of as *Brahman*. Through a process of moral, physical, mental, and spiritual discipline, the seeker slowly and patiently reaches a point of final preparation. Then in a single moment of blinding enlightenment the goal is reached, and the door beyond rebirth opens into an indescribable state of union with the Ultimate. After the experience one continues living in a blissful state in this world, until the effects of past actions are worked through. Then, upon death, the *Atman* is liberated, and there is no more rebirth.

Serious students of *bhakti* and *jnana yoga* believe that meaningful advancement requires placing oneself under the guidance of a spiritual teacher, usually called a *guru*. To be a *guru* one must demonstrate exceptional spiritual awareness and an ability to lead others toward the same end. The devotion shown to *gurus*, through prostrating oneself in the presence of the *guru* or offering gifts, is part of the process of gaining spiritual merit. Unfortunately, some unscrupulous religious leaders have played upon the practice of having a *guru* to manipulate and extort naive followers. Since there is no central authority to exercise discipline in Hinduism, it is very difficult to control such excesses.

One of the more controversial forms of worship in Hinduism is veneration of the cow. With so much hunger in India, why does the government not encourage the eating of the cows that wander through villages, towns, even cities? At certain times of the year in some locations, cows are venerated as deities, with garlands of flowers placed on their necks.

According to even an enlightened leader such as Mahatma Gandhi, "cow protection" is at the core of Hinduism. Why? The reasons are both symbolic

QUESTIONS OF MORALITY: WHAT ARE OUR OBLIGATIONS TO NON-HUMAN LIFE?

Cow Veneration

One of the customs of Hinduism is reverence for cows, for the cow is the "mother of life." This attitude is already found in the Vedic literature, as evidenced by the following passage from the Rig-Veda (6.28; Bose 1966: 196–97). The second passage, a verse from the Laws of Manu, lends support to a vegetarian lifestyle (5.48; Morgan 1953: 330).

The cows have come and brought us good fortune, may they stay in the stall and be pleased with us; may they live here, mothers of calves, many-colored, and yield milk for Indra on many dawns....
They are not lost, nor do robbers injure them, nor the unfriendly

frighten, nor wish to assail them; the master of cattle lives together long with these, and worships the gods and offers gifts.
The charger, whirling up dust, does
not reach them, they never take their way to the slaughtering stool, the cows of the worshipping man roam about over the widespread pastures, free from all danger.
To me the cows are Bhaga, they are Indra, they [their milk] are a portion of the first-poured Soma.
These that are cows are Indra, O people!
The Indra I long for with heart and spirit.
Ye cows, you fatten the emaciated, and you make the unlovely look beautiful, make our house happy, you with

pleasant lowings, your power is glorified in our assemblies.
May you have many calves, graze on good pastures, and drink pure water at good drinking places; may not the thief master you nor the wicked, and may the darts of Rudra leave you aside.
May there be a close mixing of up, may Soma juice mix with cow's milk and may this manly vigor be, Indra, for thy heroic might.
Without doing injury to living beings, flesh cannot be had anywhere; and the killing of living things is not conducive to heaven; hence eating of flesh should be avoided.

Excerpt from The Religion of the Hindus by Kenneth Morgan. Copyright © 1953. Reprinted by permission of John Wiley & Sons, Inc.

and practical. For Gandhi the cow represented all non-human life. Respect for her instills awareness that we humans are dependent on the non-human world for our very existence. Veneration of the cow also fosters, Gandhi believed, an attitude of giving freely to others. She is indeed a Mother of all humanity, to be honored, not slaughtered and eaten. Her protection is deeply rooted in the spiritual tradition of India, where she is associated with the mother goddess.

More practically, the cow *is* critical to survival for many Indians. For example, her dung is an essential fuel, a disinfectant, and an ingredient in mortar for building. Supporters of cow protection point out that to kill a cow would provide a few meals; to allow her to roam, with her products of milk, butter, and dung accessible to even the poorest, has enabled countless Indians to avoid starvation and homelessness.

Sacred: Many Gods and Beyond the Gods

Readers who have studied the whole section on Hinduism are now well aware that the Hindu conception of the spiritual is complex. It cannot be easily classified, for within Hinduism we find all types of theism as well as monism, dualism, and more. The clearest division in the Hindu understanding of the spiritual is between those who speak of the highest reality as beyond all distinctions and therefore impersonal, *Brahman,* and those who steadfastly hold to an understanding of the supreme as personal. Unfortunately, some of the most popular interpreters of Hinduism misrepresent the breadth of Hindu teaching by presenting the impersonalist view as "Hinduism." In describing Hinduism phenomenologically, we must simply acknowledge and respect this fundamental divergence.

RESPONSES TO CONTEMPORARY ETHICAL ISSUES

The Ecological Crisis

Certainly India has not been immune from the consequences of the environmental crisis. For example, in the eight years ending in 1987, 22 percent of the forests of India were cut down. This occurred despite the efforts of a Hindu environmental movement called *Chipko* or "hug-the-tree," which sprang up in India in the 1970s. The world's worst nonnuclear industrial accident occurred in Bhopal, India. Many of India's sacred rivers, including the Ganges, are polluted by municipal and industrial waste. Tragically disrespect for the balance of life runs counter to some fundamental Hindu teachings. The hymns of the *Rig-Veda* reflect an awareness of the presence of the sacred in nature. For example, in a hymn to Aranyani, the goddess of the forest, the spiritual nature of the forest is celebrated in these words: "The forest creaks like a cart at eventide. Who tarries in the forest-glade, thinks to himself, 'I heard a cry.' Sweet-scented, redolent of balm, replete with food, yet tilting not, mother of beasts, the Forest Deity, her have I magnified with praise" (*Rig-Veda* X.146; cited by Chaitanya 1983: 129).

Also present in the Vedic hymns is the awareness of an eternal law (*Rita*), which gave Hinduism a lasting sense of an underlying spiritual process that manifests itself in all reality. According to the Vedas, humans who desire to live balanced and productive lives must learn to respect and follow *Rita*. The wicked are those who try to spurn the eternal law, and inevitably pay a price for their disdain. But, as the Vedic poet says, "For one who lives according to Eternal Law, the winds are full of sweetness, the rivers pour sweets" (*Rig-Veda* I 90.6; cited by Chaitanya 1983: 131).

Several ethical values that crystallized during the classical period of Hinduism reflect ecological sensitivity. As we have noted, according to classical Hindu teaching, whether monistic or theistic, there is one Spiritual Reality (*Brahman* or the Supreme Person) from which or whom all other reality evolves. The cosmos is a single spiritual whole, with humans participating in Spirit along with all of life. Even that which appears to be physical is in truth manifestation of the spiritual, Hinduism teaches. The Spirit (*Atman*) that is the true nature of humans is the true nature of all reality, and therefore humans who are spiritually aware have a sense of kinship with and reverence for all living beings. The Hindu preference for vegetarianism, veneration of cows, and the general teaching of noninjury (*ahimsa*) flow from this understanding of spirituality. Anthropocentrism and its attendant attitude of the human right to exploit nature is not part of the basic Hindu worldview.

Another ecologically oriented Hindu value is restraint. It is an aspect of the Hindu ideal of renunciation of attachment to one's actions in order to break free from the effects of the law of *karma*, expressed so vividly in the *Bhagavad-Gita*. Traditional Hinduism recognizes that the pursuit of material ends (including wealth) is necessary at the student and householder stages of life for higher-caste males. However, as a man moves to the forest-dweller and renunciant stages, detachment from worldly goals becomes increasingly important. With the presence of holy men who renounce all worldly ends at an early age, along with this philosophy of the stages of life, the ideal of restraint has broad influence, even on those who are not fully committed to it. The result is an attitude of parsimony, which includes a restrained approach to the use of the elements of non-human nature.

Finally, the concept of *karma* (shared with other religions that emerged in India) has environmental implications. According to the law of *karma*, we are in a very real way the product of our past actions. It "binds [humanity] into the strongest community with natural processes and makes [humans] co-implicate, as it were, with them" (Deutsch 1989: 265).

These values are among those that contribute to a positive Hindu environmental ethic. On the negative side, we must acknowledge that Hindu spirituality and detachment from the material world has also led to an attitude of disregard for the fate of the earth. Since the ultimate objective is release from the cycle of rebirth in the material world, some would say that Hindu teaching has contributed to passivity in the face of environmental as well as other seemingly worldly concerns. However, in modern India the tendency of spiritual aloofness is not nearly as strong as it was in earlier times. Many Hindu leaders today are trying to balance concern for the well-being of all life in their own tradition with the need to develop the material resources of the land to provide adequately for people. It is a delicate balancing act!

War

Like other religions, Hinduism has an inherent ambiguity on the subject of war. On the one hand, the Aryan culture in which the Vedic literature was written was dominated by conflict. According to the *Rig-Veda,* one of the four castes present since creation was the *kshatriya* or warrior caste. As Hinduism developed, and the concept of *dharma* emerged as central, the attitude that the *dharma* (duty) of the warrior was to fight went largely unchallenged. In the *Bhagavad-Gita,* when the warrior Arjuna questions whether he should enter into a war that would result in the death of kinsmen, his charioteer Krishna (God in human form) told him that he must fulfill his *dharma* as a *kshatriya.* From this point of view, wars are an inevitable reality, especially in this final age of the present cosmic cycle, *Kali Yuga,* when hostility and tension are high among peoples.

On the other hand, the Hindu virtue of *ahimsa* or non-injury, shared with other religions in India, has contributed to a pacifist streak in India. Mahatma Gandhi turned *ahimsa* into a clever political strategy, using non-violent resistance rather than armed conflict to end British rule in India. Unfortunately, after independence not even Gandhi's charisma could thwart the internecine struggle between Hindus and Muslims, which led to many deaths. India today has become a nuclear power and has flexed its military muscles in border clashes with Pakistan and in support for the emergence of the nation of Bangladesh in what was once East Pakistan. Sporadic violence between orthodox Hindus and Muslims, as well as between Sikhs and Hindus, seems intractable. Nevertheless, many Hindus remain committed to Gandhi's philosophy of non-violence, a teaching that strongly influenced the American civil rights movement in the 1960s.

Abortion

In the late 1980s 3.9 million induced abortions were reported annually in India. Abortion has been legal in India since 1971, when the Medical Termination of Pregnancy Act was passed. It allows for abortions when "the continuance of the pregnancy would involve a risk to the life of the pregnant woman or of grave injury to her physical or mental health" or when "there is substantial risk that, if the child were born, it would suffer such physical or mental abnormalities as to be seriously handicapped." Two appendices state that when a pregnancy is caused by rape or the failure of a birth control device, "grave injury" will be assumed (Crawford 1989: 24–25).

However, traditional Hinduism opposes abortion. The Vedic literature includes an incantation against whomever causes a pregnant woman to abort: "The blood-sucking demon and him that tries to rob health, Kanva, the devourer of our offspring, destroy, O Prisni-parni" (*Atharvaveda* 2.25.4; cited by Ludwig 1987: 150). On the question of "When does life begin?" the Hindu manual on medicine, *Caraka Samhita,* says explicitly that life begins at conception, when the soul and mind enter the zygote formed by the union of the sperm and egg. This means that "a being with a human genetic code is indeed a human being" (Crawford 1989: 26). Thus, the fetus is inviolable and abortion is not an option, for it would be a violation of the moral principle of *ahimsa* (non-injury) to all living beings.

Ahimsa, however, is not absolute when the rights of humans conflict. When a woman risks "grave injury," abortion is permissible. Some Hindu scholars argue that the rights of an adult human being with familial obligations outweigh those of a human being whose *karmic* state in the current life has not yet developed. Under these circumstances a woman's right to have an abortion must be recognized, they maintain.

In cases of fetal deformity, Hindu leaders oppose abortion because it interferes with the child's *karmic* development (Crawford 1989: 27). They also consider the use of abortion for sex selection, usually used to secure male children, to be immoral. It is considered infanticide. More generally, many Hindus are disturbed by the use of elective abortion as birth control.

In the final analysis, however, Hinduism is a religion that recognizes that each person must make his or her own ethical decisions, because each person alone suffers or enjoys the *karmic* consequences.

Euthanasia

Because of belief in the cycle of rebirth and reincarnation, Hinduism is not as "anxious" about death and dying as other religions. Death is merely the gateway into another existence. In Hinduism, death is not the opposite of life; it is the opposite of birth.

Active euthanasia runs counter to the basic Hindu worldview and the principles of *dharma* and *karma*. "Actively [cutting] short a life through medical intervention would be viewed as destructive of one's dharma by interrupting the working out of karma in the patient's life. Active euthanasia would produce negative karma for both the patient and the physician" (Hamel and DuBose 1991: 97).

However, voluntary euthanasia, which does not require active intervention, is another matter. Some Hindu *sadhus* (holy men) have chosen voluntary starvation as an extreme expression of their renunciation of attachment to the material self, but the practice is not common. One of the disciples of Mahatma Gandhi, Vinobha Bhave, chose to end his life by stopping the intake of food. In keeping with the Hindu tradition of respect for individuals' right and obligation to chart their own destinies, no effort was made to stop Bhave from his act of voluntary euthanasia.

Economic Justice

Among the goals deemed acceptable in traditional Hindu society are *artha* (wealth or material prosperity) and *kama* (sensual pleasure). The notion that the things of the world are not to be enjoyed is not a Hindu concept. Apart from the holy persons who renounce all worldly attachments, Hinduism is not an ascetic religion.

According to traditional Hinduism, wealth or poverty is a result of a person's own *karma* (action). A starving "outcast" is enduring the unfortunate consequences of behavior in a past life. By contrast, a wealthy merchant is benefitting from the *karmic* influences of a previous existence or prior actions in this life. Since the caste system and the law of *karma* are rooted in the very nature of the cosmos itself, the concept of social inequities being "unjust" is a difficult one in traditional Hinduism. To the degree that traditional Hinduism still dominates life in India, what outsiders would view as oppression and injustice is seen by rich and poor alike as inevitable and unchangeable.

Everything discussed to this point has contributed to a stratified society in India, in which some enjoy considerable wealth while others are starving. The modern state of India, however, has outlawed discrimination on the basis of caste, sex, and religion, among other criteria. Indeed, the nation of India emerged out of the reform movement led by Mahatma Gandhi, which had the breaking down of barriers based on caste as one of its central themes. Whether concern for social justice in reformers such as Gandhi came from exposure to Western society or from their own reassessment of Hindu tradition, or both, is open to question. It should be noted in passing that a relatively strong Communist movement in India, as well as other types of socialist groups, have influenced social developments in some regions of India.

The Hindu teaching of *ahimsa* (non-injury) has been used by Gandhi and other reformers to press for programs designed to alleviate poverty, hunger, and homelessness in India. Adapting the tradition of renunciation to modern problems, the Ramakrishna Order (whose monks have come to the United States to lead Vedanta Society Centers—see Chapter Fourteen) has opened clinics and other social service agencies across India to respond to human suffering. Regardless of the sources, the contemporary leaders of India are committed to what they realize will be a long struggle to transform Indian society on the basis of the principles of equal rights and equal justice.

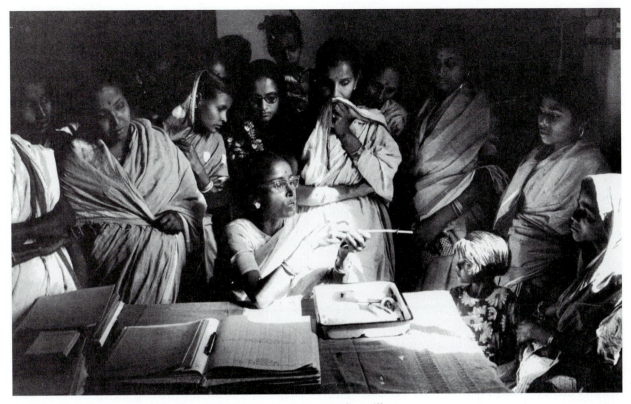

A worker illustrates the use of a birth control device to women in an Indian village.

Tremendous strides (in the face of almost overwhelming odds) are being made in the areas of distribution of food, housing, and health care, and a lower percentage of Indians live in abject poverty today than before the modern state originated. At the same time, a Hindu orthodox movement challenges much of the transformation being attempted on the grounds that the structure of the caste system is essential if Hindus are to follow the *dharma* inherent in all of life. In recent years, Hindu traditionalism has been on the rise, but without sufficient support or power to stop the government's program of reform and widening social justice.

Gender Roles and the Status of Women

The present ambiguity facing women in Hindu society is illustrated by the tension in the understanding of marriage. Traditionally, the principal *dharma* of the woman in marriage was biological, to produce large families, and especially to give birth to sons. At present, the emphasis being placed on family planning and reducing population growth has put pressure on this historic emphasis. The five traditional purposes of marriage in Hinduism include not only producing children, but also pleasure, companionship, sacrificial service, and spiritual bliss. The current challenge is to increase the importance of the other goals, as the central value of the biological function decreases (Crawford 1989: 21).

Traditional Hindu culture is deeply patriarchal. A woman's *dharma*, as it has been long understood, is to be subordinate first to her father, then to her husband, and finally to her sons. A married woman has traditionally been taught to view her husband as her god. Several practices illustrate the Hindu heritage of male dominance. One is the ancient but still very influential preference for male offspring. According to the Laws of Manu, sons alone are able to rescue the souls of ancestors from hell so that they may continue their spiritual progress toward liberation. The Laws also state that the first-born son is the only child born for the sake of *dharma;* others are the fruit of passion (Crawford 1989: 21–22).

A second tragic tradition that demonstrates the oppression of women in traditional Hindu society is the practice of female infanticide. Because a father must supply dowries for his daughters, they can become a financial drain. According to tradition, only a son can light the fires on a parent's funeral pyre, so many couples continue having children until a son is born. As one father of three daughters, whose wife had just given birth to a first son, said recently (in front of his daughters) "Now I finally feel fulfilled." Tragically, this attitude can mean doing away with female newborns (although Hindu law strictly forbids infanticide), and with a reassertion of Hindu traditionalism this practice seems to be on the rise. In lower-caste families, some "parents reluctantly poison the newborn girl, justifying it as a shortening of her suffering from one life to one hour" (Crawford 1989: 22). This practice is so common that prosecution of parents who kill their female infants is rare. In Hindu families who can afford it, female infanticide has been replaced by abortion. Amniocentesis or sonograms are used to determine the gender of the fetus. If the fetus is a girl, the woman has an abortion. In a 1992 study of 8,000 abortions for the purpose of sex selection, only one was for the purpose of giving birth to a girl. Some clinics offer "package deals"— gender determination and abortion (if the fetus is female) for one low price. Despite government efforts to discourage the practice, it is leading to a growing disparity in population. According to the 1991 census, there are now 929 females per 1,000 males in India (Young 1994: 116).

Marriages arranged at a very young age also serve to restrict opportunities for women. Traditionally, Hindu women are betrothed well before puberty, married shortly thereafter, and the mother of several children while still in the early teens. Married women are expected to be docile, even worshipping their husband's big toe. The Laws of Manu say that women are to be loyal and faithful even if their husbands are unfaithful, drunk, abusive, or deformed.

The third practice is *sati,* in which a widow immolated herself on her husband's funeral pyre, because her life symbolically ended with his death. (The name *Sati*—literally, "good woman"—refers to a goddess who committed suicide after her husband, the god *Shiva,* was insulted.) The practice was ostensibly voluntary (it is not directly enjoined in any Hindu law code), but sometimes apparently resulted from the pressure of greedy relatives who wanted the wife's inheritance. It was outlawed in 1829 under pressure from British authorities and Hindu reformers. The practice continues today only rarely, but the symbolism of a woman's identity being tied to the males in her life continues.

Women have traditionally been restricted from serving as priests, that role being reserved for male members of the *brahmin* caste. Women were for centuries forbidden from studying Sanskrit, the language in which the Hindu sacred texts are written. In some branches of Hinduism, especially some of the *bhakti* (devotional) movements, women have been accorded equal spiritual status. The influential *Bhagavad-Gita* teaches that women may become devotees of the Supreme Lord and enjoy the spiritual benefits of divine service in the same way as men. Women who have completed their household duties may become wandering ascetics, like men, but the practice is rare for women. *Tantric* movements have also allowed women an alternative to the subordination in more traditional Hindu circles (Young 1987: 88–89).

It should also be noted that, ironically, in classical Hinduism higher-caste women have traditionally been more subject to subordination by males than lower-caste women. The priestly caste, with its concern for purity, subordinated women (who, it was believed, have a natural propensity to be impure) more than the warrior and merchant castes, who placed an exaggerated value on motherhood because of a desire for large families, and the servant caste and untouchables, for whom life circumstances necessitated substantial autonomy and regard for the active role of women. Therefore, "the Hindu woman is … in the unfortunate position of either experiencing a degree of autonomy, but at the cost of lowly position on the prestigious caste hierarchy, or high-caste status but at the cost of submission to rigorous male control" (Allen 1982: 17; cited by Young 1987: 88).

Despite these traditions, many Hindu women have made remarkable progress toward equality. Mahatma Gandhi stressed equality for women in his independence movement (although he attempted to exert control over his own wife!). Civil legislation in the secular state of India now guarantees political rights for women. The 1947 Constitution banned discrimination against women in social, political, and economic settings. In India women have entered into virtually all professions. While many Western countries still have a "glass ceiling" for women in fields such as politics, women in India have moved to the top in a variety of areas. The most famous example is Indira Gandhi, who served as prime minister of India from 1966 until she was assassinated by Sikh extremists in 1984.

The Hindu concept of "female nature" derives from the understanding of feminine divinity. Female sacrality is called *shakti* in Hinduism. *Shakti* is "the energy of both creation and destruction. It is the principle of passion and change" (Carmody 1989: 42). In divinity the dark, mysterious *shakti* is balanced by the passionless, constant, intellectual male side of deity. The dangerous unpredictability of *shakti* is thought to be manifest in human female nature as well, providing a basis for the constraints placed on women in Hindu society.

The primal mother in Hindu mythology is *Adi Shakti*. According to the myths associated with her, she alone existed in the beginning. Desiring a partner, she created the male gods *Brahma, Vishnu,* and *Shiva*. Only *Shiva* accepted her proposal of marriage, and he becomes prominent, replacing her. *Adi Shakti* is still worshipped as goddess of the harvest in rural India (Carmody 1989: 42–43).

"The Great Goddess … enjoyed a reputation as a supreme deity who creates, preserves, and destroys as well as defends *dharma* by battling the demons to preserve the order of society and cosmos" (Young 1987: 90). However, there have not been many attempts to use the myth of the Great Goddess to claim a more central role for women in Hindu society. On the other hand, a myth associated with the popular goddess *Kali* illustrates how tales of the gods served to give a sacred basis for suspicion of female passion and female subordination in traditional Hindu society. After killing an evil giant and his army, *Kali* broke into a highly charged dance that threatened to shake apart the whole world. She stopped only when *Shiva* lay down at her feet, for as a devout wife she would not step on her husband. The moral of the story, according to traditional Hindu interpretation? "Unless husbands control their wives, the world will surely collapse" (Carmody 1989: 46).

At present in India tension runs high between groups and leaders who wish to preserve a modern, secular state and others who want to create a Hindu state, which would include a return to the more traditional gender relations described above. If the turn toward Hindu fundamentalism and communalism continues, "the advances of the last century for women may be endangered" (Young 1994: 133). There has even been renewed public support for the practice of *sati,* with the argument being made by Hindu communalist leaders that if suicide and even active euthanasia are increasingly accepted in the West, why should not a Hindu woman have the right of voluntary *sati* (Young 1994: 119–23)?

Homosexuality

Traditional Western scholarship on India has taken the position that there is less emphasis on homosexuality in India than in other cultures. This position reflects in part the biases of interpreters who, like A.L. Basham, state that the slight attention to homosexuality in early literature shows that "ancient India was far healthier than most other ancient cultures" (Basham 1954: 172; cited by Sharma 1993: 48). While not as judgmental, modern Indian political leaders have also taken the view that homosexuality is not very evident in Indian culture. J.L. Nehru, for example, said that "homosexuality was evidently neither approved nor at all common in India" (cited by Sharma 1993: 69). Leaders like Nehru have tended to associate homosexuality with the "vices" of minorities who occupied India, the Muslims and the British.

It is true that references to homosexuality are rare in classical Hindu texts, and where they occur the setting suggests that homosexual practice is not viewed positively. Homosexuality was seen as fundamentally incompatible with the fulfillment of the goals of *dharma* (duty) and *artha* (material well-being). However, in pursuit of the goal of *kama* (pleasure) homosexuality was seen as acceptable. According to the *kama sutra,* "the experience of physical love between two people of either the same or opposite sex is to be engaged in and enjoyed for its own sake as one of [the] arts [of love]" (Sharma 1993: 59).

Like the berdache in Native American cultures, the *hijra* in India is an institutionalized "third gender" role (Nanda 1985). *Hijras* are devotees of the Mother Goddess, *Bahuchara Mata.* Typically, *hijras* are men who live and dress as women. They often undergo a painful emasculation ritual, which leaves them incapable of sexual intercourse with women. Although *hijras* dress as women, they do not attempt to "pass" as women. There are an estimated 500,000 *hijras* in modern India, most living in communities under the leadership of a *guru.* Some *hijras* engage in prostitution, selling sexual favors to men. Others take a "husband" and live in a monogamous relationship. *Hijras* have an important ritual role and are often employed to perform at birth ceremonies and weddings. They burlesque behavior ordinarily associated with women in Hindu society and use "coarse and abusive" speech (Nanda 1985: 38).

There is considerable disdain for *hijras* among some Hindu authorities, largely because of the prostitution associated with some. A popularly held (but erroneous) belief is that *hijras* kidnap children with both male and female sexual organs and force them into their communities. Some interpreters point out that like the "contraries" in other cultures, Hindu *hijras* provide an acceptable outlet for the tensions that build up as a result of the limits of normal social interaction. For the most part, they are not only tolerated but valued in Indian society. The *hijra* role "gives religious meaning to cross-gender behavior, that is despised, punished and pushed beyond the pale of the cultural system in other societies" (Nanda 1985: 50).

In general, the fact that all the major Hindu deities, such as *Shiva,* have both feminine and masculine aspects has contributed to a more tolerant attitude in India toward homosexual and bisexual orientation. According to Hindu mythology, *Samba,* the divine son of the god *Krishna,* engaged in homosexuality and dressed as a woman to win the affections of the wives of other gods. In addition, the Hindu capacity to allow seeming contradictions to confront each other without resolution has supported a more accepting attitude toward homosexuality than has been traditionally found in Western religions.

CHAPTER SUMMARY

In this chapter we first oriented ourselves to the land, people, and history of South and Southeast Asia, an area where nearly 30 percent of the people of the world live. We then briefly surveyed the long and rich history of India as background for our study of the religions that originated in South Asia and spread to Southeast Asia.

Before turning to the religions of South and Southeast Asia, we established a framework for understanding by outlining the traditional world-view shared by these religions: the problem of desire, the law of action (*karma*), the cycle of rebirth (*samsara*), the quest for liberation from the cycle of rebirth (*moksha*), and the fulfillment of "duty" (*dharma*).

Hinduism is more a family of religions than a single religion. Our survey of the stages of development and sacred texts of Hinduism included discussion of the religion of the Indus Valley civilization (which preceded the emergence of "Hinduism"), the classical Hindu texts—the Vedas (focusing on the *Rig-Veda* and the *Upanishads*), classical Hinduism (focusing on the Laws of Manu and the *Bhagavad-Gita*), postclassical Hinduism (focusing on "devotional" Hinduism and the major deities, especially *Vishnu* and *Shiva,* and "philosophical" Hinduism). We then examined what happened within Hinduism as the influence of European culture, especially British, grew.

In our discussion of distinctive Hindu teachings, we used the framework established in Chapter One to describe the basic problem identified by Hinduism as the eternal soul (*Atman*) trapped in the cycle of rebirth (*samsara*), the cause of this problem (ignorance—*avidya*— resulting in attachment), the view of material reality (*maya*), the goal (*moksha*—liberation from the cycle of rebirth), the means to this goal (the various types of *yoga*), and the sacred (encompassing various forms of theism and monism). In discussing the teachings of Hinduism, we responded to frequently asked questions about Hinduism, such as "What is the caste system and is it still present in modern India?" and "Why are cows worshipped in Hinduism?"

We then examined Hindu teachings on contemporary ethical issues.

QUESTIONS FOR DISCUSSION AND REFLECTION

1. What were your impressions of India before you began a study of the religions that originated in India? How have they been affected by what you have learned so far?

2. Do you feel yourself (or others you know) trapped by the attachment to the material world caused by desire (craving)? Do you agree that attachment to "things" causes ignorance of the spiritual dimension of life?

3. Some have accused Hinduism of being the principal obstacle to the successful development of India into a modern nation. Is that a fair statement? How much should traditional Hinduism be altered to accommodate development?

4. Have you ever had an experience that caused you to think (in agreement with the *Upanishads* and *Bhagavad-Gita*) that the purpose of life is to come to an awareness of our ultimate oneness? What do you think it means to "see all things in Me [the Supreme Lord]"?

5. Some modern cosmologists speculate that the universe begins with a "big bang," expands, and then contracts until another "big bang" starts the process over. Compare this theory with the description of the cosmic process in Hinduism. What is the significance of any similarities you identify?

6. When Robert Oppenheimer, one of the creators of the atom bomb, saw his creation explode in the New Mexico desert, he uttered a verse from the *Bhagavad-Gita:* "Time I am, the great destroyer of the worlds, and I have come here to destroy all people. ..." Why do you think he spoke those words, and what does his use of them imply?

7. Are you aware of *dharma* in your own life and in the society in which you live? If so, what approaches do people take toward fulfilling their *dharma?* Discuss the *Bhagavad-Gita's* teaching about treating actions as sacrifices to God as a way of honoring one's *dharma.*

8. What did you think of "cow worship" before reading this chapter? Has your perspective changed after reading the discussion of cow veneration?

9. Have you ever practiced a form of meditation? If so, for how long and with what effect? If not, do you think you will ever try meditating? Do you think that meditation has the potential to lead a person to a "knowing beyond knowledge"?

10. The American writer Mark Twain said that although we in the West may consider the people of India poor and ourselves rich because of our material prosperity, in matters of the spirit we are the paupers and they are the millionaires. As we move into a new century, what are your reactions to Twain's observation?

SOURCES AND SUGGESTIONS FOR FURTHER STUDY

Hinduism

BASHAM, A.L., 1954 *The Wonder that Was India.* New York: Grove Press.

BHARATI, AGEHANANDA, 1970 *The Tantric Tradition.* New York: Doubleday.

BORMAN, WILLIAM, 1986 *Gandhi and Non-violence.* Albany: State University of New York Press.

BOSE, ABINASH CHANDRA, TRANS., 1966 *Hymns from the Vedas.* Bombay: India Publishing House.

CHAUDHURI, NIRAD C., 1979 *Hinduism.* New York: Oxford University Press.

ECK, DIANA L., 1982 *Banaras: City of Light.* Princeton, N.J.: Princeton University Press.

1985 *Darshan: Seeing the Divine Image in India,* 2nd ed. Chamberburg, Pa.: Anima Books.

ELIADE, MIRCEA, 1969 *Yoga: Immortality and Freedom,* trans. Willard R. Trask. Princeton, N.J.: Princeton University Press.

FISCHER, LOUIS, ED., 1962 *The Essential Gandhi.* New York: Random House.

GANDHI, MAHATMA,, 1958 *All Men Are Brothers.* New York: Columbia University Press.

GRIFFITH, R.T.H., 1973 *The Hymns of the Rig-Veda, Translated with a Popular Commentary.* Delhi: Motilal Banarsidass [1889].

HAWLEY, JOHN S., AND DONNA MARIE WULFF, EDS., 1986 *The Divine Consort: Radha and the Goddesses of India.* Boston: Beacon Press.

HUME, R.E., 1931 *The Thirteen Principal Upanishads,* 2nd rev. ed. Oxford: Oxford University Press.

KINSLEY, DAVID, 1982 *Hinduism: A Cultural Perspective.* Englewood Cliffs, N.J.: Prentice Hall.

KLOSTERMAIER, KLAUS K., 1989 *A Survey of Hinduism.* Albany: State University of New York Press.

KOLLER, JOHN M., 1982 *The Indian Way.* New York: Macmillan.

MACNICOL, NICOL, ED., 1938 *Hindu Scriptures.* New York: Dutton.

MORGAN, KENNETH, ED., 1953 *The Religion of the Hindus.* New York: Ronald Press.

O'FLAHERTY, WENDY, 1973 *Shiva: The Erotic Ascetic.* New York: Oxford University Press., 1980 *Karma and Rebirth in Classical Indian Traditions.* Berkeley: University of California Press.

1981 *The Rig-Veda: An Anthology.* London: Penguin Books.

PRABHAVANANDA, SWAMI, ED., 1963 *The Spiritual Heritage of India.* Garden City, N.Y.: Doubleday & Co.

PRABHUPADA, A.C. BHAKTIVEDANTA SWAMI, TRANS., 1983 *Bhagavad-Gita as It Is.* Los Angeles: The Bhaktivedanta Book Trust.

RADHAKRISHNAN, SARVEPALLI, 1964 *The Hindu View of Life.* London: George Allen & Unwin, Ltd.

RADHAKRISHNAN, SARVEPALLI, AND CHARLES A. MOORE, 1957 *A Sourcebook in Indian Philosophy.* Princeton, N.J.: Princeton University Press.

RENOU, LOUIS, ED., 1961 *Hinduism.* New York: George Braziller.

WOOD, ERNEST, AND S.V. SUBRAHMANYAM, EDS., 1974 *The Garuda Purana: Saroddhara,* Sacred Books of the Hindus, ed. B. D. Basu, vol. 9. New York: AMS Press [1911].

ZAEHNER, R.C., TRANS., 1966 *Hindu Scriptures.* Everyman's Library No. 944. New York: Dutton.

Responses to Contemporary Ethical Issues

The Ecological Crisis

CALLICOTT, J. BAIRD, AND ROGER T. AMES, ED., 1989 *Nature in Asian Traditions of Thought: Essays in Philosophy.* Albany: State University of New York Press.

CHAITANYA, KRISHNA, 1983 "A Profounder Ecology: The Hindu View of Man and Nature," *The Ecologist* 13,: 127–35.

CHAPPLE, CHRISTOPHER KEY, 1993 *Nonviolence to Animals: Earth and Self in Asian Traditions.* Albany: State University of New York Press.

DEUTSCH, ELIOT, 1970 "Vedanta and Ecology," *Indian Philosophical Annual* 16,: 3–4.

1989 "A Metaphysical Grounding for Natural Reverence: East-West," in *Nature in Asian Traditions of Thought: Essays in Philosophy,* 259–65.

LARSON, GERALD JAMES, 1989 'Conceptual Resources' in South Asia for 'Environmental Ethics,'" *Nature in Asian Traditions of Thought: Essays in Philosophy,* 267–77.

Abortion

CRAWFORD, S. CROMWELL, 1989 "Hindu Ethics for Modern Life," in *World Religions and Global Ethics.* New York: Paragon House, 5–35.

LUDWIG, THEODORE, 1987 "Incantation," in *The Encyclopedia of Religion,* ed. Mircea Eliade, New York: Macmillan, vol. 7, 147–52.

Gender Roles and the Status of Women

ALLEN, MICHAEL, 1982 "The Hindu View of Women," in *Women in India and Nepal*, ed. Michael Allen and S.N. Mukherjee, Canberra: Australian National University, 1–20.

CARMODY, DENISE, 1989 *Women and World Religions*, 2nd ed. Englewood Cliffs, N. J.: Prentice Hall.

GROSS, RITA, 1979 "The Second Coming of the Goddess: Hindu Female Deities as Resource for the Contemporary Rediscovery of the Goddess," *Anima*, 48–59.

YOUNG, KATHERINE K., 1987 "Hinduism," in *Women in World Religions*, ed. Arvind Sharma, Albany: State University of New York Press, 59–103.

1994 "Women in Hinduism," in *Today's Woman in World Religions*, ed. Arvind Sharma, Albany: State University of New York Press, 77–135.

Homosexuality

BULLOGH, VERN, 1976 *Sexual Variance in Society and History*. Chicago: The University of Chicago Press.

NANDA, SERENA, 1985 "The Hijras of India: Cultural and Individual Dimensions of an Institutionalized Third Gender Role," *Journal of Homosexuality* 11, 35–54.

SHARMA, ARVIND, 1993 "Homosexuality in Hinduism," in *Homosexuality and World Religions,* ed. Arlene Swidler. Valley Forge, Pa.: Trinity Press International, 47–80.

CHAPTER 6

Theravada Buddhism: The Middle Way

INTRODUCTION

Like "Hinduism," the name "Buddhism" is a somewhat misleading attempt to organize an array of diverse traditions. Like Hindus, Buddhists call themselves followers of the *dharma*, although for some Buddhists the typical term is the equivalent from the Pali language, *dhamma*. However, the Buddhist understanding of *dharma* is quite different from the Hindu teaching, and disagreements among followers of the Buddha about the meaning of *dhamma* are found. Buddhism is no more a unified religious tradition than is Hinduism.

Buddhism began in India in the sixth century B.C.E., and its early development occurred in South Asia. However, as we shall see, it faded away as a separate religion in India and survived because it spread from India and took root in other cultures of Southeast and East Asia.

In this chapter we will study the first phase of Buddhism, tracing its origin and early development and discussing the texts and teachings of *Theravada*—a representative school of the earliest of the two major branches of Buddhism, which flourishes today in the island nation of Sri Lanka and several countries of Southeast Asia. In Chapter Nine we will study the other segment of Buddhism, called *Mahayana*, which thrives in a variety of separate movements in East Asia.

STAGES OF DEVELOPMENT AND SACRED TEXTS

Founder: Siddartha Gautama

Buddhism had a single founder, a remarkable teacher who discovered and shared with others a path to liberation from the cycle of rebirth that is appropriately called the "middle way." Whatever their differences, all Buddhists join in honoring this man. Buddhists may differ dramatically on their understanding of the nature of the founder's teachings and the significance of his life, but a principal factor that distinguishes them from other religions is their focus on this man.

A Third Century C.E. statue portrays the Buddha while he was seeking spiritual liberation through asceticism.

Gautama was his family name; his parents called him Siddartha. He was born in about 563 B.C.E., a member of the warrior caste (*Kshatriya*), not far from the holy city of Benares in northern India. The dates of his life are uncertain, but that he was a sixth century contemporary of Mahavira, the founder of Jainism (see Chapter Seven), seems certain. We have little information about his life that historians would accept as certain beyond a doubt; legends fill the void. What follows is the religious biography his followers wrote.

Siddartha's wealthy father, a chieftain of the Sakya clan, desperately wanted him to become the emperor of India. According to one tradition, a soothsayer told his father that Siddartha was fated to become either a great political leader or a homeless monk. To ensure the former, his father raised Siddartha in luxury, protecting him from the un-pleasantness of life, which might raise reli-

A close-up of the face of a seated Buddha in a Thai shrine. The elongated ears are a symbol of an enlightened being.

gious questions in his mind. Siddartha married a lovely princess and she gave birth to a son. At the instructions of Siddartha's father, servants carefully screened the poor, sick, and dying from his sight.

Despite all the affluence, Gautama began to feel an inner longing, an emptiness he could not fill with wine and song. He began to venture out alone, without his "advance party." As his chariot journeyed through an "unsanitized" area, Siddartha experienced what Buddhist tradition calls "the four passing sights." The first was a sorrowful old man. The second was a man racked by illness. The third was a dead man being carried on a funeral pyre. For the first time in his life Siddartha had seen that life is not pleasure and joy, but includes misery, suffering, and death. And he realized that he too was destined to grow old, become ill, and die. His despair continued to deep-

en until one day he saw the "fourth sight," a monk calmly walking alone in a yellow robe.

One night Siddartha crept out of his palace, leaving behind his wife and son. This turning point in the Buddha's life is called "the great renunciation." He shaved his head, clothed himself in the robes of a monk, and set off to discover the way to escape the inevitable suffering of material existence. Thus began a six-year quest. He started out with an open mind about the teaching of the Hindu *Brahmins.* First, he tried and mastered a meditative approach such as that implied in the *Upanishads,* but to no avail. Then he tried rigid asceticism, similar to the teaching of the Jains (see Chapter Seven). For five years he denied himself, to the point that his diet consisted of a single grain of rice a day. Five other ascetics joined him, only to watch as he fainted dead away beside a stream. When he revived, Siddartha determined that self-denial would not lead to spiritual fulfillment. He accepted a meal and vowed not to deny himself to such an extreme. This left him in a quandary; neither of the commonly accepted paths to spiritual awareness had succeeded.

Not far from a place now known as *Bodh-gaya,* Siddartha sat down under a fig tree (known in Buddhist tradition as the *bodhi,* or "enlightenment tree"). He told himself he would not arise until he reached a state of spiritual enlightenment. According to Buddhist legend, as he sat, Mara, the god of desire and death, appeared to him and tempted him to turn back to his old life of pleasure. However, Siddartha remained firm in his quest. He pointed to the earth with his right hand, as if to call upon the earth to be his witness. At that moment, now aware that it was desire that had kept him entrapped, he suddenly "awakened" to a new life beyond its grip. He was now a *Buddha,* one who had "woken up." He was enlightened. The state of desirelessness he now entered was *nirvana.*

Siddartha Gautama, Buddha, now faced a decision. Should he tell others the new way of ordering life (*dhamma*) he had discovered, or should he keep it to himself, allow his existing *karma (kamma* in Pali) to dissipate, so that he could enter into the state beyond rebirth (*parinirvana*)? His fateful decision was to communicate his teaching to others, so that they too could follow the path to awakening. His first students were the five ascetics, who had left him in disgust when they saw him accept refreshment after he had fainted. In a place called the Deer Park, he proclaimed to them his teaching. That first public proclamation of *dhamma* is now known as the Deer Park Sermon. The Buddha spoke to his former colleagues of a "middle way" between the two extremes of his own life—self-denial and self-indulgence. This path, he said, had led him to the truth, and if they followed it, they too would be enlightened. (We will have more to say about the path the Buddha taught below, when we summarize the distinctive teachings of early Buddhism.)

The five ascetics were convinced. They resolved to follow the example of the Buddha and thus became the first members of the *sangha*, the Buddhist order of monks. According to Buddhist tradition, this exchange set in motion the "wheel of *dhamma*," which continues wherever the teaching of the Buddha is put into practice.

For forty-five more years the Buddha continued his work of preaching the truth of the middle way. At the age of 80 he died quietly near Benares.

According to Buddhist tradition, when he lay down he entered the state beyond the cycle of *samsara* called *parinirvana*. He would not be reborn again. His last words to his disciples were "Work out your own salvation with diligence."

Formation of a Buddhist Order of Monks and Nuns

Those who joined the early *sangha* (literally, "community" or "assembly") came from all castes. Two of the early leaders were a *Brahmin*, Sariputta, and a *Kshatriya*, Buddha's cousin Ananda. As the *sangha* grew, there was a need for rules of behavior. The "Three Refuges or Jewels" developed as the basic vows of an initiate into the *sangha*. They were "I take refuge in the Buddha; I take refuge in the *dhamma*; I take refuge in the *sangha*." The new monk was pledging to follow the example set by the Buddha, to live a life guided by the teaching of the middle way, and to accept the discipline of the order. The monks who took these vows followed the Buddha's example of wandering and preaching during the dry season, and remaining together during the monsoon season, July through October.

Statues of the Buddha reclining, such as this Twelfth Century C.E. carving in Sri Lanka, represent the moment when the Buddha entered into parinirvana.

At first, after the Buddha's death, the form of government in the *sangha* was democratic, with the assembly coming to consensus on matters of common concern. However, as the movement grew, a hierarchical ranking developed, perhaps inevitably. Permanent monasteries sprang up, and the once unified *sangha* divided into separate orders with different leaders. These monasteries became important centers of secular as well as religious power.

Although at first only men joined the *sangha*, a number of women requested initiation. After much thought, the Buddha approved allowing women to become nuns, with the same ability to pursue the path leading to liberation as monks.

For both monks and nuns the basic rules of monastic life came to be known as the Ten Precepts. Simply stated, they are:

1. Refrain from taking life (*ahimsa*).
2. Do not take what is not given.
3. Avoid unchastity.
4. Do not lie or deceive.
5. Do not take intoxicants.
6. Consume food in moderation, and never after noon.
7. Do not gaze upon spectacles such as dancing and singing.
8. Do not ornament your body.
9. Do not recline on high or wide beds.
10. Do not accept gold or silver.

The first five rules also applied to the followers of Buddha who could not leave their ordinary lives to become monks or nuns. These lay followers could also gain merit by showing kindness to the monks, offering them food when they came along with their begging bowls and listening attentively to their teaching.

The Spread of the Buddha's Teachings Beyond India

A decisive turning point in the history of Buddhism occurred when the powerful King *Ashoka* of the Mauryan Empire accepted the truth of the Buddha's teachings. Ashoka became the ruler of India in about 270 B.C.E. and ruled for thirty-five years. During his reign he instructed his subjects to observe the Buddha's teaching and sent missionaries abroad to carry the Buddha's message as far as Egypt and Greece.

The process of expansion of Buddhist teaching beyond India actually began when Ashoka's emissaries to Sri Lanka, the island nation south of India, succeeded in establishing shrines and monasteries. Sri Lanka remains one of the centers of preservation of the earliest forms of Buddhism.

Later, Buddhist missionaries spread throughout the countries of Southeast Asia—now Myanmar/Burma, Thailand, Kampuchea (Cambodia), Laos, Malaysia, and Vietnam—beginning in the third century C.E. It took centuries for Buddhism to become the dominant religion in all these countries, but for the past several hundred years all of them except Vietnam and Malaysia have been largely under the spell of the more conservative branch of Buddhism.

The Two Major Branches

The Conservative Branch: The Theravada School

The form of Buddhism King Ashoka had adopted, and which had begun to spread to Sri Lanka and beyond, has become known as Theravada (literally, "the way of the elders"), although that is somewhat anachronistic. To be precise, Theravada was actually one of a number of schools that emerged out of a complex series of debates and splits involving disputes over which were the true teachings of the Buddha. Among the conservative schools in this debate, Theravada alone survived as a representative. Therefore, it is common to generalize and call the traditionalist, conservative branch of Buddhism by the name Theravada. From the beginning, Theravada and the other conservative schools claimed to preserve in the purest form the authentic and true message of the Buddha. Attempts to reconstruct the life of the Buddha and his teachings depend on these accounts, since they provide the earliest evidence. However, we must acknowledge that these accounts reflect the biases of that tradition.

FIGURE 6-1

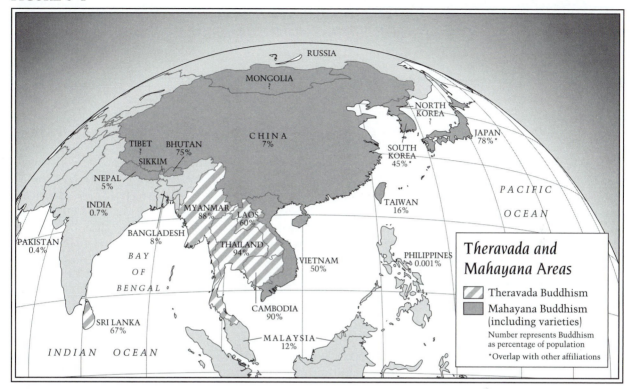

The major sacred texts of the conservative branch are known collectively as the *Pali Canon*. The term "Pali" comes from the language of the texts, which Theravada Buddhists claim was the spoken language of the Buddha. Composition of the texts in Pali is a symbol of the rejection of the authority of the Sanskrit Vedic literature. The Canon is also called the *Tripitaka* ("three baskets"): *Vinaya Pitaka* ("the basket of disciplinary regulations"), *Sutta Pitaka* ("the basket of discourses"), and *Abidhamma Pitaka* ("the basket of higher philosophy"). The thirty-one separate texts in the Pali Canon came from the first 500 years after the death of Buddha, first as oral traditions before they were written down. The first basket included guidelines for all aspects of the life of a Buddhist monk. The second basket contained the basic teachings of Buddha; whether they accurately represent the actual words of Buddha is a matter of dispute. One of the most important texts in Theravada comes from this basket. It is known as the *Dhammapada*, sayings on morality. The third basket focuses on an analysis of the nature of existence as it is understood in Theravadin teaching.

As is customary with sacred texts, commentaries arose on the Pali Canon, and some of them became important Theravadin documents. According to tradition, a Buddhist teacher from Sri Lanka named Buddhaghosa compiled the commentary into a collection known as the Way of Purifi-cation. He also turned the isolated incidents about Buddha found in the *Tripitaka* into the story of Buddha's life we have told above.

The Liberal Branch: Mahayana After the death of King Ashoka, the center of Buddhism in India shifted to northwest India. By the first century B.C.E., out of the disputes and divisions among Buddhist teachers, a new movement had coalesced. It became, in effect, the second major

COSMIC QUESTIONS:
HOW DID THE WORLD COME INTO BEING?

The Parable of the Arrow

According to the more conservative tradition, the Buddha refused to engage in speculation on such questions as cosmic origins, because he believed that they did not help a person overcome the principal human problem of suffering. This selection, the Cula-Malunkya sutta from the Majjhima Nikaya, the "Parable of the Arrow," illustrates this point (i.426-31; Warren 1896: 120-21).

"It is as if, Malunkya putta, a man had been wounded by an arrow thickly smeared with poison, and his friends and companions, relatives and kinsfolk, were to procure for him a physician or surgeon; and the sick man were to say, 'I will not have this arrow taken out until I have learned whether the man who wounded me belonged to the warrior caste, or to the brahmin caste, or to the farmers' caste, or to the menial caste.'

"Or again he were to say, 'I will not have this arrow taken out until I have learned the name of the man who wounded me, and to what clan he belongs.'

[The excuses continue with the man demanding to know the height of the man, the race of the man, the home town of the man, the type of the bow used, etc.]

"In exactly the same way, Malunkyaputta, any one who should say, 'I will not lead the religious life under the Blessed One until the Blessed One shall elucidate to me whether that the world is eternal or that the world is not eternal, [etc.]—that person would die before the Tathagata had ever elucidated this to him.'

"The religious life does not depend on the dogma that the world is eternal; nor does the religious life depend on the dogma that the world is not eternal. Whether the dogma obtain, that the world is eternal, or that the world is not eternal, there still remain birth, old age, death, sorrow, lamentation, misery, grief, despair, for the extinction of which in the present life I am prescribing. . . . "

branch of Buddhism, known to its adherents as *Mahayana* (meaning "large method, vehicle, or raft"). In the symbolism of the basic Indian worldview, "river" often alludes to the cycle of rebirth, with the far bank of the river symbolizing liberation from the cycle. *Yana* literally translates as "means," but in the context of the river analogy it can be understood as the "raft" or "vehicle" used to carry persons across the raging river of rebirth to the safe shore of liberation. From a Mahayana perspective the conservative branch of Buddhism, which we have called Theravada, is more accurately *Hinayana* (the "small vehicle or raft"). The contrast is that in the teachings of Mahayana a large vessel, with a pilot, carries many persons to liberation. (As we shall see, however, this analogy does not hold for all of the schools within the Mahayana movement.) In *Hinayana*, each person must row himself to the opposite shore in a small raft that holds only that person, having the example of the Buddha and others but with no external assistance. In Hinayana, lay people are excluded from pursuing the path to enlightenment because only monks are able to devote themselves to the necessary rigors of the passage, but in Mahayana the way is not closed in this arbitrary manner.

The Mahayana movement came into existence in India, but it flourished in the nations of East Asia when Mahayana missionaries carried their interpretation of Buddhism from northwest India into China in the first century C.E. We will discuss the various Mahayana sects and their teachings and texts in Chapter Nine.

QUESTIONS OF HUMAN IDENTITY: WHAT IS THE BASIC HUMAN DILEMMA?

The Parable of the Mustard Seed

The famous Buddhist Parable of the Mustard Seed also reflects the Buddhist view of the basic human dilemma (Rogers 1870: 271-72). In ancient India (and in modern India for many women) a woman's status was achieved by giving birth to a son.

Kisa Gotami had an only son, and he died. In her grief she carried the dead child to all her neighbors, asking them for medicine, and the people said, "She has lost her senses. The boy is dead."

At length Kisa Gotami met a man who replied to her request, "I cannot give you medicine for your child, but I know a physician who can. Go to Sakyamuni, the Buddha."

Kisa Gotami repaired to the Buddha and cried, "Lord and Master, give me the medicine that will cure my boy."

The Buddha answered, "I want a handful of mustard seed." And when the woman in her joy promised to procure it, the Buddha added, "The mustard seed must be taken from a house where no one has lost a child, husband, parent or friend."

Poor Kisa Gotami now went from house to house, and the people pitied her and said, "Here is the mustard seed, take it!" But when she asked, "Did a son or daughter, a father or mother, die in your family?" they answered her, "Alas! The living are few, but the dead are many. Do not remind us of our deepest grief." And there was no house but some beloved one had died in it.

Kisa Gotami became weary and hopeless, and sat down at the way-side, watching the lights of the city as they flickered up and were extinguished again. At last the darkness of night reigned everywhere. And she considered the fate of men, that their lives flicker up and are extinguished. And she thought to herself, "How selfish I am in my grief! Death is common to all; yet in this valley of desolation there is a path that leads him to immortality who has surrendered all selfishness."

Putting away the selfishness of her affection for her child, Kisa Gotami had the dead body buried in the forest. Returning to the Buddha, she took refuge in him and found comfort in the Dharma.

Theravada Buddhism Today

After centuries of slow decline and a recent history of suffering from active political oppression in some countries, Theravada Buddhism is in resurgence in much of Southeast Asia. (In India, where Buddhism nearly vanished into Hinduism, less than 1 percent of the population is Buddhist, and Buddhism plays a very limited role in national life.)

When Sri Lanka became independent from British rule in 1947, Theravada Buddhism became the official national religion. However, there is great instability and considerable violence because of conflict between the Hindu Tamils of northern Sri Lanka and the Sinhalese Buddhists of the south. The Tamils want an independent Hindu state, and the Sinhalese are committed to preserving Sri Lankan unity as a Buddhist nation. About two-thirds of the population of Sri Lanka is Theravada Buddhist.

Myanmar/Burma is overwhelmingly a Theravada Buddhist country, with 85 percent of the population associated with Theravada. This may contribute to the intensely self-reliant, reclusive attitude that dominates the nation. An attempt to develop a social and economic order based on Buddhist principles has been stalled by various factors, most recently a repressive regime.

Stone face of Avalokitesvara in the Bayon Temple in the Theravada complex known as Angkor Wat, in the modern nation of Kampuchea (Cambodia).

Thailand is also a Theravada country, with almost 95 percent of the population Buddhist. The greatest threat to Buddhist influence in Thailand is the lure of materialism, which has increased as exposure to modern, secular ways has grown.

Kampuchea (Cambodia) is the home of one of the most impressive Theravada complexes in the world, the twelfth-century temple called Angkor Wat. After the Communist revolution of 1976, Buddhism suffered greatly in Kampuchea; thousands of monks were driven from monasteries or killed. The horror of those days was vividly dramatized in the movie "The Killing Fields." Recent attempts to reform Kampuchea include hints, if not clear indications, of a Buddhist resurgence.

A Communist regime in Laos has also greatly damaged the status of Theravada Buddhism in that country, although there are recent signs of Buddhist restoration in Laos as well.

DISTINCTIVE TEACHINGS OF THE THERAVADA BRANCH

Some treatments of Buddhism distinguish between the teachings of Siddartha Gautama and the interpretation of those teachings in the conservative branch. However, because our knowledge of Siddartha is based largely on the Theravadin presentation of his life, such a distinction is problematic. Whether what follows is the actual teaching of the historical Siddartha is open to question. We are certain that these are the views of the Theravadin community about what the Buddha taught.

Problem: Suffering

According to the Tripitaka, Siddartha's first sermon to the five ascetics included what Theravadins (and, to a degree, Buddhists in general) consider the essence of his teaching: the Four Noble Truths. The first of these insights is called the Noble Truth of Suffering. It is a statement about the basic problem all humans face (Rhys Davids 1881: 148):

> *Birth is suffering; decay is suffering; illness is suffering; death is suffering. Presence of objects we hate is suffering; separation from objects we love is suffering; not to obtain what we desire is suffering.*

The place to begin one's spiritual journey, according to this teaching, is with admission that suffering is unavoidable. So it was with Siddartha himself. Until he removed the blinders his life of luxury had given him and faced the reality of human suffering, he could not start on his spiritual quest. He came to realize that although he was leading a life of material abundance, he was indeed suffering. Until he awoke to that reality he was lost.

According to Theravadin teaching the contention that all life is suffering is simply a statement about the way things are, not the result of a pessimistic outlook. This is a difficult concept to grasp, because in response to the Western idea of "progress" most of us try to condition ourselves to "look on the bright side" and believe that "things are not as bad as they seem" or that "things are

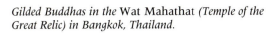
Gilded Buddhas in the Wat Mahathat *(Temple of the Great Relic) in Bangkok, Thailand.*

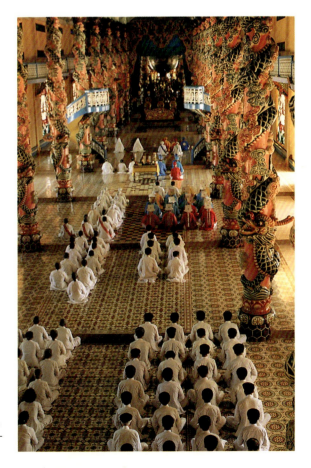

A ceremony in the Caodai Great Temple (Vietnam).

bound to get better." For the Theravadin these sentiments are wishful thinking and inhibit our spiritual quests. Even when we think we are happy, we are, in fact, in a state of suffering. For example, many of us would contend that a close relationship with a family member or friend brings joy into our lives. However, the one unavoidable fact about a relationship is that it will end. Friends leave physically or figuratively, or we leave them. The breaking of a relationship, however satisfying that relationship may have seemed, is painful. Thus its ultimate effect is suffering. From this perspective, any aspect of life, no matter how seemingly pleasant, already has the seeds of the suffering that is the common denominator for all human experience.

In order to focus their meditation on the reality of suffering (called *dukkha* in Pali), some Theravadin monks engage in what is known as "corpse meditation," gazing on bodies in various stages of decay. It is common in Theravadin monasteries to have piles of bones or skeletons displayed to drive home this point.

Cause: *Craving and Delusion*

If the basic reality of life is suffering (*dukkha*), what causes this condition? The second Noble Truth, the Noble Truth of the Causing of Suffering, gives the answer (Rhys Davids 1881: 148):

> It is that craving that leads back to birth, along with the lure and the lust that lingers longingly now here, now there: namely, the craving for sensual pleasure, the craving to be born again, the craving for existence to end.

To an extent, this is the same analysis of the cause of the human dilemma as that which is found in Hinduism (see Chapter Five) and which we will encounter in Jainism (see Chapter Seven): desire that leads to attachment. We suffer because our desire leads us to become attached to things or people and deluded as to the real nature of our situation in life. For example, we desire the pleasures of friendship, so we become attached to other persons, only to suffer when disputes arise and when the friendship ends. We would not suffer if we

were not attached, and we would not be attached if we did not desire.

Theravada Buddhism goes beyond Hinduism, however. Hinduism teaches us to direct our desire away from our physical natures toward the spiritual, to seek union with God or oneness with *Brahman*. We *should* strive for liberation, the ultimate end of human existence, according to the Hindu view. Theravadins believe that even desire for spiritual ends leads to attachment. So it was with Siddartha. It was not until he gave up his desperate quest for enlightenment that he became enlightened. As long as he desired liberation, it was denied him. His attachment to the idea of liberation was as entrapping as his earlier attachment to the material world. If, as the Second Noble Truth states, "we desire existence to end" (that is, escape from the cycle of rebirth), it will never come.

Such an insight is difficult to understand in a culture that counsels us to "go for it." "You've got to want it," we are told. On the other hand, most of us can recall a time when our desiring something actually stood in the way of our attaining it. For example, trying too hard to learn to ski can actually make it more difficult to ski. When you stop trying too hard, it sometimes "just happens." The Theravadin teaching is to extend this idea to *all* of existence. To let go of *all* desires, no matter how good they may seem, is seen as essential to authentic spiritual life.

Reality: *Impermanence and "No Self"*

If there is one basic truth, we sometimes tell ourselves, it is that nothing remains the same. Look at a photograph of yourself taken five, ten, or more years ago! According to Theravada Buddhism, this commonsense realization is the truth about *all* reality. All reality is impermanent (*anicca*). This applies both to human nature and to the nature of the cosmos.

The fundamental Theravadin teaching about human nature is that at the depth of who we are, there is no permanence. This is the opposite of the Hindu claim that beneath the changing surface of life exists the *Atman*, the eternal self that does not change. For Theravadins the truth is *anatman*

QUESTIONS OF MORALITY: WHAT IS RIGHT LIVING?

The Effects of Karma Delayed

According to the Theravadin classic, the Dhammapada, the effects of karma *are sometimes delayed (69, 71; Radhakrishnan 1950: 81).*

So long as an evil deed does not bear fruit, the fool thinks that it is like honey; but when it bears fruit, then the fool suffers grief.

An evil deed, like newly drawn milk, does not turn (at once); smouldering, like fire covered by ashes, it follows the fool.

Excerpts from The Dhammapada, *trans. Sarvepalli Radhakrishnan (1950). Reprinted by permission of Oxford University Press.*

(anatta in Pali), which literally means "no eternal self." Indeed, it is the illusion of human permanence, of an eternal substance in our nature, that creates suffering. Only when the Buddha stopped seeking some sort of permanent spiritual nature did he discover the real truth. Only when the dead boy's mother came to the realization that the basic truth about life *is* death, is impermanence, was she able to start on the path toward release from her suffering. We may wish there to be an eternal self, a part of a personal god or a oneness with the world spirit, but it is just that—wishful thinking, according to Theravada Buddhism.

We have already stipulated that all of the religions that originated in India, including Buddhism, accept the idea of the cycle of rebirth. How can Theravada Buddhists hold *both* the teaching that there is "no self" *and* the idea of rebirth? What is reborn, if there is no permanent substance to our nature, no *atman?* One of the things the Buddha refused to do, according to Theravadin teaching, was to engage in speculation about questions such as this. Instead of arguing such points philosophically, the Buddha spoke in images. When speaking about rebirth he used the example of a flame being passed from candle to candle. Nothing sub-

stantial moves between the tapers. The energy of the lighted candle causes the wick of the other candle to ignite. It is the heat that causes a new flame. So it is with human existence. As long as a life is "on fire" with desire, its influence will be passed into a new existence, "igniting" a new life. When the fire on the candle is extinguished, it no longer causes a new flame. When the flame of desire in a human life is blown out, there is no more rebirth.

This may help clarify the Theravadin understanding of the cycle of rebirth, and how it is that reincarnation is not a matter of souls passing from life to life, but it does not resolve another question. If we have no souls, then who are we as distinct human beings? What accounts for separate identities? The Theravadin answer to this question is the teaching of what are called "aggregates" or *skandhas* (*kandhas* in Pali). In this view, who we are at any given moment is actually a coming together of the five *skandhas*: form (physical factors), feelings, perceptions, volitions, and awareness or consciousness. As long as these forces are held together, a distinct and separate being exists. They are not elements, which themselves have permanence. They are nothing more than bundles of various types of energy, which result in a personality in constant flux, from moment to moment.

What holds these forces together? This is the place for *karma* (*kamma* in Pali). It is the "law of action" that accounts for the seeming permanence of the *skandhas*. When the hold of the law of *karma* is broken, the forces will dissipate. And what allows the law of *karma* to be effective? Desire. Without desire, *karma* would have no effect.

If all of this seems rather circular, it is intended to be. According to Theravadin teaching, human existence is nothing more than an always changing, interlocking circle of causes and effects. The formal expression of this view is an idea called "dependent origination" or "the chain of causation." Observation of the flow of human existence identified, from the Theravadin perspective, twelve "links" in this chain. Two of the links (ignorance and *karma*) arise from prior existence; eight account for present existence (consciousness, name

An initiation ritual for a young monk in a Buddhist monastery in Bangkok, Thailand.

and form, the six sense organs, contact, sensation, desire, attachment, existence); the last two (birth, suffering) lead to another existence.

Just as human nature is characterized by impermanence, so is the cosmos as a whole. Hinduism sees a permanent, unchanging personal God or impersonal oneness (*Brahman*) beyond the impermanence of this world. Theravada Buddhism sees no such cosmic permanence. Like the waves in the ocean, all reality is in flux, constantly in motion.

It is tempting to dismiss this teaching about human and cosmic nature as fanciful. Surely there is some kind of permanence to life. But Theravadins today point out that their theory about reality is better supported by contemporary science than the idea of permanence. Physics, for example, continues to penetrate into the nature of matter and finds not permanence but flux, no discrete entities but an interwoven field of energy. Perhaps, Theravadins would say, it is only our desire that creates the illusion of permanence!

End: Nirvana

The difference between Theravada Buddhism and some modern thinkers who deny that there is any eternal "self" is that Theravadins do not think this is the last word about our destiny. Our entrapment in an existence characterized by suffering does not need to be the final chapter in our stories. The Buddha found escape, and so can those who follow his example.

Like other religions that originated in India, the "goal" for Theravada Buddhism is liberation from the cycle of rebirth. However, the problem for Theravadins is obvious. With "no permanent self," how can there be a "goal," for who reaches it? Once again, Theravadins answer that speculation on such questions is fruitless and unproductive.

All we can know from the experience of the Buddha and others who have followed his teachings, Theravadins say, is that when craving is extinguished, suffering ends, as does rebirth. In the words of the Third Noble Truth of the Deer Park Sermon, there is a cessation to suffering.

What follows suffering? In a word, *nirvana* (in Pali, *nibbana*) arises when craving ends. *Nirvana* literally means "blowing out." Existence is ablaze with craving; that is the cause of suffering. When the flame of passion is blown out, suffering ends. One problem with the term *nirvana* is that it is not exclusively Buddhist. Hindus and Jains also use *nirvana* to describe release from the cycle of rebirth. Nevertheless, it is the most frequently used term for the state of liberation in Buddhism.

It is far easier to say what *nirvana* is not than to say what *nirvana* is. *Nirvana* is not a state of existence after death; it is a phenomenon experienced whenever a person "wakes up," as did the Buddha. In Theravada Buddhism, the person who follows the example of the Buddha and is enlightened is called an *arhant* (Pali for "worthy one"; also spelled *arhat* or *arahant*). Like Buddha, an *arhant* has overcome attachment and desire, and, once earthly life is ended, will no longer be reborn. *Nirvana* is not heaven, for that would imply a place where souls dwell. But, paradoxically, *nirvana* is also not merely negative. Descriptions of *nirvana* in Theravadin literature speak in such terms as calm, peace, joy, and bliss. Does this mean that an *arhant* continues to exist after death? A distinction is drawn between *nirvana* and *parinirvana* (that which the *arhant* enters after death), but it should not be overemphasized. Some Theravadins have suggested that *nirvana* is a state beyond both being and non-being. In the final analysis, the question of survival beyond death is one most Theravadins stubbornly reject as too speculative and not helpful in dealing with our basic problem.

Means: *The Eightfold Path*

The Fourth (and last) Noble Truth expresses the Theravadin teaching on the means to liberation. It states that the way that leads to the cessation of suffering is the "holy eightfold path." The steps in the path are:

1. right belief
2. right aspiration

QUESTIONS OF HUMAN DESTINY: WHY ARE WE HERE?

The Highest Bliss

The Buddha taught that the purpose of life is to overcome suffering, so that we can experience the bliss of nirvana *(Dhammapada 203-5; Radhakrishnan 1950: 126-27).*

Greediness is the worst of diseases; propensities are the greatest of sorrows. To him who has known this truly, *nirvana* is the highest bliss.

Health is the greatest of gifts, contentment is the greatest wealth; trust is the best of relationships. *Nirvana* is the highest happiness.

Having tasted the sweetness of solitude and the sweetness of tranquility he becomes free from fear and free from sin while he drinks the sweetness of the joy of the law *[dharma]*.

Excerpts from The Dhammapada, *trans. Sarvepalli Radhakrishnan (1950). Reprinted by permission of Oxford University Press.*

---

3. right speech
4. right conduct
5. right means of livelihood
6. right endeavor
7. right mindfulness
8. right meditation

This is the "middle way" between self-denial and self-indulgence, a moderate and focused way of living. Notably absent are rituals or expressions of devotion to a personal god. In Theravada Buddhism, adoration of deities has no place as a part of the means to reach liberation.

The eightfold path provides the guidelines, but each individual must traverse it by himself or herself. No outside assistance from gods or other humans is possible. You are on your own!

Some explanation of each of the steps may help clarify the eightfold path as a whole. These steps are not so much a set of directions to be followed sequentially as eight principles that need to be applied to the particular situation of each person.

The first step, right belief (also called "right understanding" or "right views"), means holding a correct view of the nature of reality. It includes accepting as true the Four Noble Truths and the attitude toward life associated with the Buddha. That implies recognizing what had become known as the "three marks of existence": *anatta* (no soul), *anicca* (impermanence), and *dukkha* (suffering). It also entails believing in the Theravadin notion of *dharma*. In Hinduism, *dharma* referred to right conduct in the context of the caste system, as well as one's "duty" to seek liberation. Early Buddhism redefined *dharma* (in Pali, *dhamma*) to mean (1) the truth as taught by Buddha and contained in the Pali Canon, (2) proper conduct, which applies to all regardless of caste, and (3) reality itself and the laws (such as *karma* and dependent origination), that explain how reality functions.

The second step, right aspiration, purpose, or thought, means freeing one's mind from sensual desires, greed, and malice. It also means taking on thoughts of non-violence, renunciation, and compassion. At this stage one seeks to replace cruelty and unconcern with gentleness, benevolence, and goodwill. The point is not to attach oneself to particular persons with a caring attitude, but to practice a "universal goodwill" that extends equally to all.

The third step, right speech, includes not speaking falsely, not gossiping, abstaining from harsh words, avoiding vulgar or prejudicial talk, and not falling into the habit of useless chatter.

The fourth step, right conduct or action, means not killing other living creatures; not stealing; and avoiding illicit sexual behavior, intoxicants, and gambling.

The fifth step, right means of livelihood, forbids four types of occupations: those that involve killing, those engaged in commerce or services for hire, anything that involves trickery or deception, and any work that entails astrology. In general it means earning a living in ways consistent with Buddhist ideals.

The sixth step, right endeavor or effort, refers to avoiding any sort of unwholesome action that will have a negative *karmic* influence and pursuing beneficial deeds. It requires constant alertness as to what one is doing.

The seventh step, right mindfulness or alertness, means devoting oneself assiduously to focused observation of oneself and others. Contemplation begins by focusing on one's breathing to become aware of the body and its impermanence. It also includes awareness of the ebb and flow of one's feelings, then one's mental activities, and finally the objects of one's mind. It is at this level that monks might engage in gazing on corpses. The idea is to let the reality of impermanence completely occupy your mind.

The final step, right meditation or concentration, arises as one's mind is brought sharply into focus as a result of the prior step. At this stage a calmness and peace comes as one enters the state of *samadhi*. For Hindus *samadhi* meant absorption into the spiritual; in Theravada Buddhism it is not absorption into something outside oneself, but rather a "one-pointedness" in which all attachments have been broken. Once one is at this stage, *nirvana* is at hand, and, in a flash of intuition, that state of final bliss dawns.

The steps in the eightfold path correspond to the three instructions of Theravadin tradition: morality, concentration, and wisdom. Morality (*sila*) includes right speech, action, and livelihood. Concentration (*samadhi*) encompasses right effort, mindfulness, and meditation. Wisdom (*prajna*) envelops right belief and aspiration. Since wisdom is built on concentration, and both are built on morality, the "path" is not so much linear as interconnected.

Everyone should attempt to live by the eightfold path, and theoretically enlightenment is open to anyone regardless of caste or gender, or whether lay or ordained. In practice, in Theravada Buddhism, becoming an *arhant* and reaching *nirvana* has been limited to monks and nuns who have the freedom to devote themselves fully to the path. In Southeast Asia, where Theravada Buddhism is centered, monks and nuns group together in monasteries and convents. The monks wear yellow robes, shave their heads, and own only a very few possessions, including a begging bowl.

Each Theravadin monk and nun pledges to live by the following five precepts:

1. to abstain from taking life;
2. to abstain from taking what is not given;
3. to abstain from sensuous misconduct;
4. to abstain from false speech;
5. to abstain from intoxicants, as they tend to cloud the mind.

The religious life of lay people in Theravadin countries consists of spending a limited time in a monastery (for young men especially), showing kindness to monks and nuns, receiving instruction from them, and showing reverence for the Buddha by visiting shrines where there are images of the Buddha and/or relics from the Buddha. The images are highly idealized, symbolic representations. For example, the Buddha is portrayed with long ears, a symbol of enlightenment, and a beatific gaze, to indicate that he has reached *nirvana*. A relic might be a reputed tooth of the Buddha or one of his bones. Lay people also commit themselves to a modified version of the five precepts.

The most important monuments in Theravada Buddhism are *stupas*, distinctive dome-shaped or bell-shaped structures in which are housed relics associated with the Buddha or other early leaders. Atop the dome (thought to symbolize the cosmos) one always finds three disks (to denote the umbrellas used to shield royalty). The disks represent the Buddha, who has gone beyond the attachments of this world. In India, where numerous ancient *stupas* remain, the dome shape predominates. In Southeast Asia the bell shape became more popular; it rises to a single point at the top. *Stupas* are important pilgrimage sites. Perhaps influenced by Hindu practice, worshippers come to give homage to the Buddha, circumambulating the structure and reciting verses from sacred texts. Virtually all of the *stupas* have elaborate carvings of various mythic beings adapted from the popular beliefs of the region.

The question naturally arises: Is this not worship of the Buddha as a deity? Setting up images to be venerated seems suspiciously like the worship of devotional Hinduism. The Theravada answer has always been to distinguish veneration of gods from showing reverence for the Buddha. The Buddha is *not* being worshipped as a deity; rather, followers are showing reverence to one who has attained enlightenment and symbolically committing themselves to follow his example when they show homage to an image or a relic.

Sacred: Spiritual Atheism

Theravada Buddhism is an atheistic religion, denying a central role for a personal god or gods. Theistic religions (like *bhakti* Hinduism or Christianity) focus on personal deities who have an integral role in ultimate transformation. It is not just that Theravada Buddhism is "agnostic" about the gods, without claimed knowledge concerning the existence or role of deities in human existence. Theravada Buddhism claims that gods have no role to play in human liberation, any more than any other spirits or human agencies do. Each person by himself or herself must "work out his or her own liberation."

To be precise, Theravada Buddhism, like Jainism, is atheistic in a functional rather than a theoretical sense. *Theoretical atheism* denies that gods exist. *Functional atheism* is not concerned about the question of the existence of gods; it only knows that whether they exist or not, they are irrelevant to human destiny. Theravada Buddhists simply avoid speculation on the issue of whether gods or spirits exist, because such idle thought is not productive for what is truly important—overcoming suffering.

That which is spiritual in early Buddhism is *nirvana*, the state entered when craving is extinguished. It is not a deity like Vishnu, nor a World Soul like *Brahman*, but for Buddhism *nirvana* is spiritual.

RESPONSES TO CONTEMPORARY ETHICAL ISSUES

The Ecological Crisis

Buddhism in general has been called an "ecological religion." Or, as one scholar has put it, "The fruit of Buddhism—mindful living—cultivates a view of human beings, nature, and their relationship that is fundamentally ecological. Awareness opens our perception to the interdependence and fragility of all life, and our indebtedness to countless beings, living and dead, past and present, near and far. If we have any real identity at all in Buddhism, it is the ecology itself—a massive interdependent, self-causing dynamic energy-event against a backdrop of ceaseless change" (Badiner 1990: xiv-xv).

According to the stories of the life of Buddha preserved in Theravadin tradition, he was in harmony with nature himself. He experienced enlightenment in a forest, on the banks of a river. Snails crawled on his head to protect him from the sun. In his preaching he used tales of animals, from his own past lives, implying that animals' lives were every bit as important as human. In these tales animals show great compassion. One of the principal values he taught was *metta*, loving kindness for all beings (Ho 1990: 130).

QUESTIONS OF MORALITY: WHAT ARE OUR OBLIGATIONS TO NON-HUMAN LIFE?

Compassion for All Living Beings

Theravada Buddhism holds that compassion should be displayed not selectively, but to all living beings (Metta Sutta, Khuddakapatha; Badiner 1990: 12).

As a mother with her own life guards the life of her own child, let all-embracing thoughts for all that lives be thine.

Excerpts from Dharma Gaia: A Harvest of Essays in Buddhism and Ecology, edited by A. Hunt Badiner. Reprinted with permission of Parallax Press, Berkeley, Calif. 94707.

In an essay on "Early Buddhist Views of Nature," Chatsumarn Kabilsingh summarizes Theravadin teaching on nature: "Buddhism views humanity as an integral part of nature, so that when nature is defiled, people ultimately suffer. Negative consequences arise when cultures alienate themselves from nature. . . . When we abuse nature we abuse ourselves" (Badiner 1990: 8).

The idea of the interdependence of all things, expressed in the Buddhist teaching of "dependent origination" or the "Great Wheel of Causation," accords with the Gaia theory of James Lovelock. According to Lovelock, "the entire range of living matter on Earth, from whales to viruses, and from oaks to algae, could be regarded as constituting a single living entity, capable of manipulating the Earth's atmosphere to suit its overall needs and endowed with faculties and powers far beyond those of its constituent parts" (Lovelock 1982: 9). In other words, the earth is a "homeostatic living organism that coordinates its vital systems to compensate for threatening environmental changes" (Badiner 1990: xvi). Lovelock adopted the ancient Greek name for the earth goddess, Gaia, for his thesis. This notion of a balance that occurs through constant interacting changes, however, *is* the basic Buddhist perception of reality.

One of the most significant environmental issues is the explosion in population, which threatens to overwhelm the resources of the earth. Theravada Buddhism has a unique perspective that offers a way of addressing this issue (Premasiri 1989: 55–56). Theravada Buddhism does not ground its moral teachings in a supernatural source of authority. According to Theravadin teaching, morality must be rooted in experience and reflect a concern for all of life. In other words, one of the basic moral principles of Theravada Buddhism is that we must be honest about things as they are. Another is that we must treat all beings as we ourselves would want to be treated. With its pragmatic orientation, Theravada Buddhist ethical teaching is oriented toward the results of one's actions. The prevention of unwanted pregnancies through contraception in order to respond to the population dilemma would, therefore, be considered a moral response by most Theravada Buddhists. One's duty is to the community as a whole, and birth control contributes to the welfare of society.

Theravada Buddhist awareness of the ecological community does not come from the same source as Hinduism, for the Theravadin tradition does not recognize a Spirit from which all life comes. However, the fact that all beings share in the reality of impermanence (*anicca*) creates a sense of mutuality among humans and non-human life. Just as non-human living beings have "no eternal Self," neither do humans. This value, combined with the fundamental Buddhist notion of compassion for the suffering of all, leads to a special kind of ecological awareness. In addition, like Hinduism (and Jainism), Buddhism endorses the value of *ahimsa*, with its important environmental implications.

The Theravada Buddhist attitude toward the environment is reflected in an incident observed by Lynn White in Sri Lanka. He was watching a group of Buddhists building a road. He noted that there were cones of earth left undisturbed, which, he was told, were nests of snakes the workers had discovered. They would not touch the cones until the snakes left of their own accord (Spring 1974: 4).

War

Although Theravada Buddhist texts recognize that violence sometimes results from unjust social situations, they acknowledge no circumstances under which violence can be justified in order to redress grievances. "Instead, [Theravada Buddhism] calls for a sound causal analysis of situations and circumstances in which violence and social conflicts arise and attempts to enlighten men on ways to prevent violence from ever taking place" (Premasiri 1989: 62). Violence begets violence, according to Theravadin teaching, and the only way to bring peace is through non-violence.

Abortion

According to the Theravada Buddhist interpretation of the Buddha's teachings, each person is on his or her own on the journey toward *nirvana*.

Each of us must make and take responsibility for ethical decisions, guided by the Buddha's teaching (*dharma*) and following the example of the Buddha. According to the rules stipulated for Buddhist monks, abortion would seem to be unacceptable, because it involves the taking of a human life already existent. However, in sorting through the myriad of circumstances that surround specific situations, individuals must decide for themselves what course to take. What counts from a Theravadin perspective is the "goodness of the intention," for that determines the *karmic* effect (Premasiri 1989: 56-57).

Economic Justice

The fundamental Buddhist teaching that craving must be overcome has profound economic implications. Economic systems in the West are based on the idea of insatiable consumption. What might be called "Buddhist economics" is based on "simplicity, frugality, and an emphasis on what is essential—in short, a basic ethic of restraint" (De Silva 1990: 15). From a Western perspective, development occurs as more desires are fulfilled; from a Buddhist perspective, true development is in the reduction of desires. In the words of E.F. Schumacher, writing in his now classic work *Small Is Beautiful: Economics as if People Mattered*, "the Buddhist sees the essence of civilization not in a multiplication of wants but in the purification of human character" (Schumacher 1973: 52).

Another interpreter of the Buddhist approach to economics writes (Sivaraksa 1990: 172):

> *In the spirit of Buddhist development, inner strength must be cultivated first; then compassion and loving kindness to others becomes possible. Mindful work and play would be interchangeable. Work does not have to be regarded as an obligation or a negotiation in order to get more wages or more leisure time. The work ethic could be to enjoy one's work and to work in harmony with others, as opposed to getting ahead of others and having a miserable time doing it.*

The basic Buddhist teaching of the "middle way" between self-indulgence and self-denial means that it is not wealth itself that is the problem or the enjoyment of material things. It is the attachment to wealth (or poverty) that leads people to egoism. "The keynote of Buddhist economics, therefore, is simplicity and non-violence. From an economist's point of view, the marvel of the Buddhist way of life is the utter rationality of its pattern—amazingly small means leading to extraordinarily satisfactory results" (Schumacher 1973: 54).

In terms of the issue of wealth and poverty, the Buddhist perspective minimizes the intense competition for limited resources characteristic of societies that focus on consumption as the accepted goal. Extremes of wealth and poverty develop where the quality of life is measured by the amount of material goods one possesses. Since basic Buddhism teaches people not to strive for material well-being, but to measure the quality of life on the basis of the overcoming of craving, people in traditional Theravada Buddhist societies instinctively use resources modestly. And "people satisfying their needs by means of a modest use of resources are obviously less likely to be at each other's throats than people depending on a high rate of use" (Schumacher 1973: 55).

The Buddhist approach to economic life favors self-sufficiency; local communities support themselves with the resources at hand. In the developing world this model makes people accountable for producing what they need to live, without becoming dependent on the uncertainties of being a part of large-scale trade and commerce. In this way communities are not trapped by the boom and bust cycles of such economic activity.

Since Buddhism teaches reverence for all life, it instinctively counts the cost of using up non-renewable resources. From a Buddhist perspective (Schumacher 1973: 57):

> *Non-renewable goods must be used only if they are indispensable, and then only with the greatest care and the most meticulous concern for conservation. To use them heedlessly or extravagantly is an act of violence, and while complete non-violence may not be attainable on this earth, there is nonetheless an ineluctable duty on man to aim at the ideal of non-violence in all he does …. A population basing its economic life on non-renewable fuels is living parasitically, on capital instead of income.*

Buddhism may indeed offer a middle way between unabashed materialism and traditionalist stagnation. The former has led to disastrous results— "a collapse of the rural economy, a rising tide of unemployment in town and country, and the growth of a city proletariat without nourishment

Economic self-sufficiency is an economic value based on the basic Buddhist worldview.

for either body or soul" (Schumacher 1973: 58). The latter has proven incapable of adapting to changing circumstances of life and has left people in backward conditions that have condemned them to absolute poverty. Theravada Buddhism offers an economic "middle way," which, where it has been preserved, has been characterized by "amazingly small means leading to extraordinarily satisfying results."

However, even in strongly Theravadin countries, maintaining a basic Buddhist perspective is proving difficult. Whereas traditional Theravada emphasizes purification of character and not material goals, modern Theravada is more inclined to support social reforms. Although such a shift is accompanied by the emergence of an upwardly mobile middle class, it also leads to the grinding urban poverty characteristic of other countries that have adopted materialist models of development.

Gender Roles and the Status of Women

Siddartha Gautama apparently regarded women and men as spiritual equals. According to Theravadin tradition, in speaking about the pursuit of enlightenment according to his teachings, "who-

ever has such a vehicle, whether a woman or a man, shall indeed, by means of that vehicle, come to *nirvana" (Suttanipatta I.33;* cited by Young 1987: 106). In contrast to Hindu orthodoxy, the Buddha allowed women to lead a monastic life.

However, throughout history monks have far outnumbered nuns in Theravada Buddhism, giving the religion a distinctly male orientation. Monks are, moreover, regarded as superior to nuns. The teaching of *dharma* has been a function of men, with monks teaching nuns but not typically the other way around. Nuns were taught to take on a male way of thinking in order to pursue enlightenment. Buddha is reputed to have said that the admission of women would shorten the life of the *sangha.* In short, "in all Buddhist sects throughout the Buddhist world, men have always dominated and still dominate" (Barnes 1987: 131).

The popular belief that birth as a woman indicated bad *karma* from a previous life found its way into Buddhism from Hinduism, despite the Buddha's teaching about gender equality. According to a famous story, when Buddha's disciple asked how the monks were to conduct themselves with women, Buddha answered, "As not seeing them." If a woman should see the monk he should not talk to

Buddhist monks and nuns read from texts in a New York City temple. In both major branches of Buddhism today nuns are increasingly taking leadership roles.

her, and if she speaks first, then the monk should "keep awake" (Carmody 1989: 69). The Theravadin commentator Buddhaghosa wrote graphic descriptions of women as made of "flesh that would soon decay, bodies that would rot in the grave and be foul smelling" in order to discourage monks from being seduced by women (Carmody 1989: 71). However, it may be that such texts should be interpreted as more reflective of the general early Buddhist rejection of "worldliness" than as purposefully antifeminine (Barnes 1987: 110-14).

The ambiguity of the Theravadin attitude toward women is shown in another story of two monks travelling through the forest. They came to a river swollen by spring rains and found a woman standing on the edge, debating how to cross. One of the monks offered her a ride on his back, and she accepted. On the other side of the river, the woman and the monks parted ways. Some miles later the monk who had not carried the woman criticized his companion for his intimacy with a woman. In response, the other said, "I put the woman down hours ago. Why are you still carrying her?" (Carmody 1989: 85).

In traditional Theravada areas, lay women tend shrines and, most important, earn merit by providing food for monks as they make their morning rounds. In contrast to Hindu practice, Buddhist women were given the choice whether to marry or pursue enlightenment as nuns. Married women were still expected to be docile and serve their husbands, but they were given more responsibility to manage the financial affairs of the household.

In some Theravadin countries in recent years, orders of nuns have begun to play a more prominent role (Barnes 1994: 138-45, 152-59), in some cases taking the lead in addressing social problems. In addition, Theravadin laywomen have been instrumental in leading the Buddhist revival in Sri Lanka and other countries, even taking on the role of meditation teachers (Barnes 1994: 145-46, 148-51).

Homosexuality

In general, Buddhism is neutral on homosexuality. "The principal question for Buddhism has not been one of heterosexuality vs. homosexuality but one of sexuality vs. celibacy" (Cabezon 1993: 82). Acceptance or condemnation of homosexuality in Buddhist societies has more to do with the particular norms of the host culture than the tenets of Buddhism.

In the *Jataka Tales*, which portray the previous lives of the Buddha, there is what has been interpreted as an "implicit affirmation" of homosexuality. The Buddha's affection for his disciples and theirs for him and one another at times seems, according to this view, homoerotic (Cabezon 1993: 88-89).

CHAPTER SUMMARY

Buddhism began in the sixth century B.C.E. in reaction to the perceived excesses of Hinduism at that time. Its founder, Siddartha Gautama, is known as the "Buddha." He charted a "middle way" between self-indulgence and self-denial. After his own enlightenment he initiated an order (*sangha*) of monks and nuns. Buddhism faded in India, but flourished in the countries of Southeast Asia. It divided into two main branches: Theravada ("way of the elders") and Mahayana ("the large raft").

We next surveyed the distinctive teachings of the Theravada branch of Buddhism, identifying the problem as the suffering characteristic of all existence, the cause as craving, the reality as impermanence, the goal as *nirvana*, the means as the "eightfold path," and the view of the sacred as a type of "spiritual atheism."

We concluded the chapter by examining Theravadin responses to several contemporary ethical issues.

QUESTIONS FOR DISCUSSION AND REFLECTION

1. Siddartha Gautama was spiritually blind until he saw with his own eyes the suffering of the world. Are people today who are isolated or who isolate themselves from the pain and anguish of existence necessarily spiritually blind? Draw on your own personal experience in reflecting on this question.

2. Theravada Buddhism stresses self-reliance in spiritual matters. Do you think that we are "all alone" when it comes to pursuing spiritual truth? What are the effects of such a view?

3. The Buddha said that we should not waste precious energy speculating on spiritual questions; we should instead devote ourselves to the pursuit of enlightenment. Reflect on his position.

4. Do you agree that the Buddhist teaching of impermanence provides a basis for understanding the human relationship to the environment? If not, what is your view of the human relationship with nature?

5. Would "Buddhist economics" work in a modern, industrialized society such as the United States? Do you think you could personally benefit from the Buddhist approach to the acquisition of material things? Why or why not?

6. Was the Buddha correct in saying that "all life is suffering"? Try to think of something pleasurable that does not lead ultimately to suffering in some form.

7. Why do Theravada Buddhist monks meditate on the signs of death? Do you think most people in your society need to be more aware of their own mortality? Why or why not?

8. The Buddha's "Parable of the Poisoned Arrow" makes the point that speculation on the question of cosmic origins is irrelevant to solving the real problems of life. Do you agree? What *is* the purpose of musing about how things came to be?

SOURCES AND SUGGESTIONS FOR FURTHER STUDY

General

CONZE, EDWARD, 1954 *Buddhism, Its Essence and Development.* New York:Philosophical Library.

1959 *Buddhist Scriptures.* London: Penguin.

FIELDS, RICK, 1981 *How the Swans Came to the Lake: A Narrative History of Buddhism in America.* Boulder, Colo.: Shambhala.

HUMPHREYS, CHRISTMAS, 1951 *Buddhism.* New York: Penguin Books.

LESTER, ROBERT C., 1973 *Theravada Buddhism in Southeast Asia.* Ann Arbor: University of Michigan Press.

RADHAKRISHNAN, SARVEPALLI, TRANS., 1950 *The Dhammapada.* London: Oxford University Press.

RAHULA, WALPOLA, 1974 *What the Buddha Taught*, rev. ed. New York: Grove Press.

RHYS DAVIDS, T.W., TRANS., 1881 "Buddhist Sutras" in *Sacred Books of the East*, vol. 11. Oxford: Clarendon Press.

ROBINSON, RICHARD H., AND WILLARD L. JOHNSON, 1982 *The Buddhist Religion: A Historical Introduction*, 3rd ed. Belmont, Calif.: Wadsworth.

ROGERS, T.E., TRANS., 1870 *Buddhaghosa: Buddhist Parables.* London: Trubner & Co.

SWEARER, DONALD K., 1981 *Buddhism and Society in Southeast Asia.* Chambersburg, Pa.: Anima Publishing.

THOMAS, E. J., TRANS., 1935 *Early Buddhist Scriptures.* London: Kegan Paul, Trench, Trubner and Co., Ltd.

WARREN, HENRY CLARKE, ED., 1896 *Buddhism in Translations*, Harvard Oriental Series No. 3. Cambridge: Harvard University Press.

Ethical Issues

General

PREMASIRI, P. D., 1989 "Ethics of Theravada Buddhist Tradition," in *World Religions and Global Ethics*, ed. S. Cromwell Crawford (New York: Paragon House), 36–64.

Ecological Crisis

BADINER, ALLAN HUNT, ED., 1990 *Dharma Gaia: A Harvest of Essays in Buddhism and Ecology.* Berkeley, Calif.: Parallax Press.

DE SILVA, PADMASIRI, 1990 "Buddhist Environmental Ethics," in *Dharma Gaia,* 14–19.

HO, MOBI, 1990 "Animal Dharma," in *Dharma Gaia,* 129–35.

LOVELOCK, JAMES E., 1982 *Gaia: A New Look at Life on Earth.* New York: Oxford University Press.

SANDELL, KLAS, 1987 *Buddhist Perspectives on the Ecocrisis.* Kandy, Sri Lanka: Buddhist Publication Society.

SPRING, DAVID, AND EILEEN SPRING, EDS., 1974 *Ecology and Religion in History.* New York: Harper & Row.

Economic Justice

LEISS, WILLIAM, 1976 *The Limits to Satisfaction.* Toronto: University of Toronto Press.

SCHUMACHER, E.F.. 1973 *Small Is Beautiful: Economics as If People Mattered.* New York: Harper & Row.

SIVARAKSA, SULAK, 1990 "True Development," in *Dharma Gaia,* 169–77.

WEBER, MAX, 1958 *The Religion of India: The Sociology of Hinduism and Buddhism,* tr. Hans H. Gerth and Don Martindale. Glencoe, Ill.: Free Press.

Gender Roles and the Status of Women

BARNES, NANCY SCHUSTER, 1987 "Buddhism, " in *Women in World Religions,* ed. Arvind Sharma (Albany: State University of New York Press), 105–133.

1994 "Women in Buddhism," in *Today's Woman in World Religions,* ed. Arvind Sharma (Albany: State University of New York Press), 137–69.

DIMMITT, CORNELIA M., 1975 "Temptress, Housewife, Nun: Women's Role in Early Buddhism," *Anima* 2 (1975): 52–58.

GROSS, RITA M., 1993 *Buddhism After Patriarchy: A Feminist History, Analysis and Reconstruction of Buddhism.* Albany: State University of New York Press.

MACY, JOANNA, 1976 "Perfection of Wisdom: Mother of All Buddhas," *Anima* 1 (1974): 74–80.

PAUL, DIANA Y., 1979 *Women in Buddhism.* Berkeley, Calif.: Asian Humanities Press.

Homosexuality

CABEZON, JOSÉ IGNACIO, 1992 *Buddhism, Sexuality, and Gender.* Albany: State University of New York Press.

1993 "Homosexuality and Buddhism," in *Homosexuality and World Religions,* ed. Arlene Swidler (Valley Forge, Pa.: Trinity Press International), 81–101.

CHAPTER **7**

Jainism: The Way of Non-Injury and Sikhism: Neither Muslim nor Hindu

PAKISTAN

Nanak's birthplace

•Amri

1947 partition of India and Pakistan

PUNJAB

HARYA

RAJASTHAN

GUJARAT

Bombay •

MAHARASHT

ARABIAN SEA

KARNAT

INTRODUCTION

In the history of religion we find numerous examples of religious movements that began as attempts to reform an existing tradition. In India in the sixth century B.C.E., reactions against the Vedic sacrificial system and the control of religion by the Brahmins surfaced. Two reformers became founders of major religions. The first was Siddartha Gautama, the founder of Buddhism. The other was Nataputta Vardhamana, better known as Mahavira, the founder of Jainism.

Jainism is a relatively small religion in terms of numbers of adherents. Today, fewer than 4 million persons are Jains, and they are concentrated around Bombay, India. However, the impact of Jainism on other religions and its uncompromising commitment to its own ascetic ideals make Jainism far more important than its relatively small size suggests.

The placement of Sikhism, the other religion to be studied in this chapter, in a survey of the world's religions poses a problem. Sikhism began 2,000 years later than Jainism, in the fifteenth century C.E. In addition, since it arose out of a synthesis of Hinduism and Islam, it would be appropriate to wait to discuss Sikhism until we have surveyed Islam. However, our method of grouping major religions is geographical, and Sikhism is a religion that originated in and still flourishes in India. Our resolution of this issue is to place Sikhism alongside Hinduism, Jainism, and Buddhism as religions of India, but with the suggestion to the reader that a look ahead at the discussion of the basic teachings of Islam in Chapter Thirteen would be appropriate at this point!

JAINISM: NON-INJURY TO ALL LIFE

The name *Jainism* comes from the Sanskrit term *jina*, which means "conqueror." Within the religion a *jina* is an honorary title given to great teachers. Jains are those who seek to follow the example of these figures and win the battle over that which keeps them trapped within the cycle of rebirth.

Stages of Development and Sacred Texts

Founder: Mahavira and the Tirthankaras

According to Jain tradition, within the current cosmic cycle, twenty-four exemplary teachers have become *tirthankaras* (literally, "crossing finders or makers"). The image is that of a person who finds the place where a river can be crossed. As we have already noted, in the religions that originated in India, a river often symbolizes the cycle of rebirth. So a *tirthankara* is someone who has found a way to cross over and go beyond the cycle. The way can serve as an example for others to follow.

Jains date the origins of their religion to the first of the twenty-four *tirthankaras*, who lived thousands of years ago. Historians recognize certain evidence for only the last man in this series (and perhaps the next to the last, a man named Parshva). The given name of the last *tirthankara* was Nataputta Vardhamana. He was born about 597 B.C.E. in northeastern India, near the modern city of Patna. Like Siddartha Gautama, the founder of Buddhism, Nataputta was born in the warrior class (the *Kshatriyas*) and raised in luxury. Legends abound about this man, making it difficult for historians to determine what is true and what is imaginary. Since we are attempting an "insider's" perspective, we will recount his story as legend has it.

Like Siddartha, Nataputta became disillusioned with his comfortable life. At age 30 he left his wife and young daughter. He then spent over twelve years wandering naked through central India, seeking to abandon the worldly fetters that he felt kept his spirit bound to endless rebirth. At first he joined with others who shared his commitment to self-denial, but ultimately he determined to avoid attachment to any other being. He rarely stayed more than one night in any place, lest he develop attachments with anyone or any location. Although he was not the first to try to live by the principle of *ahimsa*, he took it to the extreme in his own life. He carried a broom to sweep his path clean of all forms of insect life, and he strained the water he drank through a cloth so as not to consume even the smallest life form. He was not the first to try to deny his physical body, for renunciation was a common strategy of Hindu holy men.

However, he took asceticism to an extreme. He meditated uncovered in the intense heat of summer sun, and in the winter rain he shunned shelter and gladly endured the hardship for the sake of its positive spiritual effect. One tradition states that people in one village tried to light a fire under him while he meditated, in order to get him to move, but he sat still. They stuck pins in his ears; he remained oblivious.

In the thirteenth year of his quest he reached his goal. He became a *jina;* he won the victory over desire and attachment. For the remaining years of his life, he spent his time teaching his message of extreme asceticism and *ahimsa.* People began to follow him and practice the lifestyle he exemplified. In about 527 B.C.E. he died by voluntarily starving himself, the ultimate act of self-denial. His soul now dwells, with those of other *jinas,* in a state of eternal bliss at the top of the universe.

His followers, who transformed the example of his life into a world religion, call him in reverence *Mahavira* (which means "Great Man or Hero"). They proclaim him the twenty-fourth and last *tirthankara* for the present cosmic cycle.

The Jain Community

By the time Mahavira died, a movement had developed around him. At his death leadership passed to the survivors among his first disciples. The movement began to spread from central India to the south and to the northwest. During the Mauryan dynasty of the third century, the Jain movement benefitted from royal support for the ascetic lifestyle. As the movement spread, divisions inevitably occurred. The earliest split was on the issue of whether monks should wear clothes or go naked. One group thought that the ascetic ideal and Mahavira's own example supported nudity. Another group argued that allowing monks one white garment would not compromise the principle. By the first century C.E., Jains either supported monastic nudity (the *Digambaras,* meaning "sky-clad") or identified with those monks who accepted the white garment (the *Shvetambaras,* meaning "white-clad"). The latter group accepted women into their order, while the *Digambaras* did not. Over the centuries the *Shvetambaras* became prominent in the west and northwest, while the *Digambaras*

enjoyed success in central and southern India. Gradually Jainism faded in the latter areas and survives principally in northwest India, around Bombay.

The "Jain community" is more than these religious orders, however. Throughout Jain history there has been a close association between monastics and the laity. Lay persons revere the monks and nuns and provide for their basic necessities, and, in turn, receive instruction in the principles of Jain living.

The Agamas

The Sanskrit term *agamas* means "tradition" and refers to any body of teachings handed down by an unbroken succession of sages. As we have seen, in Hinduism the term covers a set of writings related to the personal deities. In Jainism, *agamas* is the most general designation for the writings considered sacred.

The sacred writings of the Jains are religious and philosophical in character. Each of the two major sects maintains its own canon. Included in the *Shvetambara* scripture are the remembered sermons and discourses of Mahavira. The *Digambaras* hold that the original teachings of Mahavira are lost, but maintain that in their texts the essence is preserved.

Scriptures do not occupy the same central place in Jainism as they do in some other religions. They are seen as helpful in guiding a person to the right path, but they do not possess the complete "truth." As we shall see below, in Jain teaching nothing in the material world, including scriptures, is capable of expressing pure knowledge.

Jainism Today

According to the Jain view of time, we are currently in a period of decline that will last 21,000 years. During this phase Jainism and other religions will fade away, as will all human virtue. Another 21,000-year period will follow, bringing an end to human civilization. This will complete the downward spiral of the cosmic cycle, and a period of ascendancy will begin.

This helps explain why Jains have never been concerned about spreading their religion. They feel no compulsion to carry their message to the ends of the earth before some end time, because time is cyclical and the place of religion in each phase of the cycle is inevitable. In addition, each person must decide alone to begin the arduous trek to liberation. Whether or not that person calls himself or herself a "Jain" (or proclaims membership in another religious movement) is irrelevant to spiritual success. Only one's own commitment to rigid self-denial matters.

Nevertheless, in the last several decades Jainism has become somewhat more open to other religions, and has spread to other countries. In the early 1970s a Jain monk for the first time left India to travel to world conferences on religion. And in recent years Jain centers have been established in the United States, Canada, and other countries. Many Jains are highly educated and have joined the migration of Indian professionals to the West, carrying their religion with them.

Jainism will never be a widespread religion, but it will continue to serve as an example of a religion that has not compromised its basic teachings for the sake of growth.

Distinctive Teachings

Problem: Souls "Weighed Down" Jains believe that every living being has a spiritual soul (called *jiva* in Jainism; note that in Hinduism *jiva,* which means "life principle" in Sanskrit, refers to a person's material nature). These souls are by nature perfect, blissful, all-knowing, eternal, and infinite in number. As in Hinduism, the fundamental problem Jainism recognizes is that souls are confined by *karma* to the cycle of rebirth. However, in contrast to Hinduism and other religions that originated in India, Jainism views *karma* as not just a law; *karma* is a form of very subtle matter. The human dilemma is that when we act, *karmic* matter attaches to and "weighs down" the *jiva*. The more *karma* a soul accumulates in a previous existence, the lower down the ladder of existence that soul is born in the next. Being born as a human indicates that the *jiva* has worked its way a long way up the scale and has a unique opportunity to rid itself of existing *karma* and stop the accumulation of more.

One of the more interesting implications of the Jain view of our human problem is its view of human knowledge. Although our souls are in

Digambara monks at the Maha Mastakabhisheka festival in Shravanabelagola, India, carry whisks to clear their paths so they will not step on any living being.

their pure nature "all-knowing," when attached to *karma* they are limited in knowledge by their particular situations. A famous parable, reputed to be of Jain origin but adopted by teachers in many other religious traditions, illustrates this teaching. It is popularly known as the tale of the blind men and the elephant. In this story three blind men encounter an elephant. Each touches a different part of the elephant. When asked to describe what they have experienced, each answers in a different way. The man who touched the side speaks of confronting a stone wall. However, to the man who felt the tail of the elephant, the "thing" is a rope. The last man, who reached out and held the ear of the elephant, was just as certain that it was a fan. Each man spoke truthfully, because his experience was limited to his own situation. The point is that as long as we are "blinded" by our particular *karmic* context, we will see things in part, and our knowledge will be limited. Thus, no one who is not yet liberated can claim to know the fullness of truth, but those

QUESTIONS OF HUMAN DESTINY: WHAT HAPPENS AFTER DEATH?

The Fates of Souls

According to Jainism, human beings are composed of distinct spiritual souls (jivas) united with particles of matter (ajiva). The innumerable souls may be born in non-human bodies, depending on the karma they have accumulated. In this passage from the Jain sutras, the plurality of souls and their possible fates are described (Uttaradhyayana III.27; Jacobi 1895: 15–16).

The universe is peopled by manifold creatures who are, in this Samsara, born in different families and castes for having done various actions.

Sometimes they go to the world of the gods, sometimes to the hells, sometimes they become Asuras (demons) in accordance with their actions.

Sometimes they become Kshatriyas (nobles) or Kandalas and Bukkasas (outcasts and untouchables), or worms and moths, or . . . ants.

Thus living beings of sinful actions, who are born again and again in ever-recurring births, are not disgusted with the Samsara, but they are like warriors (never tired of the battle of life).

Living beings bewildered through the influence of their actions, distressed and suffering pains, undergo misery in non-human births.

But by the cessation of Karman (karma), perchance living beings will reach in due time a pure state and be born as men.

---

who are liberated cannot communicate to us their knowledge!

Reflect on this parable. Do you agree with its basic point? Why or why not? Would the world be a better place if people did not claim to have complete knowledge of the ultimate truth?

Cause: Activity   For Jainism the cause of *karmic* bondage is not just desire, although the more attached one is to the material world and its pleasures, the more *karma* will be accumulated. Jains believe that all actions, no matter how well-intentioned, produce *karma* and burden the *jiva*. Therefore, only a commitment to inactivity or to activity that focuses on liberating the *jiva* will be effective in stopping the further accumulation of *karmic* matter.

Reality: Matter and Spirit   According to Jain teaching, reality is divided into only two categories: matter (*ajiva*) and spirit (*jiva*). In each of these categories an infinite number of individual particles exists. In the spiritual realm, as noted, an infinite number of discrete souls are present. According to Jain teaching, these souls were not created by a personal god, nor do they emanate from some cosmic Spirit like *Brahman*. They have eternally existed as individual units, all of the same nature—pure knowledge and goodness. Souls are further classified in terms of the number of senses they possess. Humans, gods, animals, and other spiritual beings have five senses; at the other extreme, plants have but one sense (touch). Matter is by nature evil and, when attached to souls, obscures their purity and goodness. It is composed of gross matter but also space, time, motion, and rest. As noted, *karma* is a particularly subtle form of matter. Jain philosophers have noted that this "atomistic" approach to describing reality accords well with what modern science is discovering about the composition of matter.

End: Becoming an "All-knowing One"   The "goal" in Jainism is for the soul to be liberated from its bondage to *karma* so that its true nature can be realized. In Jain cosmology, liberated souls rise to the top of the universe (a place called *loka*), where they dwell eternally in full consciousness, knowledge, and bliss. The liberated soul is a *kevalin*, an "all-knowing one." Through liberation one's soul joins Mahavira and others who have escaped the bondage of *karma* to become themselves *jinas* (conquerors). In effect, they attain a state higher than the gods, who remain bound by an invisible form of *karma*. However, unlike Hindu monism there is no state of unity realized upon liberation; the individual souls remain separate. And there is no ultimate communion with a personal god as there is in the *bhakti* traditions in Hinduism.

Means: Asceticism   Jainism is a religion of self-reliance. Jains believe that in the quest to become *jinas,* they are on their own. The gods cannot help, for they too are working out their own liberation. Priests cannot invoke any special powers. The Vedas (and all scriptures, even the Jain writings) are limited by the point of view of their writers, so they have no ultimate authority.

The key word in the Jain teaching about the path to liberation from the cycle of rebirth is *asceticism*. Only through a lifestyle of active self-denial can one hope to work off existing *karma* and avoid accumulating more *karma,* and only through ridding the soul of *karma* can liberation be attained. Asceticism can be considered a form of vigorous spiritual exercise, which "burns off" *karma* and controls one's appetite for more, just as physical exercise reduces calories and curbs one's desire for food.

For the Jain the ideal way of living is to follow Mahavira's example and avoid all attachments. Although according to Jain teaching, the path to liberation is open to all regardless of caste, gender, or membership in a religious organization, in practice only monks and nuns can maintain the extreme discipline required. For the laity some attachments in family life and in the community are inevitable.

Of the Five Great Vows, the first (*ahimsa*) is the hallmark of Jainism. Monastics are obligated to go to extremes to avoid taking life, consciously or unconsciously. When walking, a Jain monk sweeps the path before him so as to avoid inad-

This thousand-year-old statue of the revered Lord Bahubali at Karnataka in Shravanabelagola is anointed every twelve to fourteen years in the Maha Mastakabhisheka festival.

vertently stepping on living creatures. Like Mahavira, he strains the water he drinks and wipes out his begging bowl (if he has one; *Digambara* monks use only their hands for begging). The great gift Jainism has shared with the rest of the world is this unqualified commitment to non-injury. Others may judge it impractical, but it is an ideal that calls forth the nobility in others. It had a great impact on Mahatma Gandhi, who was influenced by the Jain community in Bombay, where he spent his early years. He transformed it into a highly successful political strategy, which was then adopted by Dr. Martin Luther King, Jr., and other leaders of the American civil rights movement.

For the Jain laity a modified set of principles evolved. Jains are to avoid taking life knowingly. Hence, they may not work at occupations, such as

QUESTIONS OF MORALITY: WHAT IS RIGHT LIVING?

The Five Great Vows

The basic ethical guidelines are the "Five Great Vows" for monks and nuns, applied in modified form to lay people. The list begins with the most important Jain virtue—non-injury (ahimsa), *which was adapted by other religions originating in India* (Acaranga Sutra 24; Jacobi 1884: 208–13).

The first great vow, sir, runs thus: I renounce all killing of living things, whether subtle or gross, whether movable or immovable. Nor shall I myself kill living beings; [nor cause others to do it, nor consent to it;]. . . .

The second great vow, sir, runs thus: I renounce all vices of lying speech arising from anger or greed or fear or mirth. I shall neither myself speak lies, nor cause others to speak lies, nor consent to the speaking of lies by others . . .

The third great vow, sir, runs thus: I shall renounce all taking of anything not given, either in a village or a town or a wood, either of little or much, of small or great, of living or lifeless things. I shall neither take myself what is not given, nor cause others to take it, nor consent to their taking it.

The fourth great vow, sir, runs thus: I renounce all sexual pleasures, either with gods or men or animals. I shall not give way to sensuality, or cause others to give way to it. . . . [For lay people, sexual activity is limited to marriage.]

The fifth great vow, sir, runs thus: I renounce all attachments, whether little or much, small or great, living or lifeless; neither shall I myself form such attachments, nor cause others to do so, nor consent to their doing so.

---

farming, in which life is taken as a matter of course. They are to remain faithful to their spouses in marriage. They are to place limits on their material holdings. This ideal has inspired many Jains (who have become quite wealthy in business, law, and banking) to give away considerable sums of money for charitable causes. They are to live simply, avoiding unnecessary travel. They must observe periods of meditation and self-denial, spending days living as monks or nuns. They must support the ascetics. Their strong commitment to a moral lifestyle has often earned Jains the admiration of others in the communities where they live.

Sacred: Spiritual Atheism Like Theravada Buddhism, Jainism is at the same time atheistic, yet spiritual. Jainism is atheistic not in the sense of denying the existence of gods; in the Jain cosmology, gods exist. Jain atheism might be described as "functional atheism." Although the gods exist, they

play no role in ultimate transformation. It is fruitless to pray to them or to "put one's trust in them," because they too are seeking liberation. They exist simply as other types of *jivas,* with their own particular form of matter (which renders them invisible).

A casual observer of Jain practice is bound to be confused when visiting a Jain temple. One will see there statues that look like images of deities, with Jain laity presenting what appear to be offerings and walking around (circumambulating) the images in an apparent display of devotion. Is this not *puja,* the worship of deities we observed in Hindu devotionalism? Although Jain practice was probably influenced by Hindu *puja,* appearances can be deceiving. When Jains bow before a statue of Mahavira or one of the other *tirthankaras,* they are not worshipping a "god." Rather, they are focusing on the example given by these "crossing finders." They are pledging themselves to follow the spiritual path blazed by Mahavira and the others. This is not to deny that there is a popular piety in Jainism, in which worshippers may seek material gains through the "merit making" of revering the images or showing kindness to monastics. Tension between the ideals of a religion and popular beliefs and practices that seem to contradict them are found in all the world's religions.

SIKHISM: NEITHER HINDU NOR MUSLIM

Sikhism has been called an example of "syncretism"; that is, a religion created out of the merger of two other religions. In the case of Sikhism, these two religions are Hinduism and Islam. As we talk about Sikhism we will point out Hindu and Muslim elements. However, its syncretistic background should not be allowed to obscure the uniqueness of Sikhism. It stands as a distinct and important major religion in the world.

Stages of Development and Sacred Texts

Founder: Nanak The background of the story of the emergence of Sikhism is the Muslim invasion of India, which began in the eighth century C.E. Three hundred years later, Islam dominated all of northwest India and was spreading southward. From this time onward a series of Hindu reformers came under the influence of the strict monotheism and anti-ceremonialism of the Muslim faith (see Chapter Thirteen). They applied these ideals to the *bhakti* movements within Hinduism and proclaimed a message of liberation from the cycle of rebirth through heartfelt devotion to the one true God for anyone, regardless of caste.

One such reformer was Kabir (1440–1518). Although born as a Muslim, he accepted the Hindu analysis of the human predicament, while rejecting the authority of the Vedas in resolving it. He combined *bhakti* devotionalism with Muslim *Sufi* mysticism and taught a path of love of God, which leads to absorption into the divine. He carried his message across the north Indian plain, winning devotees to this synthesis of the two religions. He also

emphasized the need for the guidance of a spiritual teacher, a *guru,* and rejected the rituals of both Hinduism and Islam as sterile. One can still find in India today small sects that claim to follow Kabir.

One of those who came under the influence of Kabir was Nanak. He was born in 1469 to Hindu parents in the Punjab region, in an area now part of Pakistan, about thirty-five miles from the city of Lahore (see Figure 7-1). It was a time of turmoil, with recurrent hostility between Hindu and Muslim leaders.

As with other great religious leaders, the traditions that arose about Nanak tell a story of a young man who left his family and committed himself to a spiritual quest. According to his religious biography, from an early age Nanak was a poet who tended toward religious musing. His father was intent on having him follow the family tradition and become a businessman. Nanak entered business, married, and had two sons. But he showed no proclivity for commerce. Nanak left his family in order to devote himself to his spiritual quest (although throughout his life he returned to them from time to time). He spent increasing time singing hymns to God. One of his friends was a Muslim minstrel named Mardana, who joined with him in a small band dedicated to discovering the truth.

The turning point for Nanak came when he was 30. According to one tradition, he was bathing when he disappeared in the water. Those present assumed he had drowned, but he had actually been taken into the presence of God. God commissioned Nanak to go and repeat the Divine Name and tell others to do likewise. God also challenged him to remain unpolluted by the world, to practice charity, ritual bathing, service, and meditation. When Nanak reappeared, he uttered the words that were to become the theme of his message: "There is no Hindu; there is no Muslim."

Like other religious founders, Nanak wandered through the region, teaching his message to any who would listen. He travelled with his Muslim friend, Mardana, and together they sang praises to God, who had revealed himself to Nanak as the *True Name.* Nanak wore a combination of Hindu and Muslim garments. According to some traditions

FIGURE 7–1

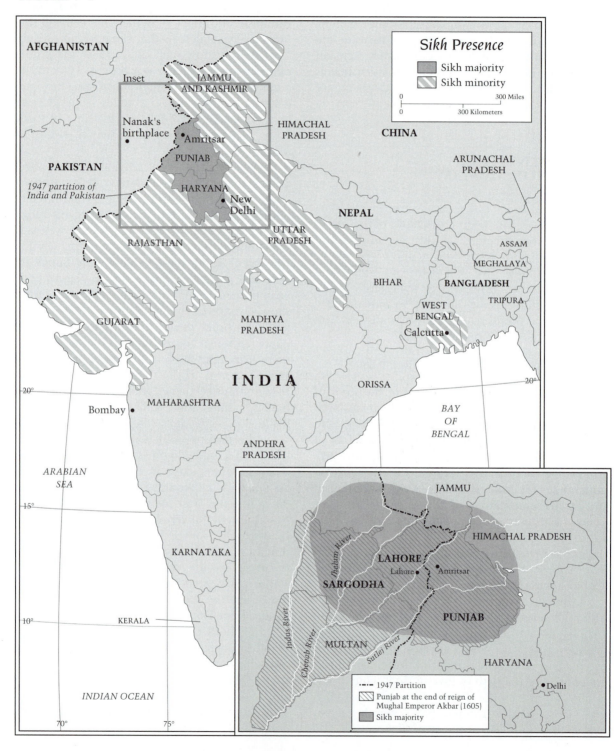

they travelled to Arabia, where they visited the holy cities of Islam, Mecca, and Medina (see Chapter Thirteen). In all his travels Nanak's greatest success in teaching came in the Punjab region of his birth.

When Nanak neared death in 1538, his Hindu and Muslim followers debated over the fate of his body. Following their heritage, the Hindus wanted to place his body on a pyre and cremate him. In accord with their tradition, the Muslims wanted to bury him. One night the dying Guru told his Hindu devotees to place flowers on his left side and his Muslim disciples to lay flowers to his right. Those whose flowers remained fresh in the morning would have the right to his body. He drew a sheet over his body. In the morning, when his followers withdrew the sheet, his body was gone and the flowers on both sides were fresh.

The Gurus after Nanak For the first 200 years after the death of Nanak, the community of his followers had a series of human leaders. The community became known as *Sikhs* (from the Sanskrit word for "disciple.") The first Guru (as the Sikh leaders were called) after Nanak was Angad (1504–1552). He composed a collection of Nanak's and his own hymns and established the custom of a communal feast for disciples known as the *langar*.

The fifth Guru, Arjan (1503–1606), compiled the Guru Granth Sahib (also called the Adi Granth), the Sikh scripture (see below). He also built a temple in the middle of a pool at a site in Punjab that became known as *Amritsar* ("the pool of immortality"). Arjan helped establish a unique Sikh identity and functioned as a political and economic leader. As a result of his political activity, Arjan was arrested, tortured, and killed by Muslims.

Arjan's son succeeded him as Guru Har Gobind (1606–1645). As the sixth Guru, he followed his father's direction and created the first Sikh army, leading it into battle against the Muslim Moghuls. The pacifism taught by Guru Nanak had fallen victim to the growing hostility between Sikhs and Muslims.

The Guru Granth Sahib at the Golden Temple in Amritsar.

The tenth and last Guru, Gobind Singh (1675–1708), created a military fraternity that still plays a prominent role in Sikh life. Called the *khalsa* (the "pure"), the members of this fraternity become through initiation *singhs* ("lions"). As their distinguishing marks they wear "five k's": *kesh*, uncut hair; *kangha*, comb; *kachh*, short pants; *kara*, steel bracelet; and *kirpan*, sword. From the beginning, men of all castes were eligible for membership; in recent times, women have been included as initiates, taking the name *kaur* ("princess"). The *singhs* were a fearsome fighting force, starting the tradition that the finest soldiers in India are Sikhs. Today, although Sikhs constitute only 1.5 percent of the Indian population, 30 percent of the Indian army is Sikh.

Guru Adi Granth   After Guru Gobind Singh's assassination, he was succeeded not by a human leader, but (at his direction) by the Sikh scripture, the Adi ("first") Granth, as Guru. Since 1708 Sikhs have venerated the Granth as their spiritual leader, considering the collection the embodiment of the ten human gurus. Each morning a copy of the Granth is symbolically enthroned and worshipped at the Golden Temple in Amritsar; at night it is put to rest. Sikh children are typically named in this manner: The first letter of the name is taken from the first letter of a verse of the Adi Granth chosen at random.

The Granth Sahib ("Book of the Lord") includes about 6,000 hymns: those of Nanak and the next four Gurus as well as compositions by Hindu and Muslim poets. Over 2,000 hymns are attributed to the fifth Guru, Arjan, who compiled the collection.

The Resurgence of Sikhism in Modern India   When the British government took control of India in 1848, the Sikhs put up the noblest resistance. They were subdued, but their fierce fighting and pledge of loyalty after defeat won the respect of British authorities. The British gave the Sikhs considerable autonomy under their rule, although this only caused many Sikhs to long for full independence. Sikhs were active participants in the movement for Indian self-determination. One of the major turning points in the struggle was the massacre by British forces of 379 unarmed persons, mostly Sikhs, rallying in the holy Sikh city of Amritsar in 1919.

When Britain withdrew from India in 1947, creating the nations of India and Pakistan, the results were tragic for the Sikhs. Their Punjabi homeland was split between the two countries. Over 2 million Sikhs had to flee Pakistan, even as Muslims flocked from India into the new Muslim state. Holy sites, including the birthplace of Nanak, were left behind in Pakistan, as were many profitable Sikh farms. Sikhs were not adequately compensated for their economic losses, and politically Sikh autonomy was thwarted by increasing centralization in the new India. One Sikh leader summarized the situation by saying, "After independence the Hindus got India, the Muslims got Pakistan; we got nothing."

Punjab is the richest agricultural area of India. Under Sikh leadership, about 80 percent of the food produced in India comes from this area. However, in a democratically elected central government the Sikhs can wield little political power. They were unable to stop, for example, the diversion of water from the Ganges River into Hindu areas.

Most Sikhs are political moderates; one of them (Zail Singh) took the symbolic office of president of India in 1982. However, frustration over their impotent political situation has led some Sikhs to call for the creation of an independent Sikh nation, to be called *Khalistan* ("land of the pure"). Drawing on their militant heritage and fired by a new spirit of Sikh fundamentalism, some Sikh extremists formed a paramilitary force, which has mounted terrorist-style assaults on Hindu civilians. In June 1984, the Indian army responded to these attacks by moving against Amritsar, where the extremists had their headquarters and arsenal. In the assault, 1,200 Sikh defenders and 200 soldiers were killed. Four months later two of Indian Prime Minister Indira Gandhi's elite Sikh bodyguards assassinated her. Her son and successor, Rajiv Gandhi, sought reconciliation with the Sikhs, and an accord was reached in 1985. However, violence has continued, including additional assaults on Amritsar and assassinations by Sikhs of government officials. Rajiv Gandhi himself was assassinated, although not by Sikhs.

Sikh worshippers wait to enter the Golden Temple at Amritsar.

In addition to the emergence of Sikh fundamentalism in India, more moderate forms of Sikhism have enjoyed a resurgence—some outside India. After 1947 many Sikhs migrated, a number to England and to the western United States and Canada. They formed communities, which in some areas have attracted converts to the healthy lifestyle of the religion.

Distinctive Teachings

Although Sikhism is an amalgamation of Hindu and Muslim teachings, it may be more accurate to say that it is a manifestation of the basic Indian worldview, expressing the Hindu *bhakti* viewpoint with certain Muslim (largely Sufi) adaptations. (If you are curious, look ahead to Chapter Thirteen. And once you have read Chapter Thirteen, look back at this discussion of Sikhism. A textbook need not be linear!)

Problem: Living Apart from God For Nanak, all humans are inherently good. Like a pearl in an oyster, we only await the shell to be opened so that the pearl may emerge. In other words, humans have a spiritual nature, which is pure and good and eternal. Unfortunately, humans choose to live in a way that distorts their spiritual nature. In short, we live apart from God and are stuck in the unending cycle of rebirth. Sikhs accept the idea of *karma* as an impersonal law that explains the entrapment of the soul. Because of *maya* (illusion), we are unaware that our true nature is hidden.

Cause: Egoism The cause of our entrapment is egoism, leading lives that revolve around the fulfillment of earthly desires. This again shows the influence of both Hinduism, with an emphasis on attachment to the self caused by desire, and Islam,

QUESTIONS OF HUMAN IDENTITY: WHY ARE WE HERE?

For Sikhism, obeying God (the True Name) is the highest purpose of human existence (Adi Granth, Japj; Macauliffe *1909:126*).

The condition of him who obeys God cannot be described.

Whoever tries to describe it shall afterward repent.

There is no paper, pen, or writer.

To describe the condition of him who obeys God.

So pure is his name—whoever obeys God knows the pleasure of it in his own heart.

with an emphasis on idolatry (worshipping earthly things rather than God). Egoism involves lust, anger, greed, attachment, and pride.

Reality: Penetrating the "Wall of Falsehood"
According to Sikh teaching, God created the material world by drawing the veil of *maya* around himself. Thus the world has reality, but it is a snare, a "wall of falsehood" by those seeking spiritual liberation. It must be penetrated by those who would see true Reality. The true Reality is One, like the Advaitan teaching, but true Reality is the personal God, as Islam and *bhakti* Hinduism hold.

End: Absorption Like other Indian religions, Sikhism envisions release from the cycle of rebirth as ultimate transformation. For Sikhs the image of liberation is absorption into God, blending our light with the eternal light. This reflects the influence of both Hindu devotionalism and the mystical teachings of Muslim Sufism. The bliss of absorption into God can be reached in this life, by those who follow the right path.

Means: Praise and Compassion Like many Hindu *bhakti* schools, Sikhism teaches that the way to reach

liberation is through devotion to the one true God and that in the current evil age the best way to show devotion is through repetition of the name of God. Praising God's name must not be mindless repetition. It must be a kind of meditation, which focuses and stills the mind and which takes root at the depths of one's being. The prayer of repetition of God's name is far better than pilgrimages to shrines, worshipping images, or practicing asceticism. Devout Sikhs rise before dawn, bathe, and recite the *japji*, a poem that expresses the essence of Sikh faith.

Each individual must learn to discipline himself or herself; there is no one formula for all to follow. The guidance of a guru is essential, however. Without a guide we will only wander aimlessly, unable to rein in our egos. The most important guru is the Granth Sahib, but human gurus are also important.

In addition to the repetition of God's name, Sikhs believe that lives of compassion are critical. Sikhism does not subscribe to the social barriers of the caste system, and men and women are treated equally. The symbol of Sikh compassion is the *langar*, the feast of the Sikh community. When a *langar* is held, it must be opened to everyone, especially those who are hungry. The Sikh places of gathering (known as *gurdwaras*, "gateways to the guru") are also to serve as way stations for travelers in need of a place to rest.

Sacred: The True Name According to Sikhism, God is one, supreme, the uncreated creator of all things, the all-knowing and all-compassionate. God's love is inexhaustible. God is the True, the ultimately Real. God is beyond our ability to describe or name. When speaking of God, Sikhs prefer "True Name," because all other, specific names are limiting. Sikhism is monotheistic, for the True Name is personal, both transcendent and immanent, the creator of all.

RESPONSES TO CONTEMPORARY ETHICAL ISSUES

Due to space limitations we will confine our discussion of responses to contemporary ethical issues in this section to Jainism.

At Sikh services worshippers show their reverence for the Guru Granth Sahib.

The Ecological Crisis

It could be argued that given the depth of the environmental crisis, the Jain approach to ecological responsibility offers the best hope for resolution. Jainism introduced the ideal of *ahimsa* into Indian culture and has always exemplified it most vividly. The ideal Jain lifestyle is one of respect for all life forms, even those that most people would find offensive. For example, in some Jain communities "rat hospitals" nurse creatures others consider nuisances at best, and serious health risks at worst. However, from a Jain perspective, rats have souls, too, and "non-injury" must be applied to them as well as to humans and other animals. Since plants have souls, human consumption of them should be eliminated or minimized. And, of course, eating animals of any type is out of the question.

Euthanasia

On the one hand, Jainism would seem to advocate euthanasia, since Mahavira and other heroes of the faith committed voluntary euthanasia as a way of overcoming their *karmic* build-up. However, when euthanasia is understood to mean the compassionate relieving of suffering of another, Jainism opposes euthanasia. Since suffering is caused by one's own *karma*, no one else can relieve the cause of suffering. Moreover, *ahimsa* forbids the taking of another life, even when that being is near death. Therefore, Jainism is opposed to the practice of euthanasia, but not to the practice of self-starvation if chosen by an enlightened being who is ready to rise to the top of the universe (Jain 1989: 83).

QUESTIONS ABOUT THE SACRED:
WHAT IS THE SACRED?

There Is But One God, Whose Name Is True

The sacred, according to Sikh teaching, is the personal God, known as True Name, who transcends all particular names and descriptions. This passage from the japji, *which Sikhs silently repeat each morning, begins with the Mul (root) Mantra (Adi Granth, Japji; Macauliffe 1909, vol. 1: 195–96).*

There is but one God whose name is true, the Creator, devoid of fear and enmity, immortal, unborn, self-existent; by the favour of the Guru.

Repeat His Name

The True One was in the beginning;
The True One was in the primal age.
The True One is now also, O Nanak;
The True One also shall be.
By thinking I cannot obtain a conception of Him, even though I think hundreds of thousands of times.

Even though it be silent and keep my attention firmly fixed on Him, I cannot preserve silence.
The hunger of the hungry for God subsideth not though they obtain the load of the worlds.
If man should have thousands of devices, even one would not assist him in obtaining God.
How shall man become true before God?
How shall the veil of falsehood rent?
By walking, O Nanak, according to the will of the commander as preordained. . . .

Economic Justice

The Jain virtue of *aparigraha* (non-attachment) is particularly relevant to a discussion of economics and social justice. According to this virtue, "one should set a limit to one's own needs and whatever surplus one may accumulate beyond these needs should be disposed of through charities" (Jain 1989: 80). It thus provides for the equitable distribution of wealth without the necessity of government intervention or revolutionary struggle on the part of the dispossessed. Jains view it as the only peaceful way the growing gulf between the rich and the poor can be bridged.

Gender Roles and the Status of Women

The equal status of men and women has been implemented more fully in Jainism than in Theravada Buddhism. In the early religious order of the founder, Mahavira, women outnumbered men. In the legends of Jainism, women play central and important roles. Throughout Jain history, women have been recognized for their learning and contributions in all fields.

CHAPTER SUMMARY

Jainism is an ascetic religion through which members seek to liberate their souls from attachment to matter. We first studied the life of the principal founder, Mahavira. We then discussed the basic branches within Jainism, Jain scriptures (the *Agamas*), the status of Jainism today, and the distinctive teachings of Jainism.

We concluded this chapter with an analysis of Sikhism, which began in India in the fifteenth century C.E. It was an attempt to synthesize Hinduism and

Islam. Unfortunately, the early pacifism turned to militancy and Sikhs sought to defend their community from persecution. The Sikh scripture, known as Guru Granth Sahib, replaced human gurus as the center of Sikhism. In modern India, Sikhs have struggled to maintain autonomy in their Punjabi homeland, sometimes with violent consequences.

We suggested to readers that they look briefly at the discussion of Islam in Chapter Thirteen in order to understand more fully Sikh teaching, which draws on both devotional Hinduism and Islam (especially its mystical branch).

We then surveyed Jain responses to some contemporary ethical issues.

QUESTIONS FOR DISCUSSION AND REFLECTION

1. Many Jains are quite successful business leaders. What in their religion accounts for this tendency to prosper? What problems might success raise for Jains?
2. Some Jains have established hospitals for rats. Discuss what their reasoning for doing this might be. Does it make sense to you?
3. Discuss and respond to the Jain view of the relativity of human knowledge. Would other religious persons benefit from adopting this perspective?
4. Is the extreme Jain teaching of *ahimsa* the "strong medicine" needed to address the ecological crisis? How could this principle be adapted by people of other religions?
5. Nanak tried to reconcile Hinduism and Islam. Did the creation of the separate religion of Sikhism mean he succeeded or failed?
6. Do Sikhs deserve a land of their own? Why or why not? What do you think should be done to end the hostility and violence between Sikh and Hindu radicals?

SOURCES AND SUGGESTIONS FOR FURTHER STUDY

Jainism

CHAPPLE, CHRISTOPHER KEY, 1993 *Nonviolence to Animals, Earth and Self in Asian Traditions.* Albany: State University of New York Press.

CHITRABHANU, GURUDEV SHREE, 1980 *Twelve Facets of Reality: The Jain Path to Freedom.* New York: Dodd, Mead, and Co.

JACOBI, HERMANN, TRANS., 1884 *Gania Sutras,* Part I. *The Sacred Books of the East,* ed. F.M. Mueller, vol. 22. Oxford: Clarendon Press.

    1897 *Gaina Sutras,* Part II. *The Sacred Books of the East,* ed. F.M. Mueller, vol. 45. Oxford: Clarendon Press.

JAIN, PREM SUMAN, 1989 "The Ethics of Jainism," in *World Religions and Global Ethics,* ed. S. Cromwell Crawford (New York: Paragon House), 65–88.

JAINI, PADMANABH S. 1979 *The Jaina Path of Purification.* Berkeley: University of California Press.

Sikhism

COLE, W. OWEN, AND PIARA SINGH SAMBHI, 1978 *The Sikhs: Their Religious Beliefs and Practices.* London: Routledge and Kegan Paul.

MACAULIFFE, M.A., 1909 *The Sikh Religion: Its Gurus, Sacred Writings and Authors,* 6 vols. Oxford: Oxford University Press.

McLEOD, W.H., 1989 *The Sikhs.* New York: Columbia University Press.

SINGH, HARBANS, 1964 *The Heritage of the Sikhs.* New York: Asia Publishing House.

SECTION IV

Religions of East Asia

Commentators have already labelled the next hundred years the "Pacific Century." The fastest-growing economic powers in the world are on the Pacific Rim, among the nations of East Asia—Japan, China, and Korea. Study of East Asian languages and cultures has rapidly expanded in American and European colleges and universities, as students prepare themselves for international careers oriented across the Pacific rather than the Atlantic.

Anyone seeking to understand East Asia ignores at his or her peril the religions that have developed in these cultures. The values and customs of China, Japan, and Korea are rooted in the religions we will study in Chapters Eight and Nine—Taoism, Confucianism, Shinto, and Mahayana Buddhism. We will begin our study in Chapter Eight with a general orientation to the region and a brief survey of the history of China and the traditional Chinese worldview. We will then examine the stages of development, sacred writings, basic teachings, and responses to contemporary ethical issues of the religions of Taoism and Confucianism. In Chapter Nine we will provide an overview of the history of Japan and Korea and the traditional Japanese worldview, then give an analysis of the various schools of Mahayana Buddhism influential in Japan and Korea today and the native religion of Japan, known as Shinto.

CHAPTER 8

Taoism: The Way of Nature and Confucianism: The Way of Virtue

Hami

Ximing

PEOP

Darlag

REPU

O

Markam

CHI

Xichang

Kunming

Ha

LAOS

Vientiane

Khon Kaen

THAILAND

Bangkok

Phnom Per

AN ORIENTATION TO EAST ASIA

The Lands and Peoples

The five independent nations in modern East Asia are China, Japan, North and South Korea, and Taiwan (see Figure 8–1). China covers 90 percent of the land and about 85 percent of East Asia's population of about 1.5 billion people. Japan is a series of islands to the east of China. Korea is on a peninsula located between China and Japan. Taiwan is a small island nation south of Japan, just off the Chinese mainland. East Asia is the most crowded region in the world, with a population density almost five times the world average.

In addition to its geographic and population dominance, China has exercised great cultural influence over the entire area. For example, the Confucian ethics developed in China plays an exceedingly important role in the everyday life of people throughout East Asia. The Confucian emphasis on proper decorum and obedience to authority are hallmarks of East Asian society.

Politically, China and North Korea are among the handful of countries still dominated by Communist regimes. Since the end of World War II, Japan has been a parliamentary democracy. Taiwan is largely ruled by Chinese who left the mainland when the Communists took control in 1949. South Korea has a constitutional form of government and democratically elected leaders, but opponents have claimed systematic abuse of human rights by the regime. Efforts to unify Korea after World War II failed, leading to an armed conflict in the early 1950s that drew in the United States (under the flag of the United Nations) and many other countries.

Economically, China and North Korea still have the central planning characteristic of a Communist state, but China has allowed a great deal of free enterprise in recent years. Japan's industrial and trade success has made it a world economic superpower and brought its people one of the highest standards of living in the world. South Korea and Taiwan have also adopted the capitalist system, which has brought significant economic growth, although many workers complain of low wages and poor working conditions.

A Brief History of China

The history of East Asia is long and complex, and largely unknown to most in the West. Full treatment is far beyond the scope of this work. However, to provide a framework for the study of the religions of East Asia, let us survey at least superficially the history of China in this chapter. In the next chapter we will give a brief overview of the history of Japan and Korea.

The Shang dynasty emerged in central China about 1750 B.C.E. During the Shang dynasty a highly organized society developed the Chinese form of writing still in use.

The next dynasty was the Chou (ca. 1122–222 B.C.E.), begun when the Chou people of western China gained control. Their power centered in the north and west, with semi-independent states in the east. In the late Chou period (a time often called the Warring States Period) these states fought one another continuously, creating a great deal of political and social chaos. This was the context for the emergence of some of the great schools of Chinese thought, including Confucianism and Taoism.

The shortlived Ch'in dynasty (221–206 B.C.E.) brought the first strong central government to China. Before this dynasty collapsed, its rulers had begun work on the 4,000-mile Great Wall of China.

During the Han dynasty (202 B.C.E.–220 C.E.) Confucianism became the foundation for the government and educational system. Chinese influence began to spread into other countries, and the first trade with Europe occurred. Late in the Han dynasty Indian missionaries brought Buddhism to China.

With the breakup of the Han dynasty China split into three competing kingdoms, and a series of short dynasties took power in the north and south. Buddhism spread, with monasteries established through the land. This is the period during which the various Chinese schools of philosophical Buddhism originated.

The next major dynasty, the Tang (618–907), brought prosperity to China. The capital, Ch'ang-an (now Sian), was a great cultural center. Chinese schools of Buddhism such as Ch'an (the Meditation

FIGURE 8–1

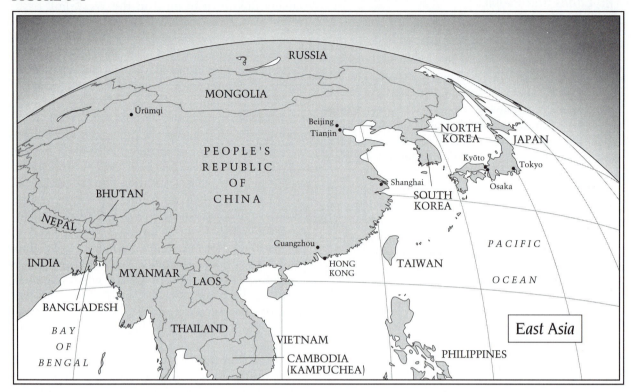

School) and Ching-t'u (the Pure Land School) developed and gained influence. However, Confucianism enjoyed a revival during the ninth century.

During the Sung Dynasty (907–1279) Confucian-educated civil servants dominated the government. The Neo-Confucian school, combining Confucian ethics with Buddhist and Taoist philosophy, received state endorsement.

During the thirteenth century Mongol invaders swept into China from the north. The Mongol leader Kublai Khan established the Yuan dynasty (1279–1368), the period during which the Italian trader and explorer Marco Polo (ca. 1254–1324) reached China.

The Ming dynasty (1368–1644 brought stability and prosperity, with Chinese influence spreading throughout East Asia. Viewing themselves as culturally superior, Ming leaders rebuffed European trade efforts and Christian missionaries.

The Ch'ing dynasty (1644–1911) brought China under the rule of Manchuria. The island of Taiwan came under Chinese control in 1683. A period of order and wealth extended until rapid population growth caused decline in the late eighteenth and nineteenth centuries. In the 1800s China began to export massive amounts of tea and silk to Europe, but still sought to limit European influence. The Opium War (1839–1842) between China and Great Britain, caused by Chinese resistance to the smuggling of opium into China, ended in a British victory. The treaty of Nan-ching gave Hong Kong to Great Britain, and opened some Chinese ports to the British. Special privileges were soon secured by other European powers and the United States. (A treaty restoring Hong Kong to China will soon take effect.)

China was weakened by the Taiping Rebellion (1851–1864) and a war with Japan (1894–1895). In the face of growing Western political, economic, and religious influence, a secret Chinese society (known as the Boxers by Westerners) led a rebellion in 1900.

A nationalist movement led by a Western-educated physician, Sun Yat-sen, mounted a successful revolution that established a republic. The last emperor of China, a 6-year-old boy, surrendered the throne in 1912. A period of struggle ensued. Chiang Kai-shek succeeded Sun Yat-sen as head of the Nationalist Party in 1925 and united China in 1928.

The Japanese conquest of China began in 1931, when Manchuria was seized. By 1938 the Japanese controlled most of China. When World War II ended in 1945, a civil war broke out between the Nationalists and Communists (who had already begun an insurgency), led by Mao Tse-tung.

The victorious Communists established the People's Republic of China in 1949, and the Nationalists fled to Taiwan. Religions were repressed by the Communists, especially after the Cultural Revolution of 1966. Since the death of Mao in 1976, greater freedom has been allowed religious groups, but government control continues. Pressure for more political freedom increased as China opened its markets and increased contact with the West. However, a student-led democracy movement was suppressed in 1989 and its leaders executed or jailed.

The Traditional Worldview and Indigenous Religion of China

The traditional worldview of China forms the basis for popular, indigenous Chinese religion still widely practiced in Taiwan and other Chinese communities (although it has largely disappeared in the People's Republic as a result of Communist suppression). In addition, elements of this worldview had an important influence on the classical Chinese and Japanese religions, as we shall see. We will blend at this point a discussion of the traditional Chinese worldview with a discussion of the major characteristics of indigenous (or popular, as it is sometimes called) Chinese religion.

Problem: Disharmony If there is a key word in the traditional Chinese worldview, which influenced the rest of East Asia, it must surely be *harmony*. The perception of an underlying harmony that humans

The public expression of respect for one's elders or superiors is a basic value in East Asian societies.

The yin/yang *symbol manifests the opposite, but complementary forces in the cosmos. The* yin *(the light side) is passive, soft, and feminine, while the* yang *(the dark side) is active, hard, and masculine.*

For example, a dry stick would seem clearly *yin,* since it is passive. However, once ignited the *yang* qualities of the stick become evident.

Humans also are a manifestation of these two energy forces. Men are predominantly *yang,* whereas women are mostly *yin.* However, men have *yin* qualities and women *yang,* and a healthy person seeks to maintain a balance between them. During one period of a person's life the *yin* force may be prominent, while the *yang* recedes, or vice versa. For example, a person may ordinarily have a dominant *yin,* and thus be a quiet, reserved person, but at times of arousal the *yang* takes precedence.

In the indigenous Chinese religion, which predates the great philosophies, the spirits that are present everywhere are either the earthly *yin (shen)* spirits or heavenly *yang (kwei)* spirits. Each person has both spirits. At death the *shen* soul (*hun*) becomes an ancestral spirit, while the *kwei* soul (*p'o*) merges with the ground when the body dissolves.

In nature the five basic elements are either *yang* or *yin.* Wood and fire are *yang,* while metal and water are *yin.* Earth belongs to both. The interaction of *yin* and *yang* (and the five elements) can be seen in the changing seasons. *Yin* is dominant in winter, gradually to be replaced, as spring and summer come, by *yang.* As the ripened fruit falls to the ground, so the *yang* gives way to *yin,* and as new life emerges from the cold ground *yang* comes to prominence again.

The symbol for *yin* and *yang* together is a circle, cut in half by a curving line. One side of the circle is dark, with a white spot, while the other is white, with a dark spot. The curving line symbolizes the dynamic interaction between the two forces within all reality (represented by the circle). The two dots indicate that the *yin* is present in the *yang,* and vice versa.

Traditionally, wisdom in China is associated with understanding and conforming with the *yin* and *yang* forces in their interaction. There is a strong sense that there is a right (auspicious) time for actions and a right place to build structures, which are in proper harmony with the interacting forces. The alternation between growth and decline, waxing and waning of the moon, and success and failure all reflect the cosmic interaction.

End: Harmony in this Life Harmony is, in the Chinese worldview, primarily a this-wordly phenomenon. The ideal of families living in harmony, and a society ruled and inhabited by virtuous persons living harmoniously, is an important part of the "goal" in popular Chinese religions and the others as well. Although life beyond death is a facet of this worldview, the emphasis is placed on the desired transformation occurring within life on earth. In indigenous Chinese religion, as in popular religions of other cultures, the specific goals are health, a full lifespan, prosperity, harmony within the family, continuity of the family lineage, and protection from natural and human disasters.

Means: Discerning and Living in Harmony
Popular Chinese religious practices are not the domain of one social class or geographic setting. They may be found in both villages and cities, observed by educated and uneducated alike. The means of realizing harmony, at the level of popular religion, are ancestor veneration; the maintenance of worship of gods at temples, shrines, and family altars; and divination. First we will briefly introduce, however, the important concepts of *te* ("virtue") and *hsiao* (filial piety).

Te (pronounced "day") means inherent power or virtue. In a sense, it is the principle that allows or creates harmonious human life. Where virtue is valued, there is harmony; where it is absent, there is chaos. Although Confucianism and Taoism developed quite different teachings about virtue, as we shall see, they both focus on the question of how to lead virtuous lives, and that concern is deeply imbued in the Chinese way of life.

Although the specific virtue of *filial piety* (*hsiao*) rose to prominence as one of the principal Confucian virtues, it is a principle deeply instilled in China as well as other East Asian cultures. Specifically, filial piety refers to the loyalty shown by a son to his father. More generally, it is the respect and reverence anyone in an inferior social position shows for superiors. It is at the root of the Asian respect for authority that even the most casual observer in China, Japan, Korea, or Taiwan notices at once. It is principally seen at the family level, but has at times been transferred or extended to the emperor, the nation, a political party, or, in modern Japan especially, the corporation. It should be noted that even as juniors are to show loyalty to elders, elders are to treat their juniors with courtesy and concern.

Reverence to elders extends to ancestors, who play an exceedingly important role in the worldview of the cultures of East Asia. Traditionally, the ancestors have been considered spirits who continue to play an important role in family life. If proper respect is shown to them, they will assist the family. If veneration is not shown to the ancestors, their displeasure can bring hardship.

Many of the popular deities of indigenous Chinese religion are particularly important ances-
tors who have been accorded the status of gods. For example, the deity *Ma-tsu*, goddess of fishermen, was at first the soul of a young girl who died before her marriage. Other deities were gods and goddesses associated with natural elements such as the soil. Proper worship of these deities determined whether there would be good crops and fertility in general. In each location a mound of earth represented the spirit of the soil (*she*). In addition, each region, city, village, and family had its own particular gods. We will have more to say about other popular deities below under the category of the sacred in the indigenous Chinese worldview and when we discuss ritual Taoism, which incorporated many of the popular Chinese deities into its pantheon. What we must note is that proper worship of these deities (and other ancestral spirits) through the periodic offering of incense and food in temples, shrines, and home altars is an important facet of popular Chinese religion.

Divination is the "deciphering" of reality in order to determine the significance of present or future events. In China divination was practiced from the earliest times. At first diviners read cracks on heated bones and tortoise shells. Over time the cracks were identified with the *yin* and *yang* forces: an unbroken line (—) with the *yang*, and a broken line (— —) with the *yin*. Lines may be arranged in triads eight different ways to form the "eight trigrams." The trigrams may be paired to yield sixty-four possible hexagrams. These patterns were interpreted in the classic manual of interpretation for Chinese divination, the *I Ching* ("Book of Changes"). Diviners drop sticks on the ground to form the trigrams (or hexagrams), and then, using the *I Ching,* interpret their significance in relation to the particular concern being addressed. Use of the *I Ching* has become popular in the West, and the manual and instructions for its use are available in many bookstores. Other forms of divination have developed in China, including geomancy (reading the signs found in the earth) and palmistry.

Sacred: A Fundamental Harmony According to the Chinese worldview, and throughout East Asia, there is a strong perception of an underlying order in the cosmos as a whole, in nature, and in human societies. What accounts for that order? Different religions in East Asia speak of this fundamental harmony in distinct ways at different times. However, no East Asian religion is immune from the influence of this perception of a harmony that is the underlying reality all must recognize. Taoists speak of the fundamental harmony as the mystical Tao; early Confucians saw the harmony manifest in the well-ordered , smoothly functioning society; devotees of the various schools of Mahayana Buddhism identified a central cosmic reality; Neo-Confucians talked of the rational principle at the heart of things; even supporters of the adapted Marxist ideology of Mao Tse-tung have had their own view of the perpetual revolution that orders life; and, in Japan, practitioners of Shinto have sought to live in harmony with the multitude of *kami*.

Early in Chinese history emerged two concepts concerning the spiritual world that have had a strong influence on the understanding of government in China. During the Shang dynasty a deity who went by the name of *Shang Ti* ("Ruler on High") became the object of worship. He was thought to determine when and if crops would grow and whether human projects would be successful. The emperor's diviners consulted him, for example, to find out when to go to war or sue for peace. Like the Indian Vedic deity *Varuna* (see Chapter Five), *Shang Ti* was the guarantor of the moral order. He ruled over a celestial hierarchy, modelled after the government bureaucracy, with deities in charge of the "ministries" of Thunder, Epidemics, Fire, etc. *Shang Ti* evolved into the Jade Emperor, the central deity in popular Chinese religion to this day.

During the Chou dynasty, a more impersonal designation for the concept of a heavenly power developed—*T'ien* (Heaven). Until the last emperor left the Chinese throne in 1912, the emperor was known as the Son of Heaven. He conducted special ceremonies intended to maintain the harmony between Earth and Heaven.

According to the traditional Chinese world-view, rulers maintain power only as long as they retain the *mandate of heaven.* First expressed in the twelfth century B.C.E., this concept has influenced the attitude toward government in China ever since, especially during periods of imperial rule. It holds that when rulers fail to exercise their responsibility to maintain harmony in society through the promotion of virtue, they lose their right to govern, and not only is a revolution in order, it is inevitable. The concept places a heavy burden on any government to create a strong sense of moral order in the society, which the people can recognize and endorse. It also lends support to the view that revolutions are a necessary ingredient in the cosmic order. This concept was invoked by the most recent Chinese revolutionaries, the Communists under Mao Tse-tung.

TAOISM: THE WAY OF NATURE

The name "Taoism" is ambiguous. It may refer to the philosophical tradition traced to the legendary sage Lao Tzu and first expressed in the collection of poems called the *Tao-te-ching* ("The Classic of the Way and Its Power"). Since the Han dynasty this tradition has been called *Tao-chia* ("the philosophy of the *Tao*"). This is the Taoism most widely known in the West today, mostly because of widespread exposure to translations of the *Tao-te-ching.* Philosophical Taoism has faded as a distinct movement in East Asia, but it did have an influence on the Meditation School of Buddhism (Zen), which continues to exercise considerable influence in Japan. It also had a profound influence on the arts and literature in both China and Japan.

However, the Taoism as currently practiced in Taiwan and other Chinese communities (but still largely dormant in the People's Republic) is more closely associated with a tradition known as *Tao-chiao* ("the teaching of the *Tao*"). Specifically, *Tao-chiao* involves the worship of deities and the propitiation of spirits through rituals carried out by hereditary Taoist priests. It is one facet of a popular religious movement that, as we shall now see, evolved from philosophical Taoism, transforming some of its basic teachings.

In our presentation of Taoism we will trace its development from a mystical philosophy of life that did not focus on gods and had no use for rituals, to a popular religious system with a pantheon of deities and a plethora of rituals.

Stages of Development and Sacred Texts

***The Legendary* Lao Tzu**   The legendary founder of philosophical Taoism is known to tradition as *Lao Tzu* ("the Old Master"). Some interpreters question if a man called Lao Tzu ever existed as a historical person; others see a real person behind the legends. A biography from the second century B.C.E. says Lao Tzu was born in 604 B.C.E. According to this biography, Lao Tzu was highly educated and took a government post. However, he left his position as an archivist because he came to the realization that governments with their laws and bureaucracies distort the simplicity by which humans should live. He withdrew from society and resolved to live a solitary life. He was besieged by visitors (including Confucius, according to the legend) and decided to leave society altogether. According to tradition, as he travelled by, the gatekeeper at the pass into the western regions persuaded him to write down his philosophy of life. In short, enigmatic poems he wrote a treatise on how to live, calling it the *Tao-te-ching*. The earliest name for the *Tao-te-ching* was *Lao Tzu*, so it is entirely possible that the legend of the "Old Master" arose to provide a specific author for this ancient book.

***The* Tao-te-ching**   Regardless of who wrote this work, the *Tao-te-ching* stands alongside works such as the *Bhagavad-Gita* of India as one of the great classics of religious literature. Many contemporary interpreters think that it was actually written sometime between 350 and 275 B.C.E. during the latter days of the Warring States Period. Like other literary classics, however, it is timeless in its basic meaning.

The *Tao-te-ching* is a short work, with eighty-one brief chapters including only about 5,500

The legendary Lao Tzu *is portrayed riding into the mountains after composing the poems of the* Tao-te-ching. *Source: The Mansell Collection.*

words (this chapter, by comparison, has nearly 18,000 words!). The short, enigmatic poems that constitute its chapters have been the subject of hundreds of commentaries and translations. The *Tao-te-ching* has become the most widely known Chinese writing. It may have been written originally as a political work, a manual to instruct those who would aspire to the art of governing, but like all great literary works it has various levels of meaning.

Today the basic political theme of the *Tao-te-ching* would be called libertarian in the West, for its teaching is that "the state that governs best governs least." Politically, it must be considered a failure. No Chinese government, or probably any other in history, has made a serious attempt to implement on a large scale its philosophy of passive government. Its lasting impact has been at other levels. The *Tao-te-ching's* teaching of natural, simple living has inspired millions of readers to examine their own lifestyles and to let go of that which has been forcing them into uncomfortable, even destructive patterns. It has also served to inspire many spiritually with its teaching of that mystical, harmonious process which it envisions as true reality.

Since the *Tao-te-chign* is the basis for Taoist philosophy, we will discuss its teachings more fully in the next section.

Chuang Tz   Another important Taoist philosopher was a teacher in the fourth century B.C.E. named *Chuang Tzu* ("Master Chuang"), legendary author of a work that goes by the same name.

The *Chaung Tzu,* second in importance in Taoism only to the *Tao-te-ching,* argues against other philosophical schools popular at the time to show that the *Tao* cannot be understood rationally and that one must let go of dependence on knowledge and words in order to live harmoniously. It distinguishes between the *Tao* and the words used to describe the *Tao,* saying that the two belong to different orders of understanding just as footprints differ from the shoes that make them. We must, the *Chuang Tzu* says, give up all thoughts about the *Tao* in order to experience oneness with the *Tao.*

The *Chuang Tzu* also argues that there is an original, natural equality of all things, which humans lose sight of as they accumulate knowledge and build civilizations. The *Chuang Tzu* is much less political than the *Tao-te-ching,* emphasizing instead a natural, spiritual freedom to which we must seek to return.

Most scholars today think that the principal sections of the *Chuang Tzu* were written about the same time as the *Tao-te-ching.* The two philosophical traditions represented by these two works were combined in the third century C.E. into the movement that became known as "philosophical" Taoism.

The Development of Taoist Rituals and Magical Practices   In speaking of the eternal *Tao,* sections of both the *Tao-te-ching* and *Chuang-Tzu* seem to suggest that whoever is in harmony with the *Tao* lives forever. This intimation of immortality in the classic texts and the popular concern for health, happiness, and long life became the basis for a new branch of Taoism, often called in the West "religious" or "magical" Taoism. By the second century C.E. there was an organized Taoist "religious" movement, focusing on the pursuit of immortality and well-being; it continues today. The facet of this movement dealing with rituals of cosmic renewal carried out to renew the community's relationship with deities and spirits is called *Tao-chiao.*

The cosmological background for this movement is the teaching (common to many religions) that humans are a microcosm, reflecting in their natures the structure of the cosmos as a whole. According to philosophical Taoism, the unmanifest *Tao* is the source of all reality; the manifest reality of this world, including humanity, is the result of the interaction between the *yin* and *yang* forces. "Magical" Taoism emphasizes the teaching that the "breath" (called the *ch'i*) of the *Tao* creates the *yin/yang* dynamic. However, when *ch'i* divides into *yin* and *yang,* death and dissolution enter into reality, because these forces tend to become imbalanced. In humans this results in the deterioration of the body and eventually death. If the creative balance can be restored, then *ch'i* will not dissipate and humans can avoid death and decay. Whoever attains the perfect balance becomes a *hsien* (immortal being). The quest for immortality can be documented in China by the third century B.C.E.

In a village in modern China, Taoist priests make offerings.

A variety of paths to immortality developed. One was alchemy, the search for some elixir that could be taken to preserve the vital force. Another was a hygienic and dietary regime, in which foods with energies thought to correspond to the five basic elements were eaten, and foods that caused the vital essence to dissipate were avoided. Breath control techniques and physical exercises (the basis of the popular exercise regime *tai-ch'i*) also developed as a means to preserve the *ch'i*. Sexual practices (similar to Indian *tantrism*) involving the suppression of orgasm were thought to contribute to maintenance of the original creative balance. Finally, living a life of virtue was thought to be essential to becoming an "immortal."

In addition to becoming a *hsien*, this branch of Taoism also responded to the popular desire for assistance with confronting the dilemmas of everyday living. Thus arose a hereditary priesthood, which could be called upon to conduct rituals to aid people in all sorts of circumstances.

The second-century Taoist movements, which developed to assist individuals in the pursuit of immortality, had a political dimension. They envisioned the coming of a new age of the *Tao,* and some of the Taoist communities resorted to military means to achieve it. Various Taoist schools, with numerous individual communities, organized and competed with one another for influence.

Associated with this branch of Taoism is an elaborate array of hierarchically arranged spiritual beings, organized on the bureaucratic model of the Han dynasty. Highest is the unmanifest Tao; next, the primordial chaos or breath (*ch'i*); followed by the Three Officials (or Three Heavenly Worthies). These were the Jade Emperor, Lao Tzu, and the Marshal of supernatural beings. Temples and shrines, in which Taoist priests conducted rituals to honor these deities and seek their blessing, sprang up all over China. Below them are the various divine ministries, inhabiting nine heavens. Still lower are the spirits of demons, humans, ancestors, and animals. The popular practice of Taoism approached a type of animism in which everything was thought to be inhabited by spirits who must be properly respected. Some of the

Discovering the harmony in the everyday, reflected in this Shanghai craftsman's work, is a basic Taoist principle.

and simple life (8), seeing both life and death as a part of the eternal *Tao* (16, 33). To lead this life is to live the ideal life, that of the Sage (22, 33, 47). In one sense, then, the goal of Taoism is at both an individual and a communal level, for if those who are leaders practice the life of natural goodness, then society will be in harmony with the *Tao*.

The notion of a goal is ironic in Taoism, for the goal is to realize the natural, cosmic process that is already present. "Goal" implies striving, and that is the problem we must overcome. Therefore, in a sense, the real goal in Taoist philosophy is to stop having a goal! Does that make sense to you? What are the risks and benefits in such an approach to life?

Means: Action without Assertion   What is the simple life through which one experiences harmony with the *Tao*? The term *wu wei* ("inaction" or "non-purposiveness") expresses it most clearly. To practice *wu wei* is to act without asserting oneself (2, 47). On the one hand, *wu wei* means to have no

ambitions, no desire for fame or power, no need to influence or dominate others. It is to be not what others think you should be, but to simply "be yourself" in the most basic and natural sense. Such a person may seem weak-willed, passive, even stupid to those who live by desire and striving. However, such a person "achieves without achieving." How can that be? By living spontaneously, the person is allowing the *Tao* to come to its true expression, and "virtue" (*te*) will be natural rather than contrived (18, 38). Rather than seeking to "do good" for others, goodness will naturally emanate from the person in non-manipulative acts of kindness. Others will be positively influenced not by an *effort* to influence them, but by the power of the *Tao* being actualized. As we will see, this attitude toward the "virtuous life" is much different than that taught by Confucian ethicists. Do you think such an approach to "virtue" has merit, or is it (in your view) hopelessly naive?

In governments the best course is non-interference (60). In education it is best not to seek

QUESTIONS OF HUMAN DESTINY: WHAT HAPPENS AFTER DEATH?

Chuang Tzu on Birth and Death

The Taoist philosopher Chuang Tzu here describes the life process and how birth and death fit into it (Chuang Tzu 23; Legge 1891²: 85).

He comes forth, but from no root; he re-enters, but by no aperture. He has a real existence, but it has nothing to do with place; he has continuance, but it has nothing to do with beginning or end. He has a real existence, but it has nothing to do with place, such as his relation to space; he has continuance, but it has nothing to do with beginning or end, such as his relation to time; he has life: he has death; he comes forth; he enters; but we do not see his form;—all this is what he is called the door of Heaven. The door of Heaven is Non-Existence. All things come from non-existence. The (first) existences could not bring themselves into existence; they must have come from non-existence. And non-existence is just the same as non-existing. Herein is the secret of the sages.

knowledge actively, but to be passively open and receptive (47). You cannot learn what is truly important from those who would presume to have the knowledge to teach you (19). Far better than knowing the world outside is knowing who you truly are (72, 33). Do you agree? If so, why are you reading this book? Are you learning anything?

To sum it all up, "in letting go, it all gets done" (48).

***Sacred: The Nameless and Eternal* Tao** We have spoken frequently already of the *Tao* ("Way"), but we have avoided trying to explain what the *Tao* means. That is because the *Tao* that can be named is *not* the *Tao* (1).

We should first clarify what the *Tao* is not. The *Tao* is not God, at least in any personal sense (4, 60). The *Tao* is not a being of any sort.

The best we can do is mention the metaphors the *Tao-te-ching* uses to try to point us toward the *Tao*. One of the most frequent images is the flow of water (78). Like a stream, the *Tao* is in constant motion, and over time wears down all that opposes it. Reality itself is the flow of the *Tao*, and those who are "truly real" are those who are going with that flow.

Feminine images point us toward the *Tao*. The *Tao* is the Mother, the source of life (1, 25). The *Tao* is the Womb of all reality. The *Tao* is also like a valley (6), for it is the emptiness of the valley that

QUESTIONS OF MORALITY: WHAT IS RIGHT LIVING?

Planted in the *Tao*

Philosophical Taoism rejected the idea of trying to conform oneself to moral principles or virtues. Our only obligation is to be rooted in the Tao. *Then a moral life will naturally follow, as is suggested in Chapter 54 of the* Tao-te-ching *(Legge 1891¹: 97–98)*

> What (Tao's) skilful planter plants
> Can never be uptorn;
> What his skilful arms enfold,
> From him can ne'er be borne.
> Sons shall bring in lengthening line,
> Sacrifices to his shrine.
>
> Tao when nursed within one's self,
> His vigour will make true;
> And where the family it rules
> What riches will accrue!
> The neighborhood where it prevails
> In thriving will abound;
> And when 'tis seen throughout the state,
> Good fortune will be found.
> Employ it the kingdom o'er,
> And men thrive all around.

COSMIC QUESTIONS: WHAT IS THE DESTINY OF THE COSMOS?

All Things End in the *Tao*

According to the Tao-te-ching *(Chapter 32), the end of all reality is the* Tao. *(Legge 1891[1]:75).*

The relation of the *Tao* to all the world is like that of the great rivers and seas to the streams from the valleys.

gives it reality. Stated more philosophically, the *Tao* is the "non-being" from which all "being" comes (40, 25), yet the *Tao* is also everything that is! The *Tao* is also like a block of wood, from which the carved images emerges, the course of creativity (15, 32), the Void (11), or a deep pool (4).

None of these *are* the *Tao*, for the *Tao* cannot be named. If one is intent on defining the *Tao*, then perhaps the following will serve that purpose: the cosmic mode of action through which non-being becomes being and being reverts to non-being. But, remember, those who talk do not know!

CONFUCIANISM: THE WAY OF VIRTUE

Some interpreters suggest, somewhat whimsically but with a grain of truth, that if philosophical Taoism is the *yin* of East Asia, then Confucianism is the *yang*. After your study of both, consider whether this is an apt description.

While Confucianism, like "religious" Taoism, officially "died" in China, and is preserved institutionally only in pockets outside the Chinese mainland, its influence on East Asian culture is difficult to overemphasize. Many would attribute the miraculous postwar recovery of Japan, Korea, and Taiwan (not to mention the resurgence of China) to an innate commitment to Confucian ideals. Others,

however, would suggest that commitment to Confucian virtues results in a social stagnation that is keeping East Asia from truly entering the modern world.

Stages of Development and Sacred Texts

Founder: Master K'ung (Confucius)   As was the case in other great movements, the followers of the man known in the West as Confucius created biographies that blended actual history with legend. Nevertheless, we can reconstruct the basic aspects of his life with some confidence.

Confucius was born in the ancient feudal state of Lu, now the area known as Shantung, in about 551 B.C.E. The name Confucius is a Latinized version of *K'ung fu-tzu*, which means "Great Master K'ung." K'ung was his family name; his given

QUESTIONS ABOUT THE SACRED: WHAT IS THE SACRED?

The Eternal *Tao*

The Taoist classic, the Tao-te-ching, *begins with an enigmatic poem (Chapter 1) about the mysterious* Tao *(Legge 1891[1]: 47–48).*

The Tao *that can be trodden is not the enduring and unchanging* Tao.
The name that can be named is not the enduring and unchanging name.
Having no name, it is the Originator of heaven and earth; having a name, it is the Mother of all things.
Always without desire we must be found,
If its deep mystery we would sound;
But if desire always within us be,
Its outer fringe is all that we shall see.
Under these two aspects, it is really the same;
but as development takes place, it receives the different names.
Together we call them the Mystery.
Where Mystery is the deepest is the gate of all that is subtle and wonderful.

name was Ch'iu. Shortly after his birth, his father died, and his mother had to sacrifice to provide him with an education, helping to instill in him the value of learning. As a young man, Confucius had several minor government posts in the state of Lu. At about the age of 50 he was appointed to a high office in the administration of the Duke of Lu. However, his policies were not adopted and he resigned or was forced out of office. He was about 55 when he began a thirteen-year period of wandering from state to state, teaching a program of political and social reform. At age 67 he returned to Lu and spent the rest of his life teaching, and (according to tradition) editing the Confucian classics. When he died, in about 479 B.C.E., he was discouraged at his failure to have more influence on government. However, he left a band of followers committed to his teaching.

The Analects and Other Texts The *Analects* (*Lun Yu*) of Confucius are the reputed sayings and conversations of Confucius. They were compiled after the death of Confucius over a long period of time, in various layers. However, the major Confucian teachings are present in the Analects, making them an important source for the ideas of Confucius himself and his early disciples. The Analects became the principal cornerstone of the Chinese educational system and the examination system for government officials. It has also continued to serve as an inspiration for personal reflection, much as the *Bhagavad-Gita* has in India.

The Analects are one of the Four Books, which serve as a basis for our understanding of Confucian teaching. The Great Learning (*Ta Hsueh*) was a chapter from the Book of Rites (39), which served as an introductory text for students beginning their study of Confucian ethics. The Doctrine of the Mean (*Chung Yung*) was also excerpted from the Book of Rites (Chapter 28). It deals with the relationship between humanity and the moral order. The Book of Mencius is the third-century-B.C.E. collection of the sayings of one of Confucius's principal disciples. It is the first attempt at a systematic philosophical statement of Con-fucius's teachings.

An 18th Century C.E. portrait of Master Kung (Confucius).
Source: *Charles Phelps. Cushing/Photoedit.*

The tradition that Confucius himself wrote the Five Classics is not considered historical by scholars today, but they are nonetheless important in the study of Confucianism. The Five Classics include the *Shu Ching* (the Book of History), the *Shih Ching* (the Book of Poetry), the *Li Chi* (the Book of Rites), the *I Ching* (the Book of Changes), and the *Ch'un Ch'iu* (the Annals of Spring and Autumn). It is quite possible that these anthologies existed by the time of Confucius, and that he made use of them in his own teaching, perhaps even editing them.

Formation of the Confucian School and Confucianism as State Teaching According to tradition, the principal disciples of Confucius became teachers themselves. In addition to the Four Books, the disciples produced the popular Book of Filial Piety (*Hsiao Ching*). Although it was not rigidly organized in this early period, they formed what we may call a Confucian School.

These were turbulent times. The feudal order was breaking up, and many rival schools emerged. In addition to Confucianism and Taoism, other schools included the Mohists (who sought to unite all people in a loving community) and the Legalists (who argued for a strict law, administered by force, as the basis for society).

Two of the leaders of the Confucian School deserve special mention. *Mencius* (ca. 371–289 B.C.E.) emphasized the Confucian virtue of humaneness (*jen*), but rejected the Mohist notion of a universal goodwill with no regard for kinship or social standing. He taught that humaneness must interact with righteousness (*i* or *yi*), so that how one expresses concern for others is related to their relative position in society. He said that rulers must place the needs of others before their own; if they do not, they lose the mandate of heaven. His most famous teaching is that humans are by nature good, and this became one of the principal themes of Confucian teaching. Mencius observed that anyone who sees a child fall into a well will save the child without considering the personal consequences, and he concluded that each of us must have a natural tendency toward goodness. However, this natural humaneness must be cultivated.

Hsun Tzu (ca. 297–238 B.C.E.) was the most important Confucian teacher in the Han dynasty. He taught that the most important virtue is *li*, propriety (see below). He also rejected Mencius's view of human nature, saying that humans are basically evil. Hsun Tzu claimed that goodness requires strict education, and an important element in training is participation in the rituals of the society.

The turning point for the official acceptance of Confucianism came in 136 B.C.E., when Confucians were given the responsibility for educating youth for positions in government. For the next 2,000 years, until 1905, Confucianism remained the basis for the educational system of China. It also heavily influenced the subject matter taught in other East Asian countries.

Confucius also became the object of state piety. As early as 195 B.C.E., a Han dynasty emperor had performed a sacrifice at the grave of Confucius. This practice continued, and Confucius was posthumously awarded titles of nobility and veneration. Temples dedicated to Confucius were built, and the sacrifices offered to Confucius became ever more involved. The temples included images of Confucius, and he became, in effect, a deity. About the same time as the Protestant Reformation in Europe (see Chapter Twelve), the state cult of Confucius was simplified and he became known as "Master K'ung, the Perfectly Holy Teacher of Antiquity."

Neo-Confucianism During the Sung Dynasty (960–1279 C.E.), the movement that became known as Neo-Confucianism evolved. Neo-Confucianism represented not only a return to the basic principles of Confucianism in response to the growing influence of Buddhism and Taoism in China, but also an incorporation of some of their philosophical ideas into Confucian teaching. The two principal branches of Neo-Confucianism were the School of Principle and the School of Mind. *Chu Hsi* (1130–1200) was the main figure associated with the former, and *Wang Yang-ming* (1472–1529) was the chief proponent of the latter.

Chi Hsi was successful in winning acceptance for Mencius's view that humans are essentially good. He also made popular the concept of the Great Ultimate, the rational principle that is at the essence of all reality and that is evident to any who objectively study nature. He thus transformed the principle of *li* into a cosmic force. Each human being also has such a principle at the core, he taught, working itself out as goodness. The influence of philosophical Taoism, influenced by traditional Confucian values, is evident. Chu Hsi advocated, and modelled in his own life, a method of introspection (somewhat similar to Buddhist meditation) as a means of bringing oneself into a way of acting that is in harmony with the Great Ultimate.

Wang Yang-ming emphasized that the underlying rational principle is discovered less from an investigation of nature than from an examination of one's own mind. He came to the conclusion that it is the mind that shapes the objects we perceive. The rational principle we discover within, he said, is a guiding light, an innate bearing toward goodness. He taught that our minds are like mirrors. When polished by proper instruction, the natural ability of the mind to reflect virtue is manifest. Like Chu Hsi, Wang Yang-ming taught that sitting quietly is the effective method of awakening to this inner principle.

Is Confucianism a Religion?

As we shall see, Confucian teaching is ambiguous on the question of religion. Confucius himself seems to have taught that it was important to conduct rituals to ancestors and other spirits, but the value of these rituals seems to lie in ordering society rather than as a means of *spiritual* transformation. Assuming the definition of religion introduced in Chapter One, we can consider early Confucianism a *secular* religion. The ultimate transformation Confucius and the early disciples envisioned related to secular society rather than any kind of spiritual reality.

Confucianism, however, according to our use of terminology, *became* a spiritual religion, rooting ultimacy in a force that undergirds the secular world of self and society. However, we must acknowledge that Confucianism is a good example of a movement that makes our distinction between "spiritual" and "secular" religions somewhat arbitrary. As we have seen, Neo-Confucianism revived Confucian teaching about the importance of human virtue as a means to create social harmony, but also incorporated Buddhist and Taoist philosophy to give Confucianism a stronger spiritual basis.

In addition, as we have already noted, the worship of Confucius transformed the teacher into a spirit to be venerated. This is not to say that Confucius was thought to be a god, any more than any venerated ancestor is a god. It does show that there was more of a spiritual dimension to Confucianism as it developed.

Is Confucianism a religion? The answer, like the question, is ambiguous. From our perspective, the most appropriate answer is that the Confucian ethical system may function as a secular religion, and Neo-Confucianism may be considered a religion with spiritual ultimacy.

Confucianism Today

With China's turn to the West in the early twentieth century, Confucianism as state orthodoxy faded. Confucianism no longer served as the foundation for the educational system, and the worship of Confucius faded. After taking power in 1949, the Communist government in China outlawed sacrifices to Confucius and banned the study of Confucian classics. Confucius was considered an advocate of the feudal system that Communism was rebelling against.

Despite these external signs of the demise of Confucianism, it is in fact alive and doing well in East Asia today. In the People's Republic of China, Confucius has been "rehabilitated." His ancestral home has been rebuilt, and Confucian moral teaching is not attacked as it once was. Worship of Confucius as a spirit continues in Taiwan and other Chinese communities outside China. And, most important, the Confucian virtues still form the basis for family life and social relations throughout East Asia. Let us now turn to an examination of these virtues.

Distinctive Teachings

The emphasis here is on the basic Confucian teachings as attributed to Confucius, developed by Mencius, and reaffirmed in the Neo-Confucian development of that teaching.

Problem: Social Chaos

Like Siddartha Gautama, Confucian teachers based their analysis of the fundamental human problem on observation of human experience. For Siddartha, suffering caused by craving was the dilemma humans must confront. For Confucius and Mencius, the predicament was manifest in the social chaos of the Warring States Period, brought on by the collapse of the feudal system.

Cause: A Breakdown of Virtue

What caused the social chaos? Confucian teaching observed that when rulers and the educated elite did not live virtuous lives, a social breakdown occurred. In particular, this breakdown occurred because people failed to follow their social roles. For example, princes failed to behave as princes should, and

QUESTIONS OF HUMAN IDENTITY: WHO ARE WE?

Humans as a Microcosm

Like other religions that originated in China, Confucianism views humanity, like other aspects of reality, as characterized by the interaction of yin and yang forces. The shen and kwei souls of mankind reflect this interaction; in this passage, they are called the "animal" and "intelligent" souls. Humans are also composed of the five basic elements, like all reality. In other words, humans are a microcosm of the cosmos as a whole, as this passage from the Confucian Book of Ritual states (Book of Ritual *[Li Chi] 7.3.1–7; Legge 1885: 381–82*).

[Humanity] (is the product of) the attributes of Heaven and Earth, (by) the interaction of the dual forces of nature [*yin* and *yang*], the union of the animal and intelligent (souls), and the finest subtle matter of the five elements.

Heaven exercises the control of the strong and light force [*yang*], and hangs out the sun and stars. Earth exercises the control of the dark and weaker force [*yin*], and gives vent to it in the hills and streams. The five elements are distributed through the four seasons, and it is by their harmonious action that the moon is produced, which therefore keeps waxing for fifteen days and waning for fifteen. The five elements in their movements alternately displace and exhaust one another. Each one of them, in the revolving course of the twelve months of the four seasons, comes to be in its turn the fundamental one for the time.

The five notes of harmony, with their six upper musical accords, and the twelve pitch-tubes, come each, in their revolutions among themselves, to be

the first note of the scale.

The five flavors, with the six condiments, and the twelve articles of diet, come each one, in their revolutions among themselves, to be the first note of the scale.

The five flavors, with the six condiments, and the twelve articles of diet, come each one, in their revolutions (in the course of the year), to give its character to the food.

The five colors, with the six elegant figures, which they form on the two robes, come each one, in their revolutions among themselves, to give the character of the dress that is worn.

Therefore Man is the heart and mind of Heaven and Earth, and the visible embodiment of the five elements. He lives in the enjoyment of all flavors, the discriminating of all notes of harmony, and the enrobing of all colors.

---

fathers no longer performed the roles they should play. At the same time, Mencius observed that people were not corrupt by nature, and that virtue seemed to depend on how people were educated. Confucian teaching pointed to an earlier age when rulers naturally displayed virtue (*te*) and sought to recover that kind of society.

Reality: Life-giving, Relational, Harmonious

According to Confucian teaching, the universe is "fundamentally oriented toward the production and promotion of life" (Kelleher 1987: 136). All

reality is relational, beginning with the hierarchical relationship between heaven and earth. It matters not which in any relational pair is superior, but that they function effectively and promote life in the relationship. Moreover, in all reality "each part seemed patterned to work for the good of the whole and yet at the same time to realize its own nature" (Kelleher 1987:137). There is a given pattern to which things should conform, both in our human nature and in society. When we accept our role and seek to live in conformity with it, then reality is harmonious. You might say, from a Confucian perspective, "We *are* our relationships."

Moreover, the harmony of the cosmos depended on an ordered, virtuous society. In an age when we are seeing what the lack of virtue can do to the environment and to human relationships, the Confucian view of reality has a certain appeal.

End: A Harmonious Society   The goal Confucius sought was the restoration of the harmony of the feudal order and the right pattern of human relationships. Like Lao Tzu, Confucius felt that the harmonious society would be created by sages, "ideal persons" who lived virtuous lives, and that they would do so by the force of their moral character. The "gentleman" (*chun tzu*) Confucius envisioned would remain committed to virtue through all of life's hardships. *Chun tzu* had meant an aristocrat, a person of noble birth. Confucius taught that anyone could become an "ideal person" through a process of moral formation. For Confucius the ideal was not to withdraw from the world, but to realize one's inherent human potential for goodness, immersing oneself in human life—first in the family, but also in society through public service. *This is the Confucian way to achieve identification with the cosmic order (Kelleher 1987: 139).

According to the Master, the gentleman was the son always filial, the father ever just and kind, the official unfailingly loyal and faithful, the husband completely righteous and judicious, and the friend always sincere and tactful. Confucius directed his efforts to the education of young men, so his pronouns were male. Many interpreters have observed that there is nothing gender-specific about the basic ideal.

Means: The Virtuous Life   For Confucius the path to the harmonious society and the "ideal persons" who would create it by the force of their moral character lay in education in specific virtues. The gentleman would maintain a balance between what we might call "inner" virtues (relating to one's basic attitude and orientation) and "outer" virtues (having to do with how one behaves toward others).

The primary "inner" virtue is *jen* (humaneness). The humane person is not concerned about self-gain or recognition, but desires to seek the good of others as an end in itself. The Chinese character for *jen* is composed of the character for "person" and the character for "two." This suggests that in all one's considerations, the other person is included naturally. The humane person instinctively recognizes the inherent worth and value of every person, from the highest in society to the lowest. For rulers this meant a concern for the needs of every person.

Related to *jen* is *shu* ("reciprocity"), the Confucian equivalent to the "golden rule." *Shu* means not doing to others what you would not have them do to you.

Another "inner" virtue is *hsueh*, translated as "self-correcting wisdom." A person with *hsueh* is constantly evaluating his or her behavior against the standard of moral excellence of the "ideal person." In the process one realizes that the goal has not yet been reached; *none* of us ever reaches the ideal. We all have room to grow. This leads to an attitude of humility, rather than pride about one's character. Contrast this attitude with the "I'm number one!" perspective common in contemporary American culture. Which is the best for society? for the individual?

These "inner" virtues need to be balanced by "outer" virtues. It is not enough to be a person of good character; one must put goodness into action. The most basic external virtue is *li* ("propriety, good form"). *Li* has a variety of meanings in different contexts. It can refer to the rites and rituals of a society. It can mean courtesy in human interaction, or treating others with reverence and respect. In general *li* is a right and proper order to be followed in any circumstance. According to Confucian teaching, without *li* a society loses sight of how to conduct proper worship. The right relationship between the genders is confused. Children and parents do not know how to treat one another. In short, human relationships lose their compass. What is the status of *li* in the society of which you are a part?

In the area of human interaction, *li* manifests itself in the "five human relationships": between

QUESTIONS OF HUMAN DESTINY: WHAT HAPPENS AFTER DEATH?

The Two Souls

Rather than developing a separate concept of life after death, Confucian texts echo the traditional Chinese teaching of two spirits, united as a complementary pair in life. Upon death the animal spirit (kwei) returns to the ground, and the intelligent spirit (shen) continues to live. More important for Confucianism than speculating on life after death, however, is conducting the proper rituals for the spirits so that society may be harmonious (Book of Ritual 21.2.1; Legge 1885: 220).

Ts'ai-wu said, "I have heard the names kwei and shen, but I do not know what they mean." The Master said, "The [intelligent] spirit is of the shen nature, and shows that in fullest measure. It is the union of kwei and shen that forms the highest exhibition of doctrine.

"All the living must die, and dying, return to the ground; this is what is called kwei. The bones and flesh molden below, and, hidden away, become the earth of the fields. But the spirit issues forth, and is displayed on high in a condition of glorious brightness. The vapors and odors which produce a feeling of sadness [and arise from the decay of their substance], and the subtle essences of all things, and also a manifestation of the shen nature.

ruler and subject, father and son, husband and wife, the eldest son and his younger brothers, and elders and juniors in general. Where there is *li*, people recognize this ordering of society and know how to treat one another with courtesy and respect within these relationships.

Li includes religious rituals, which in China meant ancestor veneration and worship of the deities and other spirits. For Confucius, therefore, the real value of these rites and the other ceremonies of society was that they maintained social harmony when properly conducted. He also taught that to find the proper way to conduct the rituals we must look to the past, to that time when society was in harmony.

Two other "outer" virtues deserve mention. One is *hsiao* ("filial piety"), which we have already identified as a characteristic of the underlying East Asian worldview. Confucianism is the principal carrier of this virtue, however. Filial piety means respect for one's elders, especially within the context of the family. In modern, secular societies, reaching maturity usually means leaving home and no longer accepting the authority of one's parents. In traditional Confucian societies, a child never "leaves home." Respect and reverence for elders continues throughout life, and, with the veneration of ancestors, beyond. You will not find many nursing homes in societies rooted in Confucian values, because keeping one's elders within the context of the family is seen as a basic, social obligation. Not only are they kept physically, but they are valued and honored. Confucius emphasized respect for elders and others in authority, but it is important to emphasize that filial piety also includes parents' treating their children and those in authority treating people in their charge with respect and courtesy. Could our society use more "filial piety"? Why or why not?

Confucian tradition also speaks of a virtue known as the "rectification of names" (*cheng-ming*). In general, this is to say that words are important. When they are degraded and lose their meaning, society suffers. In particular, titles must be respected. If one carries the title "prince," then behavior must be in conformity with the best that title

QUESTIONS ABOUT THE SACRED: HOW MANY THE SACRED BE KNOWN?

The Power of Spiritual Forces and Absolute Truth

Later Confucian commentators were more explicit than Confucius himself on the question of spiritual forces. These selections are from the Doctrine of the Mean (Chungyung), a work attributed to Tsesze, grandson of Confucius and teacher of Mencius. It provides a foundation for later Confu-cian philosophy. In the first selection, the author asserts that although spiritual forces cannot be known, they are implied by the existence in all cultures of religious rituals. Through these rituals the unseen Powers are felt. In the second selection, the author reflects on the nature of absolute truth and its unseen manifestation (Doctrine of the Mean, 16 and 24–25; Yutang 1938: 75, 86).

Confucius remarked, "The power of spiritual forces in the universe—how active it is everywhere! Invisible to the eyes and impalpable to the senses, it is inherent in all things, and nothing can escape its operation."

It is the fact that there are these forces which makes men in all countries fast and purify themselves, and with solemnity of dress institute services of sacrifice and religious worship. Like the rush of mighty waters, the presence of unseen Powers is felt; sometimes above us, sometimes around us. In the Book of Songs it is said,

> *"The Presence of the Spirits:*
> *It cannot be surmised,*
> *How may it be ignored!"*

Such is the evidence of things invisible that it is impossible to doubt the spiritual nature of man.

Thus absolute truth is indestruc- tible. Being indestructible, it is eternal. Being eternal, it is self- existent. Being self-existent, it is infinite. Being infinite, it is vast and deep. Being vast and deep, it is transcendental and intelligent. It is because it is vast and deep that it contains all existence. It is because it is infinite and eternal that it ful- fills or perfects all existence. In vastness and depth it is like the Earth. In transcendental intelli- gence it is like Heaven. Infinite and Eternal, it is the Infinite itself.

Such being the nature of absolute truth, it manifests itself without being seen; it produces effects without motion; it ac-com- plishes its ends without action.

---

implies. In the contemporary idiom we might speak of "roles." Each of us has a number of social roles. You might define yourself as student, daughter, sis- ter, friend, and worker, for example. Each name implies a code of moral behavior. If you fail to act in conformity with what is expected of you as a "sister," then the social setting in which "sister- hood" is important will become confused and chaotic. The same applies to all roles. What are the benefits and limitations of seeking to live through conformity to roles, for individuals *and* for society?

Whoever lives a "balanced" life in a Confucian sense displays a force of character, a moral charis- ma (*te*) that has a positive, constructive influence on others. If the ruling class manifests *te*, then citi- zens will follow their example, and the "good soci- ety" will exist without resort to force. In an impor- tant sense, all of Confucian teaching is oriented toward *te*, for when we learn to manifest the virtue that is natural to our human character and shaped by the social roles in which we find ourselves, the result will be inner harmony for each of us and har- mony for society.

Sacred: Making the Tao Great Like Siddartha, Confucius sidestepped issues such as "What is the nature of the spiritual?" He is reputed to have said that you cannot treat spirits and divinities properly before you learn to treat your fellow human beings properly (*Analects* 11:12). He advised his followers to treat the spirits "as though they were real" (3:12). Some have called his teaching a "spiritual agnosticism." He professed no knowledge of the spiritual, but still felt that maintaining religious rituals was critical to his central concern: social harmony.

Confucius spoke of the *Tao,* but not like a philosophical Taoist. The saying, It is humans who make the *Tao* great, not the *Tao* that makes human great, is attributed to him (*Analects* 15:29). In other words, if there is to be a "way" for things to go, an underlying harmony, it will be because humans manifest it in their commitment to virtue. For philosophical Taoists, the way to virtue is to let the *Tao* happen. Striving to be virtuous results in a lack of virtue, they argued. For Confucians, the way to the *Tao* is to seek virtue actively. From this perspective, perhaps Confucians *is* the *yang* and philosophical Taoism the *yin* of East Asian culture!

RESPONSES TO CONTEMPORARY ETHICAL ISSUES

The Ecological Crisis

Interpreters of Taoism have noted that the basic concepts of philosophical Taoism have clear implications for the present ecological crisis. Among them are "reversion, the constancy of cyclical change, *wu wei* (actionless activity), and the procurement of power by abandoning the attempt to 'take' it" (Goodman 1980: 73).

As we noted, the *Tao* is the eternal process whereby everything comes into existence and passes out of existence, or moves from non-being to being to non-being to being, and so forth. This is sometimes called the principle of *reversion* (*Tao-te-ching,* Chapter 40). It can be observed in such natural phenomena as the changing of the seasons and indeed in the birth, life, and death of all living beings. It can be argued that "much of our ecological crisis is caused by our failure to understand the simple truth of reversion." We pretend that we can simply throw things away and they will be gone forever, hiding from the simple truth that "things

are only moved around; sooner or later they will be back" (Goodman 1980: 75). For example, medical wastes dumped into the ocean have begun to turn up on many beaches, making the beaches unfit and dangerous to human and other forms of life. Apparently those who dumped this hazardous material into the sea thought that it would simply disappear. A greater appreciation of the Taoist "law of reversion" would help us face up to the terrible problem of pollution.

The Taoist ideal is to use the natural cycles with a minimum of human involvement. Industrialized societies have moved to the opposite extreme, trying to improve life by maximizing human manipulation of nature. For example, a farmer may seek to increase productivity by using chemical fertilizers. However, fertilizers sometimes increase short-term productivity but interfere with the natural processes, with negative long-term results. Taoist agriculture is suspicious of such intervention and would seek to control pests through organic means, accepting poor crops as a result of weeds or insects as a part of the natural process; they are secure in the knowledge that nature will take care of the situation in a balanced way.

Paradoxically, Taoists believe that *wu wei* ("actionless activity"), or non-intervention with the ways of nature, is a means of control. *Wu-wei* is not passivity in the face of the forces of nature, but learning to respond to them, rather than trying to coerce them. For example, by closely observing the natural flow of water in a given area, the irrigation ditches a farmer builds will work by harmonizing with the way of nature.

In its approach to energy production, Taoism would seek the path of generating power naturally. Ideally, there should be no waste, no residue. Long before heating and air conditioning, people learned to build houses with thick walls and windows facing to the south; the house is therefore naturally insulated and heated. Such "passive solar" heating accords well with Taoist principles. In addition, Taoism would be suspicious of large-scale energy production, with massive power plants and energy grids. Taoism is suspicious of too much organization and centralization. The point is not to do without

QUESTIONS OF MORALITY: WHAT ARE OUR OBLIGATIONS TO NON-HUMAN LIFE?

Chuang Tzu on Nature and Humanity

Chuang Tzu expressed succinctly the fundamental environmental warning long ago (Chuang Tzu 17; Chan 1963: 207).

A horse or a cow has four feet. That is Nature. Put a halter around the horse's head and put a string through the cow's nose, that is man. Therefore it is said, "Do not let man destroy Nature. Do not let cleverness destroy destiny [the natural order]. And do not sacrifice your name for gain." Guard carefully your nature and do not let it go astray. This is called returning to one's nature.

Excerpt from **A Sourcebook in Chinese Philosophy**, *trans. Wing-Tsit Chan. Copyright © by Princeton University Press. Reprinted by permission of Princeton University Press.*

technology, but to let nature guide the technology needed.

Taoism did not treat nature in general, but in the concrete. From a Taoist perspective, we will never resolve the environmental crisis merely "by appeal to universal principles." Instead, we "must apply ourselves to the aesthetic task of cultivating an environmental *ethos* in our own place and time, and recommending this project to others by our participation in their environments" (Ames 1986: 348).

On the surface, Confucianism would not appear to be concerned about the environment. Confucian teaching focuses on humans and their relations with one another. However, by extension Confucianism makes an important contribution to the quest for ecological responsibility. Confucian teaching views humans in the context of their social relations, never atomistically as Westerners tend to do. "Confucius posits a social model of human individuality which is an analogue of ecology's model of species adapting to niches in the economy of nature and thus acquiring their specific characteristics" (Callicott 1987: 129). From this perspective, humans are members of a biological community, in which they must practice the Confucian virtues of propriety, reciprocity, and concern for others.

Confucianism (like Taoism) reflects a Chinese worldview that holds that "all of the parts of the entire cosmos belong to one organic whole and that they all interact as participants in one spontaneously self-generating life process" (Wei-Ming 1989: 67 [citing Frederick Mote]). This notion of organic continuity and dynamism, echoed by modern ecologists, is, many argue, one of the principal starting points for developing a responsible environmental ethic today.

War

The *Tao-te-ching*, the basic text of philosophical Taoism, expresses the view that wars do more harm than good, as is the case with all unnatural exertions of force. The thirtieth poem reads (Legge 1891: 72):

> He who would assist a lord of men in harmony with the Tao *will not assert his mastery in the kingdom by force of arms.*

War was a fact of life in ancient China, as it has been in all civilizations. Confucius does not seem to have been a pacifist, but he did urge that if people are asked to go to war, they must have an understanding of the reasons for it and the potential cost. For example, in the *Analects* (13: 29–30), Confucius is purported to have said (Ware 1955: 88), "If an able man were to instruct the people for seven years, they could indeed be used in warfare immediately thereafter. Leading an uninstructed people to war is to throw them away."

Capital Punishment

Confucian teaching endorses capital punishment. A passage from the writings of the early Confucian scholar Mencius provides the basis for Confucian teaching (cited in Tse 1989: 116):

When men kill others, and roll over their bodies to take their property, being reckless and fearless of death, among all the people there are none but detest them— thus, such characters are to be put to death, without waiting to give them warning.

The justification for capital punishment implied in this passage is that some people choose to deny their own human nature (characterized by *jen* or "humaneness") when they commit acts such as murder and robbery. Such people have separated themselves from humanity and therefore "ought to be removed from the human world" (Tse 1989: 116).

Economic Justice

As with Buddhism, for Confucianism the goal of economic activity is not material prosperity but moral development. From a traditional Confucian perspective, individuals and societies must place morality ahead of material gain. As Mencius said, "If righteousness be put last, and profit be put first, they [i.e., government and common people alike] will not be satisfied without snatching all" (cited by Tse 1989: 112). Societies should be structured on moral relationships, rather than business relationships.

Confucianism also recognizes that in order to have the personal security necessary to develop morally, a person must be free from poverty and be able to own the goods necessary to provide for basic needs. Therefore, it is not opposed to the market economy and free trade.

The role of the government in the economy, in the Confucian model, is neither direct ownership of business nor a completely *laissez-faire* approach. Rather, government should supervise the conduct of business to guard against monopolies and exploitation (Tse 1989: 112–13).

As we have already mentioned, the success of the economies of East Asian countries that have a Confucian heritage may be taken as evidence that this approach is practical. When the pursuit of wealth is not the primary end, prosperity seems naturally to follow.

Gender Roles and the Status of Women

"The concept 'woman' as an independent entity over against 'man,' possessed of her own interests, which may be in conflict with those of the men in her life, and entitled to her own independent agency and to the means toward the fulfillment of her interests, was not a part of the discourse of traditional China" (Levering 1994: 174). In this section, we will both illustrate this claim and witness the extent to which women have been able to assert themselves in China despite the dominant, largely Confucian worldview, which discouraged independence.

In the Taoist and popular traditions, women were not as subordinated as this statement implies. In the earliest religion of China, women functioned alongside men as shamans, who made the power of the sacred accessible to their communities. In fact, the Chinese word for shaman—*wu*—referred originally to a woman (Reed 1987: 170).

Chinese society was and is patriarchal, but there is a strong feminine presence in the Chinese understanding of reality. According to Chinese teaching, "male" and "female" are functional expressions rather than biological classifications. In all reality both the male (*yang*) and female (*yin*) are present; they are complementary, with no distinction of superiority and inferiority. For the well-being of the whole, both are necessary (Reed 1987: 165–66).

In the *Tao-e-ching*, feminine imagery is prominent in the poems that point to the fundamental cosmic reality—the *Tao*. For example, Chapter Six of the *Tao-te-ching* speaks of the *Tao* as "the female mystery" (Legge 1891[1]: 51). The womb is another symbol of the *Tao*, as is a nurturing breast. The *Tao* is seemingly docile, like the woman's role in society, yet through the quiet and hidden "it all gets done." The successful way is not the aggressive style associated with the male role, but the responding and apparently submissive mode of the female. This is true power, the way of the *Tao*. For Taoist thinkers, the Confucian subordination of women was one of the social pretensions that must be discarded in order to allow life to occur naturally and spontaneously.

Although Chuang Tzu did not use female imagery to speak of the *Tao*, he did refer to "a myth of a utopian matrilineal society in which people knew their mothers, but not their fathers" (Reed 1987: 164).

In the other branch of Taoism, the "religious," women have functioned as shamans, opening themselves to the divine power. In the Taoist religious orders, women became masters and alchemists, and were ordained as priests. They participated in the esoteric *chiao* ritual tradition. A primary deity in Taoist mythology, the Jade Mother, is worshipped as the mother of the legendary Lao Tzu, who creates the world. Communities of Taoist women formed, in which women pursued the Taoist paths to "immortality." In the Taoist temple in modern Taiwan, laywomen perform faith healing rituals, laying their hands on the sick or their clothing (Reed 1987: 180).

The role of women in society, as structured by Confucian values, was quite different. In the traditional Confucian understanding, women are to be docile and subordinate to the men in their lives. According to the early Confucian texts, "the female was inferior by nature, she was dark as the moon and changeable as water, jealous, narrow-minded, and insinuating. She was indiscreet, unintelligent, and dominated by emotion" (Guisso 1981: 59). The subordination of earth to heaven was applied to the dominant status of men over women. The basic relationships of Confucian ethics place the man in the position of superiority over the woman in the family and in society. As girls, they were to obey their fathers; as mature women, their husbands; and as old women, their elder sons (Kelleher 1987: 140). The Chinese symbol of "wife" includes a broom, indicating the priority of her domestic status. In traditional Confucian society, there was simply no place for women in government and commerce. Women's education, under the guidance of the Confucian ethic, was limited to practical skills such as sewing and how to care for men. Women were taught to treat husbands with utter devotion in order to win their love. They were to be the keepers of the morals of the home, treating all, including the husband's concubines, with respect (Carmody 1989: 96–98).

With the development of Neo-Confucianism came increased emphasis on the importance of chastity and asceticism for women. Models for women included a woman who resists being raped by throwing herself off a high cliff and another who mutilates her body rather than remarry and dishonor her dead husband (Kelleher 1987: 156).

By the nineteenth century this had led to severe oppression of women, and inspired a reform movement within Chinese society. Women played key roles in attempts to modernize China. One traditional practice that was a symbol of the subordination of women, the footbinding of baby girls, was a particular target of reformers. The practice had left many women hobbled and unable to walk naturally. Feminist reformers also opposed arranged marriages and supported increased educational opportunities for women.

In the 1940s the Communist revolution highlighted the Confucian subordination of women as an example of the inequities of traditional Chinese society that needed to be overturned. The Communists included women in the unions organized to further workers' rights. When Mao Tsetung came to power, arranged marriages were outlawed and steps were taken to curb female infanticide (Levering 1994: 176–88). However, the traditions of treating women as inferiors did not disappear, and the Communist system has been dominated by patriarchal attitudes (Levering 1994: 188–91).

It has been in the resurgent Chinese religions that women have been most active as leaders in recent years (Levering 1994: 191–221). The democratic movement that climaxed in the occupation of Tienanmen Square in 1989 has also involved many women student leaders, who argue that the Communist Party has not lived up to its promise to liberate women in Chinese society.

In Taiwan traditional Confucian values still dominate, but there are signs of change, brought by educated, economically independent women challenging their traditional subordination on the basis of a reassertion of the egalitarian nature of basic Confucian virtues and by the upsurge of interest in new religious movements (Reed 1994).

Homosexuality

Jesuit missionaries and other early Western visitors were shocked to find widespread acceptance, even promotion, of same-sex relations in Chinese society. When missionaries expressed moral outrage to their Chinese acquaintances at this tolerance of homoerotic behavior, they were met with surprise and were told that no one had ever said such behavior was wrong. Because of gender segregation, homosexuality, both male and female, was quite common in Chinese history before modern times. Historians think it reached its peak during the northern and southern Sung dynasties (960–1279).

This cultural toleration of homosexuality is not, however, the whole story. Both Confucian and Taoist teachers developed arguments against same-sex relations (Wawrytko 1993: 204–10). Many Confucian teachers have argued that homosexuality poses a threat to social solidarity by undermining the propagation of the family line. Taoist rejection of homosexuality has been rooted in the assumption that it leads to an imbalance in *yin* and *yang* energies. In male-female sexual relations there is a balance of *yin* and *yang*; in same-sex relations there is an imbalance. The double *yang* energy in male-male relations is most dangerous, because the two assertive forces are more likely to conflict.

Under Communist rule active oppression of homosexuals has been the official policy. At its most extreme, homophobia led to the execution of homosexuals in "re-education" camps at the height of the Cultural Revolution. "In present-day China, homosexuals still pursue their proclivities at the risk of their lives, although discretion is more likely to be rewarded by official blindness" (Wawrytko 1993: 206).

CHAPTER SUMMARY

After orienting ourselves to the lands and people of East Asia, we surveyed the history of China. The traditional worldview includes a view of reality as composed of the complementary interaction of balancing forces (*yin* and *yang*); the use of divination; social relationships based on loyalty and deference to those in a superior role, and respect and courtesy for those in an inferior position; a sense of an underlying harmony; the importance of virtue; and a fatalism based on a sense of the moral and political consequences of this harmony.

We then encountered Taoism, first tracing its development from a mystical philosophy that taught a life of harmony with the mysterious *Tao*, to a religion aimed at attaining physical immortality and material well-being through propitiation of gods and spirits. We summarized the distinctive teachings of philosophical Taoism, drawing on the *Tao-te-ching* as our principal source.

While philosophical Taoism teaches a way of cosmic harmony, Confucianism is preoccupied with social harmony. The founder, Master K'ung, taught aspiring leaders a way of virtue that he believed would create harmony in society. Confucianism gained prominence as the official state philosophy in China, taught for centuries in schools. Later Confucians developed a religion that revered Confucius as a saint, if not a god. Early Confucianism seemed to have been a secular religion, but later Confucianism adopted a spiritual understanding of ultimacy. Today Confucianism has suffered in China as a result of a campaign against it in the early decades of the People's Republic. However, in all the cultures of East Asia Confucianism continues to strongly influence family life and social relations in general. Confucian ethics seeks the cultivation of virtues such as *jen* (humaneness) and *li* (propriety and righteousness), with the "ideal person" manifesting a balance between "inner" and "outer" virtues.

The chapter concluded with a discussion of Taoist and Confucian teachings on ecology, war, capital punishment, economic justice, the status of women, and homosexuality.

QUESTIONS FOR DISCUSSION AND REFLECTION

1. Do you think that all things manifest the two complementary opposite forces (the *yin* and *yang*)? Can you identify what the Chinese call *yin* and *yang* aspects of your personality or in the personalities of others you know?

2. Have you had any experience with divination? If so, did you find it helpful?

3. Do you agree with the observation that philosophical Taoism and Confucianism are the *yin* and *yang* of Chinese culture? Why or why not?

4. Would you rather live in a society based on philosophical Taoism or Confucianism? What are the reasons for your preference?

5. What do you think accounts for the appeal of philosophical Taoism and Zen Buddhism to many highly educated people in Europe and the United States? (*Note*: If the potential impact of a Zen/Taoist approach interacting with Western philosophy and literature interests you, take a look at Robert Pirsig's *Zen and the Art of Motorcycle Maintenance*. For a more lighthearted reading experience, try *The Tao of Pooh* and *The Te of Piglet*.)

6. Although Confucian teachings could form the basis for ecological responsibility, East Asian countries where Confucianism is influential have not been immune from the modern exploitation of the environment. Discuss the possible reasons for this apparent contradiction.

7. Why, according to Taoism, will we never solve the environmental crisis by appealing to universal principles? What is the Taoist alternative? Do you agree with it?

8. Do you agree with the *Tao-te-ching* that when people try to be virtuous, the result is chaos? Is the basic problem that we do not allow ourselves to "go with the flow"? Try to respond as a Confucian to these questions. Do you consider yourself more "Taoist" or "Confucian"? How about your friends? the members of your family?

9. Many people today agree with the *Tao-te-ching* that death should be accepted as part of the process of life, and speculation on what is after death should be avoided. Why do you think this is the case?

10. If the *Tao* that can be named is not the true *Tao*, can we say anything meaningful about the *Tao*?

SOURCES AND SUGGESTIONS FOR FURTHER STUDY

General

CHAN, WING-TSIT, COMP. AND TRANS., 1963 *A Sourcebook in Chinese Philosophy*, Princeton, N.J.: Princeton University Press.

JOCHIM, CHRISTIAN, 1986 *Chinese Religions: A Cultural Perspective*. Englewood Cliffs, N.J.: Prentice Hall.

SMITH, D. HOWARD, 1971. *Chinese Religions*. New York: Holt, Rinehart and Winston.

THOMPSON, LAURENCE G., 1979. *The Chinese Religion: An Introduction*, 3rd ed. Belmont, Calif.: Wadworth.

Taoism

CHUNG-YUAN, CHANG, 1970 *Creativity and Taoism*. New York: Harper & Row.

CREEL, H.G., 1982 *What Is Taoism?* Chicago: The University of Chicago Press.

GILES, HERBERT A., TRANS., 1926 *Chuang Tzu: Mystic, Moralist, and Social Reformer*, 2nd ed. Shanghai: Kelly and Walsh Ltd.

LAGERWEY, JOHN, 1987 *Taoist Ritualism in Chinese Society and History*. New York: Macmillan.

LEGGE, JAMES, TRANS., 1891[1] The Sacred Books of China: The Texts of Taoism, Part I, in The Sacred Books of the East, vol. 39.

1892[2] The Sacred Books of China: The Texts of Taoism, Part II, in The Sacred Books of the East, vol. 40.

MITCHELL, STEPHEN, 1988 The Tao te Ching: A New English Version. New York: HarperPerennial.

WELCH, HOLMES, 1965 Taoism: The Parting of the Way. Boston: Beacon Press.

Confucianism

CREEL, H.G., 1960 Confucius and the Chinese Way. New York: Harper.

EBER, IRENE, ED., 1986 Confucianism: The Dynamics of Tradition. New York: Macmillan.

HALL, DAVID, AND ROGER AMES, 1987 Thinking Through Confucius. Albany: State University of New York Press.

LEGGE, JAMES, TRANS., 1885 The Sacred Books of China: The Texts of Confucianism, part 4. The Li Ki: A Collection of Treatises on the Rules of Propriety or Ceremonial Usages, in The Sacred Books of the East, vol. 27, ed. F.M. Mueller. Oxford: Clarendon Press.

WARE, JAMES R., 1955 The Sayings of Confucius. New York: New American Library.

YUTANG, LIN, ED. AND TRANS., 1938 The Wisdom of Confucius. New York: Random House.

Religion in Communist China

BUSH, RICHARD C., 1970 Religion in Communist China. Nashville, Tenn. Abingdon Press.

WELCH, HOLMES, 1972 Buddhism Under Mao. Cambridge: Harvard University Press.

Responses to Contemporary Ethical Issues

General

TSE, CHUNG M., 1989 "Confucianism and Contemporary Ethical Issues," in World Religions and Global Ethics, ed. S. Cromwell Crawford (New York: Paragon), 91–125.

The Ecological Crisis

AMES, ROGER T., 1986 "Taoism and the Nature of Nature," Environmental Ethics 8 (1986): 317–49.

1989 "Putting the Te Back into Taoism," in Nature in Asian Traditions of Thought: Essays in Philosophy, ed. J. Baird Callicott and Roger T. Ames (Albany, NY: State University of New York), 113–44.

CAPRA, FRITJOF, 1983 The Tao of Physics: An Exploration of the Parallels Between Modern Physics and Eastern Mysticism, 2nd ed. New York: Random House.

GOODMAN, RUSSELL, 1980 "Taoism and Ecology," Environmental Ethics 2 (1980): 73–80.

HALL, DAVID, 1989 "On Seeking a Change in Environment," in Nature in Asian Traditions of Thought: Essays in Philosophy, 99–111.

IP, PO-KEUNG, 1986 "Taoism and the Foundations of Environmental Ethics," in Religion and Environmental Crisis, ed. Eugene Hargrove (Athens: The University of Georgia Press), 94–106.

SMITH, HOUSTON, 1972 "Tao Now: An Ecological Testament," in Earth Might Be Fair: Reflections on Ethics, Religion, and Ecology, ed. Ian Barbour (Englewood Cliffs, NJ: Prentice Hall),162–8.

TUAN, YI-FU, 1968 "Discrepancies Between Environmental Attitude and Behavior: Examples from Europe and China," Canadian Geographer 12 (1968): 176–83.

WEI-MING, TU, 1989 "The Continuity of Being: Chinese Visions of Nature," in Nature in Asian Traditions of Thought: Essays in Philosophy, 67–78.

Economic Justice

REDDING, S. GORDON, 1990 The Spirit of Chinese Capitalism. New York: W. deGruyter.

Gender Roles and the Status of Women

GIUSSO, RICHARD, ED., 1981 Women in China. New York: Philo.

KELLEHER, TERESA, 1987 "Confucianism," in Women in World Religions, ed. Arvind Sharma (Albany: State University of New York Press), 135–59.

LEVERING, MIRIAM, 1994 "Women, the State, and Religion Today in the People's Republic of China," in Today's Woman in World Religions, ed. Arvind Sharma (Albany: State University of New York Press), 171–224.

REED, BARBARA, 1987 "Taoism," in Women in World Religions, 161–81.

1994 "Women and Chinese Religion in Contemporary Taiwan," in Today's Woman in World Religions, 225–43.

Homosexuality

CHIA, MANTAK, AND MICHAEL WINN, 1984 Taoist Secrets of Love: Cultivating Male Sexual Energy. Santa Fe, N.M.:

Aurora Press.

VAN GULIK, R.H., 1974 *Sexual Life in Ancient China: A Preliminary Survey of Chinese Sex and Society from ca. 1500*

B.C. till 1644 A.D. Leiden: E.J. Brill.

WAWRYTKO, SANDRA A., 1993 "Homosexuality and Chinese and Japanese Religions," in *Homosexuality and*

CHAPTER 9

Mahayana Buddhism: The Great Vehicle and Shinto: The Way of the Kami

CHINA

NORTH
KOREA

SOUTH
KOREA

Hiroshin

Kitakyūshū

Fukuoka

SHIKO

Nagasaki

KYUSHU

INTRODUCTION

In this chapter we continue our discussion of the religions of East Asia. In Chapter Eight we provided an orientation to the lands and people of East Asia and a brief history of China. We noted there that the schools associated with the Mahayana branch of Buddhism (see Chapter Six) that took root in China migrated to Korea and then to Japan, where they became influential. In this chapter we will briefly survey the histories of Japan and Korea. We will then examine two of the Chinese Buddhist movements (Pure Land and Meditation) as they developed in Japan, one distinctively Japanese school of Buddhism (Nichiren), and the form of Buddhism that flourished in the mountain nation of Tibet (the Tantric School). Then we will describe the multifaceted native religious tradition that emerged in the island nation of Japan, a tradition that became known as Shinto.

A BRIEF HISTORY OF KOREA AND JAPAN

Korea

Although the Korean peninsula was inhabited nearly 30,000 years B.C.E., we will begin this overview with the Chinese invasion of 108 B.C.E. Three of the four provinces established in Korea by the Chinese were liberated by 75 B.C.E., but much of northwestern Korea remained under Chinese control for centuries. This contact resulted in heavy Chinese influence on the development of Korean civilization. The classical three kingdoms of Korea (Paekche, Koguryo, and Silla) were formed by 300 C.E. During the fourth and fifth centuries C.E., Buddhism entered Korea from China and became the major religion. In the late seventh century C.E., Silla gained control of the entire peninsula. From this time on, the Confucian educational system and values had a profound impact on Korea. The name "Korea" (from *Koryo*) is the product of tenth-century developments. After a century of Mongol occupation, Koryo regained its independence in the late

fourteenth century. The Yi dynasty, which took control in 1392 and renamed the country *Choson,* lasted until the early 1900s. Buddhism's dominance gradually lessened. After successfully resisting Japanese and Chinese attacks, the country was closed to foreigners in the seventeenth and eighteenth centuries. Christian missionaries were rebuffed when they began to enter Korea in the nineteenth century, but their success after World War II has resulted in a large Christian minority in Korea today. Japan forced Korea to reopen some of its ports by 1876, and took total control of the peninsula in 1910. In 1945, after the defeat of Japan in World War II, Japanese domination of Korea finally ended; the United States occupied the southern half of the country; and Soviet troops, the north. After failed attempts to unite the two halves of the country, and the withdrawal of American and Soviet forces, troops from North Korea invaded South Korea in 1950. A war began that involved U.S. and other forces in defense of South Korea under the United Nations flag. The war ended in 1953, but there has been tension between North and South Korea ever since. Under often strict constraints on civil liberties, South Korea has become a regional economic power. North Korea is one of the last nations under strict Communist control.

Japan

The early history of Japan is clouded in mystery. The mythological version of Japanese origins is recounted in the *Shinto Myth*. As we shall see, traditional Japanese religion (Shinto) traces its roots to the divine creation of the Japanese islands.

Historians speculate that the ancestors of the modern Japanese came to the islands originally from Korea, Mongolia, and Malay, possibly as early as 6000 B.C.E. Until the fourth century C.E., the land was divided into independent tribes and clans, who practiced indigenous religions that had many of the attributes described in Chapter Three. Then the Yamato clans took a central role, claiming that their leader was a descendant of the sun goddess.

Historians, however, know remarkably little about Japan until the Chinese introduced writing,

209

The Daibutsu ("Great Buddha"), famed statue of Amida Buddha, Lord of the Western Paradise (Kamakura, Japan).

Amitabha Buddha. Her devotees believe that she will lead the faithful to the Western Paradise of Amitabha.

Finally, in contrasting Mahayana with Theravada Buddhism, we should stress the teaching of *sunyata* ("emptiness"), introduced above. The concept appears in Theravadin texts, where it seems to mean the absence of value in the changing flux of existence. In Theravada it had a pragmatic function, helping a monk or nun overcome attachment to worldly life. In Mahayana, *sunyata* became an important concept for those schools more philosophical in their orientation. We have already mentioned Nagarjuna's use of *sunyata* and his argument that *nirvana* and *samsara* are without meaningful distinction. A later Mahayana school of philosophy in India, called *Yogacara,* expressed the concept in a more positive vein. This school stressed that if one experiences the "emptiness" of all distinctions in the perceived world, this leads to an awareness of Pure Mind, or Mind-in-itself, which is freed from the entanglements of our ordinary minds. The only way to discover this Pure Consciousness is to explore one's own mind and probe to its depths, ultimately beyond all ordinary "knowing." As we shall see, this teaching had a profound influence on the development of the

school of Mahayana Buddhism most widely known by its Japanese name, Zen.

Major Mahayana Schools in East Asia and their Distinctive Teachings

The doctrine of "emptiness" became the basis for more than one of the schools that emerged in China and Japan. Besides Zen, the school known in China as *T'ien-Tai,* and in Japan as *Tendai,* taught that there is no distinction between *sunyata* and this experienced world. According to this school, founded in China in the sixth century C.E. and brought to Japan about 200 years later, all the Buddhas are present in one grain of sand, and Buddhahood can be manifest in the ordinary life of lay people as much as in the heavenly Buddhas or monks.

T'ien-Tai/Tendai is but one of a number of separate Mahayana movements that emerged in China and then took root in Japan and Korea. We will focus here on two of the most significant Chinese schools, which have had a profound influence not only in Japan but in America—the Pure Land and Meditation schools. We will also discuss a movement that began in Japan and has spread to America—Nichiren Buddhism. All three were influenced in different ways by *T'ien-Tai/Tendai.* Finally, we will examine what happened to Mahayana Buddhism when it was introduced in Tibet.

Pure Land: The Devotional School   This school is based on a Sanskrit text that tells the story of the heavenly Buddha, *Amitabha* ("infinite light"), who resides in a celestial region known as the Western Paradise or Pure Land. The text describes the Pure Land as a rich, fertile, heavenly place, with jeweled palaces, inhabited only by gods and men, not by ghosts or demons. It teaches that any human can attain Buddhahood through faith in Amitabha. The first stage in this process is rebirth in the Western Paradise, where one receives preparation for *nirvana* and Buddhahood.

When this teaching reached China by the fourth or fifth century C.E., it was adapted to the view that we live in the last of the three declining periods of Buddhist teaching. In this perverse age people must rely on the grace of Amitabha rather than their own ability. This "easy path" of reliance on a "god" for help in attaining liberation contrasted with austere self-reliance of traditional Buddhist monks and the rigorous meditative techniques of the Meditation school. It met with wide acceptance among lay people. The Chinese Pure Land school taught that merely by calling on the name of Amitabha in faith at death, one could experience rebirth in the Western Paradise.

The real success of the school, however, came in Japan, where it was introduced first as an element within the Tendai tradition. Amitabha is known as *Amida* in the Japanese Pure Land tradition. By the twelfth century, however, the Pure Land teaching became the basis of a separate Japanese Mahayana school, known as *Jodo-shu* ("Pure Land school"). *Jodo-shu* taught that the way to express faith in Amida was by chanting his name over and over again. The chant *Namu Amida Butsu* ("I place my faith in Amida Buddha"), called simply the *nembutsu,* became the basis for a devotional tradition that is still extremely influential.

The most popular Pure Land school is an offshoot of *Jodo-shu* known as *Jodo-Shinshu* ("true Pure Land school"). Its innovation was to say that if a person has a true attitude of humility and faith in Amida, then repetition of the chant is not a prerequisite for rebirth in the Pure Land. Instead, one should chant in response to having received Amida's grace, rather than as a means of attaining his compassion. Faith comes as a freely bestowed gift from Amida, not as something generated by the believer.

Pure Land Buddhism came to America with Chinese and Japanese immigrants. The first official *Jodo Shinshu* missionaries arrived in 1899 and formed the North American Buddhist Mission. After the imprisonment of Japanese Americans during World War II, the name was changed to the Buddhist Churches of America to symbolize a commitment to adapt to American culture.

The teaching of the Pure Land schools is straightforward and simple, making it especially attractive to those impatient with the more esoteric teachings of other Buddhist movements such as the one we will now discuss—Zen.

Zen: The Meditation School   The school of Buddhism most widely known in the West is the Meditation school, known in China as *ch'an* (based on a Chinese rendering of the Sanskrit term for meditation—*dhyana*) and in Japan as *Zen.* As we shall see, Zen teaches skepticism about ordinary language and mocks attempts to explain truth rationally. Therefore, we preface this discussion of Zen with the same sort of warning given before the section on philosophical Taoism: Those who talk do not know! Although the same might be said of other religious traditions, it is especially true for Zen.

The roots of Zen can be traced to the meditation practiced by Siddartha Gautama and his followers, and the Indian philosophical schools that stressed the doctrine of *sunyata* or "emptiness" (see above). According to Zen tradition, the Buddha once held a lotus before his disciples, smiled, and said nothing. Only one of his followers experienced the truth of his silent sermon, while the rest remained confused. This disciple smiled in return, showing the Buddha he had awakened to the truth beyond words. Hence began the tradition of "mind-to-mind" teaching from a master to a disciple.

Zen tradition has focused on an Indian monk, called *Bodhidharma* (ca. 470–543), as the one who brought this insight to China. According to legend, when Bodhidharma was brought before the Chinese emperor, the monk chastised the emperor, telling the emperor that all his temples to the Buddha and copying of Buddhist texts were worthless. He is reputed to have sat in rapt mediation before a wall for nine years. Bodhidharma is often portrayed as having no eyelids, because he cut them off so he could avoid falling asleep and spend more time meditating. He is regarded as the First Patriarch of Zen in China.

Regardless of the precise method of introduction, when Buddhist meditative practice and the idea of *sunyata* reached China, they found a receptive audience among philosophical Taoists.

Bodhidharma was followed by subsequent Patriarchs, the most famous among them the sixth, *Hui-neng* (ca. 638–713). He was an illiterate kitchen laborer, who nevertheless experienced enlightenment. He is the traditional author of the Platform Sutra, which helped the Meditation school in China establish its own basis apart from the Indian texts. It popularized an approach to meditation known as "sudden enlightenment," in which radical techniques such as shouts, slaps, and even cutting off a student's finger were used to try to shock students out of their dependence on ordinary thought. This led to the creation in China of a southern school that emphasized "sudden enlightenment," as opposed to the more scholarly approach in the north, where quiet meditation and study of philosophical texts was thought to lead to a "gradual awakening." Advocates of the southern school apparently burned Buddhist scriptures and destroyed images of the Buddha. One teacher of "sudden enlightenment" is reputed to have said, "If you meet the Buddha, kill him!"

The Chinese Meditation school took root as a distinct movement in Japan in the late twelfth and early thirteenth centuries C.E. Two major movements, *Rinzai* and *Soto,* continue today, with the latter the larger and the former the more well-known for its teaching techniques. *Rinzai* emphasizes seated meditation on the word puzzles known as *koans* to lead to the experience of enlightenment. *Soto* puts more emphasis on the practice of seated meditation itself as the means of enlightenment.

The influence of Zen in Japanese culture has been very significant. According to Zen teaching, the ultimate truth is found in the tiniest detail of nature and amidst ordinary activities. Therefore, seemingly mundane activities such as the serving of tea become rituals that manifest the underlying harmony behind the seeming distinctions of this world. Under the influence of Zen, a Japanese approach to beauty developed in which the spontaneous and natural are appreciated over the ordered and conventional. Ink painting in which the artist quickly draws the brush over the paper, leaving flowing marks that cannot be changed, is one example. Another is the *haiku* poetry, through which in a single breath the poet expresses an immediate experience of a single moment. One famous haiku poem illustrates the technique:

> An age-old pond—
> A frog leaps out
> Sound of splashing water.

Ironically, in the arts influenced by Zen there *is* convention (such as the haiku pattern or the elements of the tea ceremony), but within the seeming limitation there is spontaneity and immediacy.

A Japanese rock garden reflects the influence of Zen Buddhist teaching.

QUESTIONS OF HUMAN IDENTITY: WHAT IS THE BASIC HUMAN DILEMMA?

Blinded by their Own Sight

For Zen teachers, one of the fundamental problems to be overcome is rational thinking, which causes us to view ourselves as separate from that which we are observing. This passage from the ninth-century-C.E. Zen master, Hsi Yun, is an example of such teaching (Blofeld [Chu Ch'an] 1958: 36).

The Pure Mind, the source of everything, shines forever and on all with the brilliance of its own perfection. But the people of the world do not awake to it, regarding only that which sees, hears, feels, and knows as mind. Blinded by their own sight, hearing, feeling, and knowledge, they do not perceive the spiritual brilliance of the source-substance. If they could only eliminate all conceptual thought in a flash, that source-substance would manifest itself like the sun ascending through the void and illuminating the whole universe without hindrance or bounds. Therefore, if you students of the Way seek to progress through seeing, hearing, feeling, and knowing, when you are deprived of your perceptions, your way to Mind will be cut off and you will find nowhere to enter.

Excerpt from Zen Teachings of Huang Po *by John Blofeld. Copyright © 1958 by John Blofeld. Reprinted with permission of Grove Press.*

The forms represent the presence of the absolute truth in a single moment. Japanese painting and gardens, in which elements seem to come to their own natural expression in a fluid beauty, with much space left empty, also reflect the Zen understanding.

Zen also influenced the development of the martial arts of China and Japan. The various schools share the insight that you should not try to overwhelm your opponent with aggressive, self-exerted force. Rather, when one moves with the existing flow of energy, the advantage comes naturally.

In Japan today Zen is still quite popular. The *Rinzai* school has over 2 million adherents, while about 7 million follow the *Soto* school. A smaller movement founded in the seventeenth century, called *Obaku,* combines Zen with Pure Land teaching.

Zen has become very popular in the United States. A number of Zen centers offer the opportunity to practice Zen techniques of meditation for a short time or for extended periods. They are typically led by Westerners who have studied under a Japanese master and reached enlightenment. The regimen is very similar to that in Japanese monasteries. In addition, Zen has been popularized by a number of books that offer a critique of Western, American culture from a Zen perspective.

According to Zen teaching, every individual has the nature of the Buddha. The problem is that we deceive ourselves into thinking we are *not* the Buddha. It is as though the Buddha is the sun and our nature is a calm pool that perfectly reflects the Buddha, but the surface of the water is disturbed and the perfect light breaks up into a myriad of seemingly separate particles. We deceive ourselves through becoming attached to the pleasures of this world and the diversity of objects we think we see. But we also deceive ourselves through becoming attached to the desire to escape attachment to the world. We are trapped both by our normal consciousness of the world and by our desire to be liberated from it.

How can we find our way our of this dilemma? Like early Buddhist teaching, and in contrast to the Pure Land school, Zen emphasizes that one cannot rely on forces outside oneself to discover the truth. The truth lies within, for only there can we awaken to the reality that there is no distinction between ourselves and the rest of reality. The journey is one of self-discovery, as one turns inward to penetrate to the depths of one's own existence to experience the "emptiness" or "voidness" that is at the heart of everything.

Through meditation one can overcome the illusion of "duality," that there is an "I" who stands over against the "world." The goal of Zen is the

At the center of Tibetan Buddhism are the *lamas* ("superior ones"). Although the term is sometimes used to refer to all Tibetan monks, lamas are more specifically monks (or lay people) who possess special magical powers, revealing that they are incarnations of Buddhas and bodhisattvas. In each monastery there is a hierarchy of lamas.

In the fourteenth century a reform movement in Tibetan Buddhism led to the creation of a new school. It became known as the Yellow Hat school, because the monks (called Yellow Hats) wore the color yellow to symbolize a return to the pure teachings of Buddha, and to distinguish themselves from those who resisted reform, who wore red (those monks were called Red Hats). The reform imposed a stricter discipline on monks (reintroducing celibacy, for example), but did not abolish all signs of Tantrism.

Because of the celibacy rule in the Yellow Hat order, the succession of leadership could not be hereditary. To meet this need the theory of the reincarnation of the abbots (heads) of monasteries developed. According to this concept the grand lamas of each monastery were the incarnations of Buddhas. After their deaths, they were reborn in another human form. After the death of the abbot an elaborate search for his successor began. It might take years. The goal was to find a young child, born forty-nine days after the abbot's death, who demonstrated clear familiarity with some of the abbot's belongings and who had the magical marks of the abbot on his body. Other magical signs were sought through divination. The child was then taken from his family, raised in the monastery, and installed as abbot.

In the sixteenth century the Grand Lama of the monastery at the main city of Tibet, Lhasa, took the name the *Dalai Lama.* The head lama of Lhasa had been considered an incarnation of the Buddha *Avalokita* (Avalokitesvara). According to one tradition, as a result of his work in revitalizing Buddhism in Mongolia, he was given the honorary title Dalai ("sea"), to symbolize the infinite wisdom of the Buddha he incarnated. The Yellow Hat school gained more power and influence; it not only became the dominant Buddhist movement in Tibet but spread into Mongolia, Russia, and Siberia.

A Tibetan refugee in India places an offering before a picture of the Dalai Lama.

Beginning in the seventeenth century, the Dalai Lama became the symbol of the nation of Tibet, considered both its temporal and its religious leader. By this time one-fifth of the people of Tibet lived in monasteries, which were great fortresses in addition to being religious centers.

The fourteenth and present Dalai Lama was identified as a 5-year-old child in 1940. When the Chinese took control of Tibet in 1951, he tried to work within the framework of the Communist regime. After a revolt in 1959 the Dalai Lama escaped to India, where he established a center for the preservation of Tibetan culture. He has traveled extensively to make known the plight of the Tibetan people and to call for understanding among world religions and peace among the nations of the world. For his work he was awarded the Nobel Peace Prize.

The most famous text in Tibetan Buddhism is the *Bardo Thodol* ("the between state in which there is liberation through hearing"). It is popularly known in the West as the *Tibetan Book of the Dead*. The work focuses on the liberation of a person during the period from the moment of death until the next incarnation, which lasts forty-nine days. This period is the *bardo*, the "time between." The book gives elaborate instructions to those who are attending a dying person. Typically, a lama sits at the head of the person and chants magical formulae that are intended to help the person be reborn in the Western Paradise of Amitabha rather than on earth. As death approaches, the dying person is given instructions on how to attain liberation. After death the corpse is placed in a seated position for four days, and the instructions continue. Then, after the funeral, during the entire bardo, a picture or effigy of the deceased may become the focus of further instruction. The Bardo Thodol has become popular in the West, and has been subjected to extensive psychological and philosophical interpretation.

SHINTO: THE NATIVE RELIGION OF JAPAN

At this writing, the news is full of stories of "Japan bashing"—Americans' blaming the economic problems their country is facing at least in part on Japan. At the same time one senses a begrudging admiration for the work ethic, family values, and dogged commitment to the national well-being in Japan. Matching the American ambivalence toward Japan is a similar attitude toward America in Japan. Americans read of Japanese politicians talking about the laziness of American workers and the lack of national will, while many Japanese citizens yearn for the freedom of expression and individuality they see in American culture. One conclusion seems safe: More understanding of Japanese culture is needed in America, and vice versa. One popular book of the early 1990s, *The Coming War with Japan*, sounds an ominous, if perhaps overblown, warning about the cost of a failure to understand.

Shinto, the traditional religion of Japan, played a critical role in the formation of Japanese culture and the Japanese national identity. Despite reports of its demise in recent decades, Shinto continues to be a significant force in Japanese life today.

Stages of Development and Sacred Texts

The Names "Shinto" and "Kami-no-michi"   Like Hinduism and other native religious traditions, Shinto defies easy classification. Its very name reflects the problem. "Shinto" comes from two Chinese words we have already encountered: *shen* and *tao*. Therefore, Shinto is the "way of the spirits." "Shinto" was in fact the name developed to try to understand the native traditions of Japan when Buddhism was introduced, just as the name "Hinduism" came out of a need to distinguish indigenous Indian beliefs and practices from Islam, when the Muslims entered India. Indeed, in the early stages of the development of religion in Japan there was no Shinto, only a variety of indigenous religious traditions.

The same Japanese characters pronounced *shen tao*, can also be pronounced (when the two characters are separated) as *kami-no-michi*, "the way of the kami." We will discuss the meaning of *kami* more fully below, but in general *kami* refers to anything or anyone inspiring awe, respect, and devotion. It is the Japanese word for "the sacred." The

Rising above Lake Kawaguchi, Mt. Fuji is revered as a kami *in the Shinto worldview.*

goal of life, according to Shinto teaching, is to live in harmony with the *kami*.

The Shinto Myth: Japan as the Land of the Kami

The roots of Shinto are found in the myth of the origins of the Japanese islands. The *Shinto Myth* probably had a long oral history, but it was first compiled in written form in 712 C.E., in a work known as the *Kojiki* ("Chronicle of Ancient Events"). The *Kojiki* was a complete history of the world from the creation down to the middle of the seventh century. Together with the *Nihongi*

("Chronicles of Japan"), written down by 720 C.E., these two documents form the core of the traditional Japanese understanding of national identity and history.

According to the *Kojiki,* (See Insert) the Japanese islands were created at the beginning of time by two *kami*, the original male, *Izanagi* ("Male-Who-Invites") and *Izanami* ("Female-Who-Invites") . A story of the pollution and cleansing of Izanagi foreshadows the central role of ritual purification in Shinto. From the left eye of Izanagi came the deity most revered in Japan, the sun goddess,

The Shinto Myth's story of the union of the original couple, Izanagi *and* Izanami, *is symbolized in these paired rocks near the Ise Shrine*

Amaterasu. A long list of other deities also came into being in Japan. For example, the storm god, *Susano-wo,* emerged from the nostrils of Izanagi, and subsequently engaged in a series of struggles with Amaterasu. Later, concerned about the disorder on the islands, Amaterasu sent her grandson to rule. According to legend, his great-grandson, *Jimmu Tenno,* was the first human emperor of Japan, and the ancestor of all subsequent imperial houses. The traditional date for his ascendancy is 660 B.C.E.

Therefore, according to the Shinto Myth, the emperor of Japan is a descendant of the sun goddess herself. The Japanese islands were the center of creation, and the Japanese people are all descended from the *kami.* Indeed, Japan is "the land of the *kami.*"

Medieval Shinto: Theoretical Amalgamation with Buddhism We will discuss the beliefs and practices associated with traditional Shinto below. At this point, as we examine the development of Shinto, we need to look at the period during which traditional Shinto was influenced most strongly by Buddhism, which by the mid–sixth century C.E. had been introduced from China by way of Korea. From this time on, Buddhist and Shinto teachings had influenced one another. Our

interest here is the theoretical amalgamation of the two.

As Buddhist influence spread outside the Japanese court into the villages, Shinto priests adapted by erecting Buddhist temples within the Shinto shrines. As a result, theoretical teachings developed about the relationship between Buddhist deities and the Shinto *kami.* The most common was the idea of "original substance, manifest traces." Shinto scholars argued that the original substance was found in *kami,* and the manifest traces were the Buddhist deities (if you're wondering how we can speak of Buddhist "gods," given what we said earlier about Buddhism, please be patient, we're getting there), while Buddhist teachers argued the opposite. Buddhism seemed to have the better of the debate. In any event, several different schools of "mixed Shinto" emerged, each trying to resolve the question of the relationship between the *kami* and Buddhist deities in different ways. The most popular was *Ryobu* ("two-sided") Shinto, which treated the two as manifestations of the same reality. For example, Amaterasu was said to be the same as the very popular Sun Buddha, *Vairocana.* During the Kamakura period Buddhism nearly supplanted Shinto through a process of absorption and redefinition.

COSMIC QUESTIONS: HOW DID THE WORLD COME INTO BEING?

Creation by the Kami

The Shinto Myth, preserved in the ancient chronicle known as the Kojiki, *includes the story of creation by the* kami, *making clear that Japan is at the center of creation and is the land of the* kami *(Kojiki, Book One, ch. 1, 3-4, Philippi 1968: 47-51).*

At the time of the beginning of heaven and earth, there came into existence in Takama-no-Para a deity named Ame-no-mi-naka-nusi-no-kami; next, Taka-mi-musubi-no-kami; next, Kami-musubi-no-kami. These three deities all came into existence as single deities, and their forms were not visible.

Next, when the land was young, resembling floating oil and drifting like a jellyfish, there sprouted forth something like reed-shoots. From these came into existence the deity Umasi-asi-kabi-piko-di-no-kami; next, Ame-no-toko-tati-n-kami. These two deities also came into exis-tence as single deities, and their forms were not visible.

The five deities in the above section are the Separate Heavenly Deities. [Next came into existence the Seven Generations of the Age of the Gods, including Izanagi-no-kami and his spouse Izanami-no-kami.]

At this time the heavenly deities, all with one command, said to the two deities Izanagi-no-mikoto and Izanami-no-mikoto: "Complete and solidify this drifting land!"

Another feature of medieval Shinto and its amalgamation not only with Buddhism but also with Confucianism deserves special attention: the *bushido* ("military-warrior-way") of the *samurai* warrior. It was developed in the Kamakura period, and systemized in the Tokugawa period. Although it has been compared to the medieval European knight's code of chivalry, it has a decidedly East Asian character. The unwritten code bound the samurai to their feudal lords with loyalty and to nature with reverence. Some of the virtues associated with bushido in addition to loyalty and reverence are courage, truthfulness, respect, and justice. However, the most famous bushido virtue is honor, to the extent that death is preferable to disgrace for the true samurai. The warrior always carries two swords, one to do battle with the enemy and another, shorter sword to commit ritual suicide (*seppuku*) if honor requires. Bushido reflects the influence of Confucianism with its emphasis on filial piety, loyalty, and the five basic relationships; Zen Buddhism in its focus on self-discipline and spontaneity of action;

and Shinto in its aesthetic appreciation of nature and pride in one's ruler.

In the twentieth century the bushido still has a strong influence in Japanese life. The legendary courage of Japanese *kamikaze* pilots and other Japanese combatants during World War II is a modern version of bushido, with loyalty to the feudal lord transferred to the emperor and nation. Today, some have called the Japanese businessman the modern samurai. He gives absolute obedience to his corporation, whose well-being is more important than his own. Occasionally, even today there are examples of ritual suicide carried out by a man (*harakiri*) and his wife (*jigai*). The spiritual aura of the martial arts, still evident in modern Japan, can be traced in part to the bushido.

The Revival of Shinto Efforts to restore Shinto as the central religion of Japan began as early as the fourteenth century, but it was during the Tokugawa period, beginning in the seventeenth century, that the revival became an important

Giving them the Heavenly Jeweled Spear, they entrusted the mission to them.

Thereupon, the two deities stood on the Heavenly Floating Bridge and, lowering the jeweled spear, stirred with it. They stirred the brine with a churning-churning sound, and when they lifted up [the spear] again, the brine dripping down from the tip of the spear piled up and became an island. This was the island Onogoro.

Descending from the heavens to this island, they erected a heavenly pillar and a spacious palace.

At this time [Izanagi] asked his spouse Izanami, saying: "How is your body formed?"

She replied, saying: "My body, formed though it be formed, has one place which is formed insufficiently."

Then Izanagi-no-mikoto said: "My body, formed though it be formed, has one place which is formed to excess. Therefore, I would like to take that place in my body which is formed to excess and insert it into that place in your body which is formed insufficiently, and [thus] give birth to the land. How would this be?"

Izanami-no-mikoto said: "Then let us, you and me, walk in a circle around this heavenly pillar and have conjugal intercourse."

.... They commenced procreation and gave birth to a leech-child. They placed this child into a boat of reeds and floated it away.

Next they gave birth to the island of Apa. This also is not reckoned as one of their children.

[As the story continues, Izanami dies giving birth to fire and descends to the underworld. Izanagi follows her, and unsuccessfully tries to bring her back to life. When he escapes from the underworld, he purifies himself, and creates many *kami*, including the sun goddess, Amaterasu.]

Excerpt from Kojiki, trans. Donald Philippi. Reprinted with permission of University of Tokyo Press.

---

force. This was the time when Japan's military leaders tried to close Japan to foreign influence. They joined with Shinto scholars in promoting a return to the "ancient way." The leading scholar, Motoori Norinaga, taught that Japan was superior to other countries, which are bound to give allegiance to the Mikado, the Japanese emperor. This ideology was to play an important role in the promotion of Japanese expansionism in the mid–twentieth century.

Shinto as a State Religion (1868–1945)

The introduction of Western values that followed the forced re-opening of Japan by American naval forces under Commodore Perry in 1853 led to a reaction that sought to secure Shinto as the national ideology. During the Meiji period (1868–1912) and until the end of World War II in 1945 this effort continued. For example, the Constitution of 1881 stated in Article III that "the emperor is sacred and inviolable." This was an abstract endorsement of the Shinto Myth's contention that the emperor was the manifest *kami*, a descendant of the sun goddess.

At first, an attempt was made to force Buddhism and Christianity out of Japan. Failing in the effort to purge foreign religious influences from Japan entirely, the strategy shifted to the creation of a state Shinto ostensibly separate from religious practice. State Shinto (*Jinja-Shinto*) included most of the rituals and shrines, placing them under the control of a government Bureau of Shrines. All Japanese were required to register at a shrine.

The Shinto Myth's teachings concerning the sacredness of Japan and its centrality were ordered to be taught in schools. The Imperial Rescript on Education (1890), the basis for the educational system, called the Imperial Throne "coeval with heaven and earth" and the Way of the Ancestors "infallible for all ages and true in all places." Until 1945 this is what every Japanese schoolchild was taught to accept without question. Students bowed daily before a picture of the emperor. A 1911 order required teachers to take their students to Shinto shrines for festivals, in order to teach them the reverence that is the foundation of national morality. Whether there is a substantial difference between these practices and the civic rituals conducted and observed in the schools of other nations is an interesting topic of discussion.

The government listed over 100,000 shrines during this period. Some were run by the government, but most were local shrines. Sixteen thousand priests served the major state shrines. They were instructed not to carry out overtly religious ceremonies, but the national rituals conducted by these priests were hard to distinguish from religious rites.

State Shinto was officially non-religious. The spiritual side of the Shinto Myth was de-emphasized. The *kami* of the Myth were said to be human beings who had attained legendary status. However, from our perspective state Shinto *was* a religion, albeit a secular one. Loyalty to the nation and to the emperor as its symbol became the goal. Transformation was through giving oneself fully to the nation and to the emperor, making "His august will" one's own. The *kokutai-ni-hongi* (1937) tells citizens that when they go to the shrines to perform rituals, they will be "'dying to self' to become one with the State."

With the creation of state Shinto, an officially religious branch of Shinto was recognized. Sectarian Shinto (*Kyoha-Shinto*) included thirteen separate Shinto sects that had developed by the late nineteenth century. Some focused on *kami* in nature, making prominent features such as the magnificent Mount Fuji the object of worship. Others tended toward the individual desire for health and well-being. The most prominent among this group was *Tenri-kyo*, which emphasizes faith-healing and is still a popular movement in postwar Japan. Still other Shinto sects tried to maintain the spiritual side of the Shinto Myth and the traditional rituals of purification.

State Shinto played an important role in the fostering of support in Japan for the expansionist policies that led Japan into war with the United States, Britain, and other Western powers. The most dramatic example of its influence is the phenomenon of the *kamikaze*, the Japanese pilots who crashed their planes into the enemy ships approaching Japan toward the end of the war. They were named after the "divine wind" that had turned back another foreign invasion in 1281. They manifested the idea that if the people were loyal, Japan would remain inviolable.

Shinto Today   In December 1945, four months after the dropping of the atomic bombs on Hiroshima and Nagasaki and the unconditional surrender of Japan to the Allied powers, the occupation government arranged for the publication of a "Shinto Directive." It required the abolition of government support, sponsorship, perpetuation, dissemination, and control of state Shinto. It also included the mandate that the Shinto Myth be withdrawn as the basis of Japanese education.

A month later the Emperor's Rescript stated that the emperor was not divine, Japan was not the center of the universe, and the Japanese people were not superior to any other people. Emperor Hirohito called on the Japanese people to work toward the improvement of all humanity, not just their own country. A new constitution guaranteed religious freedom and forbade state involvement in religious activities.

In this changed environment a host of "new religions" gained popularity (see Chapter Fourteen). A few (especially Soka Gakkai) have become quite influential in modern Japan and have spread to other parts of the world.

After World War II, shrine Shinto replaced the now forbidden state Shinto. The number of shrines dropped to about 85,000, with control of them at the local level. Because of land reform, shrines lost their holdings and were forced to either close or provide other services, such as pre-schools or kindergartens, for support. Many priests, accustomed to receiving government support, had to take at least part-time jobs. Still, the custom of a hereditary priesthood associated with different shrines continued. A private shrine association formed to provide coordination and support for the formerly government-controlled shrines. We will discuss the layout of a typical shrine and other aspects of the practice of Shinto at the national, local, and family levels when we discuss Shinto teachings.

Some Japanese today consider Shinto an anachronism in the secular, materialistic society

Japan has become. However, reports of the death of Shinto have been greatly exaggerated. Even though relatively few Japanese consider Shinto their "religion" in a formal sense, the role of Shinto in the actual life of the Japanese people continues. For many, Shinto still provides a way to express patriotism and national identity, as well as to strengthen family ties, and is a source of consolation at times of crisis. Whether Shinto still provides "transformation in response to perceived ultimacy" for more than a relative handful of Japanese today is an issue worthy of a more extended study.

Distinctive Teachings

In this summary of Shinto teaching we will focus on the traditional beliefs and practices associated with the historic shrines. As in other Asian religions, there is no central authority establishing an orthodoxy in Shinto. Shinto has different meanings for different people. It is also important to realize that allegiance to Shinto is not veiwed as exclusive. In the mid-1980s, over 80 percent of the Japanese people surveyed indicated an *association* with Shinto. However, 75 percent also considered themselves Buddhist, and about 15 percent identified with the "new religions."

Problem: Impurity   For the traditional Shinto associated with the shrines, the basic dilemma to be overcome is impurity brought on by disharmony with the *kami*. Failure to maintain harmony with the *kami* leads to chaos for individuals, families, and the nation as a whole. According to Shinto teachers, one manifestation of this state is individualism—when people promote themselves over their families, their clans, their companies, or their nation.

Cause: Lack of Reverence   People will naturally follow the path of harmony with the *kami*, unless they lose their reverence for the *kami*. When nature is viewed as lifeless material to be used however people please, rather than as alive, beautiful, and inspiring, people lose reverence for the *kami*. When the ancestors and ancient heroes are

The present emperor and empress of Japan.

forgotten, and people pursue individual pleasure rather than the good of family and society, they lose reverence for the *kami*. If they lose their pride in being Japanese and living in the land of the *kami*, they lose reverence. Lack of reverence results in a state of pollution, from which people must be transformed through rituals of purification and forgiveness.

Reality: The Land of the Kami   Under the influence of Buddhism, Shinto scholars developed an interest in the nature of reality, and searched for the "original essence" that is the foundation of all that is. However, we find a distinct understanding of reality in the Shinto Myth. The Myth teaches the Japanese that their islands are the center of the universe, that Japan is the land of the *kami*, and that all nations are destined to bow before the manifest *kami*, the emperor. This is what might be called an organic conception of reality, in which humanity, nature, and the spiritual all interact in one balanced whole. In a word, the linchpin of this organism is "Japan."

QUESTIONS OF HUMAN IDENTITY: WHAT IS THE BASIC HUMAN DILEMMA?

The Threat of Western Individualism

The following excerpt from the Kokutai no Hongi, *"The Cardinal Principles of the National Entity of Japan" (1937), illustrates the perspective of state Shinto that the basic dilemma facing the Japanese during this period was the influence of Western (Occidental) individualism (Gauntlett and Hall 1974: 82).*

Of late years, through the influence of the Occidental [Western] individualistic ideology, a way of thinking which has for its basis the individual has become lively. Consequently, this and the true aim of our Way of loyalty which is "essentially" different from it are not necessarily [mutually] consistent. That is, those in our country who at the present time expound loyalty and patriotism are apt to lose [sight] of its true significance, being influenced by Occidental individualism and rationalism. We must sweep aside the corruption of the spirit and the clouding of knowledge that arises from setting up one's "self" and from being taken up with one's "self" and return to a pure and clear state of mind that belongs intrinsically to us as subjects, and thereby fathom the great principle of loyalty ....

Excerpt from **Kokutai no Hongi: Cardinal Principles of the National Entity of Japan,** *trans. John Owen Gauntlett and ed. Robert King Hall, Reprinted with permission of Harvard University Press.*

In addition, the *kami* manifest themselves in particular places, creating sacred space. Virtually any place may become such a manifestation, as is evident by the number of shrines. Within homes, the *kami* are present on the *kami* shelf (see below), sanctifying and purifying the home. They are present in the village, in the region, and in national shrines. Therefore, in daily life, communal life, and national life, those who seek purification and live in harmony with the *kami* will live out their lives in sacred space.

In recent years, the traditional understanding has reappeared in a new form. Few Japanese take the Myth's portrait of reality literally today, but there is still a strong belief that "true reality" means the land and people of Japan, and everything and everyone else is outside sacred space. Even when not explicitly stated, this attitude lies behind the suspicious way others are viewed, and the difficulty outsiders (including foreign businesses) have in breaking into Japanese circles. A similar attitude is found in many cultures, including American, but Japanese ethnocentrism may be unique. It has served the Japanese well, enabling them to maintain their strong sense of national identify for centuries, and most recently to experience an amazing rebirth from the ashes of World War II.

At the same time, the Japanese have a remarkable ability to absorb the ways of others and incorporate them into their own culture. From the introduction of Confucianism and Buddhism centuries ago to the fascination with American popular culture today, the Shinto heritage supports openness to new ideas. Two Shinto principles reflect this attitude. One is *musubi* ("creativity and production"), which reflects a pragmatic attitude always ready to draw upon new ideas that have promise, whatever their source. The other is *chuto-hanpa* ("a little of this, a little of that"), which implies a willingness to combine ideas from different sources.

End: Purity   Like Taoism, Shinto has as its ultimate goal cosmic harmony, with all elements in balance. As with Confucianism, the focus of Shinto harmony is this-worldly and social. The ideal for Shinto is a Japanese people living harmoniously in their land, with one another, with the land, and, at the root of it all, with the *kami*. Such is the life of purity toward which all Japanese should strive, according to traditional Shinto teaching.

A practical accommodation has been worked out between Shinto and Buddhism in Japan. Shinto is concerned with life before death, maintaining harmony and purity in the here and now. Buddhism enables people to deal with the impermanence of life and the reality of death, offering a path to deliverance from the suffering of life in this world.

Means: Shinto Temples and Rituals The principal path to harmony and purity in traditional Shinto is through participation in temple rituals. Some rituals are national, others are local, and some are for clans and families. At each level Shinto priests perform the ceremonies of purification.

The most popular national shrine is now, as it has been for centuries, the Grand Imperial Shrine of the sun goddess Amaterasu located at *Ise*, about 200 miles from Tokyo. To some extent Ise is like Mecca for Muslims; every Japanese who takes seriously the Shinto traditions tries to visit Ise at least once. Like most Shinto shrines, the shrine at Ise is a simple structure, made of unpainted cedar. The symbols of Amaterasu are not pictures or statues, but objects associated with the myth of the goddess—a mirror, sword, and string of stone jewels. As part of the concern for purification and renewal, the central shrine buildings are torn down and rebuilt every twenty years.

Virtually every Japanese village has a Shinto shrine, at which the rituals passed down from ancient times are still carried out. Typically the rectangular compound is surrounded by a fence, to demarcate the "sacred space." A sacred threshold, a gateway called the *torii*, marks the entrance to the shrine. A path leads from the *torii* to the outer shrine, called the *haiden*. As the worshipper approaches the *haiden*, the person washes his or her hands and mouth with water for purification. Then the worshipper bows, claps hands to get the attention of the *kami*, rings the bell, drops an offering in a box, leaves a prayer on a piece of paper, and then departs while bowing low. Beyond the outer shrine one finds the inner holy place, called the *honden*. This shrine is not entered by worshippers, for it contains the sacred object associated with the *kami* of the shrine. The object is never seen, except once a year at an annual festival when it is taken and carried through the village.

In addition to the local festival associated with the *kami* of each shrine there are a series of nation-

A large camphor-wood torii *marks the entrance from the sea to the Shinto shrine of Itsukushima.*

al rites that are still widely observed. Twice each year the Great Purification is held, in June and December. Before World War II the emperor, as the manifest *kami*, would pronounce forgiveness for the sins of the nation. The type of cleansing wand used in this ceremony to symbolize the "wiping away" of impurities is used by Shinto priests in other, less formal settings. Someone who has bought a new car, for example, might bring it to the priest to be purified with the cleansing wand and thereby made safe.

Other important national Shinto festivals include New Year's, which begins at midnight on December 31 and continues for three days. This is a time when ordinary life in Japan comes to a standstill, and millions of people travel to their ancestral homes to visit local Shinto shrines and Buddhist temples. Gifts are exchanged, and children typically receive envelopes full of money from relatives.

Of particular importance for family life are the Girl's (Doll's) Festival on March 3 and the Boy's Festival on May 5. The famous Chrysanthemum Festival is held on September 9. The agricultural year is also observed in rural areas in a series of festivals linked to the phases of the cultivation of rice. Shinto's ability to adapt to change and absorb new traditions is seen in the rising popularity of treating Christmas as a Shinto festival, replete with festively decorated shopping malls.

People visit Shinto shrines not only at prescribed occasions, but at times of family importance. The rites of passage of birth, puberty, and marriage are conducted by Shinto priests. In the case of birth, the rite is at the shrine, where the family presents the child to be received as part of the "family of the *kami*." Traditional marriages are elaborate, expensive affairs in which priest and bride wear traditional dress, while the groom wears a Western-style morning coat. People also visit shrines to seek the *kami's* blessing and intercession at special times of family concern. The exception is at death, when the funeral rites are conducted by Buddhist rather that Shinto functionaries.

In addition to shrine Shinto, the practice of Shinto continues in other contexts. One is the home, where many families still maintain a *kami-dana* ("god shelf"). The ancestors of the family and other *kami* special to the family are memorialized on wood or paper tablets with their names inscribed. Miniatures of the special symbols of Amaterasu or other major *kami,* and objects or pictures of ancestors, are also found. Devout families practice daily rituals, involving offerings of food and a prayer. Many others turn to the home shrine at times of special concern or crisis in the family.

Families often have both a shelf for Shinto *kami* and a shelf for Buddhist deities and the names of ancestors (*butsu-dan*).

Sacred: Kami We have spoken frequently of the *kami,* for they are at the heart of Shinto, but the reader is probably still wondering just what the *kami* are. Interpreters of Shinto have long struggled with a simple way to describe the *kami*. As we have already indicated, the *kami* are not just deities, although some are gods. According to Shinto tradition, 8 million (or 800,000) *kami* exist. This is a symbolic way of saying that the number of *kami* is infinite. *Kami* may be family ancestors, national or local heroes, persons with extraordinary spiritual powers, celestial bodies such as the sun or moon, topographical features such as mountains or rivers, natural forces such as the wind and thunder, particularly inspiring natural objects such as rocks and trees, animals (foxes and horses

A Shinto priest purifies a new automobile.

are particularly honored), Buddhas and bod-hisattvas, and, of course, the manifest *kami,* the Emperor. Natural features considered *kami* are often designated by being surrounded or connected with a straw rope.

In sum, anything or anyone is potentially a *kami. Kami* symbolize the sacred quality of human existence, nature, and the cosmos as a whole. All reality is infused with *kami,* but some *kami* are transcendent, making Shinto in its traditional form similar to the understanding of the spiritual in indigenous religions of other cultures.

RELIGION IN MODERN EAST ASIA

Having completed the historical survey of the religions of East Asia begun in the last chapter, we will now look briefly at the situation of religions in several of the countries of modern East Asia: China, Japan, and South Korea.

China: The Impact of Communism

In 1937 the Nationalist leader Chiang Kai-shek erected a shrine with a tablet of Confucius surrounded by busts of Western scientists such as Galileo and Newton. It was intended to symbolize a new China synthesizing the best of Chinese tradition with the best of Western science and technology. Near the end of the twentieth century, events in China seem to suggest a similar attempt, but now the "best of Chinese tradition" includes fifty years of Communist rule.

When Mao Tse-tung led the successful Communist Revolution that created the People's Republic of China in 1949, he established as a goal the weeding out of all religion and philosophical idealism from Chinese life. According to the Marxist doctrine he accepted as ultimate, religion and other forms or ideology were weeds that choked the ability of people to solve the problems of the material world. Until 1966 the official policy of the Communist government was that religion would die a natural death. The new socialist democracy would choke religion's social roots—its

function as a tool of exploitation by the ruling classes. Education and improved living standards of the masses would choke its cognitive root—ignorance of the real forces causing their misery.

The Communist government recognized as religions Buddhism, Christianity, and Islam. In 1949 there were about 100 million Buddhists in China, 25 million Muslims, and 4 million Christians. The Chinese Constitution of 1951 allowed freedom of individual religion, but placed all religious institutions and leaders under strict government control. Separate associations were created to oversee the activities of each religion and to make certain that they were supportive of the Communist goals. For example, the Chinese National Patriotic Movement was the government agency that administered Catholicism. Religious leaders who refused to demonstrate the proper "socialist spirit" were sent to special re-education camps.

Confucianism was considered an idealistic philosophy, and Confucius a sponsor of the feudal order that oppressed the people. Religious Taoism was dismissed as a superstition that should be actively repressed.

In 1966 the Great Proletarian Cultural Revolution initiated a period of severe repression of all religions. Religion had not died a natural death, so government policy changed to "pull up and destroy all its poisonous roots." All churches, mosques, and monasteries were ordered closed, and the buildings were given over to more "socially useful" purposes; they were turned into museums, schools, and warehouses. Religious leaders and all vestiges of religion became the target of the fanatical Red Guard, who sought to eliminate from Chinese life the "four olds": old ideas, old customs, old habits, and old culture. The constitutional right to private free expression of religion was ignored, and even home altars became the target of Red Guard attack.

Mao died in 1975, and the new leadership discredited the Cultural Revolution. In 1978 the constitutional guarantee of free, private religious expression was reintroduced. In recent years, religious institutions have been allowed to reopen, including schools to train a new generation of religious leaders. The numbers of Christians,

In a 1989 protest in Tiananmen Square in Beijing, students erected a "goddess of liberty" as a symbol of their hope for democratic reform.

Muslims, and Buddhists are steadily growing, and there are even signs of a resurgence of Taoism and folk religion. The status of Confucianism is changing as well. The ancestral home of Confucius, destroyed during the Cultural Revolution, has been restored. The current Chinese Communist leadership seems to be trying to draw on the Confucian heritage of respect for authority and commitment to moral virtue to balance the rising tide of individualism and consumerism, especially among the youth. As many have observed, from the outset Mao Tse-tung and other Communist leaders adapted Confucian virtues to their teaching of loyalty to "the people" and to the Communist Party.

Whether or not this new receptivity to religion is part of an effort to improve the image of China in the West or a sincere change of heart is open to question. The Chinese leadership is still officially committed to the Communist philosophy, which, as

we will see in Chapter Fourteen, may be considered a secular religion. As long as it is the "state religion of China," openness to other religions will be limited. While individual freedom of religion is recognized, attempts to spread religion are still controlled, and only the right to propagate atheism is constitutionally guaranteed. The democratic reforms essential to the creation of a society that respects religious pluralism have been thwarted.

Modern China seeks openness to the best of Western science and technology while maintaining its fifty-year-old heritage of Communism. A Chinese traditionalist might point out that the current government will only remain in power as long as the "mandate of heaven" continues. Then another revolution will occur, and a new government committed to preserving the moral order will emerge. For a traditionalist there are signs that this process has begun.

Japan: The Impact of Materialism

The irony of religion in modern Japan is that while the majority of Japanese consider themselves non-religious, religions (especially Shinto, Buddhism, Confucianism, and the "new religions" to be discussed in Chapter Fourteen) have a continuing impact on Japanese life. Many people still participate in Shinto and Buddhist rituals at least periodically, and although the number of home altars has declined, they are still present (if not regularly attended) in many homes. Confucian virtues still have a strong impact on the way Japanese view themselves and treat others.

Has Japan become a secular, materialistic society, with spiritual traditions preserved only in vestigial form? If so, the argument could be made that the effective religion for most Japanese (as is the case in other affluent societies) is *materialism*. The perceived ultimacy may be simply wealth and the comfortable lifestyle wealth brings, and the transformation the frantic commitment to the accumulation of material things so evident in Japan today.

As in other societies that have gone through a period of modernization, there are growing numbers of Japanese traditionalists calling for a recommitment to the heritage of Shinto, with its strong sense of nationalism. And the new religions, with their varied approaches to individual spirituality, have attracted growing numbers of persons for whom materialism has left a void in their lives, or who see one of the religions as a vehicle for improving their position in society.

Whatever happens, it will be interesting indeed to observe the future of religion in the "land of the *kami.*"

South Korea: The Impact of Christianity

More than in other East Asian societies, Christianity has taken root and grown significantly in South Korea, to the extent that it is a significant force in modern Korea. Like Japan, South Korea has become a quite secular society. Only about 25 percent of the population of about 45 million people acknowledge a religious affiliation. Of this number, about 70 percent claim Buddhism, and 30 percent Christianity. However, this gives the Christian churches a much stronger voice than in other East Asian societies. Some Christians have been leaders in the efforts to bring greater respect for human rights and protection for the rights of workers. As in Japan and China, Confucian virtues continue to have a very strong impact in South Korea.

North Korea is still an officially Communist state, with few signs of the change in attitude being observed in China. However, in both North and South Korea, Confucianism continues to be the dominant force in social relations.

RESPONSES TO CONTEMPORARY ETHICAL ISSUES

The Ecological Crisis

Shinto   In an article on "The Japanese Experience of Nature," David Edward Shaner has highlighted two of the central themes in the Japanese attitude toward nature that expressed themselves in both Shinto and the Mahayana schools of Buddhism: ecocentrism (as opposed to anthropocentrism) and cultivation.

One symbol of the "ecocentric" principle is the *torii*, the gateway outside a Shinto shrine. The freestanding, open gateway indicates the lack of separation and the necessary balance between the man-made and the natural.

The paper walls of Japanese houses, which are sensitive to changes in light, wind, and temperature, also reflect a sense of the participation of nature in that which humans create (Shaner 1989: 166).

The theme of "cultivation" (*shugyo*) refers to the importance of the development of character in Japanese culture. Cultivation "depends upon an emotional engagement with nature and others" (Shaner 175). From this perspective, as we seek to develop ourselves we must always realize that we are part of a larger social and natural whole. There is a long tradition in Japanese culture of seeking "a keen emotional sensitivity to and empathy with the natural environment" (Shaner 177).

Shaner summarizes the Japanese attitude toward nature as a basis for ecological action in these words (179):

> From the beginning of recorded history, the Japanese world view seems to be one characterized by an intimate, prereflective, and emotional encounter with the natural world. Emotion thus served as the basis for a type of interspecies awareness. By cultivating one's sensitivity towards one's surroundings, one could more effectively intuit feelings of identity with the environment as a whole. . . . When these intimate feelings occur, they are free from moralistic reflection; yet, they serve as a ground for later remembrance and assertive action.

Mahayana Buddhism   Among the Mahayana schools, Zen has the most important environmental implications. If all reality is , in truth, the Buddha-nature, as Zen teaches, then the attitude of egoism that contributes to abuse of the environment is undermined. Zen teaching—as expressed, for example, in the art it inspires—emphasizes the harmony of nature and the place of humans within the processes of nature. The mystical experience of *satori* is of a harmony beyond description, which leads to a calm and peaceful lifestyle of balance, with all of the "grasping" that has created the environmental crisis overcome. Zen students seek to awaken to an identity with all beings, thus emptying themselves of awareness of separate self. A Korean Zen master, Samu Sunim, has said: "Everything depends on others for survival and nothing really exists apart from everything else. Therefore, there is no permanent self or entity independent of others. Not only are we interdependent, but we are an interrelated whole. As trees, rocks, clouds, insects, humans and animals, we are all equals and parts of our universe" (cited by Donegan 1990: 197).

Robert Aitken, an American prisoner of war of the Japanese during World War II, learned about Zen during his captivity and went on to establish a Zen center in Hawaii. Aitken has drawn out the implications of Zen for environmental awareness, stressing that according to Zen, "there is no barrier between human and non-human," and that all beings, even the grasses, are "in the process of enlightenment." He says that those who want to practice responsible environmental ethics must begin with "the cultivation of intimacy with all things" (cited in Nash 1989: 116).

Another environmental interpreter of Zen and other Mahayana teachings to the West has been Gary Snyder, a Pulitzer Prize–winning nature poet. Snyder reflected on the ecological consciousness of Mahayana Buddhism: "Avatamasaka (Kegon) Buddhist philosophy sees the world as a vast interrelated network in which all objects and creatures are necessary and illuminated. ... The hawk, the swoop and the hare are one. From the 'human' standpoint we cannot live in those terms unless all beings see with the same enlightened eye. The Bodhisattva lives by the sufferer's standard, and he must be effective in aiding those who suffer" (Snyder 1969: 91–92).

The Mahayana Hua-yen Sutra uses the image of the Net of Indra to illustrate the interdependence of all reality (Cook 1977). According to this text, in the abode of the god Indra there is a net that stretches infinitely in all directions, with a jewel on each point or "eye" of the net. Each jewel in the net reflects and contains all other jewels. And in each jewel is another net. The image symbolizes a cosmos in which all members are interrelated and infi-

---

QUESTIONS OF MORALITY: WHAT ARE OUR OBLIGATIONS TO NON-HUMAN LIFE?

Harmony with All

The harmony of nature is a basic Shinto principle. Here family imagery is used to speak of the harmony that needs to be maintained (Oracle of the God of Atsuta; *Aston 1905: 370*).

All ye men who dwell under Heaven. Receive the just commands of the Gods. Regard Heaven as your father, Earth as your mother, and all things as your brothers and sisters. You will then enjoy this divine country which excels all others, free from hate and sorrow.

---

nite. What affects one member affects all. There is no hierarchy, no center (for all are at the center). In this universe everything is needed, everything valuable: "It is not just that 'we are all in it' together. We all *are* it, rising or falling as one living body" (cited in Callicott and Ames 1989: 229).

Many philosophers of Western science are beginning to point to the congeniality between the basic Buddhist concept of impermanence and the emerging ecological understanding that all reality is in process. Yale biophysicist Harold Morowitz has noted that "although Buddhist syntax is entirely different from that of modern science, the notion is clearly present that everything is process—a process which only persists by virtue of some universal kind of energy flowing through the world.. ...As originally presented this must have been a very mystical idea, but a similar kind of idea seems to emerge from modern science. Everything we know of is indeed process, which is mediated on the surface of our planet by the flow of solar energy through all organized structures" (cited in Callicott and Ames 1989: 47).

The leader of Tibetan Buddhism, the Dalai Lama, speaking at the Global Forum of Parliamentary and Spiritual Leaders in 1988, captured the Buddhist attitude of compassion for all living things in these words: "Our mother planet is telling us, 'My dear children, behave in a more harmonious way. Please take more care of me!' " (Vittachi 1989). In 1990 he wrote hopefully that "if we develop good and considerate qualities within our own minds, our activities will naturally cease to threaten the continued survival of life on Earth. . . . If we care for nature, it can be rich, bountiful, and inexhaustibly sustainable" (Badiner 1990: v).

Euthanasia

Zen Buddhist masters instruct their disciples to live naturally. Presumably, this means that life should be allowed to take its course, without undue interference. One master expressed the Buddhist position by saying, "Buddha said, 'Don't kill all life.' Many machines and drugs are not necessary. Let all beings live in a natural way. When you die, where do you go?" (Serng Sahn; cited in Larue 1985: 135). When one dying Buddhist teacher was offered drugs to alleviate his pain, "he told them not to worry about that. He sat with one of the attendants supporting his head. A doctor began to give him oxygen, but with a wave of his hand he motioned him away" Kapleau 1967: 68; cited in Larue: 136).

As in Hinduism, the Buddhist belief that life and death are merely stages in a cycle that continues until enlightenment mitigates against euthanasia becoming a contentious issue.

Economic Justice

One recent interpreter has suggested that Mahayana Buddhism can provide the religious basis for the emergence of a new, global order, just as Protestantism was once the motivating force for the development of "modernism" (Thompson 1989: 25):

> *Just as once before Reformation Protestantism was the transformation of Christianity in the shift from medievalism to modernism, so now is Reformation Buddhism part of the transformation from European to planetary culture. Precisely because Buddhism is not,*

> *strictly speaking, a religion, it is more relevant to the spiritualization of everyday life than the conservative modes of consciousness that are crystallized in Hinduism and the Abrahamic religions [Judaism, Christianity, Islam].*

Another interpreter looks to Mahayana Buddhist philosophy for support of identification with the poor, which will be necessary if the gap between the rich and the poor is to be overcome (McDaniel 1985: 197):

> *The Buddhist idea of pratitya samutpada (the nonsubstantial activity of which all sentient beings are a manifestation—emptiness), particularly as interpreted in a process context, can offer further support to the liberation idea that God suffers with all that suffer, and that this suffering is part of the divine life. To say that God exemplifies pratitya samutpada can be to say that within the depths of God's existence there is an openness to influence from without through which God experiences, and is identified with, the feelings of all who suffer. ... The pain of the world is the pain of God.*

From a Mahayana perspective (Batchelor 1990: 179–81):

> *Buddhist economics has to start from the premise of nonduality—recognizing that at root the distinction between agent, act, and object is merely conceptual. It is nothing but a grammatical convenience that has been tragically mistaken to represent three intrinsically separate entities or substances. In fact there are no things apart from the agents that act upon them, and no agents apart from the things upon which they act. Whether we are admiring a tree or cutting it down, we stand in a dynamic, unbroken, and unrepeatable relationship with that tree. Each situation of life is an interdependent, seamless whole, entirely devoid of the divisions imposed on it by our alienated and anxious consciousness.*

Gender Roles and the Status of Women

Shinto In early Japanese history, female spiritual functionaries called *miko* occupied an important role. At the center of Japanese mythology is Amaterasu, the sun goddess and ancestress of the Japanese imperial family. Today a female priesthood continues at Shinto shrines, including Amaterasu's Grand Shrine a Ise, and in popular Shinto practice many women are spiritual mediums and ascetics. Therefore, in traditional Japanese culture and religion, women have had a central role. Shinto tries to harmonize life with the natural, and thus the beauty, fertility, and spontaneity associated with the feminine has highlighted women. However, the hard, uncompromising, disciplined aspects of nature (considered "masculine") have caused Shinto also to support the subordination of women (Carmody 1989: 125).

With the introduction of Chinese cultural influence and Confucian values, the subordination of women took firm hold in Japan and continued until modern times. During the long feudal period, when militarism was dominant, women married to samurai warriors were expected to carry a dagger and commit suicide in a variety of circumstances. For example, if passion for a wife was keeping a samurai warrior from complete devotion to his lord, the wife's duty was to take her own life (Carmody 1989: 118).

Leadership by women in many of the Japanese "new religions," which manifest both Shinto and Buddhist influences (see Chapter Fourteen), has increased the status of women, restoring the shamanic role of early times (Barnes 1994 : 146–50). In most of these religions a woman who suffered emotional or physical trauma had a vision that healed her. She then became a source of healing for others, and a religious movement formed around her (see, for example, Nakamura 1989).

The phenomenon of the *geisha* is also important to understand. Geishas are women who provide entertainment and companionship for men, while the wife cares for the home and family. When geishas themselves marry, they cease to be geishas. While geishas seem to most outsiders to be merely a symptom of a male-dominated society that reserves some women as "playthings" for men and restricts the wife to the home, this has not been the view taken by most women in Japan traditionally. In fact, geishas are more economically independent than other Japanese women. The teahouses run by geishas are women's worlds. Men are customers, but women are in charge. Geisha families provide a warm and supportive atmosphere for the young women who are accepted as apprentices. At the same time, wives are freed from the necessi-

ty of playing a romantic role with their husbands and can dedicate themselves to the management of the household and the nurturing of children. This division of the feminine role may seem insidious to persons of other cultures, but it has been willingly accepted by generations of Japanese women. However, this division does support male domination in Japanese society. Both geishas and wives are expected to have the well-being of men as their principal concern, meeting their needs so that they may be freed to perform in the world of business and industry.

An emergent women's movement in Japan is just beginning to challenge male dominance and discrimination. For example, the "glass ceiling" phenomenon is still a major problem for Japanese women seeking careers. The worst example is the tradition of hiring women in offices for "adornment" and then firing them when they reach their mid-thirties and are no longer thought to contribute to the pleasant surroundings men need to be productive. Women are expected to retire to their role as household managers when they marry, and especially when they begin bearing children. In the early 1980s, 72 percent of Japanese women surveyed agreed that they should be more concerned about their families than themselves (compared with 17.6 percent in the United States) (Carmody 1989: 129). Thus, the traditional attitude that women must be subordinate to men and concern themselves with the well-being of their families rather than any individual career aspirations still dominates in Japan. Whether this should change, and what the effects on Japanese society will be if it does, is a fascinating topic to discuss.

Mahayana Buddhism   In Mahayana Buddhist tradition, women may take the bodhisattva vow and become objects of devotion; there are also feminine Buddhas (Barnes 1987: 121–23). The most famous bodhisattva is Kannon, the popular goddess of mercy in Japan (Kuan-Yin in China). Women often turn to her for assistance in becoming pregnant and giving birth to healthy children. Kannon and other feminine Mahayana "deities" embody the compassion that is at the heart of Buddhist teaching.

A little girl "feeds" a dragon during one of the many annual Shinto festivals.

Buddhist worshippers in Kamakura, Japan, pray before the Daibustu ("Great Buddha"), a fifty-foot tall bronze statue of Amida Buddha, cast in 1252.

One famous Mahayana test focuses on a nun named Lion's-Yawn (enlightenment is sometimes called "the Lion's Roar" in Mahayana schools), who offers sophisticated instruction to seekers after enlightenment (Paul 1979: 94–105).

Another key feminine figure in Mahayana teaching is Queen Srimala, who is portrayed in *The Sutra of Queen Srimala Who Had the Lion's Roar* as "the ideal layperson whose teaching about the Tathagatagarbha [the womb of suchness or reality] greatly helps those desiring Buddhist salvation" (Paul 1979: 289–302). Queen Srimala teaches her hearers to give birth to the buddha nature within them.

The Lotus Sutra has a prominent role for *nagas,* female beings with lovely human faces and the bodies of snakes. The nagas continually shed their skin, constantly renewing themselves. The princesses among the nagas were the model of wit and beauty and had reached the state of *prajna-paramita.*

The very important concept of *prajna-paramita* ("the wisdom which goes beyond") is also known as the Mother of All Buddhas, representing the enlightenment that enables reality to be seen as it truly is. The association of the wisdom that gives meaning to all reality with feminine symbolism is a characteristic of other religions as well. The Chinese Tao and the Christian Holy Spirit and Wisdom, for example, have feminine overtones (Carmody 1989: 77).

In the Tantric Vajrayana ("Diamond Vehicle") school of Mahayana Buddhism popular in Tibet, women played a prominent role (Barnes 1987: 127–28; 1994: 159–60). Among the teachers (*siddhas*) who were thought to have reached perfect enlightenment were women. They taught their followers to stop thinking of themselves as concrete enough to be bound by social conventions. Thus, adherents engaged in various forms of "crazy wisdom," in which ordinary dietary and sexual taboos were purposefully broken. In this school, *taras* (goddesses) were portrayed as consorts of the buddhas and played an important role in popular piety (Carmody 1989: 83).

A nun's order established in China in the fourth century C.E. has continued in an unbroken tradition to the present time, providing an opportunity for women to live active, respected lives outside the typical family structure. They are particularly noted as teachers of the Buddhist scriptures (Barnes 1987: 123–27).

Buddhist teaching has also supported women's claims for political authority and independence. For example, in the nineteenth century women silk workers in Guangdong refused to marry and lived together, the lay equivalent of an order of nuns (Barnes 1987: 132).

In the United States, Buddhist women have played a prominent role in the spread of Mahayana teaching (Barnes 1994: 161–62). For example, the founder of the famous Shasta Abbey in California, a Soto Zen institution, was Jiyu Kennett Roshi, an Englishwoman who became a Zen master in Japan and founded Shasta Abbey in 1970.

Pointing to a shared concern in the overcoming of the dualistic thought patterns linked to patriarchy and Western religions, there are signs at present of Buddhist and feminist thinkers joining together (Barnes 1994: 168–69).

Homosexuality

Japan may very well be the most permissive society in terms of prevalent attitudes toward homosexuality. The general cultural attitude toward sexuality in Japan is summed up well by Edwin Reischauer, one of the most respected experts on Japan in the West (Reischauer 1988: 175; cited by Wawrytko 1993: 211):

> *The Japanese do not share Western views about the sinfulness of sexual relations. To them they have always seemed a natural phenomenon, like eating, which is to be enjoyed in the proper place. Promiscuity is in itself no more of a problem than homosexuality. Their attitudes have thus in a sense been permissive. But at the same time, they have a stronger awareness than contemporary Westerners of the necessity of bending the desires of the individual to the surrounding environment.*

Both Buddhism and Shinto have contributed to this acceptance. The most famous expression of male homosexuality in Japan was the pederasty common in the samurai class during the Kamakura period (1192–1336). Indeed, transgenerational homosexuality was valued in the feudal order of Japanese society, which did not end until the Meiji era, which began in 1868. Shoguns and samurai often kept young male lovers for emotional support as well as sexual expression. The attitude was that women were for producing heirs, whereas boys were for pleasure and companionship (Herdt 1987: 448). It was also common for Buddhist monks to take a younger male lover during this period (Cabezón 1993: 91). A famous seventeenth-century work, *The Great Mirror of Male Love,* by Ihara Saikaku, extolled male homosexuality.

Likewise, lesbianism has been quite common in Japan. According to one interpreter, women in Japan have been drawn together "by the alienating social climate as well as by prevailing misogyny" (Wawrytko 1993: 213).

Shinto concern for pollution has also contributed to the acceptance and promotion of male homosexuality in Japan. Two of the three main sources of ritual pollution (childbirth, menstruation, and death) are linked exclusively to women. Women are excluded from key Shinto rituals, which encourages a high degree of male bonding (Wawrytko 1993: 219).

CHAPTER SUMMARY

In this chapter we first surveyed the histories of Japan and Korea as background for further discussion of the religions of East Asia. We then touched on the popular religion of Japan and the role of shamanesses (*miko*).

Although the Mahayana branch of Buddhism is based on sutras mostly written in India, it grew to maturity in East Asia. In this chapter we outlined the spread of Buddhism from India into East Asia, identified the major Mahayana texts, contrasted Mahayana with Theravada, and briefly surveyed the major Mahayana movements: the Pure Land school, the Meditation school (better known as Zen), the Political school (Nichiren), and the Tantric school (in its Tibetan form).

Shinto, the native religion of Japan, is rooted in a mythic account of the creation of Japan as the center of the cosmos and the land of the *kami. Kami* are gods, persons, places, or things that inspire rev-

erence and awe. *Kami-no-michi,* the Japanese self-designation for Shinto, teaches a way of harmony. We traced the development of Shinto from the emergence of the Shinto Myth; through a period of amalgamation with Buddhism and then a Shinto revival; to the modern era, when an attempt to distinguish Shinto as a national ideology from "religious Shinto" was made. We highlighted the role of state Shinto in Japan before and during World War II and discussed the fate of Shinto after the war.

Like other East Asian religions, Shinto seeks harmony. In the case of Shinto, the harmony is with the *kami.* An elaborate system of shrines and rituals provides the means for maintenance of harmony.

We touched on the impact of Communism on religion in China, the effect of materialism on religion in post–World War II Japan, and the influence of Christianity in Korea.

We concluded with a discussion of responses to contemporary ethical issues in Mahayana Buddhism and Shinto.

QUESTIONS FOR DISCUSSION AND REFLECTION

1. Do you agree with the Zen Buddhist teaching of developing "an intimacy with all things"? How can this be done today?
2. Societies such as Japan, Korea, and Taiwan, which are rooted in Confucian values, have enjoyed economic success in recent decades. Compare the role Protestantism has played in countries such as Germany, Great Britain, and the United States with the role of Confucianism in the East Asian societies. Has the impact been essentially positive or negative?
3. Do you agree with the Shinto teaching that there is "neither divine nor human"? What do you think this teaching means?
4. State Shinto labelled Western-style "individualism" as the basic factor disrupting the way of harmony with the *kami* that Shinto teaches. To what degree is individualism a root problem in the world today, because it keeps us from attaining harmony?
5. Why does Zen Buddhism teach that "rational thinking" is the fundamental problem we must overcome? To what extent do you agree?
6. React to the Zen teaching that "heaven" and "hell" are products of the mind that must be overcome if real bliss is to be experienced.
7. How can a conception such as the Zen view of "heaven" and the Pure Land description of the Western Paradise co-exist in the same religion? Is this a sign of the confused state of Buddhist teaching, or a sign of its depth?
8. Some researchers studying the dying process have pointed to similarities between the descriptions of people who have "died" and returned and the Tibetan Book of the Dead's description of the state of *bardo*. How much should be made of this similarity?
9. In Japan, why do many people consider themselves participants in both Shinto *and* Buddhism? Do you understand and agree with the idea of identifying with more than one religion at the same time? Would it be good or bad for more people to adopt this practice?
10. Compare and contrast what you know about Judaism and/or Christianity with what you have learned in this chapter about Pure Land Buddhism. Do you think it is inevitable for a devotional approach, with worship of a personal god, to arise in a religious tradition? Why or why not?
11. Which Mahayana Buddhist teachings seem to conflict with Theravada Buddhist concepts? Does this inclusion of seeming opposites make Buddhism as a whole a stronger or weaker religious tradition?
12. Contemplate and respond to the Japanese art illustrated in this chapter. Write down and share the thoughts and feelings you have as you ponder this art.
13. What does the Shinto Myth suggest about the traditional self-understanding of the Japanese people? The Myth was "outlawed" after World War II by the occupying forces. Was such an action justified?

SOURCES AND SUGGESTIONS FOR FURTHER STUDY

Mahayana Buddhism

General

CONZE, EDWARD, ED. AND TRANS., 1964 *Buddhist Texts Through the Ages.* New York: Harper Torchbooks (1954).

WILLIAMS, PAUL, 1989 *Mahayana Buddhism: The Doctrinal Foundations.* New York: Routledge.

Zen

ABE, MASAO, 1985 *Zen and Western Thought.* Honolulu: University of Hawaii Press.

BLOFELD, JOHN [CHU CH'AN], TRANS., 1958 *Zen Teachings of Huang Po: On the Transmission of the Mind*. New York: Grove Press.

HABITO, RUBEN L.F., 1989 *Total Liberation: Zen Spirituality and the Social Dimension*. Maryknoll, N.Y.: Orbis Books.

KAPLEAU, PHILIP, ED., 1967 *The Three Pillars of Zen*. Boston: Beacon Press.

MOU-LAM, WONG, TRANS., 1992 *The Sutra of Hui Neng*. Phoenix: H.K. Buddhist Book Distributor (1930).

SUZUKI, D.T., 1959 *Zen and Japanese Culture*. Princeton, N.J.: Bollingen.

SUZUKI, SHUNRYU, 1970 *Zen Mind, Beginner's Mind*. New York: Weatherhill.

WATTS, ALAN, 1974 *The Way of Zen*. New York: Random House.

Pure Land

BLOOM, ALFRED, 1965 *Shinran's Gospel of Pure Grace*. Tucson: University of Arizona Press.

Nichiren

ANESAKE, MASAHARU, 1966 *Nichiren, The Buddhist Prophet*. Gloucester, Mass.: Peter Smith.

SOOTHILL, W., 1987 *The Lotus of the Wonderful Law*. Atlantic Highlands, N.J.: Humanities Press (1930).

Tibetan Buddhism

BATCHELOR, STEPHEN, TRANS., 1979 *A Guide to the Bodhisattva's Way of Life: The Bodhissatvaacharyavatara*. Dharamsala, India: Library of Tibetan Works and Archives.

BLOFELD, JOHN, 1987 *The Tantric Mysticism of Tibet*. Boston: Shambhala Publications.

FREMANTLE, FRANCESCA, AND CHOGYAM TRUNGPA, TRANS., 1975 *The Tibetan Book of the Dead*. Boston: Shambhala Publications.

GYASTSO, TENZIN (FOURTEENTH DALAI LAMA), 1975 *The Buddhism of Tibet and the Key to the Middle Way*, trans. Jeffrey Hopkins and Lati Rimpoche. New York: Harper & Row.

WADDELL, L. AUSTINE, 1972 *Tibetan Buddhism*. New York: Dover Publications.

Buddhism in the United States

FRIEDMAN, LENORE, 1987 *Meetings with Remarkable Women: Buddhist Teachers in America*. Boston: Shambhala Publications.

PREBISCH, CHARLES S. , 1979 *American Buddhism*. Belmont, Calif: Wadworth.

TUCK, DONALD R., 1987 *Buddhist Churches of America*. Lewiston, N.Y.: The Edwin Mellen Press.

Shinto

ASTON, W.G., 1905 *Shinto: The Way of the Gods*. London: Longman, Green & Co.

EARHART, H. BYRON, 1974 *Japanese Religion: Unity and Diversity*, 2nd ed. Encino, Calif.: Dickenson.

1974 *Religion in the Japanese Experience: Sources and Interpretations*. Encino, Calif.: Dickenson.

ELLWOOD, ROBERT S., JR., AND ROBERT PILGRIM, 1985 *Japanese Religion: A Cultural Perspective*. Englewood Cliffs, N.J.: Prentice Hall.

GAUNTLETT, JOHN OWEN, TRANS., AND ROBERT KING HALL, ED., 1974 *Kokutai no Hongi: Cardinal Principles of the National Entity of Japan*. Newton, Mass.: Crofton Publishing Corp. (1949).

KITAGAWA, JOSEPH M., 1987 *On Understanding Japanese Religion*. Princeton, N.J.: Princeton University Press.

PHILIPPI, DONALD L., TRANS., 1968 *Kojiki*. Tokyo: University of Tokyo Press.

WOODWARD, W., 1972 *The Allied Occupation of Japan and Japanese Religions*. Leiden, Netherlands: E.J. Brill.

YAMAMOTO, YUKITAKA, 1987 *Way of the Kami*. Stockton, Calif.: Tsubaki America Publications.

Ethical Issues

The Ecological Crisis

BADENER, ALLAN HUNT, ED., 1990 *Dharma Gaia: A Harvest of Essays in Buddhism and Ecology*. Berkeley, Calif. Parallax Press.

COOK, FRANCIS, 1977 *Hua-yen Buddhism*. University Park: Pennsylvania State University.

DONEGAN, PATRICIA, 1990 "Haiku & the Ecotastrophe," in *Dharma Gaia*, 197–207.

FIELDS, RICK, 1981 *How the Swans Came to the Lake: A Narrative History of Buddhism in America*. Boulder, Colo.: Shambhala.

LAFLEUR, WILLIAM R., 1978 *Sattva*: Enlightment for Plants and Trees in Buddhism," *Co-evolution Quarterly* 19 (Fall 1978): 47–52.

LEVITT, PETER, 1990 "An Intimate View," in *Dharma Gaia*, 93–96.

NASH, RODERICK, 1989. *The Rights of Nature: A History of Environmental Ethics*. Madison: the University of Wisconsin Press.

PAUL, DIANA Y., 1980 *The Buddhist Feminine Ideal*. Missoula, Mont.: Scholars Press.

SHANER, DAVID EDWARD, 1989 "The Japanese Experience of Nature," in *Nature in Asian Traditions of Thought: Essays in Philosophy*, ed. J. Baird Callicott and Roger T. Ames (Albany: State University of New York Press),163–82.

SNYDER, GARY, 1969 *Earth House Hold: Technical Notes Queries to Fellow Dharma Revolutionaries.* New York: New Directions Publishing.

TELLENBACH, HUBERTUS, AND BIN KIMURA, 1989 "The Japanese Concept of 'Nature," in *Nature in Asian Traditions of Thought: Essays in Philosophy,* 153–62.

VITTACHI, ANURADHA 1989 *Earth Conference One: Sharing a Vision for Our Planet.* Boston: New Science Library.

Euthansasia

LARUE, GERALD A. 1985 *Euthanasia and Religion: A Survey of the Attitudes of World Religions to the Right-to-Die.* Los Angeles: The Hemlock Society.

Economic Justice

BATCHELOR, STEPHEN, "Buddhist Economics," in 1990 *Dhurma Gaia,* 178–182.

MCDANIEL, JAY 1985 "The God of the Oppressed and the God Who Is Empty," *God and Global Justice: Religion and Poverty in an Unequal World,* 191–200.

THOMPSON, WILLIAM IRWIN 1989 "Pacific Shift," in *Nature in Asian Traditions of Thought,* 25–36.

Gender Roles and the Status of Women

BARNES, NANCY SCHUSTER, 1987 "Buddhism," in *Women in World Religions,* ed. Arvind Sharma (Albany: State University of New York Press), 105–33.

1994 "Women in Buddhism," in *Today's Woman in World Religions,* ed. Arvind Sharma (Albany: State University of New York Press), 137–69.

CARMODY, DENISE LARDNER, 1989 *Women and World Religions.* 2nd ed. Englewood Cliffs, N.J.: Prentice Hall.

DALBY, LIZA CRIHFIELD, 1983 *Geisha.* Berkeley: University of California Press.

NAKAMURA, KYOKO MOTOMOCHI, 1989 "No Women's Liberation: The Heritage of a Woman Prophet in Modern Japan," in *Unspoken Worlds: Women's Religious Lives,* ed. Nancy A. Falk and Rita M. Gross (Belmont, Calif.: Wadsworth), 134–44.

PAUL, DIANA 1979 *Women in Buddhism.* Berkeley, Calif: Asian Humanities Press.

Homosexuality

CABEZÓN, JOSÉ IGNACIO, 1992 *Buddhism, Sexuality, and Gender.* Albany: State University of New York Press.

1993 "Homosexuality and Buddhism," in *Homosexuality and World Religions,* ed. Arlene Swidler (Valley Forge, Pa.: Trinity Press International), 81–101.

WATANABE, TUNEO, AND IWATA JUN'ICHI, 1989 *The Love of the Samurai: A Thousand Years of Japanese Homosexuality in Japan.* London: GMP Publishers.

WAWRYTKO, SANDRA A., 1993 "Homosexuality and Chinese and Japanese Religions," in *Homosexuality and World Religions,* 199–230.

Religions of the Middle East and Beyond

Three of the world's major religious traditions (Judaism, Christianity, and Islam) originated in the geographic area known as the Middle East. Another, smaller religion, Zoroastrianism, which influenced the development of the other three, also began in the Middle East. We will devote the next four chapters to a study of these religions.

Because all four of the religions named above share a belief in one all-powerful, personal deity, they are also known as the monotheistic religions. These religions also distinguish between good and evil and identify the ways of living that are good or "right." Therefore, some interpreters place this group of religions under the heading "ethical monotheism."

These religions all moved beyond the region where they originated. Christian and Muslim missionaries carried their religions into all areas of the world and made them the two largest and fastest-growing religions of the world. Judaism spread from its birthplace in Israel largely through a process known as the Diaspora (the "dispersion" of Jews throughout the world as a result of exile, persecution, and migration). Because Christianity, Judaism, and Islam have profoundly influenced the Western world, they are sometimes called "Western" religions. Zoroastrianism spread beyond the land of its birth (the modern Iran) to India (where Zoroastrians are known as Parsis) and then through natural migration to create small communities in other parts of the world.

Christianity is the majority religion in Europe, the Americas, Australia, and New Zealand. Outside the Jewish state of Israel, Islam is the major religion in the Middle East. Islam is also the majority religion in areas beyond the Middle East—in Central Asia especially. In Africa, Islam and Christianity were introduced as missionary religions, and have had significant but by no means total success in displacing indigenous religions (see Chapter Three).

247

CHAPTER 10

Introduction
and Zoroastrianism:
Good versus Evil

Before we turn to the histories and distinctive teachings of the Middle Eastern religions in the next several chapters, we will survey the geography, demography, and history of the region where they originated. As we have done with the other families of religions, we will also provide an orientation to the traditional worldview that is an important part of the background necessary for understanding these religions.

AN ORIENTATION TO THE MIDDLE EAST

The Lands and Peoples

The present-day countries included in the area called the Middle East (see Figure 10-1), which includes parts of three continents, are Egypt and Sudan in Africa; Saudi Arabia, the two Yemens (Aden to the north and Sana to the south), Oman, the United Arab Emirates, Qatar, Bahrain, and Kuwait in the Arabian peninsula; Iraq and Iran in southwestern Asia; and Israel, Lebanon, Jordan, Syria, Cyprus, and Turkey in the eastern Mediterranean. Most of the people who live in the Middle East are Arabs, but one also finds Africans, Armenians, Copts, Greeks, Iranians, Jews, Kurds, and Turks. There is a real ethnic and cultural diversity in the region, the source of much conflict over the centuries. Most of the Middle East is desert; the population is concentrated along the seacoasts and river valleys. The discovery and exploitation of huge deposits of oil in the region have brought much development in the last half-century, creating pockets of great wealth amidst widespread poverty.

A Brief History

About 4000 B.C.E., two of the world's earliest civilizations emerged in the Middle East—the Egyptian civilization along the River Nile in northeastern Africa, and the Sumerian in the area known as Mesopotamia (the land between and along the Tigris and Euphrates rivers). Another great civilization, the Hittite, developed in what is now Turkey by 1900 B.C.E. In the area between, a number of

societies, including Israel (the nation out of which Judaism arose and which became known as the Holy Land), emerged in subsequent centuries.

Beginning in 800 B.C.E. the great civilizations and other societies were occupied and destroyed by invaders. Alexander the Great conquered most of the Middle East by 331 B.C.E. He brought Hellenistic (Greek) culture, which spread throughout most of the region. The Romans took control of most of the Middle East 300 years later. During Roman rule, Christianity emerged.

In the 600s, followers of the founder of Islam, the prophet Muhammad, swept out of the Arabian peninsula and conquered much of this region, which was also holy to them. Introduced as a result were Muslim culture and the Arabic language, which still dominate the area. In the 1000s, the Seljuk Turks came from Turkestan in Central Asia and seized control of Asia Minor (modern Turkey) and Arab Syria, including in 1071 Jerusalem and the rest of the Holy Land.

When the Turks began to restrict the access of Christian pilgrims to the sacred places in Jerusalem and elsewhere, the Crusades began. In the twelfth and thirteenth centuries, successive Christian armies from Western Europe mounted invasions that succeeded in recapturing Jerusalem and other portions of the Holy Land for a time. But eventually the Europeans were driven from the area by Muslim armies.

The Ottoman Empire began about 1300 and took control of much of the Middle East as a portion of its vast holdings. The Ottoman Empire was at its pinnacle during the sixteenth and seventeenth centuries. During the nineteenth century, European powers began to exert increasing influence on the Middle East. After World War I, much of the area was placed under British or French control. Independence was later granted, and separate nations such as Syria, Jordan, and Lebanon were created.

Growing immigration by Jews seeking to return to their ancestral homeland created tension with the Palestinians who resided in Palestine and considered it their homeland. In 1947 the United Nations tried to divide Palestine into a Jewish state

FIGURE 10–1

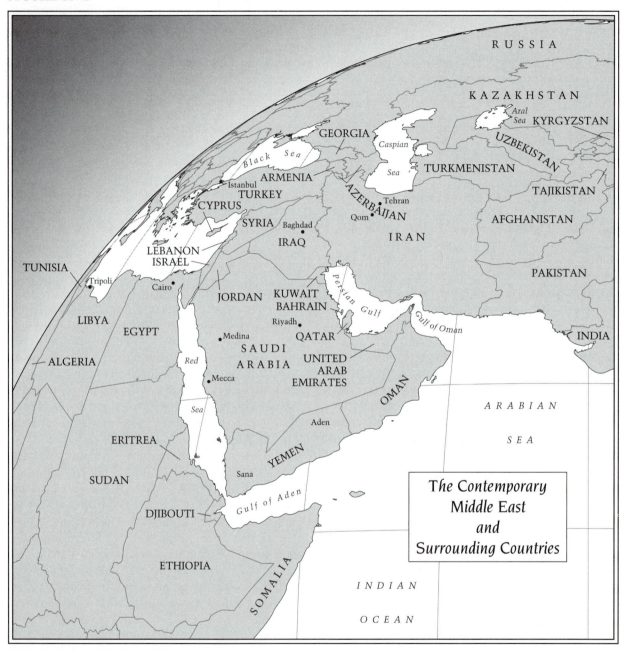

The Contemporary
Middle East
and
Surrounding Countries

(Israel) and an Arab state (Palestine); this was rejected by the Palestinians. The Palestinians were supported by Arab states in the region, while the Israelis received the backing of European nations and the United States. A series of wars (in 1948, 1956, 1967, and 1973), an ongoing Palestinian uprising, and diplomatic efforts have failed to resolve the dispute, although a direct dialogue between Palestinians and Israelis begun in 1993 offers new hope.

An Islamic revolution in 1979 led to the creation of a traditionalist Islamic Republic in Iran. A war between Iraq and Iran began in 1980 and continued for most of that decade. In 1990 Iraq invaded Kuwait, as a result of a disagreement over oil rights and other issues. Because of the threat posed to the large oil reserves in the area, a coalition of nations led by the United States drove the Iraqis from Kuwait in 1991.

The Traditional Worldview

The religions that originated in the Middle East share a worldview that distinguishes them as a group from the religions of South and East Asia and the indigenous religions. We should note that this represents the *traditional* worldview; especially in Judaism and Christianity (as we shall see in Chapters Eleven and Twelve), there are movements that have adapted elements of the traditional worldview in response to developments in the modern world.

Problem: Tension with the Creator   The religions that originated in the Middle East share a belief in one, all-powerful Creator who has revealed a path for humans to follow in life. When humans fail to follow the divinely revealed way of life, tension with the Creator results. At these times humans engage in actions that express indifference or hostility toward God and the path God has revealed, and they suffer the consequences of their turning away from God.

Who are we as humans? These religions share the understanding that humans are spiritual beings, created by God. These religions emphasize the special place of humans in the created order. From their perspective, humans are superior to other living beings, existing in a special relationship with God not shared with other creatures. This perspective is called *anthropocentric,* because it places humanity at the center of the created order. Because of their unique spiritual status, humans have a special responsibility. In fact, the status of the rest of creation is dramatically affected by the human situation. When humans stray from the divinely ordained path other beings suffer.

Cause: Turning the Wrong Way   What causes the tension in the divine/human relationship? The human problem, according to these religions, is brought on by a turning away from God. An important aspect of the special relationship humans have with God is the availability of knowledge concerning the way God desires humans to live. To varying degrees, these religions think that humans are free to choose whether to follow the path God has revealed. Unfortunately, humans often (or inevitably, some would say) choose to disobey the will of God, causing the alienation from which transformation must be sought.

Why do humans go astray? In tension with the emphasis on human freedom to choose is the common belief in these religions that there is a force of evil in the cosmos that seeks to draw humans away from the path established by God. This personified force is not equal in power to God, but can tempt people to disobey God. In addition, in their desire for independence and power, humans often (or always) choose the path in conflict with the divine will.

Reality: A Beginning and an End   These religions understand time from a perspective seemingly diametrically opposed to the view of time in the indigenous religions and most of the religions of South and Southeast Asia. For those religions, time is cyclical; individual humans and the cosmos as a whole experience time as having no ultimate beginning and no end. There are simply cycles that are repeated for individuals and the entire cosmos, which is created, destroyed, and created again.

In the worldview of the religions that originated in the Middle East, time has a beginning and an end. The cosmos began at a specific moment in time and it will end with the creation of a final, timeless state of being. This linear conception of time has a number of implications that affect these religions and the cultures for which they provide the myths. For example, it places a great deal of importance on both the beginning and the end of time. There is a strong sense of destiny, of things being oriented toward a final culmination. Reflection on the "end time" is known as *eschatology.* These religions share an eschatological orien-

Oil wells burn in the Ahmadi oil fields, Kuwait, during the 1991 Persian Gulf War.

tation. There is also a great deal of interest in what happened at the beginning of time and how what happened at the beginning affected what followed.

A linear view of time combined with emphasis on the special place of humans in creation results in more concern in these religions with human history than we find in other religions. In Judaism, Christianity, and Islam especially, historical events take on an importance equal to the place accorded to the events of the mythic era at the beginning or end of time. In fact, in these religions historical occurrences take on a mythic meaning. For example, each religion has a calendar determined by a particular event of foundational signifi-

cance, such as the birth of Jesus or the migration of the prophet Muhammad from Mecca to Medina.

The linear trajectory also applies to individual humans. According to these religions, humans "only go around once." You are born once, you live once, and you die once. This increases the urgency to participate in ultimate transformation in this life, and may help explain why at least two of these religions (Christianity and Islam) are so intent on spreading their messages and converting others to their religion. These religions share a special concern with what happens to humans after they finish their linear journeys—life after death is an exceedingly important concern.

How did reality come into existence? All these religions consider the ultimate source to be the God who is the only reality beyond time and space. At a specific moment God created the cosmos; God will also bring the cosmos to an end. What will happen at the eschaton (the end time) has been or will be determined by God.

End: Restoration   The goal in these religions is to overcome the tension brought on by humans turning away from God. The metaphor of health applies. Humans lose the state of spiritual health when they turn from the will of God. Restoration of a healthy relationship may be thought of as healing or "salvation."

Restoration relates both to individuals and to society. Some of these religions emphasize more the salvation of individuals, while others stress the healing of societies; within these religions, different movements emphasize one or the other. For individuals the experience of restoration may occur before death, but it is the state of existence after death that attracts the most attention. Typically, these religions in their traditional expressions include the idea that those who experience salvation enter into a state of eternal well-being after death, while those who do not remain alienated from God beyond this life (whether eternally or not is a matter of dispute).

A formulation of the idea of life after death found in these religions is the image of a time of judgment by God at the end of history. In general, at this end point those who have been reconciled with God enter into their final reward and those who have not been restored are condemned. Accompanying this concept is the belief that at this end time, the dead will be raised from their graves and participate with those still living in the final judgment and new life beyond. We need to note that each of the religions develops a much more complex portrayal of life after death than this brief summary suggests, with different points of view among different branches (especially in Judaism and Christianity).

The state of wholeness and well-being at the end of time is a restoration of the harmony with God that existed at the beginning. At the beginning there was a paradise in which humanity, God, and nature were in an ideal relationship. The imagery of the original paradise is used to picture the state of existence that is the destination for those who respond to the will of God.

Restoration occurs not just for individuals, but for communities and the entire cosmos. The idea that God acts within history to bring salvation to groups of people is common. One way to look at the coming end is to stress a state of restoration for people together. Sometimes this restoration of society in which everyone together is living in obedience to God is pictured within history. You can find imagery within these religions that paints a picture of a restoration of the entire cosmos to a state of well-being. Sometimes it is seen as a state beyond death.

Means: The Way   What brings about the restoration of individuals and communities? Each religion, of course, has its own distinct prescription for what must happen for renewal to occur. What they share in common is the image of a "way" revealed by God, which leads to restoration. The way is revealed through a person and includes the concept of living in obedience to God. Typically, the way of obedience is contrasted with the way of disobedience. The image of a need to turn away from the path of disobedience and embrace the path of obedience is common. The way includes guidelines for individual and social morality. In each of these religions, sacred writings play a central role in making known God's way to salvation.

Sacred: Monotheism   Among these religions there is consensus that the ultimate is a personal God who is the sole source of all life and who has no equals. According to their traditional teachings (except perhaps for Zoroastrianism), God is all-powerful and all-knowing. Nothing can occur unless it is caused or allowed to happen by God. Emphasis is placed on the "will of God" being absolute. From this perspective God is separate from the creation, transcendent. God cannot be portrayed in a picture or a statue, because God is beyond all forms. However, God is personal in the sense that God relates to the creation, with characteristics such as love and anger. These religions share the view that God loves the world and the creatures of the world.

God is beyond gender, but it is most common to read in the sacred writings of these religions

QUESTIONS OF HUMAN DESTINY: WHY ARE WE HERE?

As One Desires Bliss

Like other monotheistic religions, Zoroastrianism teaches that meaningfulness comes as a gift from the one God, either received in gratitude and obedience or rejected in favor of the path of evil (Avesta, Yasna 43.2; Mills 1887:99).

And do thou likewise (Thyself) reveal thine own (gifts) through thy most bountiful spirit, O Mazda! (And do thou teach us) Thy wonderful thoughts of wisdom, those of Thy Good Mind, which Thou hast revealed (to us) by Thy Righteousness (within us) with the happy increase of (our joy) and on a long life's everyday.

about God in male terms. God is pictured as a heavenly Father, a divine king, or a warrior. The traditional model for God's relationship to creation is hierarchical. God stands above creation and gives orders that are carried out. These religions typically envision spiritual intermediaries (e.g., angels) between the one God and creation.

Given the monotheism in these religions, two issues require special attention. If God is fundamentally separate from the creation, then how may God be experienced and how is God known? In each of the religions that originated in the Middle East, schools developed that emphasized means for experiencing the divine presence. And, in general, the image of God's spirit, everywhere present is found. Further, the religions all place importance on God's *revelation* to humans. God chooses to make known to humans the divine existence and the way humans may follow God's path.

Another issue these religions must confront is sometimes called the "problem of evil." If God is all-powerful and loves the creation, why does God allow evil to occur? For example, why did God allow someone like Adolf Hitler to come to power

and bring about such terrible suffering, including the murder of millions of innocent people? Why does God allow thousands of people to die each day from hunger and malnutrition? Why does God allow a young child to die from cancer? One answer is that there are divine forces that cause evil. The myth of a spirit who rebelled against God and who is the direct force behind much evil in the world is found in these religions. In addition, humans are seen as having freedom to decide between good and evil, with much of the evil in the world caused by human decision. However, these religions share the view that while evil is present in the creation, God will ultimately triumph over it.

QUESTIONS OF HUMAN DESTINY: WHAT HAPPENS AFTER DEATH?

The Bridge of the Separator

According to Zoroastrian belief, the soul of a dead person remains near the corpse for three days. On the fourth day the soul faces judgment on the "Bridge of the Separator" (Cinat Bridge). If the soul's good thoughts, words, and deeds outweigh the bad ones, the soul is led by Ahura Mazda's angels across the bridge to heaven. If evil thoughts, words, and deeds are found heavier, then the soul is judged wicked and is dragged to hell. At the end of time all souls are raised for a final judgment (Avesta, Yasna 46.10–11; Mills 1887:140-41).

Whoever, man or woman, shall give to me those gifts of life which Thou hast known as best, O Mazda! and as a holy blessing through Thy Righteous Order, a throne (established) with Thy Good Mind, with these I shall go forth; yea, those whom I shall accompany and so incite, to the homage of such as You on earth, forth to the Judge's Bridge (itself) with all of them shall I lead on at last. . . . And when they approach there where the Judge's Bridge extends, unlike the believing ones of God, who go firmly forth with me as guide and helper, these shall miss their path and fall, and in the Lie's abode for ever shall their habitation be.

<table>
<tr><td>

COSMIC QUESTIONS: HOW DID THE WORLD COME INTO BEING?

The First Begetter

With Zoroastrianism we encounter the view that all reality is the result of the purposeful creation of the one and only God. The answer to the rhetorical questions posed in this poem is Ahura Mazda, the Wise Lord (Avesta, Yasna 44.3, Mills 1887:113).

This I ask Thee, O Ahura! tell me aright:

Who by generation was the first father of the Righteous Order within this world? Who gave the recurring sun and stars their undeviating way? Who established that whereby the moon waxes, and whereby she wanes, save Thee? These things, O Great Creator! would I know, and others likewise still.

</td></tr>
</table>

ZOROSTRIANISM: GOOD VERSUS EVIL

Zoroastrianism is not a large religion today. It continues to exist primarily in a small community of people known as Parsis (from the word "Persia"), who live principally in India. Only about 150,000 to 200,000 Zoroastrians remain today.

Why devote separate attention to such a minor religion? As we shall see, Zoroastrianism is an intriguing religion in its own right, with a rich heritage deserving of study and appreciation. It played a role in the religion of the grand Persian Empire, which ruled over the Middle East at a critical time in world history. Today Zoroastrians tend to be highly educated and influence the societies in which they live in a manner out of proportion to the size of their religion. In addition, Zoroastrianism very likely had a significant influence on the development of the major monotheistic religions. An understanding of Zoroastrianism is helpful and important background for a study of Judaism, Christianity, and Islam.

Stages of Development and Sacred Texts

Background: The other Aryans   As we noted in Chapter Five, sometime early in the second millennium B.C.E., Indo-European nomads entered India and introduced a new culture and a new religion. They are known as the Aryans ("noble ones"), and they developed a polytheistic religion that is now remembered in the hymns of the *Rig-Veda*. At about the same time as these Aryans were establishing themselves in India, another branch from the same Indo-European tree settled into the region to the west of India now known as Iran (which probably derives from the word "Aryan").

Like the Aryans of India, the Aryans of Iran worshipped a pantheon of deities. Some were associated with the sun, moon, earth, fire, and water. Higher in the pantheon were gods who can be directly compared to some of the Vedic deities. *Intar* (like *Indra* in the *Rig-Veda*) was the god of war. *Uruwana* (like *Varuna*) was the god of the sky who watched over the moral order. *Asha* (like the Vedic *Rita*) was a personification of the cosmic order. For these Aryans, however, the highest god was *Mithra* (*Mitra* in the Vedic hymns), the god of light who watched over human affairs and maintained the moral order, and who inspired loyalty and obedience. Later *Mithra* became the focus of a Roman mystery cult especially popular among soldiers.

We may surmise that the religion of these Aryans, like their counterparts in India, was sacrificial, with offerings to the deities in rituals presided over by a priestly class. Both fire and a sacred liquid (like the Vedic *soma*) probably played a role in the worship.

Founder: Zoroaster   Like the sixth-century reformers of Vedic religion, Siddartha Gautama and Mahavira (see Chapters Six and Seven), whose work led to the formation of new religions in India, the founder of Zoroastrianism was a prophet who both reacted against the religion of his time and incorporated elements of it into a new teaching, which became a distinct religion. Westerners know him by the Latinized name Zoroaster; within the tradition he is Zarathustra.

Controversy surrounds the date of Zoroaster's birth. The only real source of information about

This devotional portrait of Zarathustra shows him in communion with the Wise Lord, **Ahura Mazda.**

Zoroaster is Zoroastrian scripture. The dispute is over how to interpret references to him in these texts. According to Zoroastrian tradition, he was the first human prophet, born around 4000 B.C.E. Other traditions from Iran place his birth at 660 B.C.E. Greek historians dated his birth to the period between 1000 and 600 B.C.E. More recent scholarship places his life between 1500 and 1000 B.C.E.

Regardless of the date of his birth, he was probably a member of a warrior clan. He is remembered as a compassionate young man, who at the age of 20 left his family to undertake a spiritual quest. Ten years later he had the first in a series of visions. In the vision the head of the angels, *Vohu Mana* ("Good Thought") told him that there is only one central God, *Ahura Mazda* ("Wise Lord"), and that Zoroaster was to be his messenger on earth.

Zoroaster was taken in the vision into the heavenly throne room of Ahura Mazda. The visions continued, and Zoroaster began to proclaim what he was told. At first he had no success. He was condemned as a heretic, and besieged by evil spirits who tried to dissuade him from his mission.

Zoroaster was persistent. His travels took him to eastern Iran, where he spent several years in the court of an Aryan ruler named Vishtaspa. Vishtaspa's corrupt priests rallied against Zoroaster and succeeded in having him imprisoned. The prince, however, was finally convinced (according to tradition, after the prophet healed his favorite horse) and accepted the teaching of allegiance to the one and only true God, Ahura Mazda.

From this point on, increasing numbers of Aryans embraced this new faith, and it spread rapidly. One tactic apparently used was military conquest followed by an ultimatum to convert. During one of these "holy wars" Zoroaster, now 77, was killed. His followers proclaimed him to be a *saoshyant,* a deliverer who leads people to the path of righteousness.

Sacred Text: The Avesta   The sacred writings of the Zoroastrians are known as the *Avesta* ("basic text"). The Avesta is a collection of hymns, prayers, and formulae for use in liturgy and a manual of instruction for worship and moral behavior. The *Gathas* are the most important texts within the Avesta, for these five hymns are the best evidence of the actual teachings of Zoroaster. Some of the hymns in the Avesta give us evidence of the religion of Iran before the time of Zoroaster, which we have described above. According to Zoroastrian tradition, all of the Avesta represents the truth received by Zoroaster in his visions and written down by him.

The Spread and Influence of Zoroastrianism
During the Achaemenid dynasty (559–330 B.C.E), famous rulers such as Cyrus the Great, Darius I, and Xerxes succeeded in spreading Persian influence throughout the Middle East. Although there is no mention of Zoroaster in the extant texts from the period, the Persians did worship Ahura Mazda as one of the deities in their pantheon (though not as the one true God). Fire was used in worship, and the priests were called *magi,* as they were in the Avesta.

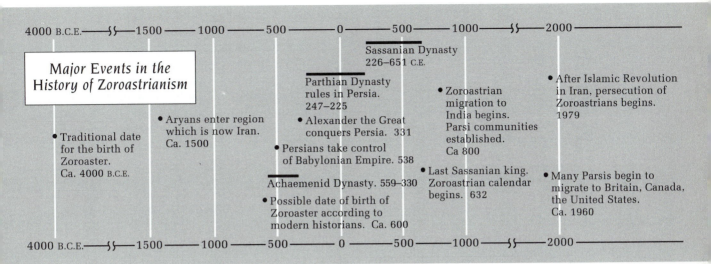

Major Events in the History of Zoroastrianism

4000 B.C.E. —⧸⧸— 1500 — 1000 — 500 — 0 — 500 — 1000 —⧸⧸— 2000

Sassanian Dynasty
226–651 C.E.

Parthian Dynasty
rules in Persia.
247–225

• After Islamic Revolution
in Iran, persecution of
Zoroastrians begins.
1979

• Zoroastrian
migration to
India begins.
Parsi communities
established.
Ca 800

• Aryans enter region
which is now Iran.
Ca. 1500

• Alexander the Great
conquers Persia. 331

• Traditional date
for the birth of
Zoroaster.
Ca. 4000 B.C.E.

• Persians take control
of Babylonian Empire. 538

Achaemenid Dynasty. 559–330

• Last Sassanian king.
Zoroastrian calendar
begins. 632

• Many Parsis begin to
migrate to Britain, Canada,
the United States.
Ca. 1960

• Possible date of birth of
Zoroaster according to
modern historians. Ca. 600

4000 B.C.E. —⧸⧸— 1500 — 1000 — 500 — 0 — 500 — 1000 —⧸⧸— 2000

Although the evidence is circumstantial, it seems clear that during this period Zoroastrian and other Persian teachings had direct influence on the development of Judaism (and therefore on Christianity and Islam). When the Persians took control of Babylon in 538 B.C.E., there were many Jewish exiles from Israel living in captivity in Babylon. What historians of the religion of ancient Israel point out is that ideas not evident or emphasized before the Babylonian exile, which began in 586 B.C.E., are found in sections of the Hebrew Bible written during and after the exile. For example, the figure Satan (from a Persian word) appears in several post-exilic writings. In addition, post-exilic Biblical writings introduce the notion of resurrection from the dead and a final judgment at the end of history. Therefore, teachings concerning an end time and life after death, which were to become so important not only in Judaism but in Christianity and Islam, may very well have been introduced or at least strongly influenced by contact with Zoroastrianism. It must be acknowledged that this theory of Zoroastrian influence on the other religions of the Middle East is not shared by all interpreters, largely because the evidence is so limited.

During the Hellenistic period, Zoroaster was highly respected by both Greek and Roman authors. One tradition says that Plato had intentions to go to Persia to study Zoroastrianism, but was prevented by the war with Sparta in 396 B.C.E. The Parthians, who came to power in Iran a century after the conquest of Alexander the Great and ruled from about 247 B.C.E. until 225 C.E., turned to the worship of Mithra as the centerpiece of their religion.

It was not until the Sassanian dynasty (226–651 C.E) that Zoroastrianism became the official religion of Iran. The Avesta was collected and translated into the contemporary language (*Pahlavi*), and Zoroastrian fire temples spread throughout the land. The Zoroastrian calendar dates from 632 C.E, the year the last Sassanian king came to power. Legends developed about Zoroaster, to the extent that he was venerated himself, and Zoroastrian teachings were refined. These were the "glory years" for the Zoroastrian religion.

The Decline of Zoroastrianism   The conquest of the Sassanian dynasty by Muslim armies marked the beginning of the decline of Zoroastrianism. For a time the Zoroastrians were tolerated by the Muslim conquerors, for they were a "people of the book" who worshipped one God and had a written scripture, like Jews and Christians (see Chapter Thirteen). Gradually, some Zoroastrians began to convert to Islam, and tension increased between the followers of the two religions.

Already by the eighth century, even before the persecution in Iran became serious, a migration of Zoroastrians to India had begun. The Hindus of India called the immigrants *Parsis* ("Persians") and treated them with the same toleration extended to other religions that did not try too actively to proselytize. The Parsis were soon recognized for their hard work and ingenuity, and many attained prosperity as merchants and business leaders. When the British took control of India, they favored the Parsis because of their industriousness and the relative absence of the caste system in their communities. Eventually, most Parsis settled in Bombay and the surrounding area.

Some Zoroastrians remained in Iran, and became known to the Muslim majority as *Gabars* ("infidels"). They called themselves *zartoshti* ("Zoroastrian") or *behdin* ("people of the good religion").

Zoroastrianism Today   Zoroastrianism is kept alive today principally by the Parsi community of India and Parsi immigrant communities in other lands. A number of Parsis have in recent decades migrated from India to establish communities in Great Britain, Canada, and the United States in particular. They tend to live in major business centers, where they continue to be very successful in a variety of commercial endeavors. The Parsis constitute about three-quarters of the Zoroastrian population of the world, and their numbers are estimated to be from about 100,000 to 150,000.

The *Gabars* of Iran cling stubbornly to their ancient dress, lifestyle, and rituals in a remote rural area of central Iran. Today their community numbers somewhere between 10,000 and 30,000. Their isolation is their main protection against pressure by the conservative Muslim majority.

Distinctive Teachings

We are fortunate to have the Gathas to provide evidence of the basic teachings of Zoroaster. We will emphasize these fundamental views in the following summary, but we will also include some of the aspects that reflect later interpretation. In many cases it is difficult to distinguish between the two.

Problem: The War between Good and Evil   Zoroaster taught that humans are free to choose between the competing forces of good and evil in the world. He described these forces as two eternal spirits: a good spirit (*Spenta Mainyu*) and an evil spirit (*Angra Mainyu*). Both emanate from Ahura Mazda and exist in a balance, and both are necessary for life. Angra Mainyu is also known as *Satan* ("accuser"). He has an entourage of demons who tempt human beings under his direction. One of the principal demons is *Aeshma*, who travels the earth spreading death and disease. The principal human problem humans face, then, is to avoid the lure of the forces of evil that seek to thwart their taking the path of goodness.

Cause: Human Accountability   Humans have only one life in which to choose the path of righteousness. Zoroastrianism emphasizes human accountability: Each individual is completely free to choose the path of goodness or the path of evil, to resist the forces of evil or succumb to them. Humans will suffer or enjoy the consequences of their decisions. In the ethical dualism of life, truth (*asha*) stands against falsehood (*druj*). It is up to the individual to recognize the distinction and to choose and honor the truth.

Humans have bodies and souls. The rational quality of the soul enables humans to evaluate the difference between good and evil and choose the good.

Reality: The Emergence of Eschatology   Zoroastrianism advances a linear understanding of time, with existence moving from its creation by Ahura Mazda to a final culmination. The world is real; it is not an illusion. It is the proving ground for humans. Their response to that which happens within time will determine their destiny when the time of fulfillment comes.

Zoroastrianism considers the basic elements of earth, fire, water, and air to be sacred. To pollute them is a wicked act for which perpetrators will be held accountable.

End: Paradise for All?   The goal for Zoroastrians is a life after death in paradise, a place of beauty where all who have followed the path of right-

A Bombay, India Parsi Fire Temple. The image over the door represents Ahura Mazda, holding a ring symbolizing authority. The guardian figures reflect the Persian background of Zoroastrianism.

eousness will spend eternity. According to the eschatological teaching concerning the destiny of individuals, after death the individual soul remains with its body for three days. On the fourth day the soul goes to the place where judgment takes place. The image of a scale is used. If the deeds of evil outweigh good deeds, then the person is sentenced to punishment. If good deeds predominate, even slightly, then the person's soul is destined for paradise. In the Gathas, judgment takes place at the *Chinvat* ("separation") Bridge. The righteous pass over the bridge easily and are met by a beautiful maiden. The wicked meet ugly hags on the bridge and topple to their doom: a

place called the House of the Lie, a dark region below the bridge in which the person is left alone to suffer forever.

The souls continue their existence in paradise or hell until the end of time. When the world comes to an end, Ahura Mazda will wipe away all evil and all souls will be raised for a final judgment. Both the good and evil are subjected to an ordeal of fire and molten metal. The souls of the righteous are not burned by the fire. The souls in hell are purified in the terrible ordeal, and those that survive this process will join with the souls of the righteous, and a new age in which there is no evil, death, or disease will begin.

COSMIC QUESTIONS: WHAT IS THE DESTINY OF THE COSMOS?

The Zoroastrian Messiah

The Zoroastrian Messiah who will appear at the end of history to initiate a new age is called the saoshyant. This text shows that his coming will restore the physical universe (Avesta, *Farvardin Yasht 129; Darmestetor 1883:220-221*).

Whose name will be the victorious Saoshyant and whose name will be Astvat-ereta. He will be Saoshyant [the Beneficent One], because he will benefit the whole bodily world; he will be Astvatereta [he who makes the bodily creatures rise up], because as a bodily creature and as a living creature he will stand against the destruction of the bodily creatures, to withstand the Drug of the two-footed brood [humans], to withstand the evil done by the faithful.

Means: Ethical Purity   In Zoroastrian teaching the world is not evil; it is good and intended for the enjoyment of humans. Zoroastrianism is not an ascetic religion. However, enjoyment must be guided by the ethical teachings revealed by Ahura Mazda to Zoroaster. The Gathas do not spell out in detail the standards to be followed; later texts, however, do become quite specific about the way of ethical living expected of the righteous.

The general ethical principles are good thought, good word, and good deed. Zoroastrians are to practice the virtues that follow from these principles: truthfulness, charity, justice, and compassion.

In keeping with the sacredness of the elements, Zoroastrians are to avoid their pollution. Traditionally, Zoroastrians were expected to practice what today might be called an ecological approach—farming wisely without unnecessary damage to the earth and caring for animals (especially the cow).

The rituals in Zoroastrianism reflect these basic principles. At the center of worship is the offering of prayers to Ahura Mazda for help in leading a life of goodness, free from impurities and pollution. The prayers are offered by priests in Avestan (the name given to the language of the sacred text), since it is believed that the sound has itself a sacred quality.

QUESTIONS OF HUMAN IDENTITY: WHAT IS THE BASIC HUMAN DILEMMA?

The Twin Spirits

For Zoroastrians, the basic conflict all humans face is the war between good and evil spirits, with a fateful choice between them (Avesta, Yasna *30.3–5; Mills 1887:29-31*).

Thus are the primeval spirits who as a pair combining their opposite strivings, and yet each independent in his action, have been framed of old. They are a better thing, they two, and a worse, as to thought, as to word, and as to deed. And between these two let the wisely acting choose aright. Choose ye not as the evil-doers!

Yea when the two spirits came together at the first to make life, and life's absence, and to determine how the world at the last shall be ordered, for the wicked Hell, the worst life, for the holy Heaven, the Best Mental State.

Then when they had finished each his part in the deeds of creation, they chose distinctly each his separate realm. He who as the evil of them both chose the evil, thereby working the worst of possible results, but the more bounteous spirit chose the Divine Righteousness; yea, He chose who clothes upon Himself the firm stones of heaven as His robe. And He chose likewise them who content Ahura with actions, which are performed really in accordance with the faith.

Instead of offering sacrifices of animals or even vegetables, Zoroastrian priests (dressed in white to symbolize purity) preside over the offering of sandalwood to the sacred flames that burn unceasingly in the fire temples, the Zoroastrian houses of worship. The fire symbolizes the divine presence, power, and purity. There is no regular, weekly observance. The priesthood is hereditary, but most priests have other occupations to help support them. Many Zoroastrians maintain a sacred flame in their homes. Only Zoroastrians are allowed to enter the temples and participate in the rituals.

The most famous Zoroastrian rite of passage is performed at death. To avoid the contamination of the elements, the corpse of a deceased person is not buried or burned. Instead, traditionally it was exposed in a special enclosure called a *dakhma* ("tower of silence"), a round structure open to the sky. Vultures that stayed near the tower quickly stripped the body. Since this practice is increasingly frowned upon, especially in urban areas, alternatives have developed, such as placing the body in a sealed casket so that it will not contaminate the elements, or cremating it with an electrical heat that does not involve a flame.

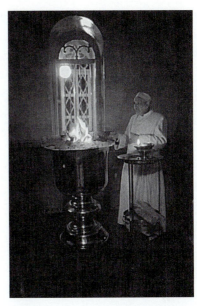

A Zoroastrian priest offers sandalwood to the sacred flame. His white garments symbolize purity. The mask is worn to prevent contamination of the fire by his breath.

Sacred: Ahura Mazda The pre-Zoroastrian religion recognized a high god known as Ahura Mazda, who was the withdrawn creator. Zoroaster's innovation was to restrict worship to the Wise Lord and call Ahura Mazda, in effect, the only god. Ahura Mazda is the invisible, eternal ruler of the universe. In later Zoroastrian writings Ahura Mazda is called by the Pahlavi name *Ohrmazd*.

Zoroaster also taught that Ahura Mazda manifests his will through Spenta Mainyu ("Good Spirit") and six "Immortal Holy Ones." These six are called either angels or modes of divine or ethical action. The six are Good Thought or Mind, Best Order or Right, Absolute Power, High Devotion or Piety, Perfection, and Immutability. Since the first three of the modes are masculine and the other three are feminine, the immortals reflect a balance between the two genders.

Zoroastrians stress that Ahura Mazda is the Supreme Lord of the universe, who has no equal; Ahura Mazda simply allows the Evil Spirit to function. Angra Mainyu opposes Spenta Mainyu; the dualism seems to be more ethical than cosmic.

RESPONSES TO CONTEMPORARY ETHICAL ISSUES

The Ecological Crisis

Like the other religions that originated in the Middle East, Zoroastrianism teaches that the Supreme God has given humanity special responsibility for the care of the creation. With its emphasis on not polluting the basic elements (earth, fire, water, and air), Zoroastrian has an inherently ecological perspective. The following selection from the Zoroastrian sacred writings indicates how important purity of the elements is in Zoroastrian teaching (*Avesta, Khorshed Yastz*; Darmesteter 1883: 86):

And when the sun rises up, then the earth, made by Ahura, becomes clean; the running waters become clean,

Vultures await the exposure of a corpse in a Zoroastrian **dakhma** *(tower of silence).*

the waters of the wells become clean, the waters of the sea become clean, the standing waters become clean; all the holy creatures, the creatures of the Good Spirit, become clean.

Although the primary context for purity is ritual, Zoroastrianism does teach that those who pollute the elements are liable to judgment.

Zoroastrian concern for other animals is shown in a passage from the Yasna, in which an ox cries out to Ahura Mazda for justice. The ox is told that Zoroaster will be his protector (*Avesta, Yasna* 29:1–9).

Economic Justice

In one short verse from the Zoroastrian sacred writings—"Let one practice here good industry; let one make the needy prosperous" (*Avesta, Visparad* 15:1; Mirza 1991: 713)—we find a good indication of the Zoroastrian attitude toward economic justice. On the one hand, those who choose to live ethically are to work hard. In this world we benefit or fail as a result of our own choices, freely made. Zoroastrians are expected to do business with integrity, keeping the promises they make to non-Zoroastrians as well as to fellow believers. As long as we avoid occupations that involve pollution of the basic elements, our labor is blessed by Ahura Mazda. On the basis of these values, Parsis in India have attained a high level of prosperity. There is also a strong orientation toward compassion for the needy in Zoroastrian teaching. Those who have prospered because of their hard work are expected to share their bounty with those who have not been as fortunate. Parsis have a reputation in India and elsewhere for their generosity and compassion for the poor.

Gender Roles and the Status of Women

According to Zoroastrian teaching, there is no distinction between the souls of men and women. Both genders are invested with the sacred thread at initiation. However, in conflict with this basic tradition of gender equality are some of the other beliefs and practices in Zoroastrian teaching. With the religion's heightened concern for purity, menstruating women have been considered particularly impure. Leadership of Zoroastrian ritual has been reserved for men.

CHAPTER SUMMARY

This section begins our study of four major religions that originated in the Middle East: Zoroastrianism, Judaism, Christianity, and Islam. We briefly surveyed the land, peoples, and history of the Middle East and then described the basic elements of the fundamental worldview shared by these religions (in their traditional form).

In our survey of Zoroastrianism, we traced the history of Zoroastrianism from its origins in what is now Iran to the present situation, in which the religion is preserved primarily by the Parsi community centered in Bombay, India. We also described what is known about the life of the founder, Zoroaster; the Zoroastrian scriptures (the Avesta); and the basic teachings of the religion.

Finally, we examined briefly some of the Zoroastrian responses to three contemporary ethical issues: the ecological crisis, economic justice, and the status of women.

QUESTIONS FOR DISCUSSION AND REFLECTION

1. Are humans free to choose between good and evil? To what extent are our choices determined by circumstances beyond our control? Evaluate the Zoroastrian position on these questions.
2. What have been the positive results from the Western assumption that humans are at the center of the created order? What are the drawbacks of an anthropocentric perspective? What are the alternatives to anthropocentrism?
3. Do you agree that at the end of history the harmony present at the beginning will be restored? If so, how will it occur? Do you think a divinely sent savior (like the Zoroastrian *saoshyant*) will be necessary to bring about this new age? How important is human effort in the creation of the new age?
4. Evaluate the Zoroastrian practice of not directly polluting the elements with a dead body.

SOURCES AND SUGGESTIONS FOR FURTHER STUDY

BOYCE, MARY, 1979 *Zoroastrianism: Their Religious Beliefs and Practices* Boston: Routledge & Kegan-Pauls.

1982 *A History of Zoroastrianism,* 2 vols. Leiden: E.J. Brill.

1984 *Textual Sources for the Study of Zoroastrianism.* Towota, N.J.: Barnes & Noble.

DARMESTETER, JAMES, TRANS., 1883 *The Zend-Avesta,* Part II in *Sacred Books of the East,* vol. XXIII ed. F.M. Müller (Oxford: Clarendon Press).

MILLS, L.H., 1887 *The Zend-Avesta,* Part III. in *Sacred Books of the East* vol. XXXI, ed. F.M. Müller (Oxford: Clarendon Press).

MISTREE, KHOJESTE, 1982 *Zoroastrianism: An Ethnic Perspective.* Bombay: Zoroastrian Studies.

PANGBORN, CYRUS R., 1982 *Zoroastrianism: A Beleaguered Faith.* New Delhi: Vikas.

Zaehner, R.C., 1961 *The Dawn and Twilight of Zoroastrianism.* New York: Putnam.

CHAPTER 11

Judaism:
The Way of Torah

MEDITERRANE
SEA

MODE
ISRAE

Te

GAZA
STRIP

Suez Canal

EGYPT

Gulf of Suez

INTRODUCTION: WHAT IS JUDAISM?

The way to begin a discussion of Judaism is with an attempt to clarify the meaning of the terms "Judaism" and "Jew." Judaism is, of course, the name of a religion, and our focus in this chapter will be on Judaism as a religion.

However, Judaism also designates the culture, civilization, way of life, and shared story of the Jewish people. Within Judaism, in this more expansive sense, are found not only people who affirm the spiritual teachings of the religion of Judaism, but others who are steadfastly secular in their orientation yet still associate themselves with Jewish culture and the Jewish story.

It is critical to make clear that although it is appropriate to speak of the "Jewish people" as those who identify with the religion, culture, and/or story of Judaism, "Jew" is *not* a racial designation. There is no factual basis for the pseudo-scientific theory of a "Jewish race," which was developed in the nineteenth century, exploited by the Nazi Party of Germany in its program of extermination of the Jewish people of Europe during World War II, and resurrected by various neo-Nazi groups today. Jews come from every racial group.

Jews are those who by birth or by conscious decision and action identify themselves with the heritage and continuing experience of the Jewish people. And Judaism is the shared story of the Jewish people. Therefore, to understand Judaism both in its narrower sense as a religion and in its broader sense, we must begin with the story of the Jewish people.

STAGES OF DEVELOPMENT AND SACRED TEXTS

The People of Ancient Israel, the Tanak, and the Origins of Judaism

The story of Judaism begins with a people remembering their past. These memories are recorded in an anthology of sacred writings that became known as the *Tanak*, an acronym formed from the first letters of the three sections of the text in Hebrew— *torah* ("law, instruction"), *nevi'im* ("prophets"), *kethuvi'im* ("writings"). The collection is also called the Hebrew Bible, Jewish Bible, or (by Christians) the Old Testament. We will use the names of the books of the Tanak most frequently used today in modern English translations. Our intent here is simply to review the story the Tanak itself tells and to describe very briefly the books of the Tanak. A full historical analysis and literary study of the Tanak takes us beyond the scope of the present work (see Hauer and Young 1994).

Origins and Ancestors The Tanak begins by recounting the creation of the universe by the one God (Genesis 1–2). The emphasis is on God as the sole creator, the goodness and order of creation, and the special place of humanity (created in the "image of God") in the creation. Next is the primal history of humanity (Genesis 3–11).

Then the story focuses on the relationship between God and the one nation God chose to be a special people with a unique role in history: the nation Israel. First, the story of the ancestors of Israel and the special covenant God entered into with Abraham and Sarah and their descendants is recounted (Genesis 12–50). The term "covenant" refers in general to agreements between two or more parties. It is often used in the Tanak to refer to various pacts initiated by God and entered into with Israel. Sometimes the covenant is a promise made by God; on other occasions the covenant includes specific stipulations for the people of Israel to follow. After having an encounter with God and being told that his descendants will become a great nation in a land of their own as well as a source of blessing to other nations, Abraham and his wife Sarah journeyed from Mesopotamia to the land that was to become Israel. This promissory covenant is then renewed with the son of Abraham, Isaac, and his wife Rebecca. The name "Israel" relates to Jacob, the son of Isaac, with whom the Abrahamic covenant is also renewed. Jacob is also called Israel ("he who strives with God"). The etymology given for the name "Israel" in Genesis (32:28) is "You have striv-

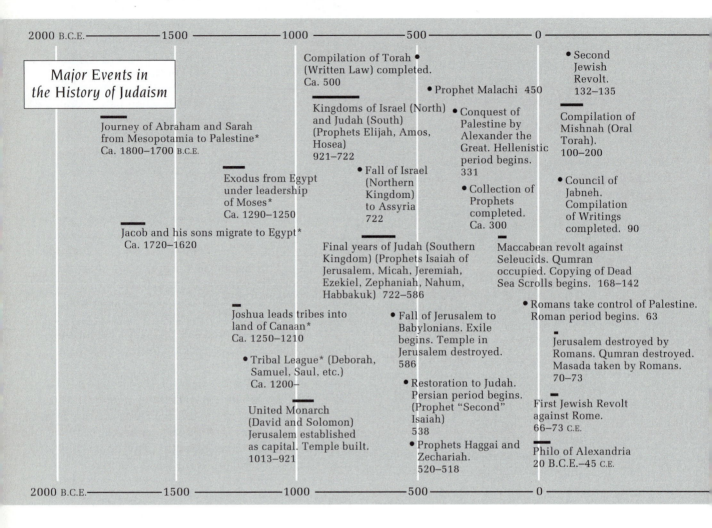

Major Events in the History of Judaism

2000 B.C.E. —— 1500 —— 1000 —— 500 —— 0 ——

Compilation of Torah (Written Law) completed. Ca. 500

Prophet Malachi 450

Second Jewish Revolt. 132–135

Journey of Abraham and Sarah from Mesopotamia to Palestine* Ca. 1800–1700 B.C.E.

Kingdoms of Israel (North) and Judah (South) (Prophets Elijah, Amos, Hosea) 921–722

Conquest of Palestine by Alexander the Great. Hellenistic period begins. 331

Compilation of Mishnah (Oral Torah). 100–200

Exodus from Egypt under leadership of Moses* Ca. 1290–1250

Fall of Israel (Northern Kingdom) to Assyria 722

Collection of Prophets completed. Ca. 300

Council of Jabneh. Compilation of Writings completed. 90

Jacob and his sons migrate to Egypt* Ca. 1720–1620

Final years of Judah (Southern Kingdom) (Prophets Isaiah of Jerusalem, Micah, Jeremiah, Ezekiel, Zephaniah, Nahum, Habbakuk) 722–586

Maccabean revolt against Seleucids. Qumran occupied. Copying of Dead Sea Scrolls begins. 168–142

Joshua leads tribes into land of Canaan* Ca. 1250–1210

Fall of Jerusalem to Babylonians. Exile begins. Temple in Jerusalem destroyed. 586

Romans take control of Palestine. Roman period begins. 63

Tribal League* (Deborah, Samuel, Saul, etc.) Ca. 1200–

Jerusalem destroyed by Romans. Qumran destroyed. Masada taken by Romans. 70–73

United Monarch (David and Solomon) Jerusalem established as capital. Temple built. 1013–921

Restoration to Judah. Persian period begins. (Prophet "Second" Isaiah) 538

First Jewish Revolt against Rome. 66–73 C.E.

Prophets Haggai and Zechariah. 520–518

Philo of Alexandria 20 B.C.E.–45 C.E.

2000 B.C.E. —— 1500 —— 1000 —— 500 —— 0 ——

en with God and with humans, and have prevailed." The twelve sons of Jacob/Israel by his wives, Rachel and Leah, and his concubines are remembered as the ancestors of the twelve tribes that would make up the nation Israel. The Book of Genesis ends with the sons of Jacob having gone into Egypt where one of them, Joseph, who had been sold into slavery by his brothers, has become a chief officer of the Pharaoh.

Moses and the Torah In the Book of Exodus, the narrative next focuses on a man named Moses who led the descendants of Abraham out of bondage in Egypt. The descendants of Abraham

have become slaves, and they cry out to God to deliver them. To Moses God reveals the special name *Yahweh* (written in most English translations of the Hebrew Bible as LORD). Yahweh instructs Moses to confront Pharaoh and demand that he set the people free. It is important to note that beginning late in the biblical period and continuing throughout most of Jewish history the name "Yahweh" has never been uttered out of reverence for God. Various circumlocutions such as "the Lord" and "the Name" are used instead. The people miraculously escape from Egypt (in a series of events remembered in the festival of Passover) and begin a journey toward the land God had promised

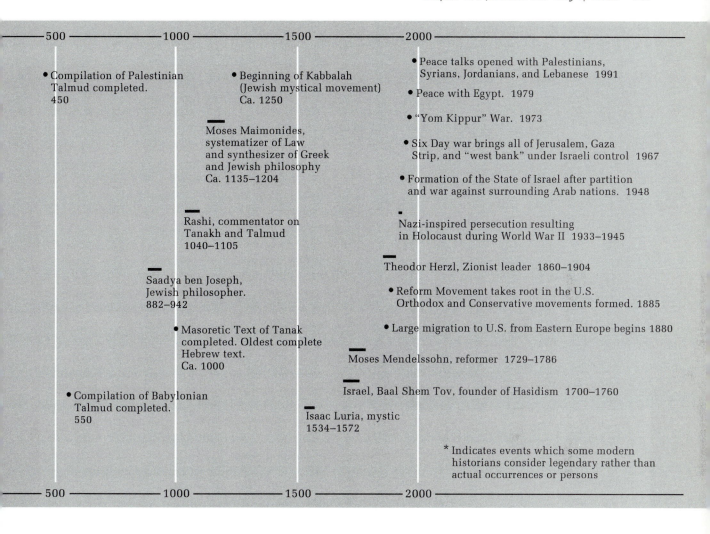

─── 500 ─────── 1000 ─────── 1500 ─────── 2000 ───

• Peace talks opened with Palestinians, Syrians, Jordanians, and Lebanese 1991

• Compilation of Palestinian Talmud completed. 450

• Beginning of Kabbalah (Jewish mystical movement) Ca. 1250

• Peace with Egypt. 1979

• "Yom Kippur" War. 1973

Moses Maimonides, systematizer of Law and synthesizer of Greek and Jewish philosophy Ca. 1135–1204

• Six Day war brings all of Jerusalem, Gaza Strip, and "west bank" under Israeli control 1967

• Formation of the State of Israel after partition and war against surrounding Arab nations. 1948

Rashi, commentator on Tanakh and Talmud 1040–1105

Nazi-inspired persecution resulting in Holocaust during World War II 1933–1945

Saadya ben Joseph, Jewish philosopher. 882–942

Theodor Herzl, Zionist leader 1860–1904

• Reform Movement takes root in the U.S. Orthodox and Conservative movements formed. 1885

• Masoretic Text of Tanak completed. Oldest complete Hebrew text. Ca. 1000

• Large migration to U.S. from Eastern Europe begins 1880

Moses Mendelssohn, reformer 1729–1786

• Compilation of Babylonian Talmud completed. 550

Israel, Baal Shem Tov, founder of Hasidism 1700–1760

Isaac Luria, mystic 1534–1572

* Indicates events which some modern historians consider legendary rather than actual occurrences or persons

─── 500 ─────── 1000 ─────── 1500 ─────── 2000 ───

to give to the descendants of Abraham (see Figure 11–1). At the mountain called Sinai the Lord gives to Moses the Ten Commandments and other laws as the basis of a new covenant relationship with the people of Israel. The earlier covenants had been unconditional—promises made by God. This covenant, often called the Sinai covenant, is conditional. The Lord promises to be the God of this nation and protect them if the people will agree to follow the guidelines he had revealed through Moses.

The revelation of God to Moses on Mount Sinai is the root of *Torah*. Because of the centrality of Torah in Judaism, its range of meaning must be clarified at this point. "Torah" is often translated today simply as law, for God revealed to the people commandments they were to keep. However, "law" is misleading, reflecting the influence of the Greek translation (*nomos*) of the Hebrew word *torah*. Torah is more appropriately translated from Hebrew into English as the "teaching" or "instruction" given by God to the people. Torah is also the name given to the first five books of the Tanak (Genesis, Exodus, Leviticus, Numbers, and Deuteronomy) because these books recount the giving of the Torah. This section of the Tanak is also called the Books of Moses (because of the traditional belief that Moses is their author) and the Pentateuch ("five books," after the Greek transla-

Rembrandt's painting of Moses breaking the tablets of the Torah (see Exodus 32) is an example of the myriad of Biblical scenes portrayed throughout history by many of the world's finest artists.

Source: Art Resource.

tion). However, Torah may also be used when speaking of the Tanak as a whole. More broadly, Torah refers to the total revelation from God as understood by classical Judaism: the Tanak (written Torah) and the related authoritative commentary (called the oral Torah). We will discuss the oral Torah more fully later in the chapter.

After the encounter with God at Mount Sinai recounted in Exodus, the rest of the Books of Moses tell the story of the people's wandering in the wilderness and the instructions that the Lord wanted them to follow in order to prosper. The guidelines cover both their relations with one another and their relationship with God. They also spell out how the Lord is to be worshipped. The people were to carry with them the Ark of the Covenant, in which the tablets of the Ten Commandments were kept. The Ark was the symbolic throne of God; it was to be kept in a tent that is meticulously described in the Torah. Despite their persistent grumbling and lack of trust, God continues to provide for the people's needs and protect them. The tribes they encounter are defeated with the help of the Lord. The people are told by Moses (according to the Book of Deuteronomy) that if they followed the covenant they had made with the Lord, they will have a good life in the land God was about to give them. However, if they failed to obey the laws, they will die.

The Rise and Fall of Ancient Israel   In the next section of the Tanak, the story of the history of the people of Israel continues. The "former prophets" (Joshua, Judges, First and Second Samuel, First and Second Kings) form a historical narrative that traces the story of the people of Israel from their occupation of the land of Canaan through a series of conflicts with the inhabitants of the land (Book of Joshua); the exploits of various charismatic leaders who mobilize some of the tribes in continuing wars (Book of Judges); the leadership of Samuel and the tragic story of King Saul (First Samuel); King David, who draws the northern tribes (called Israel) and the southern tribes (called Judah) together into a unified state and creates a mini-empire with its center in the city of Jerusalem (First and Second Samuel, First Kings 1–2); the united kingdom under the leadership of David's son, Solomon (First Kings 2–11); and finally the story of the breakup of the united monarchy and the subsequent divided kingdoms of the north (Israel) and the south (Judah), ending with the defeat of the northern kingdom by the Assyrian Empire by 722 B.C.E. and the southern kingdom by the Babylonians by 587 B.C.E. (First Kings 12–22, Second Kings). The Babylonian conquest of Jerusalem and destruction of the Temple (597–587 B.C.E.) is a watershed event in the history of ancient Israel. It marked the beginning of the Babylonian exile (which lasted until 538 B.C.E.).

The narrative in the former prophets is not a mere recounting of events, but a theological history told from the perspective that when people were

FIGURE 11-1

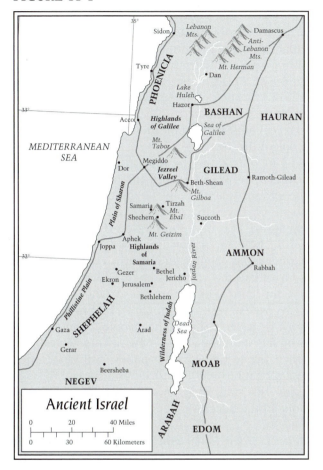

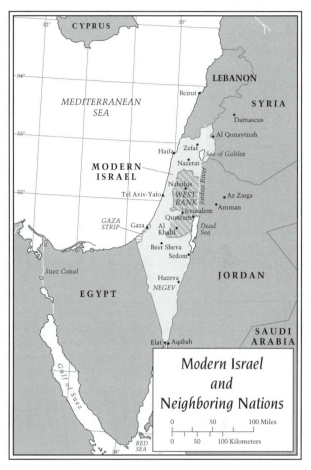

obedient to God, the nation flourished; but when they were not loyal, catastrophe struck. We also note in the former prophets a tension on the question of kingship in Israel, perhaps reflecting the presence of both pro- and anti-monarchical schools in ancient Israel. Of particular importance in the narrative is the building of a Temple of the Lord in Jerusalem under Solomon. This First Temple and the city of Jerusalem were destroyed during the Babylonian invasion, and Davidic kingship ended.

Prophets of Ancient Israel Interspersed with the story of political leaders in the historical narrative are accounts of prophets—men and women who confront the people and their leaders with God's warnings about violations of the covenant, including the worship of other deities. The prophets are not so much predictors of the future (as the term in modern usage implies), but emissaries commissioned by the Lord to challenge the people to obey the covenant and to warn them of the dire consequences if they do not.

The other section of the prophets is called the "latter prophets." These books are largely the collected utterances and writings of some of the prophets of ancient Israel. The "major prophets" are Isaiah, Jeremiah, and Ezekiel.

According to most modern Biblical scholars, the long book of Isaiah includes the sayings and poems of two or more prophets during a several-hundred-year period. The so-called "First Isaiah" or Isaiah of Jerusalem was active in Jerusalem from about 742 B.C.E. until about 701 B.C.E. Like other prophets, he felt called to serve as an emissary from the court of the divine king to the king and people of Israel and other nations (see Isaiah 6). His message was one of judgment on Israel and other nations for failure to enact justice, especially for the poor and weak. His utterances have been preserved in the first thirty-nine chapters of the Book of Isaiah. The "Second Isaiah" (author of Isaiah 40–55) wrote during the Babylonian exile (sometime between 587 and 538 B.C.E.). The long, complex poems of this prophet are among the most polished literary works in the Tanak. They herald the restoration of the nation of Israel after the punishment of the exile in a "new exodus" and praise the Lord as the only God, the Creator of the heavens and earth. Second Isaiah also speaks of an enigmatic "servant" in several poems. It is likely that a "Third Isaiah" (Isaiah 56-66) prophesied from Jerusalem after the return of some of the exiles and the rebuilding of the Temple, around or after 515 B.C.E.

Jeremiah prophesied before, during, and after the Babylonian conquest of Judah, from sometime before 609 B.C.E. until sometime after 587 B.C.E. Through this tumultuous period, he announced divine judgment and envisioned a restoration. The Book of Jeremiah, probably edited by the prophet's secretary, Baruch, includes narratives about the prophet's encounters with religious and political authorities, poems that reflect the anguish Jeremiah felt about his prophetic role, and collected oracles of judgment and hope.

Ezekiel lived in exile in Babylon and prophesied there from 597 B.C.E. until the 570s. Ezekiel describes visions in which he saw the chariot of Yahweh and was taken by the Lord to Jerusalem. His message was also one of judgment on the sins of Israel and other nations as well as the restoration of Israel after divine punishment. Among his more famous visions was one of the coming to life of "dry bones" in Chapter 38 (symbolizing the enlivening of the nation Israel) and another of a new Jerusalem and a reconstructed Temple (Chapters 40-48).

The so-called "minor prophets" or "Scroll of the Twelve" are works that relate to prophets active in both the northern kingdom and the southern kingdom from the ninth century B.C.E. well into the period after the Babylonian exile. They include the books of Hosea, Joel, Amos, Obadiah, Jonah, Micah, Nahum, Habakkuk, Zephaniah, Haggai, Zechariah, and Malachi. Discussion of their particular circumstances and messages is beyond the scope of this work.

In general, all the Biblical prophets stress the covenant between the Lord and Israel and interpret the various calamities in the life of the nation as a result of covenant disobedience. But they also emphasize that God, the creator of the ends of the earth, chose the nation Israel and will not give up easily on the people. Judgment is certain on those who violate the commandments of the covenant, but the Lord will restore those who repent and deliver those who remain faithful (although it will only be a remnant of the people). Some of the prophets look ahead to a new, eschatological age, when the fortunes of the nation will be restored and all nations will live together in peace. In some cases, this time of renewal is associated with the hope of the restoration of the Davidic kingship.

Return from Exile and the Birth of Judaism
Before we turn to the third section of the Tanak, the *kethuvi'im* ("writings"), we will briefly recount what is known of the remainder of the Biblical period in the history of Judaism. The Babylonian exile ended when the Persians defeated the Babylonians and allowed some of the exiled leaders to return to Israel, beginning about 538 B.C.E. Many remained in Babylon, which became an important center of Jewish life and scholarship for the next thousand years. Those who returned rebuilt the Temple and the walls of Jerusalem. The new Temple, constructed on the site of the Temple built by Solomon, is known as the Second Temple.

Also during the Second Temple period the Torah or some portion thereof was embraced as the national constitution of the Jewish people. It is likely that already during the Babylonian exile, when there was no access to the Temple, places of gathering emerged for the hearing and study of the teaching (Torah) believed to be revealed by God to Moses on Mount Sinai. Herein lies the root of an institution that was to become focal as Judaism developed—known by the Greek term transliterated as *synagogue* ("assembly"). We will return to the place of the synagogue in Jewish life later. Scribes and Torah-teachers, who copied and interpreted the now written Torah, were important religious leaders during this period. With the restoration of the Temple, priests also played an important role in Jewish life once again.

The period of Persian control of Israel, which had begun in 538 B.C.E., continued until Alexander the Great conquered the region in 333 B.C.E., beginning the Hellenistic period. Hellenistic (Greek) culture was to exert significant influence on the Jewish community, both in the homeland and throughout the *Diaspora* (from the Greek word used to translate the Hebrew *galut,* referring to the dispersion of the Jewish people from their homeland in Israel throughout the world). The result was, on the one hand, adaptation of Jewish teachings and life to Hellenistic ideas (evident in some of the later writings in the Tanak and the Deuterocanon–sacred writing found in later translations of the Tanak but not part of the Hebrew canon) and, on the other hand, resistance to such incursions by defenders of observance of the Torah-teachings.

After the death of Alexander, control of the Persian province of Judea fell first to a dynasty centered in Egypt known as the Ptolemies, but by the second century to the Seleucid dynasty based in Syria. The Seleucid emperor Antiochus Epiphanes enacted a particularly ruthless policy of Hellenization. He even converted the Temple in Jerusalem to the worship of the Greek god Zeus. In reaction against Antiochus's policy of oppression some Jews mounted a revolt, led by the Hasmonean family. It became known as the Maccabean revolt (from the epithet *Maccabeus,* meaning "hammerer," assigned to the first of the Hasmonean military leaders, Judas). In December of 164 B.C.E. Judas' forces liberated the Temple, an event commemorated annually in the celebration of the Feast of Hannukah. After their victory over the Seleucids, the Hasmoneans created a dynasty that gave Israel a century of political and religious independence. However, a weakened Hasmonean dynasty officially ended in 63 B.C.E., with the

A model of the restored Jerusalem Temple, which stood from the sixth century B.C.E. until its destruction by the Romans in 70 C.E.

entry of the Roman general Pompey into Jerusalem. For the rest of the Biblical period Israel was under Roman control. A watershed event during the Roman period was the destruction of the Second Temple by the Romans after a Jewish revolt in 70 C.E.

We return now to our overview of the final section of the Tanak, the writings. The writings contain a variety of types of literature. Included are narrative books that parallel the story told in the former prophets (First and Second Chronicles). The narrative books of the writings also extend the account into the post-exilic period of the history of ancient Israel (Second Chronicles, Ezra, Nehemiah), when the Persians allowed some of those who had been taken into exile in Babylon to return to Jerusalem, to rebuild the city and the Temple (the Second Temple). Together the Books of Chronicles, Ezra, and Nehemiah constitute what is often called the Chronicler's History.

Also found in the writings are two short stories or novellas that focus on the role played by women at critical times in Israel's history (Ruth, Esther). A unique work is the Book of Daniel. It is an apocalyptic writing, meaning that it purports to reveal the mysteries of the end of history and the beginning of a new age. Its original context is the Maccabean revolt (167–164 B.C.E.), but its symbolism has been applied throughout history to other time periods.

The other books of the writings are largely poetic. They include a collection of hymns associated with worship in the Jerusalem temple and other poems (Psalms); wisdom books, which are both practical and speculative in nature (Proverbs, Job, Ecclesiastes); an anthology of love poetry (Song of Songs); and a collection of poems of sorrow occasioned by the destruction of Jerusalem by the Babylonians (Lamentations). Within the writings are some of the most profound and artful literary works in the Tanak. Unfortunately, we are not able to do justice to them in this short section.

The background of the religion of Judaism is found in the Tanak's story of the ancient nation of Israel, the people who "wrestled with God." The Tanak, however, is only the beginning of the story of the Jewish people. Even as the writings that comprise the Tanak were being collected as a canon

of sacred writings, new developments were underway that helped to shape the religion of Judaism.

The name "Judaism" actually came into existence after the nation Israel was conquered and the people had lost their national identity as "Israel." Judaism referred originally to the religion of the people of the Persian province of Judea. The term Jew also originated after the Babylonian exile to refer to the people of Judea and other descendants of the people of Israel who lived in communities dispersed around the Mediterranean world.

Classical Judaism and the Oral Torah

Even before the end of the Biblical period, institutions that were to become especially important in the next phase of Jewish history were emerging.

Synagogue The Jews of the Diaspora were cut off from the Temple, the center of worship in Biblical Judaism. To fill the void the synagogue ("assembly") developed, perhaps as early as the Babylonian exile, as we have noted above. Synagogues were local centers of study and prayer. Since Jews in the Diaspora could not perform the sacrificial ritual prescribed in the Torah, they instead focused on services of prayer and intense study of the written Torah. When the Second Temple was destroyed by the Romans in 70 C.E., the synagogue became even more important. It continues today as the central religious institution beyond the family for many Jews.

In the post-Biblical period, rabbis gradually became the most important leaders in the practice of Judaism. The term *rabbi* ("my master") itself probably emerged in the first century C.E. to designate a person of learning who could interpret to others Jewish teaching. Rabbis were skilled in the interpretation of the written Tanak, and they were also instrumental in the development of the body of tradition known as the Oral Torah. Their precursors were the scribes or Torah teachers of the early Second Temple period.

Mishnah and Midrash The origins of the *Oral Torah* are found in the Jewish communities' need to apply the commandments of the written Torah to changing times and new situations. For example,

The Wall of the Old City, Jerusalem.

A Hasidic Jew in, Boro Park, New York, in a prayer shawl and black leather tefillin *(phylacteries). The* tefillin, *containing passages from the Tanak, are worn by observant Jewish men on the head and left arm during the morning daily prayer (see Deuteronomy 6:4-9).*

the written Torah stipulates that to obey the covenant with Yahweh, people must keep the sabbath holy. However, what specifically does that mean? A series of guidelines, which emerged out of deliberations among Jewish teachers of the law, developed over time to make clear how to determine what Jews could and could not do on the sabbath in order to keep the basic commandment. Interpretation of Torah had already begun in the Biblical period and is reflected in the Tanak itself (see Fishbane 1989). By the second century C.E., a large body of these legal instructions had come into existence in oral form. Near the end of the second century or the beginning of the third, one collection was written down by a teacher who lived in a Jewish academy near the Sea of Galilee in Palestine (the Romans had given this name to the land of Israel). His name was Rabbi Judah, and the collection of about 4,000 legal instructions was called the *Mishnah* ("repetition"). There were various mishnahs, passed down in oral form, which collected discussions among Torah teachers on how best to implement the instructions in the written Torah in particular circumstances. Rabbi Judah's Mishnah became the authoritative written collection.

The Mishnah gave not only the decision that resulted from the Torah deliberations, but the conflicting opinions as well. It included the discussions of many of the most respected legal scholars of the previous 400 years (called the *tannaim*). Some were quite conservative in their interpretations, others more liberal in adapting the legal principles of the Tanak to changing times. The Mishnah was divided into six sections, with guidelines for seasonal festivals and fasts; prayers, agricultural laws, and the rights of the poor; marriage and divorce; civil and criminal law; ritual offerings and sacrifices; and purification. The tradition was accepted that the laws of the Mishnah carried the same authority as the Tanak. It was therefore the first stage in the development of what is known as the Oral Torah (in contrast to the written Torah).

In addition to the Mishnah, another category of "rabbinic literature" developed. The body of material called the *Midrash* ("search, interpret") consisted mostly of interpretation of the Tanak by rabbis during the first five centuries C.E. Some of the commentary was legal in nature; some was not. The legal interpretation was called *halakhah* ("path"), a term to which we will return; the rest was non-legal commentary or *haggadah* ("telling"), which was intended to inspire readers with stories and sayings.

Talmud   These writings did not end the process of reflection and deliberation over the meaning of God's instruction and the development of the Oral Torah. The focus of discussion shifted from Palestine to the Jewish community in Babylon, which had been in existence since the Babylonian exile and which was swelled by those fleeing Roman persecution (which climaxed with the destruction of the Temple in 70 C.E.). The continued discussions among leading rabbis were committed to writing over the next 200 years and compiled by the fifth century in two versions, one in Palestine and the other in Babylon. These extensive collections of both halakhah and haggadah were called *gemara* ("tradition," "completion"). The Palestinian Gemara was combined with Rabbi Judah's Mishnah to create the Palestinian *Talmud* ("learning," "teaching") by about 400–425 C.E. The Babylonian Gemara was added to the Mishnah to form the Babylonian Talmud by 500–525 C.E. Both Talmuds are indeed libraries of volumes so immense that the phrase "sea of Talmud" was coined to describe their extent and depth.

The Babylonian Talmud attained widest acceptance by the Jewish community. Therefore, the Jewish sacred texts are not only the Tanak (the written Torah) but also the Talmud and the ever-growing body of Oral Torah associated with them. The development of the Talmud represents the culmination of the development of classical Judaism and the emergence of a style of teaching and learning that continues to define the traditional practices of Judaism. Commentary on Talmud continued into the medieval period and yielded collections that function among Jewish interpreters as part of the Oral Torah. With ongoing interpretation of the application of the tradition to new circumstances by contemporary rabbis, in a sense Oral Torah continues to be created.

The dominant characteristic of rabbinic teaching was and continues to be that the authoritative text, the Tanak, has many legitimate meanings appropriate to different occasions. The Tanak offers patterns for living, expressed through a variety of literary forms: stories, pronouncements, and law codes among them. However, finding the relevant meaning requires careful, artful study and interpretation. Even the Biblical law codes do not yield direct, unambiguous directives. They are authoritative but indefinite, yielding not only law but also ethics, mysticism, politics, poetry, and folklore. The rabbis whose deliberations are recorded in the Talmud offer extensive discussion on how to derive legal and moral instruction, but they leave to the individual and to future rabbis the specific decisions on how to enact a particular principle.

Sadducees, Pharisees, and Other Movements   Let us now turn back the clock 500 years to the beginning of the Common Era. If we could enter a time capsule and visit the Jewish world of this earlier period we would encounter a number of different "schools." To understand the development of Judaism we need to examine these groups.

During the period of the Second Temple, the High Priest of the Jerusalem Temple became the civil as well as religious head of the Jewish community. His decisions were to some degree subject to the oversight of the *gerousia,* a community of elders that later became known as the *Sanhedrin.* The High Priest and priestly families allied with him formed a party known as the *Sadducees* (from the name for the leading family of priests, *Zadokites*). This wealthy, aristocratic movement distanced itself from some of the popular religious ideas of the time (such as the apocalyptic expectation of a new age in which the dead would be raised from their graves). They rejected the emerging Oral Torah and maintained that only the five books of Moses (the Pentateuch) had authority over the life of the community. The priestly slant of the Pentateuch may have played a role in that emphasis. The Sadducees tended to favor cooperation with the Roman authorities, who by this time had taken control of Palestine, as the best way to maintain stability.

They were also more willing to adopt the Hellenistic cultural values the Romans embraced. After the destruction of the Temple in 70 C.E., they faded.

Another party, opposed to the Sadducees, acquired the name *Pharisees* (possibly "separatists"). Popular understanding of both the Sadducees and the Pharisees is obscured by the portrait painted of these movements in the Christian New Testament. In the New Testament Gospels the Pharisees are pictured as legalistic hypocrites. Today the term "pharisee" is used to describe a particularly overscrupulous person. This stereotype of the Pharisees is a prejudiced exaggeration of some of the characteristics of this party. In the context of the times, the Pharisees were liberals. They emphasized the need to adapt the guidelines of the written Torah to changing circumstances in order to maintain righteousness. This placed them in opposition to the Sadducees. They also were more open to new teachings such as the resurrection from the dead and the hope of the coming of a messiah to restore the nation Israel. They stressed righteous living, maintaining ritual and moral purity and opposing those external authorities who would compromise the integrity of the Jewish law. Rather than teaching a narrow, sterile legalism, the Pharisees emphasized living in joyful obedience to the gift of the Torah. The Pharisees came from the middle ranks of society, including both lay people and the lower ranks of the priests. The rabbis typically came from the ranks of the Pharisees. After the destruction of the Temple they became virtually the ruling party within the Jewish community. Because they were not literalists, when the sacrifice at the Temple ended they were able to replace it with worship of "the lips and the heart." The Talmud is a product of the Pharisaic movement. Classical Judaism—or rabbinical Judaism, as it is also known—can also be considered Pharisaic Judaism.

The Sadducees and Pharisees were not the only parties in Judaism at this turbulent time. Another was the *Zealot* party, which favored a violent revolution to overthrow the Romans. Their stronghold was in northern Galilee. The Zealots believed that by taking up arms they could hasten the coming of the messiah. It was a Zealot revolt, which broke out in 66 C.E., that led to the Roman destruction of the Temple in 70 C.E.

The Jewish historian Josephus and other authorities also identify a party known as the *Essenes*. They lived in monastic communities, preparing for the coming of the new age. They considered the other schools of Judaism corrupt. It has been widely assumed that the community along the shores of the Dead Sea, which produced the Dead Sea Scrolls, were Essenes. The Dead Sea Scrolls, which began to be discovered in 1947, included both Biblical texts in Hebrew (1,000 years older than the next oldest Hebrew manuscripts of the Tanak) and sectarian documents that described the lifestyle and beliefs of the community that produced them. The latter writings portray a community that considered itself the elect of God, who would emerge triumphant in a final battle between the Children of Light and the Children of Darkness. They had their own version of the Torah, and considered themselves the true priesthood because the priesthood of the Jerusalem Temple had become corrupt. They anticipated not one messiah but two, perhaps more.

Whether the members of the Dead Sea community were Essenes is a matter of intense scholarly debate at present, but in any case the diversity within Judaism at the time is documented by the existence of this community.

We should also mention Jewish communities that were heavily influenced by Hellenistic culture. Two results of Jewish Hellenization are particularly important. One was a philosophical tradition that used Greek philosophy to interpret Jewish teachings. Philo, a Jewish philosopher who lived in Alexandria, Egypt, was a particularly important representative of this movement. In addition, the translation of the Tanak into Greek resulted in the *Septuagint* ("seventy," from the tradition found in the Letter of Aristeas that seventy-two scholars chosen by the High Priest participated in the translation), making the Hebrew Bible available to the Greek-speaking world.

Out of this crucible two Jewish movements had ultimately prevailed by medieval times. One was the Pharisaic, which defined the form of Judaism that represents the dominant expression of Judaism as it was passed through the centuries. The other was the *Nazarean*, for it was composed of followers of a rabbi from Galilee named *Yeshua* in Hebrew (or, in Greek, Jesus) of Nazareth. We will devote the next chapter to the religion that emerged from this group—Christianity. Now we will pursue the development of classical or Pharisaic Judaism.

Judaism from the Middle Ages through the Enlightenment

During the Middle Ages the Jews of the Diaspora were largely at the mercy of the two religions that had come to dominance in the Middle East and Europe: Christianity and Islam.

When Christianity became the official religion of the Roman Empire in the fourth century C.E., the antagonism that had characterized the attitude of many Christian leaders toward Jews rigidified (because of the Jews' unwillingness to recognize Jesus as the messiah).

By contrast, when Muslims took control of areas in the Middle East in which Jews lived, they treated Jews with greater tolerance (until the Turkish dynasty instituted a policy of oppression). In the tenth and eleventh centuries many Jews fled from the Middle East to Spain, where there was a thriving Jewish community. Thus began an era of great achievement in all areas of Jewish life. For example, the twelfth-century physician and scholar Moses Maimonides wrote works that reconciled the best in contemporary science and philosophy with Jewish themes.

One of the most fascinating medieval developments in Judaism was a mystical movement that goes by the name *Kabbala* ("tradition"). In a thorough study of Judaism we would be able to examine the mystical practices that are as old as the Tanak (as in the visions of the prophet Ezekiel). This mystical tendency exploded in the Middle Ages, particularly in situations of persecution. In particular, exponents of Kabbala drew on numerology to probe the hidden meanings of the text of the Hebrew Bible. A mystical work written in the late thirteenth century, called the *Zohar* ("splendor"),

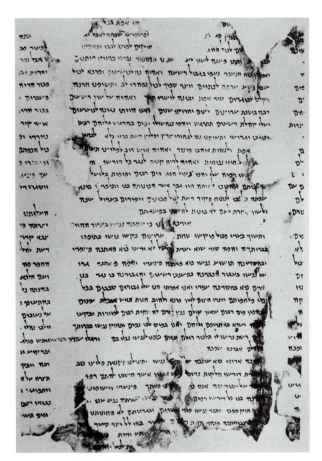

A section of the "Thanksgiving Scroll," one of the ancient scrolls associated with the Dead Sea community at Qumran.

became as popular and influential as the Tanak and Talmud among many Jews. The *Zohar* portrays God as a boundless energy (*ein sof*) from which emanate ten spheres, such as wisdom, beauty, and strength. The forces are male and female, in interaction with one another. One aspect of the Kabbalistic enthusiasm was a heightened messianic expectation, which resulted in a number of claimants.

When the Crusades began, one consequence was wholesale Christian attacks on Jews throughout Europe. Jews who refused to convert to Christianity were expelled from England in 1290, from France in 1394, and from Spain in the year Columbus left on his voyage of discovery, 1492.

The Jews who remained in Italy, Germany, and Austria were forced to live in segregated areas called ghettos. The term "ghetto" is Italian, arising from the practice decreed by Pope Paul IV in 1555 that Jews living in the papally controlled areas of Rome had to live in separate quarters. Catholic authorities also forced Jews to wear "Star of David" badges, a precursor of the practice adopted by the Nazis during World War II.

The Jews who fled Spain into the Middle East have become known as the *Sephardim* ("Spanish"), while those who fled to Poland and surrounding areas became the *Ashkenazim* ("Germans"). The Ashkenazim developed a dialect combining German and Hebrew, which is called *Yiddish*. They were able to flourish by becoming successful in trade and money lending.

In addition to these developments in the history of Judaism in Europe, throughout these centuries Jewish communities continued to exist and often flourish in the Muslim world in North Africa and the Middle East and in areas as far away as Asia.

When the Protestant Reformation swept across Europe, it appeared that Christian intolerance toward Jews might change. Martin Luther spoke warmly of the Jews in his early writings, defending them against the popular "blood libel" charge that Jews murdered Christian children and used their blood in the Passover ritual. However, when most Jews refused to convert to a reformed Christianity, as they had also declined to convert to the Catholic Church, Luther in one of his later writings (*Concerning the Jews and their Lies,* 1543) called the Jews "poisonous bitter worms" and suggested that the German princes of the day rid the land "of this insufferable devilish burden—the Jews."

In Eastern Europe a series of *pogroms* (spontaneous attacks on Jews) in the seventeenth century resulted in the death of 500,000 Jews. The blood libel accusation was widely accepted in both Christian and Muslim lands. The persecution inspired a new round of messianic excitement. One messianic claimant, Sabbatai Zevi, was widely acclaimed, but enthusiasm was crushed when he was arrested in Turkey while on his way to Jerusalem in 1665. He converted to Islam when faced with a choice of conversion or death.

An eighteenth-century movement called *Hasidism* has had a lasting impact on Judaism. Hasidic communities can still be found throughout the Jewish world. The founder of Hasidism was a delightful story-telling faith healer who became known as the *Baal Shem Tov* ("Master of the Good Name"). He became convinced that God should be enjoyed as well as studied. He rejected overemphasis on study of the Talmud and taught people to dance in joy in addition to their study. He said God is everywhere present. Hasidic communities formed around charismatic leaders called *tzadikim* ("righteous ones").

The European Enlightenment of the eighteenth century had a profound effect on Jewish life. Jewish leaders such as the German intellectual Moses Mendelssohn urged Jews to leave the ghetto and assimilate to the newly forming societies based on reason and respect for human rights. The American and French revolutions promised freedom and justice for Jews as for other citizens. Jews were admitted to universities and to the professions. Many Jews, like their Christian neighbors, gave up their distinctive religious traditions to live a new, secular life.

The Branches within Modern Judaism

Reform The attitude that Judaism should adapt to a changing world was strongest in nineteenth-century Germany. In German synagogues rabbis began reading the sabbath liturgy in German rather than Hebrew. Emphasis was placed on Jews' being loyal citizens of the countries in which they lived. A famous phrase in the early Reform movement was "We know no homelands but the land of our birth." Some rabbis contended that rigid adherence to the strict dietary laws of the written and oral Torahs was no longer as necessary as commitment to the ethical teachings of the Torah. All of this led to the creation of the *Reform* movement, dedicated to the preservation of the basic principles of Judaism by adapting them to changing circumstances. The Reform movement spread from Germany throughout Europe and to the United States, where today it is particularly popular.

Orthodox In response to the liberalism of the Reform movement, other rabbis formed what became known as *Orthodox* Judaism. Orthodox Jews reacted particularly strongly to the Reform contention that the written and oral Torahs were not the direct word of God, that their guidelines are not all of equal importance. The Orthodox were and are most concerned about observance of the Torah. Judaism could survive different ideas, they believed, but not Jews' giving up the keeping of the instructions that reflected obedience to God and distinguished them as a people. For the Orthodox community, strict adherence to the traditionally stated commandments of the Torah is a matter of Jewish survival.

Conservative Some Jews looked for a middle ground between the Reform and Orthodox approaches and found it in the *Conservative* movement, which was also founded in the nineteenth century. Conservative Jews are willing to use the vernacular in worship and apply historical study to traditional teachings. Therefore, Conservative Jews combine a commitment to observe the commandments of the Torah with a recognition that the legal tradition continues to evolve. Like Reform Jews, Conservative communities ordain women as rabbis (a practice not adopted by Orthodox Jews).

Reconstructionist A fourth branch of Judaism is *Reconstructionism*, which emerged out of the Conservative movement in the 1920s and '30s. It stresses that Judaism is a civilization, and that the maintenance of Jewish culture is the key to Jewish well-being in the modern world. Its founder, Mordecai Kaplan, called Judaism "an evolving religious civilization." This movement has created "Jewish Community Centers" as places where Jewish culture can be celebrated and continued by Jews of differing religious orientations. The particular position of Reconstructionism on religion is that Judaism must be interpreted in a modern scientific framework. For example, the idea of "God" must be seen in the light of evolving human experience.

We should also note the *Havurah* ("fellowship") movement in the United States, which holds its meetings in individual homes instead of synagogues or temples. Another potent force, particularly in Judaism in the United States, is a Jewish feminist movement. Some of the leaders and effects of that movement will be noted later when we discuss the status of women in contemporary Judaism.

Zionism

The new toleration and acceptance of Jews in nineteenth-century Europe was shortlived and superficial. In 1894 a young Austrian journalist named Theodore Herzl was covering the trial of Alfred Dreyfus, a French officer and a Jew who had been charged with being a spy. Dreyfus' conviction on the basis of very weak evidence convinced Herzl that Jews were not as safe in Europe as they thought. He joined the emergent movement called *Zionism* ("Zion" is a symbolic name for Jerusalem) and became its chief negotiator. The Zionist goal was to find a homeland for Jews where they would be safe from persecution. The preference was Palestine, and the Zionists started buying land and opening Jewish settlements there in the early 1900s. By 1909 a new Jewish city (Tel Aviv) had been established, and by 1920 there were 50,000 Jews in Palestine. The Jewish immigration caused the Arabs of Palestine, who had lived in the land for centuries (but without independence), to fear that they would lose their homeland. The British, who after World War I exercised authority over Palestine, at first encouraged then—under Arab pressure—limited Jewish settlement. In 1939 the British established a quota of 15,000 Jews per year to be allowed into Palestine.

The Holocaust

The final reversal of the acceptance of Jews into European society was the coming to power of the Nazi regime in Germany under Adolf Hitler. Drawing upon pseudo-scientific racial theories developed by some German academics, and the long history of Christian persecution of Jews, Hitler announced a goal of making Germany and all of Europe *Judenrein* ("free of Jews").

When Hitler took power in 1933, the first stage of his plan began. Jews were forced out of their positions of responsibility in German society, and Jewish property was expropriated. In 1935 laws were passed that identified categories of "Jewishness," ranging from full Jew to mixed Jew, and the discriminatory policies were institutionalized. Many Jews fled to other countries, after they paid an exorbitant exit fee and left all their property, but strictly enforced immigration quotas in most countries (including the United States) closed the door to many Jews trying to escape.

With the onset of World War II in 1939, Germany quickly began a policy of killing Jews. At first special squads followed the advancing German army and shot many of the Jews in the area "liberated." As the war progressed, more "efficient" killing centers were built in Poland. In areas under German control, Jews had been forced into ghettos, from which they were rounded up and transported to killing centers such as Auschwitz (see Figure 11-2). Most were taken directly to chambers (ostensibly for a disinfecting shower) and gassed with a pesticide, Zyklon B.

By the time the war had ended, about 6 million Jewish men, women, and children had been exterminated by the carefully orchestrated plan of genocide. Two-thirds of the Jews of Europe had been killed. In Poland the Jewish population before the war was 3.35 million; in 1945 there were 50,000 Jews left in Poland. The name *Holocaust* (*Shoah* in Hebrew, the term for a "total burnt offering") was used to describe what the Nazis had done in effectively wiping out most European Jews. It also refers to the killing of millions of non-Jews (including such groups as Communists, homosexuals, and gypsies), who were murdered by the Nazis during this same period merely because of their being labelled as socially inferior.

Surveys suggest that a disturbing number of people in the 1990s believe the neo-Nazi allegations that the Holocaust never happened and that the story of the annihilation of 6 million Jews is a hoax. The opening of the impressive and moving United States Holocaust Memorial and Museum in Washington, D.C., in 1993 was one attempt to

FIGURE 11-2

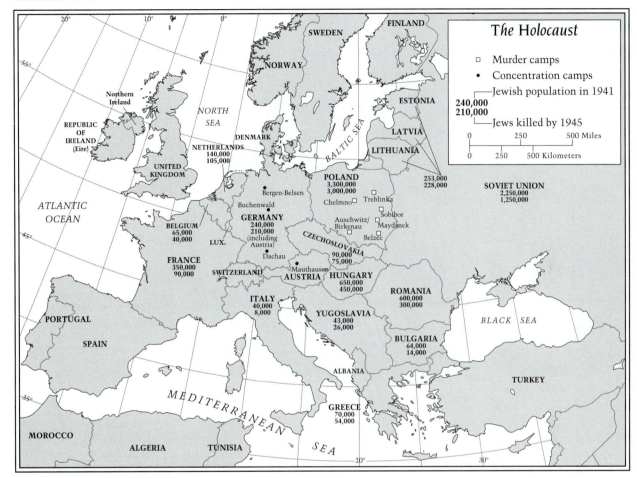

keep alive the story of what actually happened during the Holocaust so that it will never happen again.

The State of Israel

The Zionist dream of a homeland for Jews was finally realized with the birth of the modern state of Israel in 1948. The centrality of Israel in Jewish life must be recognized if we are to understand modern Judaism. Except for the most assimilated Jews, Jewish life is now seen by most Jews of the Diaspora as having a proper context both in the countries where they live and in Israel. For most Jews today, to say that Israel is merely the product of the political movement known as Zionism is misleading. "Israel" is more than a political state; it is a place where Jews are free to live as Jews—a Jewish homeland. It is a refuge against the revitalization of anti-Semitism, a place where Jews will protect other Jews from those who seek to destroy the Jewish people. Israel is a critical expression and symbol of Jewish identity as a people.

The state of Israel recognizes a "right of return" to the Jewish homeland for all the Jews of the world. In recent years a flood of Jewish immigrants from the former Soviet Union and other places where anti-Semitism is on the rise has

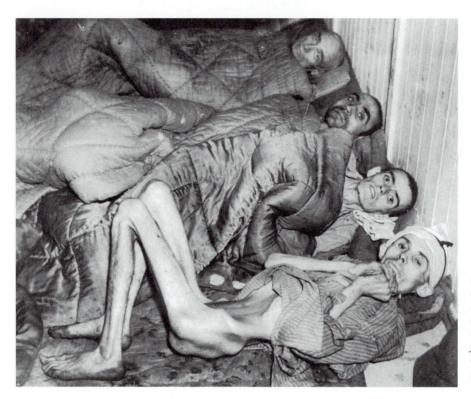

Survivors of the Holocaust awaiting transfer from the Buchenwald Camp after its liberation in 1945. These prisoners had probably survived selection for extermination at the death camp at Auschwitz and a long, tortuous march to Buchenwald.

arrived in Israel. Many Reform Jews in the United States and elsewhere, who before World War II opposed the creation of a state of Israel and the Zionist movement, have become strong political and financial supporters of Israel.

The state of Israel is officially non-religious. In fact, for many Israelis it may be argued that Zionism functions as a secular, civil religion, in which the nation fulfills the role of ultimacy (see Chapter Fourteen on civil religions). However, within Israel, Orthodox groups exercise considerable influence, as is evident in the strict policy of shutting down state-run transportation and all Jewish stores on the sabbath.

The wars with neighboring Arab states and resistance by Palestinians inside Israel and the "occupied territories," as well as those in refugee or exile status outside Israel, have created a great deal of tension within Israel. In Israel today and among Jews worldwide there is a wide spectrum

of opinion on how best to deal with the issues raised by the presence of the Palestinians. Some Israelis and other Jews want to restore the land of Israel as "Judea and Samaria," the Israel envisioned in the Biblical period. They reject the alleged right of Palestinians to a homeland of their own within the traditional boundaries of Israel. They point out that, unlike the Jews, Palestinians never had a separate homeland in the past, and assert that they should be absorbed into surrounding Arab countries. On the other extreme are those Jews who say that Israel should withdraw from all the land taken in the wars with Arab states and cooperate fully in the creation of a Palestinian state within these borders. In between there are a variety of opinions. A peace process, including a direct dialogue between the state of Israel and the Palestinian Liberation Organization (P.L.O.) begun in 1993, may lead to a resolution of this seemingly intractable problem.

Judaism Today

Since the Holocaust some Jewish theologians have questioned the traditional Jewish belief in a God who acts in history for the Jewish people. Some Jews are atheists or agnostics, and consider their Judaism simply a matter of cultural identity. They are representative of those who might be called "secular Jews," for they continue to affirm identity with Jewish history and the Jewish people but not the spiritual teachings of Judaism. Other Jews have developed new understandings of God and God's relationship with humans, and drop the notion that God has the power to intervene at will in history. However, after the Holocaust many Jews committed themselves even more strongly to the traditional Jewish ways and belief in a providential God. Regardless, the Holocaust is considered by most Jews the single most important event in the history of Judaism, especially in the modern world. Its impact is still unfolding.

Two other critical issues face Judaism today. One is *assimilation*, the threat posed to the perpetuation of Judaism by people giving up their Jewish heritage for the sake of "fitting in" to the larger culture. In the United States today many Jews are marrying outside their religion and failing to raise their children as Jews. Some Jewish families have simply faded away from the Jewish community and lost contact with Jewish tradition. Jewish authorities point out that if this trend continues, the survival of a distinct Jewish community is threatened.

Another issue of growing concern, to which we have already alluded, is the resurgence of anti-Semitism. In the early 1990s a world economic recession and the breakup of the former Soviet empire in Eastern Europe provided a context for the reappearance of the historic pattern of looking for scapegoats to blame. Jews and other minorities are again being singled out for hate campaigns in Eastern Europe and other areas of the world, including the United States. Charges such as the blood libel and allegations of a worldwide Jewish conspiracy to gain political power are re-emerging.

Today there are approximately 18 million Jews in the world. Of these, about 8.2 million live in North America, 3.5 million live in Israel, and just under 3 million reside in the former Soviet Union. The remainder live in Western Europe and throughout the world.

DISTINCTIVE TEACHINGS

Judaism as a religion has not traditionally emphasized conformity to a set of beliefs. At the heart of traditional Judaism is not so much belief but practice.

One Jewish scholar, a rabbi in the Conservative movement, has distinguished among three methods of interpretation of the revelation of the Oral Torah at Mount Sinai, which many interpreters are starting to adopt as a way of understanding the variety within Jewish teaching today (Weiss Halivini 1990). The methods are the maximalist, minimalist, and intermediary. The *maximalist* believes that because God revealed at Mount Sinai the solutions to all problems of interpreting the Torah, only learned rabbinic authorities know how Jews should live. The *intermediary* position is that at Mount Sinai God revealed specific issues or problems, not solutions. Rabbinic authorities know the methods of determining how Jews should live, but the applications to particular situations remain to be worked out. The *minimalist* asserts that God only revealed general directions and principles for how to live, but no specifics. Rabbinic authorities are able to identify the basic principles of Jewish life, but how they translate into specific decisions is up to individual interpreters. Reform Judaism and Reconstructionism take the minimalist perspective; Conservative Judaism is intermediary, but ranges within that position; and Orthodoxy reflects a range from maximalist to intermediary.

Until the emergence of the Reform movement in the nineteenth century there was not much disagreement that the common denominator that united the diverse movements within Judaism was observance of all the commandments (although what exactly observance means in particular circumstances has *always* been a subject of discussion and debate in even the most orthodox circles). Today, however, the challenge of the minimalists in the Reform and Reconstructionist movements to this pattern and the reinterpretations offered with-

QUESTIONS OF HUMAN IDENTITY: WHAT IS THE BASIC HUMAN DILEMMA?

The Two Tendencies

In rabbinic teaching we find two tendencies (not spirits), one evil and one good, competing for dominance. The evil tendency (here, desire) is constantly trying to draw humans into sin. The struggle to resist it is a daily one and is successful only with God's help, as the following selection from the Talmud illustrates (Talmud, Kiddushin 30b; Freedman 1959: 147).

Our Rabbis taught: The Evil Desire is hard [to bear], since even his Creator called him evil, as it is written, for that the desire of man's heart is evil from his youth. Rabbi Isaac said, "Man's Evil Desire renews itself daily against him, as it is said, 'Every imagination of the thoughts of his heart was only evil every day.' [Genesis 6:5]" And Rabbi Simeon ben Levi said, "Man's Evil Desire gathers strength against him daily and seeks to slay him ... and were not the Holy One, blessed be He, to help him, he could not prevail against him ...."

Excerpts from The Babylonian Talmud. *Unable to locate current copyright holder.*

---

in the Conservative movement must be taken into account in any discussion of distinctive Jewish teachings. For example, Reform Judaism has typically encouraged considerable *individual* deliberation in deciding the degree to which the keeping of the commandments (especially those involving ritual and diet) is important to one's Jewish identity.

Problem: Missing the Mark

All branches of Judaism agree that humans have freedom to decide whether to follow the will of God or to rebel against it. Classical Judaism spoke of two contrasting tendencies (*yezers*) that are at war in each

human's nature: a good impulse and an evil impulse. These impulses are not external forces, but internal tendencies that are present in every human being. Those who choose to follow the evil impulse inevitably engage in deeds that "miss the mark."

Traditional Judaism has emphasized both the intention behind acts that violate the will of God and the acts themselves. The rabbis distinguished between acts that were particularly heinous and those that were not as severe, but all violations of the commandments were considered a break with God.

Reform Judaism has tended to focus more on the ethical commandments, to the extent that many Reform Jews believe that ignoring the dietary and ritual guidelines is permissible. They argue, for example, that the dietary law was appropriate when it was formulated for health reasons and to maintain a distinctive Jewish identity, but that in the modern world the law has become irrelevant. They believe that Jewishness should not be seen as a matter of the food you eat or the type of prayers you say, but rather in terms of one's fundamental orientation toward the ethical lifestyle found in the Jewish tradition. However, it should be noted that with increasing concern about assimilation, many in the Reform movement are returning to observance of the guidelines they once considered dispensable, *because* they are distinctive.

Cause: Disobedience

Like other monotheistic religions, traditional Judaism teaches that God has revealed the way people are to live. Our choice is to obey God and follow the path (in Judaism the *halakhah*), or to disobey God. The dimension added by Reform Judaism is a certain flexibility to reflect the different circumstances people face.

Reality: "It Is Good!"

The first chapter of the Book of Genesis is the basis for the Jewish understanding that the created order is good, not evil. God has created the world as a place of harmony and abundance to be enjoyed. God has created humanity in the divine image and charged us to respect and maintain the creation. Judaism has steadfastly avoided a dualism that says that matter (including the human body) is evil and spirit (including the human soul) is good. It is not our bodies that are evil, but the acts that we commit when we follow the evil impulse within us. Not only has God created the world, God sustains the world day by day, and therefore is present in the world.

God is not only present in the natural order. Traditional Judaism teaches that God acts within human history and that history is moving toward a time of fulfillment. Especially in light of the Holocaust, belief in God as a being or power who intervenes directly in history has been questioned by some Jews in recent decades.

End: *Next Year in Jerusalem*

In the formative period of classical Judaism we find a variety of beliefs about the future fulfillment for those who keep the Torah. In particular, there was no consensus on the role of a messiah in the future and the fate of people after death. With the emergence of the Pharisaic view as normative, the following emerged as one widely held understanding, although it has sometimes been misrepresented by Christian interpreters seeking a precursor for Christian teaching about the messiah. According to this viewpoint, sometime in the future—at a time known only to God—a messiah will appear and enter into Jerusalem. The messiah will restore the nation Israel, with Jerusalem at the center. This belief is expressed in the toast that is part of the Passover liturgy, as the participants look with anticipation and hope to the coming of the messiah: "Next year in Jerusalem!"

When the messiah comes, a new age, the "age to come," will begin, bringing universal peace, harmony, and justice for all nations. Those who have died before the coming of this age will be raised from their graves. All will be judged by the messiah. Those Jews who have been obedient to the Torah and those Gentiles (non-Jews) who have followed the minimal commandments given by God to all humanity after the Flood will enter into this new Kingdom of God. The ideal place of burial for

many traditional Jews is the cemetery on the Mount of Olives near Jerusalem, where they will be ready to meet the messiah when he returns to Zion.

On the basis of this teaching, many Orthodox Jews opposed the creation of the state of Israel because the messiah has not come, and it is not time yet for the nation to be restored. The belief that the messiah will not come until all Israel is living obediently is widespread, as is the accompanying belief that Jews can "force" the coming of the messiah by their faithfulness. This has been a motivating force in the work of some Orthodox groups to try to encourage Jews who have never kept the Torah or who have stopped keeping it to live observant lives.

Reform Judaism has tended to interpret the teaching about the messiah symbolically rather than literally. Rather than expecting a messianic figure, the Reform movement has emphasized that a "messianic age" of universal peace and justice will only come if humans cooperate with God in bringing it about. The role of the Jewish community, according to this view, is to model the commitment to ethics that will bring humanity into the new age. There is no one teaching in the Reform movement on whether individual humans survive death, or, if they do, what form that life takes.

Means: *The Way of Torah*

At the heart of all branches of Judaism is the Torah, the instruction from God on how to live obediently, which includes both the written Torah and the oral Torah. Disagreement comes on what following the way of Torah should mean in particular circumstances. You can find heated debate within any of the branches of Judaism on the way in which specific situations are affected by the teachings of the Torah. However Torah is interpreted, there is consensus that following the way of Torah is not a burden, but a joy. Torah is God's gift to the Jewish people, and being obedient to Torah is a way of showing gratitude. As one rabbi said, "The reward for keeping one *mitzvah* ["commandment"], is another!"

Orthodox Jews believe that the authority of the Torah resides in its origin. They hold that the

QUESTIONS OF HUMAN DESTINY: WHY ARE WE HERE?

Life's Meaning

This passage from the Talmud suggests that the meaning of life is found in bringing joy to others, and making peace between opposing parties (Talmud, Taanit 22a; Petuchowski 1982: 112).

Rabbi Baruqa of Huza often went to the marketplace at Lapet. One day, the prophet Elijah appeared to him there; and Rabbi Baruqa asked him, "Is there anyone among all these people who will have a share in the World to Come?" Elijah answered, "There is none...." Later, two men came to the marketplace; and Elijah said to Rabbi Baruqa, "Those two will have a share in the World to Come!" Rabbi Baruqa asked the newcomers, "What is your occupation?" They replied, "We are clowns. When we see someone who is sad, we cheer him up. When we see two people quarreling, we try to make peace between them."

Excerpt from Our Masters Taught: Rabbinic Stories and Sayings, trans. and ed. Jakob Petuchowski. Reprinted with permission of Crossroad/Continuum Publishing.

whole Torah, written and oral, was revealed by God to Moses on Mount Sinai. The commandments of the written and oral Torah are therefore the actual word of God to the Jewish people. The only exception for keeping particular commandments is when a person's life is at stake. For example, if a Jew is threatened with death, then it is acceptable to break the commandments in order to avoid being killed. This was the traditional basis for defending the public conversion of Jews to other religions at times of persecution.

From an Orthodox perspective, a Jew should keep a *kosher* ("ritually correct") diet, not simply for practical considerations, but because God has clearly instructed Jews to do so. The kosher guidelines govern which foods may be eaten, how the allowed foods are to be prepared, and the acceptable man-

ner of consumption. The Talmud contains a large collection of such instruction, based on verses in the Tanak. All forms of vegetation are permissible, but only animals that have both cloven hooves and dual digestive tracts. Fish must have both fins and scales. Birds of prey and those that lack a crop, gizzard, and talon are also forbidden. Allowed fish may be eaten when caught, but fowl and the other allowed animals must be ritually slaughtered. The rules of slaughter are so complex that specially trained butchers perform this function in traditional Jewish communities. Once an animal is slaughtered, every effort must be made to remove all blood from the meat. In serving the food, meat and dairy products must not be mixed. Separate dishes are maintained for the two.

According to Reform Judaism the keeping of a kosher diet is a matter of individual conscience. Those Jews who believe that it is a valuable practice in enabling them to lead a Jewish lifestyle should maintain a kosher diet, but those who do not recognize its value should not maintain the tradition for its own sake.

A calendar of festivals is also critical to the way of Torah. At the center of the Jewish calendar is the weekly *sabbath*, the twenty-five-hour period beginning Friday at sundown. As with the other holidays, the basis of the sabbath is a scriptural tradition about the key moments in the history of God's involvement with the nation Israel. The sabbath is a re-enactment of the creation myth, the seventh day when God rested (Exodus 20:8–11), as well as a remembrance of God's mercy in delivering the people from bondage in Egypt (Deuteronomy 5:12--15). In the observance of sabbath at home, the day of rest is greeted as a guest, with a blessing for the day (*kiddush*) said over bread and wine at the sabbath meals and the lighting of the sabbath candles. Two loaves of sabbath bread are served as symbols of the double portion of *manna* from heaven that fell in the Sinai wilderness on Friday. Special prayers are said, and at the conclusion of the sabbath a *havdalah* ("separation") ceremony is held to bid farewell to the sabbath and to distinguish this holy day from the rest of the week.

Orthodox and Conservative Jews attend sabbath services in the synagogue on Saturday morn-

At a Passover seder, *the oldest male present reads from the* haggadah, *a liturgy based on the story of the deliverance of the Israelites from slavery in Egypt. (See Exodus 3-15).*

ing, where selections from the Torah are publicly read as part of a yearly cycle. Reform Jews read the Torah on Friday evening, after sundown, in houses of worship called temples. Temples typically hold less well-attended services on Saturday mornings. Calling the local places of worship a "temple" is a symbol of the Reform view that the temple is in whatever place the Jewish community gathers, not just in Jerusalem. For the Orthodox the *only* temple is the one in Jerusalem, which will be rebuilt when the messiah comes.

Orthodox observance of the sabbath requires abstention from all forms of labor (except where health is at stake), including riding in automobiles, lighting or extinguishing lights, or even carrying money. Conservatives attempt to keep the commandments, but with some adaptation (such as allowing the driving of automobiles to the synagogue on the sabbath). In Reform communities individuals decide for themselves which of the sabbath restrictions or observances have spiritual meaning.

Although the sabbath is set aside as a day of rest, according to traditional Judaism individuals should participate in services of prayer and praise three times daily, including the sabbath. The sabbath morning service is made special because of the reading from the Torah in the synagogue at this service.

Throughout the year a series of other festivals remember and re-enact other central historical events. The spring celebration of *Passover* or *Pesach* ("lamb") is an eight- (or seven-) day commemoration of the deliverance of the Israelites from Egypt. It occurs in March or April. Passover refers to the angel of death "passing over" the homes of the Hebrew families, when the firstborn of the Egyptians were killed. On the first night or (first two nights) of the celebration families gather for *seder* ("order") meals. The Passover haggadah is read at the seder, recalling the Egyptian bondage and deliverance. The participants remember the time when "we" were slaves in Egypt, making present the experience of deliverance and expressing the solidarity of the Jewish community. The foods eaten at the seder recall the exodus experience: *matzah* ("unleavened bread"), bitter herbs, roasted meat, and greens.

In ancient times Passover was one of the three annual pilgrimage festivals during which Jewish males were required to come to Jerusalem for special Temple rituals. Fifty days after Pesach is the celebration of *Shavuot* ("weeks"). It is also known as the festival of first fruit. It remembers both the bringing of first fruits of the harvest to the Temple and the receiving of Torah from God.

The third pilgrimage festival was *Sukkot* ("booths"). A celebration of the autumn harvest, it also recalls the time when the Israelites wandered in the wilderness and lived in portable dwellings called sukkot. It takes place in September or October and lasts for seven days.

The "high holy days" of the Jewish calendar are *Rosh Hashanah* ("new year") and *Yom Kippur* ("day of atonement"). Rosh Hashanah is celebrated in September or October each year. It begins with the sounding of the ram's horn (*shofar*) as a call to repentance and initiates a ten-day period of penitence when Jews review their lives during the past year and prepare for a new year of Torah obedience. During Rosh Hashanah sweets are eaten as a symbol of the hope for a pleasing year. This ends with Yom Kippur, traditionally a day of abstinence from work and fasting, with prayers for forgiveness and reconciliation. Many Jews spend the entire day in the synagogue. In the Bible and Talmud an elaborate temple ritual for Yom Kippur is described in which the High Priest entered the Holy of Holies in the Temple for the only time in the year. A goat was sent into the wilderness, carrying the sins of the people (hence the "scapegoat").

Other festival days on the Jewish yearly calendar include the Feast of Dedication (*Hannukah*), remembering the rededication of the Temple after it had been profaned by the Seleucids and liberated during the Maccabean revolution. It takes place in November or December and involves the lighting of a candle each day, for eight days. Thus it is called the Festival of Lights. The Feast of Lots (*Purim*), celebrated in February or March, recalls the Jewish victory celebrated in the Book of Esther.

Lighting the candles on the menorah *during the celebration of the festival of* Hannukah.

QUESTIONS OF MORALITY:
WHAT ARE OUR OBLIGATIONS TO OTHERS?

The Way of Torah

Judaism affirms the basic ethical principle of "love of neighbor" as the fundamental directive to be followed in relations with others. We include here the Tanak's version of the "golden rule" (Leviticus 19:18, NRSV); the last six commandments of the Ten Commandments, which establish norms for relating to others (Exodus 20:1, 12–17, NRSV); and rabbinic reflection on the commandments (Shabbat 31a; Freedman (vol. 3, pt.1) 1959: 140).

You shall not take vengeance or bear a grudge against any of your people, but you shall love your neighbor as yourself: I am the LORD.

Then God spoke all these words: .... Honor your father and your mother, so that your days may be long in the land that the LORD your God is giving you.

You shall not murder.

You shall not commit adultery.

You shall not steal.

You shall not bear false witness against your neighbor.

You shall not covet your neighbor's house; you shall not covet your neighbor's wife, or male or female slave, or ox, or donkey, or any thing that belongs to your neighbor.

A certain heathen came before

Shammai and said to him, "Make me a proselyte, on condition that you teach me the whole Torah while I stand on one foot." Thereupon he repulsed him with the builder's cubit which was in his hand. When he went before Hillel, he said to him, "What is hateful to you, do not do to your neighbor: that is the whole Torah, while the rest of it is commentary thereof; go and learn it."

Excerpts from the New Revised Standard Version *of the Bible. Copyright © 1989 by the Division of Christian Education of the National Council of the Churches of Christ in the USA. Used with persmission.*

Source: The Way of Torah. From The Babylonian Talmud: Shabbat, *trans. H. Freedman. The Rebecca Bennet Publications.*

The Jewish rite of passage into adulthood is called the *Bar (Bat) Mitzvah* ("son or daughter of the commandment"). Traditionally, when a boy reached the age of 13 he became an adult member of the community, and could be counted among the minimum of ten adult males (*minyan*) required for a synagogue. He prepared for this passage by studying Torah and learning to read Hebrew. After his first public reading from the Torah a celebration is held. In Reform and Conservative communities the ceremonial reading of the Torah has been extended to girls, while in Orthodox communities the Bat Mitzvah includes public presentation, but not Torah reading. In all branches the Bat Mitzvah typically occurs when the girl is 12.

Another rite of passage is the ritual of circumcision (removal of the foreskin of the penis) of a male infant on the eighth day after birth (or of an adult male Jewish convert). This ritual is known by the Hebrew name *berit* ("covenant"), because the ritual is the symbol of the covenant made by God with Abraham and his descendants (see Genesis 17:10–12).

Other rites of passage occur, as they do in other religious traditions, at marriage and death. At death the body of the deceased is ritually cleansed and buried (never cremated), because of the belief in resurrection of the body. During a seven-day period following the death (called *shiva*), those closest to the deceased refrain from normal activities.

Traditionally, Jews have believed that in their relations with others they are to imitate the characteristics of God. Just as God cared for the poor and needy, so do God's people. In the Biblical legislation, care for the stranger and the widow is especially enjoined. In general the Torah requires not only love of God but also love of neighbor. It also requires personal piety. The ideal is to sanctify all of life. As noted, Reform Judaism has placed greater emphasis on the ethical over ritual and dietary laws.

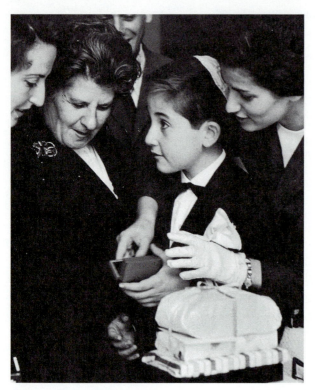

A thirteen-year old boy opens presents during the celebration of his bar mitzvah.

According to rabbinic teaching all people may manifest the love and justice of God, each in their own way. The particular Jewish obligation is to manifest the love and justice of God by following the Torah.

All branches of Judaism agree that to live a life of obedience to Torah study is critical. Synagogues are places not only of prayer but of study. In Talmudic times the centers of Jewish leadership were academies where scholars gathered to study and interpret Torah. In Orthodox communities today *yeshivas* (schools) offer instruction in the Talmud.

Sacred: The Great "I Am"

When God appeared to Moses in the fire of a bush that burned but was not consumed (Exodus 3:2), the sacred name for the deity (called the *tetragrammaton,* because it has four Hebrew consonants—YHWH) was revealed. It is usually rendered as Yahweh. For Jews it symbolizes the holiness and transcendence of God. Traditionally, the tetragrammaton is not pronounced. Instead, the more common Hebrew name for lord (*adonai*) is said, when the consonants YHWH appear in the Biblical text. When vowels were added to the consonantal text of the Hebrew Bible in the tenth century C.E., the vowels of *adonai* were written with the tetragrammaton, to remind readers that they were not to speak the sacred name. The transcendence of God is also emphasized in Judaism by the commandment against any images of God and the circumlocutions used in prayers, such as "the Holy One of Israel," "Blessed be He," and "Master of the Universe."

The clear distinction between the creation and the Creator also underline that God is far above us. However, Jewish tradition also makes room for the immanence of God. For example, the *shekinah* ("presence") is God's in-dwelling nature, said to reside in Israel and the Torah. God is the transcendent Creator, but also the ever-present sustainer of the universe. For Judaism the transcendent and immanent God is one and indivisible. At the heart of Judaism is the oft-repeated *shema:* "Hear, O Israel! the Lord is our God, the Lord alone!"

This traditional portrait of God has been subject to much reinterpretation by modern Jewish scholars seeking to reconcile the idea of God with the contemporary scientific worldview of natural causes and effects and the horrible reality of the Holocaust, which seemed to challenge the idea of a compassionate God who acts in history to deliver Israel. Some are willing to give up entirely the concept of a supernatural, personal deity in favor of an understanding of God as a personification of natural and/or human qualities.

RESPONSES TO CONTEMPORARY ETHICAL ISSUES

The Ecological Crisis

Some environmentalists today charge that the monotheistic religions that developed in the Middle East (Judaism, Christianity, and Islam) are to a significant degree responsible for the current ecological crisis. Their reasoning is that these religions have distanced the sacred from nature and created the attitude that humans may exploit nature at will, since this prerogative has been given to humans by God. In their view, the result has been unchecked abuse of the environment in the West. Since this discussion has arisen largely in the context of Christianity, we will examine it in more detail in the next chapter. In response to this criticism, Jewish, Christian, and Muslim leaders have sought to search within their own traditions for a responsible environmental ethic that will help lead the way out of the current ecological crisis.

In developing a contemporary Jewish ethic for the environment, four themes are being highlighted: divine ownership, respect for the natural order, maintenance of harmony, and reverence for the sacred quality of the natural world (Shapiro 1989: 180–181; Helfand 1986: 40–50).

The theme of divine ownership of nature derives from the Biblical affirmation that "the earth is the Lord's and the fullness thereof" (Psalm 24:1). Although humans have a special place in creation as God's partners, the earth does not belong to humans to do with as we please. Some texts may imply human ownership of the earth (e.g., Psalm 115:16). However, the Tanak in general makes clear that, as Yahweh asserts, "The land is mine" (Leviticus 25:23). This principle is also expressed in the oral Torah. For example, the Tosefta asserts, "Anyone who derives benefit from this world without a [prior] blessing is guilty of misappropriating sacred property" (Tosefta, Berakhot 4:1; cited in Helfand 1986: 41).

Therefore, humans must follow the divine plan in their treatment of nature, according to the Torah. And the divine plan is that the natural order be preserved. In this regard, attention has been drawn by Jewish interpreters to the Biblical precept that "in case you lay siege to a city many days by fighting against it so as to capture it from them, you must not ruin its trees by wielding an axe against them; for you should eat from them, and you must not cut them down .... " (Deuteronomy 20:19). According to rabbinic interpretation of this precept, unnecessary destruction of nature is not permissible (Kasher 1989: 148). This law "has been expand-

---

QUESTIONS OF HUMAN DESTINY: WHAT HAPPENS AFTER DEATH?

Resurrection of the Dead

There is surprisingly little reference in the Tanak to life after death. For the most part, texts speak of Sheol, *the place for all the dead, where they exist as "shadows" cut off from the worship of God. Some texts may acknowledge a belief in life after death with God (e.g., Psalms 16:10–11, 49:15, 73:24). However, it is in this excerpt, from the Book of Daniel, that we find the clearest statement of a belief in an individual resurrection of the dead at the end of history (Daniel 12:1–3 [NRSV]).*

At that time Michael, the great prince, the protector of your people, shall arise. There shall be a time of anguish, such as has never occurred since nations first came into existence. But at that time your people shall be delivered, everyone who is found written in the book. Many of those who sleep in the dust of the earth shall awake, some to everlasting life, and some to shame and everlasting contempt. Those who are wise shall shine like the brightness of the sky, and those who lead many to righteousness, like the stars forever and ever.

---

ed to form a protective legal umbrella encompassing almost the entire realm of ecological concerns" (Helfand 1986: 44). This attitude extends to a concern for the protection of endangered species in Jewish tradition (Helfand 1986: 45).

In the Talmud and among commentators, the principle of *yishuv ha-aretz* ("settlement of the land") has been applied to create an ethic of maintaining the harmony of the earth. For example, the Mishnah forbade the raising of goats and sheep in the land of Israel because of their propensity to defoliate the land. The fourteenth-century code of Jacob ben

so that he could negotiate with the Roman general Vespasian to be allowed to set up an academy of Jewish learning at Yavneh in Galilee. Of these situations, one was defiance and the other was accommodation. In this case, the "surrender" of Yohanan ben Zakkai secured the future for Judaism by preserving the traditions of the past and passing them on (Shapiro 1989: 179).

Today, many Jews take inspiration from Masada, which was seized by the state of Israel from Jordan during the 1967 war. The slaughter of 6 million Jews during the Holocaust (1933–1945) has imprinted the lesson that Jews must be prepared to defend themselves and not depend on others. Therefore, the fanatic resistance of Masada is a symbol of the defiance against enemies characteristic of the state of Israel today. These policies have caused tension in the Jewish community, with some uneasy about the state of Israel's firm retaliatory policy.

Capital Punishment

The legislation found in the Tanak provides for capital punishment in a number of circumstances, based on the principle of *lex talionis*—"life for life, eye for eye, tooth for tooth" (Deuteronomy 19:21). After the great flood, capital punishment seems to be established as a basic commandment for all humanity: "Whoever sheds the blood of man, by man shall his blood be shed" (Genesis 9:6). Jewish (and Christian) supporters of capital punishment point to these seemingly clear calls for the death penalty to defend their position. However, opponents argue that the law of retribution was actually a step toward the limitation of unwarranted revenge rather than a sanction for it. They also point out that provisions for the death penalty in the Tanak are balanced by calls for mercy, such as this passage from the Book of the Prophet Ezekiel: "As I live, says the Lord God, I have no pleasure in the death of the wicked, but that the wicked turn from their ways and live; ..." (33:11).

The Talmud significantly limited the conditions under which capital punishment could be imposed. In general, the Talmud substitutes financial payment for literal application of the principle of "an eye for an eye." Jewish opponents of the death penalty claim that this general principle and specific restrictions effectively abolished capital punishment in the Jewish community. Testimony in capital cases had to be presented by two eyewitnesses of the crime, who were required to acknowledge that they knew the one they were testifying against could be put to death. Another stipulation was that in capital cases the seventy-one-member Great Sanhedrin, the Jewish supreme court before the Temple was abolished, had to be in session. When the Great Sanhedrin moved out of the Temple in 30 C.E., capital punishment by Jewish authorities effectively ended. From this point on, executions were carried out only for treason in local orthodox communities.

The Mishnah includes a statement that suggests that the debate over capital punishment continued: "A Sanhedrin which sentences a person to death once every seven years is called damaging. R. Elazar, son of Azariah, says: once every seventy years. R. Tarfon and R. Akiba say: If we have been members of the Sanhedrin, no one would ever have been sentenced to death. Rabban Simeon, son of Gamaliel, says: They, too, increase the number of blood-shedders among the people of Israel" (Makkoth, 1:10; cited in Kasher 1989: 147).

Jewish opponents of the death penalty argue that it has a brutalizing effect, and that since Judaism is committed to reverence for life, it cannot support capital punishment. The Union of American Hebrew Congregations, an association of Reform Jewish rabbis, has issued the following statement: "We appeal to our congregants and to our co-religionists and to all who cherish God's mercy and love to join in efforts to eliminate this practice [of capital punishment] which lies as a stain upon civilization and our religious conscience."

The state of Israel eliminated the death penalty, except in the cases of treason and genocide. It has been applied only once, in the case of Adolf Eichmann, who was convicted of coordinating much of the implementation of the Nazi plan for the extermination of the Jews during the Holocaust. He was hanged in 1962.

The Orthodox, Reform, and Conservative branches of American Judaism have joined in opposing capital punishment both on the grounds that it is incompatible with the standards of American democracy and because of Jewish tradition.

Abortion

There is broad consensus among branches of Judaism on two aspects of the abortion question. First, human life *is* sacred. Therefore, abortion is a serious moral issue, not just a matter of convenience. Second, when a mother's life is at stake or even threatened, the life of the mother must have priority and the fetus must be aborted (Goldman 1978: 35).

Beyond these two points, however, there is considerable disagreement. The only explicit statement in the Tanak on abortion can be interpreted to support either side of the debate. The Covenant Code in the Book of Exodus states: "When people who are fighting injure a pregnant woman so that there is a miscarriage, and yet no further harm follows, the one responsible shall be fined what the woman's husband demands, paying as much as the judges determine. If any harm follows, then you shall give life for life, eye for eye, tooth for tooth, hand for hand, foot for foot, burn for burn, wound for wound, stripe for stripe" (Exodus 21:22–25).

The "pro-life" interpretation of this passage is that it cannot be used to justify abortion because the injury is accidental, not intentional. The abortion is spontaneous, not induced. Opponents of allowing induced abortions also point out that even though the abortion was accidentally induced, it was still punished. Just because the punishment was a fine does not mean that the fetus is not human! Only premeditated murder is outside the provision that a ransom be paid in similar circumstances.

The "pro-choice" interpretation is that the passage does not view the fetus as a person with rights. The concern is for the life and well-being of the mother. Even though the passage deals with a spontaneous abortion, the basic principle applies to induced abortions: The mother *is* a person and an injury to her must be taken seriously, but the fetus is *not* a person.

Pro-life advocates point to a number of other texts in the Tanak that they think show God's concern for the unborn (e.g., Numbers 35:33, Psalm 51:5, Psalm 139:13, and Jeremiah 1:5), while pro-choice supporters quote a passage from Ecclesiastes that suggests that there is a radical distinction between life before and after birth (Ecclesiastes 6:3).

Perhaps the most quoted passage from the Hebrew Bible by opponents of abortion is the fifth commandment, "Thou shalt not kill" (Exodus 20:13). Since they consider the unborn child to be a human being, they believe the commandment applies to the killing of the child through abortion. Supporters of the right to abortion claim that since the fetus is not a person, the commandment is irrelevant to abortion. Further, they point out that the Bible does not rule out all killing, only the unjustified taking of life. Therefore, according to this argument, in cases where the abortion is justified, abortion is not a violation of the commandment even if the fetus is considered a person. In response, pro-life advocates claim that the commandment applies to the taking of innocent life, and no life is more innocent than an unborn child's.

The Mishnah (Oholot 7,6) does allow for abortion to save the life of a mother: "If a woman has difficulty in childbirth, one dismembers the embryo within her limb from limb because her life takes precedence over its life. Once its head (or the greater part of it) has emerged, it may not be touched, for we do not set aside one life for another" (cited in Connery 1977: 15). Once again, however, the text is interpreted differently. The pro-choice position is that this text clearly establishes a Jewish woman's moral right to have an abortion. A pro-life interpretation holds that "it may be readily inferred from this statement that destruction of the fetus is prohibited in situations not involving a threat to the life of the pregnant mother" (Bleich 1981: 407).

There is obviously no *single* Jewish position on abortion. Individual Jewish communities must struggle with the conflicting interpretations of their legal tradition and come to their own understanding of what the Torah teaches them on this controversial issue. In general, the three major branches within Judaism take the following positions (Goldman 1978: 49–59):

1. *Orthodox.* The unborn child has a right to life. Even if a pregnancy is the result of rape or incest, of if tests reveal abnormalities, that right may not be abridged unless the life of the mother is threatened.

2. *Conservative.* The mother has power over the fetus, but she must have valid and sufficient reasons for depriving it of potential life. Therapeutic abortions are permissible when the basic health of the mother, psychological as well as physical, is threatened. Rape or incest is a sufficient cause for an abortion to be sought. Where deformity is a certainty, abortion is allowed, but not if it is only a possibility. Abortions for convenience, however, are not acceptable.

3. *Reform.* Most Reform rabbis affirm the Conservative position and add that social and economic factors may be taken into account in determining whether an abortion is moral.

In summary, the Jewish position is that abortion is moral only when the life of the mother is threatened on the basis of the duty of self-preservation (*pikuah nefesh*). However, within Judaism there is wide disagreement about what constitutes a legitimate threat to the life of the mother (Biale 1984: 219–38). The strictest interpretation is that abortion is acceptable only if the mother's physical life is in danger. More lenient interpreters include in the principle of self-protection other threats, such as physical pain, mental anguish, or even social disgrace.

Euthanasia

The Tanak establishes precedents for Jewish (and Christian) acceptance of euthanasia, but not without raising questions about it. According to the Book of Judges, Abimelech initiated voluntary euthanasia, asking his armor-bearer to kill him after he had been fatally wounded by a millstone dropped by a woman during a siege. He said to him, "Draw your sword and kill me, so people will not say about me, 'A woman killed him'" (Judges 9:54). The man killed Abimelech, and was not punished or even reprimanded for his action. However, the death of King Saul, who also requested a servant to kill him after he had been wounded in battle, is problematic (Second Samuel 1:6–10). The man who killed Saul was put to death by King David, indicating that this case of euthanasia was deemed a capital crime (although political considerations are also implied as the basis for David's action).

Most Jewish authorities today reject "active euthanasia" on the grounds that no human has the right to take another's life, even in cases of extreme suffering. However, there is disagreement on the validity of "passive euthanasia." The Biblical legislation that most Jewish interpreters think rules out active euthanasia includes Genesis 9:6, Exodus 21:14, Leviticus 24:17, Numbers 25:30, and, of course, the sixth commandment: "Thou shalt not kill" (Deuteronomy 5:17).

The Talmud recognizes a state called *goses* in which death was imminent (when a person could no longer swallow his or her saliva). Even in this state a person must be considered a human being, and it is immoral to hasten death. The medieval *Mishneh Torah*, compiled by Moses Maimonides, sums up the Talmudic teaching in this way (Judges, Laws of Mourning 4:5; cited by Hamel and DuBose 1991: 55):

> *One who is in a dying condition is regarded as a living person in all respects. It is not permitted to grind his jaws, to stop up the organs of the lower extremities, or to place metallic or cooling vessels upon his navel in order to prevent swelling. He is not to be rubbed or washed, nor is sand or salt to be put upon him until he expires. He who touches him is guilty of shedding blood. To what may he be compared? To a flickering flame, which is extinguished as soon as one touches it. Whoever closes the eyes of the dying while the soul is about to depart is shedding blood.*

However, other sources acknowledge that actions that prolong dying should be avoided (Sefer Hasidim, nos. 234 and 723; cited in Larue 1985: 22–23). The sixteenth-century rabbi Moses Isserles of Cracow, wrote: "If something causes a delay of demise, it may be removed" (cited in Kasher 1989: 150).

The positions of the three major branches of Judaism today on euthanasia may be summarized as follows (Goldman 1978: 177–81):

1. *Orthodox.* Active euthanasia is condemned as murder by all Orthodox authorities. However, there is disagreement on the circumstances under which the withdrawal of treatment or use of drugs that may hasten death while relieving suffering are appropriate.

2. *Conservative.* There is no consensus, but Conservative rabbis tend to be more liberal than Orthodox scholars in assessing when the artificial prolongation of life may be terminated in order to allow a patient to die naturally.

3. *Reform.* Leading Reform Rabbi Solomon B. Freehof took the position that the act of killing a patient, no matter what the motivation, is absolutely forbidden. However, there are circumstances, he said, when death may be allowed to come. The Reform community is more willing to recognize a "right to die" that must be respected.

During the Holocaust the term "euthanasia" was applied to the Nazi policy of killing "undesirables," which included all Jews. Therefore, the toleration of any practice that could be construed as active euthanasia is out of the question for serious Jewish ethicists. Whether more Jewish legal interpreters are willing to broaden the definition of what constitutes passive as opposed to active killing remains to be seen.

Economic Justice

The Tanak contains no economic theory on the distribution of wealth. However, the practices suggested in the legal sections, many of the utterances of the prophets, comments in the historical sections, and observations in the Psalms and wisdom writings show an unmistakable bias in favor of those on the economic margins of society.

The laws of the Torah again and again admonish the Israelites to provide for the widow, orphan, and sojourner in their midst (e.g., Exodus 22:21–24). The system of sabbatical years provided for the needs of the poor, that they might have access to food (Exodus 23:11, Leviticus 19:9–10) and their debts cancelled (Deuteronomy 23:24–25). According to the Book of the Covenant, the poor are to receive equal justice (Exodus 23:6).

Prophetic sayings calling rulers and people to bring justice to the poor because of their oppression can be found in virtually all of the prophetic books (e.g., Ezekiel 22:29, 31). The Book of Amos is a good place to begin a study of the Hebrew prophets' attitudes toward the rich and poor. This eighth-century-B.C.E. prophet indicts the northern kingdom of Israel for its treatment of the poor, identifying the needy as the righteous (2:6–7, NRSV):

> Thus says the LORD:
> For three transgressions of Israel
> and for four, I will not revoke the punishment;
> because they sell the righteous for silver,
> and the needy for a pair of sandals—
> they who trample the head of the poor into the dust of the earth,
> and push the afflicted out of the way; ...

Other indictments of the rich for their treatment of the poor are found throughout the collected sayings of the eighth-century-B.C.E. Israelite prophets (e.g., Isaiah 1:23, 2:7, 5:8, and Micah 2:2).

The Psalms portray God as having a special concern for the poor and chastising the arrogant wealthy. For example, Psalm 10 appeals to God's caring for the poor to motivate the Lord to act, and calls those who are "greedy for gain" the wicked (10:2–4). By contrast, Psalm 112 speaks of wealth righteously earned by those who "have distributed freely, [who] have given to the poor; ..." (v. 9, NRSV). According to Psalm 82, God intends that justice for the poor be a basic law, for the Lord challenges the members of the divine court to "give justice to the weak and the orphan; maintain the right of the lowly and the destitute. Rescue the weak and the needy; deliver them from the hand of the wicked" (vv. 3–4, NRSV).

The Book of Proverbs chastises individuals who are poor because of their laziness (e.g.,

Proverbs 6:11, 13:8, NRSV), but makes clear that many are poor because of the social system in which they must live (Proverbs 13:23, NRSV). Another proverb says simply, "Those who oppress the poor insult their Maker, but those who are kind to the needy honor him" (Proverbs 14:31, NRSV). In a poem celebrating a righteous woman, it is said that she "opens her hand to the poor, and reaches out her hands to the needy" (Proverbs 31:20, NRSV).

The Talmud calls for employers to treat their workers justly, saying that "whoever withholds an employee's wages, it is as though he has taken the person's life from him" (Bava Metzia 112a; cited in Shapiro 1989: 172).

Because capitalism favors "individual autonomy and dignity, the free exercise of reason and intellectual curiosity, the adaptation of scientific knowledge to the practical world via technological innovation, freedom from and of religion, and human creativity," it has been favored by many Jews, especially those in the Reform movement of Western Europe and the United States. It was in countries that adopted capitalism that Jews were allowed to participate in the economic system and achieve emancipation (Shapiro 1989: 174). Many Jews have flourished in the open competition of capitalist economies, largely because of the Jewish heritage of hard work, study, and attention to detail. However, their success has made Jews easy and convenient targets at times of economic disruption. Anti-semitism continues to be a serious problem in countries with capitalist economies, although (as evidenced in the former Soviet Union) command economies can also foster prejudice against Jews. In addition, Jewish teachers are well aware of the potential for abuse in a capitalist economy, and many Jewish groups and individuals have been active in efforts to assist and empower those left out in the competition.

Gender Roles and the Status of Women

The Torah portrays God's intention as equality among men and women. In the first creation account in Genesis, both male and female are created in the image of God (1:26), with no hierarchi-

cal ordering. In the second creation narrative, woman is created from the flesh of man, not as a subordinate but in order to fulfill him. In the Garden, Eve is portrayed as intelligent and practical. However, when Adam and Eve together violate the command of God not to eat of the fruit of the tree of the knowledge of good and evil, the situation changes. Their relationship of equality and mutuality is broken. Therefore, gender inequality is, according to the Torah, the result of the human rebellion against God's will.

The legislation in the Torah assumes male dominance. A girl was the property of her father; when she married, she became her husband's chattel. Her most important role was to produce sons to perpetuate her husband's name. Adultery was treated as a violation of the property rights of a woman's father or husband (Leviticus 20:10–11). A woman was expected to come to marriage as a virgin, and if her husband could prove that she was not, he could have her stoned (Deuteronomy 22:13–21). A woman had no right to initiate divorce, but she was not to be divorced without a substantial basis (Deuteronomy 24:1–4).

While the legislation in the Tanak supports women's subordination, the narratives are replete with stories of women who are wise and powerful. In the Book of Ruth, for example, two women (Ruth and Naomi) take charge in a situation stacked against them and defend their own rights and interests. Female sexuality is viewed positively in the Song of Songs, without a hint of male dominance and female subordination. The wife celebrated in the poem in Proverbs 31 is a woman of influence and power in her community, as well as a loving wife and mother in her home. Although the dominant imagery in the Tanak for God is masculine, texts such as Jeremiah 31:20 show that feminine metaphors could be used by Biblical authors to speak of God.

According to the traditional point of view, the Talmud treats the male as normal, with the female capable of being only a marginal Jew. Since her time was given over to husband and family, she was not expected to recite the morning prayer or attend the synagogue service on the sabbath. Her purpose was to support her husband and sons' efforts to study and keep the Torah in the community, and to ensure that the dietary laws and sabbath restrictions in the home were observed. Her greatest fear was infertility, for to be childless was in effect to be "dead." The *minyan* or minimum number for a synagogue was ten men; women did not count in defining the presence of a Jewish community. Women are silent participants in the traditional Jewish wedding ceremony, with the ritual action involving the men. The Talmudic attitude toward women is summed up in the famous phrase "Happy is he whose children are sons and woe to him whose children are daughters."

Recent studies, however, have begun to question this interpretation of the Talmudic teaching about women. Judith Romney Wegner's careful study of the Mishnah (Wegner 1988), for example, shows that women are treated as chattel only in specific circumstances, as when the woman's biological function was assumed to be under the control of the principal male in her life. Otherwise, the Mishnah treats women as full persons, with legal status and rights.

Despite a women's movement's efforts to advance equality for women, Orthodox Judaism largely continues today the traditional practices regarding the genders. It should be noted that most Orthodox women find in their allegiance to the traditional guidelines on women's roles an affirmation of not only their Jewish but also their feminine identity (Carmody 1994: 248–49).

Since the emergence of the Reform movement in the nineteenth century, however, male dominance has been challenged. In 1846 a conference of Reform Jews called for full equality for women in all areas of religious life (although this idea was largely ignored at the time). The Reform movement introduced a rite of passage for Jewish girls (*bat mitzvah*) so that they could symbolically become members of the Jewish community, just like boys. Since 1972 Reform Judaism has ordained women as rabbis, and the Conservative branch has followed suit. A Jewish women's group, called *B'not Esh*, meets annually to address feminist concerns and to join in common rituals.

A woman rabbi reads from the Torah Scroll in a synagogue service.

In the state of Israel there is tension between the law of the state, which gives full equality to women, and the rulings of the religious courts, which follow the Talmudic directives. For example, women can be frustrated in their attempts to obtain a divorce or to gain equality in the workplace (Carmody 1987: 204–5)

Among the feminist critics of patriarchy in religion are Jewish women such as Naomi Goldenberg, Rita Gross, Judith Plaskow, and Ellen Umansky, who have written movingly of the need for the empowerment of women in Jewish life and thought (Carmody 1994: 262–66). They have found in traditional Jewish sources glimpses of a spirituality to which Jewish women can relate, and through their own creative imaginations they have begun to explore and renew that spirituality. As Judith Plaskow has written in defense of her work in attempting to recover a "primordial Torah" that is not distorted by patriarchy (Plaskow 1989: 41, 49):

> *Knowing that women are active members of the Jewish community in the present, we know we were always part of the community, not simply as objects of male purposes but as subjects and shapers of tradition. To accept androcentric texts and contemporary androcentric histories as the whole of Jewish history is to enter into a secret collusion with those who would exclude us from full membership into the Jewish community. . . . Beginning with the conviction of our presence both at Sinai and now, we rediscover and invent ourselves in the Jewish communal past and present, continuing the age-old process of reshaping Jewish memory as we reshape the community today.*

Homosexuality

In a long list of forbidden sexual relations, the Holiness Code in the Book of Leviticus includes the following: "You shall not lie with a male as with a woman; it is an abomination" (18:22, NRSV). In the penalty section for violating the rules of the community we find: "If a man lies with a male as with a woman, both of them have committed an abomination; they shall be put to death; their blood is upon them" (Leviticus 20:13, NRSV). Some interpreters note that in ancient Israel cultic prostitution involving male homosexual activity was an issue of great concern, and claim these strident statements must be understood in that context. Others say the laws are clear and speak for themselves, condemning homosexuality as an abomination in the eyes of God.

In the story of the destruction of Sodom and Gomorrah in the Book of Genesis (Genesis 19:1–38), the desire of the men of Sodom to have sexual relations with the young men visiting Lot's home (19:5) is apparently one of the sins for which the city is destroyed. The modern term "sodomy," which refers to homosexual acts and engaging in sexual activity with animals, derives from this story. Interestingly,

Talmudic interpretation focused not on homosexuality but on the "Sodomites as mean, inhospitable, uncharitable, and unjust" (Eron 1993: 109).

In the Talmud the implicit prohibition of male homosexual behavior in the Tanak is reinforced and stated explicitly (B. San. 58a). In the medieval code of Maimonides, female homosexuality is also condemned, but is not regarded as seriously as male homosexuality (Mishneh Torah Melakhim 9:5–6 and Issurei Biah 21.8 and B. Yer. 76a). The clearest explanations for the prohibition of male-male sexual behavior is that it thwarts procreation, which is the purpose of human sexuality (Sefer ha-Hinnukh 209) and destroys family life (Ahseri, Ned 51a). Many commentators have noted the meager references to homosexuality in both the Tanak and Talmud and suggested that in Biblical religion and early Judaism, it was simply not a very important issue (Kahn 1989: 49–50), either because homosexual behavior was not widely practiced or because homosexuals were discreet about their sexual orientation and their expression of it.

Unambiguous condemnation of homosexuality has continued to the present in Orthodox Judaism. David Feldman, an authority on Jewish law and sexuality, has expressed the view that "the elements of the Jewish legal-moral-social view of homosexuality are simple. The practice is condemned as sinful, an 'abomination'" (Feldman 1983: 426). Feldman points out that for Jewish law, the modern debate over the causes of homosexuality is irrelevant. What is condemned are homosexual acts, regardless of the reasons behind them. Jewish law, he says, condemns homosexual behavior not only because it thwarts procreation and undermines family life, but because it runs counter to the very structures of creation as described in the Book of Genesis (Feldman 1983: 428). In defending the traditional perspective, many interpreters have distinguished condemnation of homosexual behavior and rejection of persons who experience homosexual preferences (e.g., Kahn 1989: 53).

Scholars of the Conservative movement have appealed to the concept of "constraint" to respond to the issue of homosexuality (Kahn 1989: 56). The *halakhah* recognizes that "constraint" may be "an excusing factor in circumstances beyond one's control." This is the *halakhic* basis for judging a person not guilty of a violation of the law because of the threat of punishment or temporary mental illness. If modern research is correct in the view that homosexuality is not a matter of choice, but of basic sexual orientation, then homosexuals are "constrained" by this orientation and their violation of the *halakhah* must be excused.

The Reconstructionist and Reform Jewish communities have tended to take a more liberal attitude toward homosexuality. Some scholars in these communities repudiate the traditional condemnation by invoking the authority of fundamental moral principles such as love, respect for the dignity of persons, and the value of commitment in human relationships (Umansky 1985: 9–15). Others argue that *halakhah* has always been interpreted in the particular social context of the affected Jewish community (Kirschner 1988: 452). A 1990 resolution adopted by the Reconstructionist Rabbinical Association states that congregations are expected not to discriminate when placing rabbis on the basis of "gender, marital status, sexual orientation, birth-religion, age, race, national origin or physical disability" (Eron 1993: 125).

For many in the Jewish community, especially in Reform and Reconstructionist congregations, the approach to be taken toward homosexual persons is clear: "to rescind the ancient denunciation of homosexuals and to recognize that all persons, in their unique sexual being, are the work of God's hands and the bearers of God's image" (Kirschner 1988: 458; see also Soloff 1983: 417–24).

Taking advantage of this new attitude of openness, the first gay and lesbian synagogues were opened in 1973 on the American West Coast. The Reform movement's Union of American Hebrew Congregations accepted four homosexual congregations into membership. Soon the movement spread to other parts of the United States. One participant in Congregation Beth Simchat Torah, a synagogue for gays and lesbians in New York City, writes: "My involvement in Congregation Beth Simchat Torah over the years has helped me form my own theology; I have only one identity, one self. The feeling of two conflicting identities, one gay and one Jewish, was a false consciousness. I need to be part of a Jewish community. For me, CBST is that community" (Rabinowitz 1983: 435). By 1989, thirty groups of Jewish gay men and lesbian women had formed a World Congress of Gay and Lesbian Jewish Organizations (Cooper 1989: 83).

The emergence of these gay and lesbian synagogues caused a "backlash" in the Reform community, as many lay people and some rabbis stepped forward to challenge acceptance of the open practice of homosexuality. For example, respected Reform Rabbi Solomon Freehof stated that homosexual marriages are "a contravention of all that is respected in Jewish life" (Lehrman 1983: 393). One Reform interpreter attempted to counter the use of modern research to justify acceptance of homosexuality by pointing out that the traditional rejection "is based on the empirical lesson of history: that permanent, joyous, sexually faithful bonding between men and women produces stable families and societies and is, thus, fundamentally important for human survival and growth" (Lehrman 1983: 394).

To defend an attitude of tolerance toward homosexual persons, some Jewish scholars have noted the parallel between treatment of Jews and gays in European history. In his study of the history of the treatment of homosexuals in Europe, one scholar noted: "The fate of Jews and gay people has been almost identical throughout European history, from early Christian hostility to extermination in concentration camps. The same laws which oppressed Jews oppressed gay people; the same groups bent on eliminating Jews tried to wipe out homosexuals. ..." (Boswell 1980: 15). In response, some defenders of the traditional Jewish rejection of homosexuality point out that Jews can and should vigorously defend the human and civil rights of gay people without condoning homosexual behavior.

CHAPTER SUMMARY

 Judaism is a religion that traces its origin to a covenant (agreement) made between the one God (known in Judaism by the special, sacred name Yahweh) and a couple named Abraham and Sarah. The history of God's interaction with the descendants of Abraham and Sarah is told in the long historical narrative found in the Hebrew Bible (Tanak or written Torah). In this chapter we provided an overview of this narrative and the other writings in the Tanak, the birth of Judaism as a religion in the period after the Tanak, the oral Torah, the various movements within early Judaism, the emergence of Pharisaic Judaism as the tradition that survived and was transmitted, developments in Judaism during the Middle Ages, and Judaism in the modern world. We highlighted the three major movements within Judaism today (Orthodox, Conservative, and Reform); the Holocaust and its impact on Judaism; Zionism and the emergence of the state of Israel; and issues facing Jews today, such as assimilation and anti-Semitism.

Our summary of distinctive Jewish teachings portrayed the common commitment to obedience to the Torah as God's distinctive gift, but also the tension between traditionalists and modernists in the Jewish community on just how the Torah should be kept today. We also briefly discussed the major Jewish festivals. We concluded with a survey of Jewish responses to contemporary ethical issues.

QUESTIONS FOR DISCUSSION AND REFLECTION

1. Have you ever experienced the stereotyping of Jews (or members of other religions)? Have you ever challenged such stereotyping or participated in it? Discuss or reflect on what occasioned the stereotyping and why it is still so common.
2. Try to put yourself in the place of an Orthodox Jew, a Reform Jew, and a Conservative Jew. Try to understand why each chooses his or her approach to living a Jewish life. Try to respond to issues such as eating a kosher diet and marrying within the Jewish religion from these different perspectives.
3. Do you see any ties that link all Jews together, whether they be Reform, Orthodox, Conser-

vative, Reconstructionist, or totally secular? If so, what are they?
4. Do you agree with the statement that the Holocaust is the single most important event in Jewish history? Why or why not? Discuss or reflect on the impact of the Holocaust on the world today.
5. Discuss the current policy of the government of Israel on retaliating or making preemptive strikes against forces deemed hostile. To what degree does the slaughter of innocent Jews during World War II justify this policy?
6. Is fulfilling the Torah for its own sake morally superior to following the Torah in order to reach a particular goal? Is the former possible for humans?

SOURCES AND SUGGESTIONS FOR FURTHER STUDY

General Works on Judaism

BAECK, LEO, 1975 *The Essence of Judaism*. New York: Schocken.

BUBER, MARTIN, 1966 *The Origin and Meaning of Hasidism*, trans. and ed. Maurice Friedman. New York: Harper Torchbooks.

BULKA, REUVEN P., 1983 *Dimensions of Orthodox Judaism.* New York: KTAV.

DANBY, HERBERT, TRANS., 1933 *The Mishnah.* London: Oxford University Press.

DIMONT, MAX I., 1978 *The Jews in America.* New York: Simon and Schuster.

FISHBANE, MICHAEL, 1987 *Judaism.* Hagerstown, Md: Torch., 1989 *Biblical Interpretation in Ancient Israel.* New York: Oxford University Press.

FREEDMAN, H., TRANS., 1959 *The Babylonian Talmud,* ed. I. Epstein. vol. 3 and 17. New York: The Rebecca Bennet Publications.

GARBER, ZEV, AND BRUCE ZUCKERMAN, 1989 "Why Do We Call the Holocaust "the Holocaust"? An Inquiry into the Psychology of Labels," *Modern Judaism* (May): 197–211.

GILBERT, MARTIN, 1985 *The Holocaust: A History of the Jews of Europe during the Second World War.* New York: Henry Holt and Company.

GREENBERG, IRVING, 1988 *The Jewish Way: Living the Holidays.* New York: Summit Books.

HAUER, CHRIS E., AND WILLIAM A. YOUNG, 1994 *An Introduction to the Bible: A Journey into Three Worlds.* 3rd ed. Englewood Cliffs, N.J.: Prentice Hall.

HERFORD, R. TRAVERS, ED. AND TRANS., 1930 *Pirke Aboth: The Tractate "Fathers" from the Mishnah.* New York: Jewish Institute of Religion Press.

HESCHEL, ABRAHAM, 1959 *Between God and Man: An Interpretation of Judaism,* ed. Fritz A. Rothschild. New York: Free Press.

HOLTZ, BARRY, ED., 1984 *Back to the Sources: Reading the Classical Jewish Texts.* New York: Summit Books.

MONTEFIORE, C.G., AND H. LOEWE, EDS., 1963 *A Rabbinic Anthology.* New York: Meridian Books.

NEUSNER, JACOB, 1984 *The Way of Torah: An Introduction to Judaism,* 4th ed. Belmont, Calif: Dickenson.

PETERS, F.E., 1982 *Children of Abraham: Judaism/ Christianity/Islam.* Princeton, N.J.: Princeton University Press.

PETUCHOWSKI, JAKOB J., TRANS. AND ED., 1982 *Our Masters Taught: Rabbinic Stories and Sayings.* New York: Crossroad.

ROTH, CECIL, AND GEOFFREY WIGODER, EDS., 1972 *Encyclopedia Judaica,* 16 vols. Jerusalem: Keter Publishing.

SCHACHTER, JACOB, TRANS., 1959 *The Babylonian Talmud,* ed. I. Epstein, vol. 24. New York: The Rebecca Bennet Publications.

SCHOLEM, GERSHOM, 1961 *Major Trends in Jewish Mysticism.* New York: Schocken.

SIMON, MAURICE, TRANS., 1959 *The Babylonian Talmud,* ed. I. Epstein, vol. I. New York: The Rebecca Bennet Publications.

WEISS HALIVNI, DAVID, 1990 *Peshat and Derash: Plain and Applied Meaning in Rabbinic Exegesis.* New York: Oxford University Press.

WIESEL, ELIE, 1972 *Souls on Fire: Portraits and Legends of Hasidic Leaders,* trans. Marian Wiesel. New York: Random House.

1976 *Messengers of God,* trans. Marian Wiesel. New York: Random House.

Ethical Issues

General

KASHER, AVA, 1989 "Jewish Ethics: An Orthodox View," in *World Religions and Global Ethics,* ed. S. Cromwell Crawford (New York: Paragon House), 129–54.

KELLNER, MENACHEM MARC, 1978 *Contemporary Jewish Ethics.* New York: Sanhedrin Press.

SHAPIRO, RAMI M., 1989 "Blessing and Curse: Toward a Liberal Jewish Ethic," in *World Religions and Global Ethics,* 155–87.

SHERWIN, BYRON, 1990 *In Partnership with God: Contemporary Jewish Law and Ethics.* Syracuse, N.Y.: Syracuse University Press.

Ecological Crisis

BUBER, MARTIN, 1970 *I and Thou,* trans. Walter Kaufmann. New York: Simon and Schuster.

EHRENFELD, DAVID, AND JOAN EHRENFELD 1985 "Some Thoughts on Nature and Judaism," *Environmental Ethics* 7(1985): 93–95.

HELFAND, JONATHAN, 1986 "The Earth Is the Lord's: Judaism and Environmental Ethics," in *Religion and Environmental Crisis,* 38–52.

Abortion

BIALE, RACHEL, 1988 "Abortion in Jewish Law," *Tikkun* 4: 26–28.

BLEICH, J. DAVID, 1981 "Abortion and Jewish Law," in *New Perspectives on Human Abortion,* ed. Thomas W. Hilgers, Dennis Horan, and David Mall (Frederick, Md: University Publications of America, Inc.), 405–19.

CONNERY, JOHN, 1977 *Abortion: The Development of the Roman Catholic Perspective.* Chicago: Loyola University Press.

DAVIS, DENA S., 1992 "Abortion in Jewish Thought: A Study in Casuistry," *Journal of the American Academy of Religion* 60 (1992): 313–24.

FELDMAN, DAVID, 1967 *Birth Control in Jewish Law: Marital Relations, Contraception and Abortion as Set Forth in the Classic Texts.* New York: New York University Press.

GOLDMAN, ALEX J., 1978 "Abortion," in *Judaism Confronts Contemporary Issues.* (New York: Shengold Publishers), 35–62.

Euthanasia

CYTRON, BARRY D., AND EARL SCHWARTZ, 1986 *When Life Is in the Balance: Life and Death Decisions in Light of Jewish Tradition.* New York: Youth Commission, United Synagogues of America.

FELDMAN, DAVID, AND FRED ROSNER, EDS., 1984 *Compendium on Medical Ethics,* 6th ed. New York: Federation of Jewish Philanthropies of New York.

GOLDMAN, ALEX J., 1978 "Euthanasia," in *Judaism Confronts Contemporary Issues,* 171–91.

HAMEL, RON, AND EDWIN R. DuBOSE, 1991 "Views of the Major Faith Traditions," in *Choosing Death: Active Euthanasia, Religion, and the Public Debate.* (Philadelphia: Trinity Press International), 51–102.

LARUE, GERALD A., 1985 *Euthanasia and Religion: A Survey of the Attitudes of World Religions to the Right-to-Die.* Los Angeles: The Hemlock Society.

ROSNER, FRED, 1979 "The Jewish Attitude Toward Euthanasia," in *Jewish Ethics,* ed. Fred Rosner Jr. and David Bleich (Brooklyn: Hebrew Publishing).

Gender Roles and the Status of Women

BIALE, RACHEL, 1984 *Women and Jewish Law: An Exploration of Women's Issues in Halakhic Studies.* New York: Schocken.

CARMODY, DENISE, 1987 "Judaism," in *Women in World Religions,* ed. Arvind Sharma (Albany: State University of New York Press), 183–206.

1994 "Today's Jewish Women," in *Today's Woman in World Religions,* ed. Arvind Sharma (Albany: State University of New York Press), 245–66.

GREENBERG, BLU, 1981 *On Women and Judaism: A View from Tradition.* Philadelphia: The Jewish Publication Society of America.

GROSS, RITA M., 1979 "Female God Language in a Jewish Context," in *Womenspirit Rising: A Feminist Reader in Religion,* ed Carol P. Christ and Judith Plaskow (San Francisco: Harper & Row), 167–73.

PIRANI, ALIX, ED., 1991 *The Absent Mother: Restoring the Goddess to Judaism and Christianity.* London: Mandala (HarperCollins).

PLASKOW, JUDITH, 1979 "The Coming of Lilith: Toward a Feminist Theology," in *Womanspirit Rising; 198–209.*

1989 "Jewish Memory from a Feminist Perspective," in *Weaving the Patterns: New Patterns in Feminist Spirituality.* San Francisco: HarperCollins, 39–50.

1990 *Standing Again at Sinai: Judaism from a Feminist Perspective.* San Francisco: Harper & Row.

SWIDLER, LEONARD, 1976 *Women in Judaism.* Metuchen, N.J.: Scarecrow Press.

UMANSKY, ELLEN M., 1989 "Creating a Jewish Feminist Theology," in *Weaving the Patterns: New Patterns in Feminist Spirituality,* 187–98.

WEGNER, JUDITH ROMNEY, 1988 *Chattel or Person: The Status of Women in the Mishnah.* New York: Oxford University Press.

Homosexuality

BALKA, CHRISTIE, AND ANDY ROSE, EDS., 1989 *Twice Blessed: On Being Lesbian, Gay, and Jewish.* Boston: Beacon Press.

BOSWELL, JOHN, 1980 *Christianity, Social Tolerance and Homosexuality: Gay People in Western Europe from the Beginning of the Christian Era to the Fourteenth Century.* Chicago: The University of Chicago Press.

COOPER, AARON, 1989 "No Longer Invisible: Gay and Lesbian Jews Build a Movement," *Journal of Homosexuality* 18 (1989–90): 83–94.

ERON, LEWIS JOHN, 1993 "Homosexuality and Judaism," in *Homosexuality and World Religions,* ed. Arlene Swidler (Valley Forge, Pa: Trinity Press International), 103–34.

FELDMAN, DAVID, 1983 "Homosexuality and Jewish Law," *Judaism* 32 (1983), 426–29.

Goldman, Alex J., 1978 "Homosexuality," in *Judaism Confronts Contemporary Issues,* 192–210.

Kahn, Yoel H., 1989 "Judaism and Homosexuality: The Traditionalist/Progressive Debate," *Journal of Homosexuality* 18 (1989–90), 47–82.

Kirschner, Robert, 1988 "Halakhah and Homosexuality: A Reappraisal," *Judaism* 37: 450–58.

Lehrman, Nathaniel S., 1983 "Homosexuality and Judaism: Are They Compatible?" *Judaism* 32: 392–404.

Rabinowitz, Henry, 1983 "Talmud Class in a Gay Synagogue," *Judaism* 32: 433–43.

Soloff, Rav A., 1983 "Is There a Reform Response to Homosexuality?" *Judaism* 32: 417–24.

Umansky, Ellen M., 1985 "Jewish Attitudes Towards Homosexuality: A Review of Contemporary Sources," *Reconstructionist* 51: 9–15.

CHAPTER **12**

*C*hristianity:
The Way of Jesus Christ

Ptolemais

Caesarea

SAM

An

Joppa

Lydda

Emmau

Jamnia

Jer

Azotus   Be

Ascalon

JUDAEA

Gaza

Jorda

IDUMAE

INTRODUCTION

Christianity has more followers than any religion of the world—over 1.8 billion, or about one of every three persons on earth. The admonition of Jesus to his disciples at the end of the New Testament Gospel of Matthew (28:19–20), to go into all the world and make disciples of all nations, has been largely fulfilled: Christianity has reached every continent and virtually every country.

With so many adherents, it is not surprising that there is a great deal of diversity in the Christian movement. The major historical divisions are reflected in the Roman Catholic, Eastern Orthodox, and Protestant branches.

Like other religions with a "founder," the various Christian movements are linked by their profession of faith in Jesus of Nazareth, whom they proclaim to be the Christ, the *messiah*. Christians all share the belief in a transformation wrought by Jesus Christ's life, death, and resurrection from the dead. However, how they understand the meaning of these events differs. Many also share the rituals of baptism for the forgiveness of sins and a meal that re-enacts the last meal Jesus ate with his disciples. Christians have a linear view of time; they look forward to a life beyond this life for individuals and a new age of peace for humanity.

In this chapter we will study the development of Christianity from the time of Jesus to the present, the distinctive teachings of Christianity as expressed traditionally and as reinterpreted by some contemporary Christians, and the responses of Christians to contemporary ethical issues.

STAGES OF DEVELOPMENT AND SACRED TEXTS

Founder: Jesus of Nazareth

It has been said that today Jesus of Nazareth is the best-known person in the world. The same could not be said at the time in which he lived or in the decades thereafter. Jesus was a Jew from the region of Galilee in the first century C.E. who attracted a small band of followers through a career of healing and teaching. After a short ministry he was executed by Roman authorities. Historians would have paid him little notice, but his followers made the astounding claim that Jesus had been raised by God from the dead. They kept alive his teachings and the stories of his life, and eventually began to write them down in different versions. They also proclaimed the message that through the death and resurrection of Jesus, God had made a new covenant with humanity; and that through Jesus, God offered redemption to all, both Jew and Gentile (from the Greek word for "the nations," referring to all non-Jews). The term gospel refers to the "good news of the salvation brought through Jesus". Several decades after the death of Jesus the term began to refer to narratives about Jesus.

As with other "founders," the stories of the life of Jesus told in the four Gospels of the New Testament reflect both historical events and beliefs about the significance of the founder's life. The Gospels were not written as biographies in the modern sense, but rather as affirmations of faith in who Jesus was and what his coming meant. Interpreters disagree on how much of the Gospel accounts are actual historical remembrances of the words and deeds of Jesus, and how much is the creation of faithful followers. The Gospel stories are, however, almost our only source of information about the life of Jesus. The following is a reasonable reconstruction of the basic events in the life of Jesus, based on what the Gospels tell us.

The legends about the birth of Jesus (preserved only in the Gospels of Matthew and Luke) agree that Jesus, the son of Mary, a young virgin, was born in Bethlehem, a small town several miles from Jerusalem in Judea. Her husband, Joseph, was a carpenter from Nazareth in Galilee.

All of the Gospels agree that Jesus grew up in the village of Nazareth, but they tell us almost nothing about his childhood. Jesus was about 30 when he left Nazareth and ventured to the Jordan River, where he encountered a prophet named John the Baptizer. John was proclaiming a message of repentance. Jesus was baptized by John in the Jordan, apparently culminating a period of spir-

Source: (opener photo) M. Granitsas/The Image Works.

itual awakening. (For locations of prominent New Testament sites see Figure 12.1.)

Following his baptism Jesus spent time in the wilderness of Judea, fasting and reflecting on what he should do next. Three of the four Gospels portray this as a forty-day period of testing when Jesus was tempted by Satan. He then returned to Galilee, where he began to challenge people to repent, telling them that the Kingdom of God was at hand. The "Kingdom of God" was a symbol in Jewish apocalyptic teaching of a radically new age, in which people would live in harmony with God and with one another. "Apocalyptic" refers to the revealing of the secrets of the coming end of history and beginning of a new age of universal harmony. Jesus called together a group of close disciples, the Gospels say twelve. The number seems symbolic of the twelve tribes of Israel and reflects the view of his followers that the disciples of Jesus were a "new Israel" with whom God was entering into a new covenant. In addition to these twelve men, a number of women were in the close band of followers of Jesus, according to the Gospels.

The length of the ministry of Jesus is disputed. Only the Gospel of John implies a three-year period; the other Gospels portray events that could have taken place in one year. Nor is it clear how many trips Jesus made to Jerusalem during his ministry.

Jesus taught people that more important than meticulous observance of all of the commandments of the Torah was compassion for others. He warned people of the perils of wealth and the importance of being ready for the coming Kingdom of God. The Gospel of John, in particular, says that Jesus taught that he was the Son of God who was "one" with the Father. It is in the Gospel of John that Jesus says, "No one can come to the father except through me." Scholars disagree on whether this reflects the actual sayings of Jesus or the developed interpretation of the significance of Jesus among his followers. Jesus often taught using the rabbinic device of parables, sayings and stories drawing on events and characters with which people could easily identify.

Jesus also worked miracles, according to the Gospels. He healed the sick, the blind, and the lame. He fed the hungry and cast out demons. He walked on water and calmed stormy seas. He even raised the dead. These claims may seem amazing to modern ears, but such miracles were associated with prophets and charismatic teachers in Judaism in the first century C.E.

More amazing at the time, to those particularly concerned with righteous living, was the tendency of Jesus to associate with known sinners and social outcasts. He maintained that his message was especially intended for those who were not considered righteous.

FIGURE 12–1

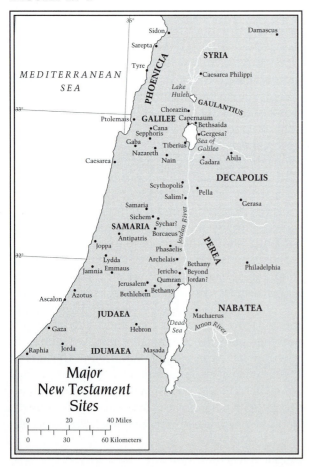

Major New Testament Sites

A minister (right) prepares to baptize a convert to Christianity. Baptism is a ritual that marks for Christians the transformation that God offers through faith in God's only Son, Jesus Christ.

Opposition to Jesus among some religious leaders and political authorities grew, and, according to the Gospels, he withdrew from his public ministry to spend time with his closest followers. He then went to Jerusalem for the Passover. The Gospels say that he was enthusiastically greeted when he entered Jerusalem and was proclaimed to be the messiah. He also taught at the Temple and challenged the religious authorities. After a last meal with his disciples, he was arrested and condemned to death by Pontius Pilate, the Roman procurator of Judea.

Jesus died on a Friday, and by Friday evening his body had been placed in a rock tomb. On Sunday morning several of the women among his disciples came to the tomb and found it empty. According to the Gospels, Jesus had been raised from the dead. In several different legends recorded in the Gospels, Jesus appeared to his disciples at various times during the next forty days before he ascended into heaven.

The New Testament and the Birth of Christianity

The New Testament preserves virtually the only evidence about the life of Jesus, and it is also the primary source for the birth of Christianity.

The New Testament is actually a library of twenty-seven separate sacred writings that came into existence over an extended period of time. Most scholars think that the earliest writings in the New Testament (the first letters of the Apostle Paul) were written fifteen to twenty years after the death of Jesus. The latest books in the New Testament were probably composed in the mid-to-late second century C.E. In addition to the New Testament canon there are a number of apocryphal Christian writings that were written throughout the period. The name "testament" is another word for covenant.

The Christian compilers of the New Testament believed that these writings were witness to a new covenant that God had made, extending the "old" covenant with the nation Israel to include all people. Some of the prophets of Israel had envisioned a "new covenant" between God and Israel (e.g., Jeremiah 31:31–34). The writers of the New Testament thought that through Jesus, whom they proclaimed as the messiah, God had initiated this new covenant. They believed that the people who responded to Jesus' call to discipleship and to the message about him were a "new Israel" God had assembled for a new age. There are a number of works available that will introduce readers to the

Located just outside the Damascus Gate into the old City of Jerusalem, this tomb is believed by some Christians to be the place where the body of Jesus was placed after his crucifixion.

critical interpretation of the New Testament (e.g., Hauer and Young, 1994). Detailed examination of the individual books of the New Testament is beyond the scope of our study.

Historians have sifted through the historical references in the New Testament and drawn on other Christian and non-Christian literary works, as well as archaeological evidence, to reconstruct the origins of Christianity. As in all scholarly endeavors, there are a variety of theories, and the work continues. What follows is a very general overview emphasizing the broad consensus of the majority of historians.

Their spiritual encounters with the risen Christ gave the immediate followers of Jesus both a message and the courage to proclaim it. The earliest church in Jerusalem centered around the Galileans who had come to Jerusalem with Jesus and remained there after his death. The community organized itself like other sectarian Jewish groups (including the group that produced the Dead Sea Scrolls). There was apparently an inner circle of leadership—Simon Peter and the two sons of Zebedee, James and John. After the execution of this James, another James (a brother or cousin of Jesus) apparently took his place as a leader of the Jerusalem community. Peter became a missionary, taking the message of the crucified yet risen Christ to Jewish communities in Palestine and the surrounding area. According to Acts, the Jerusalem followers shared their material goods in common. They met in homes on Sundays to commemorate the resurrection of Jesus, but they also continued to observe the Jewish calendar and worshipped at the Temple. As the Christian message spread, the Jerusalem community was looked upon with respect and reverence.

The early Jewish followers of Jesus understood the message they were proclaiming mostly as a fulfillment of Jewish expectations. The messiah had come, and even though he had been killed by his enemies, God had raised him from the dead. He would return soon to usher in the full realization of the reign of God on earth. As the message began to spread into non-Jewish circles, the focus inevitably shifted. Paul and other missionaries committed to winning Gentiles to faith in Christ naturally drew on imagery from the wider Hellenistic culture to interpret to those not familiar with Jewish tradition the meaning of God's sending the Christ, his Son, into the world. The message became more one of a personal salvation from a decaying world, from death, and from the evil powers of the world. Even more important, Paul and other Gentile missionaries taught that Gentiles did not have to live under the commandments of Torah in order to experience the redemption God offered. This led to friction with Jewish Christian leaders such as Peter, and a rift between Paul and Peter is evident in the New Testament. The reconciliation of this conflict portrayed in the Book of Acts reflects both the accommodation that ultimately occurred and also probably a bit of wishful thinking. According to Acts, the movement first called itself simply "the Way," and acquired the

The Illumination of St. Paul as portrayed by Italian artist, Benozzo Gozzoli (1420–1497), in a painting on display at the Metropolitan Museum of Art in New York.

Source: Religious News Service.

name "Christians" for the first time in Antioch, Syria, probably (as with the names of other religions) from outsiders seeking to understand this new group.

Through the efforts of missionaries such as Paul, Christian communities began to spring up around the Mediterranean world in both Jewish and Gentile settings by the middle of the first century C.E. Many of the contexts were urban, and Christianity seemed to emerge as a movement principally among disadvantaged city dwellers and idealistic civic leaders who turned to the new faith not only for spiritual consolation but also because of its potential political impact. Although it was probably overdramatized in the sources, the first Christians suffered persecution both at the hands of the Sadducean leaders in Jerusalem and from Roman authorities. The proclamation of Jesus as Lord was seen as a challenge to imperial prerogative. By the time of Paul's death in Rome (ca. 62 C.E), however, Christianity had a foothold in the Roman Empire.

Worship within the earliest Christian communities apparently revolved around gatherings in homes in which the last meal Jesus ate with his disciples was re-enacted as a way of experiencing his presence. The practice of baptizing converts to the faith (borrowed from Judaism and based upon the remembrance of the baptism of Jesus) continued. Paul speaks of a number of "gifts of the Spirit" present among the followers of Christ, including both "ecstatic" gifts, such as speaking in tongues and prophesying, and more ordinary gifts, such as teaching and administration. He said, and others undoubtedly agreed, that it was most important for the followers to share the unconditional love for one another that God had shown in sending his Son into the world. Emphasis was placed on giving up the "old life" dominated by sinful desire and behavior, and taking on a "new life, a new nature" in Christ, in which the fruits of the Spirit would be manifest.

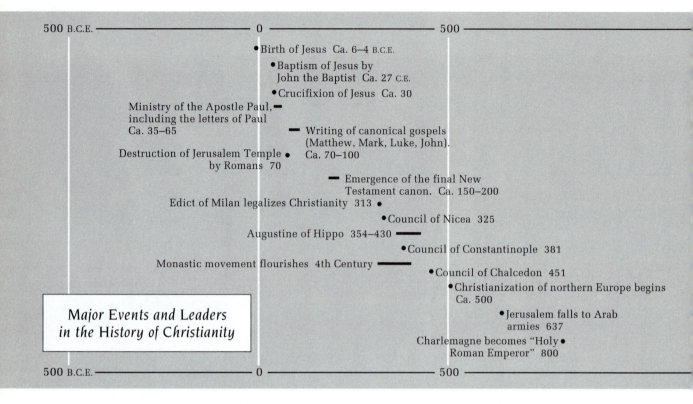

500 B.C.E. ——————————————— 0 ——————————— 500 —————————————

• Birth of Jesus Ca. 6–4 B.C.E.

• Baptism of Jesus by
John the Baptist Ca. 27 C.E.

• Crucifixion of Jesus Ca. 30

Ministry of the Apostle Paul, ▬
including the letters of Paul
Ca. 35–65

▬ Writing of canonical gospels
(Matthew, Mark, Luke, John).
Destruction of Jerusalem Temple • Ca. 70–100
by Romans 70

▬ Emergence of the final New
Testament canon. Ca. 150–200

Edict of Milan legalizes Christianity 313 •

• Council of Nicea 325

Augustine of Hippo 354–430 ▬

• Council of Constantinople 381

Monastic movement flourishes 4th Century ▬

• Council of Chalcedon 451

• Christianization of northern Europe begins
Ca. 500

• Jerusalem falls to Arab
armies 637

Charlemagne becomes "Holy •
Roman Emperor" 800

**Major Events and Leaders
in the History of Christianity**

500 B.C.E. ——————————————— 0 ——————————— 500 —————————————

The year 70 C.E. was a watershed in both the Jewish and Christian traditions. It marked the Roman destruction of Jerusalem and the Second Temple after a Jewish revolt. In Judaism, it sealed the fate of the Sadducees and their priestly supporters, and set the stage for the culmination of the Pharisees' gaining of central control. These events also hastened the estrangement of the early Christians from their Jewish heritage. Before 70 C.E. it was advantageous for Christians to claim that they were part of a group within Judaism, because Roman authorities accepted the legitimacy of Judaism.   After 70 C.E. association with Judaism was less beneficial, because of the Roman response to the Jewish revolt. Unfortunately, the growing hostility between Christians and Jews distorts the New Testament portrayal of Jews, because the New Testament was being written in the context of the increasing alienation and separation that caused Christianity to become a unique religion.

The period before 70 C.E. is called the apostolic age in Christian history; the period from 70 to ca. 125 C.E. is called the post-apostolic age. It was inevitably characterized by growing institutionalization, as the Christians organized their movement. This process accelerated as the initial expectation of an imminent end to history and the return of Christ began to fade. Bishops oversaw the churches of a region, while elders and deacons (who were already functioning during the apostolic period) exercised leadership in individual churches. The term "church" translates the Greek *ekklesia* ("gathering, those called together") and refers at this stage to the people in the Christian community, either locally or all together, never to a physical structure or a "denomination." The process of separation from Judaism continued, as did tension with Roman authorities, which led to more persecution.   By the second century, however, increased numbers of Romans of higher social status were attracted to the Christian message, and its acceptance began to improve.

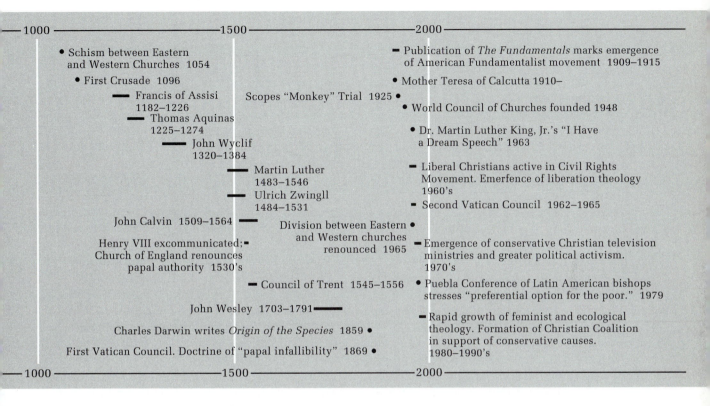

— 1000 ———————————— 1500 ———————————— 2000 —

- Schism between Eastern and Western Churches 1054
- First Crusade 1096
— Francis of Assisi 1182–1226
— Thomas Aquinas 1225–1274
— John Wyclif 1320–1384
— Martin Luther 1483–1546
— Ulrich Zwingll 1484–1531
John Calvin 1509–1564 —
Henry VIII excommunicated; Church of England renounces papal authority 1530's
Scopes "Monkey" Trial 1925 •
Division between Eastern and Western churches renounced 1965 •
— Council of Trent 1545–1556
John Wesley 1703–1791 —
Charles Darwin writes *Origin of the Species* 1859 •
First Vatican Council. Doctrine of "papal infallibility" 1869 •

— Publication of *The Fundamentals* marks emergence of American Fundamentalist movement 1909–1915
• Mother Teresa of Calcutta 1910–
• World Council of Churches founded 1948
• Dr. Martin Luther King, Jr.'s "I Have a Dream Speech" 1963
— Liberal Christians active in Civil Rights Movement. Emerfence of liberation theology 1960's
— Second Vatican Council 1962–1965
— Emergence of conservative Christian television ministries and greater political activism. 1970's
• Puebla Conference of Latin American bishops stresses "preferential option for the poor." 1979
— Rapid growth of feminist and ecological theology. Formation of Christian Coalition in support of conservative causes. 1980–1990's

— 1000 ———————————— 1500 ———————————— 2000 —

We should not leave an impression of uniformity of belief and practice in the early stages of the Christian movement. The New Testament itself reflects differing points of view and ways of expressing the faith. It took several centuries for Christian "orthodoxy" to emerge, and not long thereafter for differing interpretations of it to begin to lead to the divisions still evident in Christianity. Some of the early disagreements were over the "natures" of Jesus. Was he a human being, called by God to special work? Was he divine, and in his appearances on earth only apparently human? Or was he both human and divine, and if so, how were these natures related? A variety of groups linked together by historians under the title "Gnostics" claimed that Jesus was a divine savior who only appeared to be human. Marcionism, named after a second-century theologian named Marcion, held that there are two gods: one of justice, who created the world, and the other of goodness, the father of Jesus Christ, who redeemed the world. Marcion taught that only

a truncated version of the Gospel of Luke and ten Pauline epistles should be considered canonical. Another second-century teacher, Montanus, emphasized the freedom of the Holy Spirit that is manifest in the ecstatic gifts of the Spirit among Christians. His followers were called Montanists.

In response to such movements, other Christian leaders sought to develop standards of belief among Christians. One of the earliest expressions of this tendency is the Apostles' Creed, recited by converts to Christianity upon baptism and still used by many Christian communities as a statement of faith.

The Institutionalization and Spread of Christianity

As the Christian church grew, each of the major cities of the Roman Empire had a Christian community headed by a bishop. Over time the Bishop of Rome became the principal bishop. According to tradition, the Apostle Peter was the first Bishop of Rome, and

Peter's centrality among the apostles and in the Jerusalem church supported his leadership. The Roman church and its supporters claimed that among the successors to the apostles the first was the Bishop of Rome, the successor to Peter. By the end of the fourth century the title *pope* was in use to describe the Bishop of Rome. The term "apostolic succession" refers to the principle that the authority of church leaders derived from their historical connection with the apostles of Jesus. That authority passed to those ordained by the apostles and their successors.

Among the Eastern churches there was no one central bishop like the Bishop of Rome. In the East, ultimate authority resided in the gathering of bishops in ecumenical ("general") councils. The different understanding of the role of Christian bishops in the government of the church (compounded by still other views after the Protestant Reformation) continues to be a source of important division in Christianity.

In 313 C.E. the Emperor Constantine, after the latest in a series of persecutions of Christians, ordered in the Edict of Milan that Christianity be protected alongside other religions. Twelve years later he convened the Council of Nicea to reconcile disputes among Christian leaders over the vexing question of the natures of Christ. The Council produced the Nicene Creed, which affirmed that Christ was "begotten, not made, of the same substance with the Father. . . ." The Nicene Creed is still an official and integral part of the liturgy of a number of Christian churches. On his deathbed Constantine accepted baptism and became a Christian himself. Under the reign of Theodosius (379–395 C.E.) Christianity completed its amazing rise from outlawed sect to the official religion of the Roman Empire. In 451 C.E another ecumenical Council at Chalcedon in Asia Minor attempted to resolve the dispute over the two natures of Christ by affirming that Christ is "truly God and truly man."

Among the early theologians of Christianity, the one with the greatest influence on the subsequent shape of Christianity was Augustine, Bishop of Hippo in North Africa (354–430 C.E.). His autobiographical *Confessions*, which tells the story of his rebellious childhood and eventual conversion to Christianity, is a literary as well as spiritual classic. Augustine's conceptualization of the transcendence of God, the Trinity, original sin, divine grace, faith, the sacraments, and the role of the church in history all helped shape orthodox Christian teaching as it is still expressed today. His *City of God* is an inspired defense of the Christian understanding of history against the charge that Christianity had caused the defeat of Rome by the Goths.

Beginning in the third century C.E., a monastic movement institutionalized the Apostle Paul's emphasis on celibacy and the New Testament warning against dependence on material wealth. From Egypt monasticism, this movement with its emphasis on self-denial, prayer, and a secluded life, spread throughout the Christian world.

In 330 C.E. the Emperor Constantine moved the capital of the Roman Empire from Rome to Byzantium. This accentuated a natural division in Christianity between the West (centered in Rome) and the East (focused in Asia Minor). The Bishop of Rome evolved into a political as well as spiritual power, but the patriarchs of the East refused to recognize his primacy in either area. In addition, a variety of theological and liturgical differences divided East and West. For example, the churches in the East tended to emphasize more strongly the divinity of Christ and allowed clergy to be married. The date usually given for the split between Eastern and Western Christianity is 1054, when the Pope excommunicated the Patriarch of Constantinople, and the Patriarch returned the favor. Attempts were made over the centuries to heal this "Great Schism," but they ended when the Muslim Turks took Constantinople in 1453. The Roman Catholic Church in the West and the Orthodox churches of the East went their separate ways. An atmosphere of mistrust continued until 1965, when Patriarch Athenagoras and Pope Paul VI officially overturned the excommunications of 1054.

By the Middle Ages Christianity had become by far the major religion in Western Europe. Except for Muslim dominance in Spain (under the Moors), Europe has remained Christian until the present. Accommodations were made to indigenous religions (as, for example, in the dating of Christmas and the naming of Easter), but Christianity succeeded in supplanting native religions and withstanding the Muslim attempts at invasion. The papacy was the firm anchor during a period that saw the decline and fall of the Roman Empire. Like any power without competition, the Western church became corrupt. Papal power was often used for material gain, and ordinary people were often viewed as a source of wealth to be exploited.

Despite institutional corruption, Christian theology continued to develop and thrive in the Middle Ages. The writings of Thomas Aquinas (ca. 1225–1274), in particular, had a lasting influence. His major contribution was to draw upon the philosophy of the Greek philosopher Aristotle to defend rationally such basic Christian conceptions as the claim that God is the creator of the universe so that they could be accepted on the basis of reason, not just revelation. His writings came at a time of re-emergence of the writings of Aristotle, which posed a threat to the acceptance by intellectuals of some traditional Christian doctrines. Thomas set out to show that Christian revelation fulfills rather than contradicts the rational pursuit of truth. The depth and profundity of works such as his masterpiece, *Summa Theologica*, make them still fertile ground for those seeking to reflect rationally on Christian teachings.

An illustration of Martin Luther (1483–1546), the Protestant Reformer.
Source: National Museum, Stockholm.

Reform Movements in Christianity

Beginning in the late Middle Ages, a variety of efforts began to reform Christianity and restore its original vitality and teachings. These efforts continue to the present.

The first full-scale reformation of the Christian Church is called the Protestant Reformation. The Reformation was foreshadowed by scholars such as John Wyclif in England (ca. 1320–1384), who started the work of translating the Bible into the language of ordinary people so that they could read or hear it for themselves and be influenced directly by its teachings.

The first major Protestant reformer was the German Martin Luther (1483–1546). Luther became convinced through his study of Scripture that every Christian was a priest and that salvation was not for the church to dispense through the sacraments; rather, it was God's free gift received by each individual in faith. He challenged the corruption of the Roman Catholic Church, most famously through the posting of "95 Theses" on the door of the castle church in Wittenberg in 1517.

Other reformers quickly emerged. In Switzerland, Ulrich Zwingli (1484–1531) followed Luther's lead, but split with him on the issue of whether Christ was spiritually present in the bread and wine of communion (Luther's view, in opposition to the Roman view of actual presence through transubstantiation) or merely memorialized. John Calvin (1509–1564) re-emphasized the Augustinian doctrines of the sovereignty of God and depravity of humanity. In his role as minister of the church in Geneva, Switzerland, Calvin exercised a great deal of influence in both secular and religious affairs. He discouraged frivolity and stressed hard work and industry. He encouraged the development of businesses through the use of money loaned at interest.

The role of "Calvinism" in the development of capitalism in Europe has been widely acknowledged.

Besides the Lutheran and Reformed (Calvinist) wings of the Protestant Reformation, another group of reformers were the impetus behind the Anabaptist movement. Among them were Jacob Hutter (d. 1536) and Menno Simons (ca. 1494–1561), the founder of the Mennonites. The name Anabaptist ("baptism for a second time") comes from the practice of baptizing people as adults rather than as infants, as was the case not only in the Roman Catholic Church but also in the other Protestant churches. Anabaptists took a stricter view of Scripture, saying that only those things expressly stated in the New Testament should be allowed. The Anabaptist movement is also known as the "Radical Reformation." Anabaptists are perhaps best known for their advocacy of pacifism and the strict separation of church and state. Many Anabaptist groups have been persecuted for their beliefs.

In England a formal break with Rome came in 1533, when Henry VIII refused to accept the Pope's denial of his request for an annulment of his marriage. Henry then founded the Church of England, with himself as its head. In Scotland a follower of John Calvin, John Knox, led a movement that ultimately resulted in the creation of the Church of Scotland, which in turn inspired Presbyterian movements in England and later the United States. "Presbyterian" comes from the New Testament word for "elders," and refers to the belief that the government of the church should be vested in elders chosen by the people rather than bishops. In France Protestant Huguenots tried to establish a Calvinist church, but were eventually driven from France by persecution.

The Roman Catholic Church responded to the various Protestant reforms by instituting a reformation of its own, called the Counter-Reformation. The Council of Trent (1545–1563) set forth positions in opposition to those taken by the Protestant reformers. While Protestants emphasized that Scripture alone was the standard by which teachings of the church should be judged, the Council of Trent stated that the tradition of the Catholic Church had equal authority with Scripture. The Council reaffirmed that several books of the Old Testament were

An engraving of John Calvin (1509–1564), the Protestant reformer whose theology inspired the wing of Protestantism that includes the Presbyterian churches.
Source: New York Public Library.

indeed Scripture (calling them the Deuterocanon—"Second Canon"). Most of the reformers had rejected this idea because the books were not part of the Hebrew canon. Most Protestant churches call these works, which include Tobit, Judith, First and Second Maccabees, the Wisdom of Solomon, the Wisdom of Jesus ben Sirach (Ecclesiasticus), Baruch, and supplements to Esther and Daniel, the Apocrypha ("hidden writings"). The Council of Trent also reaffirmed the seven sacraments of the Catholic Church, because most reformers claimed that only two (the Lord's Supper and Baptism) were Scriptural.

We do not have space to cover each subsequent reformation movement in the history of Christianity. We will, however, attempt to describe the diversity within contemporary Christianity.

Major Christian Movements

In this section we will summarize briefly the modern histories and some of the major emphases of the three major branches of Christianity: Roman Catholic, Eastern Orthodox, and Protestant (see Figure 12–2 on page 323).

Roman Catholicism From the Council of Trent until the nineteenth century, the teachings and structure of the Roman Catholic Church remained fairly stable. Papal authority had been challenged in the wake of the French Revolution of the late eighteenth century and the rationalist spirit that swept across Europe after the Enlightenment. However, a nineteenth-century movement called Ultramontanism ("across the mountains") strengthened the power of the papacy. In the nineteenth century several major papal proclamations affected church teaching. In 1854 Pope Pius IX proclaimed the doctrine of the Immaculate Conception of Mary, which established as church teaching the view that the mother of Jesus was freed from original sin and filled with God's grace from the first moment of her existence. In 1869 the First Vatican Council promulgated the doctrine of papal infallibility, which said that under certain conditions the utterances of a pope are without error. The conditions were that the pope must be speaking *ex cathedra*—that is, while discharging the office of pastor and doctor of Christians—and speaking to the universal church on matters of faith and morals in his full capacity as successor of St. Peter.

At the end of the nineteenth century a movement called Catholic Modernism tried to examine church teaching in the light of the modern study of the Bible and the accepted theories of contemporary science, such as evolution. The movement was condemned by Pope Pius X in 1907, but its influence continued among many Catholic scholars. The movement called neo-Thomism had more success in winning official acceptance for its interpretation of the teachings of Thomas Aquinas using modern developments in philosophy and science.

In 1950 Pope Pius XII proclaimed the doctrine of the Bodily Assumption of Mary, the teaching that the mother of Jesus was assumed bodily into heaven "when she had finished the course of her life." The doctrine expresses the belief that it was

Pope John Paul II is shown here on a 1986 visit to France. Since becoming pope in 1978 he has traveled throughout the world to promote peace and justice.

by God's gift that Mary participated in the resurrected glory of her Son, not her own initiative.

The most transforming event in the history of Roman Catholicism since the Council of Trent began in 1962, when Pope John XXIII opened the Second Vatican Council. The Council sought to modernize the church in response to positive developments in the world at large. Among the many changes brought about by the Council were increased use of the vernacular languages in worship, the sharing of papal authority among all the bishops, an increased role for laity in the government of local parishes, acceptance that members of other churches share in God's work of salvation and are legitimate Christians, recognition of the validity of non-Christian religions, and the declaration that Jews were not to be held responsible for the death of Jesus. Pope John XXIII's successor, Paul VI, presided over the last three sessions of the Second Vatican Council.

The present pope (John Paul II) is the first non-Italian pope in modern history. He became pope in 1978. He has particularly identified with the plight of the poor and oppressed of the world, and has also been a strong supporter of traditional teaching on birth control and other matters of personal morality. He has opposed the ordination of women and any modification of the tradition that priests who seek ordination before marriage must remain celibate.

Eastern Orthodoxy   The Eastern Orthodox branch of Christianity (sometimes called simply the Orthodox churches) consists of a number of independent churches, such as the Russian Orthodox Church and the Greek Orthodox Church. Most of these countries were once part of Byzantium, the eastern part of the Roman Empire. Each church is led by a patriarch, metropolitan, or archbishop. There are patriarchates today in Constantinople (Turkey), Alexandria (Egypt), Antioch (Syria), Jerusalem (Palestine), Russia, Romania, Bulgaria, Serbia, and Georgia. Other Orthodox churches are in Greece, Cyprus, Poland, the former Czechoslovakia, and Finland. Immigrants have brought the Orthodox Church to Western Europe, the Americas, Japan, and Australia. Until the invasion of the Turks in

1453, the Patriarch of Constantinople was the spiritual leader of all these churches. This role then effectively passed to the Patriarch of the Russian Orthodox Church, although the symbolic primacy of the Constantinople patriarch is still recognized. The ideal of unity among the Orthodox churches is thus preserved, despite their essential independence as a result of different political histories.

A great deal of unity in doctrine and liturgy among the Orthodox churches has also been maintained, in part (many interpreters claim) because the Muslim invasion of many Orthodox areas in the eighth century "froze" their development. Unity has also been maintained because the Orthodox churches accept as infallible the creeds and dogmas of the seven ecumenical councils.

Justice cannot be done here to the complexity and beauty of Orthodox doctrine and worship. The Orthodox emphasis is on the incarnation of the invisible God in the liturgy and devotional practices of the church. The point is the *experience* of God's holy presence in the sacraments, icons, prayers, and pageantry of the church. The energies of God, such as glory, light, grace, and love, fill the world and can be personally experienced. Doctrine is not so much expressed in words as it is sung and lived in the richness of the liturgy. Orthodox worship services are virtual works of art.

Through a life of devotion, individuals can become "partakers of the divine nature." The famous icons (from the Greek for "image" or "likeness") found in Orthodox churches and homes are stylized paintings on wood or canvas of Christ, Mary, angels, saints, and Biblical scenes. The icons often represent those who have experienced "deification," and now serve to inspire others on that same path. Like the Bible (a verbal icon), the painted icons manifest God's presence, but they are to be venerated rather than worshipped. In Orthodox teaching, the honor given to the icon is "passed over" to that which it manifests.

At the close of World War II, every national Orthodox church except the Greek found itself in a hostile political environment. The Russian Orthodox Church, for example, was forced to cooperate with an officially atheist Communist government.

After a long struggle, the Russian and other Eastern European Orthodox churches were permitted to send delegates to the World Council of Churches in 1961. As already noted, in 1965 the Patriarch of Constantinople met with Pope Paul VI and officially renounced the schism of 1054. Ecumenical dialogue with both Protestants and Roman Catholics has continued since then.

With the demise of Communism in the former Soviet Union and Eastern Europe, a new day of openness and opportunity has dawned. In the United States nineteen parallel Eastern Orthodox jurisdictions continue to reflect the ethnic diversity of these immigrant churches. However, there are signs of increased cooperation that may someday lead to unity.

Protestantism   All but one of the major branches of Protestantism active today began during or shortly after the Protestant Reformation.

The Lutheran branch of Protestantism was established in Germany and the Scandinavian countries (Denmark, Norway, and Sweden) and has been carried into other areas by immigrants from those countries. The Reformed branch derives from the teachings of John Calvin. The largest among the Reformed churches is the Presbyterian; others include various national Reformed churches (such as the Dutch Reformed). Splitting from the Presbyterians in America were the Disciples of Christ denomination and various others.

Another branch is the Baptist, united by the common acceptance of believer baptism. One expression is the Anabaptist wing, including the Mennonites and a famous offshoot of the Mennonites, the various Amish churches. Another expression includes the Baptist churches that trace their roots to the Puritan movement in England during the sixteenth and seventeenth centuries. Among the Puritans who settled in the United States were Baptists, including Roger Williams, who established the first Baptist church in the "new world" in Rhode Island in 1639. Today the Southern Baptist Convention is both the largest Baptist church and the largest Protestant denomination in the United States. One of the other major Baptist groups is the American Baptist Churches in the United States of America.

The Anglican Communion, including the Church of England and the Episcopal Church in America, is often called a branch of the Protestant movement because, as we have seen, its origins trace to a break from the authority of the pope in the sixteenth century. However, Anglicanism technically remains Catholic in its own self-understanding and in many of its doctrines, and therefore it is misleading to call it a wing of Protestantism. The Methodist movement split from the Church of England under the leadership of John and Charles Wesley in the eighteenth century, and spread into other countries. The Congregationalist movement, which emphasizes that the true church is a gathering of people together in a particular place, not an association of local churches or a hierarchy, also emerged out of the Anglican Church in England, as did the Quaker movement (the Society of Friends). Like the Baptist movement, they arose in the religious turmoil of seventeenth-century England, when the Puritan movement was at its strongest.

The final branch of modern Christianity is the Pentecostal, including such denominations as the Assemblies of God. This movement began in late nineteenth- and early twentieth-century America and emphasizes the literal interpretation of Scripture, a "baptism of the Spirit," and the manifestation of the ecstatic gifts of the Spirit, such as speaking in tongues.

In the nineteenth century, Protestants were instrumental in a revitalized emphasis on missions, resulting in a missionary movement that enabled Christianity to spread worldwide. The Catholic Church had long before sent missionaries to South America, Central America, Japan, and the Philippines, and various Protestant groups had begun work in other parts of the world. However, during the nineteenth century the pace accelerated, and Christian missionaries spread out into virtually every country and culture to proclaim the Christian gospel. This has involved not only trying to "win individuals to the Gospel" but ministering to the full range of physical, social, and spiritual needs of people. Christian missionaries established schools, hospitals, and other institutions of social welfare. As we noted in Chapters Three and Four, Christian missionaries have often attacked the religions of indigenous peoples and sought to replace the cultures of the native peoples as well as their religions. Many Protestant churches and the Roman Catholic Church have changed their understanding of mission work in recent decades to emphasize the development of local leadership and respect for the cultures of other peoples. The movement has come full circle with missionaries from churches begun by nineteenth-century European and American missionaries being invited to bring their understanding of the Gospel to the countries of the original missionaries!

In the twentieth century, Protestantism has been particularly affected by the emergence of an American movement known as fundamentalism. In response to growing openness in some churches to developments in modern science, such as evolutionary theory in biology and the application of critical methods to the study of the Bible, some Christians reacted by reasserting doctrines they saw as threatened. These included belief in the inerrancy and verbal inspiration of the Bible, creation in six days, the virgin birth of Christ, the bodily resurrection of Christ, and the second coming of Christ. Each of these doctrines had been reinterpreted by Christians who sought to adapt Christian teaching to the new scientific worldview. Some fundamentalists have remained within traditional denominations and tried to influence the leadership and doctrine of the church, while others have rejected "denominationalism" and started independent churches (often called "ministries" or "fellowships"). The term "fundamentalist" is now being widely applied to traditionalist movements in other religions.

Another important twentieth-century development in Christianity is the charismatic movement. The term "charismatic" comes from the New Testament term for "gift of the Spirit." It has a more specialized meaning than the general understanding of "charismatic" as the ability to inspire people. This movement emphasizes the "baptism of the Holy Spirit," in which persons experience what they believe to be the power of the Spirit in their lives. The presence of the Spirit is particularly manifested in the ecstatic gifts. Charismatics believe that they can call upon the power of God in faith, and God will respond with physical healing and other forms of divine assistance. Within virtually all Protestant denominations (and Roman Catholicism), charismatic fellowships have formed. Local charismatics often seek to revitalize individual congregations through prayer and openness to the Spirit. In addition, independent charismatic churches and ministries have formed. Often a leader who has had a powerful spiritual experience forms a fellowship group, which becomes a church and sometimes a ministry. The charismatic movement is sometimes called neo-Pentecostalism, and the older Pentecostal churches are known as exponents of "Classical Pentecostalism."

The ecumenical movement is another important twentieth-century development that has principally involved Protestants, but has affected Roman Catholics and the Eastern Orthodox churches as well. The term *ecumenical* derives from a Greek word that means "the whole inhabited world." The ecumenical movement seeks to increase cooperation among Christian churches, particularly in mission to the world. The movement seeks to heal the historical divisions among churches. It also tries to mobilize Christians to confront social problems of poverty and injustice. Nineteenth-century movements such as the Young Men's and Young Women's Christian Associations were examples of Christians (especially Protestants) coming together in cooperative work. These and other organizations paved the way for the creation after World War II of the World Council of Churches, which now has nearly 300 member churches. These churches come from the Protestant and Eastern Orthodox branches of Christianity, but do not include the more conservative Protestant churches. National movements such as the National Council of Churches of Christ in America also try to increase cooperation. At the local level, there has been increased cooperation among congregations, particularly in mission work. Since the Second Vatican Council, the Roman Catholic Church has been very open to ecumenical cooperation. Finally, related to the ecumenical movement is the trend toward union among Protestant denominations. Negotiations among Protestant churches have led to over fifty such unions since World War II. Some have

FIGURE 12–2

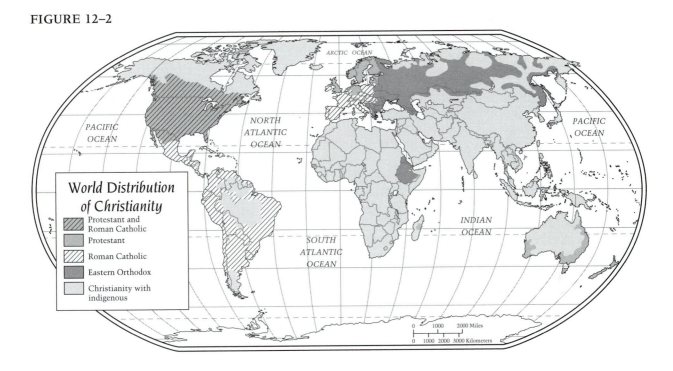

been the reunion of denominations that split over doctrinal or political disputes, while others have brought together separate churches for the first time.

Christianity Today

The issues facing Christians today have evoked responses that cross the traditional demarcations of Roman Catholic, Eastern Orthodox, and Protestant. As we have seen already, phenomena such as the charismatic movement and the ecumenical movement not only include members of the Protestant churches where they originated but involve the other branches as well. In general, Christians today are divided among three broad perspectives:

1. those who think that emphasis should be placed on adapting traditional Christian teaching and practice to the new insights, methods, and situations emerging in our rapidly changing modern, scientific, and increasingly secular world;

2. those who argue that traditional teachings (whether derived from the Bible, the church,

or an inspired leader) should be even more strongly affirmed in the face of the challenges posed by the modern, secular world; and

3. those who seek a middle ground, affirming both the core of traditional teachings but also some aspects of the modern perspectives and approaches.

Although they are not expressed institutionally in the same way, these patterns in Christianity today parallel to some degree the Reform, Orthodox, and Conservative movements in Judaism: the minimalist, maximalist, and intermediary positions. Other labels that might apply are "liberal, conservative, and moderate," "left-wing, right-wing, and centrist," or "modernist, traditionalist, and accommodationist." However, these labels are so loaded by their modern political usage that they must be used carefully. As with all abstract categories, these should only be considered a means of encountering the range and diversity of expressions of contemporary Christianity, not rigid compartments into which all

Christians must be neatly or simplistically fit. Within each branch of Christianity may be found proponents of each of these three approaches.

On the "minimalist" side are those who think that too much emphasis on traditional teachings risks making Christianity increasingly irrelevant in the modern world. For example, the traditional Christian teaching that premarital and homosexual sexual relations are immoral flies in the face, many modernist Christians believe, of accepted modern practices and scientific findings. Christians toward the left on our hypothetical spectrum also think that Christianity has traditionally placed too much emphasis on individual, private morality and the spiritual fate of individuals and not enough on transforming society in response to the fundamental principles of justice and love taught in the Bible. Like those in the Reform movement in Judaism, liberal Christians believe that their position is actually a reaffirmation of basic Christian principles, with some of the more moralistic, legalistic, and ritualistic aspects added through the years to the basic teachings pruned away.

For example, during the American civil rights movement of the 1950s and '60s, reform-minded Christians took an active role in bringing Christian teaching to bear on the struggle to overcome discrimination against blacks and other minorities. More recently, liberal Christians have been active in the movement for gender equality, justice for oppressed peoples, and environmental responsibility (as we will see later in the chapter).

On the more radical side of liberal Christianity, some movements provide a theological basis for militant political action to redress social injustices. Black theology arose during the civil rights movement to challenge the perceived racial bias of traditional Christian theology. Some black theologians call for a totally new black Christianity, which recognizes that "God is black." Others have sought to work within existing church structures to overturn teachings and practices rooted in racism.

Similarly, feminist theologians have sought to overcome the masculine orientation present in Christianity, including the limiting of talk of God to masculine language and the refusal to allow for the ordination of women in some churches. Some feminist theologians argue that a complete break with traditional Christianity is necessary in order to affirm feminine imagery for God and the role of women in religion. Others have sought to reinterpret traditional Christian teaching from a feminist perspective.

Black theology and feminist theology are sometimes considered branches within a larger theological movement called liberation theology. In general, liberation theology stresses that the fundamental activity of God is the liberation of humans from whatever keeps them in bondage. Drawing heavily on Biblical stories such as the Exodus, the prophets of ancient Israel who spoke of God's demand for social justice, and the sayings and work of Jesus, liberation theologians say that God is to be found today on the side of the poor and oppressed of the world. Liberation theology began as a movement within the Catholic Church in Third World countries, but it has spread to the other branches of Christianity. Some liberation theologians have even argued that violent revolutions are necessary to overturn oppressive regimes, and that Christians should be involved in them (as they were in the American Revolution). Others have emphasized non-violent means to liberate the poor, means they believe are more in keeping with Christian principles.

Environmental theologians emphasize that God's redemptive work is neither limited to, nor necessarily focused on humanity, but rather includes the entire cosmos. Some see the basis for an "ecological Christianity" sensitive to the well-being of the whole environment in the Biblical tradition and in the teachings of selected Christian leaders throughout history.

More conservative Christians have emphasized the message of personal salvation. The fundamental role of the church and individual Christians, they believe, is worship and praise of God and work to spread the gospel of Jesus Christ to individuals, offering them salvation from their sinfulness so that they can have eternal life. Many Protestants on the right side of the spectrum believe in a literal interpretation of Scripture. Conservative Christians point out that Jesus did not try to change society; rather, he challenged individuals to repent and prepare themselves for the Kingdom of God (which is typically understood in the conservative camp as heaven). Many conservative Christians also point out that the Apostle Paul taught Christians to respect political authorities. Some conservatives emphasize the imminent return of Christ to transform this sinful world, making attempts by Christians to alter society not only unnecessary but a sign of a lack of faith in God's promises.

In recent decades, many conservatives have come to the conclusion that they too must be politically active, because, in their view, society is too dominated by secularists and religious liberals who have too little respect for "traditional values." For example, with the legalization of abortion in the United States, conservative Protestants and Catholics have joined together to work to overturn what they view as a direct violation of the teaching of Christianity about the "sanctity of life." Some conservative Christian leaders have allied themselves with conservative politicians, or entered politics directly, in order to fight for their understanding of Christian principles. On the more radical side of the conservative wing, there is talk of creating a "theocracy" ("rule by religious leaders") in the United States to protect Christian values.

Some conservative Christians have become particularly adept at the use of television to spread their message and to win support. A host of "television ministries" now have a worldwide audience. In recent years a variety of scandals have cast a pall over some of the "televangelists," but broad interest in and support of these often quite dynamic ministers continues. The Christian Broadcasting Network, headed by former presidential candidate Pat Robertson, offers interpretation of contemporary events and issues from a traditionalist perspective.

In the current atmosphere, there does not seem to be much room for the "moderate" camp in Christianity. Moderate Christians are those who see merit in both the liberal concern for Christian involvement in righting social wrongs and the conservative emphasis on personal salvation and traditional values. They may be involved in some of the activities of both wings, but they reject the more radical stances that so often seem to gain attention. For example,

moderate Christians might support a woman's right to have an abortion, as do liberals, but agree with traditionalists that abortion has inappropriately become a method of birth control that devalues life. Christians in the center are not well-organized; ironically, however, they probably constitute the majority of Christians today. They often provide the support and leadership necessary for maintaining churches, and feel somewhat alienated amidst the cacaphony generated on the Christian left and right.

DISTINCTIVE TEACHINGS

In summarizing Christian teaching we will emphasize traditional doctrines, but also acknowledge the differences in their interpretation on the various points of the Christian spectrum we have identified.

Problem: Separation from God

Like other religions that originated in the Middle East, Christianity teaches that the fundamental problem of humanity is alienation from God. Among the religions in this family, Christianity has tended to emphasize most strongly the underlying state of existence that separates humanity from God. This state of existence is called "sin" and refers to a perceived basic orientation of humans to turn away from God. Acts of disobedience ("sins") follow from this state, but the real dilemma that needs to be addressed is the underlying quality of being ("sinfulness") that causes sinful acts.

Traditionally, Christianity has emphasized the problem as an individual matter. Individual persons are "sinners," and the resolution is personal transformation. Biblically, however, sin is also seen as a "corporate" concern. Nations may be sinful, as may other human communities. Liberal interpretation has focused on this dimension of sin, to argue that persons need to be liberated not only from their own "sin," but from their entrapment in and by sinful social structures. Moreover, environmental theologians point out that life beyond humanity is endangered by the effects of human sin, and any doctrine of sin must include its ecological dimensions.

Cause: Original Sin?

The doctrine of *original sin* developed in Christianity to explain the pervasiveness of sin. This doctrine holds that humans are by nature sinful. Although it is never directly stated in the Bible (and not accepted by Jewish or Muslim interpreters, or even all Christians), some Christian teachers saw in the story of Adam and Eve the basis of original sin. Moreover, there are passages in the New Testament (e.g., Romans 5:12–19) that may be considered as support for the teaching. The early Christian theologian Augustine was the first to express clearly the view that humans inherit the sin of Adam. It should be noted that Augustine developed the theory of inherited original sin to counter another Christian theologian's view that all humans are born free from sin, and may choose between good and evil. These same opposing points of view are found among contemporary Christians.

This traditional view that all humans inherit the sin of Adam is still widely held in Christianity, especially among those on the more conservative side. Other Christians have rejected the literal interpretation of Scripture and, consequently, do not view Adam and Eve as actual historical persons whose sin is passed on naturally through the human generations. Some Christians today reject entirely the notion that humans are by nature sinful; they assert that humans are fully free to choose whether to sin or not. Others accept original sin as a symbolic way of expressing the reality that all humans share an inclination toward sinfulness by placing "self" over God and others.

In addition, traditional Christianity accepts the existence of Satan and his demonic forces and teaches that Satan seeks to draw persons into sinful behavior. Minimalist interpretation tends to view Satan as a symbol for the reality of evil in the world, rather than as a literal being or power.

Reality: Creation and the Cosmic Christ

Like the other religions that originated in the Middle East, Christianity views reality as the creation of the one God, who transcends the created order. The creation is "good," as created by God. Humanity has been charged with the care of the creation, and the responsibility for maintaining the divinely wrought harmony. However, human sinfulness leads to the abuse and corruption of creation.

Christianity introduces the notion that Christ, as fully divine (as well as fully human), participates in the creation. The New Testament portrays Christ not only as the agent of divine creation but as present in creation, bringing harmony and unity to all reality.

Like the other religions in this family, Christianity is eschatological in its view of time. Christian teaching is that time began with God's creation of the world. Since Christians believe Christ is God's agent in the ordering of reality and is present in all reality, then the Christian measurement of time naturally is calculated on the basis of the historical manifestation of Christ. Christians traditionally have looked ahead to a time of fulfillment, when God will again send Christ into the world to restore the original harmony (the *Second Coming*). Christians sometimes speak of already living in the end time, because with the first coming of Christ they believe the new age has broken into time. This helps explain the Christian sense of living in tension with the "world," by which is meant reality corrupted by sinfulness and evil. Christians believe that through faith in Christ they have already experienced a foretaste of the new age, and therefore they feel alienated from the "world" even while they still live in it.

Many liberal Christians, like many Reform Jews, have reinterpreted the traditional eschatological teaching. Rather than looking forward to the literal return of Christ, they see the teaching of Christ's Second Coming as a symbolic way of saying that God's intention is for the terrible mess humans have created on earth to be cleaned up. If this is to happen, however, modernist Christians tend to believe that humans must cooperate with this divine intention and create through their efforts the new age of harmony.

End: The Kingdom of God in Heaven and on Earth

Many Christians believe that "life after death in heaven" is the chief goal toward which Christian life should be oriented. "Heaven" is seen as a spiritual realm in which God dwells and to which those who experience salvation will go after death to live in eternal blessedness. This is the Kingdom of God, in their view. "Hell" is a state of torment in which the damned are destined to spend eternity. Traditional Catholic teaching adds "purgatory," a state of final purification for those who die while still in a condition of sin. It is believed that prayers for the souls of the dead can help them attain purification and pass from purgatory into heaven.

According to traditionalist understanding of Biblical teaching, entrance into heaven or hell will occur at the end of time, after the resurrection of the dead and a final judgment. This emphasis on the fate of individuals after death has been challenged by interpreters on the Christian left (as well as some Christians on the right, who view it as a

---

QUESTIONS OF HUMAN IDENTITY: WHAT IS THE BASIC HUMAN DILEMMA?

No One Is Righteous

Both of the following passages are from the Apostle Paul's Letter to the Romans in the New Testament. Note the influence of rabbinic teaching concerning the two inclinations on Paul's soul-searching words about his sinful nature (Romans 3:9–12 and 7:15–20 [NRSV]).

What then? Are we any better off? No, not at all; for we have already charged that all, both Jews and Greeks, are under the power of sin, as it is written:

> There is no one who is righteous, not even one;
> there is no one who has understanding,
> there is no one who seeks God.
> All have turned aside, together they have become worthless;
> there is no one who shows kindness,
> there is not even one.

I do not understand my own actions. For I do not do what I want, but I do the very thing I hate. Now if I do what I do not want, I agree that the law is good. But in fact it is no longer I that do it, but sin that dwells within me. For I know that nothing good dwells within me, that is, in my flesh. I can will what is right, but I cannot do it. For I do not do the good I want, but the evil I do not want is what I do. Now if I do what I do not want, it is no longer I that do it, but sin that dwells within me.

---

distorted reading of the Bible). Liberal Christians tend to agree with non-Christian critics, who point out that Christian teaching about life after death has often been used to convince oppressed people that they should accept passively their horrible con-

COSMIC QUESTIONS:
HOW DID THE WORLD COME INTO BEING?

In the Beginning Was the Word

Christian teaching affirms that the Word of God, through whom God created the world, became flesh and dwelled on earth. The prologue to the Gospel of John is perhaps the primary New Testament text in establishing the basic Christian view of creation (John 1:1–14 [NRSV]).

In the beginning was the Word, and the Word was with God, and the Word was God. He was in the beginning with God. All things came into being through him, and without him not one thing came into being. What has come into being in him was life, and the life was the light of all people. The light shines in the darkness, and the darkness did not overcome it.

There was a man sent from God whose name was John. He came as a witness to testify to the light, so that all might believe through him. He himself was not the light, but he came to testify to the light. The true light, which enlightens everyone, was coming into the world.

He was in the world, and the world came into being through him; yet the world did not know him. He came to what was his own, and his own people did not accept him. But to all who received him, who believed in his name, he gave power to become children of God, who were born, not of blood or of the will of the flesh or of the will of man, but of God.

And the Word became flesh and lived among us, and we have seen his glory, the glory as of a father's only son, full of grace and truth.

dition on earth because they are going to a "better place." The goal of Christianity, they say, is not so much to prepare individuals for life after death, but to transform life in this world, so that people can experience the fullness of life God intends here and now. They point out that Jesus instructed his disciples to pray for the coming of the Kingdom of God on earth as it is in heaven. In their view, the teachings of Jesus have a this-worldly, rather than an other-worldly, emphasis, which contemporary Christianity needs to reaffirm. "Heaven" and "hell" are symbols of life in harmony with God's intentions or life apart from them, rather than actual states of existence after death, some modernist Christians have contended.

Means: Grace, Faith, and the Sacraments

A basic Christian teaching is that humans are powerless to save themselves from sin. Humans have hope for salvation only because of God's *grace*.

God sent his son into the world to deliver the world from sinfulness. According to traditional Christian teaching, Christ's death on the cross has atoned for human sinfulness, and his resurrection opens the way for humans to enter into eternal life. Anyone who responds to God's free gift of divine grace enters into a new, spiritual life in Christ, which is manifest in a new way of life characterized by love, joy, peace, and hope. The process of growing in this new spiritual life is called *sanctification*.

How is grace made available to humans? In traditional Catholic and Orthodox teaching, Christ established the church; through the church, humans have access to grace. In particular, the *sacraments* of the church are seen as one of the instruments of divine grace. In 1439 the Council of Florence declared that there are seven sacraments: baptism, confirmation into the church, penance (the rite of forgiveness), Eucharist (Holy Communion, the Lord's Supper), marriage, holy orders

The New Testament's account of the last supper of Jesus with his apostles is the basis of the Christian sacrament of Holy Communion. Leonardo da Vinci's painting of the Last Supper (1495–1498) is justifiably the most famous artistic interpretation of the meal.

Source: Alinari/Art Resource.

(ordination), and anointing of the sick (unction). These were reaffirmed by the Council of Trent.

The Protestant reformers challenged both the number of sacraments and the Catholic interpretation of their significance. The Reformers claimed that the only two sacraments instituted by Christ are baptism and the Lord's Supper. The Reformers also said that the sacraments are signs, not instruments of grace. God's grace is received by individuals when they respond in faith to what God has done in Christ, not through the mediation of the church, they argued. They re-emphasized the Apostle Paul's teaching of *justification by faith* to describe what enables humans to overcome sinfulness. The "radical reformers" of the Anabaptist movement rejected the notion of sacraments as related to divine grace altogether, preferring to call baptism and the Lord's Supper "ordinances" instead. Division over the nature and meaning of the Sacraments is one of the

most significant obstacles to the overcoming of the divisions among the Christian churches.

Christianity is still divided over the meaning of the sacrament of the Eucharist (also called Holy Communion or the Lord's Supper). The term "Eucharist" comes from the Greek term for "thanksgiving" and refers to the thanksgiving Jesus offered at his last meal with his disciples. The teaching of the Catholic and Orthodox churches is called *transubstantiation,* meaning (in its traditional formulation) that the eucharistic elements of bread and wine are converted into the substance of the body and blood of Christ. The Lutheran position is called *consubstantiation,* meaning that the substance of the body and blood are present *with* the elements. Other Protestants either follow the Reformed view that Christ is symbolically present when the church gathers for Communion, or believe that the meal is merely a memorial of the Last Supper. Some Catholic and Protestant theologians have begun to find common ground in the seemingly opposed traditional teachings.

As we have already noted, the issue of whether to baptize Christians at infancy or when they become themselves believers is a source of division. In addition, the meaning of baptism is also disputed. In Catholic tradition it is necessary for salvation.

Liberal Christian interpreters have tried to move the discussion of the "means of salvation" away from both the subjective individualism of Protestantism and the instrumentality of the church in traditional Catholicism. Participation in the work necessary to bring about the world of peace and justice God intends is seen as a major way Christians manifest that they have accepted God's grace. This work is the compassionate alleviation of suffering and political action to transform the sinful social structures and institutions.

For most Christians, the day set aside in the week for worship is Sunday, called the Lord's Day. It commemorates, they believe, the day when Jesus rose from the dead, and thus the new beginning for all humanity. In the Catholic and some Protestant traditions the worship on Sunday is called the mass (from the Latin *missa,* derived from *dimissio,* meaning "dismissal"). It is a celebration of the Eucharist, with a prescribed order that ends with the words "Go, the mass is ended." Until the Second Vatican Council, the Catholic mass was said by a priest in Latin. Since the Second Vatican Council, the mass has been said in the language of the people for whom it is being celebrated. Protestant worship puts less emphasis on the drama of the mass and more on the reading and interpretation of Scripture. In the Pentecostal tradition, worship is more spontaneous, with the outpouring of the Spirit manifest in speaking in tongues, healings, and prophesying. Some Protestant groups (notably the Seventh-Day Adventists—see Chapter Fourteen) observe the Jewish Sabbath as their day of worship, claiming that Jesus and the early Christians followed this practice.

Roman Catholics, Eastern Orthodox believers, and many Protestants observe a liturgical calendar, celebrating the various festivals of the Christian year with prescribed readings from Scripture and ritual observances. The two central cycles in this calendar

QUESTIONS OF MORALITY: WHAT ARE OUR OBLIGATIONS TO OTHERS?

Love of God and Love of Neighbor

According to the Gospels, Jesus reiterated the Jewish teaching that love of God and love of neighbor are at the heart of righteous living (Matthew 22:34–40 [NRSV]; parallel passages are found in Mark 12:28–34 and Luke 10:25–28).

When the Pharisees heard that he [Jesus] had silenced the Sadducees, they gathered together, and one of them, a lawyer, asked him a question to test him. "Teacher, which commandment in the law is the greatest?" He said to him, "'You shall love the Lord your God with all your heart, and with all your soul, and with all your mind.' This is the greatest and first commandment. And a second is like it: 'You shall love your neighbor as yourself.'   On these two commandments hang all the law and the prophets."

Excerpts from the New Revised Standard Version of the Bible. *Copyright © 1989 by the Division of Christian Education of the National Council of the Churches of Christ in the USA. Used with permission.*

revolve around the celebration of the resurrection and birth of Jesus. The New Testament sets the date of the resurrection in relation to the Jewish Passover. At first, the celebration was determined by the date of Passover. However, this came into conflict with the celebration of Sunday as the Day of Resurrection. The dispute was resolved by the Council of Nicea in 325 C.E., which set the annual date for the celebration of the feast of the resurrection as the Sunday following the first moon after the vernal equinox. Various reforms of the calendar have led to a different calculation of the dates in Western (Catholic and Protestant) and Eastern (Orthodox) traditions, so the Orthodox Easter falls from one to four weeks after the Western Easter. Over time the

QUESTIONS ABOUT THE SACRED: WHAT IS THE SACRED?

Jesus and the Father Are One

Christian teaching affirms the basic Jewish teaching of the one God, Creator of all that exists, but adds the concept that Jesus of Nazareth, the Messiah (Christ), is the Son of God, who is one with God. This be-came the basis for speculation that ultimately resulted in the Christian teaching of a divine and human na-ture of Christ and the doc-trine of the Trinity (John 14:8–11; Matthew 28:18–20 [NRSV]).

Philip said to him [Jesus], "Lord, show us the Father, and we will be satisfied." Jesus said to him, "Have I been with you all this time, Philip, and you still do not know me? Whoever has seen me has seen the Father. How can you say, 'Show us the Father'? Do you not believe that I am in the Father and the Father is in me? The words that I say to you I do not speak on my own; but the Father who dwells in me does his works. Believe me that I am in the Father and the Father is in me; but if you do not, then believe me because of the works themselves.

And Jesus came and said to [his disciples], "All authority in heaven and on earth has been given to me. Go therefore and make disciples of all nations, baptizing them in the name of the Father and of the Son and of the Holy Spirit, and teach-ing them to observe everything that I have commanded you. And remember, I am with you always, to the end of the age."

---

tradition developed of a forty-day preparation for the celebration of Easter, called Lent (from the "length-ening" of the days during spring). On the fortieth day after Easter the Ascension of Christ into heaven is celebrated, and on the fiftieth day Pentecost (com-memorating the descent of the Holy Spirit on the Apostles in Jerusalem), the traditional date of the founding of the Christian Church.

A second cycle of festivals developed around the indigenous celebrations of the winter solstice. The earliest was the feast now called Epiphany ("appear-ance") on January 6 (an Egyptian date for the sol-stice), commemorating both the birth and baptism of Jesus. In Rome the celebration of the birth of the Invincible Sun (December 25) became the date for the celebration of the birth of Jesus. The Roman Church adopted January 6 as a day of commemora-tion of the arrival of the wise men in Bethlehem. The four-week preparation before Christmas became known as Advent ("coming"), and celebrated not only a time of getting ready for celebration of the birth but anticipation of the Second Coming of Christ.

In addition to these cycles the Christian liturgi-cal calendar includes festivals commemorating saints, typically on the dates of their deaths. The process of "canonizing" saints developed to regulate the calen-dar. Many Protestant churches de-emphasized this aspect of the calendar. For example, All Saints' Day (following "All Saints' Eve" or Halloween), which itself had been an adaptation of an indigenous obser-vance, was transformed by many Protestant church-es into a commemoration of the Reformation (which had discouraged the veneration of saints). Finally, theological concepts (such as the Trinity) have become the basis for special days of observance.

More conservative Protestant churches have rejected some or all of the liturgical calendar of observances because, in their view, it lacks clear Scriptural authority. The reaction in Christianity in general, but particularly within Protestant circles, to a perceived overemphasis on rituals and doctrines is called *pietism*. A movement called pietism began in Germany in the seventeenth and eighteenth cen-turies in response to what was called Protestant scholasticism, which stressed right belief and worship. The pietistic movement taught that personal spirituality is the key to Christianity. Personal prayer and study of the Bible is, in the pietistic tradition, more important than participation in public worship or assent to doctrines. Pietism spread to England and the United States through the English Puritan movement and is evident among some of the Christians on the conservative side.

Sacred: One God, Three "Persons"

The traditional Christian understanding of the sacred is expressed in the doctrine of the *Trinity:* one God, three "persons." The New Testament does not directly express a trinitarian view of the nature of God, but it does sow the seeds for the doctrine by portraying Christ with the qualities of divinity and emphasizing the role of the Holy Spirit. In particular, the commandment of Jesus to baptize "in the name of the Father, Son, and Holy Spirit" (Matthew 28:19) and Paul's use of the threefold formula in a doxology (Second Corinthians 13:14) are the scriptural basis for the doctrine of the Trinity. It took until the fourth century, however, for the theory to be formulated in a final, orthodox version. The Council of Nicea in 325 C.E. stated that the Son is "of the same substance" as the Father. The Council of Constantinople upheld the divinity of Father, Son, and Holy Spirit, but said that within the Godhead the Father is "unbegotten," the Son is "begotten," and the Spirit proceeds from the Father. In a move that contributed to the growing hostility between the Eastern and Western churches, the Western church later added the word *filioque* ("and the Son"), expressing as dogma the teaching that the Holy Spirit proceeded from both the Father *and* the Son.

This formulation hardly resolved the arguments, however. Christian theologians have wrestled with ways to explain how Christians can maintain the unity of God (and avoid tritheism, the worship of "three gods"), yet preserve the humanity of Jesus (and avoid Docetism, the view that Christ only appeared to be human) and the relationship of the Spirit to the Father and Son (and avoid pantheism, the view that God is present in all reality). Christians consider the Trinity a mystery that defies

logical explanation or proof, but that when accepted in faith can be understood as revealing the truth about God.

Some contemporary Christian theologians have rethought the doctrine of God in light of the modern worldview and challenges to the traditional view posed by events such as the Holocaust. A movement known as "process theology" has, for example, sought to reinterpret the traditional notion that God is a power external to the world who causes events to happen in strict accordance with a pre-existent divine plan.

RESPONSES TO CONTEMPORARY ETHICAL ISSUES

The Ecological Crisis

In 1966 an interpreter of the history of science and technology in the medieval world, Lynn White, dropped the first bombshell in the modern debate over the role of Christianity in the ecological crisis. White argued that Western civilization had exploited nature to the extent that the quality, if not the very survival, of life was threatened. The reason, White said, was a dualistic ethical system that sharply discriminates between humans and nature. That ethic, he wrote, is based on the biblical tradition that informs Judaism and Christianity. Because of biblical texts, such as the first chapter of Genesis, these religions have assumed that humans are separate from, rather than part of, the natural community. Moreover, humans are told by God, according to Genesis, that nature exists solely for their benefit. White concluded that "Christianity is the most anthropocentric religion the world has seen" (White 1967: 1205). He argued that meaningful change in the treatment of nature would not occur in the West "until we reject the Christian axiom that nature has no reason for existence save to serve man" (1207). White also pointed to the Christian hostility toward animism as another basis for the attitude that nature is mere matter for humans to use as they choose, rather than living reality to be revered. He concluded that "since the roots of our [ecological] trouble are so largely religious, the remedy must also be essentially religious, whether we call it that or not. We must rethink and refeel our nature and destiny" (1207).

Other interpreters have highlighted other aspects of traditional Christianity's hostility toward nature. One is the attitude that the wilderness is a cursed land, which must be subdued and "humanized." Some assert that Christianity has also emphasized otherworldly concerns, which leaves the earth as merely a place of testing and preparation for heavenly existence (Nash 1989: 91). A consensus emerged among many interpreters that pointed to the following aspects of the Christian view of nature (Callicott and Ames 1989: 3–4):

1. God—the locus of the holy or sacred—transcends nature.

2. Nature is a profane artifact of a divine craftsman-like creator. The essence of the natural world is unformed matter.

3. Man exclusively is created in the image of God and is, thus, segregated, essentially, from the rest of nature.

4. Man is given dominion by God over nature.

5. God commands man to subdue nature and multiply himself.

6. The world is hierarchically organized: God over man, man over nature.

7. The image-of-God in man is the ground of man's intrinsic value. Since nonhuman natural entities lack the divine image, they are morally disenfranchised. They have, at best, instrumental value.

8. The rest of nature exists as a means to support human ends.

While White and others may be right in laying a degree of responsibility for the modern ecological crisis on the attitude of abuse and exploitation derived from the biblical admonition to "subdue the earth," White acknowledged that Christian teaching could also lead to environmental responsibility.

In modern times a number of Christians have sought to develop a Christian ecological ethic that could inspire environmental responsibility. Some Christian interpreters of the Bible have pointed out that in addition to the "domination of nature" theme of Genesis, there are other Scriptural injunctions and images that support Christian environmental responsibility. Richard Cartwright Austin summarizes positive biblical teachings on the environment in these words: "The Bible's ecological perspective is remarkable, for it brings nature within the community of covenant love and moral responsibility. The Lord tends a landscape which, though often injured by human oppression, yearns to flourish under just treatment and, beyond that, to respond compassionately to humans' needs" (Austin 1988: 18).

When we turn to the New Testament we find a number of ecologically related themes. The first is an important aspect of the message of Jesus, according to the first three gospels—the Kingdom of God. The Kingdom is God's new beginning, a time of the renewal of the covenant that extends to all of creation (Austin 1988: 115–126).

Another source of Christian ecology is the New Testament concept that Christ is present in the entire cosmos, with the implication that if Christ is divine, then all reality is sacred (Colossians 1:15–17).

The Apostle Paul envisioned all creation participating in God's redemption (Romans 8:21, NRSV): " ... The creation itself will be set free from its bondage to decay and will obtain the freedom of the glory of the children of God."

During the Middle Ages St. Francis of Assisi (1182–1226) addressed non-human beings as "brother" and "sister" and the earth as "mother." St. Francis "implicitly accorded to all creatures and natural processes a value entirely separate from human interest. Everything had a direct relationship with God" (Nash 1989: 93).

Early in the twentieth century, Albert Schweitzer (1875–1965) not only espoused a philosophy of life rooted in Christianity, which he called "reverence for life," he modeled it in his work in Africa and his theological writings. According to Schweitzer, "the great fault of all ethics hitherto has been that they believed themselves to have

Albert Schweitzer gave up a promising career in music, medicine, and theology in Germany to put into practice his philosophy of "reverence for life" as a medical missionary in Africa. His views helped inspire the modern Christian ecological movement.

to deal only with relations of man to man" (cited in Spring 1974: 1).

Catholic scientist and theologian Pierre Teilhard de Chardin (1881–1955), who lived in China for many years studying human origins, developed a vision of a process of cosmic redemption that has inspired a great deal of ecological reflection. The process philosophy of Alfred North Whitehead (1861–1947) has also influenced many theologians to take seriously the reality of God as a dynamic presence amidst, rather than separate from, nature. One "process theologian," Daniel Day Williams, wrote in 1972: "Our modern experience of nature leads many theologians to affirm more emphatically the divine immanence in the world. God ... is the creative spirit and the ultimate order that makes process possible and order intelligible" (cited in Barbour 1972: 58).

The first papal statement specifically on the environment came in 1971 when, in an apostolic letter (*Octogesima Adveniens*), Pope Paul VI warned that industrial society was causing "dramatic and unexpected changes in the natural order" (Jakowska 1986: 134). On the fifth World Environment Day in 1977, Paul VI said that the fulfillment of the Kingdom of God on earth includes an ecological dimension: "Nature will regain the lost balance and will participate in the liberation of all God's children" (Jakowska 1986: 135). Pope John Paul II continued the strong environmental statements of his predecessor. For example, on the eight-hundredth anniversary of the birth of St. Francis of Assisi in 1982, he warned that "we cannot continue as predators, destroying what was provided through God's wisdom; we must respect nature in order to preserve a suitable environment for future generations" (Jakowska 1986: 136).

By the 1980s many other church leaders had signed on as Christian environmentalists. For example, in 1988 Archbishop Robert Runcie of the Anglican Church made a statement that increasing numbers of Christians could endorse (cited in Vittachi 1989: 93).

> *At the present time, when we are beginning to appreciate the wholeness and interrelatedness of all that is in the cosmos, preoccupation with humanity can seem distinctly parochial. We need now to extend the area of the sacred and not to reduce it. . . . The nonhuman parts of creation would then be seen as having an intrinsic value of their own rather than being dependent for value on their relation to human beings.*

By the later 1980s evangelist Billy Graham had publicly expressed the view that "we Christians have a responsibility to take a lead in trying to take care of the Earth" (Stone 1989: 79).

However, a reaction against what has become known as "ecotheology" has sprung up among both Catholic and Protestant leaders who see it as an undermining of Christianity's central teachings (Nash 1989: 120). For example, in 1973 Bishop Robert Dwyer of Los Angeles warned that such views were "anti-human" and could lead to human self-extinction. And then-Protestant minister (now Catholic priest) Richard Neuhaus claimed that those who advocated the rights of nature were deflecting Christianity from its proper concern for the plights of humans. Nevertheless, by the 1990s most Christians were giving at least lip service to, and many were becoming much more involved in, the movement to preserve the environment and restore the balance of life.

Other Christians who support the goals of the environmental theologians question whether simply teaching people about the spiritual nature of creation and appealing to human goodness is sufficient. In the tradition of "Christian realists" such as American Reinhold Niebuhr (1892–1971), these critics point out that "our present environmental crisis is due not only to the wrongheaded thinking and mistaken feelings present in individuals ... but also to the perceived vested interests, the collective egoism, of groups, social, economic, political, and religious. For example, in his better moments an individual executive of an industry might be persuaded of the need to be concerned about the environment, and yet, because of his own ego interests and the vested interest of the firm, he might be unable to restrain this industry from polluting the environment" (Ayers 1986: 166). From this point of view, both moral persuasion and coercive action are necessary to meet environmental challenges.

Careful readers will have noticed that all of the Christian environmentalists mentioned in this section have been men. A number of feminists have taken exception not only to the anthropocentrism of traditional Christianity, but to its male-centeredness (androcentrism) as well. They have drawn a close connection between the recovery of a feminine spirituality and the emergence of a new spiritual ecology. Many feminists point out that it is understanding of the sacred as Mother that is the foundation for an appreciation of the presence of the sacred in nature. They blame the lack of an ecological sensitivity in traditional Christianity not so much on a fixation on human concerns, but on the dominance of men and male concerns (patriarchy). Both women and nature have been the victims of male subjugation, they argue, and both most be liberated from patriarchy. As one feminist, Ynestra King, put it, "ecology, feminism, and liberation for all of nature, including ourselves, are joined" (Nash 1989: 145). One contemporary Christian theologian

who has developed her theological position on the basis of insights derived from a feminist ecology is Sallie McFague (McFague 1993).

War

Within Christianity we find positions on the morality of war ranging from the pacifism of the Anabaptist "Peace Churches" (such as the Mennonites and Church of the Brethren) to the ideology of "holy war," which equates a particular war with the will of God.

There is no one, inclusive teaching on war in the New Testament. Some texts seem to support pacifism. In the Sermon on the Mount, Jesus teaches his disciples to practice non-resistance in the face of violence: "Do not resist an evildoer. But if anyone strikes you on the right cheek, turn the other also; ... " (Matthew 5:39). Some Christians extend this teaching to wars, arguing that Christians are not allowed to participate in acts of violence against any evildoers. However, others point out that Jesus seemed to accept the inevitability of war (Matthew 5:44). Yet Jesus apparently *did* rebuke those who tried to advance his cause through violence (John 18:36, Matthew 26:52–54).

The Apostle Paul instructed Christians to accept the authority of the state (Romans 13:1–7). Many Christians have argued that this passage means that Christians must participate in wars authorized by the legal authority in the nations in which they live.

In the early centuries of the Christian Church most believers refused to serve in the Roman army, and Christian theologians such as Origen warned Christians not to "take up the sword." However, when Christianity became the official religion of the Roman Empire, Christian leaders found a basis to justify the participation of Christians in war.

The fifth-century theologian Augustine developed the theory of "just war," which has dominated Christian teaching on war ever since. Augustine said that to be just a war must be authorized by legitimate rulers, fought to restore peace and to obtain justice, and motivated by Christian love. For Augustine no one should participate in war who has not overcome hate in his own heart. Wars should be conducted without unnecessary violence, indiscriminate killing, endangering innocents, or looting.

In the eleventh century, in response to an appeal from the Eastern emperor at Constantinople, Pope Urban II urged Christians to undertake a crusade to liberate the Holy Land from "pagan" control. This began a process in the church that made war sacred, and viewed the enemy as a demonic force. The enemies (in this case Muslims) were portrayed in the imagery of the Book of Revelation as the forces of the Antichrist. In other cases the "infidels" have been Native Americans in the nineteenth century, the North Vietnamese and Viet Cong during the Vietnam War of the 1960s and '70s, or Saddam Hussein and the Iraqis during the Persian Gulf War of the early 1990s. Some Christians have expressed the view that God is on the side of "Christian nations" against "infidels." They point to the various holy wars of the biblical tradition to support their claim that God fights on the side of "his people."

Christians took positions of leadership in revolutionary wars such as the American War of Independence, but the pacifist movement gained strength as warfare became ever more bloody and the ideology of "total war" became the accepted military doctrine. After the slaughters of World War I, the "war to end all wars," a mood of pacifism swept through Christian churches in Europe and the United States. Unfortunately, the world again erupted in violence and the cycle did not end until atomic bombs had been dropped by the United States on Japanese civilians, thousands of non-combatants had been killed in the devastating fire-bombing of British and German cities, and millions of Jews and others had been slaughtered in German death camps. Ironically, nuclear weapons accomplished what politics could not, by creating a situation in which all-out conflict was too terrible to be allowed to happen. The Cold War began after World War II; the doctrine of "mutually assured destruction" (MAD) kept an uneasy truce between the superpowers, the Soviet Union and the United States, while a series of proxy wars and localized conflicts (such as the Vietnam War) continued. Many Christians became active in the nuclear disarmament movement and in opposition to other

conflicts, but the majority of Christians have continued to affirm the teaching of "just war." Other Christians used the tactics of non-violent resistance in the American civil rights movement. Leaders such as the Rev. Dr. Martin Luther King, Jr., drew on Mahatma Gandhi's teachings and blended them with the New Testament admonitions about peaceful methods of bringing about social change.

Today, then, Christians take one of four basic positions on war (Clouse 1981): *non-resistance,* with a willingness to serve in non-combatant roles such as the medical corps; *pacifism,* in which Christians refuse to cooperate in any way with the state's prosecution of wars, including for some the paying of taxes used to support the military; *just war,* following the historical criteria established by Augustine and affirmed by many Christian teachers since; and *crusade or preventive war,* in which the utter depravity of the enemy is thought to justify the prosecution of war by Christians in the most violent way possible.

The Christian attitude toward war is complicated by the teaching found in the Bible (especially the apocalyptic books of Daniel and Revelation) about a great conflict between God and Satan at the end of history. Those Christians who believe that the apocalyptic passages in the Bible should be interpreted literally believe that Armaggedon is inevitable, and associate particular modern nations with the forces of goodness and evil. In Chapter Fourteen, in our discussion of the Branch Davidians, we will examine one such Christian apocalyptic group. Other Christians, who reject a literalist view of Scripture, contend that the Bible's apocalyptic imagery is symbolic and should not be used to try to predict the future. They say that Christians should be motivated by the apocalyptic books to work cooperatively to achieve the divine plan of bringing the peaceful and just Kingdom of God to earth.

Capital Punishment

Surveys indicate that most Christians in the United States support capital punishment. When asked to draw upon their religious tradition to defend their viewpoint, most name the Old Testament principle of "an eye for an eye" and the New Testament teaching that Christians should support the efforts of the legitimate civil authority to maintain order.

Christian opponents of the death penalty most often cite the teaching of Jesus concerning forgiveness and his rejection of the law of retribution. In the Sermon on the Mount, for example, Jesus said, "You have heard that it was said, 'An eye for an eye and a tooth for a tooth.' But I say to you, Do not resist an evildoer. But if anyone strikes you on the right cheek, turn the other also; ..." (Matthew 5:38–39). Supporters counter by pointing out that this applies to the Kingdom of God, which has not yet fully arrived. In the meantime, the laws of the state must remain in force. Christian critics of the death penalty also draw on the Apostle Paul's statement on the need to leave vengeance to the Lord (Romans 12:17–21). Supporters point out that this verse is followed by Paul's admonition for Christians to accept the authority of the state.

Opponents also cite Jesus's opposition to capital punishment in a specific case when he told those who were about to stone a woman caught in adultery, "Let anyone among you who is without sin be the first to throw a stone at her" (John 8:7). Finally, they claim that the sacrifice of Jesus on the cross removes the necessity of capital punishment. "Christ died that others may live. By trading places with the guilty and the enemy, by dying in the place of the murderer Barabbas, Christ closed off the Old Testament reason for the death penalty" (Zehr: 21).

Since the reinstitution of the death penalty in the United States, a number of Protestant churches have expressed opposition. A statement of the Christian Reformed Church in North America adopted in 1981 is typical (National Coalition 1988):

> *Given that human life is sacred, that the magistrate is fallible, that time for repentance is desirable, and that imprisonment will normally satisfy the demand for justice, we conclude that, though judicial executions may sometimes be divinely sanctioned and be in society's best interests, it is not desirable that capital punishment be routinely inflicted upon persons guilty of murder in the first degree. Only under exceptional circumstances should the state resort to capital punishment.*

In 1980 the U.S. Roman Catholic bishops issued a statement on capital punishment that expressed opposition on the same grounds the bishops cite in opposing abortion; namely, that all life, from conception onward, is sacred and must be protected (National Coalition 1988):

> *... Abolition of capital punishment is ... a manifestation of our belief in the unique worth and dignity of each person from the moment of conception, a creature made in the image and likeness of God. It is particularly important in the context of our times that this belief be affirmed with regard to those who have failed or whose lives have been distorted by suffering and hatred, even in the case of those who by their actions have failed to respect the dignity and rights of others. ... We do not wish to equate the situation of criminals convicted of capital crimes with the condition of the innocent unborn or of the defenseless aged or infirm, but we do believe that the defense of life is strengthened by eliminating exercise of a judicial authorization to take human life.*

Abortion

Roman Catholic The present teaching of the Roman Catholic Church on abortion is quite clear. Abortion is murder, even if it is carried out with the best of intention.

The teaching of the Church is that life begins at conception, and no artificial means of birth control may be used to interrupt the natural development of life. According to Church teaching, to do so would be for humans to substitute their judgment for God's will. Thus, the Catholic Church opposes artificial methods of birth control as well as abortion.

Historians point out that the teaching of the Church has not always been so clear-cut on abortion. Until 1588 Catholic theologians and popes condoned abortion up to eighty days for a female fetus and up to forty days for a male. In 1588 Pope Sixtus V outlawed all abortions; however, in 1591 Pope Gregory XIV overruled his predecessor's decree and allowed abortions up to forty days for both male and female fetuses. "That is how the matter stood till 1869 when Pius IX forbade all abortions at any time ..." (Gregory 1983:36).

Opposition to abortion was reaffirmed by the Second Vatican Council and a subsequent series of papal pronouncements and other Church statements, including the 1974 Declaration on Procured Abortion. In the Church's view, abortion is an attack on the principle of the "sanctity of life," which is essential to the Christian faith.

Mother Teresa, famous for her care of the dying in Calcutta, India, and her strong stand for the sanctity of life in all circumstances, is probably the most effective Catholic spokesperson for the unborn. In 1989, she told a forum of global spiritual leaders, " ... Every second so many little ones are being aborted. ... We in our mission are fighting abortion by adoption. We see now those little ones have brought so much joy into homes where the family cannot have a child. ... Natural family planning is something very beautiful, very simple. We are teaching it to our leper families, to our beggars, to our street people. ... " (cited in Vittachi 1989: 64–65).

Although the church hierarchy strongly opposes abortion, polls indicate that most Catholics in the United States support a woman's right to choose. They find support among Catholic leaders who think that the church's teaching does not accurately reflect Catholic tradition. These "pro-choice" Catholics point out that the theologian whose views most shaped Catholic doctrine, Thomas Aquinas, believed that "the embryo is certainly not a human being during the early stages of pregnancy, and that, consequently, it is not immoral to terminate pregnancy during this time, provided there are serious reasons for such an intervention" (Father Joseph F. Doncell, cited in Gregory 1983: 33).

Another Catholic "pro-choice" leader, Father Joseph O'Rourke, has written, "If the church was to stand sincerely against abortion, it would re-orient its social and relief services to stop the 100 spontaneous abortions (miscarriages) for every 200 live births in the Third World, attacking the malnutrition, poverty and medical ignorance that is the cause of this hidden plague, rather than lobbying against the rights of American women" (Gregory 1983: 34).

Sister Donna Quinn, former president of the National Coalition of American Nuns, speaks for a number of Catholic women in the United States when she says, "We are tired as women in society and in the church to hear these decisions being made by men [politicians and bishops] and not from the faithful and not coming from us as a group. You just can't make a law that forces consensus on a moral conscience issue" (Gregory 1983: 34). Despite such strong American voices questioning the church's teaching on abortion, Pope John Paul II has reaffirmed the church's ban and shows no signs of reconsidering it.

Protestant   Protestant Christians have *no* consensus on the question of abortion. All positions, ranging from the most extreme "pro-life" to the most radical "pro-choice," may be found in Protestant circles. We will first summarize some of the arguments made by Protestant opponents of abortion, then look at the points made by supporters of abortion rights.

Protestants claim that the principal, if not sole, source of authority on matters of faith and practice is the Bible. Therefore, the debate among Protestants about what the Bible has to say about abortion is important.

The passages from the Tanak cited in our discussion of Jewish attitudes toward abortion figure in the Protestant discussion. "Pro-life" Protestants add a feature in the interpretation of Exodus 21:22–25. The Greek translation says that a death penalty is to be imposed on the perpetrator if the fetus is "perfectly formed." This translation suggests that when fully formed, the fetus is a human being, and the forced miscarriage is murder (Gregory 1977: 18, 306).

On the commandment not to kill, one "pro-life" Protestant has written, "The command 'You shall not kill' cannot simply be pushed aside because of the woman's right to choose, the child's right to be wanted and healthy, or because of the possible effects of unwanted pregnancies. All the socioeconomic factors, including the population issue advanced to justify abortion, do not invalidate the basic principle of life being inherently good" (Overduin 1981: 372–73).

There is no explicit reference to abortion in the New Testament, but that has not stopped Christians on both sides of the abortion argument from appealing to the New Testament for support. Abortion opponents, for example, cite Luke 1:44, in which Elizabeth, the mother of John the Baptist, says "...The child in my womb leaped for joy." "Pro-life" advocates make the point that in the New Testament there is no distinction between a child in the womb and a child after birth (Brown 1977: 120). The various passages that speak like the Old Testament of humanity made in the image of God (e.g., Ephesians 4:24) are taken as evidence that even before birth humans have a unique worth and value that must be protected. The account of the birth of Jesus (e.g., Matthew 1:20–21) shows, according to this perspective, that conception rather than birth marks the beginning of a person's life and that God has a plan for persons before they are born. Protestant opponents of abortion often argue that the special concern Jesus showed for the weak and powerless naturally extends to the unborn, and is made even stronger by the love Jesus showed for children.

The Protestant "pro-life" community draws on the statements of the early "Church fathers," who spoke out forcefully against abortion. The early second-century Christian documents Didache and the Epistle of Barnabas say explicitly, "Thou shalt not murder a child by abortion." The late second-century church leader Athenagoras wrote, "The fetus in the womb is ... an object of God's care." In the fourth century, Basil said, "Those ... who give drugs causing abortions are [deliberate murderers] themselves, as well as those receiving the poison which kills the fetus" (cited in a pamphlet "Historical Christian Perspectives," prepared by Presbyterians Pro-Life).

Protestant opponents of abortion also cite the leaders of the Protestant Reformation in support of their position. John Calvin, for example, wrote, "... The fetus, though enclosed in the womb of its mother, is already a human being, and it is almost a monstrous crime to rob it of the life which it has not yet begun to enjoy" (Calvin 1950: 3: 41, 42).

Major twentieth-century Protestant theologians have also spoken strongly against abortion, according to the "pro-life" community. For example, Dietrich Bonhoeffer, a German Lutheran pastor martyred during World War II because of his opposition to the policies of Adolf Hitler, wrote, "The simple fact is that God intended to create a human being and that this human being has been deliberately deprived of his life. And that is nothing but murder" (cited in Brown 1977: 127, 128).

The basis for Protestant support for abortion rights can be summarized in this statement: "[Women] are recognized as creative, loved and loving human beings who have achieved full per-

sonhood. In the sight of most Protestant denominations, to equate personhood with an unborn fetus is to dehumanize a woman, to consider her a mere 'thing' through which the fetus is passing. To deny this essential tenet of our beliefs—the concept of personhood—would constitute a gross violation of our Christian faith...." (Theressa Hoover, United Methodist Church; cited in Gregory 1983: 40–41).

In response to the "pro-life" argument that the Bible regards the fetus as a person, "pro-choice" interpreters of the Bible point to several biblical texts that support the view that personhood does not begin before birth. One is Genesis 2:7: "then the LORD God formed man from the dust of the ground, and breathed into his nostrils the breath of life; and the man became a living being." Also cited are Genesis 1:26–28, with the view taken that "image of God" is a spiritual rather than physical understanding of human nature, and Genesis 3:22. "The Biblical portrait of person, therefore, is that of a complex many-sided creature with god-like abilities and the moral responsibility to make choices. The fetus hardly meets those characteristics. ... The one who unquestionably fits this portrayal is the woman. ... The abortion decision focuses on the personhood of the woman, who in turn considers the potential personhood of the fetus in terms of the multiple dimensions of her own history and the future" (Simmons: 7, 8).

"Pro-choice" interpreters claim that the silence of the Bible on elective abortions could mean either that it did not occur to Hebrews or Christians to terminate problem pregnancies or that "abortion was a private, personal and religious matter, not subject to civil regulation" (Simmons: 23). Because the Bible gives more status to women than surrounding cultures (some of which outlawed abortion) and shows respect for women as equal bearers of the divine image, the Bible may, they claim, be understood as supportive of the freedom of women to choose abortion.

Statements in support of a woman's right to choose an abortion have been made since the 1970s by the American Baptist Churches, U.S.A.; the United Methodist Church; the Lutheran Church in America; the United Church of Christ; the Presbyterian Church (U.S.A.); the Christian Church (Disciples of Christ); the Church of the Brethren; the Moravian Church in America; the

Protestant Episcopal Church; and the Reformed Church in America.

Ethicist John M. Swomley expressed the viewpoint of many Protestant advocates of the "pro-choice" position when he wrote, ". . . Protestants generally do not believe that a human person is present at conception. The soul is not infused. Instead, the fetus is a *potential* person. . . . The mere fact of conception does not mean that God wills a childbirth. The occurrence of miscarriage and stillbirths suggests that every conception is not intended to result in the birth of a baby" (Gregory 1983: 56–57).

For abortion-rights advocates the issue is at its heart one of religious liberty. When "personhood" begins is a religious issue, they argue, and any law that imposes one understanding of this complex issue on all people is a violation of the freedom of religion of those who do not agree.

Some Christians have sought to move beyond the rhetoric of the "pro-life" and "pro-choice" camps to search for common ground. For example, these advocates of a "middle way" focus on providing better access to prenatal care for women who choose to bring a child to term. They also work to provide care for children to increase their opportunities to grow into healthy adults. More and better information on birth control needs to be made available, they agree. If steps such as these were taken, perhaps the "abortion epidemic" would be curbed (as abortion opponents desire), without imposing too many restrictions on women's access to legal, safe abortions (as supporters of abortion rights want to ensure).

Euthanasia

Roman Catholic The teaching of the Roman Catholic Church on euthanasia is most clearly expressed in the Vatican's 1980 Declaration on Euthanasia, approved by Pope John Paul II (fully cited in Larue 1975: 35–43 and DuBose 1991: 58–59). The Declaration begins by recalling the Second Vatican Council's affirmation of the "right to life" and its condemnation of crimes against life "such as any type of murder, genocide, abortion, euthanasia, or willful suicide." Its central assertion is that (cited in Larue 1985: 38):

. . . No one can in any way permit the killing of an innocent human being, whether a foetus or an embryo, an infant or an adult, an old person, or one suffering from an incurable disease, or a person who is dying. Furthermore, no one is permitted to ask for this act of killing, either for himself or herself or for another person entrusted to his or her care, nor can he or she give consent to it, either explicitly or implicitly. Nor can any authority legitimately recommend or permit such an action. For it is a question of the violation of the divine law, an offence against the dignity of the human person, a crime against life, and an attack on humanity.

However, the Declaration does allow for passive euthanasia when "death is imminent." Then "it is permitted in conscience to take the decision to refuse forms of treatment that would only secure a precarious and burdensome prolongation of life, so long as the normal care due to the sick person in similar cases is not interrupted" (Larue 1985: 42).

The American Catholic bishops affirmed a similar position when, in a 1976 Pastoral Letter, they wrote, " ... It is a grave moral evil deliberately to kill persons who are terminally ill or deeply impaired. Such killing is incompatible with respect for human dignity and reverence for the sacredness of life. Something different is involved, however, when the question is whether hopelessly ill and painfully afflicted people must be kept alive at all costs and with the use of every available medical technique. Some seem to make no distinction be-tween respecting the dying process and engaging in direct killing of the innocent. Morally there is all the difference in the world. While euthanasia or direct killing is gravely wrong, it does not follow that there is an obligation to prolong the life of a dying person by extraordinary means" (cited in Horan and Mall 1977: 288–89).

Protestant In its deliberations on euthanasia, the Lutheran Church (Missouri Synod) has raised the issue of the appropriateness of such distinctions as "passive" and "active," suggesting that they only serve to confuse. A 1979 document of this denomination stipulates that euthanasia should be understood to mean "direct intervention, the killing of a human being, with or without his knowledge or consent" (Larue 1985: 66). It is therefore, according to this Protestant denomination, "contrary to

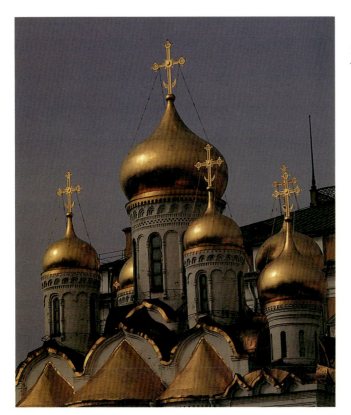

The distinctive gilded domes of the Russian Orthodox Annunciation Cathedral in the Kremlin, Moscow.

A fisherman on the Sea of Galilee. According to the New Testament of gospels, some of the first followers of Jesus of Nazareth were Galilean fisherman.

God's Word and will and cannot be condoned or justified;..." (Larue, 1985: 64).

Other Protestant churches may or may not use the phrase "passive euthanasia," but the ethical stance is virtually the same: Active euthanasia is not acceptable, but the withholding or withdrawing of treatment may be permissible. A United Methodist statement, adopted in 1980, is typical (Larue 1985: 87):

> *We applaud medical science for efforts to prevent disease and illness and for advances in treatment that extend the meaningful life of human beings. At the same time, in the varying stages of death and life that advances in medical science have occasioned, we recognize the agonizing personal and moral decisions faced by the dying, their physicians, their families, and their friends. Therefore, we assert the right of every person to die in dignity, with loving personal care and without efforts to prolong terminal illnesses merely because the technology is available so to do.*

Some Protestant Christian ethicists have pointed out the ambiguity in the position that extraordinary means of treatment may be withheld from a dying patient. What is ordinary treatment in one circumstance (for example, antibiotics to treat bronchitis in a healthy person) may be extraordinary in another (antibiotics used to treat pneumonia in a dying person). This has led some Christians to advocate what they call "situational" or "contextual" ethics, in which the basic Christian principle (love God and your neighbor as yourself) is applied, taking into account the unique dynamics of the particular situation. This opens the door for deciding that in some cases "active euthanasia" may be the moral decision for a Christian.

In part in reaction to "situational" positions, some Protestant bodies have spoken out firmly against *any* form of active euthanasia. In 1988 the Southern Baptist Convention stated that "efforts shall be undertaken ... to oppose infanticide and active euthanasia, including efforts to discourage any designation of food and/or water as 'extraordinary' medical care for some patients" (Hamel and DuBose 1991: 63–64). However, other Protestant groups, such as the United Church of Christ, have begun to explore whether there should not be a greater concern for the rights of individuals to decide to end their lives. A 1990 statement of the Rocky Mountain Conference of this denomination affirms "the right of persons under hopeless and irreversible conditions to terminate their lives and emphasize[s] that Christian understanding and compassion are appropriate with regard to suicide and euthanasia" (Hamel and DuBose 1991: 90).

Economic Justice

In this section we will survey a range of responses within modern Christianity to the reality of economic injustice in our world, in the context of the history of Christian responses to this issue.

On the one hand, some Christians indict the capitalist system as a manifestation of sinful selfishness and call for an economic transformation based on biblical principles. For example, one evangelical Protestant Christian, Ronald Sider, has written: (Sider 1977: 88, 114):

> *God requires radically transformed economic relationships among his people. Sin has alienated us from God and from each other. The result has been personal selfishness, structural injustice and economic oppression. Among the people of God, however, the power of sin is broken. The new community of the redeemed begins to display an entirely new set of personal, social and economic relationships.*
>
> *From the perspective of biblical revelation, property owners are not free to seek their own profit without regard for the needs of the neighbor. Such an outlook derives from the secular laissez-faire economics of the deist Adam Smith, not from Scripture.*

This negative reference to the leading theorist of modern capitalism, Adam Smith, would be challenged, however, by other modern Christians, who believe that Christianity not only is compatible with *laissez-faire* capitalism, but is best supported in such an economic system because of its commitment to individual liberty (Preston 1993: 77–80). Some preliminary reflection on the relationship between what the reader understands to be Christian teaching and capitalism would be a good idea at this point.

Protestant Christian interpreters such as Sider have based their contention that Christians should seek economic relationships ordered to ensure that the needs of the poor are addressed on an analysis of the teachings of the Bible.

References to the poor are found on almost every page of the New Testament. Here is a representative selection of passages cited to argue that Christians must place a high priority on responding to the material needs of the poor: Matthew 25: 31–46; Mark 10:21 and parallels in Matthew and Luke; Luke 1:46–53, 4:16–21 [cf. Matthew 11:4–6], 6:20, 6:24, 10:29–37, 12:13–21, 14:12–24, 19:1–10; John 12:6, 13:29; Acts 2:44–45, 4:32; 1st Corinthians 11:17–22; 2nd Corinthians 8:9, 8:13–15; 2nd Thessalonians 3:10; James 1:27, 2:2–4, 5:3–5.

Despite the seemingly unequivocal and extensive New Testament evidence that in its origins Christianity was especially concerned with the poor and suspicious of unwarranted and excessive wealth, many interpreters over the years have tried to suggest that several key passages show that Christians should not try actively to challenge the underlying causes of poverty.

The most famous such passage is a statement that appears in the gospels of Mark (14:7), Matthew (26:11), and John (12:8). Interestingly, the statement does *not* appear in a similar story in Luke's gospel (7:36–50). It is a comment of Jesus's (quoting Deuteronomy 15:11), in response to the disciples' complaint that the expensive oil a woman was using to anoint him could be sold and the money given to the poor: "... You always have the poor with you, and you can show kindness to them whenever you wish; but you will not always have me" (Mark 14:7, NRSV). For countless Christians this has been understood as endorsement of a permanent social stratification in which some are rich and others poor. They extrapolate that Christians should not feel compelled to work to liberate the poor and oppressed and transform the economic and social order, because poverty is an inevitable fact of life. However, biblical scholars have called this interpretation into question by pointing out that the statement is speaking to the particular circumstance of the time, not to the inevitable situation for all times. "The statement," comments New Testament scholar Vincent Taylor, "is not intended to assert that poverty is a permanent social factor" (cited in Miranda 1982: 59).

In the period after the writing of the New Testament, other Christian teachers dealt with the distribution of wealth. For example, St. Ambrose wrote, "What you give to the poor you do not take from your own property; rather you give back to him what is already his. It is common property, given for the use of all, which you claim for yourself. The earth was given to all, not only to the rich" (cited in Ferré and Mataragnon 1985: 114).

In the Constantinian era the care of the poor became a comprehensive enterprise, as Christianity became the dominant religion. The Christian Church felt an obligation to help the whole of society. During the Middle Ages the church was embroiled in a dispute among religious orders on the question of Christ's attitude toward wealth, and consequently the issue of how much of the world's goods religious people should keep for themselves instead of giving to the poor.

As the church emerged from the Middle Ages, and the Protestant Reformation dawned, the Reformers took an active interest in the needs of the poor. Martin Luther, for example, rejected an individualistic approach to solving poverty and demanded that "Each city should start caring for the poor by first abolishing begging" (cited in Schwarz 1985: 181). He also said that "If you preach the Gospel in all aspects with the exception of the issues which deal specifically with your time you are not preaching the Gospel at all" (Sider 1977: 57).

The British reformer and founder of Methodism, John Wesley, said that any Christian who takes for himself anything more than the "plain necessaries of life, lives in an open, habitual denial of the Lord." He has "gained riches and hell-fire!" Wesley lived what he preached. He earned £1,400 a year on the sale of his books, spent about £30 on himself and gave the rest away. "If I leave behind me 10 pounds," he said, "you and all mankind bear witness against me that I lived and died a thief and a robber" (Sider 1977: 172–73).

As we have already mentioned, Max Weber advanced an argument accepted by many today that Protestantism (especially in its Calvinist form) provided the motivation for the development of capitalism through emphasizing (1) work as a way of life, (2) worldly asceticism, and (3) rationalism (see Weber and Tawney).

Let us move now to the contemporary situation in Christianity and explore the responses to the gap between the rich and the poor. The Roman Catholic Church has not avoided wrestling with this dilemma. In a series of encyclicals (see Levi 1989), beginning a century ago, all modern popes have responded.

For example, in *Laborem exercens* (1981) and *Sollicitudo rei socialis* (1988), Pope John Paul II summarized the evils of the modern world and the misery brought upon people. He said there must be an "effective search for appropriate transformation of the structure of economic life" in a Christian spirit. He further claimed that the abolition of poverty has taken on a world dimension requiring the transformation of unjust structures to which the masses have no access. He said that employers and labor unions should work together for the common good. Also in *Sollicitudo* he asserted that "The motivating concern for the poor ... must be translated at all levels into concrete actions, until it decisively attains a series of necessary reforms" (Levi 1989: 45).

In addition to the official teaching of the Catholic Church, as exemplified in the encyclicals, a movement has emerged in Catholicism in recent decades that takes a more activist approach to the problem of poverty. Called "liberation theology," this movement has had a profound effect not only on Roman Catholicism but on virtually all Christian churches.

According to liberation theology, the God of Christian revelation is a God of the oppressed. This means both that God shares in the suffering of the poor and also that God is involved in their struggle to be liberated. The liberation is not merely spiritual; it is also liberation of human lives from economic inequality and political repression.

By 1980 church teaching (guided by Pope John Paul II) and most liberation theologians had agreed that at the root of the problem of excessive wealth amidst grinding poverty was a global capitalism in which "internal colonialists" cooperated with external capitalists (multinationals and developed world organizations such as the International Monetary Fund) to repress the poor. As Protestant liberation theologian José Miguez Bonino put it, "We are simply facing the normal and unavoidable consequences of the basic principles of capitalist production as they work themselves out in our global, technological time. The concentration of economic power, the search for higher profits, the efforts to obtain cheaper labor and to avoid higher costs are of the very essence of that system" (Bonino 1975: 29). However, some on the radical side of the liberation theology movement took exception to the "catch phrase" that had emerged from several bishops' conferences "preferential option for the poor." As one said, "The struggle for a society in which there will be no rich or poor is not a 'preferential option for the poor,' It is not an option, it is an obligation" (Miranda 1982: 69).

Christian critics of liberation theology counter by charging that "the blanket indictment the liberationists ascribe to capitalism is part of the universal human condition and fails to recognize that *every* social system is afflicted with the same vices.... While poverty and underemployment are still with us and probably always will be, it is nevertheless true that capitalism has produced the greatest and most widely distributed material well-being of any economic system" (Williamson 1979: 11).

Influenced by the willingness of the pope and their counterparts in the developing world to address boldly the economic situation, the U.S. Catholic bishops issued a pastoral letter in 1986 entitled "Economic Justice for All." In this document the bishops defended American capitalism's commitment to creativity and invention, enterprise, economic growth, and job creation. However, they strongly attacked the neglect of the poor at home and abroad and the growing disparity of wealth in the United States, and blamed the American capitalist system. They called for strong government action through progressive taxation of income, changed spending priorities, and heightened foreign aid to developing countries to address this situation.

The growing concern of many American Catholic lay leaders at the bishops' endorsement of what they viewed as an impractical and flawed economic and political agenda was expressed in responses such as a pamphlet entitled "Liberty and Justice for All." It was produced by the Lay Commission on Catholic Social Teaching and the U.S. Economy, headed by former Treasury Secretary William E. Simon and Catholic ethicist Michael Novak. The bishops, these Catholic lay leaders said, failed to understand the unique "American experiment in economics," which holds the promise of improving the living standards for poor people around the world; this experiment should not be attacked, it should be exported.

Other modern Christian analysts of economics react against both global capitalism and communism and suggest a truly new economic order that emphasizes sustainability and equitable distribution on a regional basis: " ... Whereas we have pursued universal affluence chiefly by increasing the total quantity of goods and services available, and we have concerned ourselves only secondarily about their distribution, the goal of living within renewable resources forces a reversal. Since global growth will be limited, and since in many areas there must be substantial reduction of production, appropriate distribution of goods to all becomes the primary concern" (Cobb 1986: 173).

For many Christians, the most important issue is what can be done practically. For Ronald Sider, the mandate is clear for American Christians. "We Christians need," he writes, "to make some dramatic, concrete moves to escape the materialism that seeps into our minds via the diabolically clever and incessant radio and TV commercials. We have been brainwashed to believe that bigger houses, more prosperous businesses and more luxurious gadgets are worthy goals in life. As a result, we are caught in an absurd, materialistic spiral. The more we make, the more we think we need in order to live decently and respectably. Somehow we have to break this cycle because it makes us sin against our needy brothers and sisters and, therefore, against our Lord" (Sider 1977: 175).

However, is it enough for individuals and churches to change their behavior and model a lifestyle of sharing? Do we not need to transform the social structures that perpetuate the problem of maldistribution of wealth? On the other end of the Christian spectrum, conservatives ask whether the only viable solution is for individuals to take more responsibility for their own economic well-being, pointing out that attempts at interfering with market forces only lead to shared misery (as the experience of modern socialist states has demonstrated). As you reflect on the range of Christian responses to questions of economic justice, what role, if any,

do you think Christian churches and individuals should play in this area?

Gender Roles and the Status of Women

In the history of Christianity, from its origins until the present, there has been tension between two perspectives, "one affirming the equivalence of man and woman as human persons and the other defining women as subordinate to men" (Radford Ruether 1987: 208). In this section we will trace this tension through the history of Christianity, and try to listen to some of the current voices of women reflecting on this issue.

Within the New Testament many Christian interpreters have noted an ambiguity with regard to the role of women. The Apostle Paul acknowledged spiritual equality when he wrote, "In Christ there is neither male nor female" (Galatians 3:28). However, Paul also seemed to endorse the subordination of women in the home and Christian community. Women were, for example, not to speak in worship, according to the Apostle (First Corinthians 14:34–36).

In the Gospels women are not among the formal inner circle or apostles of Jesus, but play important roles among the disciples, including being the first to witness the resurrection of Jesus, the defining moment in Christian history. In a recent study the attitude of Jesus toward women, as portrayed in the Gospels, is summarized in this way (Witherington 1984: 127):

> ... Jesus broke with both biblical and rabbinic traditions that restricted women's roles in religious practices, and ... rejected attempts to devalue the worth of a woman, or her word of witness. Thus, the community of Jesus, both before and after Easter, granted women together with men (not segregated from men as in some pagan cults) an equal right to participate fully in the family of faith. This was a right that women did not have in contemporary Judaism or in many pagan cults.

In the rest of the New Testament women are described in a number of leadership roles (e.g., Acts 18:14–26; Romans 16:6, 12; Philippians 4:2–3), even as stipulations are given about their subordinate status (e.g., Colossians 3:18–4:1, First Timothy 2:11–15).

In recent decades growing numbers of women have been ordained as ministers in many Protestant churches. Here a Native American woman celebrates the sacrament of communion.

There is considerable evidence to support the view, advanced by feminist scholar Elisabeth Schüssler-Fiorenza, that the earliest Christian community was "radically egalitarian" in its treatment of men and women (see Schüssler-Fiorenza 1983). However, with the growing influence of Hellenistic (Greek) ideas on Christianity, the situation changed. Most influential was the incorporation of the dualistic conception of body and soul borrowed from Greek culture. Women were thought to be more "carnal" and thus, like other things of the body, should be kept subordinate. Church "fathers" such as Tertullian, Chrysostom, Jerome, and Augustine all joined in warning of the dangers posed by women to the virtue of men. The notion that women are chattel was reintroduced and accepted as the Christian norm.

Over time the ideal spiritual woman came to be the virgin, who resisted bodily desires. That idealization of virginity had a profound effect, many believe, on the development of the relations between men and women in Western culture in general. The ideal Virgin, of course, was Mary, who became venerated as the Mother of God, who could intercede for sinners with her son.

The growth of monastic movements for women in the Middle Ages did, it must be noted, provide a refuge for women from dominance by men, since many convents were led by women and provided women creative outlets denied to them in secular society. In the larger society, however, women were likely to be blamed as the source of all ills because of their seductive powers. The leading medieval theologian, Thomas Aquinas, followed his mentor Aristotle, calling female nature essentially defective, a "misbegotten manhood". If a medieval woman displayed any spiritual power herself, she was likely to be branded a witch and burned alive at the stake.

The Protestant Reformation ostensibly restored the spiritual equality of the genders found in the New Testament. Each believer stood before God, saved by the grace of God received in faith. Women and men had equal access to the throne of grace, according to Reformation leaders. However, the subordination of women in society continued. According to Martin Luther, a woman's role was determined by her procreative function (Tavard 1973: 172; cited in Carmody 1989: 174–75). Luther also held that women bore a greater portion of the curse of original sin than men, thus justifying their subordination. Jean Calvin said that election by God was irrespective of gender (or social status), but at the same time he affirmed the Augustinian view of the subordination of women as part of the original order of creation (Radford Ruether 1987: 222).

Despite their leadership roles in the New Testament communities, women were denied early official status as ordained church leaders. That practice continues in the Roman Catholic Church, Eastern Orthodoxy, and a number of Protestant churches. Among the Reformers only the "radicals" of the Anabaptist wing allowed women to have leadership roles. However, beginning in recent decades many other Protestant denominations have opened ordination to women. Women's movements, pressing for full access for women to all roles of leadership and equal treatment in all areas of church life, have developed in most Christian churches in the West.

A feminist critique and reformulation of Christianity from within has emerged in recent decades. One of the first feminist Christian theologians was Rosemary Radford Ruether. She has emphasized the need to face up to the oppression of women within Christian history, alongside the subjugation of racial and ethnic minorities, as a starting point in a fundamental rethinking of Christian faith. Her radical reformulation includes speaking of divinity as God/ess, who liberates us from the distortions and alienations of patriarchal-hierarchical society (Radford Ruether 1983).

For insights into feminist theological reflection in the Jewish and Christian communities and beyond (now called by some the*a*logy), see the anthologies edited by Judith Plaskow and Carol Christ in 1979 (*Womenspirit Rising*) and 1989 (*Weaving the Visions*).

Another of the many feminist reformulations of Christian imagery is Sallie McFague's *Models of God* (1987). McFague calls her approach a "metaphorical theology" in which she is "trying out" new ways of speaking of the mysteries of Christian thought. She uses the image of God as Mother to speak of the creative activity of God.

Some Christian feminists, frustrated with the slow pace of change or resistance in traditional churches, have creating their own worshipping communities called "women-church." They provide an opportunity for women to express feminist experience in worship, study, and reflection (Radford Ruether 1994: 284).

Many feminists have found the description of God in Alice Walker's novel *The Color Purple* a moving expression of the spiritual immanence they are claiming (Walker 1989: 103):

> God is inside you and inside everybody else. You come into the world with God. But only them that search for it inside find it. And sometimes it just manifest itself even if you not looking, or don't know what you looking for. ...
> It? I ask.
> Yeah, It. God ain't a he or a she, but a It.
> But what do it look like? I ask.
> Don't look like nothing, she say. It ain't a picture show. It ain't something you can look at apart from anything else, including yourself. I believe God is everything, say Shug. Everything that is or ever was or ever will be. And when you can feel that, and be happy to feel that, you've found It.

Alice Walker also coined the term "womanist" to refer to the distinctive perspective of African-American women. It comes from the black folk expression, "You acting womanish," and refers to being "responsible, in charge, serious" as well as "want-ing to know more and in greater depth than is good for one" and "committed to survival and wholeness of entire people, male and female" (Williams 1989: 179). Womanist theology is emerging as the distinctive contribution of a group of African-American women reflecting on the meaning of God in terms of their own experience. Most womanist theologians place themselves within the Christian tradition.

Some feminist and womanist writers, however, have found Christianity incompatible with feminine spirituality. For example, Daphne Hampson, a historian of Christianity who had been a Christian lay person seeking ordination in the Church of England, came to the conclusion that Christianity is inherently patriarchal and therefore is "neither true nor moral" (Hampson 1990). She has developed a new theology that draws on the insights of feminine spirituality rather than Christianity.

At the other extreme from those feminists who look beyond Christianity for a meaningful spirituality are Christian traditionalists who agree that feminism and Christianity *are* incompatible, but who conclude that feminism is neither moral nor true and that persons like Hampson *should* leave Christianity. Their ire is particularly directed against those who are engaged in the process of using feminism to restructure Christian teaching.

In many cases today 60 to 75 percent of active churchgoers are women (Radford Ruether 1994: 267). We may safely assume that, although there is no one "women's perspective" in modern Christianity, the significant majority of active Christians will speak out more forcefully and clearly, and that more women will be taking leadership roles in churches across the theological spectrum in the years ahead.

Homosexuality

The teaching of Christian churches today on homosexuality ranges from full acceptance of homosexual orientation and practice within committed relationships by the Society of Friends (the Quakers) and the Moravian Church, to vigorous denunciation of homosexuality however approached among such conservative Protestant denominations as the Southern Baptist Convention, to a variety of positions in between. A Christian denomination that is dominated by persons of homosexual orientation, the Metropolitan Community Church, has provided a place of acceptance for persons who were forced out of or did not feel comfortable in "straight" churches. We will here summarize the contemporary teaching of the Roman Catholic Church, conservative and so-called "mainline" Protestant churches, and the dispute over the New Testament texts that deal with homosexuality.

Roman Catholic   The urban culture that dominated early Christianity, until the fall of Rome in 430 C.E., was tolerant of gay and lesbian Christians. Then, with the exception of a brief period of tolerance in the eleventh and twelfth centuries, repression was more characteristic. However, for the most part, homosexual activity was not singled out from other sexual "vices" for attack (Boswell 1980). The primary basis for condemnation of homosexuality was that the purpose of sexual expression is procreation, and thus same-sex relations are "unnatural." In the words of the *New Catholic Encyclopedia* (1967): "The homosexual act by its essence excludes all possibility of transmission of life; such an act cannot fulfill the procreative purpose of the sexual faculty and is, therefore, an inordinate use

Radically different attitudes toward homosexuality are found among contemporary Christians. Some (like these protesters of a "gay pride" march at the University of California, Irvine) cite Biblical denunciations of homosexual acts.

of that faculty. Since it runs contrary to a very important goal of human nature, it is a grave transgression of the divine will" (Harvey 1967: 117).

The hierarchy of the Roman Catholic Church continues to advocate rejection of homosexual practice, while being less clear on the issue of "homosexual orientation." In 1986, for example, the Roman Catholic Congregation for the Doctrine of the Faith sent to the bishops of the church a statement entitled "On the Pastoral Care of Homosexual Persons." This followed a 1975 document called the "Declaration on Certain

Questions Concerning Sexual Ethics." The 1975 statement drew on the natural law tradition of the church to condemn homosexuality on the grounds that it violates the fundamental human duty to procreate life. The 1986 utterance drew more heavily on the teachings of Scripture, concluding that the Church's rejection of homosexual behavior is based on "the solid foundation of a constant Biblical testimony" (Williams 1987: 260). It went on to make the controversial claim that homosexuality must be considered an "objective disorder" while at the same time strongly affirming the intrinsic dignity of gay persons. In the language of the statement, "Although the particular inclination of a homosexual person is not a sin; it is a more or less strong tendency toward an intrinsic moral evil; and thus the inclination itself must be seen as an objective disorder. Therefore special concern and pastoral attention should be directed toward those who have this condition, lest they be led to believe that the living out of this orientation in homosexual activity is a morally acceptable option. It is not" (Williams 1987: 264). This clarification was in response to the 1975 statement's distinction between homosexual orientation and behavior, which many Catholics had interpreted to mean, "It's okay to be gay; just don't act on it." This led to moral confusion, because if it is okay to "be" homosexual, then why is it not acceptable to engage in homosexual behavior? Defenders of the 1986 statement have tried to make clear that it is not a condemnation of homosexual persons, any more than saying that a person has a tendency toward the moral evil of irascibility is a rejection of the person. "One's personality cannot be reduced to sexual orientation" (Williams 1987: 268).

Catholic critics of the 1986 statement have pointed out that it fails to acknowledge sufficiently the modern advances in understanding homosexuality. The Bible assumes the norm of heterosexuality and treats homosexuality as a voluntary choice that thwarts what is normal. The 1975 declaration had accepted the modern recognition of a "homosexual orientation." Therefore, the later statement is a step backward, critics charge, in Catholic teaching on homosexuality (Coleman 1987: 728–31).

The Roman Catholic Church in the United States has tended toward a more open attitude on the question of homosexuality. For example, in 1983 the senate of priests of the Archdiocese of San Francisco published a pastoral plan that said that homosexuality must be addressed not only by church teaching but also in terms of the results of modern research and the real experiences of homosexual persons. It said that the feelings of many homosexual persons that their sexuality is right and good must be considered. Also in 1983 the bishops of the state of Washington took a strong stand against antihomosexual prejudice and discrimination in the Church and society (Nugent and Gramick 1989: 27).

Protestant   Conservative Protestant churches have based their teaching on homosexuality almost exclusively on the Bible. For most, the New Testament's clear rejection of homosexual behavior makes obvious that there is no basis for Christians to condone it today. The passage cited most frequently is from the Apostle Paul's letter to the Romans. In speaking of the human tendency not to honor God, although God is clearly revealed in the ordering of creation, Paul uses homosexual behavior by women and men as an example (1:26–27 [NRSV]): "For this reason God gave them up to degrading passions. Their women exchanged natural intercourse for unnatural, and in the same way also the men, giving up natural intercourse with women, were consumed with passion for one another. Men committed shameless acts with men and received in their own persons the due penalty for their error." In his list of "wrongdoers" in First Corinthians 6:9, Paul mentions both male prostitutes and sodomites (from the men of Sodom who demanded that Lot allow them to attack sexually the angels he has taken into his home [Genesis 19], and more broadly applied to anyone who engages in "unnatural" sexual acts). First Timothy 1:10 includes sodomites among examples of "the godless and sinful." These texts, combined with the Old Testament passages cited in Chapter 11, clearly leave no room, many conservative Protestants argue, for tolerance of homosexual activity. It is a sin for which affected people must seek repentance.

In 1988 the Southern Baptist Convention

adopted a resolution condemning homosexuality as "an abomination in the eyes of God, a perversion of divine standards, and a violation of nature" (Nugent and Gramick 1989: 25). In 1992 two Southern Baptist congregations that had ordained an openly homosexual person into the ministry and blessed a homosexual union were expelled from the Convention. Programs designed to help homosexual persons repent and be delivered from their presumed sinfulness have been developed by some conservative Protestant churches as a form of pastoral ministry to gays.

Some conservative Protestants have cautioned against singling out homosexuality for condemnation. They point out that although homosexual behavior is clearly a sin according to the Bible, it is not given special prominence. They warn that too much emphasis on homosexuality by Christians has helped create a climate in which homosexual persons are themselves sinned against and subjected to unwarranted restrictions in society. They maintain that the moral rejection of homosexual behavior should not be the basis for laws that discriminate against homosexual persons (Smith 1969).

Moderate-to-liberal or "mainline" Protestant Christian churches have attempted to balance the traditional understanding of the biblical teaching on homosexuality with the emergent modern understanding that homosexuality is not necessarily "abnormal." As in the Reform community in Judaism, a variety of responses have emerged. The discussion has tended to focus on the issue of whether openly gay persons should be allowed to be ordained as ministers. In 1992 the United Church of Christ became the first "mainline" Christian denomination to ordain a self-proclaimed gay. Other churches, such as the United Methodist, Presbyterian, and Episcopal, have attempted to draw on the modern research in developing a more tolerant and accepting attitude toward homosexuals in society and as church members, while still refusing to ordain openly gay persons because of the seemingly clear biblical denunciation of homosexual behavior. For example, in 1988 the United Methodist Church reaffirmed a ban on the ordination of self-avowed, practicing homosexuals (Nugent and Gramick 1989: 26). In most of these denominations lobbying groups of gay and lesbian members have organized and tried hard to change church teaching, while groups defending the traditional view have developed to thwart such efforts. It is safe to say that homosexuality is one of a number of issues that have contributed to an atmosphere of suspicion and tension between "traditionalists" and "modernists" in Protestant churches.

In recent years some Protestant scholars have begun to question the traditional understanding of the Bible's teaching on homosexuality (see, for example, Brooten 1983). In a study of the New Testament and homosexuality, Robin Scroggs (1983) concluded that the social contexts in which the New Testament was written must be taken into account in evaluating particular texts. Scroggs pointed out that committed homosexual relationships between adults were unknown in New Testament times. Therefore, Scroggs argued, the biblical denunciation of particular types of homosexual acts, such as male prostitution and man-boy relationships, should not be turned into an absolute standard used to condemn all forms of homosexual behavior today. This becomes a basis for a position that holds that in the context of loving and committed relationships, homosexuality meets the New Testament criteria for what is moral sexual behavior just as much as heterosexuality. Such scholarship has not yet been accepted into church teaching by most "mainline" denominations.

In summary, the attitudes found among Christian churches and individuals today toward homosexuality may be categorized as follows (Nugent and Gramick 1989: 31–42):

1. *Rejecting-punitive.* According to this view both homosexual behavior and the homosexual condition/orientation are sinful. The basis is the clear biblical teaching, which, at its extreme, treats homosexual behavior as a capital crime. Although only the most extreme proponents of this view think that homosexual behavior today should be punished with the death penalty, most believe that the legal sanctions against "sodomy" should be retained. Some who take this position go so far as to argue that the "plague of

AIDS" is God's punishment on homosexuals-for their sinfulness. Within this framework it is believed that all homosexuals who are truly repentant are able to go through a process of spiritual conversion, leaving their sinful condition and behavior behind.

2. *Rejecting-nonpunitive.* This perspective rejects homosexual acts but not homosexual persons. The behavior is regarded as "intrinsically evil," often because it seems to those who take this view an affront to the biological differences between the two sexes. Many supporters of this position are willing to acknowledge that some persons have a constitutional homosexual orientation that cannot be changed. Those persons unable to change their orientation must, however, remain celibate or else they violate God's law, advocates of this point of view argue.

3. *Qualified acceptance.* This position is that while homosexual activity may, in some instances, be acceptable for Christians, it is always inferior to heterosexual expression. It is based on endorsing the research that homosexual orientation is not a matter of choice, while maintaining the authority of the Christian teaching that the norm for human beings is heterosexuality. Homosexual marriages may be, from this viewpoint, necessary accommodations to the reality of homosexuality, but not of the same moral quality as heterosexual unions.

4. *Full acceptance.* According to this position, homosexuality is as much a part of the divine plan for creation as heterosexuality. Indeed, homosexuality is an expression, it is held, of the rich diversity of creation. The standard for sexuality should not be procreation or the male/female union, it is argued, but the quality of the relationship of the two persons regardless of gender. In this view, sexual behavior is morally neutral by itself. What makes it moral or immoral is the extent to which self-giving love is present. For advocates of this position, Christian churches should recognize homosexual marriages as just as valid as heterosexual unions and sanc-

tion rituals for both. The most extreme advocates of this position argue that the church should recognize "recreational sex," whether homosexual or heterosexual, as a legitimate expression of human sexuality when it is between consenting adults.

An often missing ingredient in discussions of Christian perspectives on homosexuality is the voice of gay and lesbian Christians. Those who are heard often speak of the deep anguish they feel as they seek to be true to themselves and try to find a place within the Christian community. Chris Glaser, a Presbyterian who has tried unsuccessfully to convince his church to overturn its ban on the ordination of self-affirming homosexuals, has this to say: "Usually, for most gay women and men, coming out *in* the church has meant coming out *of* the church. . . . The church has meant more than just a closet. . . . The church has become for them a giant tomb, smelling of death rather than life" (quoted in Ellison 1993: 150). National support groups of gays and lesbians have formed in most Protestant churches (in the Roman Catholic Church, the support group is known as Dignity). They wait for changes in teaching and practice that will be more accepting.

Christians are often taught to ask, when faced with a moral dilemma, "What would Jesus do?" Unfortunately, the New Testament records no words of Jesus on the subject of homosexuality, nor is Jesus described as interacting with a gay or lesbian person (unless the mysterious "beloved disciple" of Jesus described in the Gospel of John was gay). However, advocates for greater acceptance of homosexual persons within Christian churches suggest that the love Jesus showed for persons rejected on moralistic grounds gives a strong indication of "what Jesus would do." He would, at the very least, they argue, reach out to those victimized by the fear and hostility that result in so much rejection of homosexual persons in the church and in society. Many today feel that Jesus would welcome homosexual persons into his inner circle of friends and disciples, and that the church that bears his name today should do no less.

CHAPTER SUMMARY

In this chapter we introduced readers to the largest religion in the world today—Christianity. Its nearly 2 billion adherents make it almost twice as large as the next biggest religion—Islam. Given its size, we should not be surprised that Christianity is a complex religion.

To introduce Christianity we told the story of its development from the life of its founder, Jesus of Nazareth, until modern times. We surveyed the life of Jesus on the basis of the evidence found in the New Testament, the early history of the movement that proclaimed Jesus to be the Christ (messiah) and the crucified and risen Lord, the institutionalization and spread of Christianity through the Middle Ages, the various reform movements that began with the Protestant Reformation, and the branches of modern Christianity (Roman Catholic, Eastern Orthodox, and Protestant). We concluded our historical survey with discussion of various movements such as the ecumenical and charismatic movements and the tension between "traditionalists"

and "modernists" in contemporary Christianity, especially in the United States.

In our discussion of the distinctive Christian teachings we highlighted both the traditional understanding of doctrines such as sin and salvation and efforts to reinterpret these doctrines in response to modern developments.

We devoted considerable attention to Christian responses to contemporary ethical issues: the ecological crisis, war, capital punishment, abortion, economic injustice, the status of women, and homosexuality. We discovered on all these issues a spectrum of responses ranging from conservative traditionalists on one side, modernist liberals on the other, and a large group of moderates in the middle. Our discussion was extensive for several reasons: the complexity of Christian views on all these issues, the wealth of material available for those who seek to study these perspectives, and the likelihood that a majority of the readers of this book associate themselves with Christianity or have been exposed to it and therefore have heightened interest in Christian positions on these issues.

QUESTIONS FOR DISCUSSION AND REFLECTION

General

1. What image did you have of Jesus of Nazareth, the person, before reading the survey of his life in this chapter? Did the portrait of Jesus in this chapter alter your understanding? If so, how?
2. Do you think the splits within Christianity among Roman Catholicism, Eastern Orthodoxy, and Protestantism will ever be fully healed? If so, how? If not, why not?
3. Would you like to see "Christian values" have more impact on modern society? If so, which values? How might they have more impact? How involved should Christian churches and individuals be in politics in order to advance the Christian values they espouse?

4. Do you think there is too much or not enough emphasis in Christian teaching today on life after death?
5. According to the New Testament, Jesus told his followers to go into all the world and make disciples of all nations. Do you think that means that Christians today should try to convince people to convert from other religions to Christianity?

Ethical Issues

The Ecological Crisis

1. You have read the arguments on the controversial issue of whether the Christian attitude that humanity dominates nature is responsible for

the current ecological crisis. What is your position on this question?

2. Has "Christian environmentalism" restored basic principles of the religion or imposed new ideas that clash with fundamental Christian values?

3. Can an ecological, feminist spirituality be developed within the context of Christianity or other major religious traditions? Or are these religions too "androcentric" and "patriarchal" to provide a setting for appreciation of the presence of the sacred in nature? Or do you think that "feminist spirituality" itself is the product of the loss of the traditional values essential for human well-being?

War

1. With which of the four positions on war in Christian teaching do you find yourself most in agreement: non-resistance, pacifism, just war, or preventive war?

2. Under what circumstances, if any, could a Christian support the use of nuclear weapons?

Capital Punishment

1. Reflect on the various points of view taken by Christians on capital punishment. With which do you find yourself most in agreement?

2. Do you think it is possible for capital punishment to be fairly imposed, or is its imposition inevitably biased against the disadvantaged in society?

Abortion

1. Reflect on the various points of view taken by Christians on abortion. With which do you find yourself most in agreement?

2. To be consistent, should Christians who oppose abortion also oppose euthanasia and capital punishment? If not, what are the distinctions?

Euthanasia

1. Reflect on the various points of view taken by Christians on euthanasia. With which do you find yourself most in agreement?

2. Are there any circumstances in which a Christian could support "active euthanasia," in your opinion?

Economic Justice

1. What have you learned from this chapter about the biblical teaching concerning wealth and poverty? How much impact do these teachings have (or should they have) on the modern world?

2. Is *laissez-faire* capitalism compatible with Christianity? If so, are other economic systems also compatible with Christianity? If not, why is the capitalist economic system the one most frequently adopted in the nations where Christianity dominates?

3. Respond to the argument that Christianity favors a "communist" approach to the distribution of wealth.

Gender Roles and the Status of Women

1. Do you think that women should be eligible to be ordained as Christian ministers or priests? How does your perspective on the New Testament roles of women affect your attitude?

2. Do you agree that throughout Christian history women have been victims of "patriarchy"? If you agree, do you think women should withdraw from the Christian church because of this history of oppression? If you disagree, why do you think that "patriarchy" has become an issue today?

Homosexuality

1. With which of the four modes of responding to homosexuality found in Christianity today do you most agree? Why?

2. Do you think openly gay and lesbian persons should be eligible for ordination as Christian ministers or priests? Why or why not?

3. How much should contemporary Christian teaching on homosexuality be influenced by the Bible? By modern scientific research on the causes of homosexual orientation?

SOURCES AND SUGGESTIONS FOR FURTHER STUDY

General

BALY, DENIS, AND ROYAL W. RHODES, 1984 *The Faith of Christians: An Introduction to Basic Beliefs.* Philadelphia: Fortress Press.

BROWN, ROBERT McAFEE, 1965 *The Spirit of Protestantism.* New York: Oxford University Press.

CARMODY, DENISE LARDNER, AND JOHN TULLY CARMODY, 1990 *Roman Catholicism: An Introduction.* New York: Macmillan.

HAUER, CHRISTIAN E., AND WILLIAM A. YOUNG, 1994 *An Introduction to the Bible: A Journey into Three Worlds,* .3rd ed. Englewood Cliffs, N.J.: Prentice Hall.

HICK, JOHN H., AND BRIAN HEBBLETHWAITE, EDS., 1980 *Christianity and Other Religions.* Philadelphia: Fortress Press.

MEYERDORF, JOHN, 1981 *The Orthodox Church: Its Past and Its Role in the World Today,* 3rd ed. Crestwood, N.Y.: St. Vladimir's Seminary Press.

SCHÜSSLER-FIORENZA, ELIZABETH, 1983 *In Memory of Her: A Feminist Theological Reconstruction of Christian Origins.* New York: Crossroad.

VERMES, GEZA, 1981 *Jesus the Jew: A Historian's Reading of the Gospels.* Philadelphia: Fortress Press.

WARE, TIMOTHY 1984 *The Orthodox Church.* Baltimore: Penguin.

WIGGINS, JAMES B., AND ROBERT S. ELLWOOD, 1988 *Christianity: A Cultural Perspective.* Englewood Cliffs, NJ: Prentice Hall.

Ethical Issues

The Ecological Crisis

AUSTIN, RICHARD CARTWRIGHT, (four volumes in a series entitled *Environmental Theology*).

1987 *Baptized into Wilderness.* Atlanta: John Knox Press.

1987 *Hope for the Land: Nature in the Bible.* Atlanta: John Knox Press.

1988 *Beauty of the Lord: Awakening the Senses.* Atlanta: John Knox Press.

1990 *Reclaiming America: Restoring Nature to Culture.* Abingdon, Va.: Creekside Press.

AYERS, ROBERT H., 1986 "Christian Realism and Environmental Ethics," in *Religion and Environmental Crisis,* ed. Eugene Carmody (Athens, Ga.: The University of Georgia Press), 154–71.

BARBOUR, IAN, 1972 *Earth Might Be Fair: Reflections on Ethics, Religion and Ecology.* Englewood Cliffs, N.J.: Prentice Hall.

BERRY, THOMAS, 1988 *The Dream of the Earth.* San Francisco: Sierra Club Books.

BERRY, WENDELL, 1990 *What Are People For?* San Francisco: North Point Press.

CALLICOTT, J. BAIRD, AND ROGER T. AMES, ED. 1989 *Nature in Asian Traditions of Thought: Essays in Philosophy.* Albany: State University of New York Press.

CARMODY, JOHN, 1983 *Ecology and Religion: Toward a New Christian Theology of Nature.* New York: Paulist Press.

FOX, MATTHEW, 1991 *Coming of the Cosmic Christ.* San Francisco: HarperSanFrancisco.

JAKOWSKA, SOPHIE, 1986 "Roman Catholic Teaching and Environmental Ethics in Latin America," in *Religion and Environmental Crisis,* 127–53.

McFAGUE, SALLIE, 1993 *The Body of God: An Ecological Theology.* Minneapolis: Fortress Press.

NASH, RODERICK, 1989 *The Rights of Nature: A History of Environmental Ethics.* Madison: The University of Wisconsin Press.

SANTMIRE, H. PAUL, 1985 *The Travail of Nature: The Ambiguous Ecological Promise of Christian Theology.* Philadelphia: Fortress Press.

SITTLER, JOSEPH, 1972 *Essays on Nature and Grace.* Philadelphia: Fortress Press.

SPRING, DAVID AND EILEEN SPRING, EDS., 1974 *Ecology and Religion.* New York: Harper & Row.

STEWART, CLAUDE Y., 1983 *Nature in Grace: A Study in the Theology of Nature.* Macon, Ga.: Emory.

STONE, PAT, 1989 "Christian Ecology: A Growing Force in the Environmental Movement," *Utne Reader* 36 (1989): 78-79.

VITTACHI, ANURADHA, 1989 *Earth Conference One: Sharing a Vision for Our Planet.* Boston: New Science Library.

WHITE, LYNN, JR., 1967 "The Historical Roots of Our Ecological Crisis," *Science* 155 (1967): 1203-07.

War

BAINTON, ROLAND, 1960 *Christian Attitudes Toward War and Peace.* Nashville: Abingdon Press.

CLAUSE, ROBERT G., ED., 1981 *War: Four Christian Views.* Downers Grove, Ill.: InterVarsity Press.

DOMBROWSKI, DANIEL A., 1991 *Christian Pacifism.* Philadelphia: Temple University Press.

RAMSAY, PAUL, 1961 *War and the Christian Conscience.* Durham, N.C.: Duke University Press.

YODER, JOHN, 1972 *The Politics of Jesus.* Grand Rapids, Mich.: Eerdmans.

Capital Punishment

NATIONAL COALITION TO ABOLISH THE DEATH PENALTY, 1988 *The Death Penalty: The Religious Community Calls for Abolition.* Washington, D.C.: National Interreligious Task Force on Criminal Justice.

ZEHR, HOWARD, n.d. *Death as a Penalty: A Moral, Practical and Theological Discussion.* Elkhart, IN: Mennonite Central Committee.

Abortion

CALVIN, JOHN, 1950 *Commentaries on the Last Four Books of Moses.* Grand Rapids, Mich.: Eerdmans.

BROWN, HAROLD O.J., 1977 *Death Before Birth.* Nashville: Thomas Nelson Inc.

CONNERY, JOHN S., 1977 *Abortion: The Development of the Roman Catholic Perspective.* Chicago: Loyola University Press.

GREGORY, HAROLD, ED., 1983. *The Religious Case for Abortion.* Asheville, NC: Madison and Polle.

NICHOLSON, SUSAN, 1978 *Abortion and the Roman Catholic Church.* Knoxville, Tenn.: Religious Ethics, Inc.

OVERDUIN, DANIEL CH., 1981 "The Ethics of Abortion," in *New Perspectives on Human Abortion,* 357–86.

SIMMONS, PAUL D., n.d. "Personhood, the Bible, and the Abortion Debate." Washington, D.C.: The Religious Coalition for Abortion Rights.

Euthanasia

DUBOSE, EDWIN R., 1991 "Views of the Major Faith Traditions," in *Choosing Death: Active Euthanasia, Religion, and the Public Debate,* ed. Ron P. Hamel (Valley Forge, Pa.: Trinity Press International), 51–102.

FLETCHER, JOSEPH, 1969 "The Patient's Right to Die," in *Euthanasia and the Right to Death: The Case for Voluntary Euthanasia,* ed. A.B. Downing (London: Peter Owen), 61–70.

HORAN, DENNIS J., AND DAVID MALL, 1977 *Death, Dying, and Euthanasia.* Washington, D.C.: University Publications of America.

LARUE, GERALD A., 1985 *Euthanasia and Religion: A Survey of the Attitudes of World Religions to the Right-to-Die.* Los Angeles: The Hemlock Society.

Economic Justice

BOFF, LEONARDO, AND CLODOVIS BOFF, 1987 *Introducing Liberation Theology.* Maryknoll, N.Y.: Orbis Books.

BONINO, JOSÉ MIGUEZ, 1975 *Doing Theology in a Revolutionary Situation.* Philadelphia: Fortress Press.

COBB, JOHN B., JR., 1986 "Christian Existence in a World of Limits," in *Religion and Environmental Crisis,* ed. Eugene Hargrove (Athens, Ga: The University of Georgia Press), 172–87.

GUTIERREZ, GUSTAVO, 1974 *A Theology of Liberation: History, Politics, and Salvation,* trans. and ed. Caridad Inda and John Eagleson (Maryknoll, N.Y.: Orbis Press).

LEVI, WERNER, 1989 *From Alms to Liberation: The Catholic Church, the Theologians, Poverty, and Politics.* New York: Praeger.

MCDANIEL, JAY, 1985 "The God of the Oppressed and the God Who Is Empty," in *God and Global Justice: Religion and Poverty in an Unequal World,* ed. Frederick Ferré and Rita Mataragnon (New York: Paragon House), 185–204.

MIRANDA, JOSÉ PORFIRIO, 1982 *Communism in the Bible,* trans. Robert R. Barr (Maryknoll, N.Y.: Orbis Books).

NIEBUHR, REINHOLD, 1932 *Moral Man and Immoral Society.* New York: Harper.

PRESTON, RONALD H., 1993 *Religion and the Ambiguities of Capitalism.* Cleveland: Pilgrim Press.

SAXBY, TREVOR J., 1987 *Pilgrims of a Common Life: Christian Community of Goods through the Centuries.* Scottsdale, Pa.: Herald Press.

SCHWARZ, HANS, 1985 "God's Cause for the Poor in Light of the Christian Tradition," in *God and Global Justice: Religion and Poverty in an Unequal World,* 169–84.

SIDER, RONALD J., 1977 *Rich Christians in an Age of Hunger: A Biblical Study.* New York: Paulist Press.

SIMON, WILLIAM E., AND MICHAEL NOVAK, 1986 "Liberty and Justice for All," a report on the final draft of the U.S. Catholic Bishops' Pastoral Letter "Economic Justice for All" by the Lay Commission on Catholic Social Teaching and the U.S. Economy. Notre Dame, Ind.: The Brownson Institute.

TAWNEY, R.H., 1962 *Religion and the Rise of Capitalism: A Historian's Study.* Gloucester, Mass.: P. Smith.

WEBER, MAX, 1930 *The Protestant Ethic and the Spirit of Capitalism,* trans. Talcott Parsons (London: G. Allen and Unwin).

WILLIAMSON, RENÉ DE VISME, 1979 *The Integrity of the Gospel: A Critique of Liberation Theology.* Media, Pa.: The Presbyterian Lay Committee.

Gender Roles and the Status of Women

CARMODY, DENISE LARDNER, 1989 *Women and World Religions,* 2nd ed. Englewood Cliffs, N.J.: Prentice Hall.

DALY, MARY, 1973 *Beyond God the Father.* Boston: Beacon Press.

1978 *Gyn/Ecology: The Metaethics of Radical Feminism.* Boston: Beacon Press.

HAMPSON, DAPHNE, 1990 *Theology and Feminism.* Cambridge: Basil Blackwell.

HELLWIG, MONIKA K., 1985 *Christian Women in a Troubled World.* New York: Paulist Press.

JOHNSON, ELIZABETH A., 1993 *She Who Is: The Mystery of God in Feminist Theological Discourse.* New York: Crossroad.

McFague, Sallie, 1987 *Models of God: Theology for an Ecological, Nuclear Age.* Philadelphia: Fortress Press.

Mollenkott, Virginia, 1983 *The Divine Feminine: The Biblical Imagery of God as Female.* New York: Crossroad.

Ruether, Rosemary Radford, 1974 *Religion and Sexism: Images of Women in the Jewish and Christian Traditions.* New York: Simon and Schuster.

1983 *Sexism and God-Talk: Toward a Feminist Theology.* Boston: Beacon Press.

1987 "Christianity," in *Women in World Religions,* ed. Arvind Sharma (Albany: State University of New York Press), 207–33.

1989 "Sexism and God-Language," in *Weaving the Visions: New Patterns in Feminist Spirituality,* eds. Judith Plaskow and Carol Christ (San Francisco: Harper & Row). 9, 151–62.

1994 "Christianity and Women in the Modern World," in *Today's Woman in World Religions,* ed. Arvind Sharma (Albany: State University of New York Press), 267–301.

Tavard, George, 1985 *Women in Christian Tradition.* Notre Dame, Ind.: University of Notre Dame Press.

Trible, Phyllis, 1978 *God and the Rhetoric of Sexuality.* Philadelphia: Fortress Press.

1984 *Texts of Terror.* Philadelphia: Fortress Press.

Walker, Alice, 1989 "God Is Inside You and Inside Everybody Else," *Weaving the Visions: New Patterns in Feminist Spirituality,* 101–4.

Williams, Delores S., 1989 "Womanist Theology: Black Women's Voices," *Weaving the Visions: New Patterns in Feminist Spirituality,* 179–86.

Witherington, Ben, 1984 *Women in the Ministry of Jesus.* Cambridge: Cambridge University Press.

Homosexuality

Boswell, John, 1980 *Christianity, Social Tolerance and Homosexuality: Gay People in Western Europe from the Beginning of the Christian Era to the Fourteenth Century.* Chicago: University of Chicago Press.

Brooten, Bernadette, 1983 *The New Testament and Homosexuality: Contextual Background for Contemporary Debate.* Philadelphia: Fortress Press.

Carmody, Denise, and John Carmody, 1993 "Homosexuality and Roman Catholicism," in *Homosexuality and World Religions,* ed. Arlene Swidler (Valley Forge, Pa: Trinity Press International), 135–48.

Coleman, Gerald, 1987 "The Vatican Statement on Homosexuality," *Theological Studies* 48: 727–34.

Ellison, Marvin M., 1993 "Homosexuality and Protestantism," in *Homosexuality and World Religions,* 149–80.

Glaser, Chris, 1988 *Uncommon Calling: A Gay Man's Struggle to Serve the the Church.* San Francisco: Harper & Row.

Gramick, Jeannine, and Pat Furvey, eds., 1988 *The Vatican and Homosexuality.* New York: Crossroad.

Harvey, J. F., 1967 "Homosexuality," in *The New Catholic Encyclopedia,* vol. 7 (New York: McGraw-Hill), 117.

Hays, Richard, 1986 "Relations Natural and Unnatural: A Response to John Boswell's Exegesis of Romans 1," *Journal of Religious Ethics* 14 (1986): 184–215.

Heyward, Carter, 1984 *Our Passion for Justice: Images of Power, Sexuality, and Liberation.* New York: The Pilgrim Press.

McNeill, John J., 1993 *The Church and the Homosexual.* Boston: Beacon Press.

Nugent, Robert, ed., 1986 *A Challenge to Love: Gay and Lesbian Catholics in the Church.* New York: Crossroad.

Nugent, Robert, and Jeannine Gramick, 1989 "Homosexuality: Protestant, Catholic, and Jewish Issues," *Journal of Homsexuality* 18 (1989–90): 7–46.

Scanzoni, Letha, and Virginia Ramey Mollenkott, 1978 *Is the Homosexual My Neighbor?* New York: Harper & Row.

Scroggs, Robin, 1983 *The New Testament and Homosexuality.* Philadelphia: Fortress Press.

Smith, B.L., 1969 "Homosexuality in the Bible and the Law," *Christianity Today* 13 (1969): 935–38.

Williams, Bruce, 1987 "Homosexuality: The New Vatican Statement," *Theological Studies* 48: 259–77.

CHAPTER 13

Islam: The Way
of Submission to Allah

INTRODUCTION

Islam is both the youngest and, along with Christianity, the fastest-growing of the world's major religions. Nearly 1 billion people, one-fifth of the world's population, are Muslims. Muslims come from every race, nationality, and culture, from the southern Philippines to Nigeria. The largest Muslim community in the world is in the Pacific nation of Indonesia. Significant numbers of Muslims are also found in the nations of the former Soviet Union, North and South America, Africa, China, and Europe. Eighteen percent of the world's Muslims live in the Arab countries of the Middle East.

The very name of the religion (al-islam in Arabic) means at once submission and peace. According to Muslim teaching, the fundamental purpose of human life is to submit to the will of Allah. Submission leads to peace in this life and in the hereafter. The word *Muslim* means "one who submits."

According to Islam, Allah has spoken through a long line of prophets, but Allah's final revelation to humanity was to a man named Muhammad, who lived in Arabia in the seventh century C.E. Muslims believe that the words of Allah to Muhammad are recorded as they were heard in the holy *Qur'an*. As with the other monotheistic religions, the revelation of God laid forth an ethical lifestyle for the faithful to follow.

Our task here is to look beyond the stereotypical portrayal of Islam found in much of the Western media and attempt to understand Islam as it actually is. In this chapter we will begin by tracing the history of Islam from the time of the prophet Muhammad to the present worldwide Islamic revival. Then we will summarize the fundamental teachings of Islam before turning to Muslim responses to contemporary ethical issues.

STAGES OF DEVELOPMENT AND SACRED TEXTS

According to Muslim teaching, Islam did not begin with the revelation received by Muhammad in the seventh century C.E. The truth of Islam was revealed to all of Allah's prophets, beginning with Adam and Noah, and through them to every people throughout history. The first Muslims were not those who responded to Muhammad's teaching in Arabia, for people had been responding faithfully to Allah long before. However, because we have discussed some of the earlier revelations in the chapters on Zoroastrianism, Judaism, and Christianity, it is appropriate to begin this chapter with the final prophet, Muhammad, who received a revelation that summed up and perfected all that had been received before.

Arabia in the Seventh Century C.E.

The tribes that inhabited the Arabian peninsula (see Figure 13–1) in the seventh century C.E. had already been exposed to monotheism. The trade routes out of the Arabian peninsula connected Arabia to the Byzantine, Sassanian (Persian), and Abyssinian (Ethiopian) empires as well as to the rich diversity of religions found in these empires, including not only Judaism and Christianity but also Zoroastrianism.

FIGURE 13–1

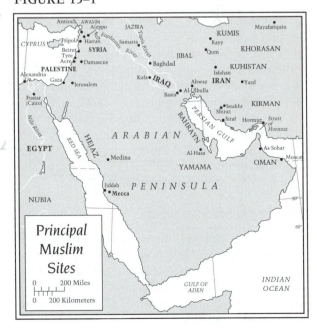

Principal Muslim Sites

0 — 200 Miles
0 — 200 Kilometers

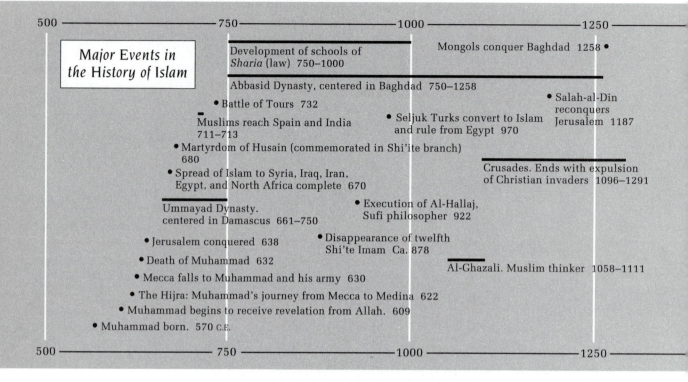

Major Events in the History of Islam

Development of schools of *Sharia* (law) 750–1000

Mongols conquer Baghdad 1258 •

Abbasid Dynasty, centered in Baghdad 750–1258

• Battle of Tours 732

Muslims reach Spain and India 711–713

• Seljuk Turks convert to Islam and rule from Egypt 970

• Salah-al-Din reconquers Jerusalem 1187

• Martyrdom of Husain (commemorated in Shi'ite branch) 680

• Spread of Islam to Syria, Iraq, Iran, Egypt, and North Africa complete 670

Crusades. Ends with expulsion of Christian invaders 1096–1291

Ummayad Dynasty. centered in Damascus 661–750

• Execution of Al-Hallaj, Sufi philosopher 922

• Jerusalem conquered 638

• Disappearance of twelfth Shi'te Imam Ca. 878

• Death of Muhammad 632

Al-Ghazali. Muslim thinker 1058–1111

• Mecca falls to Muhammad and his army 630

• The Hijra: Muhammad's journey from Mecca to Medina 622

• Muhammad begins to receive revelation from Allah. 609

• Muhammad born. 570 C.E.

However, the indigenous religion of pre-Muslim Arabia was undoubtedly animistic. The high god in the tribal polytheism was called *Allah* ("the God"); Allah was surrounded by a pantheon of other deities and spirits, including demonic spirits called *jinn*. In the Arabian city of *Mecca,* located on the major north-south caravan route, a large black meteor housed in an enclosure called the *Kaaba* ("cube") was a focus for worship. Each year time was set aside for pilgrimages to the Kaaba, and various tribes vied for control of the Kaaba.

The Prophet Muhammad

In discussing the lives of the principal figures of other religions we have been limited by the small amount of reliable historical evidence. Such is not the case with Muhammad, about whom much is known. The following summary of his life is widely accepted as historical.

Muhammad was born in 570 or 571 C.E. He was orphaned soon after his birth and adopted by his uncle, *Abu Talid,* a leader of the Quraish tribe of Mecca. Muhammad had no formal education and was unable to read throughout his life. As he grew up, he was known for his spirituality, truthfulness, generosity, sincerity, and ability to arbitrate in disputes. He was always a believer in the one God and rejected the idolatry so common in Arabia at this time.

At the age 25 Muhammad married a 40-year-old widow maned *Khadija,* whose wealth allowed Muhammad freedom for private spiritual discipline and reflection on the situation of people in the world around him. In the years after his marriage, Muhammad spent time meditating in the hills surrounding Mecca. He became convinced of the coming judgment that Zoroastrianism, Judaism, and Christianity describe, and agonized over the fate of those who worshipped idols. He was also concerned about the oppression of the poor and weak in society.

While Muhammad was meditating during the month of Ramadan on Mt. Hira in his fortieth year, an angel, whom he later learned was Gabriel,

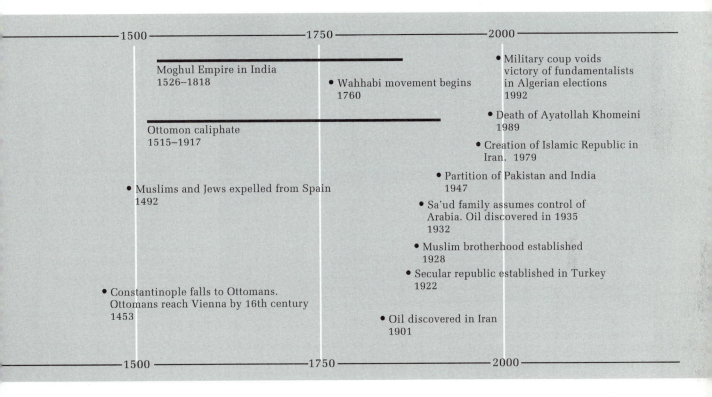

1500 — 1750 — 2000

Moghul Empire in India
1526–1818

• Wahhabi movement begins
1760

• Military coup voids
victory of fundamentalists
in Algerian elections
1992

• Death of Ayatollah Khomeini
1989

Ottomon caliphate
1515–1917

• Creation of Islamic Republic in
Iran. 1979

• Partition of Pakistan and India
1947

• Muslims and Jews expelled from Spain
1492

• Sa'ud family assumes control of
Arabia. Oil discovered in 1935
1932

• Muslim brotherhood established
1928

• Secular republic established in Turkey
1922

• Constantinople falls to Ottomans.
Ottomans reach Vienna by 16th century
1453

• Oil discovered in Iran
1901

1500 — 1750 — 2000

appeared and spoke to him. Gabriel commanded him to "Read [or Recite] in the name of thy Lord." This was the first of a number of such revelations Muhammad received during the next 23 years. He memorized what he heard, and it was written down. These recitations became the Muslim sacred text, the *Qur'an*.

Muhammad began to proclaim a message of the absolute unity of Allah. He also renounced the idolatry so prevalent in Arabia. Because the people of Mecca benefitted from the pilgrimages to the shrines at the Kaaba, they did not respond enthusiastically to Muhammad's challenge to worship Allah alone.

Muhammad's first convert was his wife, Khadija. Then his cousin *'Ali*, and a slave Muhammad had freed, *Zayd*, accepted Muhammad's call to an exclusive faith in Allah. A friend, *Abu Bakr*, converted next. Then others slowly joined them, mostly from the lower classes of Meccan society. As opposition grew, Muhammad sent some of his followers to Abyssinia (the present Ethiopia) to avoid persecution

and perhaps to prepare the way for his joining them. If so, he never went.

In 622 Muhammad did make a journey, but not to Ethiopia. Rival groups in the Arabian city of Yathrib (later called *Medina*, or "City of the Prophet") asked Muhammad to come to resolve property disputes. Opposition in Mecca had grown to the point that Muhammad's life was in danger, so he left Mecca and went north to Medina. His migration (*Hijra*) from Mecca to Medina marks the beginning of the Muslim calendar. Dates are listed A.H. (for "year of the *Hijra*"). In Medina Muhammad gathered a faithful following. Here Muhammad established the first truly Islamic society, the model for all later Islamic societies.

Only a year after his arrival in Medina, his Meccan opponents organized an attack on Muhammad. The conflicts were at first caravan raids, but gradually they escalated into a full war. By 629 the new faith Muhammad had proclaimed had become so strong that the Meccans could not resist when

The Ka'aba *in Mecca (in Saudi Arabia) is the center of the Muslim world. Muslims believe that here Allah began the work of creation and they point themselves toward it when they prostrate themselves daily in prayer. During the annual Hajj, pilgrims circumambulate the ka'aba. It houses a black meteor that was considered holy long before Muhammad received the revelation from Allah.*

Muhammad brought some of his followers to Mecca for a pilgrimage. A year later Muhammad led a force that conquered Mecca. He forgave his former enemies, but destroyed the idols in the Kaaba, leaving only the black meteoric stone and its enclosure intact. According to Muslim belief, the Kaaba had been built by the prophet Abraham and his son Ishmael. Muhammad reestablished the rite of pilgrimage to Mecca, which Muslims believe had been initiated by Abraham himself.

From this point on Islam grew steadily, and Muhammad was the undisputed political as well as religious leader of Arabia. Tribal leaders swore their loyalty to Muhammad, and he began to invite other nations to join the new "nation of Islam."

When Muhammad died in 632 at the age of 63, he had left no specific provision for succession. His friend *Abu Bakr* emerged as the first *caliph* ("successor"), but, as we shall see, the question of the rightful succession to Muhammad was to be the issue that led to the major division in Islam.

The Holy Qur'an

The *Qur'an* ("reciting, recitation") is, for Muslims, the actual Word of Allah. The analogy with Christianity is not so much the Bible, but Christ as the Word of God manifest in the world. For Christians Jesus Christ is the determinative way God has been made known in the world; for Muslims the Qur'an is the final, definitive revelation to humanity. Muslims believe that the Qur'an is the unadulterated record of God directly speaking to all humanity. The collected revelations, given directly to Muhammad and then written down, are for Muslims a holy pattern for individual and collective life and thought.

Muslims believe that the Qur'an is eternal and irrevocable. It cannot be translated, for it is God's own speech; to try to express it in another language distorts its meaning. Therefore, Muslims, regardless of their native tongue, strive to memorize the Qur'an in Arabic. Many commit all 114 *surahs* ("chapters") of the Qur'an (about the length of the New Testament) to memory. Those who do are called "guardians of the Book in the heart." The first words a baby born into a Muslim family hears are verses from the Qur'an, as are the last words a dying Muslim is told. The Qur'an is also used to teach children to read Arabic.

The surahs of the Qur'an (after the first) are organized according to length, approximately from the longest to the shortest, rather than in terms of

In Peshawar, Pakistan boys memorize passages from the Qur'an in Arabic.

topic or date of receipt of the revelation. Each sura has a name rather than a number. Some examples are "Night," "The Cow," and "Unity." Together they form a mosaic of repeated images and themes.

The content of the Qur'an ranges from hymns in praise of Allah and the myriad of "signs" of Allah in the world to warnings about the coming Day of Judgment. Many exhortations to pious living, reminders of God's involvement with people in the past through a series of prophets, and guidelines for personal as well as social morality are also found.

Muslims call the Qur'an simply "the Book." They recognize the divine origin of the Scriptures of Jews, Christians, and Zoroastrians (although they feel they were corrupted during transmission), but the Qur'an is the final and definitive Word of God. It sums up and corrects the revelations given to the earlier prophets of the other traditions. When Muslims pray, they recite verses from the Qur'an. It is chanted and meditated upon. To touch "the Book" one must be ritually pure.

The Qur'an is the principal foundation for all aspects of Muslim life. Its language sets the standard for determining grammatical rules in Arabic. Its guidelines are used as the basic laws in Muslim societies. Artists paint its verses on buildings with an elaborate calligraphy. Ordinary people pattern their speech and their behavior after it.

Because the Qur'an is accepted by Muslims as the literal Word of Allah, the Holy Book has not been subjected to the same type of critical historical and literary analysis many modern Jewish and Christian scholars have applied to their sacred writings.

The Spread of Islam

Despite the problems of succession, Islam quickly began to move beyond Arabia (see Figure 13–2). Muhammad had united the desert tribes of the peninsula into an awesome fighting force, and the Byzantine and Persian empires that controlled the Middle East were in decline.

Abu Bakr, the first caliph, died within a year of succeeding Muhammad. The second caliph, 'Umar, remained in power from 634 until 644. Under his leadership, the ancient city of Damascus fell in 635 to Muslim forces, as did most of Syria. By 637 the Sassanid Empire centered in what is now Iran had fallen to the Muslim armies. In 638 Jerusalem was conquered, and all of Palestine was soon under Arab control. Unlike other conquerors, the Muslims did not destroy Jerusalem. The Jewish and Christian inhabitants greeted the Muslims as liberators, and, in turn, the Muslim army respected these "people of the Book" and their places of worship. By 641 Egypt fell, and Muslim armies began to move across North Africa.

As a result of these conquests, the treasuries of Medina filled with tribute. When 'Umar was

FIGURE 13–2

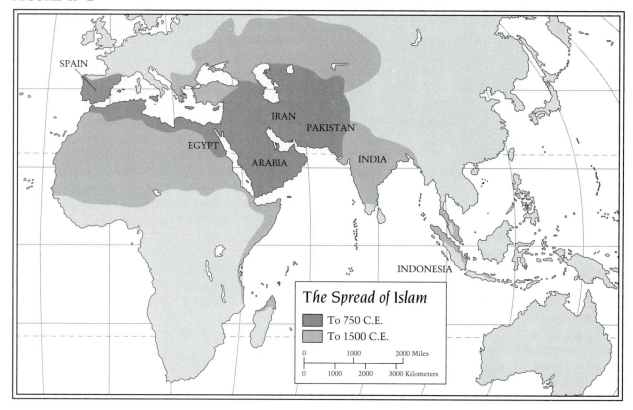

The Spread of Islam
- To 750 C.E.
- To 1500 C.E.

0   1000   2000 Miles

0   1000   2000   3000 Kilometers

assassinated by a Persian slave in 644, Muhammad's father-in-law, *'Uthman*, succeeded him. He ruled until 656. After a long campaign (640–649) Persia fell to the Muslims. Three years later, most of Asia Minor was in Muslim hands.

The next caliph was Muhammad's son-in-law *'Ali*. His two sons were Muhammad's only male descendants. 'Ali took power amidst controversy and soon was forced to flee into Iraq. In 661 'Ali was murdered.

After 'Ali the *Ummayad* dynasty began. The Ummayads were members of Muhammad's tribe, who argued that succession should be kept within the tribe but not limited to Muhammad's immediate family or associates. The Ummayads established their capital in Damascus, and ruled over a vast empire stretching ultimately from southern France to China. In 711 Muslim armies crossed the Mediterranean and entered Spain, initiating the

Moorish culture that dominated Spain for nearly 800 years. The northward expansion of Muslim political power was not halted until the Battle of Tours in France in 732. If the spread of Islam had continued into Europe, the course of history would have changed dramatically.

In 750 the *'Abbasid* dynasty replaced the Ummayad (except in Spain) and moved the center of Islamic rule to Baghdad, Iraq, where the new dynasty ruled until 1258. Baghdad became a center of culture and religious cooperation, with Jews and Muslims working together. Their scholarship preserved the works of Greek philosophers and scientists. The 'Abbasid dynasty succeeded in spreading Islam to the East, into India and ultimately into China.

In the early ninth century the unitary Muslim Empire began to split into competing factions. Spain remained under Ummayad control, and Cordoba became a great cultural center. Egypt,

Syria, and Palestine fell under the influence of the dynasties more oriented toward the *Shi'ite* branch of Islam. Then the *Seljuk* Turks gained power in the Middle East. They were the ruling power when the Christian Crusaders entered the region, beginning in the twelfth century. One of the greatest of all Muslim leaders, *Salah-al-Din,* led the resistance to the Crusaders, recapturing Jerusalem in 1187. Jerusalem was rebuilt with the massive walls that still demarcate the old city.

The spread of Islam into sub-Saharan Africa had begun early in Islamic history, with communities established in East Africa (in what is now the Sudan and Somalia). North African traders carried Islam into West Africa. By the fourteenth century a number of Muslim sultanates had been created. Also by the fourteenth century Indonesia had become a Muslim region (as it continues to be), and the Islamic faith was carried into other Pacific islands. The growth of Islam in Africa and the Pacific region continued despite the European colonization of these areas.

Mongols from eastern Central Asia invaded the Middle East in the thirteenth century under the leadership of Genghis Kahn and held power in Iraq and Persia for a century. The power of the Muslim faith proved strong, as many of the Mongols converted. The erosion of Mongol control opened the way for the emergence of new Islamic empires, including the Moghul Empire of India and the Ottoman Empire centered in Asia Minor.

The Islamic civilizations of the Middle East brought about great advances in medicine, mathematics, physics, astronomy, geography, architecture, art, literature, and history that were to have a profound influence on Western culture. Mathematical systems and innovations such as the Arabic numerals, algebra, trigonometry, and the vital concept of zero (from the Arabic word *sifr*) entered Europe by way of Islam. The navigational instruments that were to make possible the voyages of discovery by European explorers also were developed by Muslim scientists. For 800 years Arabic was the major intellectual and scientific language of the world.

Muslim armies had reached India by the eighth century, but it was the largely peaceful

A veiled Muslim woman in Zanzibar, East Africa.

migration of Muslims across the Indus River into India that led to Muslim control in parts of India by the early thirteenth century. Most of India came under Muslim control by 1526, and the Moghul Empire was created. Famous Moghul rulers such as Akbar ruled India until the British rose to power, finally abolishing the Moghul Empire in 1857.

The Ottomans, named after Othman, the first ruler of the Ottoman Empire, were nomadic Turkish tribes who had migrated from Central Asia into Asia Minor, the modern Turkey. They seized Constantinople in 1453, and the Ottoman Empire became the most powerful empire in the world during the sixteenth and seventeenth centuries. The Ottomans conquered much of Eastern Europe and almost the entire Arab world. The empire reached the height of its power under Suleiman the Magnificent, who ruled from 1520 until 1566. His armies conquered Hungary and northern Africa. Ottoman territorial expansion continued until Austrian and Polish troops turned back an assault on Vienna, Austria, in 1683. Hereafter, the power of the empire began slowly to wane. The Ottoman was the last great classical Muslim empire to fall, lasting until World War I. With the creation of the Republic of Turkey in 1922, it officially came to an end.

By the eighteenth century many parts of the Muslim world had already begun to feel the impact of European expansionism. By the nineteenth cetury and continuing into the early twentieth century, European powers (especially Great Britain, France, and Holland) had established colonies in formerly Muslim areas, from North Africa to Southeast Asia. Colonial rule replaced centuries-old Islamic institutions.

Many Muslims believed that the decline of Islamic civilization occurred not only because of external European domination but also because of a weakening of faith among Muslims. Only through a revitalization and renewal of Islam would the situation change. The stage was set for the revival of Islam that continues today, and to which we will return later. First, however, we will introduce the two major branches of Islam.

The Branches of Islam

Islam has not splintered into as many factions as other religions. There is still a remarkable unity in Islam, a testimony to its clarity of teaching and inclusiveness. However, the Muslim world is divided into two great movements—*Sunni* and *Shi'ite*—principally over the question of proper succession, but also, to some degree, on the basis of belief and practice.

Sunni: The Way of Tradition   Sunni is the larger of the two branches of the Islamic family; roughly 85 per cent of the Muslims in the world identify themselves as Sunni Muslims. The name "Sunni" comes from Sunna ("way, manner of acting"), which came to refer in Islam to the actions, words, and attitudes of Muhammad as well as the interpretation of these by the various Muslim schools of law.

The Sunni branch of Islam is committed to

following the faith and practice established by Muhammad and the four "rightly guided caliphs", the first four successors of Muhammad. The primary authority, of course, is the Qur'an, the Word of Allah revealed to Muhammad and collected by the first caliphs. However, some circumstances require guidance that the the Qur'an does not cover directly. In this case, appeal is made to the *hadith* ("speech, news"), short narrative reports of what the Prophet said, did, and allowed (or did not allow), as well as indications of his attitude while he ruled in Medina. As time passed, the validity of various Hadith—or "traditions," as we might call them—was tested on the basis of the chain of transmission through which they passed from Muhammad's time onward, as validated by Muslim scholars. For Sunni Muslims the Qur'an and Hadith serve as the primary source of guidance for all aspects of communal and personal life. If the role of the Qur'an in Islam may be compared to the role of Christ in Christianity, the analogy for the Hadith is the New Testament, which bears authoritative witness to circumstances surrounding the central revelation and its impact.

As time passed, circumstances arose for which neither the Qur'an nor Hadith gave clear guidance. To fill the void Muslim scholars appealed to two other sources to determine the proper path. One was to seek the consensus (*ijma'*) of the Muslim community, at first of Medina at the time of Muhammad, but later of the local Muslim community where a decision was needed. Another was to draw an analogy (*qiyas*) from the teachings of the Qur'an or Hadith and apply them to the new circumstance. For example, although the Qur'an does not specifically outlaw use of drugs such as cocaine, its prohibition of other intoxicants may serve as an analogy for taking a stand against illicit drug use today. *Qiyas* also opened the way for the application of reason to the determination of the right decision. The role of Muslim legal scholars (*ulama*) was enhanced by the need for authorities to determine consensus and draw analogies.

The term that developed to cover the entire body of authoritative Muslim teaching on how to live was *Sharia* ("Way"). It is often translated simply as "law," but its range of meaning (like torah in

Judaism) is wider, including personal and social morality, religion, and speculation in addition to legal matters. Today Sunni Muslims believe that both individual and communal life should be guided by the Sharia, for it is the way of life ordained by Allah. Traditionally, Islam has recognized no distinction between sacred and secular, matters of religion and civil concerns.

Four separate Sunni legal schools or traditions indicate different emphases as to the weight to be given the various sources of authority in the determination of Sharia. All four arose during the first two centuries of Islamic history.

The earliest was the *Hanifite* School, established in the eighth century in Iraq. It favors the use of analogy to determine the right path when the Qur'an is not clearly relevant. Hence, this school favors the use of rational judgment of what is best for the common good, even if (in some, very special cases) the ruling conflicts with the apparent meaning of the Qur'an. This is the basis on which scholars of this school argued that the Qur'an's directive that convicted thieves should have their hands cut off as punishment should not necessarily apply in all times and places. The Hanifite School is most influential today in Iraq, Pakistan, India, and Central Asia.

The *Malikite* School, established in Medina in the eighth century, used both the Qur'an and Hadith to determine the proper path, but turned, where necessary, first to the consensus of the community and, finally, to analogy. It is the major school in some areas of North Africa, Egypt, and eastern Arabia.

The *Shafi'ite* School also emerged in the eighth century and was the first to distinguish clearly the four sources of authority mentioned above. This school, like the Malikite, theoretically gives equal authority to the Qur'an and Hadith, but tends toward the Hadith's authority in cases of dispute. This school deemphasizes the role of reason in determining Sharia, appealing more strongly to consensus. Its influence is strongest in Indonesia, but is also felt in Egypt (the Cairo area), eastern Africa, southern Arabia, and southern India.

The last school to develop, the *Hanbalite*, arose in Baghdad, Iraq, in the ninth century and reacted against the reliance on "opinion" in other schools. This school maintains that the Qur'an holds supreme authority. Where it is clear, it must be followed. The Hadith is its only other recognized source of authority. It relies on individual responsibility to follow the dictates of the *Sharia*, refusing to use speculation to fill in the details. Saudi Arabia is the one modern country in which the Hanbalite School dominates.

All the Sunni schools are bound together by their allegiance to the Prophet, the Qur'an, and basic Muslim theology and ethics, but they differ in their understanding of how Muslims should live in the modern world. We will see more of this diversity when we discuss the status of Islam in the modern world.

Shi'ite: The Party of 'Ali   The smaller of the two major movements within Islam (comprising about 15 percent of the Muslim world) is known as the "Party (*Shia*) of 'Ali." As noted above, 'Ali was the fourth caliph. He was the cousin of Muhammad, as well as his son-in-law, the husband of Muham-mad's daughter, Fatima. According to Shi'ites, he was the *first* legitimate successor to Muhammad. The first three were "usurpers." 'Ali's youngest son, Husain, attempted to succeed his father when 'Ali was murdered, but Husain was captured at Karbala (in modern Iraq) and executed by the Ummayads in 680. The martyrdom of Husain became one of the central dates in the Shi'ite calendar, commemorated with an annual festival. The site of his execution and other key events in his life are places of pilgrimage for Shi'ites. Because of the pattern established by Husain, and an ongoing history of persecution, Shi'ites place a particular importance on martyrdom for the true faith.

The Shi'ites call the proper successors of Muhammad *imams* ("he who stands before") rather than caliphs. The use of the term "imam" has various meanings in Islam, because it is also used to refer to those who lead the community in prayer. However, for Shi'ites *the* Imam is the one endowed with supernatural authority to interpret the Sharia during the period in which he rules. 'Ali was the first Imam. Because their decisions on Muslim life carry the authority of Allah, the teachings of Imams in Shi'ite communities are regarded as infallible. Although not a "prophet" the Imam stands as Muhammad did to the people of his age, manifesting perfectly the will of Allah to the community. There is a central Imam in every age, according to Shi'ite teaching. Love and devotion for 'Ali and subsequent Imams is at the center of Shi'ite teaching.

Different Shi'ite sects recognize various numbers of Imams after Husain, before the line was broken and the principle of the "hidden Imam" began. One sect is known as the "Seveners," for they acknowledge seven Imams after Husain. Another is called the "Twelvers."

Another important Shi'ite belief, which distinguishes the movement, is the notion that the hidden Imam will return as the *Mahdi* ("the guided one"). In the Hadith the term is sometimes used to refer to a descendant of Muhammad who will restore the purity of the faith. In the Shi'ite movement it is restricted to one of the Imams. The Twelvers believe that the Twelfth Imam will return as the Mahdi. The time of the Mahdi's appearance is not known, so Shi'ites believe they must live in a constant state of preparation and expectancy, much like that expressed in the New Testament because of the anticipated return of Christ. When the Mahdi comes he will lead the entire world into a new age of justice. Many Shi'ites believe the present world is corrupt and awaits the purification of the Mahdi. There are great temptations in the present age, they believe, to turn away from the true faith.

At any time a small number of interpreters of the Sharia who are particularly learned are accorded in the Shi'ite branch the title *Ayatollah* ("Sign of Allah"). An Ayatollah is considered to be so righteous and so steeped in the true faith that he can make independent judgments that carry the authority of the Imam. The most famous of the modern Ayatollahs has been Ayatollah Khomeini of Iran.

The Shi'ite branch is in the majority in modern Iran, and is an influential minority in other Muslim countries, including Syria, Lebanon, Yemen, Pakistan, and Iraq. Smaller numbers of Shi'ites live in Saudi Arabia and India.

Sufi: The Mystical Movement

In every religion the yearning for direct experience of the spiritual comes to expression. *Sufi* ("wool clad") is the name given to the mystical movement in Islam. The name refers to the woolen garments worn by early members of the school to demonstrate their disdain for worldly things. Like the mystical branches of other religions, Sufism defies easy classification. As one Sufi teacher has observed, "Trying to describe Sufism in conventional language is like trying to send a kiss by a messenger . . . ." For Sufis the conventional teachings of Islam are like a shell, and the Sufi wisdom is the kernel inside.

Sufis trace the origin of their movement to Muhammad and the Qur'an, pointing to stories such as the account of Muhammad's ascension to heaven, the so-called "Night Journey," as indications of a hidden, mystical teaching. However, as a distinct movement it emerged in the ninth century in reaction to the materialism of the 'Abbasid dynasty. The Sufis rejected the turn toward worldly ambition that marked the caliphate, and maintained that Muhammad himself taught a simple, spiritual lifestyle.

Mansur al-Hallaj (858–922) was the most prominent and controversial of the early Sufis. He is most famous for declaring in a state of mystical union with Allah, "I am Truth!"

By the twelfth century Sufi brotherhoods, focusing on saints (*wali*) who had profound mystical experiences, had formed to initiate new members into the mystical teaching. Those initiated were called by the name *fakir* (Arabic for "poor") or *darwish* (Persian for "poor," taken over into English as "dervishes") because of the ascetic lifestyle they practiced. Members of an order called the Mawlawis, who practiced a form of ecstatic dancing in which they revolved majestically in circles, were called "whirling dervishes" by outsiders who did not understand the nature of the ritual.

Sufi saints became the object of veneration, with intercessory prayers said to them and pilgrimages to their tombs. To some Muslims this seemed like idolatry.

However, during the Middle Ages, Sufis also tried to demonstrate that they were just as loyal to the teachings of Islam as other Muslims. Al-Ghazzali (1058–1111), a Baghdad professor, succeeded in synthesizing Sunni teaching with Sufi mysticism in works such as *The Revival of the Religious Sciences.*

The Sufi contention that true religion is inward experience of holiness rather than external forms has served as a balance on the more legalistic and ritualistic aspects of Muslim life. Sufi poetry and parables are among the true gems of religious literature.

The Revival of Islam

Since the decline of European colonialism, beginning after World War I and accelerating after World War II, Islam has undergone an exciting period of reform and revitalization. In general, Muslims are seeking ways to reaffirm the integrity of their heritage in the context of the modern world. Three different types of responses may be identified (Esposito 1988: 116–61). Conservative movements have sought to purify Muslim life through a withdrawal from modern Western culture and a return to the values of the past that caused Islam to flourish. Secular movements are committed to revitalizing Muslim life through critical incorporation of the modern Western ideal of separation of the religious and secular spheres. Modernist movements have attempted to reform society through reaffirming basic Islamic values, letting go of what are viewed as unnecessary social customs of the past, and selectively adapting (Islamizing) Western ideas and technology. Some of these movements were well underway before this century; others have begun only fairly recently. In this section we will survey the range of reform and revitalization movements (conservative, secular, and modernist) that help us understand the world of Islam today.

The first movement to try to purify Islam and restore a fully Muslim society was the Sunni *Wahhabi* movement of Arabia, which adopted the Hanbilite view that the true way is found in strict adherence to the Qur'an and the ways of Muhammad as expressed in the Hadith. Its founder, Ibn 'Abd al-Wahhabi (1703–1792), rejected all guidelines based on the consensus of Muslim communities after Muhammad's in Medina and the use of rational judgment to determine Sharia. Wahhabi taught that all forms of *shirk* ("idolatry") must be rooted out and crushed, including the Sufi veneration of saints. The Wahhabis (or *muwahhidun*, "unitarians," as they have called themselves) destroyed shrines and suppressed all activities associated with them. A strict, simple lifestyle somewhat akin to the austerity associated with Puritanism in Christianity was seen as the proper way to live.

When the *Sa'ud* family, which had been in alliance with the Wahhabi movement since its creation, consolidated their control of much of the Arabian peninsula in this century, the teachings of the Wahhabi movement were used to guide the practice of Islam in the modern nation of Saudi Arabia. The wealth brought to the Saudis by the discovery of large oil reserves has brought increasing pressure to moderate the more extreme examples of Wahhabi conservatism (such as not allowing women to drive cars), but at this writing the commitment to maintaining the social values found in Muhammad's time continues amidst amazing technical modernization.

Another manifestation of the commitment to purify Islam from perceived corruption is the Muslim Brotherhood, which was founded in Egypt in 1928 and today is active in a number of countries. It is an educational and political movement with the goal of raising awareness in the Muslim world of the need to purge from Islamic societies negative, secular influences and to bring to power leaders sympathetic to this position. At times, some radicals associated with the movement have resorted to violent measures to advance their cause when they see no other recourse. When Egypt's President Anwar Sadat appeared to be accommodating himself too much to secularism, he was assassinated in 1982 by military officers associated with a faction of the Muslim Brotherhood. The Muslim Brotherhood continues to play a very important role in political life in Egypt and other Muslim countries. For example, Muslim Brotherhood candidates have

A crowd gathers on January 14, 1979 at the University of Tehran to express allegiance to the Ayatollah Khomeini, leader of the Islamic revolution in Iran.

won a number of seats in recent Jordanian parliamentary elections.

The leading example of Shi'ite efforts at purifying Islam is the Islamic Republic of Iran. After several decades of repressive rule in Iran under Shah Mohammad Reza, a revolution brought to power Ruhallah Musavi Khomeini (who was accorded the honorific title Ayatollah), whom the shah had exiled, and other Shi'ite leaders. Devoted Shi'ites saw in the shah's persecution of the Ayatollah Khomeini and other leaders a re-enactment of the Ummayad attack on Husain. The dramatic success of the revolution inspired not only Shi'ites but many in Sunni communities as well. Khomeini returned from Exile in 1979, the shah was driven from the country, and an Islamic Republic was formed. The intent of this radical revolution was to create a purified Muslim nation. Although he was not president or prime minister, Khomeini took the position of Guiding Legal Expert, which gave him power to intervene in any area where he perceived a threat to the will of Allah. The militant Revolutionary Guards were an effective force in thwarting any opposition and rooting out "heretics" such as members of the Baha'i Faith (see Chapter Fourteen). During the

1980s, war with Iraq tested the resolve of the Iranians. Thousands of young men went into battle believing that if killed they would die as martyrs in a Holy War and therefore go directly to Paradise, without having to wait for the final judgment.

Conservative Shi'ite groups in other Muslim countries, such as the *Hezballah* ("Army of Allah") in Lebanon, swore loyalty to the Ayatollah Khomeini and acted as his proxies in guerrilla warfare against American, European, and especially Israeli interests. Since the death of the Ayatollah Khomeini in 1989 there have been signs of moderation, but the radical clerics of Iran remain firmly in control.

At the other end of the spectrum, the secular response to the modern world has sought to follow the Western model by separating religion from civil affairs. In Turkey the "Young Turks," who overthrew the Ottoman Empire after World War I, abolished the religious courts and prohibited various public expressions of Islam. An effort was made to orient Turkey toward the West instead of the rest of the Muslim world. In recent decades, however, the trend toward secularization has been reversed in Turkey, with the reintroduction of the teaching of Islam in schools and other measures.

Secularization has been introduced by the Baath party in Syria and Iraq, and has also been influential in Algeria, Albania, Libya, and Egypt, although not to the same extent as Turkey. However, in all these countries conservative movements are on the rise, with intense opposition to secularization because of the threat the conservatives feel it poses to the ideal of a true Islamic society.

Other Muslim leaders have tried to steer a middle course between what they perceive as extreme conservatism and secularism. "Modernists," as we might call such leaders, have argued for a return to the basic values of Islam in order to bring democracy and justice to society, while turning away from customs (such as the segregation of women and men) that have developed over the centuries and that they do not deem essential to Muslim life. One such leader was Jamal al-Din Afghani (1839–1897), who helped spark resistance to British rule in Egypt and who campaigned for a pan-Islamic movement to unite the Muslim world across national boundaries. Another was his student Muhammad Abduh (1849–1905). Modernists say that Muslims need not turn to the West to learn of democracy and freedom, for Islam manifests these ideals. For example, the assertion of rights for women in Muslim societies, they argue, is not an imposition of Western values but a reaffirmation of the egalitarian principles of the Qur'an. Modernists have also emphasized the teaching that reason cannot contradict revelation, and called for the use of Western science, technology, and education to improve life in Muslim societies. Like conservatives, modernists argue that all of life should be in conformity with Islamic teaching, but they disagree as to what are essential Islamic values that should guide society. The modernist approach to Islamic reform continues to be influential in Egypt and some other Muslim countries such as Pakistan.

The degree to which these trends in the responses to the modern world within Islam parallel developments in Judaism and Christianity (see Chapters Eleven and Twelve) is an interesting, but very complex, topic for further investigation and discussion.

COSMIC QUESTIONS: HOW DID THE WORLD COME INTO BEING?

Allah: The Creator

The Qur'an includes numerous verses that assert that Allah is the Creator of the heavens and the earth, acting alone, without the sort of agent alluded to in Christian texts (Qur'an 32:4–7; Dawood 1956: 182–3).

It was Allah who in six days created the heavens and the earth and all that lies between them, and then ascended His throne. You have no guardian nor intercessor besides Him. Will you not take heed?

He governs the creation from heaven to earth. And in the end it will ascend to Him in one day, a day whose space is a thousand years by your reckoning.

He knows the visible and the unseen. He is the Mighty One, the Merciful, who excelled in the making of all things.

Excerpts from The Koran, *trans. N.J. Dawood (Penguin Classics 1956, Fifth revised edition 1990). Copyright © by N. J. Dawood, 1956, 1959, 1966, 1968, 1974, 1990. Reprinted by permission of Penguin Books, Ltd.*

DISTINCTIVE TEACHINGS

Despite the diversity we have noted in Islamic history, there is a common core of teaching that virtually all Muslims affirm. As we have noted, "Islam" means submission, and a "Muslim" is "one who submits" to Allah. Islam is a religion of submitting all of life, personal and corporate, to the will of Allah.

Problem: Rejecting Allah's Guidance

According to Islam, humans have been created by Allah for the purpose of submission to the divine will. Humans have the ability to reason and can determine for themselves that submitting to Allah is the purpose of life. Unlike Christianity, Islam has no doctrine of "original sin." Indeed, each child is born with an inner disposition toward virtue, knowledge, and beauty. Allah is gracious in offering humans guidance in the fulfillment of his will, especially in the gift of the Qur'an.

In his mercy Allah desires humans to submit willingly. Because God is omniscient, he knows who will respond to his will and who will not. Some passages in the Qur'an imply that God not only knows the fate of humans, he controls their ultimate destiny as well as that which happens to them day to day. This attitude is expressed in the common expression in Muslim countries, "If Allah wills . . ." (*im shallah*). The tension between free will and predestination is one that Muslim theologians have wrestled with over the centuries.

Muslims view life as a testing ground, in which humans are being given the chance to submit willingly to Allah. Muslims agree that humans who try to reject Allah's guidance will find themselves under Allah's power, one way or another. Those who reject Allah's guidance worship other powers, whether another god or something secular. Therefore, another way of stating the basic problem to be overcome is idolatry, the human tendency to worship the creation rather than the creator, for all other powers in the universe, spiritual or secular, are dependent on Allah.

Cause: Distraction

Even though Allah has sent prophets throughout history to point humans toward the righteous way to live, humans stray from this path. For Islam the cause is not so much disobedience; humans do not have the power to disobey Allah. Rather, the problem is "distraction." Humans are distracted from the path Allah has revealed by *jinn*, the evil spirits, who appeal to the earthly soul of humans, causing them to forget what their higher, spiritual soul (which is aware of Allah) is telling them to do. They are also distracted by the idolatrous tendency discussed above. Humans are not by nature corrupt, for as creatures in Allah's image that would imply some imperfection on the part of the Creator. Nevertheless, only the prophets such as Muhammad and Jesus (and, in Shi'ite Islam, the Imams) are free from distraction. They can therefore be models for others to follow to overcome this flaw.

HUMAN IDENTITY: WHAT IS THE BASIC HUMAN DILEMMA?

All Save Satan

Like traditional Judaism and Christianity, Islam teaches that an evil angel (Iblis, or, here, Satan) tries to lure people into turning away from the one true God (Surah 7.11–18; Dawood 1956: 239-40).

We created you and gave you form. Then We said to the angels:

'Prostrate yourselves before Adam.' They all prostrated themselves except Satan (Iblis), who refused.

'Why did you not prostrate yourself?' Allah asked.

'I am nobler than Adam,' he replied. 'You created me of fire and him of clay.

'He said: 'Begone from Paradise! This is no place for your contemptuous pride. Away with you! Henceforth you shall be humble.'

Satan replied: Reprieve me till the Day of Resurrection.'

'You are reprieved,' said He.

'Because You have led me into sin,' said Satan, 'I will waylay your servants as they walk on Your straight path, and spring upon them from the front and from the rear, from the right and from the left. Then you shall find the greater part of them ungrateful.'

'Begone!' said Allah. 'A despicable outcast you shall henceforth be. With those that follow you I shall fill the pit of Hell.'

Excerpts from The Koran, *trans. N.J. Dawood (Penguin Classics 1956, Fifth revised edition 1990). Copyright © by N. J. Dawood, 1956, 1959, 1966, 1968, 1974, 1990. Reprinted by permission of Penguin Books, Ltd.*

Reality: The Signs of Allah

According to Muslim teaching, reality is created by Allah. Although Allah is separate from the creation, its order and beauty are "signs of Allah" that human reason can discern. Islam has traditionally supported science, the application of human reason to the understanding of the natural world, in the

Women students engaged in research while observing the teaching of the Qur'an about modest dress exemplify the combination of commitment both to tradition and to the methods of modern science shared by many Muslims today.

belief that scientific discoveries will inevitably confirm the truth revealed by Allah.

The world is a place of goodness, to be enjoyed. Islam in general has never been ascetic or puritanical in its attitude toward life in the world.

Like the other religions in this section, Islam has a linear view of time. As noted above, Islam dates its calendar from the migration (*hijra*) of Muhammad from Mecca to Medina in 622 C.E.

As already mentioned, the strict monotheism of Islam raises the questions of predestination and fatalism in Muslim teaching. Is everything that happens preordained by Allah? Do things happen only if Allah wills them? Most Muslims seem to accept fatalism as a natural corollary to belief in Allah's power. Muslim theologians, however, have tried to maintain a balance between belief in Allah's omnipotence and the need to maintain some sense of spontaneity and freedom in the natural world. Does Allah cause innocent children to develop cancer and die before they have had the opportunity to submit to Allah? If not, how can that be reconciled with Muslim teaching about the all-encompassing power of Allah? For the vast majority of Muslims

the belief that everything happens as Allah wills, and only as Allah wills, is still comforting rather than puzzling.

End: *Paradise and the "House of Islam"*

Like Zoroastrianism, Judaism, and Christianity, Islam is eschatological. Muslims believe that Allah revealed to Muhammad the truth of the "end time," although not when it would be. The Qur'an is full of elaborate descriptions of the paradise that awaits those who submit willingly to Allah, and the torment reserved for infidels.

According to the Qur'an, after death a person's soul goes into a deep sleep. On judgment day, Allah's angel will sound the trumpet and the bodies of those who have died before the end will be rejoined with their souls. All humans are judged on the basis of whether they have lived as Allah wills. The Qur'an speaks of a heavenly book in which the deeds, large and small, of each human are recorded. Those who are judged to have been virtuous go to heaven, which is described as an oasis with cool, flowing water. Hell has the qualities of a desert storm, with fiery heat, biting winds, and foul water.

COSMIC QUESTIONS:
WHAT IS THE DESTINY OF THE COSMOS?

The Last Imam

This Shi'ite text, taken from the collected sermons (popularly known as Nahjul Balagha) of Hazrat Ali (cousin and son-in-law of Muhammad), envisions the arrival of a final Imam, called Imam Mahdi, who will come to restore the true faith and become the benevolent ruler of a world state (Nahjul Balagha, Sermons 141 and 187; Jafery 1965: 262–63).

When men will have twisted the meanings of the Holy Quran to gain their sinful desires, and will have given false interpretations to its orders to suit their vicious ways, he (the Imam of the time) will bring them back to obey the orders of the Holy Prophet (may the peace of God be upon him and his descendants), and the Holy Book.

The society will be engulfed by ravaging wars, overflowing with havoc and devastation. In the beginning the conquerors will feel very happy over their successes and booties gained therein, but it will all have a very sad end. I warn you of the wars of the future, you have no idea of the enormity of the evil which they will carry. The Imam who will create a world state will make the ruling nations pay for their crimes against society. He will bring succour to humanity. He will take out the hidden wealth from the breast of the earth and will distribute it equitably amongst the needy deserving. He will teach you simple living and high thinking. He will make you understand, that virtue is a state of character which is always a mean between the two extremes, and which is based upon equity and justice. He will revive the teaching of the Holy Quran and the traditions of the Holy Prophet (may the peace of God be upon him and his descendants) after the world had ignored them as dead letters.

Source: The Last Imam. From Nahjul Balaga of Hazrat Ali, trans. S. Jafery. Seerat-Uz-Zahra Committee.

Islam also paints a picture of the goal toward which societies are oriented. It is expressed in the oft-repeated phrase *dar al-islam* ("house of Islam or peace"). The ideal society is one that has willingly made the revelation of Allah the basis of its life. Such a society is a truly just and compassionate community. This is a goal that can be achieved before the end time. The conservative interpretation of *dar al-islam* is that the Sharia should be the only law in a society, for all areas of life must submit to the will of Allah revealed in the Qur'an and the other recognized sources of determining the right path.

Another important and related Muslim principle is *umma* ("people"). It is the ideal of a single, worldwide Muslim community. Rooted in the Qur'an, umma has been used as the basis for various pan-Islamic movements, which have sought to overcome the national and ethnic divisions within Islam.

Means: A Life of Submission

Islam has no priesthood, no intermediaries between humans and Allah. Each individual and each society is responsible for making the decision to submit willingly to Allah. Islam teaches that all those who examine life rationally will come to faith in Allah and the desire to live a life of submission. The "means" are designed to enable persons to live the lifestyle of submission.

For the individual the *five pillars* constitute the foundation of living. These are the obligations all Muslims recognize. Muslims call them the *'ibadat* ("acts of service").

The first of the pillars is affirmation of the creed: *La ilaha illa Allah; wa-Muhammadan rasulu*

During the annual Hajj, Muslims pour into the Grand Mosque in Mecca, Saudi Arabia. The sacred kaaba is visible between the minarets.

Muslims in Turkey gather for Friday prayers in observance of one of the "five pillars" of Islam: daily prayer.

QUESTIONS OF HUMAN DESTINY: WHAT HAPPENS AFTER DEATH?

Heaven and Hell

The Qur'an points to a Day of Judgment, when people will be judged on the basis of their deeds, and be led either to heaven or hell. According to the Qur'an, heaven is a luxurious garden and hell is a foul place (Surahs 56.10–27, 14.16–17; Dawood 1956: 108, 99).

Such are they that shall be brought near to their Lord in the gardens of delight: a whole multitude from the men of old, but only a few from the later generations.

They shall recline on jewelled couches face to face, and there shall wait on them immortal youths with bowls and ewers and a cup of purest wine (that will neither pain their heads nor take away their reason); with fruits of their own choice and flesh of fowls that they relish. . . .

There they shall hear no idle talk, no sinful speech, but only the greeting, 'Peace! Peace!'

Hell lies before them. They shall drink stinking water: they will sip, but scarcely swallow. Death will assail them from every side, yet they shall not die. A dreadful torment awaits them.

Excerpts from The Koran, *trans. N.J. Dawood (Penguin Classics 1956, Fifth revised edition 1990). Copyright © by N. J. Dawood, 1956, 1959, 1966, 1968, 1974, 1990. Reprinted by permission of Penguin Books, Ltd.*

Allah ("There is no God, but Allah; and Muhammad is his messenger"). Called the *shahadah* ("bearing witness"), it is recited in Arabic by all Muslims, regardless of their native tongue. We will discuss the Muslim view of Allah later; we will focus here on the Muslim understanding of Muhammad.

For Islam, Muhammad is the "seal" of the prophets, the last messenger of Allah to humanity. Allah has sent a messenger in every era, beginning with Adam and including Noah, Abraham, Ishmael, Isaac, Jacob, Joseph, Job, Moses, Aaron, David, Solomon, Elijah, Jonah, John the Baptist, and Jesus. Those who accept the revelations of these prophets as they have been written down are "People of the Book" or "People of the Covenant" and are deserving of special legal status and protection, according to the Sharia. However, as we have already noted, Muslims believe these writings have been distorted in transmission and introduce ideas (such as the divinity of Christ) that are not authentic revelations.

Only the revelation that Muhammad recited (the Qur'an) is undefiled, the pure and unadulterated Word of Allah. Muslims do not believe that Muhammad was or is *divine*, any more than any other human being. While they venerate him and seek to follow his example, they do not worship him. You will find no shrines to Muhammad, no statues or pictures to which people bow down. The important sites of his life *are* places of pilgrimage, but because they enable a Muslim to follow the pattern of life Muhammad set, not because he is an "incarnation" of Allah.

The way one becomes a Muslim is simply by reciting the *shahadah* with faith. The faithful

QUESTIONS OF MORALITY: WHAT IS RIGHT LIVING?

The Righteous Life

Personal piety and social justice are central to right living, according to the Qur'an (Surah 2.177; Dawood 1956: 339.

Righteousness does not consist in whether you face towards the east or west. The righteous man is he who believes in Allah and the Last Day, in the angels and the Scriptures and the prophets; who for the love of Allah gives his wealth to his kinsfolk, to the orphans, to the needy, to the wayfarers and to the beggars, and for the redemption fo captives; who attends to his prayers and pays the alms-tax. . .

Excerpts from The Koran, *trans. N.J. Dawood (Penguin Classics 1956, Fifth revised edition 1990). Copyright © by N. J. Dawood, 1956, 1959, 1966, 1968, 1974, 1990. Reprinted by permission of Penguin Books, Ltd.*

Muslims in Cairo, Egypt, prostrate themselves in one of the five periods of daily prayer, expressing their willingness to submit themselves totally to the will of Allah, their creator.

Muslim recites the creed every day, and it is ideally the last words on a dying Muslim's lips. Once a person has recited the creed in faith, the rest of the pillars are then his or her duty.

The second pillar is daily prayer (*salat*), which Muslims are required to perform five times a day (dawn, noon, mid-afternoon, sunset, and evening). One can always recognize a Muslim community by the sound of the *muezzin* ("crier") calling the faithful to prayer at the five appointed times. The role of muezzin may be filled by any ritually pure male. He climbs the tall *minaret* ("tower") of the *mosque* and delivers the *adhan* ("call to prayer"). Four times he calls *Allahu akbar* ("God is most Great!"), then twice the *shahadah*. Then twice each he cries "Come to prayer! Come to salvation!" The vocal call to prayer was chosen by Muhammad to distinguish Muslim practice from Christianity (in which a bell or wooden clapper is used as a summons to worship) and Judaism (in which the ram's horn is blown to call worshippers). Today, accommodation has been made to modern technology in some Muslim communities as timed tape recordings of the *muezzin* replace the human crier.

When responding to the call to prayer, Muslims first purify themselves. At mosques, water is usually available for a cleansing of the hands, face, mouth, nose, teeth, and feet. If no water is available, sand is permissible for some of the purificatory rituals. If the prayer is in the mosque, worshippers remove their shoes. The worshippers then position themselves in the direction of Mecca. The prescribed prayers are said with accompanying bending, bowing, and ultimately prostration on the knees, with heads and hands on the ground. This posture symbolizes complete and total submission to Allah. While prostrate, the worshipper cries three times in Arabic, "Glory be to my Lord, the Most High!" Most of the prayer is in praise of Allah, but it ends with an expression of concerns for others.

Friday is the day of congregational prayer in the Muslim house of worship, the mosque. The mosque ("place of prostration") is the center of the Muslim community. If possible, Muslims should come to the mosque for daily prayer. However, on Friday it is an obligation for males to come to the mosque for the noon prayer. After the prayer, led by any pious Muslim male functioning as *imam*, the assembled congregation listens to a sermon delivered by a Muslim man learned in the faith. Mosques have tended in Muslim societies to serve as community centers. Because there is no recognized distinction between religion and politics in Islam, the sermons can be calls to political action in the strongest and most unambiguous terms. In many Muslim communities, men come to the mosque for prayer and women pray at home; where women pray in the mosque they do so separately from men, usually in an enclosed area behind the men so as to avoid the distractions associated with the intermingling of men and women.

The third pillar is almsgiving (*zakat,* which means "purity, integrity"). This is, in effect, a tax on certain kinds of property, including both money and goods, which is paid at the end of each year. Its purpose is to provide for the needs of the poor of the community and for the upkeep of the mosque and other religious concerns. The *zakat* may constitute from 2 1/2 to 10 per cent of a person's disposable wealth, depending on the type of property.

The fourth pillar is fasting (*sawm*) during the entire month of *Ramadan.* All Muslims who are sane and in good health are expected to abstain from eating, drinking, smoking, and sexual intercourse during daylight hours each day of this holy month. Mothers nursing infants and travelers are exempted from the rules concerning nourishment. Muslims observing the Ramadan fast usually eat a large meal before dawn. Ramadan is the ninth month of the Islamic lunar calendar, thus its dates shift on the modern solar calendar. Muslims believe that this was the month when Muhammad received his first revelation.

The last pillar is the pilgrimage to Mecca (*hajj*). The Qur'an requires every Muslim man and woman to make the journey to the holiest city of Islam, Mecca, at least once in a lifetime. It is modelled on Muhammad's pilgrimage to Mecca a short time before his death in 632. The *hajj* always takes place in the twelfth month of the lunar calendar. As male pilgrims approach Mecca they remove their national dress, and don the simple white garments of pilgrims. This symbolizes their unity with one another as brothers, regardless of their race, nation, or economic status.

Upon arrival in Mecca, the pilgrims circumambulate the Kaaba seven times. Then the pilgrim goes to a spot where the footprint of Abraham, who built the Kaaba, is preserved. Next the pilgrim visits the well of Zamzam, a site important in the story of Hagar

Muslims pray in the main mosque in the old city of New Delhi, India, at the end of the fast of Ramadan.

and Ishmael. Hagar was a servant of Sarah, the wife of the prophet Abraham, who gave birth to Abraham's first son, Ishmael. Muslims believe that the promises Allah gave to Abraham to make of his descendants a great nation passed to Ishmael's family (rather than Isaac's, as Jews believe). According to both Muslim and Jewish tradition, Hagar and Ishmael had to flee because of Sarah's jealousy. On the hajj Muslims run between two "hills" to re-enact the flight of Hagar and Ishmael, at the point where she ran back and forth seeking help.

With these acts complete, the hajj proper begins. The pilgrims travel for several days to Mina and then to Arafat, twelve miles from Mecca. At Arafat they stand from noon to sunset asking for Allah's forgiveness, in apparent anticipation of standing before Allah at the final judgment. The next day the pilgrims return to Mina to cast stones at a pillar representing the forces of evil, commemorating Abraham's rejection of the devil's temptation to disobey God's command that he sacrifice his son Ishmael. They then sacrifice an animal, reenacting Allah's sparing Ishmael because of Abraham's faithfulness. The final acts of the hajj are the shearing of the male pilgrim's hair (and the trimming of a woman's), followed by a three-day festival and a farewell circumambulation of the Kaaba.

The individual Muslim is also expected to observe a series of dietary guidelines such as avoiding the eating of pork, drinking wine and other intoxicants (extended today by analogy to illicit drugs), and gambling.

It is difficult for persons raised in societies that assume a distinction between religious and secular institutions to understand that no such demarcation has been traditionally recognized in Islam. It was not until Muslim nations came under European influence that the pattern of separating religious and non-religious life occurred. Traditionally in Islam, all of a society's institutions and all societies must submit themselves to the will of Allah revealed through the Prophet. This has meant organizing all of life according to the dictates of the Sharia.

One of the most interesting and misunderstood aspects of the Muslim conception of submitting all of life to Allah is *jihad*. Jihad is usually assumed in the Western media to mean only "holy war" and to refer to an assumed Islamic idea that Muslims must use aggressive violence to annihilate all the enemies of Allah. In fact, jihad means "striving" or "exertion" in Arabic and refers in general to the Muslim's duty of strenuous exertion in the cause of Allah. According to Hadith, the "great jihad" is the individual Muslim's struggle against all forms of inner evil; the "lesser jihad" is the armed conflict in defense of the faith or its propagation. If

---

QUESTIONS ABOUT THE SACRED: WHAT IS THE SACRED?

Allah the Eternal

Islam is unabashedly monotheistic. The Qur'an heralds Allah as the only God in passage after passage. The Qur'an also asserts that, despite what Christianity says, Allah had no son (Surahs 2.255 and 23.91–92; Dawood 1956: 349, 218).

Allah: there is no god but Him, the Living, the Eternal One. Neither slumber nor sleep overtakes Him. His is what the heavens and the earth contain. Who can intercede with Him except by His permission? He knows what is before and behind men. They can grasp only that part of His knowledge which He wills. His throne is as vast as the heavens and the earth, and the preservation of both does nor weary Him. He is the Exalted, the Immense One.

Never has Allah begotten a son, nor is there any other god besides Him. Were this otherwise, each god would have governed his own creation, each holding himself above the other. Exalted be Allah above their falsehoods!

Excerpts from The Koran, *trans. N.J. Dawood (Penguin Classics 1956, Fifth revised edition 1990). Copyright © by N. J. Dawood, 1956, 1959, 1966, 1968, 1974, 1990. Reprinted by permission of Penguin Books, Ltd.*

---

a believer is killed while engaged in "lesser jihad," that person goes directly to Paradise, without having to wait for the last day.

Sacred: There Is No God but Allah

The Muslim creed "There is no God but Allah" and the phrase used by the muezzin in calling a Muslim community to prayer, *Allahu akbar* ("God is most great"), summarize well the basic Muslim attitude toward the sacred. Muslims are strict monotheists. Allah is personal, a supernatural being who exists separate from the creation. Allah alone is

QUESTIONS ABOUT THE SACRED: HOW IS THE SACRED KNOWN?

Muhammad's Night Journey

Surah 17 of the Qur'an refers to a journey in which Muhammad was taken by night from Arabia to the Temple in Jerusalem. An extensive tradition developed to describe what Muhammad saw when he ascended from the Temple into the heavens. Muhammad is speaking (Hadith of al-Suyuti; Jeffrey 1958: 42–43).

Now when I was brought on my Night Journey to the [place of the] Throne and drew near to it, a green rafraf [piece of brocade] was let down to me, a thing too beautiful for me to describe to you, whereat Gabriel advanced and seated me on it. Then he had to withdraw from me, placing his hands over his eyes, fearing lest his sight be destroyed by the scintillating light of the Throne, and he began to weep aloud . . . . By Allah's leave, as a sign of His mercy toward me, and the perfection of His favour to me, that rafraf floated me into the [presence of the] Lord of the Throne, a thing too stupendous for the tongue to tell of or the imagination to picture. My sight was so dazzled by it that I feared blindness. Therefore, I shut my eyes, which was by Allah's good favour. When I thus veiled my sight Allah shifted my sight [from my eyes] to my heart, so with my heart I began to look at what I had been looking at with my eyes. It was a light so bright that I despair of ever describing to you what I saw of His majesty. Then I besought my Lord to complete His favour to me by granting me the boon of having a steadfast vision of Him with my heart. This my Lord did, giving me that favour, so I gazed at Him with my heart till it was steady and I had a steady vision of Him.

There He was, when the veil had been lifted from Him, seated on His Throne, in His dignity, His might, His glory, His exaltedness, but beyond that it is not permitted me to describe Him to you.

Source: Muhammad's Night Journey. From Islam: Muhammad and his Religion, *ed. A. Jeffrey. The Library of Liberal Arts.*

Supreme. According to the Qur'an Allah has 99 names, but transcends them all. As the first surah of the Qur'an makes unmistakably clear, Allah is the transcendent, omnipotent creator, who rules and judges over all. Allah cannot be represented by any image, so you will find no statues or pictures of Allah in mosques or any Muslim home.

Since Allah is beyond direct human knowing, human knowledge of Allah depends on two sources. If humans observe Allah's creation with minds unclouded by idolatry, they will inevitably come to an awareness of the Creator. Muslims believe that all truth comes from Allah, and that study of the world cannot discover any knowledge that contradicts what Allah has made known. Therefore, they admit no contradiction between science and faith. Where science seems to contradict what Allah has revealed (e.g., that the world was created in six days), then our understanding is inadequate or incomplete. Further study will yield results that are in harmony with what Allah has made known. Allah's revelation, of course, is the Qur'an, his direct word to all humanity. Its words are Allah's words; therefore, to hear them and to recite them is the holiest of actions.

Muslims believe that Allah is the same God who spoke to Zoroastrians, Jews, and Christians. Although the prophets Allah chose to speak to these peoples fulfilled their role, Muslims believe that those who wrote down the words and transmitted them have distorted Allah's truth. For example, the Christian idea of the Trinity is blasphemous, for it implies three gods instead of the one true God.

Allah is the Supreme Lord, but there are other supernatural beings in the Muslim spiritual hierarchy. Angels exist as Allah's spiritual messengers; the most famous is Gabriel, who was Allah's envoy in delivering the Qur'an to Muhammad. Angels such as Gabriel and Michael are sent by Allah to lead people to the right path.

The Qur'an also speaks of a being who tempts humans— Iblis, the Muslim Satan or Devil. In the Qur'an Iblis is also identified as one of the jinn, (spirits), some of whom are good and others evil (although the term usually connotes evil spirits). As the chief of the evil jinn, Iblis is a creature of fire who opposes the angels, who are creatures of light. Iblis rules over hell until the final judgment. The existence of Iblis helps to mitigate the more troublesome implications of strict monotheism, giving a place for a force of evil. However, the Qur'an makes clear that Iblis has no power independent of Allah. He is Allah's servant, who may even in the end be redeemed by Allah.

RESPONSES TO CONTEMPORARY ETHICAL ISSUES

The Ecological Crisis

Islam shares with traditional Judaism and Christianity both the view that humans have a divinely given authority over other creatures and the theme of stewardship of the earth. However, there is an even stronger sense in Islam than in the other Western religions that life on earth is a time of testing and preparation for the Day of Judgment and the Paradise beyond. Thus, it is common to hear the point of view that heightened environmental consciousness is not a feature of Islam historically or in the present.

However, others have argued that Islam provides just the type of environmental ethic needed today, one that balances the need to provide for human well-being from the resources of nature with respect for the balance of nature. From a Muslim perspective, "such an approach would maintain man's position on the earth as ecologically dominant, but at the same time regulate his

---

QUESTIONS OF MORALITY: WHAT ARE OUR OBLIGATIONS TO NON-HUMAN LIFE?

Water for a Dog

Like Judaism and Christianity, Islam teaches that God has created the natural world for the benefit of humans and has given humankind the responsibility for the care of the non-human world, as this hadith illustrates (Hadith of Bukhari; Dermenghem 1958: 117).

According to Abu Hurairah, the Messenger of God [Muhammad], said "A man travelling along a road felt extremely thirsty and went down a well and drank. When he came up he saw a dog panting with thirst and licking the (moist) earth. 'This animal,' the man said, 'is suffering from thirst just as much as I was.' So he went down the well again, filled his shoe with water, and taking it in his teeth climbed out of the well and gave the water to the dog. God was pleased with his act and granted him (pardon for his sins)."

Excerpt from Muhammad and the Islamic Tradition *by Emile Dermenghem. Reprinted with permission of Georges Borchardt. Inc.*

---

behavior by clearly defined measures of reward and punishment, both in this world as well as in the other world" (Zaidi 1986: 112).

Traditional Islam has a deep sense of reverence for nature as Allah's creation. The creation is ordered harmoniously. The Qur'an makes abundantly clear that the earth belongs to Allah, and that humans are His stewards (or viceroys). Humans are held accountable for how they function in this capacity. According to the Qur'an, they are not to take actions that disrupt the environment (Surah 15:19,20; cited in Zaidi 1986: 115):

And the earth have We spread out, and placed therein firm hills,
and caused each seemly thing to grow therein [well measured].

And we have given unto you livelihoods therein, and unto those
for whom you provide not.

Creation is full of the signs of Allah, which cause reflective humans to have reverence for and respect the divine order inherent in nature. The major ecological problem is not "human dominance," from a Muslim perspective, but the materialism and greed characteristic of cultures that have turned from their spiritual roots. From the perspective of some Muslims, the modern West is such a culture. A society based on Islam accepts human control of nature, but within the limits set forth by Allah.

Because of the belief that reason and faith are not contradictory, but support one another, Muslim teaching has been traditionally supportive of science and technology. However, their use must be guided by the principle of justice, which forbids violence not only against humans but against the environment as well. Thus, long before "environmental impact statements," Muslim law required humans to measure carefully the environmental consequences of their actions. In fact, Muslim leaders have a responsibility to ensure that the programs of development necessary to better the conditions for humans do so in a way that preserves the environment (Zaidi 1986: 120–22).

War

The Qur'an clearly says that Allah approves of Muslims' engaging in war. The disagreement among interpreters rests on the issue of whether only defensive wars are permissible. The ambiguity seems to be in the text itself. For example, Surah 2.190 (Dawood 1956: 341) says, "Fight for the sake of Allah those that would fight against you, but do not attack first." That would seem to rule out Muslim participation in offensive military actions. However, the very next verse says, "Kill them wherever you find them. Drive them out of the places from which they drove you. Idolatry is worse than carnage." This has been taken to support Muslim armies moving offensively against threatening enemies.

In the early history of Islam, war played an important role. As we have seen in the historical survey above, Islam quickly expanded throughout the Mediterranean world and beyond as Muslim armies swept aside opposition. Within two centuries of the time of Muhammad, Islamic scholars had divided the world into the "house of Islam or peace" (*dar al-islam*) and the "house of war" (*dar al-harb*). Those nations not of the "house of Islam" were of the "house of war" and were the legitimate targets of war (if it was sanctioned by the proper leader) if they refused to submit willingly to the authority of Allah. Indeed, it was considered a religious obligation to wage war against the "house of war" until those within it had been brought into the "house of Islam." A Muslim ruler could not wage war against another Muslim regime unless Muslim legal authorities declared that regime's leader to be someone who had rejected the true faith.

War falls under the dictates of *jihad* ("struggle"), which, as we have noted above, refers to the Muslim's obligations to resist or struggle against evil. One Muslim scholar, Sobhi Mahmassani, has characterized the Islamic teaching on war in this way (cited in Mayer 1991: 203):

> *Islamic law.... is essentially a law of peace, built on human equality, religious tolerance and universal brotherhood.*
>
> *War, in theory, is just and permissible only as a defensive measure, on grounds of extreme necessity, namely to protect the freedom of religion, to repel aggression, to prevent injustice and to protect social order.... This defensive war, when permissible, is moreover subjected by Islamic jurisprudence to strict regulations and rules. ...*
>
> *Thus, a declaration of war has to be preceded by notification sent to the enemy. Detailed provisions are laid down for the use of humane methods of warfare and fair treatment of enemy persons and property. Acts of cruelty and unnecessary destruction and suffering are expressly proscribed. Provision is also made for the termination of war and the settlement of its consequences.*

Since the 1979 Iranian Revolution the views of the Shi'ite leader Ayatollah Khomeini have added a new dimension to discussions of Islamic teachings concerning war. As the following excerpt from a 1988 speech demonstrates, he integrated the militant ideology of modern liberation movements with traditional Islamic teaching (cited in Mayer 1991: 207):

> *We must smash the hands and the teeth of the superpowers, particularly the United States. And we must choose one of two alternatives—either martyrdom or victory, which we both regard as victory. . . .*
>
> *Our war is one of ideology and does not recognize borders or geography. We must insure the vast mobilization of the soldiers of Islam around the world in our ideological war. God willing, the great Iranian nation, through its material and moral support for the revolution, will compensate for the hardships of the war with the sweetness of the defeat of God's enemies in the world. . . .*
>
> *We say that as long as there is infidelity and poletheism [sic], there is struggle, and as long as there is struggle, we will be there. . . .*

Rhetoric such as this has inspired some groups to engage in acts of guerrilla warfare (called by opponents "terrorism"), including the taking of hostages and the bombing of civilian aircraft. In the Iran-Iraq war of the 1980s, Khomeini called Saddam Hussein an apostate from Islam who must be punished for his perversion of the faith. When the U.N. coalition drove Iraqi forces from Kuwait in the 1991 Persian Gulf War, the Iraqi leader himself tried to invoke the language of an Islamic holy war against infidels. The point should be made that the mere invoking of Islamic imagery to support a particular leader or group's actions should not be taken as an indication that they are properly representing an Islamic approach to war, and certainly not that such groups speak for all Muslims.

In fact, the vast majority of Muslims in the world today vigorously reject the idea that Islam endorses violence against civilians and wars of aggression. They are willing and eager to cooperate with people of other nations and other religions to find peaceful solutions to conflicts such as the struggle of the Palestinian people for self-determination.

Capital Punishment

Capital punishment is permissible in Islamic law. According to the Qur'an, "the only reward of those who make war upon Allah and His messenger and strive after corruption in the land will be that they will be killed or crucified, or have their hands and feet on alternate sides cut off, or will be expelled out of the land" (5.33; Pickthall 1953: 99).

As in Judaism, however, indiscriminate retaliation is not allowed. Surah 6.152 says "... Ye slay not the life which Allah hath made sacred, save in the course of justice" (Pickthall 1953: 120; cf. 17.33). This is said in the context of a statement outlawing the practice of killing children (cf. 17.31) if a family felt that it could not afford them, but it may be applied more broadly.

Abortion

According to the Qur'an (16.5), Allah ordains how long the fetus remains in the womb and when a baby is born. This would seem to imply that Muslims should not condone forced abortions, because they challenge the will of Allah. However, Surah 32.9 suggests that the fetus is not alive until "ensoulment" or "quickening" (40.68), the point at which Allah breathes the spirit into the fetus. This has opened the door for the ruling that guides Muslim teaching, that before such time as Allah breathes the spirit into a child (six weeks is the accepted time period), abortions are not in violation of the Sharia. However, the reason for the abortion must be compelling.

Euthanasia

The Qur'an teaches that Allah preordains the time of a person's birth and death. For example, Surah 6.2 reads, "He [Allah] it is Who created you from clay, and hath decreed a term for you. A term is fixed with Him. Yet still ye doubt!" (Pickthall 1953: 108). Although there is no formal Muslim position on euthanasia, the clear implication is that it would be an interference with the divine plan. Suffering is also a part of Allah's punishment for sin, and any unnatural termination of suffering would affect a person's paying the price for sin and thus finding redemption.

Economic Justice

As part of its modern revival, Islam is now engaged in a thorough soul-searching concerning its economic teachings. Islamic theorists are looking to their own tradition, especially the Qur'an and the economic practices of Muhammad during the creation of the first Muslim community in Medina, to chart a different course than either of the two dominant Western economic models: capitalism and socialism. In so doing, the issue of distribution of wealth is of critical concern. As with Christianity, there is no single point of view in Islam on economic issues. We will give here only a sense of the current discussion.

According to one expert, "... The key characteristics of the Islamic economic system are the right to private ownership of property, positive encouragement of the exploitation of resources, approval of material progress and prosperity, cooperation and mutual responsibility, acceptance of the rights of others, social justice, equitable distribution of wealth, prohibition of interest, and abstention from certain malpractices such as fraud, gambling, extortion, monopoly practices, hoarding, and the like" (Bannerman 1988: 97–98). Since Allah is the real owner of all creation (Qur'an 24:33): human ownership is as a trustee and is subject to two moral imperatives: "good management on behalf of the real owner and the requirement to apply surplus wealth productively in pursuit of social justice and the general good. . . . Although equitable distribution of wealth is deemed necessary, it is not absolute: disparities in wealth distribution are acceptable, since men are not endowed with equal intelligence, ability, and skills, and the more fortunate are not expected to hide their greater wealth" (98).

The Qur'an states that those who are able to work, and do not, deserve their poverty (4.95). However, those unable to work have a right to share in the wealth of the community (51.19, 70.24-25). Wealth itself is not unethical, but how it is acquired and distributed may be. Wealth may not be gained through cheating, robbery, or deception. As we have already noted, the *zakat*, the purifying or alms tax, requires that at least 2 1/2 percent of all acquired and held wealth must be spent on the needy each year (9:60). A series of regulations requires just treatment of debtors, widows, the poor, and orphans (90:13–16) and slaves (24:33). Additional charity beyond the tax (*sadaqa*) is high-

ly commended. People should not keep more wealth than they need for their family's present needs. Usury is strongly condemned (2.279).

Implementation of the alms tax has produced problems. Is it voluntary or obligatory? Does the state have the right to insist on payment to the central treasury? What is the proper rate? To what categories of wealth does it apply? Who qualifies as poor and needy? In Sunni practice the state usually collects. In Shi'ite communities the tax is payable to the religious authorities (Bannerman 1988: 100-101).

The main difference between Islamic economics and capitalism is the absence of interest as a source of income. The principal distinction from socialism is the recognition of private property rights. Islamic economics differs from both in the structuring of moral values into the system itself. The materialistic systems think that "livelihood" is the fundamental human problem and economic progress the ultimate end of human life. Islam recognizes these as subordinate goals (Shafi 1975: 2).

The objects of the distribution of wealth in Islam are (Shafi 1975: 7–10):

1. the establishment of a natural and practical system of economy; thus the natural force of supply and demand is recognized (see Qur'an 43:32);
2. enabling everyone to get what is rightfully due to him (including those who have not participated in the production of wealth, if Allah directs that they be cared for); and
3. eradication of concentrations of wealth (59:7).

According to capitalism, wealth is distributed only among those who have taken part in producing it through capital, labor, land, and entrepreneurship, or organization. Thus it is distributed through interest, wages, rent, or profit. Islam allows for all but the first, and adds those whom Allah directs as "secondary" recipients of wealth (Shafi 1975: 10–11).

"If the Socialist system is adopted and all capital and all land are totally surrendered to the state, the ultimate result can only be this—we would be liquidating a large number of smaller Capitalists, and putting the huge resources of national wealth at the disposal of a single big Capitalist—the State—which can deal with this reservoir of wealth quite arbitrarily. Socialism, thus, leads to the worst form of concentration of wealth" (Shafi 1975: 13). By allowing for property and rent as sources of income (in addition to wages), Islam overcomes the problems inherent in socialism. By outlawing interest and structuring in a long list of people who have a "secondary right to wealth," Islam avoids the concentration of wealth that is the great evil of capitalism (Shafi 1975: 13).

By allowing for loaning money only without interest, Islam forces the lender to share in the profit *or* loss of the borrower. "Thus, under the Islamic system of economy, Capital and Entrepreneur become one and the same, and their share in the distribution of wealth is 'Profit' not 'Interest'" (Shafi 1975: 18).

Some Muslim scholars have been critical of the gap between the Muslim ideal of social justice and the reality in many Muslim societies. As in other religious traditions, self-criticism is an important safeguard against smugness and arrogance. One Muslim teacher, Riffat Hassan, has observed that (Hassan 1982: 54):

> For hundreds of years now, Muslim masses have patiently endured the grinding poverty and oppression imposed on them by those in authority. Not to be enslaved by foreign invaders whose every attempt to subjugate them was met with resistance, Muslim masses were enslaved by Muslims in the name of God and the Prophet, made to believe that they had no rights, only responsibilities; that God was the God of Retribution, not of Love; that Islam was an ethic of suffering, not of joyous living; that they were determined by "Qismat" [fate], not masters of their own fate.

Gender Roles and the Status of Women

Before the Prophet Muhammad received his revelations from Allah, the status of women on the Arabian peninsula was desperate. Unwanted female children were buried alive, and women were treated as objects to be bought, sold, and inherited. Islam is credited with giving to women in the Arab world a status and dignity unrivalled in other regions until modern times. ". . . Islam brought legal advantages for women quite unknown in corresponding areas of the Western Christian world" (Smith 1987: 236).

Islam has been largely spared the upheaval that has occurred in Judaism and Christianity as a result of a feminist critique of male dominance. Most Muslims take this as evidence that women in Islam have an ideal status, which should be the norm for other cultures and religions. Outside critics, and some Muslim reformers, suggest that the suppression of women in Islam is so total that attempts to challenge traditional understandings of gender are very difficult to initiate and sustain.

The place to begin a study of the status of women in Islam is with passages from the Qur'an that deal with gender. Two are particularly important. Surah 4 in the Qur'an is entitled "Women," and begins with these verses (Surah 4:1–4; Dawood 1956: 354):

> Men have fear of your Lord, who created you from a single soul. From the soul He created its mate, and through them He bestrewed the earth with countless men and women.
>
> Fear Allah, in whose name you plead with one another, and honour the mothers who bore you. Allah is ever watching over you.
>
> Give the orphans the property which belongs to them. Do not exchange their valuables for that which is worthless or cheat them of their possessions; for this would surely be a great sin. If you fear that you cannot treat orphans with fairness, then you may marry other women who seem good to you: two, three, or four of them. But if you fear that you cannot maintain equality among them, marry one only or any slave-girls you may own. This will make it easier for you to avoid injustice.
>
> Give women their dowry as a free gift; but if they choose to make over to you a part of it, you may regard it as lawfully yours.

Like the Genesis account of the creation of man and woman, this text implies a complementary relationship between the two sexes, with woman created from man as "mate." One revolutionary feature is that the text assumes that women have rights that must be protected. A woman's property cannot merely be taken over when she marries. This breaks from the tradition of male "ownership" of women. The text clearly authorizes polygamy (or, more precisely, polygyny—a plurality of wives), because it is necessary for the protection of women in a society in which so many men died in battle, but places strict limits on the practice, making the welfare of the woman the primary concern. In contemporary Islam, polygyny is very rare.

A later passage in the same Surah (34–35; Dawood 1956: 358) says clearly that "Men have authority over women because Allah has made the one superior to the other, and because they spend their wealth to maintain them. Good women are obedient." Rebellious wives are to be confined to other beds and scourged, but are to be treated well if they again become obedient. The effect of this passage is to sanction patriarchy within Islam, but to place limits on male prerogative.

Surah 24:30–31 includes the text that is the basis in the Qur'an for the modest dress and veiling of women practiced in traditional Islamic societies. The verses say (Dawood 1956: 210): "Enjoin believing men to turn their eyes away from temptation and to restrain their carnal desires. This will make their lives purer. Allah has knowledge of all their actions. Enjoin believing women to turn their eyes away from temptation and to preserve their chastity; to cover their adornments (except such as are normally displayed); to draw their veils over their bosoms. . . And let them not stamp their feet in walking so as to reveal their hidden trinkets.) "The passage implores *both* male and female believers to be modest, but only women are admonished to cover themselves until they are past childbearing age. Surah 33:53 indicates that wives of the Prophet Muhammad should speak to other men from behind partitions, in the interest of propriety.

In traditional Muslim societies two practices developed to help women be modest. One is seclusion (*purdah*), under which women do not participate in the public worship in the mosque (or, if they do, they are separated from men) and do not engage in activities outside the home unless chaperoned and/or kept separate from men. The result was the creation of a woman's "life apart." The most famous example of this tradition is the harem, in which the wives of a man lived together, separate from men. The rationale for *purdah* is that it allows women to be freed from social pressures so

According to Muslim teaching, women and men are spiritual equals. Here women in Quetta, Pakistan are shown reading and memorizing the Qur'an.

that they can devote themselves to home and family. However, it has also had the effect of creating a two-tiered, gender-determined society in traditional Islamic cultures. Reformers point out that in Medina women participated with men in all worship and prayer (Smith 1987: 240).

The other practice is the veil. No specific type of veil is mentioned in the Qur'an, and the practice was actually borrowed by Muslim culture from Persian and Byzantine societies when they were conquered by the Muslim armies. It was first adopted by upper-class, urban women so that they could practice "seclusion" and still go out in public. In different cultures, different styles of covering developed. The fullest is the covering of the whole body, except for hands and feet, with the head entirely enclosed and the woman's face entirely hidden (*chador* or *burka*). More common is a veil that covers the face below the eyes or a head scarf and a long, loose-fitting dress.

SOURCES AND SUGGESTIONS FOR FURTHER STUDY

General

BUTTERWORTH, CHARLES E., AND I. WILLIAM ZARTMAN, 1992 *Political Islam.* Annals of the American Academy of Political and Social Sciences, vol. 524. Newbury Park, Calif.: Sage Publications.

CRAGG, KENNETH AND R. MARSTON SPEIGHT, 1987 *The House of Islam,* 3rd ed. Belmont, Calif.: Wadsworth.

DAWOOD, N.J., TRANS. 1956 *The Koran.* Baltimore: Penguin Books.

DENNY, FREDERICK MATHEWSON, 1987 *Islam and the Muslim Community.* San Francisco: Harper & Row.

DERMENGHEM, EMILE, 1958 *Muhammad and the Islamic Tradition,* trans. from French by J.M. Watt. New York: Harper and Brothers.

DESSOUKI, ALI E. HILLAL, ED., 1982 *Islamic Resurgence in the Arab World.* New York: Praeger.

DONAHUE, JOHN J., AND JOHN L. ESPOSITO, 1982 *Islam in Transition.* New York: Oxford University Press.

EATON, CHARLES LE GAI, 1985 *Islam and the Destiny of Man.* Albany: State University of New York Press.

ESPOSITO, JOHN J., 1983 *Voices of Resurgent Islam.* New York: Oxford University Press.

1988 *Islam: The Straight Path.* New York: Oxford University Press.

GIBB, H.A.R. ET AL., EDS., 1960 *Encyclopedia of Islam,* new ed. Leiden, Netherlands: E.J. Brill.

JAFERY, SYED MOHAMMED ASKARI, TRANS., 1965 *Nahjul Balagha of Hazrat Ali.* Pathergatti, India: Seerat-Uz-Zahra Committee.

JEFFREY, ARTHUR, ED., 1958 *Islam: Muhammad and his Religion.* New York: The Library of Liberal Arts.

KRAMER, MARTIN, ED., 1987 *Shi'ism, Resistance, and Revolution.* Boulder, Colo.: Westview Press.

LINGS, MARTIN, 1981 *What Is Sufism?* Berkeley: University of California Press.

MOMEN, MOOJAN, 1985 *An Introduction to Shi'i Islam.* New Haven, Conn.: Yale University Press.

PICKTHALL, MOHAMMAD MARMADUKE. 1953 *The Meaning of the Glorious Koran.* New York: Mentor Books.

RAHMAN, FAZLUR, 1979 *Islam.* Chicago: University of Chicago Press.

SCHIMMEL, ANNEMARIE, 1992 *Islam: An Introduction.* Albany: State University of New York Press.

Ethical Issues

General

AL FARUQI, ISMA'IL R., 1989 "Islamic Ethics," in *World Religions and Global Ethics,* ed. S. Cromwell Crawford (New York: Paragon House), 212–37.

The Ecological Crisis

ZAIDI, IQTIDAR H., 1986 "On the Ethics of Man's Interaction with the Environment: An Islamic Approach," in *Religion and Environmental Crisis,* 107–26.

War

DONNER, FRED M., 1991 "The Sources of Islamic Conceptions of War," in *Just War and Jihad: Historical Perspectives on War and Peace in Western and Islamic Traditions,* ed. John Kelsay and James Turner Johnson (New York: Greenwood Press), 31–69.

MAYER, ANN ELIZABETH, 1991 "International Law and the Islamic Tradition of War and Peace," in *Just War and Jihad,* 195–226.

Economic Justice

BANNERMAN, PATRICK, 1988 *Islam in Perspective: A Guide to Islamic Society, Politics, and Law.* London: Routledge.

BOZDAG, ISMET, 1979 *The Third Idea the World Is Waiting For: Socio Economic Model of Islam.* Karachi, Pakistan: National Book Foundation.

HASSAN, RIFFAT, 1982 "On Human Rights and the Qur'anic Perspective," in *Human Rights in Religious Traditions,* ed. Arlene Swidler (New York: Pilgrim Press), 51-65.

SHAFI, MUFTI MUHAMMAD, 1975 *Distribution of Wealth in Islam.* Karachi, Pakistan: Begum Aisha Bawany Wakf.

TURNER, BRIAN S., 1974 *Weber and Islam: A Critical Study.* London: Routledge & Kegan Paul.

Gender Roles and the Status of Women

AFSHAR, HALEH, 1987 *Women, State, and Ideology: Studies from Africa and Asia.* Albany: State University of New York Press.

AHMED, LEILA, 1992 *Women and Gender in Islam. Historical Roots of a Modern Debate.* New Haven, Conn.: Yale University Press.

AL-HIBRI, AZIZAH, ed., 1982 *Women and Islam.* Elmsford, N.Y.: Pergamon Press.

FRIEDL, ERIKA, 1989 "Islam and Tribal Women in a Village in Iran," in *Unspoken Worlds: Women's Religious Lives,* ed. Nancy A. Falk and Rita M. Gross (Belmont, Calif. Wadsworth Publishing), 125–33.

HUSSEIN, FREDA, ED., 1984 *Muslim Women: The Ideal and Contextual Realities.* New York: St. Martin's Press.

MURATA, SACHIKO, 1992 *The Tao of Islam: A Sourcebook on Gender Relationships in Islamic Thought.* Albany: State University of New York Press.

SMITH, JANE I., ED., 1980 *Women in Contemporary Muslim Societies.* Lewisburg, Pa.: Bucknell University Press.

1987 "Islam," in *Women in World Religions,* ed. Arvind Sharma (Albany: State University of New York Press), 235–50.

1994 "Women in Islam," in *Today's Woman in World Religions,* ed. Arvind Sharma (Albany: State University of New York Press), 303–25.

TABARI, ASAR, AND NAHID YEGANEH, EDS., 1984 *In the Shadow of Islam: The Women's Rights Movement in Iran.* New York: St. Martin's Press.

Homosexuality

DURAN, KHALID, 1983 "Homosexuality and Islam," in *Homosexuality and World Religions,* ed. Arlene Swidler (Valley Forge, Pa.: Trinity Press International), 181–97.

HERDT, GILBERT, 1987 "Homosexuality," in *Encyclopedia of Religion,* ed. Mircea Eliade (New York: Macmillan), vol. 6, 445–53.

SECTION VI

Conclusion

As we conclude this survey of the world's religions and their responses to basic human questions and contemporary ethical issues, two important areas of inquiry remain.

In addition to the major religions to which we have devoted separate chapters, our world today is populated by a host of new religions that deserve our attention. Many of them are familiar because they have been widely covered in the media; others are not as well-known but are fascinating nonetheless. Some of the new religions, we will study in Chapter Fourteen are movements that began within the major religions, others are unique. The large number of such religions is a good indication that we are living in an era of religious ferment and change.

Our final topic shifts our focus to the future. In Chapter Fifteen we will examine two questions about the future of the world's religions. What will be the relationship among religions in the future? We will look at three possible patterns of relationship, with examples of efforts oriented at realizing them: exclusivism, inclusivism, and pluralism. The second question will be whether religions will be able to find common ground in addressing the critical issues our world faces. As an example, we will look for evidence of cooperation among religions in the area of addressing the ecological crisis. The final word about religions and the future will come from an unlikely source.

CHAPTER 14

The New Religions

INTRODUCTION: WHY SO MANY NEW RELIGIONS?

A survey of the world's religions would not be complete without attention to religions that have sprung up in the modern era. Almost all of the religious movements discussed in this chapter began in the nineteenth or twentieth century. Some emerged from the major religious traditions discussed in the previous chapters. Others are religions that have a spiritual ultimacy, but claim no association with any of the major religions. Still others are the "secular" religions whose patterns of ultimacy rule out a spiritual dimension of existence. In selecting from among the hundreds of new religions practiced by over 150 million people in the world today, we have chosen a representative sampling of new religions that are well-established in North America.

Why are there so many new religions and why are they so popular today? There are, of course, many reasons debated by interpreters. Here are but a few possible explanations. One cause is the growing individualism in the modern world. Even in cultures with a strong tradition of group solidarity, such as Japan, people are increasingly willing to step out on their own, turn from the traditional religious commitments of their families, and join new religious movements. A characteristic of new religions is that they often provide an alternative communal atmosphere for persons who feel isolated and alone. A related reason is growing alienation from traditional religions, creating an environment in which people are more willing to turn to religions that offer alternative approaches to basic human questions and responses to contemporary ethical issues. At the same time, some new religions claim to return to the "true teachings" of a religious tradition and appeal to some people's desire to retreat from the chaos and confusion they perceive in the modern world. Other new religions appeal to many people's fears and fascination about the future, offering myths that guarantee that those who embrace them will have their futures secured when the "end" comes. The rapid development of communications technology must also be considered a factor in the rapid growth of new religions. New religions now have access to fairly inexpensive means to communicate their messages and to research that shows them how to "package" their messages effectively so that people today will respond. Many new religions have made more effective use of modern communications technology than traditional religions. Another factor is the bureaucratization of some of the major religions, which has made it more difficult for people to see them as communities responsive to the spiritual needs of persons. New religions effectively address the needs people express in a way that seems less organizationally structured than major religions. Finally, many people today yearn for clear and straightforward messages expressed by forceful leaders. A common denominator of most new religions is the presence of a charismatic leader, who has a vivid and appealing message that is delivered in an engaging style of communication.

THE "CULTS" CONTROVERSY

Once again, we face a decision about classifying a group of religions. Many of the religions discussed in this chapter are called "cults" or "sects." Speaking descriptively, a *cult* is a movement that focuses on one person or god; a *sect* is a religious group that has split from another movement or is a particular group within a larger religion. In that sense many of these groups fit these definitions. However, in common usage today the terms "cult" and "sect" have become pejorative labels to refer to religious groups in which, it is argued, fanatical loyalty to a central leader clouds the members' judgment and causes them to sacrifice their individual will and identity for the sake of the group. From this perspective cults subject people to psychologically coercive recruitment and indoctrination practices ("brainwashing") and practice rejection or hatred of the rest of society. Portrayed negatively, cults and sects are "parasitic," receiving funding through deception for the personal gain of the leadership elite, but performing no service for society.

387

A "New Age" channeler in the mountains of Peru receives spiritual energy.

After horrific events such as the mass suicide of 900 persons at the People's Temple in Guyana in 1978 and, more recently, the tragic deaths of more than ninety persons in the events surrounding the Branch Davidian community in Waco, Texas, in 1993, concern grows and questions are raised (but not resolved) as to how "dangerous cults" may be effectively monitored and controlled without endangering the religious freedom of responsible movements that are not in the religious mainstream in a society. On the other hand, how may the freedom of mature individuals to choose their own religion be preserved while susceptible persons are protected from becoming victims of insidious leaders who exploit people's desire to belong and have meaning in life? Your reflection on such questions is encouraged as you begin this chapter.

In the highly charged religious atmosphere of the late twentieth century, the debate rages over which of the new religious movements are "dangerous" and which are merely unique but legitimate expressions of the human quest for ultimate transformation. Some observers would call some, even all, of the movements to be discussed in this chapter offensive "cults," which should be exposed as such. Some parents concerned about children who have joined new religious groups have hired "deprogrammers" to kid-

nap their sons or daughters and perform psychologically coercive techniques in an attempt to "cleanse" them from what the parents view as the cults' brainwashing and restore the children to "normalcy." Defenders of freedom of religion as a basic, absolute value challenge the legality and morality of deprogramming, pointing out that the very same techniques condemned in cults are used in deprogramming. They also remind critics that some of the major religions of today (for example, Christianity) were condemned as dangerous cults or sects when they originated. Many experts on the new religions to be discussed in this chapter now contend that the term "cult" has become so loaded and devalued that it should not be used at all in serious discussions. We will honor that recommendation.

We choose the more neutral and descriptive phrase "new religions" to describe the movements discussed in this chapter in order to maintain the descriptive approach outlined in Chapter One. Our intention is to describe, not evaluate, these movements. However, where serious and apparently credible charges have been made about the negative effects contact with the religion being discussed has had on persons, these accusations will also be noted. Readers are invited to set aside their preconceptions and seek an understanding of these religions, as a basis for a personal evaluation of them.

THE "NEW AGE" PHENOMENON

Walking across hot coals without being burned. Trance channeling to communicate with the spirit world. Healing with crystals. Returning to a past life. Abduction by a UFO. These are examples of activities associated with what has become known as the "New Age." New Age does not refer to a single religious group or movement, but rather to an array of individuals and organizations who share a general perspective about the contemporary era and its spiritual significance. Proponents of the New Age perspective typically believe that we are living in a time with as much potential for transforming human culture as the Renaissance and Protestant Reformation. We are on the verge, it is believed, of a breakthrough into a new era in which there will be peace and harmony. We will, in this brief overview, survey the general New Age worldview, using the framework we have developed for studying religion, and describe a few of the groups and events that manifest this point of view. We are indebted in this section to the information on the New Age phenomenon gathered by Russell Chandler in his book *Understanding the New Age* (1988).

The New Age Worldview

Not all groups or teachers who are associated with the New Age phenomenon share the same worldview, but the following characteristics are most common. According to the New Age perspective, the basic human dilemma is blindness to our true nature. We are as humans merely extensions of a cosmic Oneness, which is spiritual. Hidden or suppressed in our physical nature is a higher spiritual nature, a true self (much like the *atman* of Hinduism). We in the West lose touch with this Oneness, according to the New Age perspective, principally because of the rationalism and individualism of modern Western culture that causes us to lead fragmented lives, in the illusion that we are sepa-

rate from one another and from reality. All reality is One, from the New Age perspective. Pure consciousness and universal energy are descriptions of this Oneness. Sources for this point of view are the monism we have encountered in Eastern philosophies such as Hindu Advaita Vedanta (see Chapter Five) and Taoism (see Chapter Eight), but also the teachings on matter and energy found in modern quantum physics. The goal in the New Age worldview is enlightenment, an intuitive experience of Oneness. However, the goal is not merely individual spiritual enlightenment, but a "paradigm shift" for humanity as a whole, a transition into a "higher consciousness." A host of methods are available to those who seek to wake to their "higher selves." These include classical techniques associated with Asian religions, such as meditation and chanting. However, the New Age perspective is not exclusive, and a variety of innovative methods of spiritual advancement are found within the broad New Age umbrella, including the use of mind-altering drugs and various devices designed to measure and assist in the process of transformation. Those who become enlightened will naturally find themselves drawn to those political, economic, and social causes that they believe will contribute to the emergence of the new "planetary consciousness" of Oneness. For example, New Age proponents are often enthusiastic participants in ecologically oriented groups.

New Age Groups and Events

The roots of the modern New Age movement in the United States are in nineteenth-century Spiritualism, which gave rise to at least one of the new religions we will discuss below (Theosophy), and the visits of spiritual teachers such as Swami Vivekananda, founder of the Vedanta Society, after the first World Parliament of Religions in 1893.

The more recent background, however, is found in the "countercultural" movements of the 1950s and '60s and the fascination with Zen Buddhism and other Eastern religions of influential writers such as Jack Kerouac and Alan Watts. The 1971 publication of *Be Here Now* by Harvard psychology professor Richard Alpert, who took the name

Baba Ram Dass after studying with a guru in India, is considered by some interpreters to mark the beginning of the contemporary New Age phenomenon.

In the 1970s and '80s a variety of gurus came from India to the United States, attracted devoted followers, and helped increase interest in the New Age. They included Swami Muktananda; Maharishi Mahesh Yogi, founder of Transcendental Meditation; Maharaj Ji, whose "Divine Light Mission" was very popular; and Bhagwan Shree Rajneesh, who established a center in Oregon before being deported and returning to India. Actress Shirley MacLaine's well-publicized belief in reincarnation and channeling also helped increase interest. J.Z. Knight, channeling for a 35,000-year-old warrior named Ramtha, told people to take responsibility for their own lives and convinced many people to move to the American Northwest to prepare for a massive destruction that Ramtha predicted would occur before the year 2000.

Elizabeth Clare Prophet, founder of the Church Universal and Triumphant and known to her followers as Guru Ma, is another New Age leader. Guru Ma claims to be God's chosen earthly messenger who receives (channels) direct messages from a variety of "ascended masters," including Buddha, Jesus, Pope John XXIII, Christopher Columbus, and "K-17," the head of the "Cosmic Secret Service." The Church is centered on a large ranch near Yellowstone National Park, where her followers are preparing for the end of history and the beginning of the new age. The teaching of her church is a complex mixture of ideas drawn from both Asian and Western religions.

One of the most famous New Age events was the "Harmonic Convergence" on August 16 and 17, 1987. Art historian Jose Arguelles convinced 144,000 believers to gather at 350 sacred sites around the world to participate in an event intended to "synchronize the Earth with the rest of the galaxy." He chose the dates because of the alignment of nine planets and his interpretation of the Aztec calendar. Arguelles believed that the 144,000 people linked together would release energy to "jump start" enough people to set in motion the new age of peace and harmony.

Among the other groups linked to the New Age phenomenon by some interpreters that will be surveyed in this chapter are Scientology, the Self-Realization Fellowship, the Unification Church, and Wicca. It should be noted that for academic interpreters, "New Age" is a media-generated label that is of limited value in a serious study of new religious movements.

CASE STUDIES

The organization of a survey of the new religions poses a problem. We could group them together in terms of their association with the major religious traditions described earlier. For example, we could discuss Wicca as an indigenous religion (since its roots may be traced to the indigenous religions of pre-Christian Europe) and the Jehovah's Witnesses as a movement obviously rooted in Christianity. However, some groups have roots in more than one of the religious traditions (e.g., the Native American Church and Baha'i). We could organize the religious movements chronologically in terms of their date of origin. However, in some cases there are differences of opinion between the movement and outside observers on when the religion started. Other types of possible classification could be on the basis of the style of leadership in the movement or the numbers of adherents. These and other approaches have legitimacy.

In this work we have decided to adopt a more neutral method of organizing our survey. We *will* make a broad distinction between new religions with spiritually oriented patterns of ultimacy and those that are secular in their focus. However, under each of these headings the "new religions" will be discussed alphabetically, using the first letter of the first word in the name the movement prefers or the name that is most common.

There are many other new religions that could be covered besides those discussed here. For example, the guru tradition in India has inspired many other charismatic religious movements in India beyond those discussed here. In addition to those associated with the New Age phenomenon mentioned above we could also include the 3HO (Happy, Health, Holy Organization); the Sikh Dharma Brotherhood of the Yogi Bhajan; the True World Order of Swami Vishnu-Devananda; the Sri Chinmoy Centers of Sri Chinmoy; the Siddha Yoga Dham movement of Gurumayi Chidvilasananda; and the movement associated with Satya Sai Baba, who lives in South India but is said to be an *avatar* of God who appears to devotees wherever they live. We could also discuss more of the religions associated with the New Thought movement in nineteenth-century America. Christian Science is one religion with a background in New Thought (see below), but there are others including the well-established Unity School of Christianity (headquartered in Lee's Summit, Missouri) and the School of Metaphysics.

Why is it important to study new religions, including those that seem most foreign to our own values and worldviews? In an address on the tragedy involving the Branch Davidians, J. Gordon Melton, a scholar who has devoted his entire career to the study of new religions, states the case plainly (Melton 1993):

> *We ... know the pleasurable feeling we receive when someone with a different myth understands us. Such is the case with small (at least right now) new religions. Instead of denigrating them, instead of ignoring them, instead of dismissing them, let us attempt to understand them. Just maybe we have something to learn from each other.*

The Baha'i House of Worship in Wilmette, Illinois, one of five in the world, one on each continent.

SPIRITUALLY ORIENTED NEW RELIGIONS

The Baha'i Faith: Toward World Unity

History and Basic Teaching In 1844 a young Iranian Shi'ite Muslim (who was also influenced by Sufi mysticism) named Mirza Ali Muhammad (1819–1850) proclaimed that he was the *Bab-ud-Din* ("Gate of the Faith"). According to the beliefs of the Shi'ite sect to which he belonged, the Bab was claiming to be the twelfth Imam who had disappeared and would return as the *Mahdi*, the messiah who would restore a purified Islam. His followers

became known as *Babis* and in 1848 withdrew from Islam. They called for significant reforms of Iranian society. For most of his ministry the Bab was imprisoned. In 1850 he was executed. Before he died he announced that another would follow him, who would be the prophet of a new, universal religion.

One of the Bab's followers, Mirza Husayn Ali (1817–1892), experienced a revelation while in prison in 1852 in which he first experienced a call to be the prophet of God for the modern age, whom the Bab had foretold. In 1863 he publicly proclaimed himself as a prophet in the succession of Muhammad, Moses, and Jesus. His followers called him *Baha'u'llah* ("The Glory of God") and the religion he established became known as the *Baha'i* ("Glory") *Faith*.

Baha'u'llah spent most of the rest of his life persecuted and under arrest, transported from one location to another, finally spending his last years under fairly liberal house arrest in Acre, Palestine. Even though imprisoned, he nurtured the Baha'i movement and wrote a number of works used today by members of the Baha'i Faith for worship and study. He also communicated with world leaders, urging that they dedicate themselves to world peace and understanding.

Upon Baha'ullah's death his son, known as Abdul Baha ("Servant of Glory"), succeeded him. Abdul Baha (1844–1921) established branches of the movement in the United States and developed the teachings of his father as they are understood in the West. Abdul Baha's grandson, Shoghi Effendi ("Guardian of the Cause") (1897–1957), succeeded him and continued his grandfather's missionary and organizational work. After Shoghi Effendi's death leadership passed to a Universal House of Justice.

The Baha'i Faith teaches that all religions are true, for they all come from the same source. In virtually every age God reveals the truth through a designated prophet. Baha'u'llah, however, as the prophet of the modern age, is the last and greatest of these messengers. God is one, and so is humanity. All prejudice must be overcome, for all humans are members of the same family. The Baha'i Faith also teaches that in the modern age science and religion must cooperate, for their teachings balance one another. Any religion that makes a claim contrary to science is distorting the truth. The freedom of each individual to pursue the truth must be protected. Equality between men and women is also stressed. The Baha'i Faith also strongly advocates world peace and calls for universal education and a universal language to help attain this goal.

The extremes of wealth and poverty must also be eliminated, the Baha'i Faith teaches, if world peace is to be realized. A universal court should be given the power to judge international disputes, so war can be avoided. The Baha'i Faith advocates a theory of work that considers it service to God. In

COSMIC QUESTIONS: WHAT IS THE DESTINY OF THE COSMOS?

The Regeneration of the Whole World

In this text Baha'u'llah prophesies the coming together of all humanity and the regeneration of the entire universe (Baha'u'llah 1952: No. 115, p. 243).

I testify that Thou art the Lord of all creation, and the Educator of all beings, visible and invisible. I bear witness that Thy power hath encompassed the entire universe, and that the hosts of the earth can never dismay Thee, nor can the dominion of all peoples and nations deter Thee from executing Thy purpose. I confess that Thou hast no desire except the regeneration of the whole world, and the establishment of the unity of its peoples, and the salvation of all them that dwell therein.

Excerpts from Gleanings From the Writings of Baha'u'llah *by Baha'u'llah. Copyright © 1952, 1976 by the National Spiritual Assembly of the Baha'is of the United States. Reprinted by permission.*

keeping with its pragmatic orientation, the Baha'i Faith rejects a literal interpretation of heaven and hell. The souls of humans are eternal, but heaven and hell are not "places" where they go, but rather states of existence measured by the degree of harmony with God the soul exhibits. Its worldview is essentially positive. No separate force of evil (such as Satan) is recognized. Evil is merely the lack of goodness.

The Muslim background of the Baha'i Faith is evident in the movement's attitude toward worship. Daily prayer is mandated, and Bahai's should fast during one of the nineteen months in the Baha'i Faith's calendar (the period between March 2 and March 20) unless they are ill, pregnant, nursing, very old, young, performing heavy labor or traveling. There is no special clergy to conduct services, which are usually held in a member's home.

Worship is uncomplicated, with prayer and readings from the writings of Baha'u'llah and Abdul Baha. Individual congregations are administered by nine-member Local Spiritual Assemblies. Each country has a National Spiritual Assembly, also with nine members. The number nine, the largest whole number, symbolizes the world unity the Baha'i Faith seeks to promote. Local communities typically do not have separate buildings in which they worship. However, magnificent Houses of Worship have been constructed on all five continents. The North American House of Worship is located on the shores of Lake Michigan in Wilmette, Illinois.

Today there are approximately 5 million members of the Baha'i Faith in the world. The nation with the most Bahai's is India, with 2 million, followed by Iran with about 300,000; the United States has 110,000 Bahai's. The movement is growing fairly rapidly in the developing world because of its commitment to universal justice and acceptance of diverse cultures. Since the 1979 Islamic Revolution in Iran, members in the homeland of the religion have been intensely persecuted by the Islamic authorities, who view the religion as a heretical departure from the true faith. More than 200 Bahai's have been killed.

Responses to Contemporary Ethical Issues

THE ECOLOGICAL CRISIS   The Baha'i Faith is very concerned with the relationship between the human and non-human worlds and the human responsibility to care for the earth. However, teachings of the Baha'i Faith also reflect the attitude of the religions that originated in the Middle East that humanity is at the center of creation (Baha'u'llah 1952: No. 27, p. 65):

> *Having created the world and all that liveth and moveth therein, He, through the direct operation of His unconstrained and sovereign Will, chose to confer upon man the unique distinction and capacity to know Him and to love Him—a capacity that must needs be regarded as the generating impulse and the primary purpose underlying the whole of creation . . . . Upon the inmost reality of each and every created thing He has shed the light of one of His names, and made it a recipient of the glory of one of His attributes. Upon the reality of man, however,*

> *He has focused the radiance of all of His names and attributes, and made it a mirror of His own Self. Alone of all created things man has been singled out for so great a favor, so enduring a bounty.*

WAR   Abdul Baha wrote in 1912 that, "When perfect equality shall be established between men and women, peace may be realized for the simple reason that womankind in general will never favor warfare. Women will not be willing to allow those whom they have so tenderly cared for to go to the battlefield. When they shall have a vote, they will oppose any cause of warfare" (Pokorny 1984: 7).

The ideal of the Baha'i Faith is a unified world in which national loyalties have been transcended and people share a commitment to the well-being of all. The task of members of the Baha'i Faith is to model the "new world order," and, by the spreading of the teachings of Baha'u'llah and other Baha'i leaders, to show others the way to find world unity.

ECONOMIC JUSTICE   Although the Baha'i Faith recognizes that wealth earned by hard work in an honorable profession is ethical, there is a great deal of concern about the disparity between the rich and the poor. According to the principles of the Baha'i Faith, the rich (which on a world scale includes the American middle class) are obligated to give of their wealth for the poor. Baha'u'llah echoed other great religious leaders when he said, "O Ye that Pride Yourselves on Mortal Riches! Know ye in truth that wealth is a mighty barrier between the seeker and his desire, the lover and his beloved. The rich, but for a few, shall in no wise attain the court of His presence nor enter the city of content and resignation" (cited in Thomas 1984: 95). He also said, "Nobody should die of hunger; everybody should have sufficient clothing; one man should not live in excess while another has no possible means of existence" (cited in Thomas 1984: 97). From the perspective of the Baha'i Faith, both societies and individuals have an obligation to respond to the needs of the poor.

GENDER ROLES AND THE STATUS OF WOMEN   One of the twelve principles of the Baha'i Faith, first enunciated in 1912, is that there is equality between men and women. Baha'u'llah had said that "the

QUESTIONS OF HUMAN IDENTITY: WHAT IS THE BASIC HUMAN DILEMMA?

Disunity

For the Baha'i Faith, the basic human problem is disunity (Messages 1976: 46).

The true cause of the ills of humanity is disunity. No matter how perfect may be the machinery devised by the leaders of men for the political unity of the world, it will not provide the antidote to the poison sapping the vigor of present-day society. These ills can be cured only through the instrumentality of God's Faith. . . . The Baha'i Community is a worldwide organization seeking to establish true and universal peace on earth.

Excerpt from Messages From the Universal House of Justice, 1968-73. Copyright © 1976 by the National Spiritual Assembly of the Baha'is of the United States. Reprinted by permission.

capacity of woman has become so awakened and manifest in this age that equality of man and woman is an established fact" (cited in Schoonmaker 1984: 142). Members of the Baha'i Faith are taught that with "the emergence of womankind as a full and coequal partner with mankind ... human civilization will take the next vital step forward" (Schoonmaker 1984: 143). It is education, according to the teaching of the Baha'i Faith, that will enable women to realize this equality.

Branch Davidians: Unlocking the Seven Seals

Introduction   Until the spring of 1993 few people had heard of a small religious movement known as the Branch Davidians. That quickly changed on February 28, 1993, when agents from the U.S. government's Bureau of Alcohol, Tobacco, and Firearms failed in an attempt to enter a hundred-member Branch Davidian community called Mt. Carmel outside Waco, Texas, to execute a search warrant for illegal weapons. Four ATF agents and a number of Branch Davidians were killed in an exchange of gunfire. Then began a siege of Mt. Carmel, headed by the Federal Bureau of Investigation. Branch Davidian leader David Koresh and his followers inside Mt. Carmel refused to surrender, and a stand-off began. Attempts to negotiate a peaceful resolution through negotiation continued for fifty-one days until Mt. Carmel burned to the ground on April 19 after the FBI had used tanks spraying a powerful chemical to try to force those inside to come out. Eighty-six members of the community (including seventeen children) died. Some of the survivors have been charged with murder in the death of the ATF agents. All charged were acquitted; but a few were convicted of lesser charges.

This tragedy raises a number of very important questions. Who are the Branch Davidians and what do they believe? Why did attempts to negotiate a peaceful resolution fail? More generally, what may be learned from this incident about interactions between government agencies and new religious movements? What may be learned about the way the media covers new religions?

History and Basic Teachings   In 1935 Victor Houteff, the founder of a group known as the Davidians, moved from California to Waco, Texas, and there opened a commune known as Mt. Carmel Center. Houteff, an immigrant from Bulgaria, had joined the Seventh-Day Adventist Church (see below) soon after arriving in the United States in 1918. A year before moving to Waco, Houteff had left the Seventh-Day Adventists and started his new movement. Basing his beliefs on the apocalyptic writings in the Bible, Houteff taught that the return of Jesus to earth was imminent, and with his return the eternal Kingdom of David, promised in the Old Testament, would begin. He gave his group the name "Davidian Seventh Day Adventists," but since it had no association with the Seventh-Day Adventist denomination, it became known simply as the Davidians. In addition to the Waco community, other Davidian groups sprang up in the United States and elsewhere in the world; for example, in England and Australia.

When Houteff died in 1955, his wife, Florence, assumed leadership of the Davidians and announced that on April 22, 1959, during the Jewish Passover, the Kingdom of David would be established on earth. Hundreds of Davidians sold whatever they owned and converged on Waco to await the Second Coming of Christ. When the end did not come, a new leader named Ben Roden and a majority of the Davidians broke off from the main group and formed a new movement, which took the name Branch Davidians. They assumed control of Mt. Carmel. When Roden died in 1978, his wife, Lois, became the leader of the Branch Davidians and initiated an effort that increased the group's international membership.

In 1987 a young convert to the Branch Davidians named Vernon Howell became the group's leader and prophet, after a bloody conflict with Roden's son, George. Howell changed his name to David Koresh, taking the name of the ancient Israel-ite King David and the Hebrew version of the Persian King Cyrus, whom the prophet Isaiah called a messiah (anointed one) of God. Eventually, David Koresh proclaimed that he was a messiah sent by God to serve as a divine teacher during the last days before the return of Christ. He fathered many children, believing that was his mission as described in Isaiah 45:4–7, 10–16. Koresh's claim was widely misinterpreted in the media to mean that he was claiming to *be* Jesus Christ. Koresh taught his followers instead that he had been chosen by God to open the Seven Seals described in the New Testament Book of Revelation. The opening of the seals would lead to the final judgment, in which the forces of evil would be vanquished and God's elect would inherit the eternal Kingdom.

Unfortunately, the attempted forced entry by the ATF was a clear indication to Koresh and the Branch Davidians that the final battle prophesied in Revelation was about to begin. Surrender to the forces of "Babylon" was, for Koresh and his followers, not in the "script" they believed they had to follow. They believed that they were living in the time of the Fifth Seal in Revelation. According to Revelation 6:9–11, they had to wait for a sign from God to Koresh. At that time they would die, only to be raised from the dead when Christ returned. The Branch Davidians lived in their own symbolic world, defined by their understanding of the apocalyptic signs in the Bible, and they believed David Koresh alone could unlock the code. The FBI negotiators could make little sense of the biblical language Koresh used when they talked with him, and they decided he was merely stalling. Several scholars of religion, who understood the apocalyptic worldview of the Davidians, engaged in dialogue with Koresh through his legal representatives during the siege, and had developed what they believed was a method whereby Koresh could surrender without compromising his understanding of the Book of Revelation (Tabor 1993). However, the scholars were unable to convince the federal authorities that their approach might be effective. Thus, once again, on April 19, 1993, a forced entry was attempted. Again, the Davidians felt they had to act according to their understanding of Revelation, and the prophesied conflagration occurred.

There are important lessons to be learned from this tragedy. First, government agencies dealing with new religions must "do their homework." In the Waco tragedy it was evident that neither the FBI nor the ATF had a very good understanding of who the Branch Davidians were and what they believed. They depended for their information on disgruntled former members who obviously presented a biased picture; psychologists who tried to fit David Koresh and his followers into secular profiles that assumed that they were not really acting on the basis of their professed religious beliefs but rather pathological drives; and groups such as the Cult Action Network, which view new religious groups such as the Branch Davidians as dangerous "cults" in which people are "brainwashed" by unscrupulous, psychopathic leaders. Amidst this clutter of information, the views of legitimate experts on new religions who could help the agencies understand the worldview of the Branch Davidians were seen as just one set of opinions among others. There obviously needs to be better communication between scholars who study the new religions and the government agencies that find themselves confronting them. Fortunately, as a result of the Waco tragedy new avenues of communication between religious scholars and the FBI and other government agencies that deal with new religions seem to have opened.

Second, the media must look beyond the sensational aspects of a new religion and try to help the public understand groups such as the Branch Davidians before condemning them. The press seized upon allegations of child abuse (which turned out to be false) and David Koresh's claim to be "Christ" as well as his fathering of many children. Like the government agencies, most in the media seemed unable to look beneath the surface to try to understand the worldview of the Branch Davidians. This led to public outcries to do something to protect the children, to liberate people from this "dangerous cult," and to capture the "madman" David Koresh.

Finally, the public needs to demand that they be provided with accurate information about new religious groups. It would be best if the public were educated about such groups before crises such as the Waco incident arise. However, at the least, when a group such as the Branch Davidians becomes the center of a controversy, we need to avoid the easy tendency to stereotype and judge before we understand. Public perception is a potent force, and had the perception of the Branch Davidians been more accurate, the pressure may very well have been to find a way to resolve the tragedy more peacefully rather than to end it quickly.

Christian Science: Healing through Faith

History and Basic Teachings In 1866 a woman named Mary Baker Eddy (1821–1910), who had been studying various forms of mental healing, experienced a miraculous healing after a serious injury. Eddy devoted the rest of her life to the promotion of Christian healing. Her book, *Science and Health with Key to the Scriptures,* the primary supplement to the Bible in Christian Science, appeared in 1875. Four years later the Church of Christ (Scientist) was organized, with headquarters in Boston, Massachusetts (home of the Mother Church). The goal of the movement was to recover original Christianity, with its emphasis on healing, which had been lost as Christianity evolved. Each congregation is expected to make available a reading room in which the public has access to

Mary Baker Eddy (1821-1910), founder of the Church of Christ (Scientist).

Christian Scientist publications, including the highly respected newspaper *The Christian Science Monitor.*

In accord with Eddy's teachings, the Bible and her book are the pastor in Christian Science, so there is no professional clergy. At services, portions of Scripture and *Science and Health* are read, and members witness to their faith experiences. Instead of ministers or priests, some lay members (male or female) function as "practitioners." They specialize in the healing ministry of the church, which takes place outside the context of the services, usually in the members' homes.

Christian Science teaches that God is the Divine Mind, the only principle that really exists. Only Mind and Spirit are real; matter is an illusion. Since sickness strikes the material body, it cannot be real. The error is in thinking it is. The same is true of sin and death. Error is overcome through prayer. As a believer develops spiritually, the error is transformed and apparent sicknesses disappear.

Christian Scientists choose themselves whether to refuse traditional medical treatment. Civil

QUESTIONS ABOUT THE SACRED: WHAT IS THE SACRED?

Infinite Mind and Spirit

In Science and Health with Key to the Scriptures, *Mary Baker Eddy defined God in the following terms. Note how Eddy draws on traditional Christian imagery and adds unique nuances (Eddy 1906: 465, 587, 256).*

God is incorporeal, divine, supreme, infinite Mind, Spirit, Soul, Principle, Life, Truth, Love.

GOD. The great I AM; the all-knowing, all-seeing, all-acting, all-wise, all-loving, and eternal; Principle; Mind; Soul; Spirit; Life; Truth; Love; all substance; intelligence.

Love, the divine Principle, is the Father and Mother of the universe, including man.

Excerpt from Science and Health with Key to the Scriptures, *by Mary Baker Eddy.*

while Christian Scientists strive to follow Jesus' commands and to fulfill his promise of abundant life, they recognize, like all Christians, how far they still have to go in this regard. And they feel only the deepest compassion for those faced with the dilemma they may feel when struggling with pain and disease, either Christian Scientists or others.

QUESTIONS OF HUMAN IDENTITY: WHO ARE WE?

Spiritual and Perfect

According to Christian Scientists humanity is spiritual and perfect. Anything that detracts from this perfection is a product of false thinking that can be corrected through purifying thought and gaining a deeper understanding of God and man in His image and likeness. This turning of thought to the spiritual truths about God and man is prayer that brings healing to the human experience. (Eddy 1906: 475).

What is man?

Man is not matter; he is not made up of brain, blood, bones, and other material elements. The Scriptures inform us that man is made in the image and likeness of God. Matter is not that likeness. The likeness of Spirit cannot be so unlike Spirit. Man is spiritual and perfect; and because he is spiritual and perfect, he must be so understood in Christian Science. Man is idea, the image of Love; he is not physique. He is the compound idea of God, including all right ideas; the generic term for all that reflects God's image and likeness; the conscious identity of being as found in Science; ... that which has not a single quality underived from Deity; that which possesses no life, intelligence, nor creative power of his own but reflects spiritually all that belongs to his Maker .... Man is incapable of sin, sickness, and death. The real man cannot depart from holiness....

Excerpt from Science and Health with Key to the Scriptures, *by Mary Baker Eddy.*

courts have sometimes held Christian Scientist parents accountable for withholding treatment from their children.

As noted, Christian Science was itself the source of other religious movements that are often grouped together under the label "New Thought." They include the Unity School of Christianity, the United Church of Religious Science, and the Spiritual Frontiers Fellowship. With Christian Science they share an abiding faith that God dwells within each human being, and through faith anything is possible.

Responses to Contemporary Ethical Issues

EUTHANASIA   As an example of a Christian Science response to a contemporary ethical issue, we include the following statement on euthanasia (cited in LaRue 1985: 115):

A Christian Scientist does not consider any disease beyond the power of God to heal. For this reason, he would not be an advocate of euthanasia. Christian Scientists realize the complexity of this issue within the context of ordinary medical practice, however. Also

The Church of Jesus Christ of Latter-day Saints (the Mormons)

History and Basic Teachings   The founder of the Church of Jesus Christ of Latter-day Saints was Joseph Smith (1805–1844). Like other religious founders, Smith was seeking for the truth amidst a variety of spiritual paths when he experienced a revelation. For Smith revelation came in 1822, when an angel named Moroni told him about golden plates containing the word of God in a language called Reformed Egyptian hieroglyphics. Moroni told Smith he had been chosen to dig up these buried plates. Smith found them a year later near Manchester, New York. He was equipped with two special stones, the Urim and Thummim, to enable him to read the plates. He eventually translated them as the Book of Mormon in 1830.

The movement begun by Smith proclaimed that Christ's kingdom would come in America. Within a year he and his wife Emma had attracted a thousand followers, mostly converts from other religions. He led his followers first to Ohio, then to Missouri. (Smith believed the New Jerusalem was going to arrive in Independence, Missouri.) Called now Mormons, Smith and his followers sparked opposition because of their attacks on the validity of other Christian groups. Driven out of Missouri, Smith established an autonomous Mormon enclave in Nauvoo, Illinois. From there missionaries spread out to carry the Mormon faith. Thousands of converts came to join the Nauvoo community. Hostility grew and Smith was killed by an angry mob in 1844.

After Smith's death the movement split. Members of Smith's family joined a remnant of other followers who had stayed in Missouri and formed the Reorganized Church of Jesus Christ of Latter-day Saints. Today the world headquarters of the RLDS movement is in Independence, Missouri. They reject the name "Mormon."

The "Mormons" are those who associate with the followers of Smith who accepted the leadership of Brigham Young (1801–1877). They retained the name Church of Jesus Christ of Latter-day Saints (LDS). From this point on, our discussion will be confined to this group. Brigham Young led the famous migration to Utah. Near Great Salt Lake, Young and his followers founded the "Zion in the Wilderness." Young's followers transformed a desolate area into a thriving region that they called Deseret, from the Reformed Egyptian word for "honey bee." When they arrived, Utah was part of Mexican Territory. When the United States took control, opposition to Young led ultimately to the dissolution of the church corporation in 1887 and the outlawing of the accepted Mormon practice of polygamy. In 1890 the church officially abandoned polygamy.

After Utah achieved statehood, Mormons settled into their roles as citizens and focused on the development of the church. The movement has grown to about 5 million members in the United States, with rapid expansion around the world through their international missionary efforts.

The doctrine of the Mormon Church is rooted in basic Christian teachings, but with some unique interpretations based on the revelation Smith received. For Mormons matter is eternal, and God is a self-created being with a material body. There are other gods of other worlds; Mormons worship the god of this world. Humans now living may one day become gods in their own worlds because of the coming of Christ. The godhead consists of three separate gods: Heavenly Father, Jesus Christ, and Holy Ghost. Jesus Christ is the eldest "spirit child" who came to earth as Jehovah (as described in the Old Testament).

Christ's kingdom will be established on earth, in America. Everyone is eligible to enter Christ's kingdom, but only through Mormon baptism by immersion by a member of the priesthood. Those who are dead may be vicariously baptized (the basis for the elaborate genealogical records kept by the church). Before the kingdom comes those who are baptized wait in heaven. There they live with material forms just like their earthly bodies.

According to Mormon belief, eternal life after death in heaven has three levels. In descending order they are the Celestial Kingdom, the Terrestial Kingdom, and the Telestial Kingdom. The Celestial Kingdom itself has three levels. The highest is reserved for married persons who have been obedient to Mormon teachings and married in an LDS temple. Males at this level become gods of their own worlds. This level is the only one in which the Heavenly Father lives and rules. The other two levels are also reserved for LDS members. The second kingdom, the Terrestial, is for those who have not yet heard the Restored Gospel as taught by the LDS church. Jesus will visit this kingdom, but not the Heavenly Father. The Telestial is for those who have heard but rejected the Restored Gospel. Beneath all these is the Second Death or Outer Darkness, reserved for the especially wicked.

Mormons consider marriages eternal; families will be rejoined in heaven. The central unit in Mormon life is the family, and a great deal of emphasis is placed on preserving and strengthening it. There is no professional Mormon clergy. Every male may become a priest. The religious status of a woman is dependent on her husband.

The organization of the church is hierarchical. All leaders are male. At the head are the Council of Twelve Apostles and a President, considered the successor to Joseph Smith. Like Smith, the President can receive revelations that define basic church doctrine. For example, a revelation given in 1978 allowed African-American males to be admitted to the priesthood. There are a number of levels of administration below the Apostles, with virtually every Mormon male participating. Only Mormon men may be ordained as priests (of the order of Aaron or Melchizedek). At the local level individual congregations form wards, headed by an appointed bishop. The world headquarters of the Mormon Church are located in Salt Lake City, Utah.

The Book of Mormon includes not only teachings on how Mormons are to live, but also a detailed account of the early history of America. According to the narrative, a group known as the Lamanites (the ancestors of the American Indians) and the Nephites (their foes) both descended from the "lost tribe of Israel" that came to America about 587 B.C.E. Christ appeared to the Lamanites after his resurrection, promising to return to America to establish his kingdom on earth. The Lamanites rebelled against the truth and attacked the Nephites. The only Nephites to survive were Mormon, who wrote the story we have just summarized on the golden plates

Temple Square in Salt Lake City, Utah, center of the Church of Jesus Christ of Latter-day Saints.

that Joseph Smith translated, and his son Moroni. As stated above, it was Moroni who, as an angel, led Smith to the plates.

Besides the Book of Mormon, two other works written by Smith, *Doctrine and Covenants* and *Pearl of Great Price*, are considered necessary supplements to the Bible by Mormons. The Bible alone does not contain the whole truth needed for salvation.

The early, intense controversies that led to the murder of Joseph Smith and the seizure of Mormon property in Utah have subsided. American Mormons have largely assimilated into the political and economic life of the United States. Their dedication to values of hard work, loyalty, and family have brought the community as a whole and many individual Mormons considerable wealth. However, criticism of the Mormons for their "additions" to basic Christian teachings, a restricted role for women, and their rejection of the validity of other Christian denominations as well as other religions continues to stir debate and sometimes hostility.

Responses to Contemporary Ethical Issues

EUTHANASIA   A statement on "Prolongation of Life and Right to Die," published in 1983 in a book of guidelines for local leaders of the Church of Jesus Christ of Latter-day Saints, has this to say about euthanasia: "The Church does not look with favor upon any form of mercy killing. It believes in the dignity of life; faith in the Lord and medical science should be appropriately called upon and applied to reverse conditions that are a threat to life. There comes a time when dying becomes inevitable, when it should be looked upon as a blessing, and as a purposeful part of mortality" (Larue 1985: 113).

GENDER ROLES AND THE STATUS OF WOMEN   The teaching of the Mormon Church is that all spirits are created by a Heavenly Father and a Heavenly Mother. Each individual spirit has an eternal gender, reflecting the male/female division in the divine. Families, with gender divisions, continue into the heavenly realm beyond this life.

Deep Ecology:
The Interconnectedness of All Life

Ecology is the scientific study of the interconnectedness of all living things in the environment. The "environmental movement" is composed of organizations that are trying to raise people's awareness of the current ecological crisis (see Chapter Two) and influence public policy to address it. The phrase "Deep Ecology" first appeared in the 1970s to refer to the spiritual dimension of the modern environmental movement and as an attempt to address the concern expressed by Lynn White and others, that the traditional spirituality of Western religions is antithetical to the preservation of the balance of nature (see Chapter Twelve).

The first exponent of Deep Ecology was the Norwegian philosopher Arne Naess, who coined the phrase in 1973. "Deep ecology goes beyond a limited piecemeal shallow approach to environmental problems and attempts to articulate a comprehensive religious and philosophical world view" (Devall and Sessions 1985: 65). Naess and those he influenced stress that they are trying to replace the Western understanding of nature with an "ecological egalitarianism." The term "biocentrism" (as opposed to anthropocentrism) is sometimes used to describe the orientation they seek. Every living being has a "right to be," which must be respected. Humans have failed to recognize the right to "self-realization" of other beings as they are expressed in natural patterns. Humans must reawaken to their place in the natural community. For Deep Ecologists, nature as a whole is ultimate and environmental activism the means to transformation in response to this ultimacy. All forms of anthropocentrism must be overcome. "Deep ecology recognizes that nothing short of a total revolution in consciousness will be of lasting use in preserving the life-support systems of our planet" (Seed 1988: 9).

On the one hand, the program of Deep Ecology is radical. According to Naess, the material standard of living in industrialized societies must be "drastically reduced" and the human population should be reduced to "no more than 100 million people" (Devall and Sessions 1985: 75–76). From this perspective, the time for gradual reformation of our approach to restoring the balance of life is past. Radical steps are necessary and they must be taken now. This attitude has inspired some in groups such as Greenpeace and Earth Now to take direct action to challenge practices they deem environmentally irresponsible.

On the other hand, Deep Ecology calls not so much for sacrifice on the part of the individual as for an expanded awareness of "self-interest." Influenced by Buddhism, Deep Ecologists speak of an "eco-self," an understanding of human identity that does not separate the "self" and "nature." As Naess has said, ecological responsibility will flow naturally and easily "if the self were widened and deepened so that the protection of nature was felt and perceived as protection of our very selves" (cited in Macy 1990: 62).

Deep Ecology is not a unified movement; it is a spiritual perspective that is emerging simultaneously in a variety of contexts. People who are active in traditional religions, as well as those who are not religious at all in a traditional sense, are becoming increasingly aware that the environmental crisis requires spiritual transformation. Some are motivated by the spiritual values of indigenous religions and the recovery of a spirituality that takes seriously the idea of Mother Earth (see Chapters Three and Four and the discussion of Wicca below). Others find a basis for Deep Ecology in the traditional religions of the Middle East, which speak of the human responsibility to be God's stewards of the earth and recognize the divine presence in nature. Some Christian theologians, such as Matthew Fox, are speaking of the "cosmic Christ," meaning that "Christ" is present in all reality. Still others see in Eastern religions such as Taoism or Zen Buddhism a spiritual awareness of the inherent harmony of all life.

Some persons base their Deep Ecology on the *Gaia* hypothesis of scientist James Lovelock, who asserted that the earth, the life on the earth, and the atmosphere surrounding the earth are one living, self-regulating being whom he called Gaia (from the Greek name for the earth as a goddess).

Ecofeminism has emerged in recent years as a movement that shares some concerns with Deep Ecology, but goes beyond it in the analysis of the roots of the environmental crisis. The term "Ecofeminism" was coined in 1974 by French writer Françoise d'Eaubonne as a focus for women's potential to take the lead in bringing on an ecological revolution. Ecofeminists join Deep Ecologists in saying that more than gradual reform of our attitude toward the environment is necessary. But they criticize Deep Ecologists for not being radical enough in their critique of the role played by male domination in creating the cultural values that led to the ecological crisis (see Zimmerman 1987). As one Ecofeminist scholar puts it, "The master-slave role which marks man's relationship with nature is replicated in man's relation with woman" (Salleh 1984: 344).

Whether these various and quite distinct proponents of Deep Ecology join together to express in a more unified way their common understanding of the spiritual relationship humans must foster with the earth and all of life remains to be seen. Some observers think that Deep Ecology has the potential to spark a universal spiritual renewal and reformation as profound as any in history. Many Deep Ecologists maintain that human survival depends on this spiritual transformation. Otherwise, extinction of the human species will inevitably occur to restore the ecological balance humans have callously disrupted.

The Holy Spirit Association for the Unification of World Christianity: The Unification Church

History and Basic Teachings   The Holy Spirit Association for the Unification of World Christianity (more widely known as the Unification Church) was established in 1954 in Korea. According to the church, Jesus appeared to its founder, the Reverend Sun Myung Moon (1920), on Easter Sunday in 1936, instructing him to establish the Kingdom of God on earth. In 1945 Moon began a movement in northern Korea, but Communist authorities imprisoned him for over two years. He was set free when United Nations forces reached the area. He then moved to South Korea, where the church was founded. It reached the United States by 1959. Eventually the offices of the world headquarters were established in and near New York City.

The church recognizes Rev. Moon's *Divine Principle*, which interprets the true meaning of the Christian Bible, as a sacred text. The work presents a history of humanity that focuses on God's efforts to establish the divine kingdom on earth. It teaches that the original harmony will be restored when a second Adam and a second Eve come to pay the price for human sin. Jesus was the second Adam, but he failed to marry, so only a spiritual restoration occurred, with the Holy Spirit as the bride of Jesus. Jesus died unnecessarily, because of the failure of John the Baptist to prepare the way for him properly, Rev. Moon contended. The

The Rev. Sun Myung Moon and his wife (left) conduct a wedding ceremony in Madison Square Garden for couples whose marriages he has arranged (1982).

material world remained under the power of Satan. The time is near, Rev. Moon wrote, when a new messiah will appear, the Lord of the Second Coming. He will come to Korea, where he will marry so that the full price of the sin of humanity can be paid and the model for the new, spiritual family can be created. The new messiah, a Third Adam, will bring God's kingdom to earth. Rev. Moon does not overtly claim to be this messiah, but he and his wife are enacting the prophecies associated with his coming.

As spiritual parents to all members of the church, Moon and his wife arrange and preside over the marriages of their "children" in mass ceremonies called Blessings. Members must themselves pay "indemnity" for human sinfulness through sacrificial good deeds. The raising of money for the church is the primary means of paying this indemnity. The church teaches that Satan is still alive and at work in the world, trying to deflect Moon and his followers from the mission given to him by Jesus himself.

The movement is strongly anti-Communist (calling Communism Satanic) and vigorously supports the role of the United States as leader of the free world. It opposes abortion, defends "family values," and supports private religious education. In 1974 the church sponsored demonstrations in favor of President Nixon during the Watergate scandal. Rev. Moon has spent time in a federal prison, after being convicted in 1984 on charges of income tax evasion. In an effort to win support for the church, conferences for scholars (under the label of the International Religious Foundation) in the area of religious studies are held to explain the legitimacy of the church's teachings. The church also purchased and publishes *The Washington Times,* a daily newspaper. The church maintains that it recognizes and supports other religions, and only asks that this openness be reciprocated. There are some indications of the influence of Confucian teaching on the Unification Church's doctrine.

Critics of the Unification Church charge that most members are treated as virtual slaves whose labor is the source of the great wealth of the movement. The church has been given the derogatory name "Moonies" and is often the target of deprogrammers hired by concerned parents whose sons or daughters have joined. The church responds that overzealous recruiting by some misguided members has been curbed, and that the church seeks only recognition and the opportunity to function as a legitimate Christian denomination. However, efforts by the church to attain recognition as a legitimate Christian church from ecumenical agencies such as the National Council of Churches have so far failed.

Responses to Contemporary Ethical Issues

ECONOMIC JUSTICE   "In the Unification Church, God is viewed as the parent of the world with all people as God's children. When we talk about rich and poor nations in relationship to theology, this concept becomes a central factor. Any discussion of the relationship between rich and poor nations necessarily involves the belief that people of all nations are siblings. The sibling metaphor denotes a relationship that goes beyond economic or military considerations" (Anderson 1985: 120).

The International Society for Krishna Consciousness: The Hare Krishnas

History and Basic Teachings   In 1966 a 70-year-old retired owner of a small Indian pharmaceutical firm named Abhay Charan De arrived in New York City. Seven years earlier he had taken the vow of a *sannyasin* (see Chapter Five). He came to the United States to fulfill a promise he had made to his spiritual teacher in 1936 to bring the teaching of "Krishna Consciousness" to the West. This humble old man became the leader of a movement, the International Society for Krishna Consciousness (ISKCON), which has been the principal point of contact with the Hindu tradition for millions of Americans and others.

Swami A.C. Bhaktivedanta Swami Prabhupada, as his followers came to know him, taught a message he believed had been passed from guru to guru for literally thousands of years. According to this tradition, in the present materialistic age (the last before the current cosmic cycle ends in destruction) persons should chant the holy names of God as the simplest and surest way to find spiritual fulfillment. Because he considered America the most influential country in the West, the Swami fulfilled his spiritual master's instruction by coming to the United States to proclaim his message of Krishna Consciousness. He arrived penniless, without followers, ending up on the Lower East Side of New York City, where he simply started chanting the names of God in Tompkins Square Park. Gradually he began to attract followers who had dropped out of mainstream American culture. Eight years later nearly seventy centers of the International Society for Krishna Consciousness had opened around the world, with twenty-eight in the United States. Devotees became known as "Hare Krishnas," because of their simple chant, heard on street corners around the world: "Hare Krishna, Hare Krishna. Krishna, Hare Hare, Hare Rama, Hare Rama, Rama, Rama, Hare Hare." Krishna and Rama are divine names in Sanskrit. Krishna is an epithet meaning "beloved" or "all-attractive." Literally, the chant translates, "Beloved Krishna, beloved Krishna, Krishna, Krishna, Lord, Lord, Beloved Rama, Beloved Rama, Rama, Rama, Lord, Lord." The official translation of the chant is "O all-attractive, all-pleasing Lord, O energy of the Lord, please engage me in your devotional service." By chanting the names of the Lord, devotees believe that they are being drawn into the presence of the Supreme Lord of the Universe.   Although

A ceremony in an International Society for Krishna Consciousness temple in Brooklyn, New York. Worshippers offer bananas and corn as spiritual food for Krishna and his attendant deities.

often condemned as a "cult," Krishna Consciousness is actually a Vaishnavite *bhakti* movement that historians trace to a sixteenth-century teacher named Chaitanya. The principal text for the movement is the *Bhagavad-gita*, which members believe to be the literal word of Krishna. Devotees have attracted a great deal of attention (and often disdain) by asking for donations for copies of their Swami's translation of the *Gita* and other movement literature at airports and other public places. Some members devote themselves entirely to the movement and maintain a rigorous lifestyle, living in the centers. Other devotees live outside the centers, and participate to varying extents in the center's cycle of group chanting before images of Krishna. All members maintain their spiritual focus through chanting the names of God on *japa* beads individually throughout the day.

After Swami Prabhupada's death, the leadership of the movement passed to a council. The movement has experienced some bitter divisions, and much negative publicity, yet continues to function as the most successful example of the *bhakti* branch of the Indian religious tradition outside India.

Responses to Contemporary Ethical Issues

THE ECOLOGICAL CRISIS   In response to a request for ISKCON positions on current social issues, Drutakarma Dasa, a member of the movement for over twenty years and an editor of ISKCON publications, including *Back to Godhead* and *ISKCON World Review*, made the following statement on the ecological crisis (1992a):

> The root of the environmental crisis is a spiritual one. The world has for several centuries been dominated by a mechanistic, materialistic, and essentially godless view of the universe. And from this has grown an industrial-consumer civilization bent on exploiting and dominating matter to the maximum extent possible. The environment has suffered from this. Responding to the environmental crisis, the International Society for Krishna Consciousness offers a new way of looking at the universe, as the energy and property of God, who offers humans an opportunity to develop their dormant God consciousness and return to their original spiritual home. Meanwhile, humans can use the resources of nature in a balanced, harmonious way, consistent with the primary goal of developing God consciousness. The movement sees the gradual adoption of voluntary simplicity in the context of a spiritual, God-centered philoso-

phy and way of life as the real solution to the environmental problems brought on by the industrial-consumer civilization.

WAR   The founder of the International Society for Krishna Consciousness, A.C. Bhaktivedanta Swami Prabhupada, advocated the position that conflicts will not end until destructive nationalism, racism, and sectarian religion are overcome. These attitudes are from this perspective, merely one of the manifestations of the ignorance of the material world. They create a sense of "enemy" and "friend," which can be transcended only through perception of the true, spiritual self. According to Srila Prabhupada, "Because people are identifying with this material world, they are thinking 'I am an Englishman,' 'I am this,' 'I am that.' But if one chants the *Hare Krishna mantra*, he will realize that he is not this material body..." (Drutakarma 1992a: 54). Only through such spiritual realization will people develop the sense of unity necessary to overcome nationalism, racism, and sectarian religion and the wars they breed.

Concerning war, the Hare Krishna movement today takes the following position, according to Drutakarma Dasa (1992a):

> *Members of the Hare Krishna movement are followers of the Vedas. In the Vedas, there is allowance for war under certain circumstances, principally self-defense and to uphold primary spiritual values. Wars were, however, carried out by members of a professional military social order (the warrior caste) away from civilian areas. In short, the state does have a right and duty to maintain armed forces and police to protect the state and its citizens. But wars should be fought by volunteer professionals, for reasons in harmony with Vedic spiritual and ethical principles, and in such a way that fighting does not endanger civilians.*

CAPITAL PUNISHMENT   Drutakarma Dasa (1992a) explains the Hare Krishna position on capital punishment as follows:

> *The Vedas and books of social codes such as the Manu-samhita sanction capital punishment. According to the laws of karma, a killer must suffer in the next life by being killed violently. But if the killer receives capital punishment in this life, the killer is freed from any further violent karmic reaction in the next life. Capital punishment is thus a legitimate resource for the state in*

its dealings with criminals, and in the context of the law of reincarnation, is in fact merciful.

ABORTION   According to Drutakarma Dasa, the Hare Krishna position is that abortions are not to be condoned. (1992a):

> *According to Vedic books of knowledge, the persons involved in abortion must themselves be aborted in future lives. The Vedas say that the soul is present in the embryo from the moment of conception. For worshippers of Krishna who become initiated by a spiritual master in the line of succession, illicit sex is forbidden. This means that there can be no abortion or contraception. Couples should engage in sex only for the purpose of procreation. If all children are wanted, there is no requirement for abortion. Procreative sex is considered spiritual sex, and is sanctioned. These rules are observed by initiated members in good standing. However, anyone may participate in Temple functions regardless of their views on abortion.*

ECONOMIC JUSTICE   Drutakarma Dasa (1992a) explains ISKCON's position on economic justice in this statement:

> *Under Vedic standards, the government has a duty to see that all members of society are employed and have adequate food, shelter, and medical care. In Vedic times, brahmanas (brahmins) trained in the Ayur-Veda system of medicine would provide free medical advice and care, living simply on charity. Srila Prabhupada, the founder-acharya of the International Society for Krishna Consciousness, said that no one should go hungry within 10 miles of any Krishna temple. In response, the movement has organized Hare Krishna Food for Life, which distributes free vegetarian meals to the poor and homeless, as well as disaster victims, on five continents. Unemployment is thought to be largely a byproduct of the urban-industrial civilization. A move back to a more simple, natural way of life on the land, in small self-sufficient villages, would solve that problem.*

GENDER ROLES AND THE STATUS OF WOMEN   According to Drutakarma Dasa (1992a), the Hare Krishna position on the status of women is as follows:

> *The Vedas teach that God, Krishna, has an eternal, equal, female counterpart, Radha, who is the personification of love of God. God is therefore worshipped in the dual Radha-Krishna form. The most perfect examples of love of God are Radha and her feminine extensions, the*

gopis. Throughout history, there have been great women devotees of the Lord, who are honored and respected.

On the spiritual platform men and women are considered equal, with the same opportunity for spiritual progress through bhakti-yoga. There were, however, different gender roles.

In an ideal Vedic society, the economy was household-based and husbands and wives were partners, according to their social status. The economic base of society was primarily agricultural and centered around households. This meant that both men and women would be part of the same economic unit, though with different roles. Generally, men would be involved in ploughing and herding cows, and women would be involved in churning butter, making yogurt, cooking and other such activities around the household. Kshatriyas would be involved in military and administrative affairs. Women would not normally be engaged in fighting and ruling, but would be loyal assistants to their husbands and play a role appropriate to their status as queens, princesses, etc. The wives of brahmanas (brahmins) would assist their husbands in the performance of religious rituals and teaching. In each case, the men and women would be partners in the particular activity of their social order, but with different roles in the partnership.

In modern Western society, ISKCON has had to make adjustments. The economy is not agricultural or household-based. So members might follow the standard patterns of either both husband and wife working at some occupation away from the household, or husband working, and wife staying home and taking care of the children. But men and women, as in Vedic society, have equal access to the bhakti-yoga process. They receive the same initiations, and perform mostly the same priestly duties in temples. There is, however, as in society in general, some debate about the role of women, their role in the family, leadership in ISKCON, etc. According to tradition and philosophy, women may take the position of guru, or spiritual master, and this is about to take place in the Hare Krishna movement. Women do not currently occupy any seats on ISKCON's Governing Body Commission, but a change in this policy is under discussion. In some parts of the world, such as Europe, women do serve as temple presidents and occupy other administrative posts.

HOMOSEXUALITY   Drutukarma Dasa (1992a) reports that the position of the Hare Krishna movement on homosexuality is that it would not be allowed for initiated members, for they commit themselves to having no illicit sex. Illicit sex involves sex outside marriage and sex within marriage not for procreation. Thus, practicing homosexuals may not be initiated, and would not be offered positions of leadership in the movement. Previous homosexual practice does not disqualify someone from initiation, and practicing homosexuals who are not initiated are not excluded from attending temple functions and practicing Krishna Consciousness as much as they can. The movement has no position on the issues of homosexual rights in society outside Krishna Consciousness communities.

Jehovah's Witnesses: Preparing for the Kingdom

History and Basic Teachings   The Jehovah's Witnesses are best known for their door-to-door and street-corner evangelism in which they distribute the denomination's magazines: *The Watch Tower* and *Awake!*. They are also the group often in the news because of members' refusal to accept blood transfusions or salute the flag. In public schools Jehovah's Witnesses children will often not participate in observances of holidays or birthdays.

The movement began in the United States with the ministry of Charles Taze Russell (1852–1916). Russell was influenced by the teaching of William Miller (1782–1849), who calculated the date for the Second Coming (advent) of Christ and the end of the world. Although Miller's prediction for the Second Coming did not come to pass, people influenced by his teaching eventually formed the Seventh-Day Adventist movement (see below). Russell did not join the Adventists, but instead developed his own interpretation of the Bible, which he promulgated in lecture tours and publications. Russell's teachings spread through the United States and to other countries such as Great Britain and Germany, and students of his method of Bible interpretation became known as Russellites.

The name Jehovah's Witnesses was not adopted for the movement until 1931, when Russell's successor, Jospeh Rutherford, reorganized it into a tightly controlled denomination led by appointed elders. Because of their refusal to express allegiance to any government, Jehovah's Witnesses were persecuted during World War II on both sides of the conflict. In Germany many were sent to concentration camps.

After World War II the movement has continued to grow, with an estimated 3 million members worldwide. Members gather for worship in local Kingdom Halls, under the leadership of persons appointed to serve by district leaders, who are themselves appointed by the World Headquarters.

Witnesses (as they call themselves) believe in the literal truth of the Bible and absolute loyalty to the one God. According to the doctrine of the church, Jesus was the Son of God, but was not God himself. He was God's first creation, through whom all else came into existence. On earth he was only a human being, although God did raise him from the dead and brought him to heaven where he is second in authority to God.

In Witness mythology Lucifer (Satan) was God's younger son, who was placed in charge of humans. He failed in his assignment, tempted Adam and Eve, and brought corruption to the earth, making it necessary for God to send Jesus, Lucifer's elder brother, to set things right. Witnesses believe that the establishment of God's kingdom on earth began in 1914, and the final consummation will come very soon. Only those who are righteous will participate in this new age on earth; the rest (99 percent) will simply be annihilated. People will be selected from all races and nationalities for the new age. A special remnant of 144,000 is now being raised to an eternal life with God in heaven.

In the current age members are told not to participate in politics or other public activities—hence the Witnesses' refusal to serve in the military, vote, or take part in other aspects of national life such as voting, or to join in celebrations such as national holidays. Other Christian denominations are considered "false religions" because they teach the doctrine of the Trinity and other inaccurate interpretations of Scripture. Since God alone is Lord, no allegiance can be sworn to any government. Blood transfusions are forbidden because of the statement in the Book of Genesis that humans are not to "consume blood." Christmas and other religious holidays are not celebrated because they are not Scriptural. Witnesses call God Jehovah because they accept as literal the King James Version of the Bible, which uses Jehovah (for YHWH) in the Old Testament.

The Nation of Islam: The "Black Muslims"

The Nation of Islam began in Detroit, Michigan, in 1930. Members of the movement are popularly known as the "Black Muslims," although this is a name not used or preferred within the Nation of Islam. The founder, Wallace Fard, proclaimed that he had come from the Islamic holy city of Mecca (see Chapter Thirteen) to reveal to black Americans that their salvation would come through self-knowledge in which they recovered a sense of their own glorious history and accepted the essentially deceptive character of whites. The charismatic Fard organized a Temple, a University of Islam, and a paramilitary force called the Fruit of Islam. He published several works, including *The Secret Ritual of the Nation of Islam* and *Teaching for the Lost Found Nation of Islam in a Mathematical Way*.

When Fard disappeared in 1934, his chief disciple, Elijah Muhammad, became the principal leader. Elijah Muhammad taught that Fard was an incarnation of Allah, and that he was Fard's messenger. He urged his fellow blacks to withdraw from white society and create their own institutions. Under Elijah Muhammad's leadership, Nation of Islam mosques were established in urban areas across the United States. The Nation created its own schools, stores, houses, and farms.

The traditional teachings of the Nation of Islam were that whites are the personification of evil in the world. Humanity was originally black; the white race was created by a black scientist named Yakub who rebelled against Allah. If blacks are to realize their destiny, they must purge themselves from all white influences. As the religion of the whites, Christianity is dangerous and must be avoided, the Nation of Islam taught. Followers are to maintain a strict lifestyle, with prayer five times a day, no intoxicants or tobacco, a pure diet, and no illicit sex.

In the 1950s Malcolm X emerged as a key figure in the movement. (Members of the nation of Islam typically drop their last name, considering it a "slave" name assigned to them by whites, and use "X" instead.) Malcolm X had been converted in prison and attributed his own salvation to Elijah Muhammad. Malcolm became a charismatic expo-

Minister Louis Farrakhan of the Nation of Islam.

nent of the teachings of Elijah Muhammad and helped win many converts to the Nation of Islam. However, after a pilgrimage to Mecca he began to question whether the Nation of Islam was in harmony with traditional Islamic teaching about universal brotherhood. Malcolm was killed by supporters of Elijah Muhammad in 1965.

After Elijah Muhammad's death in 1975, his son Wallace D. Muhammad assumed leadership. Influenced by Malcolm X's proposals to bring the Nation more into line with the racially inclusive teachings of traditional Islam, he opened the movement to people of all races and changed its name to "The World Community of al-Islam in the West." Other members of the Nation of Islam rejected this shift and sought to maintain the original ideology of racial separatism. Louis Farrakhan became the primary spokesman for this wing of the movement, which retains the original name.

The Native American Church: Peyote Religion

Peyote is a small, spineless, blue-green cactus that grows in the deserts of Mexico and certain areas in the southwestern United States. When the "buttons" that grow atop the clusters of the cactus are

dried and either chewed or consumed in a tea, the first result is often violent vomiting. Following this reaction, however, the peyote consumer typically experiences a euphoric state in which time stands still. During this state, hallucinogenic visions frequently come. For the Native American Church the consumption of peyote is a sacrament, as important as the symbolic eating of the body and blood of Christ in the Christian sacrament of communion, which the Native American Church also recognizes.

This is not our first encounter with the use of mind-altering drugs in a religion. In the religion associated with the *Rig-Veda* of India, the hallucinogenic drug made from pressing the soma plant played an important role (see Chapter Five). The use of hallucinogens for spiritual purposes is an interesting phenomenon. Should people's rights to use drugs such as peyote in religious ceremonies be protected, when the ordinary consumption of such agents is forbidden by law?

Reports from sixteenth-century Spanish missionaries speak of the importance of peyote among indigenous peoples of Mexico. The ritual consumption of peyote continued through the centuries and spread into the tribes of the American Southwest, such as the Kiowa. The visions received while under the influence of peyote were considered to be a form of communication with the spirit world, which helped the worshipper maintain harmony with the spirits. Soon after European contact, peyote users were associating consumption with Christianity, calling peyote the "flesh of God," a symbol of Christ.

When the U.S. government began to outlaw Native American religious practices, including the use of peyote, in the late nineteenth century, a group of Native Americans responded by incorporating peyote into a new religious movement that eventually became known as the Native American Church of Christ. The first efforts at organization were in Oklahoma, Indian Territory.

From Oklahoma the Native American Church spread through the western and midwestern states. When it reached Canada it became known as the Native American Church of Christ in North America. Today the church claims about 200,000 members. It has served to bring a sense of spiritual unity to Native Americans across tribal boundaries. Typically, members of the church participate in both their own tribal rituals *and* the rites of the church.

Whether the church is Christianity adapted to indigenous ways or indigenous religion adapted to Christianity is a matter of dispute within and outside the church. Two divisions within the church, the Cross Fire and Half Moon Fireplaces, reflect this tension. Both claim to be Christian. The Cross Fire Fireplace maintains a strong Christian orientation, using the Bible in the services and taking an evangelical approach to Christianity. The Half Moon Fireplace uses the name of Jesus in songs, but is not so overtly Christian.

The peyote ritual is quite formalized, with variations among the different groups and geographic areas in which it is practiced. A peyote ritual in the Southwest typically begins on Saturday evening and lasts through the night until noon on Sunday. The officiant is called the Peyote Chief, and he is assisted by a Fire Chief, Drum Chief, Road Man, and Cedar Man. After purification, the participants consume a few buttons through chewing them or drinking tea. Through the night songs are sung, and more buttons are consumed, until visions are attained. It is clear that the intent of the ritual is to communicate with the Supreme God for the purpose of receiving spiritual power, guidance, and healing. Spirit intermediaries, such as Thunderbird, carry the people's petitions to God. The ritual objects used in the all-night ritual include a gourd rattle, an iron kettle partially filled with water, the water drum; an eagle feather; cedar incense; and sage.

Even though the Bureau of Indian Affairs reversed a half-century of trying to eliminate peyote use in 1940 and recognized its legitimacy, the dispute over peyote continued. In 1946 the U.S. Supreme Court ruled that use of peyote by the Native American Church was legal. In 1961 the Native American Church was finally recognized as an official church by the federal government. A few years later, however, in reaction to the abuses of the drug culture of the 1960s, Congress listed peyote among the "dangerous drugs" (despite a lack of scientific evidence to support this claim, supporters of the Native American Church point out). In 1990 the Supreme Court reversed itself and upheld the right of states to ban the ceremonial use of peyote without violating the constitutional guarantee of freedom of religion. Deeply concerned by the implications of this decision for the rights of all Americans to practice religion, a coalition of religious groups has formed to support a national Freedom of Religion law. At this writing, twenty-three states and the U.S. government still allow for the use of peyote in the Native American Church.

Perfect Liberty Kyodan: Life Is Art

After World War II hundreds of "new religions" (*shinko shukyo*) became popular in Japan. As one interpreter said, they sprang up "like bamboo shoots after the rain." Some were movements within Shinto and Buddhism; others were new creations. All focused on one charismatic leader and emphasized an individual transformation with promises for a more fulfilling life on earth. They stood in contrast to the communal and family orientation of traditional Japanese religion. We will examine two of these "new religions" in this chapter: Perfect Liberty Kyodan and later Soka Gakkai, a lay Buddhist movement. Both have established centers in the United States.

Perfect Liberty (or simply P.L.) *Kyodan* was established by Tokuharu Taniguchi in 1926, although it did not grow rapidly until after World War II. Combining elements of Shinto and Buddhism, this movement's goal is enrichment of personality through self-expression. The twenty-one precepts taught by P.L. Kyodan begin with the assertions that "Life is art" and "Life is a succession of self-expressions." This reflects the general Buddhist view of the impermanence of the self, and the specific Zen teaching of spontaneity.

Those who join the movement are given a personally designed program to enable them to realize their fullest potential. According to P. L. Kyodan doctrine, persons suffer because they do not express themselves. Each individual is a manifestation of god, the Supreme Spirit. By expressing ourselves we create harmony with god. Each person should follow what his or her first inspiration dictates, his "art." Perfect Liberty comes to those who express their true selves.

P.L. Kyodan is sometimes called the "Golf Religion," because golf is often recommended to members as a means of artistic self-expression. A number of P.L. Kyodan centers, with golf courses, have been opened in Japan and in California.

The Ras Tafari Movement: The Black Messiah

The Ras Tafari movement (also known as Rastafarianism) began in 1930 when Crown Prince *Ras Tafari* became Emperor Haile Selassie of Ethiopia. The coronation seemed to be a fulfillment of a prophecy made by Marcus Garvey, a black nationalist leader from Jamaica. When Garvey was preparing to go to the United States from Jamaica in 1916, he told the blacks of Jamaica to look to Africa where a black king, who would be their redeemer, would be crowned. The Ethiopian king was addressed with titles associated with Christ in the Bible (King of Kings and Conquering Lion of the Tribe of Judah), adding weight to the view that Haile Selassie was the long-awaited black messiah. The Ras Tafari movement emerged out of the enthusi-

asm. Its principal leader was Leonard Howell, who organized the movement near Kingston, Jamaica.

The movement split into an old school, which emphasizes a return to Africa, and a new school, which focuses on improving the quality of life for blacks in Jamaica and elsewhere. Reggae music and artists such as Bob Marley have been associated with the new school.

Rastafarian teachings include the belief that Haile Selassie is the living God; the black man is superior to the white man; Jamaica is hell and Ethiopia is heaven; Haile Selassie has provided for the return of blacks to Africa; and blacks will one day rule the world. The Ras Tafari movement rejects modern industrial life as an evil system introduced by whites to enslave blacks, and idealizes a return to simpler, more natural ways of life in Africa. Ras Tafari men are distinguished by a unique hairstyle called dreadlocks, in which the hair is allowed to grow to look like the mane of a lion—as a symbol of the natural life. Rastafarian ritual is famous because of the smoking by some members of what members call *ganja* (marijuana).

The Ras Tafari movement spread from Jamaica throughout the Caribbean and to the United States and Canada. While he was living, Emperor Haile Selassie, who died in 1974, repudiated the claims made about him by Rastafarians, but his refusal to cooperate with the ideology did not discourage members of the movement.

Satanism: Indulging Self

The most controversial of the recently established new religions is *Satanism*. In the contemporary popular media, Satanism has become virtually synonymous with ritualized murders conducted by people described simply as "Satanists." Various groups have mobilized to challenge the influences of Satanism in popular culture, as for example in heavy metal rock music. Movies such as "The Exorcist," "Rosemary's Baby," and "The Seventh Sign" exploit a popular fascination with evil "Satanic" powers.

Few people are aware that in addition to distressing examples of what might be called "spontaneous" Satanic activities, there are organized Satanic movements, which claim absolutely no connection to lurid "Satanic" activities. Critics charge that these organized Satanic movements should not be so clearly distinguished from "Satanic" crimes because, they claim, the organizations at least tacitly encourage such behavior even if they do not officially condone it. However, no connection between the organized Satanic groups discussed here and any "Satanic" violence has been demonstrated by recognized authorities.

"Formal" Satanism is divided by three distinct orientations. Some Satanists accept the traditional Christian understanding of Satan as the evil opponent of God, the Prince of Darkness, whom they worship as the true power of the universe. They hope for a life after death in Satan's realm. A second approach accepts the idea of a personal Satan, but regards Satan as the heroic rebel against the Christian God who attempts to thwart natural human desires. His presumed evilness is a Christian distortion, designed to try to make people feel guilty, they say. More typical today is a third understanding, which holds that the personification of Satan in general is a projection of Christian guilt and insecurity. According to this perspective, the true "Satan" is the life force itself and all the natural impulses associated with life in the flesh. In this orientation, worship of Satan is a celebration of this natural life force, freed from the repressions of hypocritical Christian morality. Adherents of this understanding reject as childish and silly the view of Satan as a personal god and as wishful thinking the hope of any kind of afterlife.

There is no one, centralized Satanic movement. Instead, a number of groups have developed around charismatic leaders. They are part of a tradition that arose in the late nineteenth and early twentieth centuries in Europe. One of the key figures in that tradition of hedonistic rejection of Christian morality was Aleister Crowley (1875–1947), a magician and author who advocated that "Do what you will shall be the whole of the Law" (Ellwood and Partin 1988: 155).

The two most widely known Satanic movements in modern America endorse the view that Satan is nothing more than a symbol for humanity's carnal desires. They could just as easily be dis-

QUESTIONS ABOUT THE SACRED: WHAT IS THE SACRED?

The Nine Satanic Statements

Anton LaVey's The Satanic Bible *begins with the following statements about who "Satan" is. (LaVey 1969: 25).*

1. Satan represents indulgence, instead of abstinence!

2. Satan represents vital existence, instead of spiritual pipe dreams!

3. Satan represents undefiled wisdom, instead of hypocritical self-deceit.

4. Satan represents kindness to those who deserve it, instead of love wasted on ingrates!

5. Satan represents vengeance, instead of turning the other cheek!

6. Satan represents responsibility to the responsible, instead of concern for psychic vampires!

7. Satan represents man as just another animal, sometimes better, more often worse than those that walk of all-fours, who, because of his "divine spiritual and intellectual development," has become the most vicious animal of all.

8. Satan represents all of the so-called sins, as they all lead to physical, mental, or emotional gratification!

9. Satan has been the best friend the church has ever had, as he has kept it in business all these years!

cussed as "secular religions," since they reject the idea of a spiritual level of existence. In 1966 Anton LaVey organized the Church of Satan in San Francisco. A former animal trainer, criminologist, musician, and magician, LaVey was put off by the hypocrisy of "good Christians" whom he would see engaging in immoral behavior on Saturday night and then proclaiming their piety in church on Sunday morning. He challenged people to be honest with the fact that what they truly worship is their own natural desires. LaVey taught his followers to indulge themselves, so long as they did not hurt anyone who did not want to be hurt. The highly dramatic rituals of the Church of Satan included the traditional "black mass," in which the elements of the Catholic mass are parodied. For example, the altar would be a nude woman. Instead of praying for others, curses would be hurled, with members ventilating their anger. With the publication and notoriety of his *The Satanic Bible* in 1969, LaVey's movement was growing. Satanic churches were opened in major cities throughout the United States and Europe. The membership was never very large, probably numbering in the hundreds.

Tension developed within the movement, however. Some members believed LaVey was concerned only with the money and fame the Church of Satan was bringing to him, not with the religion itself. In 1975, Dr. Michael Acquino, a military intelligence officer and former political science professor who had been attracted to the Church of Satan because of its materialistic ideology, withdrew to form the Temple of Set (named after the Egyptian deity Seth, the source, Acquino argues, of the name Satan). In recent years the Temple of Set has largely replaced the Church of Satan as the major organized "Satanic" movement in the United States. Its headquarters are in St. Louis, Missouri. According to the Temple of Set's literature, it does not try to recruit members. In fact, those who desire to join are carefully screened to ensure that they are not mentally or emotionally unstable.

The basic principle of all forms of organized Satanism is that humans should pursue and enjoy natural pleasure and power and not feel guilty about their physical desires. Humans are animals and should simply be free to live out rather than repress their natural instincts (so long as they do not interfere with others' right to do the same). Satanists believe there is nothing wrong with individualistic egoism. Some observers say this message is frightfully similar to the idea that seems to resonate in modern Western culture that everyone should "grab as much as you can get" and "look out for number one." Dr. Acquino has contended that most people today are latent Satanists and just don't realize it!

Scientology: Total Freedom

The founder of Scientology, L. Ron Hubbard (1911–1986), was a science fiction writer. "Ron" (as Scientologists call him) claimed to have had a near-death experience while serving in the Navy during World War II, which instilled in him a message he was to share with others. In 1950 Hubbard published Dianetics: The Modern Science of Mental Health. That book served as the basis for the formation of Scientology in 1952. In Scientology ("The Study of Knowing") Hubbard combined a mythical narrative he had developed in his science fiction writing with the ideas about human nature found in Dianetics. In 1954 he established the Founding Church of Scientology in Washington, D.C.

In 1959 Hubbard moved to England and started the Hubbard College of Scientology in Sussex. He dropped out of public view in 1964 and spent most of his remaining years on board a ship. Members of the movement he started consider him a Buddha-like being who transcended the limitations of human knowledge.

After Hubbard's death, David Miscavige assumed leadership. He has tried to make the case, disputed by many critics, that Scientology is a legitimate religion. Outside observers contend that Scientology has from 50,000 to 200,000 members. Church figures run as high as 8 million members.

Members of Scientology report enthusiastically on the "total freedom" they have achieved in the religion. According to Scientology, the basic human problem is that unhappy experiences in present and past lives are encoded in the unconscious mind as mental aberrations called *engrams*. Until these engrams can be exposed and removed, we live in a state of unhappiness, called "preclear." Engrams are constantly stimulated by experiences similar to the ones that caused them. Many were incurred in the womb. The first goal in Scientology is to become a *clear*, one who is freed from the engrams. This is accomplished through a process called *auditing*. Auditing sessions are conducted by trained Scientology "auditors" who attach an "E-meter" to the subject. The "E-meter" has been described as a simplified lie detector, reading the electrical changes on the skin as the subject talks about his or her troublesome experiences. Numerous auditing sessions are usually necessary to remove all the engrams.

Once a person becomes clear, he or she is ready for the next stage, which is called that of the "operating thetan" (OT). To reach this stage (which itself has a number of levels) one must embark on a journey of self-discovery guided by someone who has already taken the path. According to the mythology Hubbard taught, thetans are spirits banished to earth 75 million years ago by a galactic ruler named Xenu. The thetan within us uses the mind to control the body and communicate with the outside environment. The thetan is entrapped not only by engrams but also by matter, energy, space, and time (MEST). An OT succeeds in escaping time and space; "out of body" experiences are common for those who reach this stage.

In addition to the science fiction mythology, Scientology makes use of imagery from Buddhism and other Eastern religions. However, its scientific mystique seems to attract the most people today. Members believe that Ron Hubbard discovered a "technology" (or "tech," as they call it) to attain what religion and philosophy had not reached in centuries of inquiry. An extensive drug counseling program is sponsored by the movement.

Scientology has attracted a number of Hollywood celebrities (including Tom Cruise, Kirstie Alley, and John Travolta), whose testimonials are used to lend credibility to the movement. Scientologists speak of a "family" atmosphere among members.

Critics charge that Scientology simply uses a religious cover to mask its primary goal: to enrich the leaders. To reach the state of clear can cost thousands of dollars for the individual auditing sessions required, critics maintain. Those seeking to become OT's can easily invest hundreds of thousands of dollars in the "journey of self-discovery." Court cases have been brought against Scientology by former members who invested their entire life's savings, before they became aware that they were, in their opinion, victims of fraud. The Internal Revenue Service withdrew Scientology's tax exempt status in 1967.

Scientology leaders have mounted intense campaigns to discredit government and journalistic probes of their affairs. Critics like to cite a statement attributed to L. Ron Hubbard to the effect that he decided to start a religion when he realized he could make a lot more money as the founder of a religion than he could as a writer of science fiction.

Seventh-Day Adventism: Living in the Final Days

The fourth of the Ten Commandments in the Bible says, "Remember the sabbath day, to keep it holy." For the Christian movement known as Seventh-Day Adventism, the commandment means that keeping holy the Jewish sabbath (from sundown Friday to sundown Saturday) is incumbent on Christians as well as Jews. Keeping the "seventh day" (rather than Sunday, the first day of the week) as the weekly holy day, and a firm belief that Jesus Christ will return soon (*advent* refers here to the Second Coming of Christ) to begin the promised Kingdom of God on earth, distinguish Seventh Day Adventism.

Seventh-Day Adventism is an example of a *millenarian movement*. In general, millenarian movements expect that supernatural powers are about to bring a new age to earth, which will totally transform life and bring restoration and salvation to the community of believers who have faithfully received the message of the coming end time. Often a messianic figure is associated with the coming of the new age. We have already seen an example of a millenarian movement in the Ghost Dance, which brought hope to many Native Americans as their lands were being taken and cultures destroyed in the late nineteenth century (see Chapter Four). The Rastafarians and Jehovah's Witnesses described above are other examples of millenarian religions. Christian millenarian movements typically draw their understanding of the coming end time from the symbolism of the Old Testament Book of Daniel and the New Testament Book of Revelation, in which a final struggle between God and Satan and the return of Christ as judge at the end time and ruler of the new age are revealed.

Although now a movement spread throughout the world, Seventh-Day Adventism (like the Jehovah's Witnesses movement) traces its roots to the biblical interpretation of William Miller, who predicted that the end would begin sometime between March 21, 1843, and March 21, 1844. When the end did not come, a follower recalculated the date to October 22, 1844. Thereafter, some of the smaller groups that had formed in response to Miller's teachings joined to form Seventh-Day Adventism. One of the principal figures was a woman named Ellen White, who was thought to be God's prophet for the present time.

The major beliefs of the movement are that in 1844 Christ began the process of judging the sins of both the living and the dead; that we are living in the final days before the end of time; that when Christ comes he will take the faithful with him to heaven to begin a thousand-year rule; and that after this "millennium" a final battle between God and Satan will lead to the creation of a new earth, which will be the eternal home of the righteous.

Self-Realization Fellowship: Practical Yoga

In 1920 a Hindu guru named Swami Yogananda (1893–1952) came to the United States to attend a religious conference. As Vivekananda, the founder of the Vedanta Society in the United States (see below), had done after the World Parliament of Religions in 1893, Yogananda remained in the United States after the conference and began a Hindu movement. He established a center in Los Angeles, and taught a type of yoga called "practical" yoga, a means of refocusing from everyday concerns to the spiritual centers within the body, with the goal of infinite joy and bliss. The movement grew to include about 150 centers throughout the world. Centers are called Churches of All Religions, because of the belief that yoga underlies all approaches to truth. Services are held on Sunday mornings (as they are in Vedanta Society Centers). Classes in yoga and on other topics are often held throughout the week. Yogananda is still called Master (because he remains guru even though he has given up his physical body), and his pictures are prominent in Self-Realization centers.

Soka Gakkai: The Society for Value Creation

History and Basic Teachings   Soka Gakkai ("The Society for Value Creation") is a lay movement within the Nichiren branch of Buddhism (see Chapter Nine). It was started by a high school principal named Tsunesaburo Makiguchi (1871–1944) before World War II. Makiguchi and some of his followers were imprisoned during the war because they rejected the call to exclusive loyalty required by state Shinto. The founder died in prison.

After World War II, Soka Gakkai's commitment to individualism and this-worldly results, as well as its separation from state Shinto, made it popular. It experienced rapid growth during the 1950s under the leadership of Josei Toda, who had been imprisoned with Makiguchi. Today, the movement has become the largest of the "new religions," with 16.5 million counted as members in Japan. The international wing, known as Nichiren Sho-shu, brings the total to over 17 million. In 1975, Soka Gakkai International, an international umbrella organization encompassing the Nichiren Sho-shu groups in various nations, was created.

Adapting the teachings of Nichiren and the Lotus Sutra to the contemporary world, Soka Gakkai stresses self-improvement for individuals leading to beauty, truth, and especially benefit. Happiness is the ultimate value in Soka Gakkai. Each person can become a Buddha through chanting "Hail to the Lotus Sutra!" (*nam-myo-ho-renge-kyo*) and meditating on a *gohonzon* ("personal worship object"), a mandala with the names of principal figures of the Lotus Sutra at the center. The chant brings members into harmony with the energy radiating from all the Buddhas mentioned in the

QUESTIONS ABOUT THE SACRED: WHAT IS THE SACRED?

The Buddha Nature in All Life

In a pamphlet produced to explain Soka Gakkai, the following statement clarifies why the movement devotes so much attention to finding worldly happiness, for it is there that the Buddha nature is to be found, according to the Lotus Sutra ("SGI": Soka Gakkai International 1992: 40–41).

The Lotus Sutra, taught the existence of an innate and universal truth known as Buddha nature, the manifestation of which enables one to enjoy absolute happiness and to act with boundless compassion. Rather than stressing impermanence and the consequent need to eliminate earthly desires and attachment, the Lotus Sutra asserts the ultimate reality of the Buddha nature inherent in all life. It is therefore a teaching which profoundly affirms the realities of daily life, and which naturally encourages engagement with others and with the whole of human society.

The Lotus Sutra is also unique among the teachings of Shakyamuni in that it makes the attainment of enlightenment a possibility open to all people—without distinction based on gender, social standing, or education.

Excerpt from "SGI: Soka Gakkai International," pamphlet published by Soka Gakkai International (1992). Permission requested.

Lotus Sutra, and the central Buddha Reality at the core of all being. Members gather in *zadankai* (discussion) groups to help one another see that which is impeding the achievement of happiness. Converts are encouraged to destroy all signs of other religions in their homes, such as Bibles and Shinto *kami* shelves.

According to Nichiren Buddhism, *now* is the time for world salvation through turning to the truth of the Lotus Sutra. Soka Gakkai recognizes the legitimacy of *shakubuku* ("break and subdue"),

in which devotees try to win converts by showing them the error of their present beliefs and the truth of the Lotus Sutra.

In addition to drawing individuals into the movement, Soka Gakkai seeks to influence the course of national as well as international events. In Japan Soka Gakkai organized the *Komeito* ("Clean Government") Party, which continues to hold seats in the Japanese Diet. On the world stage, Soka Gakkai is active in movements to achieve world peace and ultimately a "Third Civilization," in which Buddhism and society will be yoked.

The movement's center is a large temple at the foot of Mount Fuji. The temple is a pilgrimage site for members from throughout the world. Mass rallies are frequent occurrences to draw attention to the movement and increase the enthusiasm of members.

Responses to Contemporary Ethical Issues

THE ECOLOGICAL CRISIS   The following excerpt from a January 1992 address by Daisaku Ikeda, president of Soka Gakkai International, illustrates Soka Gakkai's concern to address the ecological crisis in a global context (Ikeda 1992: 18–21):

In the past twenty years, the industrialized countries have pursued material wealth to the virtual exclusion of all other concerns, racing down their chosen path in the firm belief that the doctrine of economic growth was supreme. The prosperity of one's own country has come first, and concern for the Earth's environment has been considered secondary. . . . The problem of poverty and its attendant issue of explosive population growth have been left unaddressed. In the end, this approach has led to environmental destruction within the developing countries, the accumulative effect of which has contributed to the degradation of the global environment. . . .

The three monumental problems confronting humankind—global environmental destruction, population growth, and poverty—are inextricably linked, and we are therefore confronted with the extremely difficult task of finding a simultaneous and comprehensive solution. . . .

It would seem that the 1990s have ushered in an era of pressing choices that demand our immediate response. The choices we make now could well determine the survival of the human race. By their nature, the global problems confronting us call for the combined efforts of all people, with no distinction between North and South.

The Spiritual Regeneration Movement: Transcendental Meditation

The Spiritual Regeneration Movement was created in 1959 by Maharishi Mahesh Yogi (born Mahesh Prasad Varma), a physicist turned religious leader. The movement is better known by the name of the technique the Maharishi taught: transcendental meditation.

TM (as it is called) teaches that the way to fullness of life is through reaching the ground of joy through meditation. In what some have described as a popularization of Vedanta philosophy, the Maharishi taught his followers that by going beneath the surface of reality they can experience the calmness of original consciousness. Through meditative discipline one releases the mind to pursue its natural happiness in pure consciousness. The practice is a simple period of meditation fifteen to twenty minutes per day. Each member is given his or her own sacred syllable (*mantra*) to use in the meditation.

Practitioners claim that TM is a natural process whose effects have been scientifically measured. Through meditation one slows breathing and relieves mental pressure and emotional anxiety. According to the movement's publicity, TM enables people to work more efficiently, athletes to perform more effectively, artists to be more creative, and everyone to be more happy. According to the Maharishi, if only 10 percent of the world's population meditated, wars and other social problems would end. TM advocates have gone to areas of social turmoil to meditate and claim to have had a positive effect.

TM was very popular during the 1960s, when various celebrities such as the Beatles, actress Mia Farrow, and professional football player Joe Namath became meditators. The Maharishi International University was established in Parsons, Iowa, offering undergraduate and graduate degrees in "the neuroscience of human consciousness." The movment's international headquarters are in Switzerland.

However, the movement has not maintained the same level of support and attention in recent years. In the 1970s the Maharishi made the claim that through meditation persons could levitate, bringing some notoriety but also skepticism and ridicule.

Many supporters of TM contend that it is not a religion, but a science that can be used alongside any religion or by non-religious persons. Some observers point out that the ideal state of pure consciousness seems to be an adaptation of the Vedanta teaching of Brahman and a goal for ultimate transformation. If so, it is appropriate to consider TM a spiritual religion.

The Theosophical Society: Divine Wisdom

The Theosophical ("Divine Wisdom") Society is a monistic movement that emphasizes the hidden meanings in sacred writings, which point to a unitary Truth manifest in all religions. The Truth is apprehended through mystical experience. Theosophy draws heavily on Hindu and Buddhist philosophy.

The Society was founded in New York City in 1875 by Helena Blavatsky (1831–1891) and Henry Olcott (1832–1907). Three years later they moved to India and established the Society's world headquarters in Madras. After years of interaction with a variety of Indian spiritual teachers, Blavatsky published *The Secret Doctrine* in 1888, the major Theosophical text. A complex and sophisticated work, it synthesizes themes from both West and East, presenting a cosmology in which reality emanates from the One but includes the evolution of humanity. The "secret doctrine" is manifest in all religions when their symbolisms are properly understood. It includes an elaborate hierarchy of the spiritual as well as such basic Indian concepts as karma and reincarnation. People are initiated into the doctrine by often invisible Masters called Adepts. The goal of Theosophy is to present this ancient wisdom to the modern world.

Annie Besant (1847–1933) succeeded the founders as head of the Theosophical Society. She was active in the movement for home rule in India. Theosophy in general was instrumental both in introducing Hindu and Buddhist teachings to the West and in reintroducing the Indian people to their spiritual heritage after years of colonialism. For example, Mahatma Gandhi first encountered the *Bhagavad-Gita* when it was given to him by a Theosophist.

Although Theosophy has been weakened through a number of schisms, its influence continues not only through the various Theosophical organizations, but also through the timeless work of poets such as W.B. Yeats (1865–1939), whose poetic vision was influenced by his association with Theosophy. Although he eventually separated himself from Theosophy in 1930, the noted lecturer Jiddu Krishnamurti (1895–1986) was brought up by Theosophists who were grooming him to be the next World Teacher, the manifestation of Maitreya Buddha (see Chapter Six). His philosophy of "total awareness beyond mental process" reflects his Theosophical background.

The major American centers of the Theosophical Society are located in Ojai, California, and Wheaton, Illinois.

Unitarian Universalist Association: The Unity of God

History and Basic Teachings The Unitarian Universalist Association was created in 1961 as the result of a merger between the American Unitarian Association and the Universalist Church of America. In that sense it is a new religion. However, the two movements that merged have quite a long history.

Unitarianism was a movement that rejected the orthodox Christian teaching of the Trinity in favor of an affirmation of the unity of God. The roots of Unitarianism are found in the early Christian trinitarian disputes, some leaders of the Protestant Reformation who questioned the Trinity, and the Enlightenment criticism of revealed religion. The movement spread from England to the United States, where it gained a strong foothold in New England. Inspired by the preaching of William Ellery Channing in the early nineteenth century, Unitarianism formally organized in America. Among its principal teachings were a commitment to interpret the Bible rationally, dedication to follow the example of Jesus but not claim

him as God, and a strong devotion to serve humanity and right the wrongs of society. Many of the strongest opponents of slavery in the United States were Unitarians. The idea of human perfectibility through education is also a strong tenet. Respect for the integrity of individual conscience meant that Unitarianism had no creeds to which members pledge allegiance. American Transcendentalism and authors such as Ralph Waldo Emerson gave literary expression to many Unitarian principles.

Unitarianism had always been a middle- and upper-class movement. The movement with which it merged in 1961 had its roots in a lower-class movement in England, which emphasized the love of God that will eventually restore all humanity to harmony with God and one another. Universalism was more evangelical and accepting of orthodox Christian teachings, but it did emphasize the unity of God.

Since the merger, Unitarian Universalism has been principally, but not exclusively, a movement among highly educated, middle- to upper-class Americans. However, its openness to other religions and other cultures has won interfaith admiration among people of various cultural and ethnic backgrounds. Recently a group of neo-pagan Wiccans has found a home among Unitarian Universalists, creating the Covenant of Unitarian Universalist Pagans. The basis of Unitarian Universalist teaching is the free and open search for truth, with the recognition that truth can be found among all religious traditions. However, it finds in the Judeo-Christian expression of love of God and love of neighbor the core truth needed today. Its goal is the creation of a world community of justice and peace.

There is no set liturgy for worship in Unitarian Universalism, so Protestant-style services of prayer, praise, readings, and sermons often alternate with experimental services and programs on current social issues.

Responses to Contemporary Ethical Issues

CAPITAL PUNISHMENT The General Assembly of the Unitarian Universalist Association adopted resolutions opposing the death penalty on a number of occasions. These resolutions have urged the complete abolition of capital punishment as "inconsistent with respect for human life; for its retributive, discriminatory, and non-deterrent character" (National Coalition 1988: 44).

EUTHANASIA   The Unitarian Universalist response to the dilemma posed by modern medical care is one of the most liberal statements on euthanasia, affirming each individual's right to choose his or her own form of dying. It is one of the few religious groups to support active euthanasia, asserting "the right to self-determination in dying, and the release from civil or criminal penalties of those who, under proper safeguards, act to honor the right of terminally ill patients to select the time of their own deaths" (Hamel and DuBose 1991: 86).

The Vedanta Society:
The Truth at the Heart of All Religions

The Vedanta Society is a movement brought to the United States by Vivekananda (see Chapter Five). After his success at the Parliament of Religions in Chicago in 1893, Vivekananda began a tour that attracted much interest in the *advaita vedanta* teaching of a single spiritual truth at the heart of all the world's religions. As a result, centers to teach this philosophy opened in major cities throughout the country. Called the Vedanta Society, this movement brought swamis (an Indian title of honor for a teacher or leader) from the Ramakrishna Order in India to instruct Americans in the Vedanta philosophy. Each teacher attracted a following of usually highly educated persons who came to the centers to study classical Hindu texts. The swami helped each individual develop a spiritual discipline suited to his or her particular religious background and personality. By the 1970s fourteen centers had opened in the United States.

The Society teaches that the true human nature is divine, and that the aim of human life is to manifest this divine reality through prayer, meditation, and service to others. Because of this common divine nature, mankind is bound together as one. If you help others, you are helping yourself! The Society teaches that all religions are true; they have differences because they emerged in different historical and cultural settings. However, the ultimate truth lies beyond all religions. According to the Society's philosophy, the Vedanta teaching is not a religion alongside the others; rather, it is the means to experience the truth toward which all religions point.

Wicca: The Renewal of European Witchcraft

The word "witch" conjures up an image of an old woman dressed in black with a pointed hat, stirring a cauldron, casting evil spells. Even recent scholarly treatments of witchcraft draw solely on the tradition, developed by the Christian Church in Europe during the Middle Ages, that witchcraft is "the performance of magic for evil ends" (Owen 1989: 805). However, another, more positive understanding of witches and witchcraft has been developed by a twentieth-century movement called Wicca.

Wicca (the Old English word for "wise") is the name given to a very loosely connected movement committed to restoring the witchcraft traditions of pre-Christian Europe. "Wicca" is the root of the English word "witch." Because of the negative connotations associated with "witch" and "witchcraft," the older "wicca" is preferred. Modern Wicca began in England, as a result of the work of Gerald Gardner (1884–1964), and spread to the United States by the mid-1960s. The movement is based on what can be recovered from the ancient tradition (now mostly lost or distorted, Wiccans admit, after centuries of Christian suppression), combined with newly devised rituals that reflect the basic principles of the indigenous worldview. In the last several decades Wicca has been one important element in a broad movement aimed, proponents say, at the recovery of feminine spirituality.

In the Wiccan religion all members are considered witches. It simply means that they are seekers of the ancient wisdom. There is no hierarchy, but in practice one witch assumes leadership, and is sometimes called the priestess. Members form their own groups known as *covens*, some of which are for women only (called Dianic), with others open to both men and women. The covens are small, usually limited to thirteen members, and there is no central organization among them. Other, larger groups have developed beyond the coven level to

QUESTIONS ABOUT THE SACRED: WHAT IS THE SACRED?

The Great Cosmic Mother

In their work The Great Cosmic Mother: Rediscovering the Religion of the Earth, *Monica Sjöo and Barbara Mor describe the Mother Goddess who is worshipped in Wicca and other neo-pagan religions, as well as their understanding of the Goddess' appeal today in these provocative words (Sjöo and Mor 1987: xviii):*

The Great Mother in Her many aspects—maiden, raging warrior, benevolent mother, death-dealing and all-wise crone, unknowable and ultimate wyrd—is now powerfully reemerging and rising again in human consciousness as we approach the twenty-first century. Isis, Mawu-Lisa, Demeter, Gaia, Shakti, Dakinis, Shekhinah, Astarte, Ishtar, Rhea, Freya, Nerthus, Brigid, Danu—call Her what you may—has been with us from the beginning and awaits us now. She is the beauty of the green earth, the life-giving waters, the consuming fire, the radiant moon, and the fiery sun. She is Star Goddess and Spiderwoman; she weaves the luminous web that creates the universe. As earth, the great planetary Spirit-Being, She germinates life within Her dark womb.

After thousands of years of life-denying and anti-evolutionary patriarchal cultures that have raped, ravaged, and polluted the earth, She returns. The earth's immune system is breaking down and so is ours. Her soil, atmosphere, plant life, trees, and animal worlds are exhausted beyond endurance. All beings are suffering and can take no more.

Based in matricide, the death of all nature, and the utter exploitation of women, Western culture has now run itself into the ground, and there is no other way but to return to the Mother who gives us life.

provide coordination and opportunities for networking. The only connection among covens and larger groups is a loose network of electronic bulletin boards, newsletters, other publications, and conferences that draw various covens and other groups together.

The goal of Wicca is to enable members to reestablish the harmony with the earth lost in modern civilizations. Wicca teaches the indigenous idea of the interconnectedness of all of life, and stresses that humans are part of nature, not her masters.

The Wiccan view of the sacred is that all nature is spiritually alive. However, as in other indigenous religions, there are gods. One deity is the male lord of animals, death, and the beyond, called the *Horned God,* symbolized in the sun. Increasingly, the more important deity for the practice of Wicca is the *Goddess,* who appears in three aspects reflective of the cycle of life, and, in particular, the phases of the moon: the maiden, the mother, and the crone (old woman). There is no strict distinction drawn between the gods and nature; the gods are present in nature, in everyone, and in all of life. Their energy is the energy of nature, not an energy infused into nature from outside.

Wiccan rituals are usually held outside and involve the creation of sacred space, through purification involving the four elements (fire, water, earth, and air) and the demarcating of the four cardinal directions. The creation of the space is called "casting the circle." Ritual objects such as swords, knives, wands, and chalices are used. Worshippers stand and dance in circles. In some covens, at some times, they are skyclad (naked), to manifest their sense of oneness with nature and the beauty of the natural body. The ceremonies involve the use of chanting and dancing to raise the spiritual energy within the circle, then the focusing of the energy into a "cone." When the witch in charge senses intuitively that the energy is at its peak, it is directed at a particular goal decided upon by the group. The goal usually involves the well-being of a particular person or group, or the healing and harmony of the environment. Many Wiccans today seek to apply the power politically, to effect changes in policies deemed detrimental to the well-being of Mother Earth.

Wiccan magic is "white magic," not the so-called "black magic" associated with the use of magical powers for destructive ends. The identification of witchcraft with evil is, they believe, the result of the prejudice and stereotyping of others. Wiccans point out that the image of the "witch" boiling toads in a cauldron to cast evil spells, and riding on a broomstick, is more the creation of the hysterical response by church authorities to witchcraft in Christian Europe in the eleventh and twelfth centuries than historical reality. A witch, in the Wiccan view, is anyone willing to draw upon the spiritual power of the body's senses in the pursuit of wisdom and harmony with nature.

One distinctive Wiccan ritual is the "drawing down of the moon." The moon, representing the three phases of the Goddess, is magically "drawn down" into an individual who then exhibits to the coven the force of the Goddess. The individual takes the role of the shaman of other indigenous religions, becoming "possessed" by the spirit world and manifesting the power of that world to others. The Goddess uses the person to instruct the group in the ways of wisdom.

As in indigenous religions, Wiccans have no written scriptures. They do find meaning in ancient myths such as the story of the Greek goddesses Demeter and Persephone. The chief source of revelation is nature. There is no founder, nor a single central leader.

The Wiccan calendar reflects the cycle of nature, with special rituals held at the summer and winter solstices, and fall and spring equinoxes. At the winter solstice each year the Horned God is born anew. In spring he becomes the Goddess'

lover. At Halloween he dies, and the Goddess becomes the crone of winter.

With Wicca we encounter the contemporary religious phenomenon identified by some scholars as *neo-paganism*. The term "pagan" comes from the Latin word for "countryside." In the Roman world, pagans were those who lived in the country rather than the city. In the early Christian Church, pagan became a pejorative term to refer to anyone who practiced the indigenous ways associated with rural life rather than Christianity, which had gotten its foothold in the urban populations. Eventually, pagan referred to any indigenous peoples who had not yet been exposed to the Christian gospel and therefore still practiced their traditional religions. Part of bringing Christianity to a pagan area was to root out all indigenous religious ways. Neo-paganism is the self-conscious attempt to recover these suppressed indigenous beliefs and practices. Besides Wicca, neo-paganism includes groups trying to revive ancient Egyptian or Greek religions and Druidism. Although some modern Satanic groups (see above) claim to be neo-pagan, Wiccans and other widely recognized neo-pagan groups (as well as most scholars of new religions) reject this claim. Two scholars of new religions have described the neo-pagan goal in these words (Ellwood and Partin 1988: 187):

> What Neo-Pagans seek is a new cosmic religion oriented to the tides not of history but of nature—the four directions, the seasons, the path of the sun and of the timeless configurations of the psyche. They seek not that morality which comes of imposing the will on the reluctant flesh, nor the mystical trance which is the fruit of asceticism, but the expansiveness of spirit which comes of allowing nature and rite to lower the gates confining the civilized imagination.

SECULAR NEW RELIGIONS

According to the definition of religion adopted in this text (transformation in response to perceived ultimacy), religions need not be spiritual. Secular (this-worldly, as opposed to spiritual) patterns of ultimacy may also provide the basis for religious transformation. As stated in Chapter One, from this perspective virtually anything can take on religious meaning. At an individual level, this means that a person's religion focuses on whatever he or she perceives as ultimate, whether or not that accords with the person's formal religious affiliation. At a social level it means that groups that have a secular sense of ultimacy take on religious characteristics and can indeed be considered "religions."

As the process of secularization initiated in the West spreads throughout the world, the phenomenon of people turning from traditional, spiritually oriented religions to secular substitutes should not be ignored in a study of the world's religions. As we have seen, secularization has also spawned defensive reactions as well as reform movements within the world's traditional religions.

In this section we will contend that the two most prevalent economic systems of the twentieth century, Marxism and capitalism, can be considered "secular religions." We will also focus on the phenomenon of "civil religion," in which the nation-state takes on the qualities of ultimacy. Next, the movement known as secular humanism will be discussed. Finally, we will ask whether the various self-help movements so popular today can be considered religions.

Capitalism: Material Well-Being, Individual Freedom

Like Marxism, capitalism may be, but is not necessarily, a secular religion. Like Marxism, capitalism is concerned with people's material well-being. The difference is that capitalism stresses individual freedom in making the decisions that lead to this well-being. If Marxism focuses on liberation for workers, capitalism emphasizes freedom for "consumers." When consumers are free to choose what to do with their resources, producers will respond by providing what consumers truly want, and happiness will result. Thus, according to capitalism, a "free market" system in which private companies compete to meet consumer demand is the best way to ensure economic well-being.

When does capitalism become a religion? Collectively, when the "free market" is accorded ultimacy, capitalism becomes a religion. When individuals and companies, for example, treat the bottom line as an end in itself (without regard for the social, environmental, or moral consequences of their decisions) and use "whatever it takes" to manipulate consumer demand, then capitalist theory takes on the quality of religious doctrine.

Individually, "consumerism" can rise to the level of ultimacy for people who make the acquisition of wealth for the purpose of acquiring material goods the central goal in life, without regard for the well-being of other people or other living beings, not to mention their own spiritual welfare. As a religion, capitalism becomes a form of materialistic individualism or egoism, which most of the traditional religions identify as an aspect of the fundamental human problem. When it does not take on the status of ultimacy, and when its potential excesses are self-regulated or are controlled by governments, capitalism would seem to be the most successful way yet devised to organize a society economically.

Civil Religion: The Nation as Ultimate

Rather than an organized religious movement, "civil religion" is a phenomenon found in a variety of religious, political, and educational settings. In civil religions, symbols associated with spiritual religions are used to interpret and accord ultimacy to a particular secular social group, usually a nation. We will focus here on what has been called American Civil Religion.

American Civil Religion is rooted in the belief that just as God once chose the ancient nation of Israel, God has selected the United States to be a "light to the nations." As God led Israel out of bondage, so God liberated the people who came to this country from European domination. As God gave to the Israelites a land "flowing with milk and honey," so God led Europeans who came to this country into the "promised land" that stretches from coast to coast. As God preserved Israel at times of national crisis, so God has watched over

America. God sends America into the world to fight wars to spread this freedom to other lands. In return, God expects Americans to live according to the divine law, with its personal and civic morality. When Americans turn from the divine law, the nation suffers.

Associated with this belief system are a series of rituals such as Independence Day and Thanksgiving, which re-enact the foundational events of the national myth. National leaders appeal to the American Civil Religion to legitimate their claim to power, repeating for example the creed-like statement that "America is the greatest nation on earth!"

Civil religion is not unique to the United States. Virtually every nation has a similar set of beliefs and rituals, rooted in its own history, to celebrate its national identity. Is the civil religion of the United States or any country a religion as we have defined the concept? As with Marxism and capitalism, the answer is "perhaps." When the nation becomes ultimate—as expressed, for example, in the popular slogan "My country right or wrong!"—civil religion can be a means of transformation in response to perceived ultimacy.

Some interpreters suggest that many Americans blend themes from civil religion with aspects of Christianity to create a syncretistic religion of "God and country." However, the national pride and patriotism expressed in civil religion need not take on the qualities of ultimacy. If they do not, allegiance to civil religion is qualified by that which *is* accorded ultimacy. Some would argue that American Civil Religion is, by nature, qualified by belief in a God who transcends the nation, and therefore does not conflict with Judaism and Christianity, from which its symbols are derived.

Humanism: Humanity as Ultimate

History and Basic Teachings   One result of the secular challenge to spiritual ultimacy has been the emergence of groups that consider humanity itself to be ultimate. The idea of treating humanity as a substitute for God can be traced to the French philosopher and founder of modern sociology,

Auguste Comte (1798–1857). Comte organized a *Church of Humanity* in Paris, substituting a calendar celebrating the achievements of scientists for the Catholic calendar commemorating the miracles of saints.

Comte's Church of Humanity faded away, but the notion of a humanistic substitute for traditional religion continued. In 1876 Felix Adler, who had studied to be a rabbi but turned away from traditional Judaism, organized the *Ethical Culture Society* in order to inculcate moral values without religious ritual and legalism. Today centers of the Society continue in a number of cities, supporting charitable causes and offering members worship that focuses on inspirational readings, music, and lectures in place of Jewish ritual. Members may, if they choose, retain belief in God, since there are no doctrinal requirements, but the activities of the group are non-theistic.

The *American Humanistic Association* is probably the most active secular humanistic organization today. Its origins can be traced to the 1920s, when a group of Unitarian ministers and others turned away from theism and embraced a secular philosophy based on humanism. In 1933 eleven prominent humanists (among them the educational leader John Dewey) issued "A Humanist Manifesto," which rejected supernatural explanations, calling the universe "self-existing" and regarding humanity as part of nature. The AHA formally organized in 1941. In 1973 "Humanist Manifesto II" appeared as a "consensus statement on social policy." It provides a set of principles for the Association's program.

The general goal of the AHA is "the fulfillment of human life," to be attained by humans using their creative abilities together. According to Humanist Manifesto II, "using technology wisely, we can control our environment, conquer poverty, markedly reduce disease, extend our life-span, significantly modify our behavior, alter the course of human evolution and cultural development, unlock vast new powers, and provide humankind with unparalleled opportunity for achieving an abundant and meaningful life." It then lists seventeen "positive principles rele-

COSMIC QUESTIONS: HOW DID THE WORLD COME INTO BEING?

The Universe as Self-Existing

The Humanist Manfestos I *and* II *of the American Humanist Association are an expression of the understanding popular among many in the modern world that the world and humanity are the result of a totally materialist process.* Humanist Manifesto II *included the following statement relevant to the question of cosmic origins* (Humanist Manifestos I *and* II *1973):*

Today man's larger understanding of the universe, his scientific achievements, and his deeper appreciation of brotherhood have created a situation which requires a new statement of the means and purposes of religion. Such a vital, fearless, and frank religion capable of furnishing adequate social goals and personal satisfactions may appear to many people a complete break with the past. While this age does owe a vast debt to traditional religions, it is nonetheless obvious that any religion that can hope to be a synthesizing and dynamic force for today must be shaped for the needs of this age. To establish such a religion is a major necessity of the present. It is a responsibility which rests upon this generation. We therefore affirm the following:

FIRST: *Religious humanists regard the universe as self-existing and not created.*
SECOND: *Humanism believes that man is a part of nature and that he has emerged as the result of a continuous process.*

Excerpts from **Humanities Manifestos I and II.** *Reprinted with permission of Prometheus Books.*

dings and funerals for people who prefer a "secular clergy." Approximately 20 percent of the AHA membership is composed of college students organized as the Humanist Student Union of North America.

Falling under the category of secular humanism are a host of movements that stress the realization of "human potential" apart from any spiritual claims. They are often called *self-help programs.* The literature of such movements fills the shelves of most bookstores. On your next trip to a bookstore, peruse some of the titles and glance inside a few. Do you notice any indications of self-help programs functioning as religions, in the sense the term has been defined in this text? Should these programs be viewed as a substitute for or an enhancement of traditional, spiritual religions? Why do you think they are gaining in popularity in the modern world?

Responses to Contemporary Ethical Issues

THE ECOLOGICAL CRISIS The Humanist Manifesto II, includes as one of its seventeen basic principles the following statement on the environment:

> The world community must engage in cooperative planning concerning the use of rapidly depleting resources. The planet earth must be considered a single ecosystem. Ecological damage, resource depletion, and excessive population growth must be checked by international concord. The cultivation and conservation of nature is a moral value; we should perceive ourselves as integral to the sources of our being in nature. We must free our world from needless pollution and waste, responsibly guarding and creating wealth, both natural and human. Exploitation of natural resources, uncurbed by social conscience, must end.

EUTHANASIA Leaders of humanist movements such as the Ethical Culture Society have not only endorsed passive euthanasia, like most other religions surveyed here, they have spoken in defense of active euthanasia. One leader has written, for example, "When a relative or friend or professional person is party to an act of euthanasia, every effort should be made to remove this act from the category of criminal action subject to criminal punishment—*provided* the suffering is unbearable and the illness terminal and hopeless, *and* the sufferer

vant to the present human condition," which are "a design for a secular society on a planetary scale."

In place of ministers, the American Humanist Association licenses counselors to perform wed-

has fervently requested such action in the presence of witnesses, *and* written and sworn affidavits are furnished" (cited in Larue 1985: 130).

The American Humanist Association included euthanasia, suicide, and the right to die with dignity among the freedoms claimed in its 1973 *Humanist Manifesto II*.

ECONOMIC JUSTICE   The principal current statement of principles of the American Humanist Association (*Humanist Manifesto II*) has this to say about economics and the issues of poverty and wealth:

> *The problems of economic growth and development can no longer be resolved by one nation alone; they are worldwide in scope. It is the moral obligation of the developed nations to provide—through an international authority that safeguards human rights—massive technical, agricultural, medical, and economic assistance, including birth control techniques, to the developing portions of the globe. World poverty must cease. Hence extreme disproportions in wealth, income, and economic growth should be reduced on a worldwide basis.*

Marxism: Material Well-Being, Classless Society

Karl Marx (1818–1883) would not be pleased if he knew that the system named after him appeared in a survey of the world's religions *as a religion!* Marx was a German philosopher who became convinced that traditional religion was an "opiate of the masses" that rendered people powerless to confront the real forces of economic oppression from which they needed liberation. Marxists are typically "scientific atheists" who seek to understand history from a strictly materialistic standpoint.

How can we call Marxism a religion? The argument here is that Marxism is a secular religion with its own distinctive means of transformation in response to perceived ultimacy. We cannot here give a complete history of Marxism. Instead, we will focus on its "religious" characteristics.

According to Marxism, humans are material beings, with no souls or spiritual natures. There is no God outside humanity guiding or sustaining humanity. Humans create what they are by their own labor. They use their intelligence and creative abilities to produce from the natural world the goods necessary for life. What humans deserve and desire is control over their own productive capacities and material well-being in this world. However, production is not an individual enterprise; it requires division of labor. This division leads to some people's controlling the means of production, with the rest (workers) having only their labor to sell in order to attain goods. According to Marx, history is an inevitable struggle between the ruling and working classes. At the heart of this struggle is private ownership of the means of production. Until the community as a whole controls production, social and economic inequalities will result in alienation for the workers. The ruling classes will use religion and other social institutions to control workers.

According to Marx, in the modern world the oppressive ideology is capitalism, which emphasizes the concentration of wealth in the hands of a few. Capitalists control the means of production, and use their power to exploit workers. Workers must organize and seize control of the means of production. The ultimate result will be a classless society, a utopia in which all peoples' material needs will be met through an even distribution of the wealth produced by labor.

Marx himself was vague on the best political strategy to accomplish his utopian goal. He never assumed any political or other position of power himself. It remained for Marxist leaders such as Lenin in Russia and Mao Tse-tung in China to implement Marx's vision. Marxism has led to different types of socialist systems in different countries. The common denominator has been the belief that during the revolutionary transformation to the classless society, the Communist Party should maintain political and economic control, holding it in trust for the people.

Although Marxism denies any spiritual ultimacy, it replaces it with a secular ultimacy. For Marx, his scientific theory was ultimate. For followers of Marx, the Communist Party became ultimate. Practically, the leaders of Communist revolutions such as Lenin, Stalin, Mao, and Fidel Castro in Cuba became substitute deities, with rituals focus-

People wait to pay a "ritual" visit to Lenin's Tomb in Red Square, Moscow.

ing on them (such as the obligatory pilgrimage to Lenin's tomb in Red Square in Moscow). The means of ultimate transformation are political and economic, the work of the people organized by the Party in bringing about the classless society. Therefore, it is essential for the Party to remain in power for the transformation to occur.

Our contention is not that Marxism *must* be a religion. Some Marxists use Marxism as a political and economic theory, but do not accord it ultimacy. For example, some Christians who advocate

"liberation theology" (see Chapter Twelve) draw on Marxism to diagnose the ills of their societies, but retain their allegiance to a spiritual power as the ultimate source of the needed transformation of society.

In the 1990s Marxism and the Communist Party it inspired are in serious decline. Only a few nations (prominent among them China, North Korea, and Cuba) maintain a Marxist philosophy. The dream of a utopia in which all share wealth equally has faded.

CHAPTER SUMMARY

Hundreds, perhaps thousands, of "new religions" have sprung up in recent decades. We began this discussion of a representative sampling of new religions by raising the issues of why there are so many new religions, why they are so popular, and how they should be approached. For a significant number of people, they are all "sects" and "cults," which are a danger to individuals and society. However, to judge them negatively simply

because they have only arisen recently is unfair. In this chapter we sought to describe the religions selected objectively, observing the principle stated in Chapter One that we should seek to understand religions before we evaluate them.

After discussing the controversy over "cults" and clarifying what is meant by the New Age phenomenon, we briefly surveyed a representative selection of twenty-five spiritually oriented and secular new religions.

QUESTIONS FOR DISCUSSION AND REFLECTION

1. With which of the "new religions" discussed in this chapter were you familiar before this study? What was your opinion of them? How has this chapter affected your attitude?

2. In your opinion, are any of the religions discussed in this chapter "cults" that pose a threat to you personally or to society in general? If so, which religions, what kind of threat, and to whom?

3. Do you think governments should seek to restrain any of these religions? If so, how could this be done without jeopardizing the freedom of religion?

4. React to the Baha'i Faith's teaching that "one world," with a single world government, should be created.

5. Evaluate the federal government's response to the Branch Davidians. How do you think the government and press should respond to allegations involving new religions?

6. Should children of Christian Science parents be given medical treatment against the will of their parents?

7. Why do you think the Church of Jesus Christ of Latter-day Saints is one of the fastest-growing religions in the world?

8. Will Deep Ecology become increasingly popular as an alternative to the major religions? If so, who will be attracted to it?

9. What are the possible reasons for the refusal of ecumenical Christian groups to admit the Unification Church to membership? Do you agree with the refusal?

10. In light of your study of Hinduism (Chapter Five), do you think the International Society for Krishna Consciousness is a modern manifestation of one branch of Hinduism or a totally new religion?

11. In your view, should the right of Jehovah's Witnesses to refuse to deny blood transfusions, even to children, be protected on the basis of freedom of religion?

12. If you have seen the movie "Malcolm X," directed by Spike Lee, discuss its portrayal of Malcolm and the Nation of Islam. Why do you think Malcolm X is a hero to many African Americans in the 1990s? Look up some articles about Louis Farrakhan and reflect on his role as an African-American leader. Do you think movements that emphasize separation of the races have a positive or negative impact on American society?

13. Should the right of members of the Native American Church to use the hallucinogenic drug peyote be legally protected? Why or why not?

14. Before World War II, state Shinto warned of the dangers of "individualism." After World War II, the Japanese "new religion" Perfect Liberty Kyodan emphasized individualism. Which approach do you find most convincing?

15. Why do you think the Ras Tafari movement has continued to flourish even though the central figure, Emperor Haile Selassie, denied its claims about him? If you listen to reggae music, try to determine how the lyrics reflect Ras Tafari teaching.

16. Evaluate the Satanist claim that most people are motivated by the pursuit of self-indulgence and need not feel guilty about it.

17. Scientology coins a new vocabulary with terms such as "reactive mind" and "engram." Reflect on the possible reasons for creating these new words and their value in helping diagnose the basic human dilemma.

18. Why is the idea that a new age of peace and harmony, advanced by millenarian movements such as the Seventh-Day Adventists, so compelling for many people today?

19. Why do you think Soka Gakkai has enjoyed so much success in attracting new members both in Japan and on the West Coast of the United States?

20. Should Transcendental Meditation be considered a religious movement?

21. Do you agree with the Theosophical Movement that there is one ultimate wisdom toward which all religions point?

22 Why do you think many highly educated people are attracted to Unitarian Universalism?

23. What is your view of "witchcraft"? How does your attitude affect your response to Wicca? Why do you think Wicca is gaining in popularity today, especially among women? Respond to the claim of the re-emergence of the Mother Goddess as we approach the twenty-first century. In your view, is this a positive or negative development?

24. Do you think capitalism really functions as a religion for some people? If so, what distinguishes contexts in which capitalism is "religious" from those in which it is simply an economic theory?

25. How influential is "civil religion" in the United States and in other countries? Does civil religion pose a threat to world peace and/or to spiritual religions?

26. Do you agree with the optimism of "secular humanism" about humankind's ability to cooperate to create a better future? Why or why not? Do you agree with the attitude that traditional, spiritual religions stand in the way of human progress? The Humanist Manifestos say that it is necessary to break from the traditional religious understanding that the world has an ultimate, spiritual source. Do you agree or disagree? Can self-help psychological therapies become "religions" for those who practice them?

27. Do you think that Marxism should be considered a "religion"? Why do you think so many people are turning away from Marxism today?

SOURCES AND SUGGESTIONS FOR FURTHER STUDY

New Religions in General

BECKFORD, JAMES A., ED., 1986 *New Religious Movements and Rapid Social Change.* London: Sage Publications.

CHANDLER, RUSSELL, 1988 *Understanding the New Age.* Dallas: Word Publishing.

COLLINS, JOHN J., 1991 *The Cult Experience: An Overview of Cults, Their Traditions, and Why People Join Them.* Springfield, Ill.: Charles L. Thomas.

ELLWOOD, ROBERT S., AND HARRY B. PARTIN, 1988 *Religious and Spiritual Groups in Modern America,* 2nd ed. Englewood Cliffs, N.J.: Prentice Hall.

FERGUSON, DUNCAN, 1992 *New Age Spirituality: An Assessment.* Louisville, Ky.: Westminster/John Knox.

MELTON, J. GORDON, ED., 1987 *The Encyclopedia of American Religions,* 2nd ed. Detroit: Gale Research Company.

1992 *Encyclopedic Handbook of Cults in America,* rev. ed., New York: Garland Publishing.

MILLER, TIMOTHY, ED., *When Prophets Die: The Post-Charismatic Fate of New Religious Movements.* Albany: State University of New York Press.

NEEDLEMAN, JACOB, 1970 *The New Religions.* New York: Doubleday & Co.

ROBBINS, THOMAS, AND DICK ANTHONY, ED., 1991 *In Gods We Trust: New Patterns of Religious Pluralism,* 2nd ed. New Brunswick, N.J.: Transaction Publishers.

ROBBINS, THOMAS, WILLIAM C. SHEPHERD, AND JAMES MCBRIDE, EDS., 1985 *Cults, Culture, and the Law: Perspectives on New Religious Movements.* Chico, Calif.: Scholars Press.

WILSON, BRYAN, ED., 1981 *The Social Impact of New Religious Movements.* New York: The Rose of Sharon Press.

ZARETSKI, IRVING, AND MARK LEONE, ED., 1974 *Religious Movements in Contemporary America.* Princeton, N.J.: Princeton University Press.

Spiritual New Religions

The Baha'i Faith

ANONYMOUS, 1976 *Messages from the House of Justice, 1968–1973.* Wilmette, Ill.: Baha'i Publishing Trust.

BAHA'U'LLAH, 1952 *Gleanings from the Writings of Baha'u'llah,* trans. Shoghi Effendi. Wilmette, Ill.: Baha'i Publishing Trust (1939).

1979 *Selected Writings of Baha'u'llah.* Wilmette, Ill.: Baha'i Publishing Trust.

DAHL, GREGORY C., 1984 "A Baha'i Perspective on Economic and Social Development," *Circle of Unity: Baha'i Approaches to Current Social Issues,* ed. Anthony A. Lee (Los Angeles: Kalimar Press, 1984) 155–89.

HATCHER, WILLIAM S., AND J. DOUGLAS MARTIN, 1984 *The Baha'i Faith: The Emerging Global Religion.* San Francisco: Harper & Row.

HUDDLESTON, JOHN, 1988 *The Earth Is But One Country.* London: Baha'i Publishing Trust.

PHILLIPS, ROBERT T., 1984 "The Antinuclear Movement and the Baha'i Community,"*Circle of Unity,* 21–35.

POKORNY, BRAD, 1984 "A Worldwide Movement for Peace," *Circle of Unity,* 3–19.

SCHOONMAKER, ANN, 1984 "Revisioning the Women's Movement," *Circle of Unity,* 135–53.

SMITH, PETER, 1987 *The Babi and Baha'i Religions.* Cambridge: Cambridge University Press.

STOCKMAN, ROBERT H., 1985 *The Baha'i Faith in America.* Wilmette, Ill.: Baha'i Publishing Trust.

THOMAS, JUNE MANNING, 1984 "Poverty and Wealth in America: A Baha'i Perspective," *Circle of Unity,* 91–116.

Branch Davidians

MELTON, J. GORDON, 1993 "Child Abuse, Suicide, and the Branch Davidians," paper presented at the 1993 Annual Meeting of the American Academy of Religion (Washington, D.C.).

TABOR, JAMES D., 1993 "Apocalypse at Waco: Could the Tragedy Have Been Averted?" *Bible Review* 9:5 (October): 24–33.

WOOD, JAMES E., JR., 1993 "The Branch Davidian Standoff: An American Tragedy," *Journal of Church and State,* 35: 233–40.

Christian Science

BABBITT, MARCY, 1975 *Living Christian Science: Fourteen Lives.* Englewood Cliffs, N.J.: Prentice Hall.

CHRISTIAN SCIENCE PUBLISHING SOCIETY, 1990 *Christian Science: A Sourcebook of Contemporary Materials.* Boston: The Christian Science Publishing Society.

DEWITT, JOHN, 1962 *The Christian Science Way of Life.* Englewood Cliffs, N.J.: Prentice Hall.

EDDY, MARY BAKER 1906 *Science and Health with Key to the Scriptures.* Boston: The Christian Science Board of Directors (1875, renewed 1934).

GOTTSCHALK, STEPHEN 1973 *The Emergence of Christian Science in American Religious Life.* Berkeley: University of California Press.

PEEL, ROBERT, 1988 *Health and Medicine in the Christian Science Tradition.* New York: Crossroad.

SILBERGER, JULIUS, 1980 *Mary Baker Eddy: An Interpretive Biography of the Founder of Christian Science.* Boston: Little, Brown.

The Church of Jesus Christ of Latter-day Saint

ARRINGTON, LEONARD J., AND DAVIS BITTON, 1979 *The Mormon Experience.* New York: Alfred A. Knopf.

BUSHMAN, RICHARD L., 1984 *Joseph Smith and the Beginnings of Mormonism.* Chicago: University of Chicago Press.

GOTTLIEB, ROBERT, AND PETER WILEY, 1984 *America's Saints: The Rise of Mormon Power.* New York: G. P. Putnam's Sons.

HINCKLEY, GORDON B., 1979 *Truth Restored: A Short History of the Church of Jesus Christ of Latter-day Saints.* Salt Lake City: Corporation of the President of the Church of Jesus Christ of Latter-day Saints.

McCONKIE, BRUCE R., 1966 *Mormon Doctrine.* Salt Lake City: Deseret Book.

O'DEA, THOMAS F., 1957 *The Mormons.* Chicago: University of Chicago Press.

SHIPPS, JAN, 1985 *Mormonism: The Story of a New Religious Tradition.* Champaign: University of Illinois Press.

SMITH, JOSEPH FIELDING, ED., 1976 *Teachings of the Prophet Joseph Smith.* Salt Lake City: Deseret Book.

TUCKER, RUTH A., 1989 *Another Gospel.* Grand Rapids, Mich.: Zondervan.

WHALEN, WILLIAM J., 1964 *The Latter-day Saints in the Modern Day World.* South Bend, Ind.: University of Notre Dame Press.

Deep Ecology

CHENEY, JIM, 1987 "Eco-Feminism and Deep Ecology," *Environmental Ethics* 9 (1987): 115–45.

DEVALL, BILL, AND GEORGE SESSIONS, 1985 *Deep Ecology: Living as if Nature Mattered.* Salt Lake City: Peregrine Smith Books.

FOX, WARWICK, 1984 "Deep Ecology: A New Philosophy of Our Time," *The Ecologist* 14 (1984): 194–200.

LOVELOCK, JAMES E., 1982 *Gaia: A New Look at Life on Earth.* Oxford: Oxford University Press

MACY, JOANNA, 1990 "The Greening of the Self," *Dharma Gaia,* ed. Allan Hunt Badiner. (Berkeley, Calif.: Parallax Press),: 53–63.

NAESS, ARNE, 1987 *Ecology, Community, and Lifestyle: Ecosophy T.* Cambridge: Cambridge University Press.

SALLEH, ARIEL KAY, 1984 "Deeper than Deep Ecology: The Eco-Feminist Connection," *Environmental Ethics* 6 (1984): 339–45.

SEED, JOHN, AND JOANNA MACY, PAT FLEMING, AND ARNE NAESS, 1988 *Thinking Like a Mountain: Towards a Council of All Beings.* Philadephia: New Society Publishers.

SJÖO, MONICA, AND BARBARA MOR, 1987 *The Great Cosmic Mother: Recovering the Religion of the Earth.* San Francisco: Harper & Row.

WARREN, KAREN, 1987 "Feminism and Ecology: Making Connections," *Environmental Ethics* 9 (1987): 3–20.

ZIMMERMAN, MICHAEL E., 1987 "Feminism, Deep Ecology, and Environmental Ethics," *Environmental Ethics* 9 (1987): 21–44.

The Holy Spirit Association
for the Unification of World Christianity
(The Unification Church)

ANDERSON, GORDON L., 1985 "God Is Parent: Rich and Poor Nations Are Siblings," in *God and Global Justice: Religion and Poverty in an Unequal World*, eds. Frederick Ferré and Rita H. Mataragnon (New York: Paragon House),120–35.

BROMLEY, DAVID G., AND ANSON D. SHUPE, 1979 *"Moonies" in America*. Beverly Hills, Calif.: Sage Publications.

KIM, YOUNG OON, 1980 *Unification Theology*. New York: The Holy Spirit Association for the Unification of World Christianity.

LEE, SANG HUN, 1981 *Explaining Unification Thought*. New York: Unification Thought Institute.

MOON, REVEREND SUN MYUNG, 1973 *Divine Principle*. New York: The Holy Spirit Association for the Unification of World Christianity.

SONTAG, FREDERICK, 1977 *Sun Myung Moon and the Unification Church*. Nashville,Tenn.: Abingdon Press.

International Society
for Krishna Consciousness

DRUTAKARMA DASA, 1992a Personal correspondence. June 1992.

    1992b "Peace and the New Nationalism," *Back to Godhead* (1992): 25–26, 52–54.

Jehovah's Witnesses

BECKFORD, JAMES, 1975 *The Trumpet of Prophecy: A Sociological Study of Jehovah's Witnesses*. New York: Wiley.

BERGMAN, JERRY, 1984 *Jehovah's Witnesses and Kindred Groups: An Historical Compendium and Bibliography*. New York: Garland.

PIKE, EDGAR R., 1954 *Jehovah's Witnesses: Who They Are, What They Teach, What They Do*. New York: Philosophical Library.

The Nation of Islam

LEE, MARTHA F., 1988 *The Nation of Islam: An American Millenarian Movement*. Lewiston, N.Y.: Edwin Mellen Press.

LINCOLN, C. ERIC, 1973 *The Black Muslims in America*. Boston: Beacon Press.

LOMAX, LOUIS, 1964 *When the Word Is Given: A Report on Elijah Muhammad, Malcolm X, and the Black Muslim World*. New York: New American Library.

MARSH, CLIFTON E., 1984 *From Black Muslims to Muslims: The Transition from Separation to Islam, 1930–1980*. Metuchen, N.J.: Scarecrow Press.

X, MALCOLM, 1965 *The Autobiography of Malcolm X, with Alex Haley*. New York: Grove Press.

Native American Church

ABERLE, DAVID, 1982 *The Peyote Religion Among the Navaho*, 2nd ed. Chicago: University of Chicago Press.

ANDERSON, EDWARD F., 1980 *Peyote: The Divine Cactus*. Tucson: University of Arizona Press.

LaBARRE, WINSTON, 1969 *The Peyote Cult*. New York: Schocken Books.

SLOTKIN, J. SYDNEY, 1956 *The Peyote Religion: A Study in Indian-White Relations*. Glencoe, Ill.: Free Press.

STEINMETZ, PAUL, 1990 *Pipe, Bible and Peyote among the Oglala Lakota: A Study in Religious Identity*. Knoxville: University of Tennessee Press.

STEWART, OMER C., 1987 *Peyote Religion: A History*. Norman: University of Oklahoma Press.

Perfect Liberty Kyodan

BACH, MARCUS, 1971 *The Power of Perfect Liberty*. Englewood Cliffs, N.J.: Prentice Hall.

HAMMER, R.J., 1963 "The Scripture of 'Perfect Liberty Kyodan': A Translation with a Brief Commentary," *Japanese Religions* 3 (1963): 23–24.

The Ras Tafari Movement

BARRETT, L.E., 1977 *The Rastafarians*. Boston: Beacon Press.

CAMPBELL, HORACE, 1987 *Rasta and Resistance: From Marcus Garvey to Walter Rodney*. Trenton, N.J.: Africa World Press.

SMITH, M.G., 1960 *The Ras Tafari Movement in Kingston, Jamaica*. Mona, Jamaica: University College of the West Indies.

Satanism

LaVEY, ANTON, 1969 *The Satanic Bible*. New York: Avon Books.

LYONS, ARTHUR, 1970 *The Second Coming: Satanism in America*. New York: Dodd, Mead and Co.

RICHARDSON, JAMES T., JOEL BEST, AND DAVID G. BROMLEY, 1991 *The Satanism Scare*. New York: A. de Gruyter.

RASCHKE, CARL A., 1990 *Painted Black: From Drug Killings to Heavy Metal; The Alarming True Story of How Satanism Is Terrorizing Our Communities*. San Francisco: Harper & Row.

Scientology

GARRISON, OMAR V., 1974 *The Hidden Story of Scientology*. Secaucus, N.J.: Citadel Press.

HUBBARD, L. RON, 1950 *Dianetics: The Modern Science of Mental Health.* Los Angeles: Bridge Publications.

1970 *Scientology 0-8: The Book of Basics.* Los Angeles: American Saint Hill Organization.

1972 *Scientology: The Fundamentals of Thought.* Copenhagen: Aosh DK Publications.

WALLIS, ROY, 1977 *The Road to Total Freedom: A Sociological Analysis of Scientology.* New York: Columbia University Press.

Seventh-Day Adventism

PEARSON, MICHAEL, 1990 *Millennial Dreams and Moral Dilemmas: Seventh-Day Adventism* New York: Cambridge University Press.

Soka Gakkai

BETHEL, DALE, 1973 *Makiguchi the Value Creator, Revolutionary Japanese Educator, and Founder of Soka Gakkai.* New York: Weatherill.

BRANNEN, NOAH S., 1968 *Soka Gakkai: Japan's Militant Buddhists.* Richmond, Va.: John Knox Press.

HARDACRE, HELEN, 1986 *Kurozumikyo and the New Religions of Japan.* Princeton, N.J.: Princeton University Press.

IKEDA, DAISAKU, 1987 *A Lasting Peace,* 2 vols. New York: John Weatherill.

1992 "A Renaissance of Hope and Harmony," speech delivered on January 26.

MCFARLAND, H. NEILL, 1967 *The Rush Hour of the Gods: A Study of the New Religious Movements in Japan.* New York: Macmillan.

METRAUX, DANIEL, 1988 *The History and Theology of Soka Gakkai.* Lewiston, N.Y.: Edwin Mellen Press.

MURATA, KIYOAKI, 1971 *Japan's New Buddhism: An Objective Account of Soka Gakkai.* New York: Weatherill.

SOKA GAKKAI, 1992 "SGI: Soka Gakkai International," a pamphlet published by Soka Gakkai in 1992.

THOMSEN, H., 1963 *Japan's New Religions.* Rutland, Vt.: Tuttle.

The Spiritual Regeneration Movement: Transcendental Meditation

CAMPBELL, ANTHONY, 1973 *Seven States of Consciousness: A Vision of Possibilities Suggested by the Teaching of Maharishi Mahesh Yogi.* New York: Harper Torchbooks.

FOREM, JACK, 1974 *Transcendental Meditation: Maharishi Mahesh Yogi and the Science of Creative Intelligence.* New York: Dutton.

GOLDHABER, NAT, 1976 *TM: An Alphabetical Guide to the Transcendental Meditation Program.* New York: Ballantine Books.

KROLL, UNA, 1974 *The Healing Potential of Transcendental Meditation.* Atlanta: John Knox.

WALLACE, ROBERT K., 1974 *Neurophysioloy of Enlightenement: Scientific Research on Transcendental Meditation.* New York: MIU Press.

The Theosophical Society

BLAVATSKY, HELENA P., 1920 *The Key to Theosophy.* Los Angeles: The United Lodge of Theosophy.

CAMPBELL, BRUCE F., 1980 *Ancient Wisdom Revised: A History of the Theosophical Movement.* Berkeley: University of California Press.

WESSINGER, CATHERINE LOWMAN, 1988 *Annie Besant and Progressive Messianism.* Lewiston, N.Y.: Edwin Mellen Press.

Unitarian Universalism

TAPP, ROBERT, 1973 *Religion Among the Unitarian Universalists.* New York: Seminar Press.

WILBUR, EARL, 1946 *A History of Unitarianism.* Cambridge: Harvard University Press.

1963 *Our Unitarian Heritage.* Boston: Beacon Press.

WILLIAMS, GEORGE , 1976 *American Universalism.* Boston: Beacon Press.

Wicca and Witchcraft

ADLER, MARGOT, 1979 *Drawing Down the Moon.* New York: The Viking Press.

CUNNINGHAM, SCOTT, 1990 *Wicca: A Guide for the Solitary Practitioner.* St. Paul, Minn.: Llewellyn Publications.

GARDNER, GERALD, 1970 *Witchcraft Today.* New York: Citadel Press.

MELTON, J. GORDON, 1982 *Magic, Witchcraft, and Paganism in America: A Bibliography.* New York: Garland.

MURRAY, MARGARET, 1970 *The God of the Witches.* New York: Oxford University Press.

OWEN, D.E., 1989 "Witchcraft," in *The Perennial Dictionary of World Religions,* ed. Keith Crim et al. (San Francisco: Harper & Row), 805–6.

RUSSELL, JEFFREY, 1980 *A History of Witchcraft.* London: Thames and Hudson.

SJÖO, MONICA, AND BARBARA MOR, 1987 *The Great Cosmic Mother: Rediscovering the Religion of the Earth.* San Francisco: HarperCollins.

STARHAWK, 1979 *The Spiral Dance: A Rebirth of the Ancient Religion of the Great Goddess.* London: Harper & Row.

1988 *Dreaming the Dark.* Boston: Beacon Press.

Secular New Religions

Capitalism

LAPHAM, LEWIS, 1988 *Money and Class in America: Notes and Observations on a Civil Religion.* New York: Weidenfeld and Nicholson.

PRESTON, RONALD H., 1991 *Religion and the Ambiguities of Capitalism.* Cleveland: The Pilgrim Press.

Civil Religion

BELLAH, ROBERT, 1975 *The Broken Covenant: American Civil Religion in a Time of Trial.* New York: Seabury Press.

1980 *Varieties of Civil Religion.* San Francisco: Harper & Row.

RICKEY, RUSSELL E., 1974 *American Civil Religion.* New York: Harper & Row.

ROUNER, LEROY S., ED., 1986 *Civil Religion and Political Theology.* Notre Dame, Ind.: Notre Dame University Press.

1991 *To Be at Home: Christianity, Civil Religion, and World Community.* Boston: Beacon Press.

WOOD, RALPH, AND JOHN E. COLLINS, EDS., 1988 *Civil Religion and Transcendent Experience.* Macon, Ga.: Mercer University Press.

Humanism

ADLER, FELIX, 1918 *An Ethical Philosophy of Life.* New York: Appleton-Century-Crofts.

AMERICAN HUMANIST ASSOCIATION, 1973 *Humanist Manifestos I and II.* Buffalo, N.Y.: Prometheus Books.

EDWORDS, FREDERICK, 1984 "The Humanist Philosophy in Perspective," *The Humanist* (Jan./Feb.).

HUXLEY, JULIAN, 1957 *Religion without Revelation.* New York: Mentor Books.

KURTZ, PAUL, ED., 1973 *The Humanist Alternative.* Buffalo, N.Y.: Prometheus Books.

LAMONT, CORLISS, 1982 *The Philosophy of Humanism.* New York: Ungar.

Marxism

MARX, KARL, 1977 *Selected Writings,* ed. D. McLellan (New York: Oxford University Press).

McLELLAN, DAVID, 1987 *Marxism and Religion.* New York: Harper & Row.

NEWELL, WILLIAM L., 1986 *The Secular Magi: Marx, Freud, and Nietzsche on Religion.* New York: The Pilgrim Press.

WEST, CHARLES, 1987 "Marxism," in *The Encyclopedia of Religion,* ed. Mircea Eliade (New York: Macmillan), vol. 9, 240–49.

CHAPTER 15

The Future
of the World's Religions

HOW WILL THE WORLD RELIGIONS RELATE TO ONE ANOTHER? THREE POSSIBLE FUTURES

As we complete this descriptive survey of the world's religions, we look to the future. There would seem to be at least three possible directions for the world's religions: *exclusivism, inclusivism,* or *pluralism.* At the present time, signs of each of these potential futures are apparent on the religious landscape.

Exclusivism

When proponents of each religion maintain that their religion alone is true, they are advocating a position we might call "exclusivism." Proponents of this approach usually take the position that their religion will ultimately win worldwide allegiance, either through divine intervention or successful evangelism, or both. For example, some Christian apocalyptic groups believe that the end of history is near, and that Jesus is about to return and initiate the Kingdom of God on earth (or take his followers to heaven). They often claim that they are the vanguard of this new age, and that only those who respond to their teaching will be citizens of the Kingdom.

The seemingly inevitable consequences of this attitude are, as they have been in the past, hostility that sometimes leads to violence. The major signs of exclusivism are in the growing acceptance of extreme *fundamentalism* in religions around the world. Whether in Iran, India, or Indiana, religious groups that claim to represent the only means to ultimate transformation are growing, while more tolerant movements seem to be on the decline. In secular form, some nationalist movements, especially in the former Soviet Union, have elevated a racially oriented nationalism to the status of religion.

Inclusivism

The *inclusive* attitude is that all religions will be subsumed within one universal religion. That religion could be a universalistic religion already in existence, such as the Baha'i faith or it might be some religion that has not yet developed. According to this view, as people become more aware of the need for global unity, they will seek a religion that manifests the one Truth toward which all other religions point. This is the point of view expressed by those associated with the New Age phenomenon (see Chapter Fourteen). Signs of an emerging "planetary consciousness" are usually cited as evidence that the inclusive vision is beginning to be realized. If it is, individual religions will not so much be repudiated as transcended, shed like a butterfly slipping free from the cocoon in which she has matured.

The Universe Story (Berry and Swimme 1992), a recent attempt to formulate a new "myth" appropriate for the scientific worldview of the modern world, may be seen as an imaginative example of an inclusive approach. *The Universe Story* was composed by a historian of spirituality, Thomas Berry, and a scientist, Brian Swimme. Recognizing the power of "foundational stories" within the world's cultures, Berry and Swimme have created a new sacred narrative that they believe could have the same role for people in the future as the various cosmogonic myths (such as the story of creation in the Book of Genesis in the Jewish and Christian sacred texts) had for earlier generations. The story begins with "the primordial flaring forth of the vast energies" 15 to 20 billion years ago and continues "through the galactic formations, the shaping of the solar system, of the Earth, of living beings, and of the human species, along with the historical development of humans through the ages." It is, as earlier foundational stories have been, a celebration of the mysteries of existence, and a structuring of time and space within which those who identify with the story may find meaning. *The Universe Story* sees as woven throughout time three tendencies: differentiation, inner spontaneity, and intimate bonding of each component of the universe with every other component. It envisions the new biological era into which we are now entering as the Ecozoic Era, "a period when humans would be present to the Earth in a mutually-enhancing manner" with the realization that all beings form with humans "a single community with a common destiny." Whether *The Universe Story* provides a shared sacred narrative that will be broadly

Leaders of the world's religions at the 1993 Parliament of the World's Religions.

accepted remains to be seen. It has already been criticized for being too anthropocentric and for ignoring the role of suffering in existence, but it is an ambitious attempt at an inclusive cosmic narrative by two gifted visionaries.

Pluralism

The third possible future for the world's religions is *pluralism*, in which the religions of the world will continue to be essentially separate, but grow ever more tolerant of one another. Proponents of this view argue that the first two approaches are idealistic and unlikely to come about, given the diversity of human cultures and worldviews. According to this perspective, the best that can be hoped for is mutual acceptance, in which religions continue to affirm their own truths but without feeling the need to deny the truths apprehended in other traditions. According to a pluralistic perspective, religions should continue to look for those principles upon which they agree while affirming their own unique histories and teachings.

Groups within a number of religions have moved in the direction of pluralism, and there is now quite a long history of dialogue among faiths at local, national, and world levels. World gatherings of spiritual leaders were held in England in 1988 and in association with the so-called Earth Summit in Brazil in 1992.

Another gathering of representatives of the world's religions, a Parliament of the World's Religions, was held in Chicago in 1993, to commemorate the 100th anniversary of the first Chicago Parliament of Religion. The Parliament included representatives from more than 100 of the traditional and new spiritual religions as well representatives from various secular traditions. One of the stated goals of the 1993 Parliament was to hold a celebration, with openness and respect, of the rich diversity of religions. For the most part this was the spirit of the gathering, as over 200 religious leaders shared their unique heritages and affirmed a commitment to work together to solve the world's problems.

However, the tension among religions was also evident at the 1993 Parliament. Some Christian groups withdrew because of the presence of movements that do not express a belief in a Supreme Being. Some Jewish groups left when Nation of Islam leader Louis Farrakhan appeared. And when a Sikh leader attacked the treatment of his religion by the government of India, a brief shoving match with representatives of Hinduism resulted. News coverage of the event was not very extensive, and there is no indication that world political leaders took much notice.

One of the concrete results of the 1993 Parliament was a proposal called "A Global Ethic" (see Küng 1993). This declaration addresses many of the contemporary ethical concerns we have discussed in this book. Its principal author was Hans Küng, a Ro-man Catholic Christian and ecumenical theologian. Although not yet officially endorsed by individual religious bodies, it was accepted by the leaders of many of the world's religions gathered in Chicago. The statement begins with a sense of urgency and anguish:

> *The world is in agony. The agony is so pervasive and urgent that we are compelled to name its manifestations so that the depth of this pain may be made clear.*
>
> *Peace eludes us ... the planet is being destroyed ... neighbors live in fear ... women and men are estranged from each other ... children die!*
>
> *This is abhorrent!*
>
> *We condemn the abuses of the Earth's ecosystems.*
>
> *We condemn the poverty that stifles life's potential; the hunger that weakens the human body; the economic disparities that threaten so many families with ruin.*
>
> *We condemn the social disarray of the nations; the disregard for justice which pushes citizens to the margin; the anarchy overtaking our communities; and the insane death of children from violence. In particular we condemn aggression and hatred in the name of religion.*

The declaration goes on to say that the basis for an ethic that "offers the possibility of a better individual and global order" already exists. It is present in the set of core values found in the teachings of the world's religions. It is a truth "already known, but yet to be lived in heart and action."

The declaration itself states that:

> *We are interdependent. Each of us depends on the well-being of the whole, and so we have respect for the community of living beings, for people, animals, and plants, and for the preservation of Earth, the air, water, and soil.*
>
> *We take individual responsibility for all we do. All our decisions, actions, and failures to act have consequences.*
>
> *We must treat others as we wish others to treat us. We make a commitment to respect life and dignity, individuality and diversity, so that every person is treated humanely, without exception.*

> *We must have patience and acceptance. We must be able to forgive, learning from the past but never allowing ourselves to be enslaved by memories of hate. Opening our hearts to one another, we must sink our narrow differences for the cause of the world community, practicing a culture of solidarity and relatedness.*
>
> *We consider humankind our family. We must strive to be kind and generous. We must not live for ourselves alone, but should also serve others, never forgetting the children, the aged, the poor, the suffering, the disabled, the refugees, and the lonely. No person should ever be considered or treated as a second-class citizen, or be exploited in any way whatsoever. There should be equal partnership between men and women. We must not commit any kind of sexual immorality. We must put behind us all forms of domination or abuse.*
>
> *We commit ourselves to a culture of nonviolence, respect, justice, and peace. We shall not oppress, injure, torture, or kill other human beings, forsaking violence as a means of settling differences.*
>
> *We must strive for a just social and economic order, in which everyone has an equal chance to reach full potential as a human being. We must speak and act truthfully and with compassion, dealing fairly with all, and avoiding prejudice and hatred. We must not steal. We must move beyond the dominance of greed for power, prestige, money, and consumption to make a just and peaceful world.*
>
> *Earth cannot be changed for the better unless the consciousness of individuals is changed first. We pledge to increase our awareness by disciplining our minds, by meditation, by prayer, or by positive thinking. Without risk and a readiness to sacrifice there can be no fundamental change in our situation. Therefore we commit ourselves to this global ethic, to understanding one another, and to socially-beneficial, peace-fostering, and nature-friendly ways of life.*
>
> *We invite all people, whether religious or not, to do the same.*

The Declaration makes clear that it is not claiming that religious people are better than others or have a corner on the truth, but that "as religious and spiritual persons we base our lives on an Ultimate Reality, and draw spiritual power and hope therefrom, in trust, in prayer, in meditation, in word or silence. We have a special responsibility for the welfare of all humanity and care for the planet Earth." The Declaration asserts that it is calling for pluralism, not exclusivism or inclusivism, stating that "we do not mean a global ideology or a single unified religion beyond all existing religions, and certainly not the domination of one religion over all others."

Which of these trends dominates the future (exclusivism, inclusivism, or pluralism) will depend on persons, such as the readers of this book, who, having become informed about the diversity of religions in the world, make conscious decisions not only about how they will be religious themselves, but how they will view and interact with participants in other religions.

The spreading cultural influence of the United States around the world may assist in the acceptance of pluralism. A recent study entitled *One Nation Under God* has shown that religions in the United States are much more likely to seek common ground than the same religions in other parts of the world. The cultural diversity that is a part of the American experience has shaped the religions that have taken root in American soil, causing them to be more tolerant of one another than is the case elsewhere. At the same time, there is a strong resistance to American cultural dominance, often led by those who take an exclusivist approach to their religion (whether it be spiritual or secular). Which of these two opposing trends becomes the strongest will also be an important factor in determining the future.

THE SEARCH FOR COMMON GROUND: THE ECOLOGICAL CRISIS

Making a broad declaration of general ethical principles that all the world's religions may affirm is a good starting point in the effort to face the dilemmas before us. However, as the saying goes, "Talk is cheap!" The real test of religions' abilities to work together will come in the search for shared agendas of action in response to specific issues. Before ending our discussion of the world's religions, let us make an attempt at identifying common ground in response to at least one of the contemporary ethical issues we have addressed in this work: the ecological crisis. In this area there are some hopeful signs.

Whatever the fundamental cause of the current environmental dilemma, representatives of all nations and religions are beginning to face up to it and take steps to deal with it. For example, in 1988 100 spiritual leaders from the world's religions and

100 political leaders gathered in Oxford, England, for the first Global Forum of Spiritual and Parliamentary Leaders on Human Survival (see Vittachi 1989). Its supporters enthused that the conference opened a new phase of world history, in which humans will look beyond their religious and political differences to recognize the global ecological crisis and truly begin the long-overdue process of joining together to restore the balance of life on earth. Some interpreters point to the emergence of an "ecological world view" and the emergence of a "planetary culture" that takes its cue from the holistic approach to nature (e.g., Thompson 1989: 25–36).

On May 6, 1992, Mikhail Gorbachev, former president of the Union of Soviet Socialist Republics, symbolically ended the Cold War at Westminster College in Fulton, Missouri, from the same podium at which British Prime Minister Winston Churchill, "opened" the Cold War era in 1946 when he spoke of the "iron curtain" descending across Europe. Gorbachev proclaimed that "humanity is at a turning point" and said that for the first time, "the resources of the world community can be focused on solving problems in nonmilitary areas: demography, ecology, food production, energy sources, and the like." He warned that "despite all the efforts being made to prevent ecological catastrophe, the destruction of nature is intensifying. And the effects of our poisoning of the spiritual sphere—drug addiction, alcoholism, terrorism, crime—become further ecological threats." He claimed that the ecological crisis "compels governments to adopt a world perspective and seek generally applicable solutions." Gorbachev called for the United Nations to be the forum for developing the cooperative structures for globally confronting the crisis.

In June 1992 the United Nations sponsored a Conference on Environment and Development (called the "Earth Summit") in Rio de Janeiro, Brazil, setting in motion a detailed set of steps that nations have pledged to take to restore environmental responsibility. Over 10,000 official delegates from 150 countries attended the summit, including the leaders of most of the world's nations. At the Earth Summit a set of environmental principles was adopted "with the goal of establishing a new and equitable global partnership through the creation of new levels of cooperation among states, key sectors of societies and peoples, working toward international agreements which respect the interests of all and protect the integrity of the global environmental system, recognizing the integral and interdependent nature of the earth, our home." The first of the twenty-seven principles states that "human beings are at the center of concerns for sustainable development. They are entitled to a healthy and productive life in harmony with nature." The principles recognize the rights of states to develop their material resources, but always with awareness of and attention to the environmental needs of present and future generations. They recognize that "peace, development, and environmental protection are interdependent and indivisible."

In a parallel Global Forum, 20,000 other concerned citizens met to try to launch an "Environmental Revolution," which, if it succeeds, "will rank with the Agricultural and Industrial Revolutions as one of the great economic and social transformations in human history" (Brown 1992: 174).

Many today agree that two elements must be present if ecological renewal is to occur and the "Environmental Revolution" is to be successful. First, the renewal *must* be spiritual, because the question of the human relationship to nature is essentially spiritual. As Lynn White observed in his famous article in 1967, "More science and technology are not going to get us out of the present ecological crisis until we find a new religion, or rethink our old one" (White 1967: 1206). (For a defense of the opposite viewpoint, that a turn toward the spiritual will undermine progress in facing environmental problems, see Passmore 1974.) Will those who have lost a sense of spiritual identity with nature recover that awareness? In 1949 Aldo Leopold, one of the principal "founders" of the modern environmental movement, was skeptical that such a basic change would occur, for Western religion and philosophy had then not yet heard of the environmental movement (Leopold 1949). As we have seen in Chapters Eleven and Twelve, this has changed, as more and more attention is being given, in Judaism and Christianity especially but other religions as well, to environmental issues and the basic orientation required in order for people to live in harmony with nature. With increasing respect in Western circles for indigenous and Asian religions and their attitude of reverence for all life, a new day *may* be dawning.

The second element is individual responsibility. In each community on earth we must all take responsibility for the quality of life around us. That responsibility has both a global and a local dimension. The spiritual leader of Tibetan Buddhism, the Dalai Lama, said to the participants in the Global Forum in 1988: "When we talk about global crisis, ... we cannot blame a few politicians, a few fanatics or a few troublemakers. The whole of humanity has a responsibility because this is our business. I call this a universal sense of responsibility." In her own simple and straightforward way the Roman Catholic leader Mother Teresa challenged the gathered religious and political leaders with these words: "Go back to your countries. Do what you must do to protect life." Or in the often quoted words of René Dubos, "Think globally; act locally."

The objectives adopted on Earth Day 1990 form a good basis for a concrete action agenda for those who want to act on their ecological convictions (Badiner 1990: xix):

- a worldwide ban on chlorofluorocarbons, fully implemented within five years,
- dramatic and sustained reduction in carbon dioxide emissions,
- preservation of old-growth forests, both tropical and temperate,
- strong recycling programs in every community and a ban on disposable or non-biodegradable packaging.
- transition to renewable energy resources and increased industrial and residential efficiency,
- greater protection for endangered species and habitats, and
- safeguarding of the global commons, the atmosphere, the oceans, and the Antarctic by an international agency.

The Dalai Lama, exiled spiritual head for the Buddhists of Tibet, here pictured on a visit to Finland, is one of the leaders of the movement to increase understanding and cooperation among the world's religions.

However, specific actions will not occur apart from a basic reorientation of priorities. The Worldwatch Institute's 1992 *State of the World* proposes a "fundamental restructuring of many elements of society—a shift from fossil fuels to efficient, solar-based energy systems, new transportation networks and city designs that lessen automobile use, redistribution of land and wealth, equality between the sexes in all cultures, and a rapid transition to smaller families, ... reduced consumption of resources by the rich to make room for higher living standards for the poor" (Postel 1992: 3–4).

If we fail to take action, we may be the only species, as British environmental leader Sara Parkin

has said, "to have minutely monitored our own extinction. What a measly epitaph that would make: 'they saw it coming but hadn't the wit to stop it happening' " (Postel 1992: 8). And if the religions of the world do not do a better job of teaching a spiritual ecology that makes living in harmony with all of nature a foundational principle in our daily lives and in our social policy, we may be doomed to do just this!

A FINAL WORD

The postscript for this survey of the world's religions and the points at which they engage basic human questions and some of the most compelling ethical issues we face at the beginning of a new millennium comes not from a religious leader. Instead, it is an admonition from a famous twentieth-century scientist whose work helped create the possibility for global destruction, but whose vision points the pathway to a more hopeful future:

> The more knowledge we acquire, the more mystery we find. ... A human being is part of the whole, called by us the Universe, a part limited in time and space. We humans experience ourselves, our thoughts, and feelings as something separate from the rest—a kind of optical illusion of our consciousness. This delusion is a kind of prison for us, restricting us to our personal desires and to affection for a few persons nearest to us. Our task must be to free ourselves from this prison by widening our circle of compassion to embrace all living creatures and the whole of nature in its beauty. Nobody is able to achieve this completely, but the striving for such achievement is in itself part of the liberation and a foundation for inner security.—Albert Einstein (cited in McGaa 1990: xiii–xiv and edited for inclusiveness).

QUESTIONS FOR DISCUSSION AND REFLECTION

1. When you began this study of the world's religions, which position best described your own point of view: exclusivism, inclusivism, or pluralism? How has your study affected your attitude?

2. Which of the three futures for the world's religions do you think is most likely to occur? Which do you hope for? On what basis do you make this judgment?

3. Do you think there is a need for a new "sacred narrative" such as *The Universe Story* in our age? Why or why not? If so, who should compose it?

4. Evaluate the Declaration of a Global Ethic agreed upon by representatives of many of the world's religions gathered for the 1993 World Parliament of Religions. Do you think it offers a realistic basis for continued dialogue on how the religions of the world might work together to address the common issues humanity faces? Try to think of other principles the religions of the world might affirm together.

5. What role do you think the world's religions should play in addressing the ecological crisis?

Evaluate the suggestions for action proposed in this chapter.

6. Look back over how the religions of the world are addressing other contemporary ethical issues. Individually and in groups, search for common ground the world's religions might find in seeking to confront issues such as war, capital punishment, abortion, euthanasia, economic justice, gender roles and the status of women, and homosexuality.

7. Write your own "final word" as you come to the end of your exploration of the world's religions, and share it with others. What effects do you imagine this study might have on your future?

SOURCES AND SUGGESTIONS FOR FURTHER STUDY

The Future of the World's Religions

BERRY, THOMAS, AND BRIAN SWIMME, 1992 *The Universe Story: From the Primordial Flaring Forth to the Ecozoic Era—A Celebration of the Unfolding of the Cosmos.* San Francisco: HarperCollins.

COWARD, HAROLD, 1985 *Pluralism: Challenge to World Religions.* Maryknoll, N.Y.: Orbis Books.

D'COSTA, GAVIN, 1986 *Theology and Religious Pluralism.* Oxford: Basil Blackwell.

HICK, JOHN, 1982 *God Has Many Names.* Philadelphia: Westminster Press.

KOSMIN, BARRY A., AND SEYMOUR P. LACHMIN., 1993 *One Nation Under God: Religion in Contemporary American Society.* New York: Harmony Books.

KÜNG, HANS, ED., 1993 *Towards a Global Ethic (An Initial Declaration).* New York: Continuum Publishing.

ROOF, WADE C., 1993 *Religion in the Nineties*, Annals of the American Academy of Political and Social Sciences, vol. 527. Newbury Park, Calif.: Sage Publications.

SCHUON, FRITHJOF, 1975 *The Transcendent Unity of Religions.* New York: Harper & Row.

SWIDLER, LEONARD, ED., 1988 *Toward a Universal Theology of Religion.* New York: Orbis Books.

The Ecological Crisis: The Search for Common Ground

BARBOUR, IAN, 1973 *Western Man and Environmental Ethics.* Reading, Mass.: Addison-Wesley.

BROWN, LESTER, 1992 "Launching the Environmental Revolution," in *State of the World 1992: A Worldwatch Institute Report on Progress Toward a Sustainable Society*, ed. Linda Starke (New York: W.W. Norton), 174–90.

LEOPOLD, ALDO, 1949 *A Sand County Almanac.* New York: Oxford University Press.

McGRAA, ED AND EAGLE MAN, 1990 *Mother Earth Spirituality: Native American Paths to Healing Ourselves and Our World.* San Francisco: HarperCollins.

PASSMORE, JOHN, 1974 *Man's Responsibility for Nature: Ecological Problems and Western Traditions.* New York: Charles Scribner's Sons.

POSTEL, SANDRA, 1992 "Denial in the Decisive Decade," in *State of the World 1992*, 3—8.

THOMPSON, WILLIAM IRWIN, 1989 "Pacific Shift," in *Nature in Asian Traditions of Thought: Essays in Philosophy*, ed. J. Baird Callicott and Roger T. Ames (Albany: State University of New York Press), 25–36.

VITTACHI, ANURADHA, 1989 *Earth Conference One: Sharing a Vision for Our Planet.* Boston: New Science Library.

Glossary

Abu Bakr—Muhammad's father-in-law and first political successor (caliph).

Advaita Vedanta—Sanskrit for "non-dual [interpretation of] the Vedanta [Upanishads]"; Hindu philosophical school that stresses the oneness of all reality (monism).

advent—in Christianity, refers to the Second Coming of Christ. "Adventist" groups, such as the Jehovah's Witnesses, calculate the time of and prepare for the return of Christ.

agnosticism—the view that it is impossible for humans to know whether spiritual reality exists.

ahimsa—non-injury to all life, a concept found in Jainism, Hinduism, and Buddhism.

Ahura Mazda—"Wise Lord," the Zoroastrian designation for the one God, creator and judge of the universe.

'Ali—Muhammad's son-in-law and cousin, the first after Khadija to accept Muhammad's teaching; the fourth caliph and first Imam of Shi'ite Islam.

Allah—the Arabic term for "God." According to Muslims, there is no god but Allah.

Amaterasu—in Shinto, the sun goddess.

Amitabha—in Pure Land Buddhism, the heavenly Buddha of the Western Paradise; called *Amida* in Japan.

Analects, The—the reputed sayings and conversations of Confucius.

anatman—literally, "no *atman*"; Buddhist teaching that humans have "no permanent self."

Angra Mainyu—the evil spirit in Zoroastrian cosmology.

anicca—Pali for "impermanence"; Buddhist concept that all reality is constantly changing and without any permanence.

animism—the belief that all reality is infused with spirits or a spiritual force and is therefore alive.

apocalyptic—referring to the revelation of the secrets of the end time.

arhant—Theravada Buddhist term for someone who has followed the teaching of the Buddha and attained enlightenment.

Aryans—Sanskrit for "noble ones"; in India, refers to people who migrated from Persia into the Indus Valley beginning in the middle of the second millennium B.C.E. A nomadic people who left no archaeological evidence, they are known because the Vedic literature originated when the Aryans were dominant.

asceticism—active self-denial for the purpose of spiritual fulfillment.

Ashkenazim—Jews who fled persecution in Western Europe and settled in Eastern Europe during the late Middle Ages.

Ashoka—Indian ruler (died 232 B.C.E.) who adopted Buddhism as the official religion of his reign.

Noted for tolerance and for initiating the spread of Buddhism beyond India.

atheism—the denial of the existence of a personal god (see theism) or, for some today, any spiritual reality.

atman—Hindu concept of the eternal soul.

auditing—in Scientology, the process of clearing oneself of engrams; requires a trained auditor who uses a machine called an "E-meter" to discern engrams.

avatar—Hindu concept of the incarnation or earthly manifestation of a deity.

avidya—Hindu concept of ignorance of the true, spiritual reality.

Bar (Bat) Mitzvah—Hebrew for "son (daughter) of the commandment"; the Jewish rite of passage through which one becomes an adult member of the Jewish community.

Bhagavad-Gita—Sanskrit for "Song of the Lord"; a section of the Hindu epic poem, the *Mahabharata* ("Great Epic"), which came to be considered a distinct text. The *Gita*, as it is called, is regarded as the crowning achievement of Hindu sacred literature, for it synthesizes the major strands within Hindu teaching.

bhakti—Hindu concept of devotional service to a personal god. Bhakti-yoga is one of the principal paths to liberation taught in Hinduism.

bodhisattva—Sanskrit for "a being intended for enlightenment"; in Mahayana Buddhism, one who has taken a vow to delay his or her own experience of **nirvana** in order to help others.

Brahma—Hindu god of creation.

Brahman—Hinduism the spiritual oneness of all reality.

Brahmin—In Hinduism, the spiritual oneness of all reality.

bushido—Japanese for "military warrior way"; the code of belief and conduct of the samurai warrior, synthesizing Confucian, Zen Buddhist, and Shinto teaching.

caliph—from the Arabic for "successor"; in Islam, political successors to Muhammad.

canon—a collection of sacred writings, deemed authoritative by and for a religious group.

caste—from the Portuguese *casta*, meaning "race";

the stratified system of social classes found in traditional Hindu society.

Chuang Tzu—the Taoist philosopher who, according to tradition, lived after Lao Tzu; also the name for a philosophical text.

clear—a goal in Scientology, a state achieved when engrams have been purged.

Conservative—in Judaism, the modern movement that seeks the middle path between the Reform and Orthodox positions, emphasizing the importance of keeping the commandments, but with some adaptation to contemporary circumstances.

conversion—the process of deliberate change from one religion to another.

consubstantiation—the belief that in the sacrament of Holy Communion the body and blood of Christ are actually present with or alongside of (but not replacing) the physical elements of bread and wine; associated with the Lutheran wing of the Protestant Reformation.

cosmology—the study of or a view of how the universe (all reality) is ordered. "Cosmogony" is a theory or story of how the cosmos originated.

cosmos—ordered reality as a whole. In religions, ultimacy is typically the source of cosmos.

coven—the small groups into which Wiccans are organized, and in which rituals are performed.

covenant—an agreement characterized by mutual loyalty and trust. The term "new covenant" is used in Christianity to refer to the relationship established with all humanity by God through Jesus Christ, fulfilling and superseding the "old covenant" with the nation Israel.

cult—descriptively, a movement that focuses on one person or god. Often used negatively for a religious movement deemed dangerous.

Dalai Lama—the chief spiritual and temporal leader of the Tibetan people.

dar al-islam—Arabic for "house of peace"; a symbol of the ideal of political unity established by submission to the will of Allah.

demons—spiritual beings that cause evil.

dhamma—Pali term (like the Sanskrit *dharma*) that describes the Buddha's teaching, which all who seek to lead a Buddhist lifestyle must follow.

dharma—Sanskrit for "duty" or "the way things are intended to be"; also translated as "law." In Hindu society, "social *dharma*" is determined by caste, while "eternal *dharma*" refers to one's duty to pursue the path that leads to liberation from the cycle of rebirth.

Diaspora—the dispersion (scattering) of Jews from their homeland.

divination—methods of discovering the nature and significance of events, usually future ones.

Divine Mind—the Christian Science name for God.

doctrine—a religious teaching expressed in rational form.

dogma—a doctrine accepted as true in a particular religion.

dualism—the view that reality is divided into two, and only two, basic principles or forces (one material and the other spiritual) that are mutually opposed and/or complementary.

ecumenical—from the Greek for "the whole inhabited world"; in Christianity, used to refer to the movement for increased cooperation and unity among Christian churches.

engrams—according to the teaching of Scientology, unhappy experiences in present and past lives that are encoded in the unconscious mind as mental aberrations.

eschatology—teaching about or study of the "end time," which will occur at the climax of history, according to the religions that originated in the Middle East.

ethics—principles of "right conduct" and the study of them.

fakir—Arabic for "poor;" in Sufism a seeker of the way to union with Allah.

fatalism—the view that events are predetermined.

fetish—a sacred object thought to have special powers.

filial piety—reverence for one's social superiors, coupled with respectful treatment of inferiors by superiors; expressed in five basic relationships.

five pillars—the basic obligations individual Muslims observe. They include (1) the profession of faith, (2) daily prayer, (3) the alms tax for the needy, (4) fasting during the month of Ramadan, and (5) taking the hajj at least once.

Four Noble Truths— the basic teaching of Buddhism, expressed by Siddartha Gautama in his Deer Park Sermon: (1) life is painful; (2) the cause of pain is desire; (3) there is a way to overcome this suffering; (4) the way is the eightfold path.

fundamentalism—a movement within a religion that stresses the absolute, unchanging and unequivocally true nature of the movement's teachings. First used in Christianity, but now applied to other religions.

Gabars—"infidels," the name for the Zoroastrian community in rural Iran.

Gaia—the Greek name for the earth goddess. The Gaia Principle (developed by James Lovelock) holds that the earth is one unified organism.

ganja—the Rastafarian word for marijuana; it is smoked ritually by some members of the movement.

Gathas—a set of five hymns found in the Zoroastrian scripture, the Avesta; basic source of Zoroastrian doctrine.

Ghost Dance—a ritual and associated movement that gained popularity in the late nineteenth century among a number of Native American peoples, including the Lakota. Participants believed that the dance would lead to the restoration of the glory days of Native American peoples. "Ghost" refers to the shirts worn by dancers, which made them appear as ghosts to white officials.

Goddess—in Wicca, the principal deity, manifested as maiden, mother, and crone (old woman). Her power is called upon in Wiccan rituals.

gohonzon—a "personal worship object" used by members of Soka Gakkai to help them meditate on the Lotus Sutra.

gospel—the Christian proclamation of the "good news" of salvation through Jesus Christ. As a literary term, refers to the four New Testament books that tell the story of and proclaim the "good news" about the life, death, and resurrection of Jesus.

grace—in Christianity, refers to the free gift of God's salvation through Jesus Christ.

guru—a spiritual teacher; in Sikhism, a leader of the religion.

hadith—Arabic for "speech, news, event"; refers to the narratives (or traditions) of what Muhammad said, did, or was like when he established the first

Muslim community in Medina. Next to the Qur'an, the major source for determining Muslim Sharia.

hajj—the pilgrimage to Mecca, which every Muslim must try to make at least once during his or her life.

halakhah—Hebrew for "to walk, go, follow"; a term used in Judaism to designate an authoritative instruction on the way a Jew seeking to be obedient to God should act.

haggadah—a Hebrew term referring to interpretation of the Tanak that is homiletical rather than legal in nature.

Hasidism—a Jewish movement that began in eighteenth-century Europe and emphasizes the joy of following the Torah.

heretic—someone who rejects authoritative (orthodox) teachings and/or emphasizes one teaching to the exclusion or distortion of others.

high god—in indigenous religions, a deity who is responsible for creating the world, but who then withdraws and is not directly involved in the ongoing life of the world.

hijra—Arabic for "emigration"; the emigration of Muhammad from Mecca to Medina in 622 C.E. Muslims date their calendar from this event.

Holocaust—the mass killing of approximately 6 million Jews in Europe by the German Nazis during World War II.

Horned God—in Wicca, the male god, associated with the sun.

Hsun Tzu—Confucian scholar who emphasized *li* as the central virtue, and taught that humans are not fundamentally good.

I Ching—Chinese "Book of Changes"; the Chinese classic on divination.

Iblis—in Islam, a name for Satan, who is considered to be the personification of evil and chief of the jinn. He rules over hell until the Judgment Day, after having been banished from heaven for his disobedience to God.

imam—Arabic for "one who stands before"; in Sunni Islam, the leader of worship in the mosque. In Shi'ite Islam, a spiritual successor to Muhammad who is endowed with the power to interpret the truth in the age in which he lives.

immanent—present in this world.

immortality—the belief that the soul of a person (or something about a person) survives death and continues to live in this or another world.

indigenous—originating in or pertaining to a particular area or region. Indigenous religions are those native to a geographical area, such as Native American religions.

Indus Valley civilization—a sophisticated urban culture that flourished along the banks of the Indus River in India from about 2500 B.C.E. to 1500 B.C.E.

jen—the Confucian virtue of "humaneness" or "concern for others."

jihad—Arabic for "struggle," referring to the obligation of all Muslims to struggle against error. In one sense refers to the defensive military struggle against those who would attack Muslims and subvert their faith, hence the concept of "holy war."

jina—"conqueror"; the Jain term for someone who has attained liberation.

jinn—Arabic for "spirits"; some (like Iblis) are evil, while others are good.

jiva—in Hinduism, the physical/psychological/social "self," which acts, but which is not eternal; in Jainism, the spiritual, eternal soul.

justification by faith—the Christian teaching that humans receive redemption from sin through trust in what God has done in Jesus Christ, not by any merit of their own.

Kaaba—Arabic for "cube"; the central shrine of Islam, located in the Grand Mosque of Mecca. It symbolizes the center of the world and is visited by Muslims on the hajj.

Kabbala—Hebrew for "tradition"; the Jewish mystical movement.

Kali—Hindu goddess of death, destruction, and renewal.

kami—Japanese for "the sacred"; anything or anyone that inspires awe or reverence. *Kami-no-michi* ("Way of the Kami") is the Japanese phrase used to describe indigenous Japanese religion (Shinto).

karma—Sanskrit for "action"; the law that explains human behavior as the chain of causes and effects resulting from desire. According to the religions that originated in India, *karma* binds us to the cycle of rebirth.

Khadija—Muhammad's wife and the first to accept his teaching.

khalsa—the "pure"; the members of the Sikh military fraternity, distinguished by the wearing of the "five k's": *kesh*, uncut hair; *kangha*, comb; *kachh*, short pants; *kara*, steel bracelet; and *kirpan*, sword.

Krishna—Hindu god prominent in the *Bhagavad-Gita*. Devotees of Vishnu consider Krishna to be one of Vishnu's *avatars*.

Lao Tzu—Chinese for "Old Master"; the legendary founder of Taoism and author of the *Tao-te-ching*. Also an early name for the *Tao-te-ching*.

li—the Confucian virtue of "propriety, right form," as expressed in the proper conduct of rituals. In Neo-Confucianism, the principle that orders reality.

liberal—referring to a religious movement that stress the importance of adapting the religion's teachings and practices as times change. First used in Christianity, but now applied to other religions. See "Modernist."

magic—the manipulation of other beings through spells, incantations, or other special means; in Wicca, the focusing of the five senses to effect change, always used positively.

Mahayana Buddhism—literally, "Large Raft" Buddhism; one of the two branches of Buddhism, dominant in East Asia and Vietnam. So named because of the belief that its teachings provide a "large raft" to carry people to enlightenment.

Mahdi—Arabic for "the guided one"; in Islam in general, a descendant of Muhammad who will restore justice on earth. In Shi'ite Islam, a messianic imam who will appear to end corruption.

mandate of heaven—in China, the right to rule, withdrawn when a leader fails to fulfill its terms (which are to maintain harmony and to rule justly).

mantra—a sacred syllable. In Transcendental Meditation, practitioners are given a personal mantra to use in daily meditation.

maya—Hindu concept of false or illusory reality.

Mecca—the Arabian city at the center of the Muslim world. When Muslims pray, they prostrate themselves in the direction of Mecca. At least once, Muslims are expected to make a pilgrimage (*hajj*) to Mecca.

Medina—the Arabian city to which Muhammad fled in 622 C.E. and where he established the first Muslim community.

meditation—focused, disciplined concentration intended to enable experience of the sacred.

Mencius—follower of Confucius who emphasized *jen* (humaneness) as a central virtue, and taught that humans are fundamentally good.

messiah—Hebrew for "anointed one"; the hoped-for descendant of King David who will appear to restore Israel to glory. Rooted in the promise in Second Samuel 7 that David's dynasty would be eternal.

Midrash—interpretation of the Tanak in a verse-by-verse commentary. Collection of Midrash on books of the Tanak were part of the rabbinic literature influential in shaping Classical Judaism.

millenarian—the belief that supernatural powers are about to bring a new age on earth that will totally transform life and bring restoration and salvation to the community of believers who have faithfully received the message of the coming end time.

Mishnah—Hebrew for "teaching, tradition, study;" the oral Torah as it existed in its written form in the late second or early third century C.E.

mitzvah (plural, mitzvoth)—Hebrew for "commandment"; collectively, the laws traditional Jews believe to have been revealed to Moses by Yahweh, which all Jews are to keep for all time. According to tradition, there are 613 mitzvoth.

modernist—referring to a movement within a religion that seeks to adapt the teachings and practices of the past to changing circumstances, affirming essential principles and letting go of beliefs and customs that are no longer relevant in a changed world. See "liberal."

moksha—Sanskrit for "liberation from the cycle of rebirth."

monasticism—a way of life withdrawn from the ordinary pursuits and dedicated to religious matters.

monism—the view that all reality is one, typically emphasizing spiritual unity.

monotheism—the belief in one all-powerful personal God who has created and sustains the cosmos.

Mormon—name used to refer to members of the Church of Jesus Christ of Latter-day Saints (but not members of the Reorganized Church). Mormon lived about 2,500 years ago and wrote the Book of Mormon.

Moroni—the son of Mormon, who, as an angel, appeared to Joseph Smith and directed him to the golden tablets on that the Book of Mormon was inscribed.

mosque—the communal place of prayer for Muslims.

mysticism—direct, unmediated experience of the ultimate.

myth—a story about the sacred, which is foundational, creating the basic patterns of life for people who accept the story as true for them.

neo-paganism—the movement that seeks to restore suppressed indigenous practice, especially of Europe.

nirvana—the state of bliss that comes when desire and attachment are overcome.

Ogun—the most widely worshipped orisa; the Yoruba god of war and iron, with associated powers of both formation and destruction.

Olorun—"owner of the sky"; the Yoruba high god, Lord above all, who dwells in the heavens and is the source of all life.

oral Torah—legal teachings that supplement the written Torah (the Hebrew Bible), which appeared first orally among Torah teachers but were committed to writing by the late second or early third century C.E. as the Mishnah, and grew to encompass the whole Talmud and ongoing rabbinic interpretation.

original sin—the Christian teaching that all humans are sinful at birth or are born with a tendency to sin.

orisa—the Yoruba name for spirits.

orthodox—authoritative, right beliefs.

Orthodox—in Judaism, the modern movement that stresses loyalty to Jewish tradition and strict adherence to the commandments of the Torah.

Pali Canon—the Theravada Buddhist scripture, consisting of the *Tripitaka* ("three baskets"): the basket of disciplinary regulations, that of discourses, and that of higher philosophy.

pantheism—the belief that all reality is infused with the presence of God.

Parsis—"Persians," the name for the Zoroastrian community in India.

Passover—the Jewish festival commemorating the deliverance of the Hebrew slaves form Egyptian bondage.

peyote—a small cactus that produces a drug that causes hallucinogenic visions when consumed; used as a sacrament in the Native American Church.

Pharisees—a party within Judaism, active in the last centuries B.C.E. and the first century C.E., composed of lay people dedicated to keeping the commandments of the written and oral Torahs; opposed to the Sadducees.

pietism—a Christian movement that emphasized personal spiritual devotion over corporate worship and assent to doctrine.

polytheism—belief in a multiplicity of personal deities.

pope—title for the Bishop of Rome; leader of the Roman Catholic Church.

prajna—Buddhist term for "wisdom." *Prajna-paramita* is the wisdom that goes beyond ordinary knowledge to an intuitive experience of the ultimate truth.

profane—the opposite of the sacred, that which is "unreal" for religious persons because it is apart from the ultimate.

Qur'an—Arabic for "recitation"; the collections of revelations received by Muhammed from Allah.

rabbi—Hebrew for "my master"; Jewish teachers who interpret the Torah for others and serve as leaders of Jewish communities.

Ras Tafari—the crown prince of Ethiopia, who became Emperor Haile Selassie in 1930. In Jamaica a group known as Rastafarians heralded him as a living god and the black messiah.

reality—all that is, or all that can be perceived.

Reconstructionism—in Judaism, the modern movement that views Judaism as an evolving religious civilization and interprets religious teaching in light of scientific understanding.

Reform—in Judaism, the modern movement that stresses loyalty to the essence of the Jewish tradition while adapting Jewish principles to changing times and different cultures.

revelation—the manifestation of ultimacy to humans.

rites of passage—rituals that mark and facilitate the transition from one state of life to the next, typically at birth, puberty, marriage, and death.

ritual—symbolic action in response to perceived ultimacy, based on myth.

Rosh Hashanah—the Jewish new year, which occurs in the fall; along with *Yom Kippur*, the "high holy days" in the Jewish ritual calendar.

sabbath—the Jewish holy day, beginning at sundown on Friday and ending at sundown on Saturday, commemorating the "day of rest" after the six days of creation.

sacraments—in Christianity, the signs of God's grace; rituals through which believers participate in the spiritual reality to which they point. The Lord's Supper (Holy Communion) and baptism are the two sacraments recognized by all Christians.

sacred—that which is ultimate, either of a spiritual or secular nature, hence "real" for religious person.

sacred hoop—Oglala Lakota circle symbolism. When in harmony, the nation is an unbroken "sacred hoop" with a flowering tree at the center. When the sacred hoop (probably derived from the summer camp circle that reinforced unity among the various bands) was broken, the nation suffered and eventually died.

sacred pipe—holy object, symbolizing the universe, smoked in all Oglala Lakota rituals to carry prayers in behalf of the world to *Wakan Tanka*.

sacrifice—a ritual in which worshippers present offerings to deities or spirits in exchange for certain, usually material, benefits.

Sadducees—a party within Judaism, active in the last centuries B.C.E. and the first century C.E., composed of priests and their supporters; opposed to the Pharisees.

salvation—deliverance from that which impedes transformation in response to ultimacy.

samsara—Sanskrit for "the cycle of rebirth."

sanctification—in Christianity, the process through which a person is incorporated ever more fully into the spiritual reality of Christ.

sangha—the Buddhist order of monks.

saoshyant—in Zoroastrianism, a deliverer who leads people to righteousness.

Satan—Hebrew for "adversary," from the Persian. The figure of an angel who functions in the divine court as a tempter of humans appeared for the first time in Hebrew post-exilic writings.

Second Coming—in Christianity, the expected return of Jesus Christ at the end of history to inaugurate the Kingdom of God on earth.

sect—a religious movement that split from another group; used negatively as a synonym for cult.

secular—having to do with this observable reality (as opposed to the spiritual).

Sephardim—Jews who fled persecution in Western Europe and settled in the Middle East during the late Middle Ages.

Septuagint—the Greek translation of the Tanak.

shakti—Sanskrit for "power, energy"; in Hinduism, the active energy of a deity, personified as a goddess. Shaktism is the practice of seeking to identify with this active power and draw upon it for material or spiritual pursuits.

shaman—in an indigenous religion, a holy person who, having been "taken over" by spiritual powers, becomes an intermediary between the spirit world and the people.

Shang Ti—Chinese for "Ruler on High"; central deity in ancient Chinese mythology, guarantor of the moral order and of rulers' authority.

Sharia—the path or way Muslims are to follow; hence, Muslim "law."

Shi'ite—the smaller of the two main branches of Islam; split from Sunni over the issue of rightful succession to Muhammad.

Shinto Myth—the indigenous Japanese story of creation and of Japan as the land of the *kami*.

Shiva—Hindu god of destruction and rejuvenation.

Sikh—Sanskrit for "disciple"; the followers of Nanak.

soul, spirit—that which gives life to a material being, but which has the quality of permanent, immortal reality. A "spirit" or "soul" is an entity which has this quality of "otherness" but which may be manifest and related to in this world.

Spenta Mainyu—the good spirit in Zoroastrian cosmology.

spiritual—referring to a level of existence beyond the ordinary, material, temporal reality of this world. In contrast to "secular" reality.

Sun Dance—a Lakota ritual in which participants dance around a cottonwood tree, some dragging buffalo skulls and/or connected by rawhide thongs that pierced the skin; some continue dancing until the thongs break loose. Called the Sun Dance because participants gaze at the sun as they dance.

Sunni—the largest of the two main branches of Islam; where the Qur'an is not explicit this movement appeals to *Sunna* (the manner of behavior associated with Muhammad; via *hadith*).

Sufi—the mystical movement within Islam.

sunyata—an important Mahayana Buddhist teaching regarding the "emptiness" or "openness" of all things and of all our perceptions of things.

sura—one of the divisions of the Qur'an.

sutras—collections of aphorisms, sayings.

symbol—any object, word, or action which points toward and allows experience of and/or participation in perceived ultimacy.

synagogue—Hebrew for "assembly"; a Jewish place of prayer and study. After the destruction of the Temple in Jerusalem, synagogues became the centers of Jewish worship outside the home.

taboo—some object, action, or person that must be avoided because of its potentially injurious power. For example, a warrior not yet purified after battle or a menstruating woman might be considered taboo.

Talmud—Hebrew for "learning"; in Judaism, the collection composed of the Mishnah along with further interpretation (Gemara). In Classical Judaism, the whole Talmud is considered God's instruction to Israel on how to live; it is the oral Torah.

Tanak—an acronym from the Hebrew names for the three sections of the Hebrew Bible—the law, prophets, and writings; used as a designation for the Hebrew Bible.

Tantra—Sanskrit for "that which extends, spreads." In a broad sense, tantrism is a religious practice outside the Vedic tradition, including rituals open to persons not of the Brahmin class. Practiced in Hinduism, Tibetan Buddhism, and Jainism, tantrism attempts to harness sensual energy for either spiritual or mundane purposes.

Tao—Chinese for "the way"; the underlying process of all reality that causes balance; the source and end of all reality.

Tao-te-ching—Chinese for "The Classic of the Way and Its Power/Virtue"; the basic text of philosophical Taoism.

Te—Chinese for "power" or "virtue."

theism—belief in one or more personal deities.

theology—disciplined study of and talk about God or, in a more general sense, about any spiritual or even secular ultimacy.

Theravada Buddhism—literally, "Way of the Elders"; surviving school of one of two branches of Buddhism, found in Southeast Asia. Claims to be the most ancient expression of Buddhist teaching. Called *Hinayana* ("Small Raft") by Mahayana Buddhist teachers.

Third Adam—according to the teaching of the Unification Church, a messiah who will appear to pay the full price for the sin of humanity and establish the Kingdom of God on earth; Jesus was the Second Adam.

T'ien—Chinese for "heaven"; in ancient China, the impersonal power with which the emperor was in harmony, as long as he ruled justly.

Torah—Hebrew for "law, instruction"; in general, God's revelation of the divine instruction on how to live. Specifically, the first five books of the Tanak (Genesis, Exodus, Leviticus, Numbers, and Deuteronomy). Also used to refer to the Tanak as a whole. See also *oral Torah.*

totem—an animal or something else with which a group develops a special relationship; it often takes on the characteristics of the totemic object, and becomes a taboo for the people.

tradition—the handing down of beliefs and practices, or these beliefs and practices considered as a dynamic collection.

traditionalist—referring to a movement in a religion which seeks to preserve the teachings and practices of the past; evaluating changing developments in terms of their conformity with tradition.

transcendent—removed from or "above" the secular world. In contrast to immanent.

transubstantiation—in Christianity, the belief that through the proper consecration during the sacrament of Holy Communion the elements of bread and wine become the substance of the body and blood of Christ.

True Name—the Sikh name for the one God.

umma—Arabic for "community"; the entire community of Muslims throughout the world.

untouchables—in traditional Hindu society, those "below" the caste system, and thus not members of any of the four castes. Also called members of the "scheduled castes" or "outcasts." Mahatma Gandhi called the untouchables *harijan,* "children of God."

Upanishads—Sanskrit for "to sit nearby"; philosophical utterances that, with the Vedas, are the basis of later philosophical reflections in Hinduism. They introduce such important Hindu concepts as *atman, brahman, samsara,* and *moksha.* Also called Vedanta ("end of the Vedas"). There are thirteen principal *Upanishads.*

Vedas—Sanskrit for "knowledge"; the sacred writings of the Aryans, deemed canonical by later Hinduism. Includes hymns to the gods (*Rig-Veda*), ritual materials and directions for the sacrifices and invocations for the gods (*Yajur-Veda*), verses from the *Rig-Veda* arranged musically (*Sama-Veda*), and hymns together with spells and incantations (*Atharva-Veda*). Also includes the *Upanishads.*

Vishnu—Hindu god of preservation and love; appears on earth on various forms (*avatars*) in times of crisis.

vision quest—a ritual in Lakota and some other indigenous cultures in which the participant spends time alone, often on a hill or mountain, fasting and waiting for a vision from the spirit beings that will give him or her direction for life. A "vision without lamenting" comes spontaneously and is considered especially sacred.

wakan—Oglala Lakota for "holy" or "sacred." **Wakana** is "holiness" and a *wakan* person is someone who has been given spiritual powers. **Wakan Tanka**, "Great Spirit" or "Great Mystery," is, in some senses, a deity to whom the Oglala pray.

However, *Wakan Tanka* is also a collective title for sixteen separate spiritual powers.

Wicca—Old English for "wise," from which the term "witch" derives; taken as the name for a movement that seeks to restore pre-Christian European witchcraft.

wu wei—Chinese for "inaction"; in philosophical Taoism, the concept of "action without assertion."

Yahweh—the special name for God in Judaism, revealed to Moses (according to the Book of Exodus in the Tanak). From the verb "to be," probably meaning "he causes to be what is."

Yiddish—a dialect combining German and Hebrew, spoken in Jewish communities of Eastern Europe (the Ashkenazim).

yin and yang—the complementary, opposite forces present in all reality, according to the basic Chinese worldview. The *yin* force is dark, mysterious, wet, female, etc.; the *yang* force is bright, clear, dry, male, etc.

yoga—Sanskrit for "to yoke or join"; refers to a variety of methods that seek to join the individual soul (*atman*) to the Ultimate, and thus achieve liberation from rebirth. The major types of *yoga* are *karma yoga* (the way of action), *bhakti yoga* (the way of devotion), and *jnana yoga* (the way of knowledge).

Yom Kippur—the Jewish "day of atonement." With *Rosh Hashanah,* the "high holy days" of the Jewish ritual calendar.

zadankai—Soka Gakkai "discussion groups" in which members are encouraged to admit their errors and commit themselves to the true faith.

Zionism—the political movement dedicated to the creation of a Jewish homeland; there all Jews of the world may come and live without fear of persecution.

Photo Credits

Index

	2500 B.C.E.	1500	1000	500
Indigenous (Yoruba and Lakota)			Indigenous traditions flourish	
Hinduism	• Indus Valley Civilization flourishes 2500 B.C.E.	• Compilation of Vedic literature begins 1500 B.C.E.	Great epics (*Mahabharata* and *Ramayana*) being composed. 500 •	Compilation • of Laws of Manu begins Ca. 200
Buddhism			Siddartha Gautama 563–483 ——	Spread beyond • India begins Ca. 250
				Theravada schools developing Ca. 200 •
Jainism		• The 23 Tirthankaras	——	Mahavira 597–527
Sikhism				
Taoism			Traditional date of• birth of Lao Tzu 604	"Religious" • Taoism emerges 200
Confucianism			Master Kung (Confucius) 551–479 ——	
				Becomes basis of Chinese educational system 136 •
Shinto		• Indigenous traditions 2000 B.C.E.		• Traditional date of first emperor of Japan 660
Zoroastrianism			Birth of Zoroaster 600 (?) •	State religion of Persia 130 •
Judaism		Abraham and Sarah Ca. 1800–1700 (?) ——	David and Solomon 1000–900 —— Moses Ca. 1300–1200 (?) ——	Babylonian Exile. Diaspora begins. 597–538 ——
Christianity				
Islam				
New Religions	(See Ch. 14 for key dates)			
Interfaith				